Fighting Poverty

Fighting Poverty

The Development-Employment Link

edited by
Rizwanul Islam

LYNNE
RIENNER
PUBLISHERS

BOULDER
LONDON

Published in the United States of America in 2006 by
Lynne Rienner Publishers, Inc.
1800 30th Street, Boulder, Colorado 80301
www.rienner.com

and in the United Kingdom by
Lynne Rienner Publishers, Inc.
3 Henrietta Street, Covent Garden, London WC2E 8LU

Library of Congress Cataloging-in-Publication Data
Fighting poverty : the development-employment link / editor, Rizwanul Islam.
    p. cm.
  Includes bibliographical references and index.
  ISBN 1-58826-396-7 (hardcover : alk. paper)
  1. Economic development. 2. Manpower policy. 3. Poverty. I. Islam, Rizwanul.
HD75.F54 2005 *2006*
339.5'09172'4—dc22

                                                2005018521

British Cataloguing in Publication Data
A Cataloguing in Publication record for this book
is available from the British Library.

Printed and bound in the United States of America

Contents

Tables and Figures

▦ Tables

■ Figures

Preface

The stubborn persistence of poverty remains a major challenge in many parts of the world today, despite notable successes in poverty reduction in some countries. The experiences of countries that have succeeded in reducing poverty significantly indicate the importance of sustained high growth in achieving that result. However, studies on poverty are replete with an equally important finding, that high growth alone is not adequate; the pattern and sources of growth, as well as the manner in which its benefits are distributed, are equally important from the point of view of rapid poverty reduction. Understanding the channels that link economic growth to poverty reduction is essential to the design of pro-poor policies. Employment is the key channel in that link. This book explores that channel in the context of developing countries.

Prevailing strands in the existing literature on poverty reduction focus either on economic growth or targeted micro-level interventions. Given the limitations of both, we explore here a third way, the thrust of which is on the pattern of growth—in terms of its outcome on employment and productivity—and on giving growth a pro-poor orientation through higher employment intensity. Although there is a nascent literature on this third strand of thinking about strategies for poverty reduction, it is difficult to find a systematic analysis of the nexus of economic growth, employment, and poverty reduction with in-depth empirical evidence. It is this gap in the development literature on poverty that we seek to fill. Thus we provide conceptual and analytic frameworks for examining how employment serves to link growth with poverty reduction, as well as empirical analyses of the linkages among economic growth, employment, and poverty reduction using cross-country data and in-depth country-level studies.

The main message emerging from the book can be summed up as follows: A high rate of economic growth is a necessary, but not sufficient, condition for poverty reduction. There is no fixed relationship between economic growth and poverty reduction; similar growth rates can be associated with differing poverty reduction outcomes. Developments in employment and labor markets that take place as a result of growth play an important role in producing such varying results. For economic growth to be pro-poor, it has to result in a transformation of the economic and employment structure to high-productivity activities that enable the poor to benefit through higher real wages and earnings.

This study has important implications for public policy. There can be two broad types of public policy aimed at poverty reduction. First, policies can be aimed not just at raising the rate of economic growth, but also at influencing the pattern of growth or at giving growth a more pro-poor orientation. The second category of policies includes direct interventions, some of which are often targeted at the poor. The policy implications emanating from the volume belong to both categories mentioned above. Chapter 12 discusses some of these implications.

Some of the chapters of this volume are based on papers produced under collaborative projects that the International Labour Organization (ILO) has undertaken with the Swedish International Development Cooperation Agency (SIDA) and the United Nations Development Programme (UNDP) on employment for poverty reduction. SIDA also partially funded the publication of this volume. Thanks are due to both organizations, and in particular to Per Ronnas of SIDA and Selim Jahan of the UNDP, who played key roles in initiating the collaborative projects. I would like to thank both of them for their encouragement and support. I am grateful to Per Ronnas and my colleague M. Muqtada, who kindly read an earlier version of the entire manuscript and provided valuable comments and suggestions. Nina Torm and Alan Wood provided useful support in terms of research and editorial assistance at various stages in the preparation of the book, and Evelyn Ralph was of invaluable help in putting together the various drafts. Thanks are due to all of them. However, I remain responsible for any remaining inadequacies and shortcomings of the volume.

—*Rizwanul Islam*

1

Introduction

Rizwanul Islam

If one were to cite a single problem that poses a challenge for world leaders, development practitioners (at the global as well as the national level), and policymakers alike, it would be the stubborn persistence of poverty in many parts of the world. It is only in countries of East and Southeast Asia (ESEA) that real success in poverty reduction has been achieved, although that achievement also looked rather fragile during the economic crisis of the late 1990s. Progress in poverty reduction outside that region has been rather disappointing. This has been especially so in the low-income countries of sub-Saharan Africa (SSA) and South Asia. While two-thirds of the world's poor live in Asia, South Asia is home to most of them.

For some years now the issue of poverty has been back on the development agenda. One reflection of the concern with poverty is the adoption of the Millennium Development Goals (MDGs), one of which is to reduce poverty by half by 2015 (against the benchmark of 1990). Whether one judges by this yardstick or independently of it, making a significant dent in poverty needs to be a central element in development efforts. Even if one goes by the MDGs, it is important to look beyond the global level to individual regions and countries, simply because global figures are heavily influenced by the performance of large countries (e.g., China and India). Indeed, although projections by the World Bank (World Bank 2003c) indicate the possibility of halving poverty by 2015 at the global level, doubts remain about certain regions (e.g., sub-Saharan Africa) and countries.[1]

Although economic growth is typically regarded as the major means of achieving the MDG of poverty reduction, the actual outcome in terms of poverty reduction may differ from projections made on the basis of observed relationships between growth and poverty reduction, depending on changes in the pattern of growth. For example, with an increase in income inequality the

1

degree of poverty reduction from a given economic growth will be less than what would have been with unchanged income distribution.[2] Pattern of growth, therefore, needs to be an important consideration in a strategy for poverty reduction.

There is already a nascent literature in development economics pointing to the importance of the pattern of growth in achieving poverty reduction. And the role of employment in that respect is also mentioned occasionally.[3] However, development literature has not yet fully explored the role of employment in linking growth with poverty reduction, and in making growth pro-poor.

Indeed, discussions of poverty in the literature on development policy and the world of development practitioners are still dominated by two broad strands. In one, high economic growth is regarded as the only means of achieving significant and sustained reduction in poverty. In this line of reasoning, growth is supposed to ensure all other factors that may be necessary for poverty reduction. In the second strand, benefits of growth often do not reach the poor, and hence the need for targeted interventions (e.g., through microfinance and similar micro-level programs) aimed at the poor. While both approaches have their strengths, both exhibit their limitations if applied independently. Growth, while essential, is not sufficient per se for achieving poverty reduction; the pattern of growth is extremely important. On the other hand, the impact of micro-level interventions is likely to remain limited unless opportunities for the poor are created by the process of economic growth and the macro policy environment is conducive to pro-poor economic growth.

Given the limitations of the two strands of thinking on strategies for poverty reduction, it is necessary to look for a third way, one that could add ammunition to the fight against poverty. A focus on the pattern of growth in terms of its outcome on employment and productivity and giving growth a pro-poor orientation by augmenting its employment intensity is the basic thrust of this third way. Although there is a nascent literature on the importance of the pattern of growth for poverty reduction, it is not easy to find an in-depth analysis of the nexus of economic growth, employment, and poverty reduction based on analytic rigor and empirical evidence.[4] It is this gap in the literature on poverty that the book intends to address.

Exploring the nexus of economic growth, employment, and poverty reduction is especially important in the context of strategies for poverty reduction that are being pursued at the national level in many countries. Poverty reduction strategy papers (PRSPs), which serve as the basis for debt relief for poor countries under the Highly Indebted Poor Countries initiative, have now become a commonly used framework for action at the country level. And yet the macroeconomic framework within which the PRSPs are developed does not make an explicit provision for using the employment route out of poverty and integrating employment considerations into economic policymaking.[5]

Analysis of the kind undertaken in this volume would have to be the initial step if the focus of PRSPs were to be reoriented and the employment outcomes of the underlying growth and macroeconomic frameworks were to be integrated into the poverty reduction strategies.

The book contains three types of analysis. First, there are attempts (in Chapters 2, 3, and 4) at developing conceptual and analytic frameworks for examining how employment serves to link growth with poverty reduction. Second, cross-country data are used (in Chapters 3 and 4) to provide empirical evidence on the linkages among economic growth, employment, and poverty reduction. Third, in-depth country-level studies are presented,[6] providing analysis of the employment related channels that link growth to improving the incomes of the poor. Policy implications for pro-poor growth are brought out from that analysis.

Chapters 2, 3, and 4 present frameworks for analyzing the linkages among economic growth, employment, and poverty. All of them contend that although a high rate of economic growth is a necessary condition for poverty reduction, it is not sufficient, and that there is no invariant relationship between the rates of growth and poverty reduction. In these frameworks, employment is a key element linking economic growth with poverty reduction.

S. R. Osmani (Chapter 2) starts by pointing out two channels—social provisioning and personal income—that act as mechanisms for linking growth and poverty reduction. And employment is a crucial variable that determines the functioning of the personal income channel. He identifies three sets of underlying factors that affect the incomes of the poor, for any given growth of the labor force: the growth factor, the elasticity factor, and the integrability factor. Variables relating to employment and the labor market are captured by the second and third factors. The elasticity factor represents a summary expression of the extent to which output growth leads to an expansion of employment. The integrability factor refers to the extent to which the poor are able to integrate into economic processes so that, when growth occurs and employment potential expands, they can take advantage of the available employment. The elasticity factor, in turn, depends on various features of the growth process (e.g., the sectoral composition of output, choice of technology, etc.). The integrability factor refers to the degree of correspondence between new economic opportunities and the capabilities of the poor. The latter, in turn, could be influenced by a variety of factors (e.g., education and skills of workers, lack of assets and access to credit, and discrimination in the labor market for gender and other reasons).

The framework used by Rizwanul Islam (Chapter 3) is very similar to that of Osmani in that Islam also regards employment as a key factor in linking output growth with poverty reduction. He considers the linkages among output growth, employment, and poverty at both macro and micro levels. He conceptualizes pro-poor economic growth as a virtuous circle of economic growth leading to poverty reduction via growth of employment with rising productivity, and reduced poverty creating the possibility of further increases in productivity (e.g., through higher expenditures on health, education, and skill development) and higher rates of economic growth. In this framework, for output growth to result in poverty reduction, three things need to happen: improved productivity of various sectors, a shift in the structure of employment toward sectors and occupations with higher levels of productivity, and increases in real wages and in earnings from both wage employment and self-employment.

Employment elasticity with respect to output plays an important role in Islam's framework as well; and he argues that from the point of view of poverty reduction, it is important for the overall employment growth intensity (defined in terms of employment elasticity) to be high. And the overall elasticity being a weighted average of sectoral elasticities, greater allocation of investment in more labor-intensive sectors and higher growth rates in such sectors could result in high (even rising) overall employment elasticity even with declining employment elasticities in some sectors. In order to test the impact of employment-intensive growth on poverty, Islam uses regression analysis, with employment elasticity as one of the explanatory variables (along with growth in gross domestic product [GDP]) for explaining variations in annual changes in poverty. He uses the same methodology also to examine the influence of employment and labor market variables on poverty.

In Azizur Rahman Khan's framework (Chapter 4), the linkage between employment and poverty is envisioned as a process in which economic growth induces an increase in productive and remunerative employment, which leads to a reduction of poverty. The effectiveness of the process in reducing poverty depends on the strength in each link in the process. And according to Khan (like Osmani in Chapter 2), these links consist of economic growth, output elasticity of demand for labor, and the ability of the poor to respond to increasing demand for labor, especially for more productive categories of employment.

Recognizing high economic growth as a necessary condition for poverty reduction, Khan outlines a few scenarios where such growth may fail to bring about a commensurate rate of poverty reduction; they include low output elasticity of demand for labor; employment impact of high growth offset by countervailing contraction of employment induced by economic reforms; economic growth creating employment of a kind for which the poor do not possess necessary skills; and growth taking place in a situation of highly unequal distribution of productive assets like land and capital. Indeed, growth associated with increasing inequality could result in a weak or adverse impact on poverty reduction.

Khan also outlines a set of employment-related interventions for poverty reduction that includes the following: policies, institutions, and incentives needed for rapid labor-absorbing growth; measures for transforming the poor into productive entrepreneurs engaged in self-employment; raising the productivity of poor workers in both wage employment and self-employment; improvement and adjustment in the skills of the poor—especially in line with changes in the demand for skills in a dynamic labor market; improved terms of exchange for the poor; appropriate management of unemployment resulting from economic reforms, especially from reforms of state-owned enterprises, that should include provision of protection and safety nets for the newly unemployed; and specially designed employment opportunities for the labor-disadvantaged households (e.g., female-headed).

The above discussion indicates that a few common elements run through the frameworks used by Osmani, Islam, and Khan for analyzing the linkage between economic growth and poverty reduction. In this sense, it can be said that the volume provides one framework for this purpose. In this framework, economic growth is an important prerequisite for poverty reduction, but needs to be accompanied by two other factors. One of the latter is the extent to which output growth leads to an expansion of productive employment, while the other is the ability of the poor to utilize the economic opportunities that open up in the process of economic growth. The last two factors are critical in translating the results of economic growth into poverty reduction. The country studies included in the book do actually follow, by and large, the analytic framework mentioned above.

▨ Notes

1. In sub-Saharan Africa, the percentage of people living on less than US$1 per day increased from 47.4 percent in 1990 to 49.0 percent in 1999, and is projected to decline only to 46 percent by 2015. And if China is excluded, the percentage of people below poverty for the rest of the world is projected to decline from 28.5 percent in 1990 to 15.7 percent by 2015—thus remaining at over half of the 1990 level. See World Bank 2003c.

2. The World Bank (2003c) recognizes that the relationship between economic growth and poverty reduction has weakened (that is, for the same growth rate, the rate of poverty reduction has declined).

3. See Chapter 3 for a brief review of this literature.

4. The director-general of the ILO, in his 2003 report titled *Working out of Poverty,* noted employment as "the most effective route to poverty eradication" and went on to say that "understanding the channels which link growth to improving the lives of people living in poverty is therefore essential to the design of pro-poor growth strategies." See ILO 2003a.

5. See Muqtada 2003 for a critique of the macroeconomic framework of PRSPs. It needs to be mentioned here that contents of PRSPs exhibit some variation from

country to country, and there are cases where employment has been incorporated into the strategies. However, the issue is one of integrating employment into the macro-economic framework rather than treating it as an add-on.

6. The country studies are presented in alphabetical order rather than by geo-graphical region. The simple reason is that an adequate number of country studies is not available in order to draw conclusions at the regional level. Instead of that ap-proach, each country study can be looked at on its own merits for an in-depth analysis of the nexus of economic growth, employment, and poverty reduction.

Part 1

Analytic Framework and Cross-Country Analysis

2

Exploring the Employment Nexus: The Analytics of Pro-Poor Growth

S. R. Osmani

There was a time when the growth of national income was taken to be the explicit objective of economic development. More recently, poverty reduction has come to be accepted as the explicit objective. A synthetic view is now emerging, however, contending that the two objectives are not really different, because sustained poverty reduction is not possible without sustained and rapid economic growth. A spate of recent empirical studies indeed demonstrates that persistent growth failures have invariably been accompanied by persistent failure to reduce poverty, and that, conversely, sustained and rapid economic growth has invariably been accompanied by reduction of poverty.[1]

The empirical evidence, however, also points to an important feature of the relationship between growth and poverty that is often neglected—namely that there is no invariant relationship between the rate of growth and the rate of poverty reduction.

In other words, faster growth is not always accompanied by faster rates of poverty reduction, just as slower growth does not always entail slower rates of poverty reduction. Furthermore, even if faster growth leads to faster reduction of poverty in certain cases, the extent to which poverty responds to growth—as measured by the growth elasticity of poverty[2]—varies a great deal from case to case.[3] The reasons for these variations are not yet fully understood. Why is it that rapid growth sometimes entails rapid reduction of poverty but sometimes a rather modest rate of poverty reduction? How is it possible that even relatively modest growth sometimes goes hand in hand with relatively rapid reduction of poverty? If the goal of policymaking is to eliminate poverty in the shortest possible time, then it is important to understand what lies behind these variations.

Any attempt to explain the variable relationship between the rate of growth and the rate of poverty reduction must investigate the causal mechanisms, or channels, that link growth with poverty.[4] This chapter attempts to develop an analytic framework for this purpose. At the core of this framework is the notion of the "employment nexus," which may be summarized by the proposition that employment opportunities for the poor offer the most crucial link between growth and poverty. The stronger the nexus, the stronger the effect of growth on poverty. An immediate policy implication of adopting such a framework is that it requires any pro-poor growth strategy worthy of its name to seriously explore the extent to which it creates productive employment opportunities for the poor.

After developing the analytic framework below, I draw on the insights it provides and then suggest some directions for future research.

The Employment Nexus Between Growth and Poverty

When poverty is viewed broadly to imply basic capability failures (as opposed to just low income)—such as the capabilities to be free from hunger, to live a healthy and active life, and so on—two basic channels can be identified:

- *The social provisioning channel.* Growth-generated resources are utilized by the society to provide services to the poor so as to enhance their various capabilities.
- *The personal income channel.* Growth of the economy translates into higher personal income of the poor, who then utilize their income so as to enhance their capabilities.

The workings of both the channels are subject to variations. The extent to which growth-generated resources actually get to be utilized for the purpose of social provisioning can vary from society to society. And the extent to which growth of the economy translates into higher income of the poor can also vary. Both types of variations can underlie the observed variable relationship between the rate of growth and the rate of poverty reduction.

A crucial variable that determines the functioning of the personal income channel is employment. It is the quantity and quality of employment of the poor that determine how growth of the economy would translate into higher income of the poor.[5] This might be called the "employment nexus" between growth and poverty. Explicating the nature of this nexus—that is, understanding what factors make this nexus strong and what factors make it weak—is an essential precondition for devising policies that will best serve the poor. In order to see how the employment nexus mediates between growth and poverty, it is useful to begin with some taxonomies of the poor based on the nature of their employment.

One basic taxonomy is to distinguish between the poor who are in the labor force and those who are not. Some among the latter group may have no one in the labor force to support them. For them, obviously, the employment nexus is of little relevance; some form of social provisioning will be needed in order to alleviate their poverty. However, most of the poor who are not in the labor force would actually be dependents of the first category of poor, so that their conditions will be inextricably linked with each other. For analytic purposes, therefore, it is adequate to focus only on those among the poor who are in the labor force.

The poor in the labor force can in turn be divided into two groups: the unemployed poor and the working poor. As an empirical reality, it is fair to suggest that the unemployed poor would constitute a numerically insignificant category in the poor countries. The reason simply is that the vast majority of these countries do not have any social insurance mechanism, without which the poor cannot afford to remain unemployed. Thus the working poor would constitute by far the major segment of the poor in the labor force.[6]

The working poor themselves can be further classified, along two different lines. The more traditional line of classification looks at the relationship between labor and the means of production, and accordingly classifies the working poor into the self-employed poor and the wage-earning poor. A different line of classification would look at the proximate causes of low income that make the working people poor. Two broad categories of proximate causes can be distinguished: underemployment and low returns to labor.

Those who suffer from underemployment can be of two types:

- *Open underemployed.* Those who work less than full-time and hence cannot earn enough to rise above the poverty line.
- *Disguised underemployed.* The Nurkse-Lewis-type surplus labor—those who apparently work full-time but at low intensity, within an institutional framework that permits both work sharing and income sharing.[7]

Those who suffer from low returns to labor despite working full-time and at high intensity can be classified into three categories depending on the causes of low returns:[8]

- Those who work for very low wages because they have to compete with potential entrants (comprising the unemployed and the underemployed, and constituting a pool of surplus labor) who have very low reservation wages—the *surplus labor* syndrome.
- Those who work with poor skill, or poor technology, or inadequate complementary factors—the *low productivity* syndrome.

- Those who suffer from adverse terms of trade, because of either low product prices or high input cost (including high cost of credit), or both—the *adverse terms of trade* syndrome.

The preceding typologies demonstrate that there are a wide variety of pathways through which a part of the working population can become poor. These typologies thus provide a rich analytic framework for understanding the detailed processes through which different groups of people come to experience poverty. The objective of the present discussion, however, is not to embark on a full-fledged exploration of these detailed processes, but to identify in broad terms the channels through which the employment nexus relates the proximate causes of poverty to what might be called the underlying factors that affect poverty.

As noted above, the proximate causes of poverty are unemployment/underemployment and low returns to labor—in other words, the quantity and quality of employment.[9] To see what the underlying factors are, one might begin by noting the rather trivial fact that the condition of the poor will depend on their scope of earning higher income—through either greater quantity of employment or higher returns to labor, or a combination of the two. This scope will obviously depend on factors affecting both the supply of and the demand for labor.

On the supply side, there are long-term forces affecting the growth of the labor force and there are both long- and short-term factors affecting the supply of labor of a given labor force. The present analysis will abstract from considerations of the forces that affect the growth of the labor force, which means that I will discuss only the factors that affect the incomes of the poor for any given growth of the labor force. The factors affecting the supply of labor of a given labor force, however, will be considered.

On the demand side, too, there are both long-term and short-term forces. The present analysis will abstract from considerations of short-term fluctuations of demand for labor associated with business cycles, which means that the phenomenon of Keynesian unemployment will be left out of discussion. There are a number of reasons for this. First, since the focus of this chapter is on the factors affecting the trend of poverty over time, unemployment of structural types is much more relevant for the present purpose than is the Keynesian type. Second, as an empirical reality, Keynesian unemployment happens to be much less prevalent than structural unemployment in most of the poor countries. Third, the analytics of Keynesian unemployment are quite well advanced in the existing literature, and this chapter has nothing to add in this regard.

Subject to these caveats, the ensuing discussion presents a framework for analyzing the underlying factors that affect the incomes of the poor, for any given growth of the labor force. Three sets of underlying factors can be identified:[10]

1. *The growth factor.* The rate at which the production potential of the economy expands, as represented by an upward shift of the production possibility frontier.
2. *The elasticity factor.* The extent to which an upward shift of the production possibility frontier enhances the employment potential—the latter being defined as the scope for improving the quality and quantity of employment. In other words, the concern here is with the elasticity of employment potential with respect to growth in production potential.
3. *The integrability factor.* The extent to which the poor are able to integrate into economic processes so that, when growth occurs and the employment potential expands, they can take advantage of the greater scope for improving the quality and quantity of employment.

Some brief remarks on each of these underlying factors are in order. The starting point for any program of sustained poverty reduction must be the expansion of an economy's production potential, as determined by the growth of its labor force, accumulation of human and physical capital, and technological progress. Only such an expansion can create the basis for sustained increase in the incomes of everyone, including the poor. For a while, of course, redistribution of existing income can help alleviate poverty to some extent; and to the extent that this is possible without seriously compromising the growth potential of the economy, redistributive measures should certainly be undertaken. But it is clear that sustained increase in the income of the poor must be underpinned by sustained growth of potential output.[11]

Given any shift in the production potential, the next parameter that has a bearing on the poor's income is the extent to which growth in output expands the scope for improving the quantity and quality of employment—in short, the employment potential. The expansion of employment potential will manifest itself as an upward shift of the marginal value product curve of labor. For the wage labor sector, this is nothing but the standard demand curve for labor. For the self-employed sector, however, the term *demand curve* does not strictly apply. Even so, the common feature of both cases is that an upward shift of the curve allows the workers to improve the quality and quantity of their employment. Precisely in what way the effect would be split between quality and quantity would depend on the nature of the supply curve of labor. If the supply curve is relatively flat—as in a situation of surplus labor—most of the impact would be felt as greater quantity (as reflected in reduced underemployment for the poor). If the supply curve is steep—as when surplus labor is exhausted or nearly so—most of the impact would be felt as higher quality, as reflected in higher wages in the case of wage labor and higher returns to labor in the case of the self-employed.[12]

Thus the greater the expansion of employment potential, the greater the opportunity for reducing underemployment and raising the returns to labor—the two proximate causes of poverty mentioned earlier. The growth elasticity of employment potential is therefore an important intermediate variable that shapes the extent to which the growth of the overall economy translates into higher incomes of the poor.

It should be noted that the notion of elasticity that is being used here is quite different from the standard one that is found in the empirical literature on growth and employment. The standard definition refers to the observed empirical relationship between actual growth of income and actual increase in the quantity of employment (as measured by the number of people employed). This is different from the concept used here on a number of counts. First, the concept here relates potential growth with expansion in employment potential defined as a shift in the marginal value product curve of labor. Since employment potential, as has been shown, is only partly reflected in the quantity of employment, the other part being reflected in the returns to labor, it's quite possible that a high elasticity in the present sense may be associated with little or no expansion in the quantity of employment. Second, to the extent that the concept here refers to the quantity of employment, it focuses on the intensity-adjusted amount of work rather than the number of workers. Thus a high elasticity in the present sense may well be associated with a reduction in underemployment, without actually showing up as more people being at work. Finally, and perhaps most important, the concept here looks solely at the demand side of the labor market so as to capture the ability of growth to absorb labor. By contrast, the standard definition, by relating actual growth with actual employment, looks at the net result of the interaction between supply and demand. It is thus a reduced form concept, and as such doesn't have much analytic content. Consider, for instance, a case where labor force is growing rapidly, and since open unemployment is rare in poor countries, the number of people at work is also growing rapidly. If growth of income happens to be low in this case, the standard definition will reveal a high elasticity, but it will be misleading to interpret it as indicating that growth has been highly labor-absorbing.

Of course, a high elasticity of employment does not necessarily entail higher incomes of the poor. All it does is to allow the working population as a whole to reduce their unemployment and underemployment and raise their returns to labor. In short, it expands the opportunities, generally. There remains the question, however, whether the poor are able to take this opportunity or whether it is grabbed mainly by the nonpoor workers, or even whether the opportunities are seized at all. Much depends on whether the poor possess the necessary attributes that will enable them to integrate fully into the workings of an expanding economy. This is what I have termed the "integrability" factor.

The preceding analysis shows that while economic growth is indeed essential for sustained poverty reduction, the rate of poverty reduction also depends crucially on two other parameters—the elasticity factor and the integrability factor. A comprehensive strategy for pro-poor growth will have to attach due importance to all three factors.

The importance of growth is already well recognized in the literature. It is obvious that without the growth of production possibilities there can be no sustained expansion in employment potential. The only way employment can be expanded in a stagnant economy is either by depressing the returns to labor or by increasing the rate of underemployment. Neither route is good for the poor. Only a growth-induced shift in the employment potential will enable the poor to enjoy rising income either through reduced unemployment/underemployment or through higher returns to labor. Economic growth is therefore an essential component of any employment-focused strategy of poverty reduction. The strategies for promoting growth have been discussed extensively and systematically in the literature. By contrast, the discussion of the other two factors—namely elasticity and integrability—is much less extensive and far from systematic. Since these two factors constitute the core of the employment nexus between growth and poverty reduction, they are discussed further below.

The Elasticity Factor

The elasticity factor refers to the ability of any given growth of production to stimulate the growth of employment potential, as represented by upward shift of the marginal value product of labor curve. The idea behind this concept is that any given growth rate can be associated with different degrees of shift in employment potential depending on the nature of the growth process. And the growth process that is associated with a bigger shift—that is, the one that is more employment-elastic—would be more helpful for the poor, other things remaining the same. The degree of elasticity would depend on three features of the growth process:

- *Sectoral composition of output.* The extent to which the growth of output is concentrated in the more labor-intensive sectors.
- *Choice of technique.* The extent to which more labor-intensive techniques are used, especially in the growing sectors.
- *Terms of trade.* The extent to which the internal and external terms of trade improve for the labor-intensive sectors.

One of the main reasons why economic growth did not lead to appreciable reduction of poverty in many developing countries in the past is that the growth process did not promote labor intensity either in the composition of output between sectors or in the choice of technique within sectors. The inward-looking import-substituting strategy of industrialization followed in these countries had created an incentive structure that fostered capital intensity of production at the expense of reducing the employment potential. The trend is now changing, and there is greater understanding today about the need for adopting a more outward-looking open economy strategy. In general, this change will not only enhance the "growth factor," but also impact positively on the "elasticity factor" by promoting greater labor intensity in labor-abundant poor economies. Both of these will be beneficial for the poor. Therefore, the elimination of policy distortions that create an artificial bias toward capital intensity in the pursuit of widespread import substitution must form an essential part of an employment-focused strategy for poverty reduction.

It should be noted, however, that abandoning widespread import substitution and opening up the economy will not necessarily enhance the elasticity factor in all circumstances. There are a number of reasons for this.

First, there are many poor countries—for instance, in sub-Saharan Africa—that are land-abundant rather than labor-abundant. The standard Heckscher-Ohlin theory of international trade, which predicts that labor-abundant countries will specialize in labor-intensive products as they open up their economies, also predicts by the same logic that land-abundant countries will specialize in land-intensive activities—crop production, for example.[13] The impact on employment potential will then depend crucially on the institutional arrangements that govern labor's access to land. If, for instance, land distribution happens to be highly unequal and production is dominated by a few large owners cultivating large tracts of land through mechanized means, then the impact on employment elasticity might be small.

Second, the predictions of the simple version of the Heckscher-Ohlin theorem may not hold when complications arising from the presence of multiple goods and in particular, nontraded goods, are introduced. Thus, even in a labor-abundant economy, if the labor-intensive products require complementary nontraded inputs that are scarce in supply, then comparative advantage may not actually lie in these products. Opening up the economy will not then necessarily impact positively on the elasticity factor.[14]

Third, poor infrastructure—both physical and human—may inhibit the expansion of labor-intensive activities, even if they happen to have potential comparative advantage. This is especially likely if the existing infrastructure was geared specifically toward supporting capital-intensive activities that were promoted artificially in an earlier regime of import substitution. The recognition that infrastructural bottlenecks seriously inhibit the expansion of sectors that have a potential comparative advantage is a common theme in the literature on underdevelopment in sub-Saharan Africa.

These are some of the reasons why greater labor intensity of production is not guaranteed merely by the opening up of a poor economy. An employment-focused strategy of poverty reduction would then demand that, simultaneously with the opening up, other measures be taken to overcome the bottlenecks that might inhibit labor intensity in particular circumstances.

Apart from labor intensity of production, the other factor that affects the employment potential is the terms of trade. Higher terms of trade will raise the marginal value product of labor, and thereby create greater opportunities for increasing the quality and quantity of employment. Much of the woe in sub-Saharan Africa in the recent decades stems from the fact that the primary commodities in which it has comparative advantage are experiencing sharp and sustained reduction in their terms of trade. This makes it difficult for the working poor engaged in the production of these commodities to raise their income either through greater employment or through higher returns to labor.

Internal—that is to say, intersectoral—terms of trade may also be important. The experience of China in the postreform period is especially relevant here. China has maintained a very high growth rate ever since it launched market-oriented reforms in the late 1970s, but its record of poverty reduction has varied enormously. Rural poverty was reduced sharply in the period immediately following the reforms, but since the mid-1980s there has been very little reduction (and probably even some increase in poverty for a while) despite rapid growth. This asymmetrical performance has much to do with the behavior of the terms of trade of farm products, in the production of which the majority of China's rural poor are employed. The terms of trade increased sharply up to the mid-1980s, and fell sharply thereafter. The rate of poverty reduction followed the same pattern, while rapid growth of the overall economy continued unabated (Khan and Riskin 2001).

The Integrability Factor

Rapid growth and high elasticity of the employment potential can together ensure that economic activities create greater opportunities for workers to increase their income through a combination of greater employment and higher returns to labor. However, "workers" does not necessarily mean "poor workers," and opportunities are not necessarily seized. So even a combination of rapid growth and high elasticity does not guarantee a rapid rate of poverty reduction. If the new opportunities are such that the capabilities they demand do not match the capabilities of the poor, then either nonpoor workers will seize the opportunities or perhaps the opportunities will not be seized at all. Much, therefore, depends on the correspondence between the structure of opportunities that are opened up and the structure of capabilities possessed by the poor. The integrability factor refers to the degree of this correspondence. The greater the degree of correspondence, the more extensively will the poor be able to integrate into the processes of economic expansion and the faster will be the rate of poverty reduction for any given rate of growth.

There are a variety of reasons, however, why the poor may not be able to integrate fully into economic processes so as to take advantage of any expansion in employment potential created by economic growth. One extreme case is illustrated by some recent nutrition-based theories of unemployment and underemployment. The problem stems from the physiological fact that every individual has to incur a "fixed cost" of energy expenditure simply to maintain the body (at rest) before incurring any additional energy expenditure for doing physical work. For an individual who does not have an alternative means of meeting the fixed cost—for example, an assetless laborer—the energy value of the returns to labor will have to be large enough to cover both the fixed cost and the variable cost associated with work. The sum of fixed and variable energy costs will then represent his or her reservation wage, below which he or she would not work. However, those with some asset income might be willing to work for a lower wage, since a part of the fixed cost will be met by other means. As a result, in a competitive labor market, the assetless laborers will be priced out by those who have some assets and will suffer from unemployment (Dasgupta 1993). By the same token, those who have fewer assets may be priced out by those who have more. To put it differently, the poorest among the poor may not be able to integrate into economic processes because of competition from the less poor, or perhaps from the nonpoor as well, even in the face of an overall expansion in the employment potential.

The lack of integrability may also result from market failures, especially the failure of the credit market. It is well-known that because of informational asymmetries the formal credit market often tends to resort to credit rationing in such a way that the poor, because of their lack of assets, are left out or are at least severely discriminated against. The poor entrepreneurs are then compelled to turn to monopolistic informal moneylenders. But the exorbitant rates of interest they charge may render it impossible to expand the business even if there is an overall expansion of economic opportunities. Similarly, poor infrastructure, lack of information, market thinness, and other problems of living in remote areas may make the transaction costs so prohibitive that the poor entrepreneurs of those areas may not find it worthwhile to expand business or to undertake new business activities even if new opportunities open up in the overall economy.[15]

Labor market institutions may also play an important role by creating an insider-outsider problem. Certain types of labor laws and practices of collective bargaining may create such an asymmetry of power between insiders (i.e., those already employed in the organized sector) and outsiders (i.e., those seeking entry into the organized sector) that the insiders may be able to effectively prevent the outsiders from gaining entry (Lindbeck and Snower 1989). In that case, the outsiders will find it hard to integrate into the mainstream of economic expansion. The benefit of expansion will then accrue largely to the insiders in the form of higher returns to labor, leaving little direct benefit for the outsiders. To the extent that the outsiders are likely to be poorer than the insiders, this will be detrimental to the cause of poverty reduction.[16]

Another source of limited integrability lies in a possible mismatch of skills—between the skills demanded by the expanding sectors and the skills possessed by the poor. A case in point is the current experience of many Latin

American countries. As these countries try to open up their economies, they find that, unlike the countries in East and Southeast Asia that had opened up their economies earlier, their comparative advantage does not lie in the activities that are intensive in relatively unskilled labor. The emergence of poor and populous countries such as China and India on the global scene has ensured that Latin America will not be able to compete in these types of products. Instead, it is in the relatively skill-intensive activities that most of the Latin American countries find their comparative advantage (Wood 1997). The opening up of these economies has therefore led predictably to an expansion of these skill-intensive activities, but the poor have benefited little from this expansion so far, as they do not possess the skills that are needed by the expanding sectors.[17]

A rather different kind of mismatch relates to the gender dimension of the integrability problem. The types of jobs for which demand rises may be culturally defined as men's jobs, whereas poverty may be concentrated mostly among women. This problem is especially relevant in much of Africa, where crop production has acquired a gendered pattern—with many cash crops being identified as men's crops and subsistence food crops being identified as women's crops. Trade liberalization and greater commercialization of agriculture may boost the employment potential in cash crop production, but to the extent that a gendered pattern of crop production remains a constraint, poor women will find it hard to take advantage of the new opportunities.

Yet another problem that creates difficulty for women in their efforts to integrate into economic processes is the time constraint. Poor labor-abundant economies may have a comparative advantage in labor-intensive activities; and if market distortions are removed, then such activities may indeed flourish, but many poor women may not be able to take advantage of these opportunities. There is a direct conflict between the demands of labor-intensive activities and the severe time constraint faced by poor women as they try to combine productive and reproductive activities within the household.

The preceding discussion of the integrability factor is by no means comprehensive, nor is it being suggested that the impediments that cause the integrability problem are identical in all cases. On the contrary, the nature of the problem is very likely to be context-specific. To identify the most important impediments in a specific context is an essential prerequisite of formulating a pro-poor growth strategy.

■ Some Suggested Topics for Future Research

Building on the analytic framework developed above, this section suggests some areas of future research that would pay rich dividends both in creating a better understanding of the linkage between growth and poverty and in helping to formulate policies that seek to maximize the effect of growth on poverty.

Growth and Poverty Reduction:
Explaining the Variety of Experience

One of the most obvious areas of future research emerging from the notion of the employment nexus is investigation of the observed fact that there is no invariant relationship between the rate of growth and the rate of poverty reduction. Rapid growth can be associated with both rapid and slow rates of poverty reduction, just as slow growth can be associated with both slow and at least moderate if not rapid rate of poverty reduction.[18] Four different kinds of growth-poverty episodes may be identified, referring to specific countries during specific periods of time:

1. Rapid growth with rapid poverty reduction.
2. Rapid growth with slow poverty reduction.
3. Slow growth with rapid poverty reduction.
4. Slow growth with slow poverty reduction.

An important research question concerns what lies behind this variable relationship between growth and poverty. A typical way of answering this question is to refer to changes in income distribution. It is thus commonplace to say that growth has failed to have a large effect on poverty in a particular case because income distribution has worsened (Thailand in recent years is a typical example), or the other side of the coin, that growth has succeeded in reducing poverty fast because income distribution didn't worsen (China in the early phase of its economic reform is a typical example). Statements such as these are true in an accounting sense, but not very helpful in understanding the causal relationships. The problem is that the rate of growth, the rate of poverty reduction, and changes in income distribution are all endogenous variables of a growth process. They are all simultaneously determined by the initial conditions and exogenous variables affecting the growth process within a period of time. In other words, they are all outcomes of the same process; neither of them causally determines the others. Therefore, in order to understand the causal processes underlying the relationship between growth and poverty, it is not very illuminating to refer to changes in income distribution as the explanation. Causal explanations must be found in the initial conditions and exogenous variables.

Three general types of hypothesis can be advanced as explanation. The first hypothesis is based on the statistical properties of the initial distribution of income. It is well-known that the rate of poverty reduction, as it is usually measured by the observed change in the headcount ratio, can be very sensitive to the nature of income distribution around the poverty line. If density is very high just below the poverty line (i.e., if a disproportionately large number of poor people are concentrated just below the poverty line), then even a small growth in the per capita income of the poor may lead to a very large reduction in poverty.[19] If, by contrast, density just below the poverty line is low (i.e., if a disproportionately large number of poor people are located well below the poverty line), then a similar increase in per capita income of the poor will be seen to result in a much lower reduction in poverty. Similar rates of growth can thus be associated with varying rates of poverty reduction.

The second hypothesis refers to targeted antipoverty programs operating as exogenous variables affecting the growth process. Different levels of emphasis given to such programs can lead to variable relationships between the rate of growth and the rate of poverty reduction, other things remaining the same. It is indeed conceivable that if antipoverty programs such as direct redistribution of food or cash and special employment creation programs for the poor are undertaken on a large enough scale, then even slow or moderate growth can go hand in hand with rapid rate of poverty reduction, at least for a while.

The third hypothesis rests on the idea of the employment nexus explored in this chapter. This hypothesis suggests that any given rate of growth can have variable impact on the rate of poverty reduction depending on variation in the elasticity and integrability factors. For any given rate of growth, what determines the rate of poverty reduction is the degree to which the employment potential responds to economic growth (elasticity) and the extent to which the poor are equipped to integrate into the expanding activities (integrability). Thus, according to this hypothesis, the explanation for the variable relationship between the rates of growth and poverty reduction lies in the nature of the growth process itself, as determined by the whole gamut of economic policies and the structural features of the economy, not just in a few targeted actions directed toward the poor.

An important research agenda is to ascertain, in the first instance, which of these alternative hypotheses best explains the empirical facts. To the extent that the third hypothesis is found to have some explanatory power, the next objective would be to assess the relative importance of elasticity and integrability factors. It is not being suggested here that attempts should be made to actually quantify elasticity and integrability as specific numbers. Whether such quantification is at all possible is itself a moot issue, but the relevant point is that quantification is not necessary for the purpose at hand. Rather these concepts should be used as analytic devices with which to explore systematically certain related empirical phenomena. Thus in the context of elasticity, the task is to study the production structure in order to ascertain what has happened to labor intensity of production and the terms of trade—the prime determinants of elasticity. In the case of integrability, the task is to explore the barriers that the working poor might face when trying to integrate into the processes of economic expansion. The insights generated by these inquiries could lead to useful policy conclusions on how to enhance the poverty-reducing effect of growth in specific circumstances.

Globalization and the Poor

While closer integration with the world economy has been accompanied by rapid reduction of poverty in some developing countries (e.g., in parts of Asia), it is also true that the experience has been quite different in other countries (e.g., in parts of Africa and Latin America), where poverty has not declined and may even have increased. The experience of the latter group of countries has helped foster the view in some circles that globalization marginalizes the poorest economies of the world and increases the vulnerability of the poor. This view is hotly contested by many economists, whose theory predicts that globalization should generally be a favorable force for the poor. An important research agenda is to disentangle the arguments involved in this debate and to confront the competing arguments with empirical facts. It is arguable that the idea of employment nexus explored in this chapter can help shed some useful light on this debate, which has produced more heat than light so far.

Part of the reason for continued disagreement lies in the very notion of globalization, which has many dimensions—some economic, some political, some technological, and some cultural—and as such may mean different things to different people. But even when the term is defined narrowly to mean increasing economic integration among countries brought about by trade liberalization, technology transfer, and greater capital mobility, arguments continue to persist. There are those who argue that globalization is contributing to increasing economic disparities in the world by allowing some countries and some segments of the population to become ever richer while marginalizing the poorer countries and the poorer population groups. They tend to blame globalization itself for deepening poverty in parts of the world. Others contend that if some countries and some population groups have failed to benefit from globalization, the fault lies not in globalization itself but in the fact that they have not actually embraced globalization as fully as has the rest of the world.[20]

Those who claim that globalization will help the poor in developing countries typically rely on the argument that the forces of globalization will help promote growth as well as labor intensity in labor-abundant developing countries, both of which should be beneficial for the poor. The inference they draw from this argument is that if the poor are not actually gaining, it must be because globalization has not gone far enough.

While the hypothesis that globalization has not gone far enough in many countries is a plausible one, this is not the only plausible explanation of why the poor in some parts of the world might fail to benefit from globalization. In terms of the conceptual framework proposed in this chapter, it may be argued that while globalization may help the growth factor, the benefits may fail to accrue to the poor because of unfavorable elasticity and integrability factors.

The proponents of globalization tend to argue, of course, that by forcing open the erstwhile closed economies, globalization will move the economic structure of developing countries toward more labor-intensive methods of production. If true, this will ensure that globalization will improve the elasticity factor as well as growth. But it is by no means certain that opening up the economy will bring about greater labor intensity. There are a number of reasons for this. In the first place, while labor-abundant countries are indeed likely to move toward greater labor intensity, not all developing countries are labor-abundant; some are more properly described as land-abundant. Second, the scarcity of complementary nontraded inputs may lead to a situation where even a labor-abundant economy may not be able to move toward greater labor intensity. Besides, infrastructural bottlenecks and adverse movements in the terms of trade may inhibit the translation of potential increase in labor intensity into an actual increase.

For all these reasons, it is by no means ensured that the process of globalization will automatically enhance the elasticity factor in developing countries. Then there remains the further problem that the poor might face difficult integrability problems in gaining from the new opportunities opened up by globalization.

In short, where increasing integration with the world economy has not been associated with significant reduction of poverty (even after controlling for extraneous factors), three alternative hypotheses can be advanced to explain the phenomenon:

- Globalization has not proceeded far enough—that is, the problem lies with inadequate integration with the global economy.
- Globalization has failed to create a sufficient amount of productive employment opportunities for the poor—that is, the problem lies with the elasticity factor.
- The poor have not been able to take advantage of the opportunities opened up by the forces of globalization—that is, the problem lies with the integrability factor.

The proponents of globalization who recognize that poverty has not declined everywhere tend to emphasize the first possibility. But clearly the other two explanations are also possible. The opponents blame globalization itself for the accentuation and perpetuation of poverty. But they too need to recognize that the fault probably lies in the failure to improve the elasticity and integrability factors and that, if these factors can be improved, perhaps globalization will be good for the poor after all.

Obviously, the policy implications of these alternative hypotheses are radically different from each other. Yet in much of the current debate on globalization, strong policy conclusions are made without first trying to ascertain which hypothesis actually holds in a particular situation. It is therefore essential to determine which of the three possibilities (which are not mutually exclusive, however) is actually driving the relationship between globalization and poverty. This is essentially an empirical matter, and different forces might operate in different situations. The objective of the proposed research agenda is to test empirically the validity of the alternative hypothesis, recognizing that different hypotheses might hold under different circumstances.

For testing the first hypothesis, it will be necessary to use some indicators to measure the degree of globalization for individual countries. Researchers have already developed a number of such indicators of a country's integration into the global economy, which can be used for this purpose.

The second hypothesis suggests that globalization has worsened or at least not improved the employment potential for the poor—that is, the impact on elasticity has not been favorable. Testing this hypothesis will involve investigation of the impact of globalization on the labor intensity of production and the terms of trade.

The third hypothesis focuses on the integrability factor. Testing of this hypothesis will require investigation of the attributes and capabilities of the poor where globalization has failed to make a dent on poverty and then assessing the degree of correspondence between these capabilities and the opportunities opened up by globalization.

One possible methodology of testing the relative strength of the three hypotheses is to compare a set of countries where globalization has been accompanied by significant reduction in poverty with another set where the opposite has happened. An understanding of how these two sets of countries differ in terms of the degree of globalization, the impact of globalization on the elasticity factor, and the nature of the integrability problem will enhance the ability to make globalization work better for the poor.

Enabling the Poor to Integrate into the Growth Process

I have argued in this chapter that the main rationale for adopting an employment-focused strategy of poverty reduction is that rapid growth is no guarantee of rapid poverty reduction. While rapid growth, if sustained over a period of time, will almost certainly help reduce poverty, the rate at which poverty will be reduced depends not just on the rate of growth but also on the barriers faced by the poor while trying to integrate into the expanding activities—that is, the integrability factor.

The importance of this problem in the context of poverty reduction cannot be overemphasized. I have already argued that the extent to which economic growth will contribute to poverty reduction depends a great deal on the degree of integrability of the poor. It is also important to emphasize that this factor may have a bearing on the rate of growth itself.

To consider just one possibility, suppose a labor-abundant country opens up its economy, thereby creating an opportunity for moving the production structure toward greater labor intensity. But also suppose, not unrealistically, that the new labor-intensive activities require a certain minimum level of skills that are not in plentiful supply (because of, say, lack of education or health on the part of the poor)—a case of limited integrability. Producers will then be forced to switch to activities that require fewer workers with perhaps greater skill. And if the structure of the society is such that it allows a small number of well-educated and well-nourished workers to exist side by side with a large number of uneducated and malnourished ones, then the producers will have no difficulty in doing so. But this is a second-best option since such activities would rank below the most labor-intensive activities in the scale of comparative advantage. As a result of adopting the second-best option, however, economic efficiency will be sacrificed, and to that extent growth will fall short of its potential. Limited integrability can thus inhibit poverty reduction twice—by limiting the poverty-reducing impact of any given rate of growth and by reducing the rate of growth itself.[21]

Despite its undoubted importance, it is fair to say that of the three underlying factors that affect poverty—namely growth, elasticity, and integrability—it is the last that is understood the least. It is not that there is a lack of understanding, in theory, what kind of barriers could stand in the way of the poor benefiting from growth. In fact, a number of possible barriers have been identified here—for example, a nutrition-based barrier, the insider-outsider problem, market failures of various kinds, mismatch of skills, cultural stereotyping of occupations, women's struggle to combine productive and reproductive activities, and so on. The point, rather, is the empirical one that there is an insufficient understanding of which of the barriers act as the major constraint in different parts of the developing world. Since policies cannot possibly deal adequately with all the problems at the same time, it is necessary for the sake of efficient policy formulation to identify the constraints that dominate in particular circumstances. An important area for future research is to provide this kind of detailed empirical knowledge for different countries and regions of the developing world.

This is admittedly an ambitious task but well worth pursuing. Since integrability depends on the degree of correspondence between the structure of opportunities on the one hand and the structure of capabilities of the poor on the other, this task is informationally very demanding. Macro- and meso-level knowledge of the structure of production and the associated employment potential will have to be combined with micro-level information on the attributes and capabilities of the poor.

For the micro-level information on the poor, recourse will have to be taken to various household-level surveys of income, expenditure, and employment. Fortunately, many household-level surveys of national coverage already exist in different parts of the world, thanks largely to the efforts of the UNDP and the World Bank. Many more surveys of more limited (and yet representative) coverage also exist—for example, those conducted by the International Food Policy Research Institute and the International Rice Research Institute as well as by various national research institutions. The research project will have to draw upon this rich source of information as much as possible.

The immediate objective of the exercise will be to clarify the empirical picture regarding the binding constraints on integrability in different parts of the developing world. In identifying these constraints, the research program should pay special attention to the constraints faced by poor women. Cultural stereotyping of occupations, time constraints imposed by the burden of combining productive and reproductive activities, and discrimination in various spheres of life render the integrability problem especially severe for poor women.[22]

The other, related, objective would be to study how some countries have been able to improve the integrability factor more successfully than others and to draw policy lessons from this comparative analysis. As an example of such comparative analysis, reference is often made to the greater success of the East Asian and Southeast Asian economies in improving the education and health status of their people relative to the rest of the developing world.[23] These experiences confirm that the emphasis on human development given in recent years by the UNDP and others is justified not only because human development is a worthy goal in itself but also because it can play an important instrumental role in promoting improvements in material living standards. However, as noted above, education and health are not the only variables that have a bearing on the integrability factor. There are many more, but very little is known about the comparative success in dealing with them. A more comprehensive analysis will help identify the strategic policy interventions that might be fruitfully employed in the less successful countries and regions. This type of knowledge is essential for making the employment nexus an effective tool for poverty reduction.

■ Conclusion

The analysis presented in this chapter started from the empirical observation that there is no invariant relationship between the rate of growth and the rate of poverty reduction. It has sought to explain why it is that the same rate of growth in per capita income is not always associated with the same rate of poverty reduction. One possible answer is that the poverty alleviation effect of redistributive measures or direct employment creation programs (such as food for work) makes a difference. The analysis here offers an alternative (but not mutually exclusive) hypothesis—namely that the difference is made by variations in the elasticity factor (i.e., the extent to which the quality and quantity of employment respond to growth) and the integrability factor (i.e., the ability of the poor to take up the opportunities for productive employment created by the growth process). From a policy perspective, it is important to know which hypothesis is empirically the more relevant one.

The present analysis also provides the rationale for adopting an approach to poverty reduction that is not single-mindedly obsessed with growth but does pay due regard to it. This alternative and in a sense more comprehensive approach will also pay due regard to the elasticity and integrability factors. Since these last two factors form the core of the employment nexus between growth and poverty reduction, this comprehensive approach may reasonably be described as the employment-focused strategy for poverty reduction.

It is worth emphasizing that the proposed framework is also comprehensive in a somewhat different sense. Although I have described it as an employment-focused approach, its relevance is not confined merely to those who are currently unemployed and seeking employment opportunities. It is also relevant to those who are currently working but poor, and to the new entrants to the labor force. Indeed, one of the strengths of the proposed framework is that a single analytic framework can be used to address the concerns of the unemployed (except the Keynesian variety), the working poor, and the new entrants to the labor force. For all these categories of people, the proximate determinants of income are the quantity and quality of employment opportunities open to them, which in turn depend on the same three underlying factors—namely growth, elasticity, and integrability. A pro-poor growth strategy must focus on all three factors, while recognizing that the relative importance of the three factors might vary from case to case.

▨ Notes

1. For comprehensive reviews of this literature, see, among other sources, Osmani 2000 and Srinivasan 2001.

2. Defined as percentage change in the rate of poverty for 1 percent growth in per capita income during a specified period of time.

3. See, for instance, a recent review of experiences in some Asian countries in Osmani 2004.

4. A part of the explanation may lie in the statistical properties of the income distribution in question. If there is a large concentration of the poor just below the poverty line, the rate of poverty will be more responsive to growth, other things remaining the same. But surely a large part of the explanation lies in the nature of the growth process, which is the object of study in this chapter.

5. Employment may be relevant for the social-provisioning channel as well, because in some cases a person's eligibility to claim social provisioning may depend on whether or not he or she has a job—for instance, when free or subsidized health and education services are provided by the employer.

6. For a pioneering attempt to estimate the number of the working poor in the developing world, see Majid 2001.

7. Work sharing implies that the size of the work force can be expanded while adding little to total production, while income sharing ensures that the same total output or income is distributed among more workers, thereby reducing everyone's individual income and in the extreme case pulling everyone below the poverty line. See Nurkse 1953 and Lewis 1954.

8. It should be noted that these are meant to be analytic categories, not empirical categories in which individual workers can be neatly fitted, because in practice a single worker may suffer from more than one reason for low returns to labor.

9. Strictly speaking, the quality of employment refers not just to the returns to labor but also to a host of other attributes of work that are subsumed under the notion of labor standards—namely protection against unfair dismissal, health and safety standards at the workplace, the length of the working day, the power of the workers to organize and to bargain collectively with the employers, the scope of the workers to take part in the decisionmaking processes, and so on. In this comprehensive sense, what the workers need is what the ILO describes as "decent work." The analysis here, however, abstracts from the broader dimensions of decent work, and focuses exclusively on employment and returns to labor, because a rather different framework of analysis would be needed to address those broader issues.

10. Similar ideas are also discussed in Khan 2001b, a revised version of which appears as Chapter 4 of this volume.

11. Note that I am referring here to the growth of potential output, as distinct from actual output. The reason for this lies in the methodological quest for identifying the underlying exogenous factors that determine poverty—that is, the factors that affect poverty but that are not themselves affected by it. As will be shown later, the growth of actual output is not an exogenous factor in this sense, because it may well depend to some extent on the rate of poverty reduction.

12. The latter being defined as the curve that shows, for different amounts of self-employed labor, the net value added (after deducting, from the gross value added, the wages paid to hired workers) divided by the amount of self-employed labor.

13. See Heckscher 1991 and Ohlin 1991.

14. For evidence of the diverse effects of trade liberalization on manufacturing employment, see Ghose 2000.

15. It is conceivable that in both cases of market failure mentioned here—namely credit market imperfections and high transaction costs of living in remote areas—poor entrepreneurs will find it worthwhile to expand business provided the shift in the marginal value productivity curve of labor is sufficiently large to offset the additional costs. This implies the existence of a threshold effect—this is to say, integrability will remain a problem unless the expansion in employment potential is large enough to cross a minimum threshold.

16. It must be noted, however, that if the incentives provided to the insiders can be designed so as to increase their productivity—for example, by paying them efficiency wages or by improving their working environment—then the spillover effect of higher productivity may indirectly benefit the poor outsiders. These indirect benefits must be weighed against the direct cost to the outsiders when considering the desirability of labor laws and practices that strengthen the hand of the insiders.

17. The resulting phenomenon of widening wage differentials between skilled and unskilled workers has been analyzed in Behrman, Birdsall, and Szekely 2000.

18. The variety of experience from around the developing world has been analyzed in Khan 2001b.

19. Very steep decline in poverty observed in Vietnam in the 1990s has been attributed partly to this phenomenon, although the nature of the growth process, characterized by a very high rate of growth, no doubt played a large role as well (Poverty Working Group 1999).

20. For accessible presentation of some of the arguments in this debate, see Department for International Development 2002 and World Bank 2002c.

21. It is for this reason that the actual rate of growth, as distinct from the potential rate of growth, was described as an endogenous variable earlier in the chapter.

22. The specific disadvantages faced by poor women are discussed in, among other sources, Division for the Advancement of Women and United Nations 1999, 2001; and World Bank 2001a.

23. For a review of the Asian experience from the employment perspective, see Islam 2001.

3

The Nexus of Economic Growth, Employment, and Poverty Reduction: An Empirical Analysis

Rizwanul Islam

The experiences of countries that have succeeded in reducing poverty significantly indicate the importance of sustained high growth in achieving this result. However, studies on poverty are replete with an equally important finding that high growth alone is not adequate; the pattern and sources of growth as well as the manner in which its benefits are distributed are extremely important from the point of view of achieving the goal of poverty reduction. And in that regard, the importance of employment as the key link between growth and poverty alleviation is often pointed out. While this proposition has strong intuitive appeal, there is some scattered empirical support for it too. For example, a comparison between the experience of precrisis East and Southeast Asia on the one hand and that of South Asia on the other clearly shows much higher employment elasticity of economic growth in the former, where the record of poverty reduction was also much more impressive (Islam 2001). This kind of evidence, however, needs to be compiled and analyzed more systematically in order to make a case for an employment-intensive growth strategy as a means of making economic growth more pro-poor. In other words, the nexus of economic growth, employment, and poverty alleviation needs to be fully articulated and empirically substantiated. While this would involve some analytic work, a good deal of empirical work is required to monitor the labor market outcomes from the perspective of raising the incomes of poor households, and to identify policies, programs, and interventions that could have a positive, poverty-alleviating impact on such outcomes.

The kind of work mentioned above is especially important because a large number of developing countries are currently engaged in formulating poverty reduction strategies, and yet policies for using employment as a route out of poverty are not often integrated into such strategies. Likewise, the Millennium Development Goals relating to poverty reduction do not explicitly mention employment as a means for achieving them. But given the challenge ahead, it will be necessary to mobilize and effectively employ all possible mechanisms for achieving those goals. Employment could be critical in that respect.

It is against the above background that this chapter undertakes an empirical analysis—based on cross-country data—of the nexus of economic growth, employment, and poverty reduction. The purpose behind this is to argue that for economic growth to be pro-poor, it has to be accompanied by employment growth with rising productivity. The chapter starts by providing a brief overview of the literature on the growth-poverty linkage, and pointing out a gap therein—in terms of the role of employment in that linkage. It next presents an analytic framework for examining the linkages among economic growth, employment, and poverty reduction,[1] followed by an empirical analysis of the linkage between poverty and employment-related variables, and then presentation of empirical evidence to argue that there is no invariant relationship between growth and poverty reduction, and that developments in employment and labor market are critical variables influencing the poverty-reducing outcome of growth.

■ The Linkage Between Economic Growth and Poverty Reduction: A Gap in the Literature

Analysis of the relationship between economic growth and poverty reduction has gone through various phases in the literature on development. For example, an important premise of the very early theories of development was that the benefits of economic growth would trickle down to the poor. Since then, questions have been raised on the assumption of an automatic link between growth and poverty reduction, and attempts have been made to understand the mechanisms through which the benefits of growth may get transmitted to the poor. Some of the latter categories of studies do also refer to the role of employment, and yet a rigorous analysis of the role of employment in the linkage between economic growth and poverty reduction appears to be missing.

Following on the Kuznets hypothesis (1955) of an inverted U shape of the relationship between economic growth and income inequality, Adelman and Morris 1973 was one of the earlier studies to question the automaticity of the relationship between economic growth and benefits to the poor. And then came the 1974 study by H. Chenery and colleagues, an influential contribution focusing on the importance of redistribution alongside economic growth.

Economic growth, however, came back to fashion once there were studies casting doubt on the suggestion that higher growth could be associated with increased poverty, and reasserting that growth, almost always, reduced poverty.[2] The 1980s witnessed renewed emphasis (especially on the part of the international development partners) on economic growth, but studies on growth contributing to poverty reduction have again come in good numbers during recent years.[3]

While growth has continued to occupy the center stage in development literature, there have been studies, especially in recent years, arguing that although growth is necessary for poverty reduction, it is not sufficient.[4] Some studies point out that the pattern of growth is important from the point of view of its effectiveness in reducing poverty (World Bank 1990b; Lipton and Ravallion 1995; Squire 1993; McKay 1997; Department for International Development 1997; Goudie and Ladd 1999). And while talking about the pattern of growth that could be more effective in reducing poverty, some studies mention explicitly the importance of labor-intensive growth (Department for International Development [DFID] 1997; International Labour Organization [ILO] 2003a).[5] However, none of these studies explicitly examine the employment nexus in the linkage between economic growth and poverty.[6] Lyn Squire, for example, recognizes that "economic growth that fosters the productive use of labor, the main asset owned by the poor, can generate rapid reductions in poverty" (1993, 381), and yet his empirical analysis does not include this aspect.

Thus in the literature on the linkage between economic growth and poverty reduction, there is an absence of analysis on the role of employment. Such analysis becomes particularly important in the current context, where the rate of poverty reduction needs to be accelerated and all possible means need to be found to make economic growth more pro-poor. In addressing this absence, this chapter makes an attempt to identify possible elements of pro-poor economic growth in terms of output growth coupled with growth of employment and rising productivity.[7]

◼ Linkages Among Output Growth, Employment, and Poverty: In Quest of Elements for Pro-Poor Growth

Conceptually, the linkages among output growth, employment, and poverty can be analyzed at both the macro and the micro level. At the macro level, the linkage between poverty, in its income dimension, and output growth can be conceptualized in terms of the average productivity of the employed work force, which in turn becomes reflected in low levels of real wages and low levels of earnings in self-employment. At the micro level of a household, the same linkage between poverty and employment operates through the type and low productivity of economic activities in which the earning members of a household are engaged, the low level of human capital of the members of the work force, the dependency burden that limits participation in the work force, and the mere availability of remunerative employment.

A low average productivity of the work force can be due to the deficiency of capital relative to labor and the use of backward technology. When high rates of economic growth lead to sustained increase in productive capacity, employment opportunities with rising productivity are generated. This in turn allows for a progressive absorption and integration of the unemployed and the underemployed into expanding economic activities with higher levels of productivity. In the process, the poor may be able to achieve higher productivity and increase their incomes in their existing occupations, or shift to new occupations involving higher-level skills and better technology. The results of this process could be reflected in improved productivity of various sectors and occupations; a shift in the structure of employment toward occupations with higher levels of productivity; and increases in real wages, earnings from self-employment, and earnings from wage employment.

Higher levels of earnings resulting from the process would enable workers to spend more on education and skill formation of their children, thus raising the productive capacity of the future work force and creating necessary conditions for achieving higher levels of economic growth. The process would thus complete the virtuous circle of economic growth leading to poverty reduction via growth of employment with rising productivity, and reduced poverty creating the possibility of further increases in productivity and higher rates of economic growth (see Figure 3.1). The kind of growth with such a virtuous circle in operation can be termed "pro-poor growth."

Figure 3.1   Virtuous Circle of Links Among Growth, Employment, and Poverty Reduction

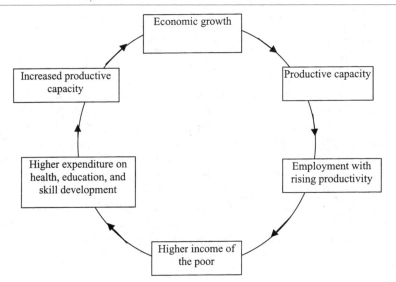

Indeed, the conceptual framework outlined above for analyzing the linkages among economic growth, employment, and poverty basically follows a demand-supply approach. The variables that are expected to influence incomes of the poor from the demand side include the employment intensity of growth, shifts in the employment structure toward higher productivity sectors, greater technology, creation of assets for the poor, and so on. From the supply side, an important factor is the ability of the poor to integrate into the process of economic growth and obtain access to the jobs that are created. Levels of education and skills of the work force are among the key variables that determine the ability of the poor to integrate into and benefit from the growth process.[8]

A summary indicator of the employment growth that is associated with a given output growth is provided by the growth of output elasticity of employment (for overall GDP, measured as the proportionate change in employment divided by the proportionate change in GDP during a given period). This implies that employment elasticity could be taken as a surrogate for the employment intensity of growth. But employment elasticity reflects the inverse of labor productivity. While an elasticity higher than unity implies a decline in productivity, an elasticity lower than unity means that employment expansion is taking place along with an increase in productivity. A rise in productivity would lead to a reduction in employment elasticity. Therefore, raising employment elasticity in individual activities cannot be the objective, as that would mean a further lowering of productivity in economies that may already be characterized by widespread low-productivity employment.

Two further questions need to be raised in the context of levels of, as well as changes in, employment elasticity. Regarding levels, the desirability of an elasticity that is lower than unity has been mentioned above. How much lower than unity it should be (i.e., the right order of magnitude for the elasticity of employment) depends on the level of development and the relative factor endowment of the country concerned. The magnitude would also have a good deal of sectoral variation. The overall elasticity being a weighted average of sectoral elasticities, greater allocation of investment in more labor-intensive sectors and higher growth rates in such sectors could yield a situation where the overall employment elasticity increases (even with declining elasticities in some sectors). And the result could be higher employment growth with given GDP growth or employment-intensive growth.

A simple illustration may be useful in indicating the magnitude of employment elasticity (and output growth) that may be desirable for an economy in order to quickly absorb its surplus labor. With a labor force growth of 2.5 percent per annum and an overall employment elasticity of 0.4, a GDP growth of 6 percent would be required merely to absorb the annual additions to the labor force. And in order to have an employment growth so as to enable the economy to absorb its backlog of the unemployed and surplus labor, the required GDP growth would be on the order of 7 percent. On the other hand, if this hypothetical economy could achieve a high growth of its more labor-intensive sectors (e.g., labor-intensive manufacturers, construction, and services), the overall employment elasticity could perhaps be raised (say, to 0.6), and a lower GDP growth (say, of 6 percent) could enable it to achieve the same objective (namely the absorption of surplus labor in modern sectors).

A few words about the estimation of employment elasticities may be in order. The overall employment intensity of growth should be measured by the GDP elasticity of employment: the proportionate change in employment divided by the proportionate change in GDP. However, it is very difficult to obtain reliable estimates of aggregate employment in many developing countries—particularly where there are large unorganized sectors for which estimates of employment at constant intensity of employment are difficult to come by. In such situations, it may be practical to focus on sectors (e.g., manufacturing industries) for which estimates of output and employment would be more reliable and more easily available. Of course, whenever possible, employment elasticities of other major sectors should be estimated in order to gauge the direction of the employment intensity of growth.

Regarding methodology of estimating the elasticities, it is important to note the availability of alternatives, ranging from the simple measurement of arc elasticity (i.e., using data from two points in time) to more rigorous econometric estimates. The choice of a particular method is often dictated by the availability of data. But whenever necessary time-series data are available, it would be advisable to use the econometric method in order to avoid problems caused by fluctuations in the data.

Even after employment elasticities are estimated, their links to poverty remain to be examined. In a cross-section study with data from a reasonable number of countries, it may be possible to examine such linkage. Doing this for a single country may not be so straightforward, especially if data on the incidence of poverty as well as estimates of employment elasticities are not available for an adequately long period of time. What should be possible, however, is to see if the level and direction of change in this statistic are appropriate from the point of view of its level of development, incidence of poverty, and existence of surplus labor. Such an analysis can be done against the benchmark of countries that are regarded as having demonstrated success in achieving employment-intensive pro-poor growth and in either abolishing poverty altogether or reducing it substantially.

The analysis of the summary indicator of the employment intensity of economic growth as indicated above would need to be supplemented by a more detailed examination of whether and how growth has led to structural changes in an economy that has benefited the poor. In that regard, the first important thing to examine would be the sectors and occupations where the poor are concentrated and the nature of the trends in productivity and earnings in various occupations. The second important task would be to examine whether there are discernible shifts in the structure of employment toward occupations with higher productivity. The third important element in the channel of transmission of benefits of growth to the poor would be real wages and earnings of wage-paid workers and real earnings of the self-employed. An examination of the linkage between real wages and productivity would enable one to examine whether the benefit of growth had reached the poor.

Just as the above discussion focuses basically on a macro-level analysis of how economic growth could contribute to poverty reduction through increases in employment in higher-productivity sectors and occupations and a rise in real wages, a similar analysis could be carried out at the micro (household) level to examine the impact of employment and labor market variables on poverty. Conceptually, it is possible to think of a number of such variables that could influence the probability of a household being poor in terms of inadequate income. The variables could be asset related (e.g., the possession of income-generating assets), human capital related (e.g., education and skill levels of the working members of a household), or employment related (e.g., the sector and quantity of employment of the workers, wages, productivity, etc.). Once necessary data are available for quantifying variables of the kind mentioned above and for identifying whether a particular household belongs to the poor or non-poor category, standard econometric methods (e.g., the estimation of a Probit model) can be applied to examine the influence of employment and labor market variables on the probability of a household being poor.

In the above discussion, pro-poor growth is conceptualized in terms of the employment outcome of growth, with employment serving as the link between growth and poverty reduction. However, a critical element in this link is the income of the poor resulting from growth and employment. Hence pro-poor growth can also be conceptualized in terms of the share of the poor in the additional output that is produced. Based on this criterion, growth can be characterized as pro-poor only when the share of the poor in the additional output increases, or in other words, when the distribution of income improves. Of course, it is possible for the income of the poor to increase (and the incidence of poverty to decline) even when the distribution of income does not change or worsens. But the poverty-reducing effect of economic growth in such cases would be lower than in the case of growth with improved income distribution (i.e., lower inequality).

Employment and Poverty: A Cross-Country Empirical Analysis

Methodology

Based on the analytic framework presented above, a number of testable relationships can be derived in order to examine the influence of employment-related variables on poverty or changes in its incidence. First, in order to examine the importance of employment intensity of growth in reducing poverty, employment elasticity can be used as an explanatory variable along with GDP growth. However, for many countries it is not easy to obtain estimates of employment elasticity for the major sectors. Therefore, employment elasticity in manufacturing has been used as an explanatory variable along with GDP growth to explain the variation in annual change in the incidence of poverty (using a headcount measure). In other words, an attempt has been made to estimate the following function by using cross-country data:

$$ACPI = F\ (GDPG,\ EETY) \tag{1}$$

where

> $ACPI$ = annual change in the incidence of poverty
> $GDPG$ = GDP growth
> $EETY$ = employment elasticity with respect to output

If the initial level of poverty is included as an explanatory variable,[9] a second formulation would be:

$$ACPI = F\ (GDPG,\ EETY,\ IPOV) \tag{2}$$

where

> $IPOV$ = initial level of poverty

As mentioned above, improvements in productivity and increases in real wages and earnings from self-employment are important explanatory variables. But it is not easy to generate the data required to quantify all these variables (especially earnings from self-employment) at the country level. Assuming that data on wage trends in major sectors (e.g., agriculture and manufacturing) are available and that movements in real wages will reflect changes in labor productivity, a third regression model that can be postulated is:

$$ACPI = F\ (GDPG,\ EETY,\ IPOV,\ GAGW,\ GMNW) \tag{3}$$

where

> $GAGW$ = growth in real wages in agriculture
> $GMNW$ = growth in real wages in manufacturing

Cross-country data have also been used to test the hypothesis concerning the impact of employment and labor market variables on the incidence of poverty. Although it is not easy to define such variables at the macro level exactly in the same way as can be done at the household level, an attempt has been made to identify several variables, at least in surrogate form. Since employment in nonfarm activities is found to influence the income of the poor, employment in agriculture and manufacturing has been used as explanatory variables. Likewise, a dependency ratio has been used as an indicator of the extent of labor force participation. Level of education and skill of the work force are hypothesized as exerting a positive impact on the income of the poor. However, at the macro level it is not easy to define this variable, and hence a surrogate in the form of adult literacy rate has been used as an indicator of the education variable. The postulated model is thus:

$$POV = \text{F } (EAG, EMA, EDU, DEP) \tag{4}$$

where

POV = headcount measure of poverty
EAG = percentage of work force employed in agriculture
EMA = percentage of work force employed in manufacturing
EDU = adult literacy rate (as percentage)
DEP = dependency ratio

Estimating a model of the kind mentioned above can involve problems, especially if the independent variables are correlated. And that is actually the case here, especially with employment in manufacturing, education, and dependency rate. In such a situation, results obtained from an ordinary least squares (OLS) regression would need to be interpreted carefully.

As mentioned above, the poverty-reducing effect of economic growth can also be affected by the degree of inequality in the distribution of income. This can be tested by regressing the incidence of poverty on per capita income and the index of income inequality. However, for many countries, instead of income distribution, data are available for expenditure distribution. In order to allow for differences in Gini coefficients based on income and expenditure distribution, the use of a dummy variable would be in order. The regression model would thus be:

$$POV = \text{F } (GPC, GIN, D) \tag{5}$$

where

POV = headcount measure of poverty
GPC = GDP per capita
GIN = Gini coefficient of income or expenditure distribution

D = dummy variable with a value of 0 for expenditure Gini and 1 for income Gini

Results

It was possible to compile figures on employment elasticities and poverty incidence for roughly similar periods for twenty-three countries (see Table 3.4). Figure 3.2 shows a scatter of the data. Although the sample is not large, it was possible to use this dataset to run OLS regression for estimating equations 1 and 2. The following results were obtained:

(1) $ACPI = -2.04 + 0.42\ GDPG^* + 1.18\ EETY^{**}$
$\qquad\qquad\quad (2.71)\qquad\quad (1.91)$

where

$R^2 = 0.27$
$F\ (2,20) = 5.08$
* = significance at the 99 percent level
** = significance at the 95 percent level
figures within parentheses represent values of the t-statistic

(2) $ACPI = -5.20 + 0.53\ GDPG^* + 1.33\ EETY^{**} + 0.07\ IPOV^*$
$\qquad\qquad\quad (3.72)\qquad\quad (2.45)\qquad\quad (2.72)$

where

$R^2 = 0.45$
$F\ (3,19) = 6.95$
* = significance at the 99 percent level
** = significance at the 95 percent level
figures within parentheses represent values of the t-statistic

It is clear from the results that the model involving GDP growth and employment elasticity as explanatory variables for annual change in poverty incidence performs quite well in terms of the sign and level of significance of the variables as well as the strength of the overall relationship.[10] Where it does not perform so well is in terms of the percentage of variation explained by the two selected variables. This is not surprising, because in the analytic framework outlined previously, it is the overall employment intensity of growth of an economy that is expected to influence change in poverty, but in estimating the regression model only employment elasticity for manufacturing could be

Figure 3.2   Percentage Decline in Poverty and Manufacturing Employment Elasticity

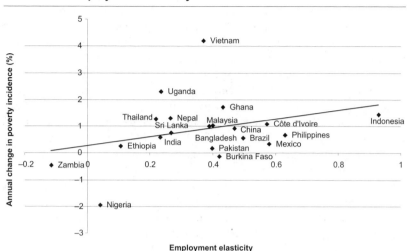

used. The fact that the coefficient of this variable has the right sign and is statistically significant despite its limitation as an indicator of overall employment intensity should be taken as support for the hypothesis of employment intensity of growth influencing the rate of poverty reduction.

It was difficult to estimate equation 3 given the difficulties in quantifying the real wage variables for all twenty-three countries for which estimates of both employment elasticity and poverty were available. Data on changes in manufacturing wages could be obtained for fifteen of these countries, and the following regression equation was estimated:

$$(3) \quad ACPI = -3.65 + 0.24 \; GDPG + 1.3.8 \; EETY^* + 0.04 \; IPOV$$
$$\quad\quad\quad (1.50) \quad\quad (4.15) \quad\quad\quad (1.13)$$
$$+ 0.18 \; MNWG^*$$
$$(2.43)$$

where

adjusted $R^2 = 0.67$
$F\,(4.10) = 7.96$
* = significance at the 99 percent level
figures within parentheses represent values of the t-statistic

It has been possible to estimate the model (equation 3) involving various employment and labor market variables using data on a larger number of countries than was the case for equations 1 and 2. The results are presented in tabular form in Table 3.1. As mentioned already, estimation of this model by OLS method faced the familiar economic problem of multicollinearity—especially as some of the variables, namely employment in manufacturing, education, and dependency, were correlated with each other.[11] Regressions were therefore run separately with each of the explanatory variables to examine their significance and explanatory power. All of them showed the right signs and had statistically significant coefficients. In fact, dependency ratio by itself explains over 50 percent of the variation in poverty incidence. Likewise, employment in agriculture and education also explain—individually—over 40 percent of the variation in poverty. When the complete model was estimated, all the variables (except employment in manufacturing) had the right sign, but only dependency ratio emerged as statistically significant. Comparison of this with the results obtained by running simple regressions raises the suspicion that the problem of multicollinearity is masking the combined effect of the selected variables in the multiple regression model.

Table 3.1   Results of Regression Exercise with Incidence of Poverty as Dependent Variable

	Specification							
	(i)	(ii)	(iii)	(iv)	(v)	(vi)	(vii)	(viii)
Independent variables								
EAG	0.43			0.12		0.38	0.07	
	(5.34)			(0.98)		(3.42)	(0.57)	
EMA		−1.84				0.30	−0.35	−0.15
		(−3.17)				(0.05)	(−0.53)	(−0.25)
EDU			−0.53		−0.20	−0.25		−0.21
			(−5.23)		(−1.26)	(−1.81)		(−1.31)
DEP				90.29	56.19	68.92		65.95
				(6.75)	(2.60)	(3.12)		(2.88)
Adjusted R^2	0.42	0.2	0.42	0.54	0.57	0.59	0.39	0.58
N	39	37	38	35	37	35	37	35

Notes: Incidence of poverty is defined as the percentage of population below the dollar-a-day poverty line. The data used in the regression are presented in Table 3.5. Figures in parentheses represent values of the respective *t*-statistic.

Based on the regression results mentioned above, the hypothesis of the impact of employment and labor market variables on poverty reduction seems to remain strong. It can be broken down into several components: concentration of workers in agriculture causes poverty; a shift of workers to manufacturing reduces poverty; education of the work force (or population as a whole) contributes to poverty reduction; and a higher dependency burden causes poverty.

Econometric exercises based on household survey data in several countries (namely Bangladesh, Bolivia, Ethiopia, India, and Vietnam) provide stronger support to the hypothesis mentioned above. Apart from asset-related variables, employment and labor market variables (e.g., the sector of employment, diversification of the sources of income, receipt of remittance income, dependency ratio, and education of the work force) are significant in explaining either the probability of a household being poor or the actual income of the poor households.[12]

For the purpose of estimating equation 4—that is, to examine how the degree of income inequality affects the poverty-reducing effect of economic growth—a poverty measure based on a dollar-a-day poverty line, GDP per capita measured in purchasing power parity (PPP) and Gini coefficient of income or expenditure distribution have been used. All these figures were taken from the World Bank's *World Development Indicators 2003* (World Bank 2003e). The result obtained was:

(4) $\ln POV = 7.24 - 0.66 \ln GPC^* + 2.17 \ln GIN^{***} - 0.37D$
$\qquad\qquad\quad (4.25)\qquad\quad (1.76)\qquad\qquad (1.30)$

where

adjusted $R^2 = 0.50$
$F (3,40) = 14.31$
$N = 41$
$*$ = significance at the 99 percent level
$***$ = significance at the 90 percent level
figures within parentheses represent values of the t-statistic

It is clear from the estimated regression that the degree of inequality has a statistically significant influence on the incidence of poverty. The positive sign associated with the inequality variable indicates that an increase in inequality leads to an increase in the incidence of poverty. In other words, an increase in inequality can counteract the poverty-reducing effect of an increase in per capita income. The coefficient of the dummy variable turned out to be statistically insignificant—thus implying that the impact of the distribution variable is not sensitive to the measure employed (i.e., income or expenditure).

■ Economic Growth, Employment, and Poverty: Some Insights on Pro-Poor Growth from Selected Country Experiences

Different Combinations of Growth and Poverty Reduction

A sustained high rate of economic growth is by now widely recognized as a necessary condition for poverty reduction. However, it is possible to demonstrate empirically that there is no invariant relationship between the rate of economic growth and the rate of poverty reduction. The poverty-reducing impact of growth depends on a variety of factors that characterize the pattern of growth. As mentioned previously, an important factor is the degree of employment intensity of the growth process, while another is the ability of the poor to benefit from the employment opportunities that are created.[13] Relevance of these two broad sets of factors for poverty reduction has already been demonstrated above. Given the importance of such factors in poverty reduction, it is quite possible to see in reality different experiences of growth and poverty reduction. While on the one hand high rates of growth can be accompanied by moderate or slow rates of poverty reduction, it is also possible to have rapid rates of poverty reduction with moderate rates of growth—if the pattern of growth is sufficiently employment-intensive and the poor can readily integrate into the growth process and benefit from the income-earning opportunities that open up.

Using data from in-depth studies of employment-poverty growth linkages in seven countries,[14] six different combinations of growth and poverty have been identified[15] (see Tables 3.2 and 3.3). High growth leading to rapid rates of poverty reduction is only one of these six combinations. What is also interesting is that the same country can have different growth-poverty outcomes in different periods—depending on the nature of policies pursued. For example, in Indonesia during the 1970s and the 1980s, high growth was associated with high rates of poverty reduction; but the rate of poverty reduction slowed down during the 1990s, although output growth rates remained high. In India, high growth during the 1990s was associated with a slow rate of poverty reduction in rural areas and a moderate rate of poverty reduction in urban areas. Given the problems involved in comparing data from different surveys in India, it is difficult to arrive at a definite conclusion as to whether higher GDP growth produced better results in poverty reduction during the 1990s compared to the earlier decade. K. Sundaram and S. Tendulkar (2002), for example, conclude that the rate of poverty reduction during the 1990s was faster than during the 1980s. Using an alternative approach for producing comparable estimates, G. Datt, Valerie Kozel, and Martin Ravallion arrive at a differ-

Table 3.2   Varying Rates of GDP Growth and Poverty Reduction: Some Examples

Rate of GDP Growth	Rate of Poverty Reduction		
	High	Moderate	Low
High	Indonesia (1970s and 1980s) Vietnam (1990s) Uganda (1990s)	India (1990s)[a] India (1990s—urban)[c]	India (1990s)[b] India (1990s—rural)[c] Indonesia (1990s)
Medium	Bolivia (1990s)	Bangladesh (1991–1996)	Ethiopia (1990s) Bangladesh (1996–2000) India (1980s)[a]

Sources: Country studies in this volume.
a. Based on Sundaram and Tendulkar 2002.
b. Based on Datt, Kozel, and Ravallion 2003.
c. Based on Deaton 2003.

Notes: The cutoff points used here to categorize countries by high and medium growth, and various rates of poverty reduction, are rather arbitrary. An annual GDP growth of 6 percent and above is here regarded as high. For poverty reduction, the following cutoff points are used: high = 2 percentage points and above per annum; moderate = 1–2 percentage points per annum; low = less than 1 percentage point per annum.

ent conclusion; according to them, the rate of poverty reduction during the 1990s was "slightly lower than India experienced during the 1980s" (2003, 360). A. Deaton and Jean Dreze regard the decline of poverty in the 1990s "as an example of *continued progress*"; they conclude that "there is, at any rate, no obvious pattern of 'acceleration' or 'slowdown' in this respect" (2002, 3743, emphasis in original). The literature on poverty in India thus does not indicate any consensus on whether higher GDP growth during the 1990s was associated with a faster rate of poverty reduction compared to the 1980s. The answer seems to depend on how the rate of progress is measured.

Bangladesh experienced a decline in the annual rate of poverty reduction from 1995–1996 to 2000, compared to the period of 1991–1992 to 1995–1996, although the rate of economic growth was higher during 1996–2001, compared to 1991–1996. Ethiopia provides another example of moderate growth producing very little reduction in poverty.

Good Growth

An understanding of the different growth-poverty combinations as mentioned above requires an in-depth examination of the factors underlying the different growth regimes, and especially the employment and labor market aspects of such regimes. Some illustrations may be helpful. First, let us look at a few cases of high growth resulting in high rates of poverty reduction (which can

Table 3.3   GDP Growth and Poverty Reduction, Selected Countries

	GDP Growth (% per annum)	Incidence of Poverty (% of population below poverty line)	Annual Percentage Point Change in Poverty
Bangladesh			
1986–1991	2.46	51.7 (1985–1986)[a]	
1991–1996	4.50	58.8 (1991–1992)	+1.18
1996–2001	5.29	53.1 (1995–1996)	−1.43
		49.8 (2000)	−0.83
India			
1970–1980	3.8		
1980–1990	5.8		
1990–1998	6.1	Sundaram and Tendulkar 2002[b]	
		46.5 (1983: URP)	
		37.3 (1993–1994: URP)	−0.92
		35.5 (1993–1994: MRP)	
		27.6 (1999–2000)	−1.32
		Deaton 2003	
		37.2 (1993–1994: rural)	
		30.2 (1999–2000: rural)	−0.70
		32.6 (1993–1994: urban)	
		24.7 (1999–2000: urban)	−1.32
		Datt, Kozel, and Ravallion 2003	
		39.1 (1993–1994)	
		34.3 (1999–2000)	−0.80
Indonesia			
1970–1980	7.5	40.1 (1976)	
1980–1990	5.7	28.6 (1980)	−2.88
1990–1996	7.3	15.1 (1990)	−1.35
		11.3 (1996)	−0.63
Vietnam			
1990	5.1	58 (1993)	
1995	9.5	37 (1998)	−4.2
2001	6.8	32 (2000)	−2.5
2002	7.0	28.9 (2002)	−1.5
Ethiopia			
1980/81–1991/92	2.3		
1992/93–2000/01	4.6	45.4 (1995–1996)	−0.33
		44.2 (1999–2000)	
Uganda			
1990	6.5		
1995	11.5	56.0 (1992–1993)	
1999	7.4	44.0 (1997–1998)	−2.4
2000	6.0	35.0 (2000)	−3.0
2002	6.0	38.8 (2002–2003)	+1.9
Bolivia			
1987–1990	3.45	57 (1989)[c]	
1991–1998	4.36	65 (1996)	
1999–2001	1.34	56 (1999)	−3.0
		64 (2001)	+4.0

Sources: Country studies in this volume; Sundaram and Tendulkar 2002; Deaton 2003; and Datt, Kozel, and Ravallion 2003.

Notes: a. Using the CBN (cost of basic needs) method.

b. URP = uniform recall period; MRP = mixed recall period. The first figure (37.3) for 1993–1994 is comparable to that for 1983, while the second figure (35.5) is comparable to that for 1999–2000.

c. Percentage of households; hence this figure is not comparable to the subsequent figures.

be called "good growth"—or, using the currently fashionable term, "pro-poor growth").

Indonesia. Indonesia's experience in the 1970s and the 1980s is notable in this context. To recall, the incidence of poverty started declining rapidly only in the second half of the 1970s. And although output growth in manufacturing was already high during the 1970s, employment elasticity in that sector remained rather low.[16] Much of the growth in employment during that period came from construction and services. Reduction in rural poverty was helped by high rates of growth in agriculture and rural nonfarm activities. Manufacturing employment started growing at a high rate during the 1980s (reaching 7.2 percent per annum during 1985–1990). Employment elasticity in manufacturing increased from 0.33 during 1975–1980 to 0.76 during 1981–1985. Real wages and earnings increased after 1978 in all sectors—although there was a reversal for a few years (1986–1989). Thus the experience of Indonesia during the second half of the 1970s and the 1980s provides a good example of high output growth associated with high rates of employment growth and growth of real wages and earnings. Moreover, growth in real wages roughly followed growth in labor productivity. That is thus a good example of "pro-poor growth" as outlined previously.[17]

Uganda. Uganda's experience, during the 1990s, of high rates of GDP growth accompanied by a rapid reduction of poverty also provides a good example of economic growth of the type that can lead to poverty reduction. In order to understand the process, it is necessary to examine the structure of the economy, the sources of its growth, as well as the institutional framework within which growth in the major sectors was achieved. In the early 1990s, over half of Uganda's GDP and nearly three-fourths of the labor force were accounted for by agriculture. Agriculture was dominated by crop production, and for a third of those engaged in agriculture cash crop was the main activity. Coffee growing was widespread, although other cash crops (e.g., tobacco, tea, and cotton) were also grown. Growing of coffee is primarily a smallholder-based activity, and the distribution of landholding is also quite egalitarian. Tobacco is grown mainly on small- and medium-scale farms, while tea is produced primarily on large-scale estates.

Agriculture as a whole played a prominent role in the high growth that Uganda achieved during the 1990s. And within agriculture, cash crops did especially well. Coffee, in particular, benefited from the boom in prices that took place in the world market. Being an activity based on smallholders, and with the liberalization of marketing, its growth and the rise in prices benefited the producers and raised their incomes significantly. There are concrete data (from the Bank of Uganda) to show that the share of farmers in the world prices of coffee increased by at least 50 percent between 1991 and 1997. The same conclusion cannot be drawn about tea, however, which is dominated by large estates using hired laborers for harvesting. In the absence of hard data on real wages of workers in that sector, it is difficult to say anything with confidence as to whether the poor have benefited from the rise in prices to the same extent as their counterparts engaged in coffee growing. Tobacco farmers also do not seem to have benefited from the growth in production because of their weak bargaining position vis-à-vis the buyers of their products, which are large enterprises enjoying monopoly power.

Another aspect of Uganda's pattern of growth and poverty reduction is that the latter was not achieved through a change in the structure of employment toward manufacturing. Indeed, the share of this sector in total employment remained virtually unchanged despite healthy growth of output in the sector and an increase in its share in GDP. The only notable change that took place in the structure of employment was a shift away from food crop to cash crop.

The above raises an important question about the sustainability of the present rate of poverty reduction in Uganda. Agriculture, of course, is relatively more labor-intensive, and this sector (especially the food crop sector) still has the highest incidence of poverty. As long as this sector can continue its healthy growth without any increase in inequality (which should be possible in a smallholder-based production), poverty reduction can continue. However, it is necessary to look at the important factor that contributed to the impressive growth and poverty reduction in agriculture: sharp increases in the prices. How long such price increases will continue is a question; the price of Ugandan coffee in the export market has already declined after the boom of the early to middle 1990s (Kabananukye et al. 2004). And it is the cash crop sector that achieved the most impressive rate of poverty reduction during the 1990s.

Indeed, in the wake of the decline in coffee prices during the late 1990s, the incidence of poverty registered an increase between 2000 and 2002–2003. The degree of income inequality also increased during that period—the Gini coefficient of income distribution rising from 0.395 in 1999–2000 to 0.428 in 2002–2003 (see Chapter 10). It thus appears that the question about the sustainability of the rates of growth and poverty reduction achieved by Uganda during the 1990s is a real one.

Vietnam. Another case of high growth leading to poverty reduction at a rapid rate is that of Vietnam. In rural areas of the country, incomes of households in the 1990s increased mainly due to improvements in farm productivity, which was made possible by intensification and diversification away from low-value outputs (e.g., staple crops) to higher-value ones (e.g., livestock, aquaculture, fruits, and perennial crops). While the shift to higher-value crops generated additional employment, the linkage effects of higher agricultural income helped create nonfarm employment. During 1993–1998, rural nonfarm self-employment increased at 6.7 percent per annum. In the urban areas, the private sector grew rapidly (in response to reforms that included strengthening of property rights, and an overall supportive policy environment), and created jobs that could (at least to some extent) absorb workers made redundant by the reform of state-owned enterprises (see Chapter 11 and Huong, Tuan, and Minh 2003). Thus the pattern of growth was, on the whole, quite conducive to poverty reduction.[18]

It needs to be noted, however, that the rate of poverty reduction in Vietnam has declined in recent years (a little over 2 percentage points per annum during 1998–2000, and 1.5 percentage points per annum during 2000–2002, compared to over 4 percentage points per annum during 1993–1998)—although it remains higher than in many developing countries. The distribution of income has also been worsening, albeit slowly. And these developments have taken place despite some positive changes on the employment side. For example, the structure of employment (i.e., the sectoral composition) has changed more noticeably—toward manufacturing—in recent years (especially since 2000). Second, job creation in the private sector has become an important factor contributing to poverty reduction. The decline in the rate of poverty reduction and a worsening of income distribution (Gini coefficient of expenditure distribution increased from 0.33 in 1993 to 0.35 in 1998) despite positive developments in the area of employment show the nature of the challenge that lies ahead for Vietnam despite the good quality of growth. It seems that the period of high growth leading to rapid increases in the income of the poor is coming to an end. Several aspects with regard to the quality of future growth will need attention. First is the spatial distribution of investment. Unless new investment goes beyond urban areas, the rural-urban divide is likely to grow, with all its accompanying consequences (e.g., migration to urban areas and an increase in urban poverty). Second, an increase in employment alone may not be an effective route out of poverty, unless the quality of jobs also improves. For example, wages in the formal private sector are lower than in the state sector, and the situation is worse in the informal segment of the private sector.

Poor Growth

Indonesia. Turning to the cases of growth not producing high rates of poverty reduction, one can contrast Indonesia's experience in the 1990s with that of the earlier decades. Poverty did continue to decline after 1990, but the rate slowed substantially compared to the 1980s, which is consistent with several findings on employment. Growth of employment in manufacturing declined from 7.2 percent per annum during 1985–1990 to 4.5 percent during 1990–1993. And overall employment growth declined from 4.1 percent during 1980–1985 to 2.5 percent during 1985–1990, and further to 1.5 percent during 1990–1993 (Agrawal 1996). Employment elasticity in manufacturing declined from 0.76

during 1981–1985 to 0.66 during 1986–1992 (Islam 2001). Indeed, employment elasticity for major manufacturing subsectors (e.g., textiles, garments, furniture, and food manufacturing) during 1993–1997 was lower compared to 1985–1988 (see Chapter 9).

A reduction in employment growth and employment elasticity may not be unusual when an economy develops and surplus labor becomes exhausted. But in the case of Indonesia, it seems to have happened earlier than warranted, because it was only in the 1990s that agriculture started shedding labor, and that the structural shift in employment away from agriculture started in a noticeable manner. And even in 1996, the year before the country was hit by economic crisis, underemployment and employment in the informal sector remained high (I. Islam 2003). Thus, although the economy continued to grow at a high rate, the rate of decline in poverty slowed down.[19]

Bangladesh. The experience of Bangladesh during the 1990s can also illustrate how with similar economic growth rates, different rates of poverty reduction can result. Indeed, during 1996–2000, despite higher growth, the rate of poverty reduction slowed down (compared to 1991–1996). Again, several employment-related observations are relevant in that context.[20]

First, the sectoral composition of employment in the country has not been changing in a direction that could support a high rate of poverty reduction. Indeed, the share of the manufacturing sector in total employment has been declining continuously since 1989; and although the trend reversed after 1996, the figure for 2000 (10.3 percent) remained well below that of 1989 (15.5 percent). Second, employment elasticity for the manufacturing sector as a whole declined during the 1990s compared to the 1980s (0.69 for 1990–1998 compared to 0.75 for 1980–1989). Third, open unemployment increased during 1996–2002 (from 2.5 percent to 4.0 percent). Fourth, higher output growth in agriculture during 1996–2001 (5.07 percent per annum, compared to 1.50 percent during 1991–1996) has not translated into higher rate of poverty reduction in rural areas. Decline in moderate poverty during 1996–2001 was 0.82 percentage point per annum compared to 1.13 percentage points per annum during 1991–1996. Fifth, the rate of real wage increase has been slower in agriculture compared to other sectors. More important, there has been a decline in real wages in agriculture after 1996–1997,[21] and this implies that agricultural workers (who form the bulk of the rural poor) have not benefited to the extent they could have from the growth in agriculture that took place during the second half of the 1990s. Finally, inequality in the distribution of income increased between 1991–1992 and 2000—at the national level as well as for rural and urban areas separately (the increase being greater for urban areas) (Bangladesh Bureau of Statistics 2002; Osmani et al. 2003). Comparison between the two subperiods of the 1990s (1991–1992 to 1995–1996, and 1995–1996 to 2000) indicates a faster rise in rural income inequality in the second subperiod and the opposite for urban income inequality (Osmani et al. 2003).

On the whole, the figures on employment and labor market developments in Bangladesh mentioned above are consistent with a slower rate of poverty reduction during the second half of the 1990s, although the rate of economic growth was slightly higher. This leads one to suspect (if not conclude) that growth in Bangladesh may have become less pro-poor in the second half of the 1990s, and that developments in the employment and labor market situation played a role.

Ethiopia. An example of moderate economic growth not producing any significant reduction of poverty is provided by Ethiopia's experience. After the introduction of economic reforms, the performance of Ethiopia's economy (as reflected in the growth of GDP) improved during the 1990s. GDP growth per annum averaged 4.6 percent during 1992–1993 to 2000–2001, compared to 2.3 percent during 1980–1981 to 1991–1992. But the incidence of poverty (anchored on a national poverty line defined in terms of a minimum calorie requirement for subsistence and basic nonfood expenditure) at the national level remained at 44.2 percent of the population in 1999–2000 compared to 45.5 percent in 1995–1996. Indeed, poverty in urban areas increased, while rural poverty registered a slight decline.

As far as overall employment is concerned, there was a decline (0.6 percent per annum) during 1994–1999. Thus, output growth during the 1990s was achieved through higher productivity alone, and there was no employment expansion. In manufacturing, employment increased by 1.8 percent during 1992–1999 while output increased by 5 percent per annum—thus indicating a low employment intensity of growth in the sector. The source of output growth was mainly productivity growth. Although real wages in manufacturing also registered a healthy growth, given the small size of the sector relative to the overall economy and the low rate of employment growth, this sector does not appear to have contributed much to poverty reduction. Indeed, manufacturing in Ethiopia remains dependent on outdated technology, and yet is capital intensive in character. Its linkages with the rest of the economy appear to be weak.

Employment in agriculture in Ethiopia appears to have declined during the second half of the 1990s, although output increased (except for years of drought like 1997–1998). So labor productivity should have risen. It is, however, difficult to say anything with confidence in this regard, because in the absence of time-series data on employment, estimates of labor productivity in the sector are based on projections, and appear to be highly volatile. Be that as it may, it can perhaps be said that the slight reduction of rural poverty in Ethiopia may have been due to an improved performance of agriculture where growth is relatively more employment intensive. Nearly 80 percent of the work force is still accounted for by agriculture, and the poor peasant households appear to have benefited from the termination of the unfavorable policies (i.e., collectivization and unfavorable compulsory procurement) of the earlier regime.

Bolivia. Bolivia's experience during the 1990s provides an example of a brief period of moderate growth associated with a fairly rapid rate of poverty reduction. But neither economic growth nor poverty reduction could be sustained after 1999. And an examination of the pattern of economic growth that took place indicates that it did not take a pro-poor character.

What is striking about Bolivia is its high level of income poverty (about 60 percent of the population in 2001) for a country of its per capita income (US$950 in 2001). In fact, there has been a reversal of the decline in poverty since 1999, and the level in 2001 was only a shade below that of 1996. Non-income dimensions of poverty also indicate high levels of poverty despite some improvement in recent years. The observed high levels of poverty co-existing with the per capita income of a lower-middle-income country could be understood in terms of a number of factors—for example, high degrees of inequality in incomes (in both rural and urban areas),[22] a large percentage of the work force (about 45 percent) still engaged in agriculture, and a rather slow transformation of the structure of the economy.

Several aspects of the pattern of Bolivia's economic growth are relevant in the context of poverty reduction. First, while the rate of overall GDP growth has been moderate, the sectors that achieved high rates of output growth (e.g., financial services; electricity, gas, and water; and transport and communication) are those with low degrees of employment intensities of output. And sectors with high employment intensity (e.g., agriculture, commerce, etc.) have achieved low rates of growth. As poverty is much higher in rural areas, growth in agriculture and other rural economic activities has to play an important role in reducing poverty in Bolivia. But this does not appear to have happened, even when overall GDP growth picked up.

Second, although the gap between the average real earnings in rural and urban areas narrowed a little during the mid-1990s, the gap widened later, and in 2001 it was higher than in 1996.

Third, the sectoral composition of employment does not show any structural shift toward sectors with higher productivity. The share of agriculture in total employment has remained between 40 and 44 percent during 1988–2001. The share of manufacturing registered a small increase during 1992–1999, only to decline in 2001. Indeed, the recent increase in agricultural employment was at the cost of declining productivity. Thus, agriculture appears to have acted as the sponge to absorb labor for whom the alternative would have been unemployment.

Fourth, the annual increase in real wages in manufacturing far outstripped the rise in labor productivity during 1991–1998 (a real wage increase of 3.8 percent per annum compared to 0.4 percent per annum growth in labor productivity). As a result of this, the manufacturing sector found itself in a weak competitive position at the end of the 1990s. When economic growth slowed down sharply during 1999–2001, the labor market adjusted mainly through the quantity mechanism—with a sharp decline in employment. Labor productivity thus increased, and it is during this period that real wage and labor productivity rose in tandem.

On the whole, it thus appears that although economic growth in Bolivia during the 1990s was associated with poverty reduction, the real pattern of growth cannot be termed "pro-poor." With the continuation of a high degree of income inequality, widening rural-urban income gap, output growth taking place mostly in the relatively more capital-intensive sectors, and very little change in the sectoral composition of employment, neither the rate of output growth nor the pace of poverty reduction could be sustained. Moreover, real wages increased in manufacturing without a corresponding rise in productivity. And the increase in agricultural employment came at the cost of reduced productivity. The basic ingredients of a pro-poor economic growth were thus absent.

India. India provides another interesting case. While it is difficult to say whether higher economic growth in India during the 1990s resulted in a faster rate of poverty reduction, it is useful to go beyond simple headcount measures of poverty (reported earlier) to an examination of the employment and labor market characteristics. There is, of course, no clear consensus among researchers on these aspects either. Sundaram and Tendulkar, for example, conclude: "Our overall assessment is one of improvement in the employment situation in India over the 1990s" (2002, 16). They arrive at this conclusion after noting and arguing the following. First, growth of employment in manufacturing was positive during the 1990s, compared to a net decline in the 1980s. Second, the reduction in the average number of days worked per person per year (for the usually employed persons on principal plus subsidiary status) is placed against the observed rise in real wages of agricultural workers to argue the possibility of a tightening of the labor market.

On the other hand, Sheila Bhalla (2003) presents data that show a clear decline in overall employment growth during the 1990s (1.05 percent per annum during 1993–1994 to 1999–2000) compared to the 1980s (2.07 percent per annum). The decline in rural areas was much sharper than in urban areas. Estimates presented in Bhalla's study also indicate a decline in the employment elasticities with respect to output—overall as well as for major sectors like agriculture and manufacturing. Based on data on differences in employment and income growth, the study also points to a deepening of the rural-urban divide in India.

Data on real wage rates in agriculture in India presented by Deaton and Dreze (2002) show a substantial decline in the rate of real wage growth during the 1990s (2.5 percent per year compared to 5 percent per year during the 1980s). Deaton and Dreze also point to an increase in income inequality during the 1990s that offset some of the poverty-reducing effects of growth. Indeed, they (like Bhalla) also discuss rising rural-urban disparity in the 1990s.

Datt, Kozel, and Ravallion (2003) argue that the sectoral pattern of growth in India during the 1990s was not particularly pro-poor: the states with higher growth in agriculture yields were not the states with initial high levels of poverty. They also point out that growth in the nonfarm sector in the 1990s was generally not any higher in the states where it would have had the most impact on poverty nationally.

An examination of the pattern of growth in India during the 1990s and of developments in the employment and labor market situation would thus point to the possibility that growth could have been more employment-friendly and pro-poor than it was.

■ Conclusion

This chapter started with an attempt to identify elements of pro-poor economic growth, and I have argued that this can be conceptualized in terms of a virtuous circle of economic growth leading to poverty reduction via growth of employment with rising productivity, and reduced poverty creating the possibility of further increases in productivity and higher rates of economic growth. Using cross-country data, the chapter has empirically demonstrated the link between poverty reduction and employment intensity of growth (defined in terms of employment elasticity with respect to output). Cross-country analysis has also been employed to show the impact of employment and labor market variables on poverty reduction. Developments that are found to make a positive contribution to poverty reduction include structural transformation of employment toward manufacturing and other nonfarm sectors, education, and lowering of the dependency burden (i.e., increase in labor force participation).

Based on the growth and poverty reduction experience in selected countries (namely Bangladesh, Bolivia, Ethiopia, India, Indonesia, Uganda, and Vietnam), I have argued that there is no invariant relationship between growth and poverty reduction. It has been demonstrated that similar growth rates can be associated with different outcomes on poverty reduction. And an examination of the experiences indicates that the patterns of growth, especially in terms of developments in employment and labor markets that take place as a result of growth, play an important role in producing such varying results regarding poverty reduction.

The experiences of countries reviewed in this chapter also give rise to a number of questions concerning the ingredients of pro-poor growth. The first relates to the role of agriculture. Given the large size of the population relying on this sector in many of the developing countries with high incidence of poverty, and the facts that labor productivity is lower and the incidence of poverty higher for those engaged in this sector relative to others, agriculture must have a prominent role in a strategy for pro-poor growth. Within the overall framework of this chapter, this strategy has been couched in terms of a structural shift of the economy (including its employed labor force) toward higher-productivity sectors capable of generating higher incomes. The empirical finding that a shift away from agriculture to higher-productivity sectors is associated with a reduction of poverty validates the importance of structural shift.[23] However, this does not mean that agriculture itself cannot contribute to the pro-poor growth process. Indeed, the experience of countries like Uganda and Vietnam points out the important role that this sector can play in reducing poverty. This is particularly the case where the distribution of landholding is relatively egalitarian and crop production is based primarily on smallholders. Where production is based on large estates and hired laborers, an important factor would be the productivity and real wages of workers. Another important factor would be the relative prices of agricultural products, especially in relation to purchased inputs, but also relative to nonagricultural products. Uganda, for example, benefited from the rise in the prices of its major crops during the 1990s; and Vietnam's agriculture also benefited from a favorable movement in its terms of trade. Structural shift within agriculture in terms of move to higher-value products can also contribute to poverty reduction. Thus, policies in support of the growth of smallholder agriculture, product diversification, and raising productivity and real wages of agricultural laborers are important for pro-poor growth.

Having recognized the importance of growth in agriculture, it is essential to point out the importance of a structural shift of employment toward higher-productivity nonfarm sectors. In countries with an abundance of labor, such structural shift should involve growth of the relatively labor-intensive sectors and subsectors—for example, labor-intensive manufactures and other nonfarm activities (in both urban and rural areas). The experience of Indonesia before the Asian economic crisis of 1998 provides a good example of high growth of the nonagricultural sectors that helped reduction of poverty. In contrast, Uganda does not appear to have achieved any noticeable shift in its employment structure (except for a slight shift toward commercial agriculture) during the period of its high growth. Likewise, Bangladesh, Bolivia, and Ethiopia are countries for which the challenge is not just one of moving to a higher growth

Table 3.4 Data Used for Regression with Employment Elasticity as Independent Variable

	Annual Average Poverty Change	Years	Initial Poverty Incidence (%)	Employment Elasticity in Manufacturing	Years	Annual Average GDP Growth (%)	Years
Bangladesh	1.00	(1991–2000)	58.8	0.390	(1991–1998)	4.7	(1990–1998)
Brazil	0.56	(1990–1995)	46.3	0.498	(1991–1998)	1.0	(1991–1999)
Burkina Faso	-0.13	(1994–1998)	44.5	0.421	(1991–1998)	3.8	(1990–1999)
China	0.93	(1980–1995)	20.0	0.470	(1980–1985)	10.0	(1990–2001)
Côte d'Ivoire	1.07	(1995–1998)	36.8	0.574	(1991–1998)	3.7	(1990–1999)
Ethiopia	0.26	(1995–2000)	45.5	0.108	(1991–1998)	4.8	(1990–1999)
Ghana	1.71	(1991–1998)	52.0	0.433	(1991–1998)	4.3	(1990–1999)
India	0.59	(1993–2000)	35.6	0.234	(1991–1998)	6.1	(1990–1998)
Indonesia	1.44	(1976–1996)	40.1	0.930	(1981–1992)	6.1	(1980–1990)
Kenya	0.41	(1992–1998)	44.8	1.401	(1991–1998)	2.2	(1990–1999)
Malaysia	1.04	(1984–1995)	19.9	0.400	(1981–1992)	5.3	(1980–1990)
Mexico	0.34	(1989–1994)	21.4	0.580	(1991–1998)	1.3	(1991–1999)
Nepal	1.30	(1995–2000)	44.6	0.266	(1991–1998)	5.0	(1990–1998)
Nigeria	-1.96	(1985–1995)	47.3	0.040	(1980–1990)	1.6	(1980–1990)
Pakistan	0.18	(1984–1990)	24.9	0.399	(1981–1990)	6.3	(1980–1990)
Philippines	0.68	(1991–2000)	39.9	0.630	(1992–1997)	3.3	(1990–1998)
Sri Lanka	0.74	(1991–1996)	30.4	0.268	(1991–1998)	5.0	(1990–1998)
Tanzania	0.36	(1992–2000)	38.6	2.670	(1991–1998)	2.9	(1990–1998)
Thailand	1.28	(1990–2000)	27.0	0.220	(1992–1997)	7.4	(1990–1998)
Uganda	2.30	(1992–1997)	55.5	0.236	(1991–1998)	7.2	(1990–1999)
Vietnam	4.20	(1993–1998)	58.0	0.371	(1990–2000)	7.6	(1990–2001)
Zambia	-0.46	(1991–1998)	69.7	-0.115	(1991–1998)	1.0	(1990–1999)
Zimbabwe	-7.40	(1991–1996)	25.0	-0.546	(1991–1998)	2.4	(1990–1999)

Sources: Compiled by the author.

Table 3.5 Data Used in Multiple Regression Exercise Involving Poverty and Employment Variables

	Poverty Incidence (%)	Annual Average GDP Growth (%)	GDP per Capita (PPP) (for same years as poverty incidence)	Employment in Agriculture (%)	Employment in Manufacturing (%)	Adult Literacy Rate (%)	Age Dependency	Gini Index (for same years as poverty incidence)
Argentina	16.5 (1991)	0.4 (1980–1990)	8,388	0.6 (2000)	14 (2000)	96	0.6	0.44 (I)
Bahamas	7.6 (1993)	n/a	14,108	3.5 (1998)	3.7 (1998)	98	0.53	0.45 (I)
Bangladesh	29.1 (1996)	4.1 (1990–1995)	1,290	62.1 (2000)	7.3 (2000)	38	0.7	0.43 (I)
Bolivia	14.4 (1999)	4.2 (1990–1998)	2,255	5 (2000)	15.3 (2000)	83	0.77	0.55 (I)
Botswana	33.3 (1985–1986)	10.3 (1980–1990)	2,857	19.7 (2000)	8.8 (2000)	70	0.8	0.56 (I)
Brazil	11.6 (1998)	3.3 (1990–1998)	6,702	24.2 (1999)	11.6 (1999)	83	0.51	0.6 (I)
Burkina Faso	61.2 (1994)	3.6 (1980–1990)	763	92 (2000)	2 (2000)	19	1	0.48 (E)
Chile	2 (1998)	7.3 (1990–1995)	8,504	13.6 (2001)	n/a	95	0.55	0.56 (I)
Colombia	19.7 (1998)	4.6 (1990–1995)	5,873	1.1 (2000)	20.2 (2000)	91	0.59	0.57 (I)
Costa Rica	12.6 (1998)	5.1 (1990–1995)	7,496	15.1 (2001)	15 (2001)	95	0.6	0.47 (I)
Côte d'Ivoire	12.3 (1995)	0.7 (1990–1995)	1,488	60 (2000)	10 (2000)	40	0.85	0.38 (E)
Dominican Republic	3.2 (1996)	3.9 (1990–1995)	4,475	19.9 (1997)	18.2 (1997)	82	0.61	0.49 (I)
El Salvador	21 (1998)	6.3 (1990–1995)	4,232	21.4 (1999)	18.8 (1999)	72	0.67	0.52 (I)
Ethiopia	31.3 (1995)	1.1 (1980–1990)	557	86 (2000)	2 (2000)	36	0.97	0.39 (I)
Gambia	51 (1998)	1.6 (1990–1995)	1,512	82 (2000)	8 (2000)	39	0.86	0.48 (E)
Ghana	44.8 (1999)	4.2 (1990–1998)	1,834	59 (2000)	13 (2000)	65	0.85	0.33 (E)
Guatemala	10 (1998)	4 (1990–1995)	3,606	26.1 (1993)	n/a	65	0.86	0.6 (I)
Honduras	24.3 (1998)	3.5 (1990–1995)	2,428	32.8 (2001)	15.2 (2001)	73	0.82	0.59 (I)
India	44.2 (1997)	4.6 (1990–1995)	2,027	61.7 (2000)	15.8 (2000)	52	0.63	0.38 (E)
Indonesia	12.9 (1999)	5.8 (1990–1998)	2,841	43.2 (1999)	13 (1999)	84	0.54	0.3 (I)

continues

Table 3.5 Continued

	Poverty Incidence (%)	Annual Average GDP Growth (%)	GDP per Capita (PPP) (for same years as poverty incidence)	Employment in Agriculture (%)	Employment in Manufacturing (%)	Adult Literacy Rate (%)	Age Dependency	Gini Index (for same years as poverty incidence)
Jamaica	3.3 (1996)	2.9 (1990–1995)	3,526	21 (1998)	8.9 (1998)	85	0.61	0.36 (E)
Kenya	26.5 (1994)	4.2 (1980–1990)	967	80 (2000)	7 (2000)	78	0.86	0.58 (E)
Madagascar	49.1 (1999)	1.3 (1990–1998)	775	78 (2000)	7 (2000)	46	0.93	0.38 (E)
Mali	72.8 (1994)	0.9 (1980–1990)	609	86 (2000)	2 (2000)	31	1	0.54 (E)
Mexico	15.9 (1998)	1.1 (1990–1995)	7,825	17.7 (2001)	18.9 (2001)	90	0.61	0.53 (I)
Nepal	37.7 (1995)	4.6 (1980–1990)	1,101	n/a	n/a	28	0.8	0.37 (E)
Nigeria	70.2 (1997)	1.6 (1990–1995)	799	43 (2000)	7 (2000)	57	0.87	0.51 (E)
Pakistan	31 (1996)	4.6 (1990–1995)	1,758	48.4 (2000)	11.5 (2000)	38	0.82	0.4 (I)
Panama	14 (1998)	6.3 (1990–1995)	5,600	16.3 (1999)	9.8 (1999)	n/a	0.58	0.58 (I)
Paraguay	19.5 (1998)	3.1 (1990–1995)	4,496	5.2 (1996)	14.3 (1996)	92	0.74	0.48 (I)
Peru	15.5 (1996)	5.3 (1990–1995)	4,353	8.1 (2001)	12.6 (2001)	89	0.63	0.46 (I)
Rwanda	35.7 (1983–1985)	2.2 (1980–1990)	816	92 (2000)	3 (2000)	n/a	0.83	0.27 (E)
Senegal	26.3 (1995)	3.1 (1980–1990)	1,251	n/a	n/a	33	0.91	0.41 (E)
Sierra Leone	57 (1989)	0.3 (1980–1990)	774	67 (2000)	15 (2000)	31	0.91	0.63 (E)
Sri Lanka	6.6 (1995)	4 (1980–1990)	2,695	41.6 (1998)	15.4 (1998)	90	0.48	0.5 (I)
Tanzania	19.9 (1993)	3.8 (1980–1990)	445	84 (2000)	5 (2000)	68	0.92	0.34 (I)
Thailand	2 (1998)	8.4 (1990–1995)	5,652	48.8 (2000)	14.5 (2000)	94	0.44	0.42 (I)
Uruguay	2 (1989)	0.4 (1980–1990)	9,628	4.2 (2001)	15.5 (2001)	97	0.6	0.42 (I)
Venezuela	23 (1998)	2.4 (1990–1995)	5,727	10.8 (1997)	13.5 (1997)	91	0.62	0.5 (I)
Zambia	63.7 (1998)	0.2 (1990–1995)	729	75 (2000)	8 (2000)	78	0.9	0.52 (E)
Zimbabwe	36 (1990–1991)	3.6 (1980–1990)	2,249	68 (2000)	8 (2000)	85	0.89	0.57 (E)

Sources: United Nations Development Programme 1998; United Nations University and World Institute for Development Economics 2000; World Income Inequality Database; World Bank 2002c; World Bank 2003f; and World Bank 2000c.

Notes: Poverty incidence represents the percentage of the population living on less than US$1 a day. The literacy rates are all for 1995. "Age dependency" refers to the number of dependents in the working-age population in 2000. For the Gini index, (I) = income inequality, and (E) = expenditure inequality.

path, but also one of achieving a shift in their employment structures toward higher-productivity nonagricultural sectors. But given the low base of modern manufacturing in many developing countries, rural nonfarm activities need to be seen as possible sources of higher-productivity employment.

Variables on the supply side of the labor market that can have significant influence on poverty include education and skills. Investment in human capital formation plays a major role in boosting economic development that could benefit the poor. One of the principal means of enhancing their ability to integrate into the growth process and their productivity is to endow them with education and skills. Analysis based on household-level data shows that poverty and education are inversely correlated. Also, a comparison of the experience of the East Asian countries that were more successful than their South Asian counterparts in terms of growth and poverty reduction shows that the former, in general, performed better in terms of human capital as well (R. Islam 2003a). Investment in human capital, in terms of both education and skill training, therefore needs to be an important ingredient in a country's strategy for pro-poor growth.

This analysis has important implications for development strategies and policies for accelerating growth and poverty reduction. While employment and labor market variables emerge as significant in making growth pro-poor, it needs to be borne in mind that if treated separately from the overall development strategy, employment cannot serve as an effective route out of poverty.[24] Employment outcomes of alternative strategies and policies must be considered as one of the major criteria in formulating them (i.e., the strategies and policies). This is particularly important when it comes to the formulation of macroeconomic policies and policies relating to specific sectors. It should be possible to integrate employment concerns into the process of formulating such policies. A pro-employment macro policy regime would take into account the possible effects of tariffs, exchange rates, and taxation policies on the growth of sectors and subsectors that are by nature more labor-intensive than others. Integration of employment concerns should be associated with the adoption of measures to track the employment intensity of growth to determine whether growth is taking on a pro-poor character.

Table 3.6   Correlation Matrix of Variables Used in Multiple Regression Exercise

	POVERTY	EAG	EMA	EDU	DEP
POVERTY	1.0				
EAG	0.620582	1.0			
EMA	−0.53929	−0.73073	1.0		
EDU	−0.6739	−0.73236	0.591592	1.0	
DEP	0.744778	0.685476	−0.69917	−0.70855	1.0

■ Notes

1. A somewhat different and more detailed analytic framework is provided in Chapter 2, and Chapter 4 presents a rich empirical-analytic study of employment policies for poverty reduction.

2. In that regard, mention may be made of Ahluwalia, Carter, and Chenery 1979 and Fields 1980.

3. A widely quoted recent study is Dollar and Kray 2001. See also Demery and Squire 1995 and Ravallion 1995.

4. See, for example, Dagdeviren, Hoeven, and Weeks 2001; Goudie and Ladd 1999; and McKay 1997. Chen and Ravallion 2001 reminds one of the importance of country-specific research on factors determining "why some poor people are able to take up the opportunities afforded by an expanding economy . . . while others are not" (p. 1813).

5. It may be noted that while the World Bank (1990) points out the importance of labor-intensive growth in reducing poverty, it does not (2000e) put the same emphasis on labor incomes as its earlier counterpart.

6. The ILO (2003a) argues the case for "decent work" as the foundation for poverty reduction, and within that framework points out the importance of employment.

7. Although the term "pro-poor growth" is used frequently in the current discourse on development, there have been few attempts to define it. One exception is White and Anderson 2001.

8. See, also, ILO 2003a in regard to promoting such an approach to poverty reduction. There are of course other factors that influence the ability of the poor to participate in the growth process; access to capital and productive assets is important in that respect.

9. The sign associated with this variable can be taken as an indicator of whether income inequality is worsening or improving in the process of development. A positive sign in the formulation here would be an indicator of poorer countries performing better (i.e., inequality not worsening). See also Squire 1993.

10. It should be mentioned that an alternative specification with per capita GDP growth rather than overall GDP growth was also tested, but produced results that are not as good as those reported here.

11. The correlation matrix is presented in Table 3.6.

12. This conclusion is based on the country studies presented in this volume.

13. Chapter 2 provides an analytic framework to bring together these two factors, along with the growth factor, in linking poverty reduction with growth and employment.

14. The countries are Bangladesh, Bolivia, Ethiopia, India, Indonesia, Uganda, and Vietnam. The following major criteria were used in selecting them: at least a moderate (preferably high) economic growth during the 1990s, and representation from the three developing continents (Africa, Asia, and Latin America). Countries that attained moderate to high rates of economic growth were selected because the purpose was to examine the contribution of growth to poverty reduction.

15. This is slightly different from the classification suggested by S. R. Osmani (in Chapter 2 in this volume, and in Osmani 2002), but follows the basic idea suggested therein.

16. Observations made in this paragraph are based on data available in Agrawal 1996; Islam 1990; and Chapter 9 in this volume. See also Islam 2002.

17. However, this is not to ignore the weaknesses that remained in the Indonesian economy and the continued existence of a high rate of underemployment and informal sector employment until the mid-1970s; see R. Islam 2003b for an assessment.

18. The estimated employment elasticity for the manufacturing sector (referencing Figure 3.2) is of course rather low, and does not reflect the overall employment outcome of growth—especially in the rural areas. There could be several possible explanations for this. First, a large part of the manufacturing is still in the state sector, which, given its background and composition, is characterized by a high degree of capital intensity. Second, recent reforms in state-owned enterprises have been associated with a good deal of labor retrenchment, thus resulting in a rise in output per worker and a fall in employment per unit of output.

19. That was before the economic crisis. During the crisis (especially in 1998), the incidence of poverty increased sharply. For a good analysis of the vulnerability of the Indonesian people at the lower end of the income scale, see Dhanani and Islam 2002.

20. The figures quoted in the rest of the paragraph, unless otherwise mentioned, are from Chapter 5 in this volume. See also Rahman and Islam 2003.

21. Part of that decline, especially in 1998 and 1999, may have been due to the severe floods that affected the country in 1998. But it remains to be seen whether real wages demonstrated a sustained increase after 1999. Although there was an increase in 1999–2000, the level of 1996–1997 was not reached.

22. According to data from the Economic Commission for Latin America and the Caribbean (2003), in 1999, Gini coefficients of income distribution in rural and urban areas were 0.64 and 0.50 respectively. These are rather high figures.

23. A structural shift within agriculture can also contribute to poverty reduction.

24. This is not to deny, of course, the role of employment creation programs in providing safety nets to the poor in specific situations (e.g., to combat chronic seasonal unemployment, provide support in crisis-affected situations, etc.).

4

Employment Policies for Poverty Reduction

Azizur Rahman Khan

Poverty is defined in many different ways and using many different standards. The essence of the concept relates to deprivation. Most simply it is measured unidimensionally as a shortfall from some minimum acceptable standard of consumption or income. Increasingly, it is being measured multidimensionally as a shortfall from minimum acceptable standards of not merely consumption and income, but also such elements of human capability as health, education, security, and empowerment. The reason that the poor are deprived of these minimum indicators of well-being is that they lack resources. The World Bank's recent report on attacking poverty identifies these resources as human assets (e.g., capacity for basic labor, good health, and skills); natural assets (e.g., land); physical assets (e.g., physical capital and access to infrastructure); financial assets (e.g., savings and access to credit); and social assets (e.g., informal or formal social security and political power).[1]

With the exception of the last element, which can typically protect only a small proportion of population from poverty on a long-term basis and possibly a larger proportion of population for very short periods, all the other elements help avoid poverty by increasing employment and its productivity. Access of the poor to land, physical assets, and financial assets helps them overcome poverty not by providing them with entitlement to rent or annuity but by creating for them the opportunity for more intensive and productive employment and for a higher value of the product of their labor.[2] Access of the landless to land enables them to employ themselves more intensively and remuneratively. Access of the poor to physical capital and financial capital helps them make productive use of their otherwise underutilized labor resources. Access to infrastructure helps increase the productivity of labor and generates higher values for the produce of labor. Access to these resources

63

makes little sustained contribution to the welfare of the poor except by increasing the intensity and the terms of utilization of their capacity to work.

Informal or formal social insurance is necessary to alleviate poverty on the part of those who have inadequate endowment of labor. These institutions are also necessary to protect population from the worst consequences of short-term emergencies that afflict also those who have adequate endowment of labor. But the proportion of households who suffer from an inadequate endowment of labor is typically small.[3] In most societies, especially the poor ones, the informal and formal institutions for social security do not have the capacity to protect a high proportion of the population from poverty without finding a way of utilizing and enhancing their capacity to work.

It is in this sense that employment is the basic route for escape from poverty. The linkage between employment expansion and poverty reduction, however, has many facets. The poor are helped out of poverty when there is an increase in wage employment, an increase in real wages due to a rise in demand for labor and/or a rise in the productivity of labor, an increase in the opportunity of the poor to employ themselves, an increase in the productivity of the poor in self-employment, and an increase in the terms of exchange of the output of the poor in self-employment. Employment policy for poverty reduction needs to concern itself with all these different aspects of the linkage between employment and poverty.

Growth, Employment, and Poverty

The linkage between employment and poverty is envisioned as a process in a market economy in which economic growth induces an increase in productive and remunerative employment, which leads to a reduction of poverty. The effectiveness of the process in reducing poverty depends on the strength of each link in the process. These links consist of the rate of growth of the economy, the output elasticity of demand for labor, and the ability of the poor members of the labor force to respond to increasing demand for labor, especially for more productive categories of employment. Simultaneous strength of each of these links promotes rapid reduction in poverty, while the weakness of any of these links weakens the poverty reduction effect of the process. In recent history the successful operation of these linkages is best illustrated by the growth of the East Asian countries, like the Republic of Korea (hereafter Korea), the Taiwan Province of China (hereafter Taiwan), and the city-states of Hong Kong and Singapore. Since about the mid-1960s, these countries achieved historically unprecedented rates of growth in their outputs. Economic growth in these countries was accompanied by a high output elasticity of demand for labor. The labor forces in these countries came to be endowed with steadily increasing levels of human capital in terms of better health and higher skills. As a result, employment increased rapidly and real wages increased roughly at the same rate as per capita output. Rapid economic growth resulted in low and stable inequality in the distribution of income and a dramatic decline in the incidence of absolute poverty. A summary of the experiences in these countries is presented later in this chapter.

Rapid economic growth is necessary for a high rate of expansion of productive and remunerative employment. Growth in productive employment is limited by the rate of growth in output. Employment growth in excess of the growth rate of output is possible only at the cost of a decline in the productivity of employment, which has an adverse effect on the welfare of the poor.[4] Thus poverty reduction by employment expansion fails in the absence of a high enough rate of economic growth. As discussed later, the persistence of poverty in sub-Saharan Africa is probably best understood as the very slow rate of the region's growth severely constraining the expansion in productive employment in recent decades.

Can the employment-poverty linkage be made to work without an adequately high rate of growth? It is possible to expand employment without growth, but it is unlikely for such an expansion of employment to entitle those employed with means to overcome poverty. This entitlement is successfully created only if employment is productive—that is, accompanied by economic growth. Contemporary development experience is full of examples of guaranteeing employment in excess of what is warranted by the growth of output and income. The most extreme example of this consists of the former socialist countries that opted for guaranteed employment as a method of social security, a system in which employment was not determined by the labor demand induced by economic growth in a market economy, but by the use of employment creation as an instrument for guaranteeing livelihood irrespective of the employees' contribution to output. This kind of employment growth had, at best, a weak effect and, at worst, an adverse effect on poverty reduction due to its unfavorable impact on economic efficiency and growth. Less extreme versions of this policy have been practiced by many nonsocialist countries as well, especially those with large public employment. As shown later, a number of developing countries, especially in Latin America, have often expanded employment at a substantially faster rate than output, with the ostensible purpose of protecting the workers. In the long run these policies are unsustainable. In pursuing the objective of poverty reduction, absence of economic growth cannot be compensated by arbitrary employment expansion.

However, high economic growth may fail to bring about a commensurate rate of poverty reduction if it is not accompanied by a rapid growth of productive and remunerative employment. Several distinct scenarios, producing this outcome, can be documented from contemporary experience:

1. *Low output elasticity of demand for labor.* Economic growth may have low employment intensity due to inappropriate economic policies and institu-

tions. Past policies in developing countries, in Latin America and South and Southeast Asia among others, often leaned heavily in favor of import-substituting industrialization, which created an unduly high incentive for capital-intensive technology due to the artificial cheapening of credit and imported capital equipment. Labor market interventions often aggravated the distortion by emphasizing the protection of the workers employed in the small formal sector at the cost of restricting the growth of formal employment. In countries with concentrated landownership (e.g., the Philippines and Brazil), the intensity of labor use in agriculture has been low due to the widely observed phenomenon of the inverse relationship between farm size and labor use per hectare and the withholding by large landowners of tracts of land from cultivation for speculative purposes, resulting in the restriction of employment and output in agriculture.[5] As a consequence of these distorted policies and institutions, employment and wages have grown too slowly to permit a reduction in poverty that is commensurate with the rate of economic growth under appropriate policies and institutions.

2. *Employment impact of high growth offset by the countervailing contraction of employment induced by economic reform under globalization, thereby resulting in a low observed output elasticity of employment.* This phenomenon is characteristic of countries that in the past resorted to artificial employment creation as an instrument of social security and have succeeded in achieving high growth in the age of globalization by gradually abandoning those policies. Rapidly growing transition economies, like China and Vietnam, represent the most outstanding examples of this case, of which numerous nontransition economies also serve as less extreme illustrations. While economic growth may lead to a rapid increase in labor use—as measured by an increase in employment at constant intensity of work—the increase in the headcount rate of employment may be very low, or even negative, because the process of growth entails reform that results in a reduction of concealed surplus labor employed in public enterprises. The phenomenon can encompass private enterprises as well, if the incentive system in the past had discouraged efficiency in the hiring of labor in these enterprises. Once the process of eliminating surplus labor is complete, employment and wages should rise rapidly once again and the transition should ultimately be beneficial to all, including the poor, because of the increased efficiency that it will instill in the economy. But the process of transition is characterized by an increase in the headcount rate of unemployment. Since the unemployed face a far greater probability of being poor than the employed, the process has an adverse effect on poverty reduction. As the evidence from many developing countries shows, the process may take decades to complete.

3. *Economic growth could lead to a high rate of growth in employment of a kind for which the poor do not possess necessary skills.* While this phenomenon may have been widely prevalent among developing countries, a

clear example of it is the United States in the 1990s, when the US economy had achieved a high rate of growth that was highly employment-intensive by the standards of the advanced industrial economies. The unemployment rate declined dramatically. The growth in employment, however, was directed much more to highly skilled workers than to the unskilled workers dominant among the poor. As a result, real wages increased much faster for the skilled workers than for the unskilled workers. Indeed, the median real wage rate in the mid-1990s was lower than what it was two decades before.[6] The result was a much slower decline in the incidence of poverty than would have been feasible if the poor workers had access to necessary skills. It appears that the same phenomenon has occurred in a number of developing countries where real wages have risen despite the persistence of high unemployment or a rise in the rate of unemployment. The rise in real wages in such cases often appears to reflect a growing inequality in the distribution of wages.[7]

4. *Growth might also fail to reduce poverty if the distribution of scarce productive resources—land and physical capital—is highly concentrated.* The scarcity of productive assets in this case dictates a very high and increasing share of income for them. Thus a very high, and continuously increasing, share of income would have a highly and increasingly unequal distribution. In this case growth would be associated with immiserizing employment, the creation and the perpetuation of the working poor. Employment would not lead to an escape from poverty, because of its low return. Growth would be associated with increasing inequality and a weak or adverse impact on poverty reduction. Indeed the preceding case may be regarded as a subcategory of this phenomenon, showing the consequences of a skewed distribution of skills. It is likely that the weak and declining impact of growth on poverty reduction in cases like Bangladesh since the mid-1980s was largely due to this phenomenon.[8]

What role does the distribution of income have in the growth-employment-poverty nexus? While there are relatively few instruments for improving the welfare of the poor except by improving the intensity and terms of utilization of their labor resources, there are many policy instruments to change the distribution of income, including numerous methods of redistribution of income from one group of nonpoor to another. Thus changes in the distribution of income need not be associated with equivalent changes in the welfare of the poor in the same direction. Strongly employment-intensive growth, leading to a high rate of absorption of the poor into productive employment with rapidly rising real wage, should be associated with undiminished or improving equality in the distribution of income, as indeed was the case, discussed later, in several East Asian countries. However, it is unnecessary for poverty-reducing growth in employment to be associated with undiminished equality in the distribution of income. While economic growth may absolutely benefit the poor by expanding their productive employment, owners of other factors of production—namely skilled labor, land, and capital—may make proportionately greater gains. The result is a reduction of poverty with rising inequality as was the case, discussed later, in countries like Chile and Thailand. The increase in inequality must in this case be viewed as a leakage that diverts resources from poverty reduction to nonpoor beneficiaries. If this leakage is very large (i.e., if inequality increases sharply), it is possible for economic growth to fail to reduce poverty at all. This might have been the case in urban China in the period of its integration with the global economy. This kind of extreme increase in inequality is typically associated with an extreme employment hostility of growth, as the case of urban China may be interpreted. As long as productive and remunerative employment for the poor continues to rise as a proportion of population, it is unlikely for the forces of inequality elsewhere in the economy to make it impossible for absolute poverty to decline. On the other hand, for growth to reduce poverty rapidly, it is essential for much of its benefit to be passed on to the poor in the form of rapidly rising remunerative employment and other methods, resulting in no more than a modest rise in inequality of income distribution.

■ Employment Policies for Poverty Reduction

The nexus of growth, employment, and poverty reduction provides a framework for the analysis of employment policies for poverty reduction. Employment-related interventions for the reduction of poverty could be classified under the following sets of policies:

1. *Rapid labor-absorbing growth providing the poor with productive and remunerative employment.* This chapter can at best discuss the rudiments of the policies and circumstances that lead to this outcome. First, the economy must succeed in ensuring a high rate of growth. This calls for comprehensive policies encompassing incentives for domestic capital accumulation and attraction of capital from abroad, policies for effective deployment of investment resources in socially productive activities and industries, and institutions conducive to the pursuit of efficiency. This is the subject matter of the literature on economic growth and development, which, though not entirely agreeing about the ingredients of a strategy, has a broad consensus about what works and what does not. It is neither necessary nor feasible for this chapter to summarize the consensus.

Growth must also be appropriately employment-intensive in the given context of resource endowment. For developing countries this means a high output elasticity of demand for labor. The basic requirement for this is the reflection of resource endowment in the system of incentives guiding economic decisions. Artificial cheapening of capital—characteristic, for example, of the development policy based on import-substituting industrialization—and the artificial increase in the cost of using labor—due, for example, to inappropriate interventions in the labor market—are two of the major factors that inhibited this process in developing countries. Labor use is also inhibited by inappropriate institutions. As discussed in the preceding section, this is often the case in agrarian systems characterized by highly unequal distribution of land. Different resource endowments of the large and small landowners lead them to use very different amounts of labor per unit of land. Speculation and the wielding of monopsonistic control on the workers can exacerbate the situation by inducing large landowners to keep land uncultivated while the landless and the small landowners are unable to fully employ themselves due to the shortage of land to work on. Industries under the influence of the demonstration effect of multinationals can advance along undesirably capital-intensive expansion paths unless economic incentives act as deterrents. Economic institutions and incentives need to be adjusted to eliminate or reduce these tendencies to make growth appropriately labor-intensive.

Macroeconomic policies affect employment of the poor through the influence they exert on the growth performance of the economy. They can also have more direct influence on the employment and welfare of the poor members of the labor force. Thus macroeconomic stabilization, retrenching public expenditure, often causes curtailment in direct employment generation through public works programs, and affects the employability of the poor by reducing public expenditure on basic education and skill development for them. Macroeconomic policies, guiding public revenue and expenditure policies, can affect the productivity of the poor and the terms of trade for the products of the labor of the poor. For example, in an agrarian economy characterized by peasant farming and limited inequality in the distribution of land, a rise in the prices of inputs and/or a fall in the prices of outputs brought about by changes in fiscal policy can reduce the welfare of the self-employed poor. While imperatives behind macroeconomic policies are complex, their effect on the employment and welfare of the poor should receive due weight in the selection of the combination of such policies.

Appropriate institutions and incentives, complemented by well-developed infrastructure supported by public investment and an enabling system of governance, should normally be enough for the promotion of an adequately high rate of employment-intensive growth. However, this may need to be supplemented by more direct public intervention for the promotion of employment-intensive growth. Examples of circumstances making this necessary are periods of adjustment when private enterprise fails to absorb labor in necessary numbers (see item 6 below); and the stimulation of growth in regions with a disproportionately high concentration of the poor that fail to attract large enough investment under market incentives even when the latter have been subjected to market-friendly methods of public intervention. In such cases public investment (e.g., public works programs for the development of infrastructure in poor regions) can directly contribute to an acceleration of employment-intensive growth. Numerous developing countries have used this instrument to provide employment to the poor. To what extent these programs have combined the objective of poverty reduction with efficient production of infrastructural capital is a matter of empirical analysis.[9]

2. *Conversion of the poor into productive entrepreneurs engaged in self-employment.* Growth-induced employment generation, as outlined above, is often perceived as a strategy exogenous to the process of poverty reduction. In contrast, the promotion of self-employment among the poor, by converting them into microentrepreneurs, could be an efficient growth strategy that is endogenous to the process of poverty reduction. Its importance derives from the possibility that growth-induced employment generation may often be an inadequate strategy for poverty reduction even though the output elasticity of employment is reasonably high. This would be the case, as discussed previously, if productive assets are scarce and distributed very unequally. In this case a small and decreasing proportion of output is shared among workers, conceivably leading to a decline in real earnings of the poor workers.

In the rural and subsistence sectors of most low-income developing countries the incidence of poverty is far higher among smallholders and self-employed categories.[10] For these households employment expansion is often a matter of enabling them to attain a more intensive and productive utilization of household labor by improving their access to productive assets. Redistribution of land and improved access of the poor to the use of land under favorable rental/tenancy arrangements are powerful methods of improving the income and welfare of the poor. Other methods are the provision of credit, infrastructure and public services for nonfarm microenterprise, and granting access to education and training that would make the poor more productive as entrepreneurs (see below). Targeted public action is essential for the promotion of the access of the poor to these resources.

Land is the most important of the resources to which access by the poor has a decisive effect on their welfare. Successful implementation of comprehensive land reform was a remarkably effective instrument of combining growth and poverty reduction during the early years of reform in Korea and Taiwan (predominantly rural at the time) and in China. Such land reforms have proven impossible to replicate. The realization of their effectiveness in alleviating poverty and the difficulty of their replication have led institutions like the World Bank to seek market-friendly methods of redistributing land by inducing large landowners to sell land to the poor, whose ability to purchase is augmented by the provision of credit. So far there is scant evidence of success of such policies in providing access to land to large numbers of the poor. The poor rarely possess the market power to gain access to such a valuable resource as land; the targeting of the poor to receive the large volumes of credit that are necessary for such transactions is likely to face overwhelming problems of leakage in the direction of the nonpoor.

A second instrument of targeted support to enable the poor to productively employ themselves is the provision of credit for microenterprise. In recent years its appeal has greatly widened, partly due to the frustration arising out of the difficulty of redistributing land and partly due to the apparent success of programs like the Grameen Bank in Bangladesh. The success of this instrument depends on the prevention of its leakage to the nonpoor and the combination of credit with complementary resources like technology, skill, and market access.

The attraction of activating the labor resources of the poor by the promotion of self-employing microenterprise also derives from the fact that this is an effective way of pushing outward the production possibilities of the economy. To the extent that these resources would otherwise have remained unused, poverty reduction in this case acts as what might be considered a vent for surplus—that is, a source of growth in output that does not require resources in a conventional sense but that can be achieved by activating productive energies and resources that are latent due to the absence of necessary incentives and institutions.[11]

3. *Increasing the productivity of the poor workers both in wage employment and in self-employment.* Increased productivity leads to an increased demand for wage labor, which is translated into increased employment or wages or both. Increased productivity of the self-employed workers directly raises their income. Increased productivity therefore enhances the prospect of the labor-dependent households to escape poverty. The principal policy to enhance the productivity of the poor is to endow them with greater human capital: skill, education, and health. This is another important area of targeted public support to enhance the productivity of employment of the poor. Skill, education, and health are of course scarce resources with high productivity. Successful targeting of these resources to the poor, without large-scale leakage to the nonpoor, faces all the problems that any program of redistribution faces in a society with undeveloped institutions of governance.

4. *Improvement and adjustment in the skill composition of the poor members of the society so that they can compete for employment in a labor market in which the skill composition of demand for labor changes rapidly.* This is closely related to, yet distinct from, the preceding policy. Endowing the poor with skills is not a once-and-for-all process. Their skills must adjust to the changes that skill composition of demand for labor periodically undergoes. Failure to do so may easily prevent the poor from benefiting from growth-induced increase in demand for labor.

5. *Appropriate terms of exchange for the produce of the poor.* Given the employment productivity of the poor, the higher the terms of trade of their output, the easier it is for them to escape from poverty. Ensuring appropriate terms of trade for the products of the microentrepreneurs and the small farmers is an effective way of alleviating their poverty. For an agriculture domi-

nated by small peasant farmers, an improvement in terms of trade is likely to favorably affect the poor, because of the greater preponderance of net sellers over net buyers of food among the poor. The effect is likely to be the opposite for an agriculture dominated by large farmers, where the latter account for most of the marketed output while the wage-earning agricultural laborers account for most of the net buyers of food. Similarly, poor microentrepreneurs in nonfarm activities are favorably affected by an improvement in the relative price of their outputs to that of their inputs. Improved access of the poor to infrastructure and public services helps them achieve better terms of exchange for their produce.

6. *Orderly dismantling of the past systems of inefficient excess employment, especially in state-owned enterprises.* For many developing countries, especially the transitional economies, this may be the most important single measure to prevent a declining impact of growth on poverty reduction. Opening up to the global economy forces these countries to abandon their past system of social protection. This leads to large-scale increase in the headcount rate of open unemployment even though the aggregate labor use in the economy, measured in units of employment at constant intensity of work, may be rising. In severe cases, as in state and collective enterprises in China, the rate of shedding surplus labor has far outpaced the growth of aggregate labor use so that the number of unemployed, those without an entitlement to income, has increased sharply. To protect the newly unemployed from poverty either some transparent system of social security (e.g., unemployment insurance) must replace the past concealed system of social security or large-scale public works programs in productive capital construction must be introduced. As noted above, these are immensely difficult tasks in a period of budgetary retrenchment that reform programs almost always impose on these countries.

7. *Specially designed employment opportunities for the labor-disadvantaged households.* Not all poor households have the ability to benefit from employment opportunities that economic growth offers in a market economy. Labor resources available in a female-headed and female-labor-intensive household would often be at a disadvantage if labor-intensive economic growth of the usual kind were the principal instrument for poverty reduction. For the benefit of increased labor demand to filter down to these poor families, special opportunities—for example, subcontracting arrangements linking enterprises in the formal sector with micro- and cottage enterprises that facilitate work for these disadvantaged households in or near their homes—should be created by appropriate incentives. Similar measures are needed to spread the benefit of increased overall demand for labor to remote and isolated communities.

8. *Caution in the design of labor market interventions in protecting vulnerable workers by ensuring security of employment at the living wage.* Concerned policymakers have often felt that in a market economy the workers are at a serious disadvantage relative to the employers in the bargain concerning

employment and earning. Those who are subject to these vulnerabilities have often been identified as groups in, or at risk of, poverty. The wish to protect them from these vulnerabilities has often led governments to adopt policies for employment security at regulated wage. Legislation of minimum wages, regulation of conditions of work, and rules for termination of employment are examples of such policies. Caution needs to be exercised in the adoption of these measures. Implementing sensible standards of safety in workplaces and protection for vulnerable workers facing monopsonistic employers in a labor market characterized by gross inequality of power can be effective as instruments for the enhancement of the welfare of the poor. But it is counterproductive and detrimental to the welfare of the poor to allow these interventions to artificially raise the cost of employment to the point of restricting a healthy elasticity of labor demand with respect to output growth.

Needless to say, comprehensive strategies for poverty reduction include policies in addition to the above. These additional policies are of two categories. The first of the two categories includes the subsidiary policies to facilitate the implementation of the above policies (e.g., providing the poor with access to efficient public services, which helps them succeed as microentrepreneurs, and quickening the pace of demographic transition, which reduces the imbalance between supply of and demand for labor, improves the prospect for increased wages, and makes it easier to provide the members of the labor force with human capital).[12] They should be subsumed under the employment policies for poverty reduction. The second category consists of policies that are independent of employment-related interventions for poverty reduction. The most important intervention of this kind consists of direct income subsidies to the poor, including relief in cash and in kind (e.g., feeding of vulnerable groups). This is necessary and effective in improving the welfare of those poor households who do not have an adequate labor endowment. Governments also resort to income redistribution through the regulation of prices, public distribution, and subsidies as an instrument to address the problem of poverty. Policymakers have made widespread use of public distribution, pricing policy, and subsidies as methods of protecting vulnerable groups of population from poverty. Thus "essential goods" have often been distributed through the public rationing system at low cost. Goods and services used by the poor for consumption and production have been kept cheap through direct and indirect subsidies. While it has been argued that these policies make the real incomes of the poor higher than they would otherwise be, there is wide recognition that targeting these interventions to the poor is extremely difficult, that their benefits are substantially appropriated by the nonpoor, and that they distort production incentives to the detriment of economic growth. The consensus seems to be that these interventions do not have an advantage over direct income subsidies to the poor. Even direct income subsidies are subject to limitations as an instrument for poverty reduction: they require budgetary resources that are difficult to find. Their targeting presupposes a degree of administrative capability and honesty that is rare among developing countries. The point of this brief discussion of poverty reduction policies unrelated to employment is to reinforce the argument that there are few effective instruments of poverty reduction that are not concerned with utilizing and improving the capacity of the poor to work.

■ An Empirical Analysis of Employment Policies for Poverty Reduction

This section is concerned with an empirical analysis of the arguments made in the preceding sections. It tries to relate the performance in poverty reduction to performance in generating productive employment with reference to actual experience in developing countries, with a view to seeking evidence for the arguments made above. It addresses the following questions: Can a clear relationship be established between employment expansion and poverty reduction? How can observed differences in the strength of the relationship between growth and employment expansion on the one hand and poverty reduction on the other be explained? What can one conclude about the effectiveness of different kinds of employment-related interventions for poverty reduction from an analysis of the experience of different developing regions and countries?

For the purpose of this analysis, indicators of performance in poverty reduction, economic growth, and the employment intensity of growth are required. Numerical estimates of long-term trends in the incidence of poverty with reference to common yardsticks are available for only a limited number of countries. Even when such estimates are available, they are often subject to controversy. At times it is hard to choose from competing estimates claiming very different outcomes. This chapter tries to avoid unnecessary controversy by settling for consensus views on trends even when disagreements prevail about actual changes. Detailed data are presented in Tables 4.7 and 4.8 for regions for which they are less readily available. Trends in poverty are discerned from estimates based on national poverty thresholds and from estimates based on the World Bank's internationally comparable PPP$ poverty threshold. Comparisons of the incidence of poverty between countries are generally based on the latter, for which changes in the incidence of poverty are available, for the main developing regions and a limited number of countries, only for the years 1987 to 1998.[13] Measurement of economic growth presents fewer problems and can be represented by the rate of growth in (per capita) gross domestic product or gross national product. Employment intensity of growth should be measured by the GDP elasticity of employment: the proportionate change in employment divided by the proportionate change in GDP. However, it is very difficult to obtain reliable estimates of aggregate employment for the developing countries, where, for the large traditional and informal sectors, it is virtually impossible to obtain reliable estimates of employment at constant intensity of work. This section often uses the output elasticity of employment in manufacturing industries, for which these measurements are more accurate and easier to interpret, as the proxy for the employment intensity of growth. Attention is mostly focused on the change in the elasticity, which should make this procedure more acceptable than it would otherwise be. One would tend to regard a fall (rise) in the output elasticity of employment in manufacturing as a good indicator of a deterioration (improvement) in the overall labor intensity of growth. The critical importance of this elasticity, despite the often small size of manufacturing in total employment, derives from the fact that manufacturing is typically the largest incremental source of employment in the earlier phases of transformation of the developing countries. Wherever possible, supplementary evidence is provided for the labor intensity of the rest of the economy. Trends in unemployment are also used at times as supplementary evidence on employment performance.

This may also be the place to consider what is the right order of magnitude for the output elasticity of employment. This obviously depends on the level of development and the relative factor endowment of the country concerned. It is expected that the output elasticity of employment would gradually fall as a country becomes more developed and relatively less labor abundant (more labor scarce). Thus the elasticity in Korea is understandably lower for the 1980s than for the 1970s. The desirable level of the elasticity can also be judged by what the countries, with best-practice policies and institutions, achieved at the time of comparable levels of development and relative resource endowment. Thus, one might argue, that Korea's elasticity of 0.7 during the 1970s represents the level that most developing countries should aim at achieving until they attain something like an upper-middle-income status. With an output growth of at least 5 percent, an elasticity of this order for the economy as a whole should enable a country to achieve an employment growth of at least 3.5 percent, which with few exceptions should allow an employment growth in excess of the growth in the labor force. This should complete the so-called Lewis transition reasonably quickly once demographic transition proceeds simultaneously.[14] This also permits a healthy growth in labor productivity, which, if properly harnessed and distributed in favor of the poor workers, can further help the process of poverty reduction. There is obviously a conflict between a high output elasticity of employment and a rapid growth in labor productivity. The right balance between the two depends on the specific circumstances of a country. In general, a country with a high incidence of poverty and a relative abundance of labor resources will help its poor by focusing more on a higher elasticity of employment than on a higher growth in labor productivity.

Another way to view this matter is to consider that in an economy with a lot of poverty, unemployment and underemployment are widespread and the elasticity of labor supply is very high. The effect of an upward shift in labor productivity in such an economy, bringing about a rise in demand for labor, principally results in an increase in employment rather than an increase in real wages. Initially, poverty reduction takes place due mainly to an increase in employment per household—that is, a reduction in dependency ratio—and to a lesser extent due to a rise in real wages per worker. As the process succeeds in reducing unemployment and underemployment, the rise in real wages begins to accelerate. An attempt to artificially accelerate the process of increasing real wages by direct interventions in the labor market can at best succeed in a limited segment of the market, typically the relatively small modern sector. This kind of segmentation of the market adversely affects the distribution of earnings among the workers and aggravates the problem of poverty reduction among the workers employed outside the modern sector.

Should the output elasticity of employment be allowed to exceed the numerical value of one, indicating a lower productivity of employment at the margin than on average? Normally a country should avoid this outcome. But this does not mean that an elasticity greater than 1.0 is necessarily a bad thing. A country initially characterized by an undesirably highly capital-intensive technology with restricted employment may benefit from a very different composition of incremental output representing a higher rate of growth in employment than in output, signifying a lower, and socially more desirable, capital intensity at the margin. However, one needs to be certain that the higher-than-unit elasticity of employment is consistent with efficient labor use.

Finally, the urgency of the drive for a high output elasticity of employment depends on the rate of output growth itself. A country with a high rate of growth can perhaps make do with a comparatively lower output elasticity of employment than a country unable to achieve a high enough rate of growth. Below a critical minimum rate of growth of output, the pursuit of a higher output elasticity of employment as an instrument for poverty reduction is futile; attention must be focused on an acceleration of the growth rate itself by policies that make growth endogenous to the process of poverty-alleviating employment expansion—that is, generating a higher output growth by utilizing otherwise redundant labor.

East and Southeast Asia

The ESEA region has been the most rapidly growing in the world since the second half of the twentieth century, averaging an annual growth in GDP of 8 percent over the past two decades. It is the largest of the regions into which the developing countries are usually classified.[15] It accounts for 31 percent of world population and 36 percent of the population in the developing world. This region, however, accounts for only 23 percent of the poor of the developing world; it is also the region that achieved the highest rate of decline in the incidence of poverty during the last decade according to the World Bank's PPP$ poverty line. Indeed, the number of people in absolute poverty thus measured in this region declined by a third between 1987 and 1998, while the number of poor in the rest of the developing world during the same period increased by a fifth. ESEA is thus the region that has achieved the fastest rate of growth and the most rapid reduction in the incidence of poverty in recent times. An understanding of the factors contributing to successful poverty reduction must necessarily focus on the experience of this region.[16]

The experience in poverty reduction in the region has not been uniform, however. Four distinct types of experience characterize the countries included in the case studies: (1) the Republic of Korea, representing the four original East Asian pioneers (the other three being Taiwan, China; Hong Kong, China; and Singapore); (2) China; (3) Indonesia, Malaysia, and Thailand, the three later imitators of the original East Asian pioneers; and (4) the Philippines, a case of poor performance in poverty reduction by East Asian standards.[17]

The Republic of Korea. In many ways the Korean case represents the broad features of the general experience of the four East Asian pioneers.[18] During the last three decades of the twentieth century the country achieved an annual average growth in GDP of more than 8 percent. A quick and early demographic transition enabled the country to convert much of this gain into increase in per capita income. Economic growth was highly labor-intensive, as illustrated by the high output elasticity of employment in manufacturing, which was 0.69 during the 1970s and declined only to 0.49 during the 1980s, when the country was left with little surplus labor. (The output elasticity of employment fell further to 0.28 after 1992, when the Republic of Korea became a labor-scarce economy.) The result of high growth and high employment elasticity in the early phase of development was not only a rapid rate of employment growth and a structural change in the composition of employment away from agriculture in favor of industries and services, but also an unprecedented rate of increase in real earnings of labor (as illustrated by the growth rate in manufacturing earnings, which was faster than the growth rate in per capita income). Rapid growth in employment and wages brought about a sharp reduction in the incidence of absolute poverty. According to World Bank estimates, less than 2 percent of the population of Korea fell into the category of poor in 1998. Rapid growth over more than three decades was associated with undiminished and high equality in the distribution of income.[19]

The case resembles the classic vision of a high rate of growth-induced expansion in employment, combined with a high growth in the productivity and earnings of workers, acting as the principal instrument for poverty reduction. With few distortions in incentives and institutions favoring inappropriate techniques of production and employment-averse behavior on the part of the employers, high economic growth was translated into a high rate of employment expansion at rapidly growing real wage. Early demographic transition helped accelerate the process.

However, it was much more than a case of poverty reduction due to growth-induced employment expansion in a market operating under conditions of laissez-faire. There were numerous employment-related policy interventions for poverty reduction in addition to the overall strategy of promoting a high rate of employment-intensive growth. Early in the growth process a thorough redistribution of land enabled the small farmers and the previously landless workers to convert themselves into productive agricultural entrepreneurs, a process that received a further positive impetus from the policy of ensuring favorable terms of trade for them and granting them access to the benefits of publicly funded research in improved technology, public provision of infrastructure, and public services.

Redistributive policies to promote productive entrepreneurship among the poor featured prominently in other East Asian pioneers as well. Taiwan implemented a highly egalitarian land reform. Singapore and Hong Kong, being city-states, avoided the need for land reforms. These countries, however, went for an egalitarian distribution of housing, perhaps the most important asset in these societies, through public housing programs. While South Korean industrialization was by and large promoted by large-scale enterprises, subcontracting with small and cottage producers was practiced widely, especially in later years. Elsewhere in the region, notably in Taiwan, industrialization itself was largely accounted for by the growth of small-scale enterprises. Another important employment-related policy that helped poverty reduction was large public investment in improving the human capital endowment of workers. Very early implementation of universal primary education was quickly followed by widespread access to secondary education and the removal of gender disparity in access to basic education. Easy access to skill acquisition has been instrumental in bringing about massive shifts in the occupational structure, which facilitated the change in the pattern of production and trade that was frequently warranted by rapid growth, without impairing the welfare of the poor.

It thus appears that the remarkable success of Korea and the other three East Asian pioneers was due to a strategy that incorporated the first five of the eight employment-related policies identified earlier in this chapter. These countries do not appear to have needed the remaining three policies: they did not face a significant problem of initial inefficiency in the form of excess employment in public enterprises. In these countries the share of the public sector in total employment has generally been small, and employment and wages in the public sector have not been far divorced from market rules. They all appear to have avoided using labor market interventions in the form of minimum wages and the regulation of conditions of employment during the early phase of their development. Indeed, there was little need for these instruments in the context of rapidly growing employment and real wage.[20] Indeed, Korea's labor laws inherited a provision that made it virtually impossible for enterprises to terminate employment. However, there is little evidence that this law prevented drastic restructuring of employment that was periodically required by the process of structural transformation. The extraordinarily high rates of growth in employment and wages made voluntary restructuring possible.

Indonesia, Malaysia, and Thailand. These countries gradually adopted the development strategy of the four East Asian pioneers during the late 1970s and the early 1980s. Like the East Asian pioneers, they succeeded in achieving high rates of growth with an emphasis on the efficiency of resource use. The incentive structure on the whole favored rapid labor absorption. These countries generally supported small-scale enterprises by avoiding the disincentive that these enterprises are subjected to, relative to the large-scale enterprises, in much of the developing world. Their performance in endowing the members of the labor force with human capital was also good. They have generally exercised caution in the use of labor market interventions. Public employment, as a proportion of total employment, has been limited. There has been little attempt to regulate the conditions of employment and its termination in the private sector. Minimum wage legislations either have been nonexistent or set wages at a sufficiently low level so that their effect was to protect the very vulnerable groups of workers rather than to affect the overall level and structure of wages. They all achieved rapid demographic transition, which made it easier to absorb the growth in labor supply into productive employment.

However, these countries differed from the East Asian pioneers insofar as their development policies have not been characterized by major redistributive programs. Malaysia resorted to some redistribution of assets, although the emphasis was on the disadvantaged ethnic group. Indonesia's agriculture was characterized by peasant landownership with limited inequality. Although land reform was avoided, public policy in Indonesia strongly emphasized investment targeted to benefit the smallholders and favorable terms of trade for agriculture. Thailand avoided land reform and, until the recent past, imposed unfavorable terms of trade on agriculture by discriminatory trade policy. Urban-rural inequality in Thailand has remained very large, and Thailand's record with respect to the change in inequality in the distribution of income is the worst among the countries in the group.

By and large, these countries were able to achieve an appropriate linkage among growth, employment generation, and poverty reduction although, as shown in Table 4.1, the linkage was not always as powerful as that in the case of the East Asian pioneers. Nevertheless the demand for labor increased rapidly in these countries until the early 1990s, resulting in the steady growth in employment and real wages. All the three countries experienced rapid reduction in the incidence of poverty in the decades preceding the crisis of 1997.

Table 4.1 Average Annual Percentage Growth Rates in Output, Employment, Earnings, Productivity, and Output Elasticity of Employment in Manufacturing in Selected ESEA Countries, 1971–1997

	Real Value Added			Employment			Real Earnings			Labor Productivity		Output Elasticity of Employment		
	1971–1980	1981–1992	1992–1997	1971–1980	1981–1992	1992–1997	1971–1980	1981–1992	1992–1997	1971–1980	1981–1992	1971–1980	1981–1992	1992–1997
Korea	16.71	11.93	8.11	11.61	5.80	2.30	10.56	8.05	5.44	5.10	6.13	0.69	0.49	0.28
Indonesia	14.56	12.09	10.35	6.49	11.19	2.55	4.30	4.72	7.87	8.07	0.90	0.45	0.93	0.25
Malaysia	11.48	10.62	12.81	10.28	4.22	3.05	2.61	2.11	4.35	1.20	6.40	0.90	0.40	0.24
Thailand	10.28	10.22	8.18	6.87	5.42	1.80	0.16	6.19	3.01	3.41	4.79	0.67	0.53	0.22
Philippines	5.93	0.90	4.47	11.13	-0.45	2.81	-3.34	5.88	-0.86	-5.19	1.34	1.88	-0.50	0.63

Sources: Estimates are based on data from the United Nations Industrial Development Organization (UNIDO). For 1971–1980 and 1981–1992 the data are from Khan and Muqtada 1997, tab. 6.11. The estimates for 1992–1997 have been updated by adopting the same method as in Khan and Muqtada 1997, to the extent it could be ascertained. The estimates are growth rates between end points and the data are from the following sources: employment, UNIDO; value added, UNIDO current price value added deflated by the implicit deflator for manufacturing value added in World Bank 2000c; real earnings, International Labour Organization 1999.

Notes: Output elasticity of employment is the ratio of employment growth to growth in value added. For real earnings, the terminal year in the last period (1992–1997) is 1996 for Indonesia and 1995 for Malaysia and the Philippines.

In the early 1990s the output elasticity of employment in these countries declined sharply. It is hard to argue that during this period these countries experienced a significant tightening of the labor market. Indeed, both Indonesia and Thailand still bore the marks of comparative labor abundance. And yet industries in these countries became less labor-absorbing than industries in Korea, which became a relatively labor-scarce country in this period.

The financial crisis of 1997 appears to have reversed the trend of poverty reduction rather seriously in Indonesia, significantly in Thailand, and modestly in Malaysia. The crisis has also raised issues about the resilience of the growth process itself in these countries, especially in Indonesia and Thailand.

China. Available estimates about levels and trends in poverty in China are often in conflict with one another. However, there seems to be broad agreement among various sources about the following two propositions: China achieved a remarkably rapid reduction in poverty in the years after it embarked on economic reforms, and since about the mid-1980s the rate of poverty reduction drastically slowed down. A detailed World Bank study estimated that the proportion of rural population in poverty in China declined by two-thirds between 1978 and 1984 and showed no further decline for the decade of the 1980s thereafter. It also found a similar break in trend in the incidence of urban poverty in the year 1984. A study based on carefully designed household surveys for 1988 and 1995 shows that the rate of reduction in rural poverty between the two years was far slower than the rate at which rural poverty is generally estimated to have declined before the mid-1980s. The study found that between the two years urban poverty did not decrease at all and, arguably, increased. It also estimated that inequality in the distribution of income increased very sharply over the period. China's economy achieved a historically unprecedented growth during the entire postreform period with a slight acceleration in the rate of growth since the mid-1980s. The evidence on the break in trend in China's performance in poverty reduction suggests a major shift in China's development policy around that time.[21]

China's remarkable growth in the immediate postreform period was led by growth in agriculture. This was based on an egalitarian access of the rural households to land; a sharp and steady improvement in agriculture's terms of trade; and the liberalization of the rural economy, including encouragement for entrepreneurship in nonfarm activities. This led to a sharp increase in the productivity and earning of rural population, who accounted for an overwhelming proportion of China's poor. The urban economy benefited from the backward linkage of rural growth. The observed output elasticity of employment in urban areas was reasonably, though not remarkably, high. During this period, China's state and collective enterprises continued the policy of supporting excess employment as a concealed method of social protection. China had a decent record of human capital endowment of the labor force. Thus there was a combination of the first five of the policies listed previously in this chapter, while the need for the sixth policy—namely an orderly dismantling of the past systems of inefficient excess employment—had not yet arisen. The result was a remarkable increase in income of the poor, especially those in the rural economy, based on the productive use of their labor.

A large percentage increase in manufacturing value added, as shown in Table 4.2, marks a change in China's development policy since the mid-1980s from rural development to industrialization, led by exports, within the overall strategy of a rapid integration with the global economy. Public resources for agriculture declined. The improvement in agriculture's terms of trade was halted and, for a period, reversed. As a result, the rate of improvement in the welfare of the rural poor sharply slowed down. But the most serious failure of the growth-employment-poverty linkage took place in the urban economy. As China opened up to private and foreign investment, its vast state and collective enterprises were forced to begin reducing the concealed surplus labor that they had carried in the past in order to regain a semblance of competitiveness. The result was a sharp fall in the observed output elasticity of employment in industries: it fell to 0.34 after 1985 and to a dismal 0.15 after 1990. Since 1995, employment in manufacturing has contracted rapidly, resulting in a highly negative output elasticity of employment. The contrast with Korea, with an elasticity of employment of nearly 0.7 during the comparable phase of development, is obvious.

How might one explain the paradox that industrialization based on the expansion of labor-intensive exports during the era of globalization resulted in such a slow—and negative since 1995—growth in employment? It is particularly intriguing that this happened despite the fact that empirical studies show that the growth of China's manufactured exports was concentrated in labor-

Table 4.2   Annual Percentage Growth in Value Added, Employment, Real Wages in Manufacturing, and Output Elasticity of Employment in Manufacturing, China, 1978–1999

	Value Added	Employment	Real Wages	Output Elasticity of Employment
1978–1980	10.6	5.2	8.0	0.49
1980–1985	9.9	4.7	4.5	0.47
1985–1990	9.2	3.1	2.8	0.34
1990–1995	17.7	2.6	.8	0.15
1995–1999	10.3	–4.6	8.3	–0.45

Source: National Bureau of Statistics 2000.
Notes: Growth rates are annual compound rates between end points. Real wages have been estimated by deflating nominal wages by the urban consumer price index. Output elasticity of employment is the ratio of growth rate in employment to growth rate in value added.

intensive products.[22] The explanation of the paradox lies in the initial conditions of manufacturing industries. The system of incentives prevailing in the period before accelerated globalization permitted an absorption of labor far in excess of requirement in the overwhelmingly dominant state and collective sector. Economic reform for integration with the globalizing world economy made it increasingly difficult to continue with this system of concealed social protection. Thus a process of shedding the concealed surplus labor began. The observed low output elasticity of employment hides the fact that it represents the sum of two effects: a fairly high output elasticity of employment measured at constant intensity of employment per worker, and a rise in the intensity of employment per worker due to a reduction of concealed unemployment in industries. It is possible to argue that reforms leading to globalization should not be blamed for the slow growth of employment in industries. Industrial employment, measured at constant intensity of employment per worker, has increased quite rapidly, but this has been outweighed by the contraction in employment brought about by the reduction in concealed surplus labor in public sector industries. Once the process of shedding surplus labor is completed, industries will become more efficient. Indeed, a continuation of concealed unemployment in industries is an inefficient method of protecting workers. A proper method of protecting surplus industrial workers is to institute either a formal system of unemployment insurance or sufficiently large public works programs during the transition period. China found it very hard to pursue either of these alternatives in an environment of macroeconomic policies emphasizing fiscal retrenchment. The problem is that poverty reduction depends on the growth of the headcount rate of employment, which in these cases was very slow and, since 1995, negative.

Inappropriate labor market interventions (e.g., the strict rationing of urban employment and the exclusion of the floating migrants from the urban labor market) further exacerbated the inequity in the labor market. No doubt the poor performance of China in poverty reduction after the mid-1980s was aggravated by many other factors: the regional concentration of development in the rich provinces in the age of globalization, the strongly disequalizing change in the distribution of public subsidies, and the weakening of public services for the poor. But much of the explanation of the phenomenon lies in the failure of the employment link in the process of converting growth into benefit for the poor. In terms of the policy interventions listed previously in this chapter, China failed to implement the fifth and sixth policies and allowed inappropriate interventions in the eighth policy area.

It is useful to note that real wages in manufacturing continued to rise in the period of rapidly growing unemployment. It is difficult to judge how this came about. Conceivably this could have been due to the replacement of the large number of previously underemployed workers by fewer workers with greater skill and higher productivity. But it is more likely that this was due to a regulated market for employment in state and collective enterprises from which the floating migrants were excluded. The result was a greater inequality between the employed urban workers and the rest. Be that as it may, the phenomenon demonstrates that rising real wage is a favorable factor for poverty reduction only when it is a part of a process of increasing labor demand in a well-functioning labor market. It is not a good indicator of the welfare of the poor when it is artificially buttressed by arbitrary regulations in a situation of falling demand for labor.

It may be useful to note that the failure of the employment linkage during reform in the age of globalization can be observed in the other major transition economy in the region. In Vietnam the annual growth in employment in industries (including construction) during 1991–1995 was 1.6 percent, while output in those sectors increased at an annual rate of 13.8 percent, yielding a dismally low output elasticity of employment of 0.12.[23]

The Philippines.   The Philippines stands out as an exception to the other major ESEA countries in that it failed to achieve a high rate of growth, thereby failing to fulfill the basic condition of poverty reduction through growth-induced employment generation. As Table 4.1 shows, employment performance in the Philippines was erratic and enigmatic: during the 1970s it expanded employment far in excess of output growth, and during the 1980s it experienced a negative output elasticity of employment. Since 1992 the output elasticity of employment has been quite reasonably high, except that the growth in employment itself remained quite low. While a distorted system of incentives and the dominance of oligopolies in industries prevented the growth of output and employment, in agriculture a highly unequal distribution of land encouraged speculative nonuse of land and restriction of employment. The poverty reduction process was further hampered by a slow rate of demographic transition that created a large imbalance between the supply of and the demand for labor and made the task of imparting human capital to the labor force difficult. The performance on poverty reduction was highly unsatisfactory.[24]

South Asia

South Asia—overwhelmingly dominated by five major countries—namely Bangladesh, India, Nepal, Pakistan, and Sri Lanka—accounts for 22 percent of world population and 26 percent of the population of the developing world. However, it accounted for a staggering 45 percent of the developing world's poor in 1998 according to the World Bank's PPP$ poverty line. Between 1987 and 1998 this region experienced the largest absolute increase in the number of poor of all developing regions. The percentage increase in the number of poor, however, was lower than that in all the other three regions (Latin America and the Caribbean, sub-Saharan Africa, and Europe and Central Asia) in which poverty increased according to World Bank estimates. These estimates also show that the proportion of population in poverty actually decreased from 45 percent in 1987 to 40 percent in 1998.

South Asia has achieved relatively steady, if unspectacular, growth in recent decades. Since the 1970s the growth rate in GDP has steadily accelerated in all countries with the exception of Pakistan. India's growth rate has increased substantially and, if the current growth rate is sustained, the country might soon be said to have made a qualitative transition to a higher growth trajectory than what it experienced in the past. The acceleration in growth in Bangladesh, Nepal, and Sri Lanka has been modest. In all these four countries the steady decline in the rate of population growth has served as an independent element in the improvement of their living standard; the growth rate in per capita GDP in all these countries rose substantially faster than the growth rate in GDP. Pakistan is the only country in the region that has experienced a reduction in the rate of per capita GDP growth, which since the late 1980s has been less than half of what it was the decade before. Belatedly, the demographic transition has started to reduce the rate of increase in the labor force.

The accelerated growth in per capita GDP should have enabled Bangladesh, India, Nepal, and Sri Lanka to achieve a faster rate of poverty reduction in the late 1980s and the 1990s than before. Even Pakistan should have achieved a reduction in the incidence of poverty, if only at a slower rate than before. Available evidence, though sometimes controversial, does not suggest that this has happened. In Bangladesh the rate of poverty reduction dramatically declined after the mid-1980s, particularly in rural areas, where most people live.[25] In India there is an intense controversy on the question of whether poverty reduction has just slowed down or been reversed in recent years. However, there appears to be little disagreement that it has at best slowed down substantially. Careful recent studies suggest that the rate of reduction in poverty since the early 1980s has been rather slow, with virtually no change in the proportion of population in poverty between the late 1980s and the middle 1990s.[26] In Pakistan the incidence of poverty is estimated to have increased since the late 1980s.[27] There are many reasons for this perverse outcome resulting in the failure of higher growth to be transmitted to an equivalently higher rate of poverty reduction. One factor that needs to be noted is the extreme employment hostility of growth in these countries since the 1980s.

Table 4.3 presents evidence on output elasticity of employment in manufacturing for each of the past three decades. Two important points emerge:

1. With only minor exceptions, these countries failed to achieve a high degree of labor intensity in manufacturing throughout the period under review. All these countries were vastly more labor abundant than Korea was during the 1970s. And yet none of them ever ap-

proached the elasticity that Korean industries achieved at that time. The elasticities for Sri Lanka for the 1970s, for Bangladesh for the 1980s, and for Pakistan for the 1990s are the only exceptions. Sri Lanka's high elasticity only highlights the opportunity that the country and the region have failed to take advantage of during the past two decades. The Bangladesh estimate for the 1980s perhaps reflects the well-known phenomenon of concealed unemployment in public sector enterprises that the country has since been struggling to rid itself of. The relatively high estimate for Pakistan during the 1990s almost certainly represents the lag in the response in the adjustment in employment during a period of sharply falling growth in output.

2. In all these countries, except Pakistan, the elasticity was dismally low during the 1990s, a period of widespread reform in the system of incentives and rapid integration with the global economy. For India, Bangladesh, and Sri Lanka the elasticity declined during the 1990s from the already low levels of the 1980s. For Nepal the estimate was extremely low by any absolute standard. Even for Pakistan the relatively high value of the elasticity during the 1990s needs to be seen in the context of low growth in employment due to the drastically lower rate of growth. The average value of the elasticity during the 1990s reflects an employment-hostile pattern of growth for the region.

The decline in the labor intensity of industries in the postglobalization period cannot be explained with reference to distorted incentives affecting the choice of techniques alone, because these incentives generally improved in this period. It appears that these countries were also faced with the kind of phenomenon that afflicted China in the form of excess employment in manufacturing. Economic reforms and privatization to ensure competitiveness in

Table 4.3   Growth and Employment Elasticity, South Asia, 1965–1998

	GDP Growth Rate (% per year)			Output Elasticity of Manufacturing Employment		
	1965–1980	1980–1990	1990–1998	1971–1980	1981–1990	1991–1998
Bangladesh	4.2[a]	4.3	4.7	0.165*	0.637*	0.390*
India	3.8	5.8	6.1	0.463*	0.272*	0.234
Nepal	2.3	4.6	5.0	0.004*	0.213*	0.266
Pakistan	5.2	6.3	4.2	0.516*	0.399*	0.615*
Sri Lanka	4.0	4.6	5.0	0.796*	0.369*	0.268

Sources: Growth rates are based on data shown in the World Bank's *World Development Indicators* and *World Development Report,* various years, excepting Bangladesh, for which national data have been used.
Notes: * = significance at the 95 percent level.
a. 1975–1980.

the process of increasing integration with the global economy must have led these countries to reduce the concealed unemployment in industries, thereby making the observed output elasticity of employment so very low.[28]

Low employment intensity of industrial growth meant declining real wages in those countries in the region for which information is available. Real manufacturing wages declined between 1990 and 1995 in both India and Pakistan by 25 percent.[29]

In Bangladesh the poor performance in poverty reduction was largely a rural phenomenon. It was due to a period of agricultural stagnation that reduced the growth of productive employment in the rural economy. As noted earlier, real wages in agriculture fell by more than 16 percent between fiscal year 1985–1986 and the second half of calendar year 1998. This demonstrates how the working poor can face increasing immiserization in case the concentration of ownership of land and other assets leads to a rising share of incremental output being distributed among nonlabor factors of production. The relatively better urban poverty performance in Bangladesh was at least partly due to the expansion of employment in the export-based garment industry, although traditional industries, mostly in the public sector until recently, faced the same problem of adjustment for excess employment that other countries faced.

The failure of the growth-employment-poverty linkage in the region must have been due to a broader failure of policies for the promotion of productive and remunerative employment, as outlined previously. The region's performance in the redistribution of land and the widening of the access to productive resources for the promotion of self-employment and microenterprise has been very poor.[30] The region's record in endowing the poor with human capital has also not been particularly good (Sri Lanka being an exception). Furthermore, it has been alleged that the region's inappropriate interventions in the labor market exacerbated the problem of employment expansion. Regulations of conditions of employment, termination of employment, and the level and structure of wages were effective only in the modern sector of the economy. These measures at best succeeded in creating small islands of protected high-cost employment and generally contributed to the low elasticity of labor demand.

Sub-Saharan Africa

Sub-Saharan Africa is home to 13 percent of the population of the developing world and, according to the World Bank's PPP$ poverty line, 24 percent of the poor of the developing world. The number of poor in SSA, thus measured, increased by a third between 1987 and 1998. It is the developing region with the highest proportion (46 percent) of population in poverty.

In terms of the framework presented here, the overwhelming reason for SSA's failure to prevent a rise in poverty was its failure to achieve growth.[31]

This is demonstrated by the contrast between those few countries that achieved reasonable growth and those that failed to do so.

Ethiopia, Ghana, and Uganda are three countries that achieved reasonable growth in the 1990s. They all succeeded in reducing the incidence of absolute poverty quite substantially. Côte d'Ivoire also achieved a similar, though less convincing, outcome. They were helped in this by high labor intensity of growth, especially in agriculture. This is particularly well documented for Ethiopia and Uganda. An important fact about their poverty-reducing growth is that it was based on a wide access to productive work. In each of these countries nearly 90 percent of the workers are principally employed in agriculture.[32] The key to livelihood for these workers was access to the critical complementary factor of production, land. In Ethiopia the distribution of land is quite equitable by the standard of the least-developed countries (LDCs).[33] The land reform of the 1970s finally brought its benefits to the poor peasant households as the oppressive and coercive villagization, collectivization, and unfavorable compulsory procurement, resorted to by the Derg regime, were finally abolished in the early 1990s. In Uganda the formal distribution of land is less equal, but approximately 97 percent of the rural households have access to land use, and land rent, under the existing system of tenancy, is very low.[34] Thus the distribution of income in the rural economy was relatively equitable. While the equality of the distribution of farm income was ensured by widespread and equitable access to land, the equality of the distribution of this primary source of income led to the equity of the distribution of nonfarm income growth that it induced. Restoration of peace and comparative security by itself was a major boost to rural incentives. This was supplemented by the abolition of compulsory procurement at unfavorable prices, as in Ethiopia, and other discriminatory practices prevalent in the past. Ghana and Côte d'Ivoire also had very rapid growth of agriculture during the 1990s.

Numerous observations about growth in African countries can be made from Table 4.4. Generally speaking, nonagricultural sectors, relatively small in absolute size, experienced very rapid growth. The output elasticity of employment in manufacturing for Ethiopia remained dismally low during the 1990s, although higher than during the 1980s. This probably indicates the adjustment for the past years of arbitrary growth of employment in industries that were almost entirely in the public sector. For Uganda the absolute rate of growth of manufacturing employment was high, and the low elasticity of employment was a reflection of an extremely high rate of output growth that probably created an opportunity to productively absorb the excess employment created in the past. In Ghana and Côte d'Ivoire the elasticity increased during the 1990s and approached a healthy absolute level. It appears that the output elasticity of employment in manufacturing in these countries during the 1990s reflects the beginning of a process of adjustment for the arbitrary expansion of employment in state-owned enterprises in the past. These coun-

Table 4.4 Economic Growth, Employment Growth in Manufacturing, and Output Elasticities of Employment, Selected African Countries, 1980–1999

	GDP Growth Rate (%)		Output Elasticity of Employment in Manufacturing	
	1980–1990	1990–1999	1980–1990	1991–1998
Countries in which poverty declined in the 1990s				
Côte d'Ivoire	0.7	3.7	0.466*	0.574*
Ethiopia	1.1	4.8	–0.001	0.108*
Ghana	3.0	4.3	0.368*	0.433*
Uganda	2.9	7.2	0.211*	0.236
Countries in which poverty increased or remained undiminished in the 1990s				
Burkina Faso	3.6	3.8	0.688*	0.421
Kenya	4.2	2.2	0.756*	1.401*
Mauritania	1.8	4.1	–0.486	–0.324
Nigeria	1.6	2.4	0.040	1.241*
South Africa	1.0	1.9	1.306*	0.850
Tanzania	—	3.1	—	2.670
Zambia	1.0	1.0	0.460	–0.115*
Zimbabwe	3.6	2.4	0.925	–0.546*

Sources: Growth rates are from World Bank 2000c. Output elasticity of employment for Tanzania is from Islam and Majeres 2001. For the other estimates of the elasticity, the method and data sources are explained in the chapter appendix.

Notes: For Mauritania, poverty increased according to the international poverty line and decreased according to domestic poverty lines. For Kenya, South Africa, and Tanzania poverty estimates are not available. For Kenya and South Africa, per capita income declined in the 1990s and there is indirect evidence to support the hypothesis of increasing poverty. Poverty figures are shown in Table 4.7.

* = significance at the 95 percent level.

tries have also started directing resources to an improvement of human capital, especially by targeting a reduction of AIDS, which affects members of the labor force in their prime.

In contrast to these favorable examples stand the experiences of Kenya, Nigeria, South Africa, Zambia, and Zimbabwe, where the absence of robust growth was the principal cause of the increasing or nondiminishing incidence of poverty. These countries also had arbitrary employment growth in industries, unrelated to efficient labor demand dictated by growth in output. This is reflected in employment elasticities greater than 1.0 for Nigeria and Kenya and negative elasticities for Zambia and Zimbabwe during the 1990s. As discussed earlier, employment expansion without growth cannot be a sustainable basis for poverty reduction. South Africa suffered from the same phenomenon during the 1980s.

Tanzania, Mauritania, and Burkina Faso also achieved moderate growth during the 1990s. Mauritania's decent overall growth clearly failed to create the right linkage for employment growth; its manufacturing industries rapidly expanded employment despite negative growth in output. Tanzania and Burkina Faso attained only modest overall growth. In Tanzania, fairly rapid growth in manufacturing employment was based on a very slow output growth. Burkina Faso experienced too slow a rate of growth in manufacturing employment.

The failure of the employment linkage in the SSA region was exacerbated by the unfavorable supply-side conditions because of the absence of a demographic transition. The annual rate of population growth during the last two decades of the twentieth century was 2.8 percent for the region as a whole as compared to an average of 1.9 percent for all low-income countries.[35] The supply-side problem was further aggravated by the high incidence of AIDS, which had a disproportionately large impact on the most productive age group of the labor force and thereby contributed to a worsening of the dependency ratio.

Latin America and the Caribbean

Latin America and the Caribbean (LAC) have a PPP$ per capita income that is almost twice as high as that of ESEA. And yet the proportion of population in absolute poverty, as measured by the World Bank's PPP$ poverty line, is slightly higher in LAC than in ESEA due to the much greater inequality of the distribution of income in the region. According to the World Bank's PPP$ poverty threshold, LAC is home to just under 7 percent of the developing world's poor as compared to 10 percent of the developing world's population. Between 1987 and 1998 the number of people in poverty increased by 23 percent. As a proportion of population, the poor in Latin America remained virtually unchanged, 15.3 percent in 1987 and 15.6 percent in 1998.

Estimates of poverty made by the Comisión Económica para América Latina (CEPAL; Economic Commission for Latin America), based on national poverty lines related to basic consumption bundles, show that the incidence of poverty—the weighted average proportion of population in poverty for eight major countries: Brazil, Chile, Colombia, Costa Rica, Honduras, Mexico, Peru, and Venezuela—declined in the period before 1980, increased during the 1980s, and declined during the 1990s. If Brazil is excluded, CEPAL estimates show no decline in the proportion of population in poverty in the aggregate of the remaining seven countries between 1990 and 1997.[36]

In the decades before 1980, Latin America had a very high rate of growth in per capita income: 4.6 percent in the eight years before the first oil shock and 2.4 percent between the first oil shock and 1980. CEPAL estimates show that the incidence of poverty declined relatively modestly during this period, from 43 percent of population in 1970 to 38 percent in 1980 for the eight countries (see Table 4.8). The rapid growth that the region experienced before 1980 might have led to a faster rate of poverty reduction if growth was more employment-friendly. As Table 4.5 shows, the output elasticities of employment in Brazil and Argentina were very low in this period. The incentive system underlying the strategy of import substitution, adopted by all the countries except Peru, was not conducive to a high demand for labor. Inequality in the distribution of land, and the consequent obstacles to the development of small peasant farming, reduced the rate of labor absorption in agriculture. The relatively low and slowly growing access to human capital, and the resulting low and slowly rising productivity of labor, contributed to both a low demand for wage labor and a slow growth of productive self-employment. Despite these adverse factors, considerable productive employment was generated to make it possible for a steadily increasing proportion of the labor force to be pulled into employment in the relatively high-paying modern sector. Employment growth served as the main link between output growth and poverty reduction.[37]

This linkage was broken during the 1980s, when per capita income in the region fell by 1 percent per year. Among the major countries, per capita income fell in Argentina, Brazil, Mexico, and Peru, making it impossible for the nexus of economic growth, employment, and poverty reduction to function. Argentina expanded employment in industries despite falling output, thereby attaining a negative elasticity of employment. Real wages fell in Argentina and Brazil, while in Mexico they fell for most of the period and recovered after 1988, a phenomenon that was almost certainly a reflection of rising wage inequality due to a rise in the wages of skilled workers. In Peru, employment in manufacturing remained unchanged over the decade, while real wages in manufacturing showed a steady rise that would be considered a perverse and unsustainable phenomenon but for the possibility that this was due to a break in the composition of data.[38] Among the major countries of the region, only Colombia and Chile experienced significant growth in per capita income during this lost decade. But in Colombia, employment failed to rise, as is indicated

Table 4.5 Output Elasticity of Employment in Manufacturing Industries, Major Latin American Countries, 1971–1998

	1971–1980	1981–1990	1991–1998
Argentina	0.441	–0.168	0.503*
Brazil	0.394*	0.739*	0.498
Mexico	0.635*	0.898	0.580

Notes: See the chapter appendix for method and data source for these estimates.
* = significance at the 95 percent level.

by a level of manufacturing employment in 1990 that was lower than that in 1980. Chile was the only country with a healthy growth of industrial output inducing a rapid growth in employment. Indeed, the growth in employment in manufacturing was a bit faster than the growth in output, perhaps signifying that growth of industrial output was concentrated in sectors and products with more than average labor intensity. Real wages fell initially—evidence that is consistent with high labor intensity at the margin—and increased later to record a rise over the decade as a whole. For Latin America as a whole, the rise in poverty during the decade largely reflects the failure of employment to rise due to the stagnation of the economy. CEPAL evidence for Chile, where the growth-employment linkage operated satisfactorily, is available only for the period after 1987, when poverty shows a decline.[39]

The 1990s witnessed a restoration of economic growth in most Latin American countries. Per capita income growth in the major countries has increased over what it was during the 1980s (Colombia being the exception), although not to the high levels prevailing before 1980, especially before the first oil shock. Has the resumption of growth in Latin America been accompanied by a healthy linkage, operating through high employment elasticity and rising productivity and real wages, to exert a substantial impact by way of reducing poverty? The evidence is summarized in Tables 4.5 and 4.6. Estimates of output elasticity of employment are shown only for the three largest countries in Table 4.5. For all three countries the estimates suggest at best a modest degree of employment friendliness of growth.

Table 4.6 shows trends in unemployment for Chile and trends in urban unemployment for the other countries. Since more than 75 percent of employment in Latin America is in urban areas, where nearly 80 percent of the people reside, variations in urban unemployment can be a good indicator of the overall employment performance of the economy. The table also shows trends in real wage rates.

As noted earlier and shown in Table 4.8, the record of poverty reduction in the 1990s has been rather poor for the seven major LAC countries (i.e., the group of eight excluding Brazil). For these countries taken together, the decline in the proportion of population in poverty between 1990 and 1994 was offset by the rise in the proportion of population in poverty by 1997. Can this unfavorable performance in poverty reduction be related to the employment performance in the period of restored growth in these countries?

Argentina succeeded in reversing its long stagnation during the 1990s by attaining a high rate of growth by its past standards. But it failed to achieve the desired impact on employment. The unemployment rate in Argentina has been high and has increased. The output elasticity of employment in manufacturing has not been high. Real wages have fallen. CEPAL data on poverty do not include estimates for Argentina, but the evidence on unemployment and real wages does not indicate the likelihood of a favorable poverty outcome.

Table 4.6   Growth, Unemployment, and Real Wages, Latin America, 1981–1999

	Per Capita Income Growth (% per annum)		Trend Rate of Change (% per annum) in 1991–1999	
	1981–1990	1991–1999	Unemployment	Real Wages
Latin America	−1.0	1.4	4.9	—
Argentina	−2.1	3.3	21.5 until 1997, 12.6 since 1997	−0.3
Brazil	−0.7	1.0	Insignificant until 1997, 3.1 since 1997	4.0 until 1997, 3.1 after 1997
Chile	1.3	4.4	−2.3 (ignoring higher rates at end points)	3.6
Colombia	1.6	0.5	11.7 (ignoring high initial rates in 1991 and 1992)	1.5
Mexico	−0.3	1.3	Insignificant; humped during 1995 and 1996	5.7 until 1994 0.2 after 1994
Peru	−3.3	2.9	0	−0.8 (ignoring rise in 1994)

Average Unemployment Rate (%), 1991–1999
Latin America   7.0 (mostly urban)
  Argentina   11.7 (urban)
  Brazil   5.7 (urban)
  Chile   7.2 (national)
  Colombia   11.3 (urban)
  Mexico   3.6 (urban)
  Peru   8.5 (capital city)

Source: Growth rates and data on unemployment and real wage rates are from Comisión Económica para América Latina 1999.

Notes: Trends are based on semilog regressions. Unless stated to be insignificant, all coefficients are significant at the 1 percent or 5 percent level, the only exception being the growth rate in real wage in Peru, which is significant at the 10 percent level. Where trends have a break, the estimates are based on equations like log $X = a + bT + cZT$, where X is the dependent variable, T is time (1 for 1991, 2 for 1992, etc.), and Z is a dummy variable set at 0 for years up to the break and at 1 for years after the break. Trend growth rate is b up to the break and $(b + c)$ thereafter. Humps and initial and terminal high levels have similarly been addressed by inserting dummy variables.

Colombia had an all-round poor performance: growth rate has fallen sharply, and unemployment has been high and increasing. Average real wages have, however, increased steadily, albeit at a modest rate. Since the rise in average real wages is backed neither by growth nor by a rising demand for labor, it is almost certainly due to either a rise in inequality in the distribution of wages or to unsustainable labor market interventions by the government. Neither can be the basis for a healthy reduction of poverty.

Mexico's recovery of economic growth was interrupted by the crisis of 1994, and the average rate of growth for the 1990s was modest. The measured unemployment rate in Mexico is low on average and, except for the rise in the years following the crises of 1994, there is no trend change within it. Real wages rose until 1994 and have been almost stagnant thereafter. The output elasticity of employment has not been particularly high. Ongoing research, however, shows a high and rising inequality in the structure of wages. The picture is one of lackluster economic growth resulting in a sluggish rate of increase in overall labor demand. It is not surprising that CEPAL estimates show that the proportion of population in poverty was higher in 1998 than in 1994.

There was a strong revival of growth in Peru in the 1990s. While the unemployment rate is relatively high, it shows no trend during the decade. Real wages have not increased; they may be said to have declined a little. The substantial reduction in the incidence of poverty that CEPAL data show must be attributed to a sharp rise in the rate of growth of per capita GDP, from –3.3 percent during the 1980s to 2.9 percent during the 1990s, and an avoidance of increased unemployment.

Chile continued to be the country with the most dynamic nexus of economic growth, employment, and poverty reduction: there was a robust increase in the rate of growth accompanied by a steady reduction in the rate of unemployment and a steady rise in real wages. CEPAL estimates show a dramatic decline in the proportion of population in poverty between 1990 and 1998.

According to CEPAL data, Brazil achieved substantial reduction in poverty between 1990 and 1996. It should be noted that in the four years leading up to 1996, Brazil's per capita income growth was quite high, approximately 3 percent per year. During this period the unemployment rate was relatively low and stable and real wages rose rapidly. The highly favorable poverty outcome for the period up to 1996 is a reflection of this positive nexus of economic growth, employment, and poverty reduction. For the entire decade of the 1990s, Brazil's performance was far less favorable: per capita income grew at a meager 1 percent per year for the decade and at a negative rate after 1997. Unemployment rose after 1997. The rate of increase in real wages fell somewhat.[40] The impact of these unfavorable performances in growth and employment on poverty is yet to be measured.

Latin America faces a long agenda of improving its performance on the links in the nexus of economic growth, employment, and poverty reduction. Foremost on the agenda is the stabilization of a decent rate of growth. It should then improve the employment intensity of growth by reforming the institutions and incentives that still serve as obstacles to high labor absorption. The extreme inequality in the distribution of land continues to be an obstacle to rural labor absorption, a serious impediment to poverty reduction in a region in which the rural society still accounts for 30 percent of all the poor. The Latin American countries generally have a poor record of redistribution and promotion of entrepreneurship among the poor through an expansion of their access to productive assets. Recently, attempts for land reform have been intensified in Brazil, although the outcome so far has been very modest. The record of Latin America in endowing the poor with human capital is also mixed: it is rather poor for Brazil, the largest country in the region, but good to reasonable for Costa Rica, Uruguay, Chile, Argentina, and Mexico. The leakage of the benefits of modestly restored growth from the poor to the non-poor is illustrated by high and rising inequality in income distribution in the region. The mean of the Gini ratios for the Latin American countries increased from 0.481 in 1988 to 0.491 in 1993.

Other Regions

According to the World Bank's PPP$ poverty threshold, the incidence of poverty in the other two developing regions—the Middle East and North Africa (MENA), and (developing) Europe and Central Asia—is very low, which in 1998 stood respectively at 1.9 percent and 5.5 percent of the population. Lack of growth was the central problem faced by these regions. MENA averaged an annual growth in GDP of 3 percent during the 1990s, much of which was eaten up by the 2.5 percent or higher rates of annual population growth that the countries in the region experienced. According to World Bank estimates, the region nevertheless succeeded in further reducing the incidence of poverty in recent years. The developing countries of Europe and Central Asia averaged an annual decline in GDP of 2.9 percent during the decade. This region also experienced widespread breakdown of the system of protection for the poor, however inefficient, insofar as the past system of guaranteed employment was abandoned without being replaced by an alternative. The catastrophic proportion of the crisis is captured by the combination of the large fall in per capita income with the sharp increase in inequality of income distribution: the mean of the Gini ratios for these countries increased from 0.217 in 1988 to 0.326 in 1993.

For the countries in these two regions, a return to the right kind of linkage among economic growth, employment, and poverty reduction must begin with the restoration of growth to a decent level. Individual countries in these regions (e.g., Syria, Tunisia, and Poland) appear to have achieved this transition. But most of the countries are stagnating or declining. The restoration of growth by itself will not establish the right kind of linkage among growth, employment, and poverty reduction in these regions. The rest of the policy agenda, outlined previously, will need careful implementation. The transition economies will have to create the right structure for their systems of incentives and institutions. They need to replace their past inefficient system of social protection, now abandoned, with an alternative system. The notion of entrepreneurship for self-employment has been comparatively unknown in these countries. Compared to their levels of income per capita, the MENA countries have generally had very low levels of human capital, a fact that is illustrated by the lower ranks of these countries in terms of the UNDP's Human Development Index than in terms of per capita income.

Conclusion

The most effective way to reduce poverty is to make growth-induced employment accessible to the poor. In other words, poverty is most effectively reduced by the greater utilization of labor, the resource that most poor households have more of than any other resource, in a way that creates for them entitlement to income and welfare. An analysis of the experience of the developing countries shows that rapid expansion of productive and remunerative employment has always been associated with rapid poverty reduction.

Growth is a precondition of sustained expansion of productive and remunerative employment. For employment to alleviate poverty it must create an entitlement to income. Without economic growth, employment expansion, in the ultimate analysis, is an inefficient method of redistribution, a concealed system of unemployment insurance. Numerous cases in contemporary development experience demonstrate the futility of seeking a way out of poverty by employment expansion without the backing of adequate growth. The Philippines in the 1970s expanded employment ahead of effective demand for labor only to pay for it later in the form of extremely low output elasticity of employment. Bangladesh in the 1970s went through a similar binge of employment expansion in public enterprises, without an increase in effective demand for labor, for which a full adjustment is yet to be made.

However, it is not useful to think of growth as a process exogenous to poverty-reducing employment generation. Indeed, in most developing countries the utilization of the capacity of the poor to work is an effective way to raise the rate of economic growth. For growth to be endogenized into the process of employment expansion for the poor, it is necessary to provide poor households with access to resources: land, other physical assets, credit, and public services. It is in this sense that redistribution of land and assets can be an effective method of ensuring complementarity between high growth and rapid poverty reduction. The experiences of countries that promoted wide access of the poor to land and other resources demonstrate the validity of this claim. It should be emphasized that access of the poor to assets rarely brings about an improvement in their welfare independently of enabling them to utilize more effectively their capacity to work. It is also worth noting that this kind of redistribution is a method of poverty reduction far superior to redistribution of consumption, which quickly runs into resource, administrative, and political constraints. Redistribution may also be a necessary condition of poverty reduction in cases where assets are so scarce that a high and increasing proportion of income is appropriated by their owners, thereby reducing the poverty-alleviating effect of employment-intensive growth.

For employment expansion to be an effective instrument for poverty reduction, it is necessary for the poor workers to be endowed with adequate human capital. The human capital endowment of the poor needs to be continuously updated in order to ensure that they can adjust to the changing composition of demand for skills that characterizes contemporary economic development.

Proper functioning of the process of poverty reduction through employment promotion also critically depends on the terms of exchange that the produce of poor labor faces in the market. Case studies show that adverse changes in the terms of trade for peasants and self-employed poor have often deprived them of the opportunity to escape poverty.

Ensuring a high rate of growth within a framework of incentives and institutions that promote appropriately employment-intensive technology may not generate a high enough headcount rate of employment creation. There may be a countervailing and offsetting reduction in employment that is often unleashed by the reform for higher and more efficient growth. This is a particularly serious hazard in the age of globalization, when existing systems of inefficient allocation of labor, resorted to in the past as an alternative to unemployment insurance, have to be dismantled as part of the reform for the promotion of efficiency and competitiveness. This puts a heavy additional burden of employment generation, or social protection, on the poverty reduction strategy. Finding resources for this kind of additional employment generation, or an alternative form of social protection, poses an enormous challenge for expenditure-retrenching reform in the process of which these problems emerge. The experiences of China and Vietnam, and to a lesser extent South Asia, are a graphic reminder of this danger.

There are groups of poor who are at a serious disadvantage to compete for employment in the marketplace. They need to be helped by special measures— for example, endowment with special skills and opportunity for work at home for the female members of poor households.

Careful interventions in the functioning of the labor market, with a view to protecting the weak members of the labor force, especially in an environment of unequal bargaining power, can improve the welfare of the poor. However, it is important to ensure that these interventions do not restrict the growth of demand for labor, which is detrimental to the welfare of the poor.

While growth-induced employment expansion is the most effective method of poverty reduction, it is necessary for policymakers to recognize its limits. For the households with inadequate labor endowment, admittedly a small minority of the poor in most societies, there must be additional policy interventions, namely income and consumption subsidies, to alleviate poverty.

Employment policies for poverty reduction must be continuously reviewed to ensure their evolution with changing circumstances. East Asia's success in eliminating much of poverty by growth-induced employment expansion, buttressed by redistribution of assets and egalitarian access to human capital, was a remarkable achievement. These countries should have reinforced this achievement by building a system of social protection for the workers, especially after they had reached high levels of income. Their failure to do so at the right time contributed to an unwarranted intensity of decline in the welfare of the workers, and to a descent into poverty for many of them, in the wake of the crisis of 1997.

▪ Appendix

This appendix discusses the method of estimation of the output elasticities of employment and shows the data on trends in poverty for those regions for which these estimates are not readily available.

Output Elasticity of Employment in Manufacturing

Data on employment and value added in manufacturing are from the United Nations Industrial Development Organization. The value-added data are at current prices. These are deflated by using the manufacturing value-added deflator from the World Bank (2000c). For the ESEA region, estimates of output elasticity of employment have been available and well-known. All that has been done for the countries of this region is to update the estimates shown in Khan and Muqtada 1997, Table 6.11, by following the methodology believed to have been followed by the authors of those estimates (see sources for Table 4.1). For all other cases the elasticities are estimated by fitting the following equation to the data described above:

$$\log EMP = C_1 + C_2 D_1 + C_3 D_2 + C_4 [\log VA] + C_5 [D_1(\log VA)] + C_6 [(D_2(\log VA)]$$

where

   EMP = employment in manufacturing
   VA = real value added in manufacturing
   D_1 = dummy variable with a value of 0 for all years from 1971 to 1980
       and 1 for all years thereafter
   D_2 = dummy variable with a value of 0 for all years from 1971 to 1990
       and 1 for all years thereafter
   C_1 to C_6 = estimated coefficients

The output elasticity of employment is C_4 for 1971–1980, $C_4 + C_5$ for 1981–1990, and $C_4 + C_5 + C_6$ for 1991–1998. For the SSA countries, only the elasticities for 1981–1990 and 1991–1998 can be estimated. An asterisk has been used to indicate that a coefficient is significant at least at the 95 percent level of confidence. If C_4 has a high enough t-value, then the elasticity for 1971–1980 is shown as significant. If the t-value is high enough for C_5, the elasticity for 1981–1990 is shown as significant (even if C_4 for the country is

Table 4.7   Population in Poverty, Selected African Countries, 1980–1999

	Incidence of Poverty (%)[a,b]				International Poverty Line (%)[c]	
	Year 1		Year 2		Year 1	Year 2
Burkina Faso	Rural	51.1	Rural	50.7	—	—
	Urban	10.4	Urban	15.8		
	National	44.5	National	45.3		
Côte d'Ivoire	—		—		17.7	12.3
Ethiopia	—		—		46	31.3
Ghana	Rural	45.8	Rural	36.2	—	—
	Urban	15.3	Urban	14.5		
	National	35.7	National	29.4		
Mauritania	Rural	72.1	Rural	58.9	31.4	37.9
	Urban	43.5	Urban	19.0		
	National	59.5	National	41.3		
Nigeria	Rural	45.1	Rural	67.8	—	—
	Urban	29.6	Urban	57.5		
	National	42.8	National	65.6		
Uganda	Rural	59.4	Rural	48.2	—	—
	Urban	29.4	Urban	16.3		
	National	55.6	National	44.0		
Zambia	Rural	79.6	Rural	74.9	—	—
	Urban	31.0	Urban	34.0		
	National	57.0	National	60.0		
Zimbabwe	Rural	51.5	Rural	62.8	—	—
	Urban	6.2	Urban	14.9		
	National	37.5	National	47.2		

Source: Islam and Majeres 2001.

Notes: a. The dates in this column correspond to several years: Burkina Faso, 1994 and 1998; Ghana, 1991–1992 and 1998–1999; Mauritania, 1987 and 1996; Nigeria, 1992 and 1996; Uganda, 1992 and 1997; Zambia, 1991 and 1996; Zimbabwe, 1991 and 1996.

b. Nutrition-based poverty lines.

c. International poverty line as defined by population living below US$1 a day. The years in this column vary among countries: Côte d'Ivoire, 1988 and 1995; Ethiopia, 1981–1982 and 1995.

not significant). If the t-value for C_6 is significant, the elasticity for 1991–1998 is shown to be significant (even if C_4 and C_5 for the country are not significant). In a few cases the initial/terminal year is different from the limits indicated above.

In using the dataset described above, several inconsistencies with other known sources were detected for countries and periods for which estimates based on these data are not used in this chapter. This nevertheless points to the need for caution in using these results. Since the real value added was somewhat indirectly derived, it is possible that occasionally the estimates do not quite conform to what direct estimates would have been.

Table 4.8 Poverty in Major Latin American Countries (percentage of population)

Brazil		Mexico		Chile		Peru		Colombia		All Latin America (Brazil included)		All Latin America (Brazil excluded)	
1970	52	1970	32	1970	15	1970	45	1970	45	1970	43	1970	35
1979	41	1984	34	1987	39	1979	46	1980	39	1980	38	1980	36
1990	43	1989	38	1990	33	1986	51	1994	45	1990	41	1990	41
1993	37	1994	34	1994	23	1995	40	1997	43	1994	37	1994	38
1996	29	1996	42	1996	20	1997	35			1997	35	1997	41
		1998	35	1998	18								

Source: Comisión Económica para América Latina 2000.

Poverty Data for Sub-Saharan Africa and Latin America

Previous estimates of trends in poverty in sub-Saharan Africa and Latin America may not be readily available and hence are reproduced in the tables. Trends in poverty in Asia are well documented and widely available, and no need is felt to reproduce them here. Also included are a detailed analysis of alternative estimates and references to their sources.

■ Notes

1. See World Bank 2000e. While this list conforms to the broad categories in the *World Development Report,* there are certain differences in the subcategories.

2. A poor person could escape poverty without using his or her capacity to work if he or she received an endowment of assets large enough to provide an annuity that is greater than the poverty threshold. Few societies in the world can afford to provide such an endowment to a significant proportion of their poor.

3. The proportion may be high in postwar societies and after natural disasters. Also, the proportion of households whose labor endowment is of such a special kind that they cannot benefit from an expansion of the usual types of employment—for example, female labor that cannot compete for employment in a market for wage employment because of the commitment to child care and household work—may be substantial in many societies. As discussed later, special measures are needed to enable them to convert their capacity to work into remunerative employment.

4. Note, however, that an exception to this is possible when the economy is initially characterized by an undesirably high degree of capital intensity. In such a case the shift toward a more appropriate technique of production would indicate a faster rate of increase in employment than in output. This kind of correction, however, is a once-and-for-all process and is unlikely to continue for long.

5. There is a large literature on the subject. A recent empirical study documenting the phenomenon for Brazil is Thiesenhusen and Melmed-Sanjak 1990, which reports that employment per hectare was 9.78 person-months for farms 1–10 hectares in size and only 0.7 person-month for farms of 50–200 hectares and 0.02 person-months for farms 10,000 hectares and above.

6. The phenomenon of widening wage inequality in US industries until the mid-1990s is documented in Galbraith and Cantu 1999, which also shows a declining wage inequality in US industries since the mid-1990s, after which the very low rate of unemployment finally improved the supply-demand balance for unskilled workers.

7. Examples of this, as a probable explanation of rising real wages with increasing unemployment in some Latin America countries, are given later in the chapter.

8. The inequality in the distribution of the extremely scarce land, and the consequent rise in its factor share, probably go a long way toward explaining the decline in real wages in Bangladesh agriculture by more than 16 percent between 1985–1986 and the second half of calendar 1998, which in turn constitutes a major explanation of the poor performance in poverty reduction in rural Bangladesh during this period (see discussion later in the chapter, and Khan 2000a). This phenomenon is distinct from the case, discussed previously, of the unequal distribution of assets restricting employment growth but not necessarily bringing about an increase in the share of these assets in total output.

9. Notable contemporary examples of this include food-for-work programs in Bangladesh and China, the Maharashtra Employment Guarantee Scheme and the

Jawahar Rozgar Yojona in India, and the Community Employment and Development Program in the Philippines.

10. See World Bank 1993 and World Bank 1998 for evidence of this for Uganda and Bangladesh respectively.

11. The term "vent for surplus," originally used by Adam Smith, was applied by Hla Myint (1959) to the utilization of otherwise unused land and labor resources of countries by their being opened to foreign trade. I am using the term in a broader sense to include all activation of productive energy and resources that are latent and unused due to the absence of incentives and institutions required to facilitate their utilization.

12. Demographic transition can also help poverty reduction in important ways that are not directly related to employment expansion—namely increasing per capita resources of poor households by reducing their dependency ratio.

13. These measurements are based on the World Bank estimates of absolute poverty defined as population living on less than US$1 a day (to be exact, US$1.08 a day at 1993 PPP$ prices). The method underlying these estimates involves many crude approximations, so that the results should be treated as no more than orders of magnitude. The source of these estimates is World Bank 2000e.

14. A Lewis transition is visualized in the context of W. Arthur Lewis's model of economic growth (1954) and indicates the turning point at which the surplus labor in a disguised unemployment in the traditional sector of the economy is exhausted.

15. In this section the regional classification is the one that the World Bank uses. "ESEA" is what is called "East Asia and the Pacific" in the World Bank classification.

16. Perhaps it is useful to note that the incidence of poverty in ESEA in 1998 reflects the worst consequences of the 1997 financial crisis, but for which the outcome might have appeared more spectacular. Poverty also declined over the same period in one other developing region—the Middle East and North Africa. This region, however, represents less than 5 percent of the population of the developing world and had a low initial incidence of poverty. Thus the absolute decline in the number of the poor was minuscule. The number of people in poverty increased in all other developing regions.

17. These six countries account for 91 percent of the population of the developing ESEA region.

18. There are many case studies of this experience. For an ILO study of the experience, see Khan and Muqtada 1997, chap. 6.

19. The World Bank (1997) shows no trend in Korea's Gini ratio of income distribution between the early 1960s and the late 1980s.

20. It has been alleged that the undeveloped system of social protection in Korea was responsible for some of the adverse consequences of the financial crisis of 1997 on the poor. This does not invalidate the argument that the country successfully eliminated almost the entire problem of poverty without resort to these policies prior to the financial crisis. However, it underlines the need for a transition in policies at the right time. These countries should have gradually instituted these systems of social protection once they had reached a high level of per capita income. The effect of the crisis and its aftermath need careful study. It is noteworthy that the crisis resulted in negative growth of very modest proportions in Korea for only one year, after which growth was reinstated at a higher than precrisis rate. The other three East Asian pioneers were far less adversely affected by the financial crisis than was Korea.

21. For sources and documentation, see Khan and Riskin 2001, chap. 4.

22. See Boltho 1994.

23. These estimates are based on the official data quoted in International Monetary Fund 1996.

24. For an analysis of the growth-employment-poverty linkage in the Philippines, see Khan 1997a.

25. See Khan 2000a for a summary of sources of the evidence.

26. See Datt 1997 and Datt 1999.

27. See Amjad and Kemal 1997, 39–68.

28. See Khan 2000c for evidence for Nepal.

29. See International Labour Organization 1999–2000. These rates of decline appear rather high. It has not been possible to ascertain the method underlying the estimates shown in this ILO report.

30. Bangladesh's much vaunted microcredit program must have helped rural income growth. Its overall impact does not appear to have been sufficiently large. Also, the targeting of the poor by the microcredit program in Bangladesh became weaker after initial years. See Rahman 2000. See also Islam 2001 for an evaluation of these direct interventions.

31. For rural sub-Saharan Africa, the problem is empirically documented in the ILO study in Khan 1997b.

32. Note that this means that for nearly 90 percent of the labor force, agriculture is the principal, not the sole, occupation.

33. International Fund for Agricultural Development 2001 shows that the Gini ratio of land distribution in the 1980s in Ethiopia was 0.47, compared to the range in which it lay for most other countries of sub-Saharan Africa, from 0.6 (Mauritania) to 0.8 (Madagascar).

34. See World Bank 1993, 94–96.

35. See World Bank 2000e, tab. 2.1.

36. CEPAL 2000; the data are shown in Table 4.8 in this chapter.

37. See Khan and Muqtada 1997, chap. 4.

38. This possibility is indicated in World Bank 1995, the data from which provide the basis for these statements.

39. Employment trends in Latin America during the 1980s are based on World Bank 1995.

40. Real wages continued to rise, however. This was clearly unsustainable in the long run without a reversal of the growth performance.

Part 2

Country Studies

5

Bangladesh: Linkages Among Economic Growth, Employment, and Poverty

Rushidan Islam Rahman and K. M. Nabiul Islam

Despite recent progress in poverty alleviation, the magnitude of poverty in Bangladesh remains high both in terms of absolute magnitude and as a percentage of the population. A rapid progress in poverty reduction is not possible without an acceleration of economic growth. In a resource-poor country like Bangladesh, economic growth hinges on the proper utilization of its labor force. The country has few natural resources, and agricultural land per rural household is low and is continuing to decline. Therefore the growth of the economy will require improved productivity of all available resources, including labor. It must be emphasized, however, that the nature of economic growth will be critical for the success of poverty alleviation. Poverty reduction requires employment-friendly and equitable growth. The growth process must generate employment opportunities for the poorer sections, and the wage rate and productivity of employment must be such as to generate adequate earning for them.

Strategies for reducing poverty in Bangladesh should therefore be based on an analysis of the linkages among economic growth, employment, and poverty. Such analysis will help to highlight how GDP growth can be made pro-poor through the growth of employment. The objective of this chapter is to examine the linkage between poverty and employment and to arrive at specific policy suggestions for poverty alleviation. This will involve analyses at both the macro and the micro level. Specific components of the analyses include the following:

- *Pattern of economic growth and poverty alleviation.* An overview of the performance of the country in terms of economic growth and poverty reduction will be presented. Real GDP growth over various subperiods will be examined. The standard measures of poverty will be used to document the trends. Poverty analysis will use data based on the "direct calorie intake" (DCI) method and the cost of basic needs method–based statistics. In addition to income poverty, the achievements in the "human development" aspects will find a place in the analysis of poverty-employment-growth linkages. The multidirectional interfaces between income poverty and human poverty need attention.

- *Sectoral GDP growth rates, employment elasticities, and labor productivity.* The objective of this component of analysis is to investigate the relationship between the changes in the elasticity of employment and the changes in the incidence of poverty. A direct analysis of such linkage between employment elasticity and poverty may be constrained by data availability and methodological problems. Therefore the chapter will examine how employment-intensive the pattern of growth in Bangladesh has been and, in turn, what type of linkage between the pattern of growth and employment creation can be identified. A large part of this analysis component will consist of separate estimates of employment elasticities and their changes for major manufacturing subsectors.

- *Trends in wage rates and their implications for poverty.* Wage income is the major source of income for about one-fifth of rural households in Bangladesh. In addition, a large percentage of the urban poor households depend on wage from unskilled labor. Trends in wage rate should therefore receive attention in the analysis of the employment-poverty linkage. Wage rates of unskilled workers in manufacturing and in agriculture will be examined. The discussion will focus on the linkages among trends in productivity, real wages, and poverty.

- *Employment-poverty linkage at the micro level.* At the micro level, employment-poverty linkage operates in both directions. Labor force and employment characteristics of a household are likely to influence the probability of its being poor. The poverty status in turn can influence the possibility of being engaged in employment with higher productivity. Factors affecting the probability of being below the poverty line will be examined.

The analyses are based on various types of information:

- Published reports of relevant national surveys, including surveys of the labor force, manufacturing industries, and household expenditures, will be used. In addition, data and findings from other published studies will be quoted.
- Household-level data from Bangladesh's 1999–2000 national labor force survey have been used for household- and worker-level analysis.[1]

The survey covered a national representative sample of 9,790 households. After excluding some cases with partially missing or inconsistent data, data for 18,983 workers from the 9,790 households have been used.

Economic Growth and Poverty

The chapter will examine the poverty trends in Bangladesh on the basis of the commonly used indicators. The headcount ratio of poverty will be presented on the basis of cost of basic needs and on the basis of calorie intake.[2] These two indexes can supplement each other. Improvement in income poverty may not be a sufficient indicator of sustained improvement in household and individual well-being, in terms of both nonincome, material indicators as well as nonmaterial achievements. In addition to the poverty estimates based on poverty lines, the importance of nonincome dimensions (e.g., education, health, etc.) should not be underemphasized. The chapter will also focus on the trend of human poverty estimates and examine whether improvements in income and nonincome dimensions are related. These links are likely to have special importance for the employment-poverty relationship and therefore deserve attention.

Income Poverty Trends: Rural and Urban

To obtain insights into the link between poverty and economic growth in Bangladesh, it will be pertinent to present a disaggregation of poverty trends by rural and urban location. Locational pattern of economic growth may then be linked with the poverty trends. Even if a strictly locational disaggregation of economic growth data is not available, the sectoral pattern of growth may provide a relevant basis for analysis.

Data on headcount ratio (HCR) of poverty incidence based on a "poverty-line income" are presented in Table 5.1. The poverty line is based on the "cost of basic needs" (CBN) method. The table provides the following features of poverty trends:

- Poverty incidence in Bangladesh continuously declined from 1988–1989 to 2000. (The decline was continuous starting in 1985–1986 if one considers the DCI-based HCR.)
- Poverty incidence (according to the CBN method) increased from 1986 to 1992.
- In the rural areas, poverty incidence increased at a higher rate. There was an 8.1 percentage point increase during this period. Among the urban households, poverty increased by 2.0 percentage points between 1986 and 1992.

- Between 1992 and 1995, both the urban and the rural poverty situation improved, but the improvement was less pronounced for the rural areas compared to the urban areas: the rate of poverty reduction was 1.1 and 2.5 percentage points per year for the rural and urban households respectively.
- A contrasting trend was observed from 1995 to 1999. Rural poverty declined by 3.7 percentage points while the urban poverty situation increased by 1.6 percentage points during this four-year period.
- Above observations are based on the moderate poverty line. Similar trends hold for extreme poverty estimates, which are shown in Tables 5.32 and 5.33.

So far we have not focused on the earlier period and have examined only the period of 1985–1986 to 1999–2000. There are methodological problems in making direct long-term comparison of poverty incidence for the earlier period. Nonetheless, the data for 1973–1974 and 1981–1982 are comparable. The extent of poverty reduction during the two subperiods is shown in Table 5.2. Even if there are methodological differences, the difference in the rate of poverty reduction is so large between the two periods that one may accept the observation that "the incidence of poverty declined at a faster rate in the first period than in the second period" (Bangladesh Institute for Development Studies [BIDS] 2001, 2). The same view has been expressed by other researchers (e.g., by A. R. Khan in his recent public lecture on globalization delivered on September 12, 2001, at the BIDS).

Direct Calorie Intake Based on Poverty. The following aspects of the trends of poverty incidence based on the calorie norms (DCI method) and the differences of the results with the CBN method (from Tables 5.1 and 5.2) are worth highlighting:

Table 5.1   Trends in Rural and Urban Poverty, Bangladesh, 1985/86–2000

	HCR Based on CBN Method (%)			HCR Based on DCI Method (%)		
	Rural	Urban	National	Rural	Urban	National
1985–1986	53.1	42.9	51.7	54.7	62.6	55.7
1988–1989	59.2	43.9	59.1	47.8	47.6	47.8
1991–1992	61.2	44.9	58.8	47.6	46.7	47.5
1995–1996	56.7	35.0	53.1	47.1	49.7	47.5
2000	53.0	36.6	49.8	42.3	52.5	44.3

Sources: Bangladesh Bureau of Statistics, various years; World Bank 1998, 2002d.
Note: Percentages are based on the upper poverty line.

Table 5.2   Comparison of Poverty Trends, Bangladesh, 1973/74–1981/82 and 1983/84–1995/96

	Percentage Point Change per Year	
	1973/74–1981/82	1983/84–1995/96
Urban	2.97	2.93
Rural	1.10	0.40
National	1.29	0.92

Source: Khan 2000b.

- Based on DCI, there was a decline in headcount ratio of poverty between 1984–1985 and 1995–1996, and between 1995–1996 and 2000. Between 1988–1989 and 1995–1996 the poverty situation remained virtually unchanged.
- Despite the difference in definition there is no disagreement that there was a decline in poverty between 1985–1986 and 2000. According to the DCI-based estimate, poverty declined by 11.4 percentage points between these years, and according to the CBN estimates, the decline was 1.9 percentage points.

The following aspects of the contrasting trend of poverty measured by CBN and DCI methods are worth highlighting:

- According to CBN estimates, the decline in HCR of poverty took place mostly between 1991–1992 and 1995–1996. Before this period, poverty increased. Estimates based on DCI show a different timing of the improvement of the poverty situation: between 1984–1985 and 1988–1989 some decline in the poverty incidence took place and after that the poverty situation remained virtually unchanged and again declined slightly during 1996–2000.
- Between 1985–1986 and 1988–1989, and between 1988–1989 and 1991–1992, the percentage of poverty increased according to the CBN method and declined on the basis of the DCI method.
- The contradiction becomes even more glaring when one compares the urban figures in the two estimates. In the CBN estimates urban poverty decreased between 1991–1992 and 1995–1996 by about 10 percentage points, whereas the DCI estimates show an increase during this period.
- Between 1992 and 1996, rural poverty showed a decline on the basis of CBN method but was almost stagnant when the DCI method was used.

It is difficult to reconcile the contrasting picture obtained by the CBN and DCI methods. The first observation mentioned above implies that the improvement in income poverty during the nineties has not been transformed into an actual improvement in the calorie consumption. The improvement in the "command" over the bundle of basic needs may not be translated into improvement in the standard of calorie intake due to a variety of social reasons. The following explanations of the difference between the poverty trends based on CBN and DCI methods are offered:

1. An obvious explanation for these contrasting pictures obtained by the two is based on the observation that the urban poor spend a significant part of income on nonbasic needs and as income increases, they may increase the proportion of income spent on the items not included in the "bundle for the poor." However, one has to stretch one's imagination to visualize a scenario where this would take place at the cost of a decline in food consumption and calorie intake. It is conceivable that a lack of education in general and absence of knowledge of balanced food may result in inadequate nutrition intake. But it is unlikely that with an upward shift in income, calorie intake will actually decline.

2. An alternative explanation for this contradiction (rising poverty in terms of calorie and falling poverty in terms of expenditure required for command over basic needs) lies in the change of prices of food and nonessential nonfood. A price index of nonfood basic needs expenditure is incorporated into the calculation of the poverty line. But the actual consumption pattern may include a much larger percentage of nonfood, particularly in the urban areas. If the prices of these items increase more than in proportion to the price index of the package of nonfood basic needs basket, and the quantity consumed remains fixed, then the income allocated for food may decline, resulting in a decline of actual calorie intake. This actually implies that a comparison on the basis of CBN is not free from the biases built into the baseline "consumption basket" and the associated price vector of this basket.

3. Another minor point that may be relevant is that household expenditure in the Household Income and Expenditure Survey (HIES) includes imputed expenditures for many items. Total expenditure may show an increase due to the increase in the value of these items. More specifically, many of the urban poor living in slums construct their own shacks on the public land. No rent is paid for these dwelling units of the "owner-occupants," whereas those who rent a room in a slum pay the "market rent." Such market price would be imputed for the owner occupants. When the market rent of these slum houses rises, so

does the imputed expenditure. But there is no possibility of converting this imputed expenditure into calories, and thus the contradictions.
4. Given the problems of contrasting results given by the two methodologies, a combination of the CBN and DCI methods should be used in poverty analysis, the former providing a hypothetical picture based on poverty-level income and the latter providing the actual, in terms of calorie intake. The DCI method provides a strictly consistent estimate of poverty, which ensures comparability over time even if the welfare implication of this index is rather narrow.

The above differences should not undermine one important achievement in the reduction of poverty. Bangladesh achieved a substantial decline in the HCR of extreme poverty. Whether the CBN or the DCI method is used, the decline was more than 10 percentage points during the entire period of 1983–1984 to 1999–2000.

Other dimensions of poverty, that is, the depth and severity of poverty, measured by the poverty gap and the squared poverty gap, are presented in Table 5.34. The trends in depth and severity of poverty are similar to the trends in the HCR. There was an overall improvement in these two measures. For the urban areas, the situation worsened by these measures during the late 1990s. The changes were more or less continuous except between 1988–1989 and 1991–1992 in the rural areas, and between 1995–1996 and 2000 in the urban areas. Depth and intensity of poverty were higher in the rural areas.

The poverty situation is linked with income inequality in urban and rural areas. The period under review witnessed increases in inequality. This is especially true for urban income (see Table 5.35). Improvement in poverty situation could have been more impressive had the degree of income inequality not increased.

A number of microsurveys provide estimates of the poverty incidence. CBN-based estimates of poverty have been provided by an analysis of poverty trends conducted by the BIDS study and by a poverty monitoring survey conducted by the Bangladesh Bureau of Statistics (BBS) (under the auspices of the Centre on Integrated Rural Development for Asia and the Pacific). According to the poverty trends analysis, rural poverty (both extreme and moderate) increased between 1987 and 1989–1990 and then declined in 1994. According to the poverty monitoring survey, the poverty incidence varied from 47 percent in 1995 to 45 percent in 1999 (BBS 2002) in the rural areas and stagnated at 44 percent in the urban areas.

The poverty trends analysis shows a significant decline in the nonincome indicators of extreme poverty over the 1990–1995 period (Hossain 1992, 1996a). For example, the percentage of rural population without basic clothing declined from 15 to 4 and the percentage of households living in extremely vulnerable housing *(jhupri)* declined from 9 to 2. Such a large improvement in housing situation may appear incompatible with the much smaller change in calorie-based poverty estimates. Nonetheless, other studies (Alam 2002) also show a significant improvement in housing condition during the recent years, with very small change in average food intake among the poor households. This shows that the rural poor have a high propensity to invest in their housing.

The above quantitative findings have been based on structured questionnaire surveys and are subject to the usual criticism against such methods. Qualitative studies on poverty, including participatory studies, utilize the poor's own perception about their situation. Such studies are also subject to a number of important problems:

- People's own perceptions are likely to set up a higher standard of living (than others' prescription of poverty bundle) as the norm.
- Intertemporal comparison is difficult because people's perceptions about poverty change with the growth and availability of consumer goods and knowledge and information.
- Participatory studies on poverty sometimes tend to combine the notions of absolute and relative poverty, and the symptoms of poverty and causes of poverty.

As a result, poverty studies based on participatory assessment provide higher figures of the incidence of poverty. For example, Shamunnay's participatory assessment (2000) shows that 75 percent of rural households were poor in 1996 (against 47 percent in the BBS survey). Another participatory study (Impact Monitoring and Evaluation Cell 1999), however, provides similar estimates of poverty obtained through quantitative surveys (in the same study). In fact, an important role of qualitative studies will be to suggest improvements in the indicators for poverty assessment, which may then be used in quantitative studies to quantify the extent of poverty.

Some of the recent studies on poverty observed that the comparison of the changes of poverty incidence is complicated, because the changes during various intervals are not consistent with evidence provided by other time-series data on trends in consumption expenditure. In particular, the changes in per capita expenditure obtained from HIES and national accounts statistics show contradictory trends. If the midpoint dataset (1995–1996) of the HIES is dropped, the above complications concerning the fluctuations of the poverty incidence and the contradictions with other evidence do not arise (World Bank 2002d; Interim Poverty Reduction Strategy Paper 2002).

Given the large intervals at which these surveys are conducted, loss of one data point on these grounds involves costs, which should be carefully considered before surveys are carried out.

Human Poverty Trends and
Comparison with Income Poverty

Income- or calorie-based measures of poverty incidence faced criticism on the grounds that these are inadequate indicators of welfare or standard of living. The Human Development Index (HDI), developed by the UNDP, incorporated a number of other aspects of improvement in the quality of life, such as education, health, mortality, and women's empowerment. The Human Poverty Index (HPI) has been defined as a corollary to the HDI and provides a measure of the percentage of households/persons below a cutoff point of the HPI.

In Bangladesh the HPI registered a sharp decline between 1983 and 1997 (see Table 5.3). A comparison of the rate of decline of human poverty and income poverty (see Tables 5.1 and 5.2) shows that an improvement in human poverty in Bangladesh has been accompanied by a much smaller decline in income poverty. This illustrates that a decline in the HPI is possible without a commensurate change in income poverty. In addition, the weak linkage implies that an improvement in human development is not being translated into higher income of the poor households.

This is likely to be due to the lack of opportunity for productive utilization of human capital. The increase in the educated unemployment rate discussed later in this chapter provides supporting evidence. Moreover, the positive impact of human development may take place with a gestation gap and therefore the income enhancement of the poor households may not be immediately observed. In addition, an increase in the HPI may have taken place through improvement in the situation of the higher-income groups compared to the poorer groups. This may have a positive impact on the income of this relatively better-off group that does not lead to a reduction of the incidence of income, or of calorie-based poverty.

Thus the increase in the average value of the HPI is not a sufficient indicator of an improvement in the situation of human capital of the households in the lowest deciles based on income.

Table 5.3   Changes in Human Poverty Index, Bangladesh, 1981/82–1995/97

	Value of Human Poverty Index (%)	Decline in Human Poverty Index (percentage points per year)
1981–1982	61.3	
1993–1994	47.2	–1.41
1995–1997	40.1	–2.37

Sources: Bangladesh Institute for Development Studies 2001; author calculations.

GDP Growth and Poverty Trends

As mentioned, a growth of mean income is essential for reduction of the number of households below poverty-level income. The positive impact of economic growth on poverty reduction has been established on the basis of cross-country studies. Such studies do not, however, establish that growth is a sufficient condition for poverty alleviation. The relationship may hold because of the special features of economic growth in the countries that have succeeded in poverty alleviation. In other words, even if the relationship is significant, there will be countries for which growth did not lead to poverty alleviation. Such cross-country studies also suggest that there can be large variations in the poverty reduction impact resulting from the same rate of economic growth (Kakwani and Son 2002). Therefore, in addition to cross-country correlation studies, individual countries should assess whether growth has been pro-poor in their particular case. A positive relationship between the two can indicate that the growth pattern that is being realized is of the right type. If the contrary result is obtained, there will be need for caution and policies must be revised to achieve pro-poor growth.

Whether growth is pro-poor will depend on the structure of growth as well as on the importance of various productive factors in the growth process. We will examine here the trends of GDP growth rate and its relationship with poverty trends. To obtain better insights into the growth-poverty linkage, GDP growth rate will be disaggregated for the major economic activities (agriculture and industry). The employment elasticity in the manufacturing sector is important in this context and will be examined below.

A discussion of the trend GDP growth rates during the past one and a half (or two) decades will provide insights into the overall economic environment, which resulted in the poverty decline during the 1990s. In addition, we will compare the extent of improvement in the poverty situation at various points of time and the trend GDP growth rates during the relevant period. Insights into the poverty-reducing impact of GDP growth may also be obtained through analysis of the links between sectoral GDP growth rates and urban and rural poverty reduction rates. More specifically, the hypothesis behind such analysis is that urban poverty may depend on growth rates in industry and service sectors, which are the dominant sources of income of poor households in the urban areas. Similarly, agricultural income growth and rural poverty are expected to be interlinked. Such analysis assumes importance especially in view of the small number of data points available for the analysis of growth-poverty linkages.

Growth Rate of GDP and Poverty Trends, 1986–2000. A number of studies (e.g., Mujeri 2001; Bhattacharya 2001) have already highlighted the high annual growth rates of GDP in Bangladesh during recent years. Annual growth rates are influenced by the growth in the previous year. The trend of GDP growth rates should therefore be examined to assess the performance of the economy during longer periods.

The trend growth rate of GDP for the three subperiods is presented in Table 5.4. The trend growth rate was 2.46 percent per annum during 1986–1991. The trend growth rate rose to 4.50 percent and 5.29 percent per annum during the first and second half of the nineties respectively. Even if there was an acceleration of the rate of growth, the growth rate achieved during the latest period was much lower than the growth rate targeted for Bangladesh's sixth five-year plan (1998–2003).

The acceleration of GDP growth between 1996 and 2001 was modest because of the devastating floods of 1998. One may therefore argue that there exist potentials of a higher rate of GDP growth. The trend rate of growth could be much higher had the flood damage of 1998 not occurred. Such a hypothetical case should not be overstretched, because natural calamities are facts of life in Bangladesh and occur frequently. Such calamities caused a downturn in economic growth at least once during each of three five-year periods: 1986–1991, 1991–1996, and 1996–2000.

The GDP growth rate shows the expected relationship with poverty reduction. During the first subperiod, growth rate was low, and the HCR of poverty increased. The GDP growth rate accelerated during the second subperiod, 1991–1996. During this period, the headcount ratio of moderate poverty declined at a rate of 1.4 percentage points per year. The decline of extreme poverty was faster, at 2.1 percentage points per annum.

During the second half of the 1990s, GDP growth was faster. The HCR further declined during this period, though the decline per year was smaller than in 1991–1996. The decline in the HCR of moderate and extreme poverty per year was 0.73 and 0.98 percentage points respectively during these two periods. The percentage point of acceleration of GDP growth was 0.79 per year during the second half of the 1990s, which was smaller than the acceleration of GDP

Table 5.4 GDP Growth Rates and Poverty Trends, Bangladesh, 1986–2001

		CBN Method–Based HCR Decline		
	GDP Growth Rate (percent per annum)	Change of GDP Growth Rate (percentage points per year)	Moderate Poverty Decline (percentage points per year)	Extreme Poverty Decline (percentage points per year)
1986–1991	2.46		+1.18	+1.48
1991–1996	4.50	1.04	−1.43	−2.08
1996–2001	5.29	0.79	−0.23	−0.98

Source: Bangladesh Bureau of Statistics, various years.

growth rate during the previous subperiod (see Table 5.4). The crucial importance of GDP growth for poverty reduction is reflected in the association of a smaller acceleration of GDP growth rate with a smaller rate of decline of poverty during this period. Nonetheless, growth appears to have been less pro-poor during the second half of the 1990s.

The above conclusion stands in contrast to the observations made in a number of other recent papers. M. Mujeri states: "It is clear that an average growth rate of around 4 per cent per year is not rapid enough to make any significant impact on poverty" (2000, 99). Such lack of recognition of the concomitant variations of GDP growth and poverty reduction has been due to a number of reasons. The 2000 HIES results were not available when Mujeri's paper was prepared, and therefore the evidence of improvement of poverty during the entire decade was not in the hands of the author. In contrast, the World Bank (2002d) recognizes that poverty declined from 1991–1992 to 2000, which is "consistent with the growth performance." But one may question the validity of such comparison on the basis of changes at two points over almost a decade. This point is discussed below.

A GDP growth rate in the range of 4 to 5 percent per annum could have led to a larger poverty reduction impact, if the inequality of income (expenditure) had declined. However, inequality increased during the 1990s. Since urban income inequality is higher and future GDP growth is likely to take place through a higher rate of growth of urban sectors, a drastic decline of income inequality in the near future is not foreseen. Therefore, poverty reduction at a rate of 1.5 percentage points per annum (which is a midterm development goal target) will require a GDP growth rate higher than 6 percent per annum.

Sectoral Growth Rates and Poverty Reduction. Given the structure of the Bangladesh economy, the role of agricultural growth in poverty alleviation deserves special attention. Poverty incidence is higher among the rural households. All sources of data show that the poor in Bangladesh live mostly in rural areas and are engaged in agricultural activities. Growth of the manufacturing sector is expected to provide the impetus of poverty reduction in the urban areas. Therefore, we examine here the links between agricultural growth and rural poverty, and follow this with an analysis of the relationship between the urban poverty trend and nonagricultural growth rates.

Agriculture's share in GDP is the highest despite the decline of this share during the past three decades: from 50 percent in the 1970s to about 25 to 30 percent at the end of the century. The share of agriculture in employment remains high, with more than 60 percent of the labor force engaged in such activities. Such employment consists of both wage employment and self-employment.

Within the rural areas, poverty incidence is higher among the wage laborers and small and tenant farmers. The link between poverty and agricultural growth follows from these features of the poor.

The poverty-reducing impact of agricultural growth works along three channels:

1. Such growth raises the demand for rural laborers, which results in a larger number of days of employment for these workers. Higher demand is also likely to raise wage rates. Both factors will contribute to increased earnings.
2. Such growth helps to raise the income of small and tenant farmers. Initially there was some controversy about the possibility of these groups of farmers participating in agricultural modernization. The doubts were based on observations that the marginal landowners and tenant farmers cannot take the risks associated with the cultivation of modern rice varieties, and that they lack access to credit and other sources of funds for investment in agricultural inputs. Subsequently, most research findings demonstrated their ability to participate in the agricultural growth process.
3. Such growth affects the prices of the staple food. A higher growth reduces the price of food grain and helps the poor households, who are often net buyers of food grain.

The above channels may work simultaneously and help in the poverty reduction process.

Data on poverty incidence in the rural and urban areas and the extent of growth in agriculture and nonagricultural sectors during the subperiods are presented in Tables 5.5 and 5.6. However, the data do not show a direct relationship between agricultural growth rate and rural poverty. The two magnitudes vary in different directions at certain periods. However, this may not signify a lack of relationship between GDP growth and poverty, which was observed to exist when total GDP instead of sectoral GDP was considered. It is plausible that the decline of poverty incidence in the rural areas is linked not only with agriculture but also with other sectors, because the growth of industrial sectors and urban service sectors draws workers from the rural areas. Such predictions have been made by a range of two-sector development models wherein the modern sector flourishes through the withdrawal of labor from the traditional rural sector. This is expected to increase the average labor productivity of agricultural workers. With the gradual withdrawal of the landless laborers and their migration to urban areas, rural wage rates will be subjected to an upward pressure.

Similarly, the growth of food production will raise the real earnings of both urban and rural wage laborers. Therefore the reduction of poverty in the relevant region—urban or rural—is not directly linked with sectoral growth rates. Rather the combined result of overall GDP growth is linked with the poverty alleviation impact of growth. This becomes clearer if one examines

Table 5.5   GDP Growth in Agriculture and Extent of Poverty Decline in Rural Areas, Bangladesh, 1986–2001

	GDP Growth Rate in Agriculture (percent per annum)	Decline of Rural Moderate Poverty (percentage points per annum)	Decline of Rural Extreme Poverty (percentage points per annum)
1986–1991	2.19	+1.35	+1.67
1991–1996	1.50	–1.13	–1.88
1996–2001	5.07	–0.82	–0.98

Source: Bangladesh Bureau of Statistics, various years.

Table 5.6   GDP Growth Rate in Industry and Extent of Poverty Decline in Urban Areas, Bangladesh, 1986–2001

	GDP Growth Rate in Industry (percent per annum)	Decline of Urban Moderate Poverty (percentage points per year)	Decline of Urban Extreme Poverty (percentage points per year)
1986–1991	5.06	+0.33	+0.57
1991–1996	7.81	–2.53	–2.40
1996–2001	6.42	+0.36	+0.71

Source: Bangladesh Bureau of Statistics, various years.

certain features of the relationship between the growth of the agricultural sector and the nonagricultural sectors.

In Bangladesh the industrial base is very small and the growth of agriculture and nonagriculture is expected to show progress in the same direction. This would lead to simultaneous improvement in both rural and urban areas. In contrast, the observed sectoral pattern of growth is the reverse (as shown in Rahman and Islam 2003, tab. A.2.6).

The annual growth rate of the two sectors moves in the reverse direction in eight years out of fifteen. In three years the growth rates of both agriculture and industry declined. Only in four years did both agriculture and industry experience positive changes in growth rate. Explanation of this inverse relationship will consist of a number of factors. Such negative association, to some extent, is a reflection of the fluctuations in the growth rates of both agriculture and industry. The fluctuations in agricultural growth have been associated with natural calamities. The fluctuations of industrial growth have been linked with a variety of factors, including both natural factors and the demand-side forces. For example, the devastating floods of 1988 and 1998 affected both agriculture and industry. Moreover, this will be the result of a natural response of the economy where the work force is involved in different occupations. When one type of activity faces a setback, the labor force automatically switches to other activities. The same argument may be extended, whereby the industrial growth is expected to accelerate, as labor is more easily available in years of downturn of agricultural growth. However, such responses are not likely to be so large in magnitude as to have a sufficient countercyclical impact. A more plausible explanation of the observed phenomenon lies in the nature of government interventions and conscious policy efforts to ensure the level of growth and to alleviate poverty. When agriculture faces a setback due to adverse weather conditions, for example, government tries to ease credit and other services for accelerating growth of industry and other urban activities. Such development encourages a movement of labor to the urban areas. Therefore, lower agricultural growth may not necessarily lead to a worsening of rural poverty. Similarly, when industry lags, the government makes more investment in agriculture and infrastructure building. Thus the interventions producing a reverse pattern of growth of agriculture and nonagricultural sectors perhaps contribute to the absence of a direct association between such sectoral growth and rural/urban poverty trends.

The lack of direct association between sectoral growth and the extent of poverty reduction (in rural or urban areas) also shows that growth is necessary for poverty reduction but not a sufficient condition. Agricultural growth during the latter part of the 1990s, especially in the aftermath of the flood year 1998, did not lead to a recovery of employment and wage rate (discussed later in the chapter). As a result, the rate of poverty reduction was slow.

Similarly, during the second half of the 1990s, industrial growth, at 6.4 percent per annum, was not accompanied by poverty reduction. Urban moderate poverty (and extreme poverty) increased by 0.36 (and 0.71) percentage points per year. This is explained by the increase in income inequality and rising urban unemployment during this period. The increase in unemployment led to a stagnation in the wage rates (especially in the informal sectors). This is also reflected in a decline in employment elasticity of most of the subsectors of manufacturing (see below). Thus industrial growth cannot reduce poverty unless growth is employment-intensive and inequality-reducing in nature.

■ Sectoral Employment Growth and Poverty

Because employment is an important variable in making economic growth pro-poor, it is important to examine what has happened to employment as a result of growth. There are two ways of looking at the issue. The first would be to ask how employment-intensive growth has been. This question can be addressed by using the concept of employment elasticity with respect to output growth; the concept can be applied to the economy as a whole or to its major sectors. The second approach (which can actually complement an analysis based on employment elasticity) would be to examine how the structure of employment has responded to economic growth. For growth to be able to contribute to poverty reduction, it must lead to a transformation of the structure of employment toward sectors characterized by higher productivity and returns. For a country like Bangladesh, this would typically imply a shift toward manufacturing and other modern sectors.

Changes in Employment Structure During the 1990s

Here we examine changes in the labor force participation rate (LFPR) and sectoral composition of employment in Bangladesh during the 1990s. Table 5.7 shows LFPR and structure of the labor force at three points during the decade. Data show a small decline in LFPR during this period, from 69.6 percent in 1991 to 64.8 percent in 1996. Subsequently, in 1999–2000, LFPR increased to 65.8 percent.

Sectoral composition of the labor force also underwent change during this period, with the percentage of the labor force employed in agriculture declining from 66.3 to 62.3. Most of the decline was compensated by an increased percentage of the labor force employed in service sectors. In fact, the percentage of the labor force engaged in manufacturing also declined during the period. This stands in contrast to the increased percentage of the labor force employed in manufacturing (including electricity, construction, etc.) from 1983–1984 to 1991 (from 9.6 percent to 18.3 percent).[3]

Growth of Sectoral Employment

Data on sectoral growth of the labor force in Bangladesh (see Table 5.8) show that the percentage of the labor force employed in manufacturing declined to a significant extent during the first half of the 1990s, from 1989 to 1995–1996. This is somewhat inconsistent with the acceleration of growth of manufacturing GDP that occurred during this period, as shown in Table 5.6.

Table 5.7   Sectoral Composition of Labor Force and Participation Rate, Bangladesh, 1991–2000

	Sectoral Composition of Employed Labor Force (%)			Labor Force Participation Rate (%)
	Agriculture	Manufacturing, Electricity, Construction, and Others	Service and Others	
1991	66.3	12.7	20.7	69.6
1996	63.2	9.5	27.3	64.8
2000	62.3	9.6	28.1	65.8

Source: Various labor force survey reports.
Note: Based on extended definition of labor force, age ten years and older.

GDP growth in industry was associated with the rapid growth in the ready-made garments sector, which employed more than 1.5 million women during this period. In contrast, labor force survey data show a decline in female manufacturing employment (see Table 5.8). A number of other forces were at work during this period, influencing employment opportunities in manufactures. For example, the loss-making state-owned enterprises (SOEs) were closed down, and the privatized SOEs retrenched excess labor. The exact magnitude of such job loss is not known. The scope for reemployment is extremely limited for the retrenched workers. Therefore, many workers may have to resort to reverse migration to the rural areas and generate self-employment in agriculture and nonfarm activities. If such a process of deindustrialization and decline in manufacturing employment had not taken place, poverty reduction could have been achieved at a faster rate.

Bangladesh's 1999–2000 labor force survey provides data on sectoral composition of employment, indicating a growth rate of manufacturing employment close to that indicated by data from Bangladesh's manufacturing-industry census. The latest labor force survey shows a 0.9 percent (0.5 percent

Table 5.8 Average Annual Growth Rate of Labor Force by Industry and Gender, Bangladesh, 1990/91–1995/96 and 1995/96–1999/00

	Annual Growth Rate (%)					
	1990/91–1995/96			1995/96–1999/00		
Major Industry	Both Sex	Male	Female	Both Sex	Male	Female
Total	1.8	2.2	1.1	3.0	1.1	14.7
Agriculture, forestry, fisheries	0.7	2.2	–0.9	4.1	0.8	41.0
Mining, quarrying	10.7	9.3	100.0	172.7	93.7	982.0
Manufacturing	–6.2	–7.8	–2.6	1.3	0.5	2.7
Electricity, gas, water	31.5	26.1	240.0	7.5	7.2	9.6
Construction	18.7	18.6	19.0	2.0	1.7	6.2
Trade, hotel, restaurant	9.5	8.1	61.8	0.7	0.5	0.6
Transport, storage, communication	5.6	6.7	6.7	3.2	3.2	5.3
Finance, business services	33.3	20.6	113.4	22.3	20.3	46.9
Community and personal services and others	–9.7	–14.8	–1.1	1.6	–0.2	4.8

Source: Various labor force survey reports.

for male and 1.4 percent for female labor) per annum growth of manufacturing employment, while employment in agriculture had grown by 0.8 percent per annum.

The manufacturing-industry census provides an alternative source of data on employment in this sector.[4] For an assessment of structural change in the economy, these census data may be more relevant, because they cover enterprises with ten or more persons. According to this source, manufacturing employment underwent stagnation during 1981–1986, when the increase was 1.3 percent per year. During 1986–1990, there was an average growth of 5.3 percent per year in employment. Employment growth declined to less than 2 percent per year during the first part of the 1990s.[5] Female employment growth during the 1990s was double that of male employment growth, which stands in sharp contrast with 1995–1996 labor force survey data.

The balance of the evidence thus shows that there was a slow and fluctuating increase in both agricultural and manufacturing employment. Other tertiary sectors (trade, etc.) also absorbed labor at a rate higher than did the manufacturing sector. Thus there is no evidence that the pattern of employment underwent a significant structural change during this period.

Employment Intensity of Growth and Employment Elasticity

The development of an economy like that of Bangladesh requires that the manufacturing sector, which is the driving force of economic development, is able to generate additional job opportunities so that it may not only offer employment to the additions in labor force of the urban sector but also absorb some people from the subsistence agriculture sector, which is characterized by disguised unemployment and underemployment.

Hence it is important to achieve a greater understanding of the responsiveness of manufacturing employment to the change in the factors that determine it. Two possible determining variables of employment are output and wage rates. However, the labor demand function may be estimated independently irrespective of wages, capital, or investment. For given complementary inputs, it is possible to hypothesize that a close relationship exists between employment and output flows. Hence the research questions here concern, first, the employment intensity of economic growth and the change in employment intensity during the 1980s and 1990s; and second, whether the output intensity of employment (or value added) in the major economic sectors played a role in poverty trends in Bangladesh. The latter may be explored through estimating the output (or value-added) elasticity of employment.

While high elasticity of employment implies an employment-intensive growth, it needs to be remembered that an employment elasticity of unity or above means employment expansion that is not accompanied by improvements in labor productivity. Hence, in order to have healthy rates of employment expansion along with improvements in productivity, the desirable employment elasticity should be well below unity. Taking into account the experience of countries that achieved healthy rates of employment expansion during their period of high growth and surplus labor (e.g., the Republic of Korea during the 1960s and the 1970s, Indonesia during the 1970s and the 1980s), it can be suggested that an employment elasticity of around 0.7 would enable reasonable rates of employment expansion as well as improvements in labor productivity.

Here we examine employment elasticities in the manufacturing sector of Bangladesh (data for undertaking a similar exercise for other sectors being limited) and changes therein over time. The analysis is carried out separately for 23 subsectors at the three-digit level, and 24 subsectors at the four-digit level of manufacturing-industry activities.[6] In all, the manufacturing-industry census generates data for 49 three-digit-level activities, from which the present analysis includes 23 categories of activities. The employment in the selected 23 categories at the three-digit level accounts for 77 percent of the total employment in the censused manufacturing activities.[7] However, because of the heterogeneous character within different subsectors, it is important that the analysis be carried out also at some further disaggregated level. Hence, a further 23 (out of 162) four-digit-level activities are selected in the present analysis, the employment of which accounts for 58 percent of the total censused manufacturing employment. Employment and value added provided by the censused manufacturing industries constitute more than half of those of the whole manufacturing sector. Thus, in terms of coverage, the analysis fairly represents the manufacturing sector. The analysis considers two subperiods, 1980–1989 and 1990–1998, referred to as approximately the 1980s and the 1990s, and any changes between these two periods are analyzed.

Table 5.9 shows employment elasticities with respect to value added and output (for total volume) for the two subperiods. It can be seen from the table

Table 5.9   Value-Added/Output Elasticities of Employment in Manufacturing-Industry Activities, Bangladesh, 1980/89–1990/98

Level	Value Added/ Output	Value Added/Output Elasticity of Employment			Percentage Change Between Two Periods
		1980–1989	1990–1998	1980–1998	
Three-digit	Value added	0.7463	0.6859	0.7580	−8.1
Four-digit	Value added	0.7848	0.7263	0.7845	−7.5
Three-digit	Output	0.7557	0.7226	0.7788	−4.4
Four-digit	Output	0.7359	0.6046	0.6929	−17.8

Source: Bangladesh's census of manufacturing industries, various years.

that employment elasticity with respect to value added for the total period 1980–1998 is estimated at 0.76 and 0.78 for the three- and four-digit-level activities respectively. Similarly, the employment elasticity with respect to output is estimated at 0.78 and 0.69 for the three- and four-digit-level activities respectively. For all the cases of value added and output, at the three-digit or four-digit level, the estimates are statistically significant, at more than 99 percent.[8]

Comparing the elasticity between the 1980s and 1990s, it can be seen that for all the selected activities at both the three- and the four-digit level (with either value added or output), the elasticities for the latter period declined. The rate of decline for value added is in the range of 8 percent for the three-digit level and 7.5 percent for the four-digit level. In the case of output, however, the picture with regard to the rate of decline is mixed: in the range of 4.4 percent for the three-digit level of activities, and as high as 17.8 percent for four-digit level. The higher values of manufacturing employment elasticity in the 1980s and the lower values of employment elasticities during the 1990s indicate that the employment-generating capacity of the manufacturing sector declined.

Tables 5.10 and 5.11 present ranges of value-added elasticities of employment at the three- and four-digit levels respectively.[9] As can be seen from Table 5.10, some 30 percent of the three-digit activities under study (7 out of 23), entailing more than 45 percent of total censused manufacturing employment, have value-added elasticities lower than 0.5. Nearly 35 percent (8 out of 23) of the activities, entailing about 14 percent of total censused manufacturing employment, have elasticities between 0.50 and 0.75, again with 35 percent (8 out of 23) of the activities, entailing 18 percent of total censused manufacturing employment, having elasticities greater than 0.75.

As can be seen from Table 5.11, the picture is somewhat different in the case of four-digit-level activities. Relatively fewer activities seem to have lower elasticities, with a greater number of activities having relatively higher elasticities. Some 17 percent of the three-digit activities under study (4 out of 23), entailing less than 2 percent of total censused manufacturing employment, have value-added elasticities lower than 0.5. Nearly 26 percent (6 out of 23) of the activities, entailing about 11 percent of total censused manufacturing employment, have elasticities between 0.50 and 0.75, with 57 percent (13 out of 23) of the activities, entailing 46 percent of total censused manufacturing employment, having elasticities greater than 0.75. It can be seen that the garments industry (the number one export subsector, which provided nearly 1.5 million jobs in 2002–2003, mostly to women), with employment elasticity of 0.96, falls into this category.

Rahman and Islam 2003 provide detailed data on employment elasticities on individual industries within the censused manufacturing categories. The estimates of elasticity are highly significant for nearly all the activities, for both value added and output and at three- and four-digit levels. That the estimates are positive for most of the activities indicates a positive association between

Table 5.10 Ranges of Value-Added Elasticities of Employment at Three-Digit Level, Bangladesh, 1980–1998

Range of Value-Added Elasticity of Employment, 1980–1998	Number of Activities Under Study	Percentage of Total Manufacturing-Industry Employment	Subsectors
< 0.50	7 (30.4)	45.5	321 Textiles manufacturing 341 Paper and paper products 352 Industrial and chemicals 353 Other chemical products 371 Iron and steel basic 382 Fabricated metal products 383 Nonelectrical machinery
0.50–0.75	8 (34.8)	13.9	312 Food manufacturing 332 Furniture and fixture 342 Printing and publishing 351 Drugs and pharmaceuticals 356 Rubber products 357 Plastic products 384 Electrical machinery 385 Transport equipment
≥ 0.75	8 (34.8)	17.8	311 Food manufacturing 314 Tobacco manufacturing 322 Textiles manufacturing 324 Leather and leather products 331 Wood and cork products 361 Pottery 369 Nonmetallic minerals 381 Fabricated metal products
Average 0.76	23 (100.0)	77.2	All twenty-three subsectors

Source: Bangladesh's census of manufacturing industries, various years.

output (value added) and employment. The estimates for some of the activities exceed unity, indicating that a 1 percent increase in output in such activities would lead to an increase in employment of greater than 1 percent.

The activities (International Standard Industrial Classification of All Economic Activities, ISIC-Rev. 2, 1968) having elasticity estimates (for value added) greater than unity at the three-digit level are food manufacturing (311), tobacco manufacturing (314), leather and leather products (324), wood and cork products (331), pottery (361), and nonmetallic minerals (369) (Rahman and Islam 2003, tab. A.3.4, p. 64). Of the three-digit-level activities (for value added), nonmetallic minerals (369) has the highest elasticity, at 1.70. Non-

Table 5.11   Ranges of Value-Added Elasticities of Employment at Four-Digit Level, Bangladesh, 1980–1998

Range of Value-Added Elasticity of Employment, (1980–1998)	Number of Activities Under Study	Percentage of Total Manufacturing-Industry Employment	Subsectors	
< 0.50	4 (17.4)	1.6	3533	Soap and all detergents
			3713	Iron and steel rerolling
			3714	Bamboo-cane
			3124	Gur
0.50–0.75	6 (26.1)	10.9	3116	Oil except hydro
			3126	Tea and coffee processing
			3211	Cotton textiles
			3321	Wooden furniture
			3611	Earthenware
			3321	Wooden furniture manufacturing
			3832	Agricultural machinery
≥ 0.75	13 (56.5)	45.7	3118	Grain milling
			3122	Bakery products
			3128	Edible salt
			3143	Bidies manufacturing
			3214	Silks and synthetic textiles
			3216	Handloom textiles
			3223	Knitwear
			3231	Ready-made garments
			3241	Tanning and finishing
			3311	Saw and planing mills
			3691	Bricks-tiles and nonclay
			3814	Furniture and fixture
			3857	Ship-breaking
Average 0.78	23 (100.0)	2	All twenty-four subsectors	

Source: Bangladesh's census of manufacturing industries, various years.

electrical machinery has the lowest elasticity, at 0.16. Among the four-digit-level activities under study, only three activities have elasticities greater than unity: bakery products (3122), tanning and leather finishing (3241), and bricks-tiles (3591) (Rahman and Islam 2003, tab. A.3.5). Among the four-digit-level industries, bakery products and bricks-tiles have the highest elasticity, at 1.19, and iron and steel rerolling has the lowest, at 0.34. Such high elasticity estimates for some of the activities seem to be consistent with conventional interpretations of relatively labor-intensive and low-productivity jobs in these subsectors.

For most of the industries, however, the estimates for value-added (and output) elasticity are lower than unity, much lower in some cases, indicating that an increase (decrease) in value added (output) would lead to a less-than-proportionate increase (fall) in employment in these activities. Such activities under the three-digit level are nonelectrical machinery (0.17), basic iron and steel (0.21), fabricated metal products (0.31), and industrial chemicals (0.35) (Rahman and Islam 2003, tab. A.3.4, p. 64). At the four-digit level, activities such as bamboo and cane (0.12), soap and detergents (0.28), and iron and steel rerolling (0.34) are among those showing very low values of elasticity (Rahman and Islam 2003, tab. A.3.5, p. 65). Returns to scale, however, are greater than unity for activities such as food manufacturing, textile manufacturing, furniture and fixture, paper and paper products, printing and publishing, drugs and pharmaceuticals, other chemical products, plastic products, fabricated metal products, and electrical machinery (not shown in the Rahman and Islam 2003 tables). The remaining activities have returns to scale that are lower than unity. At the four-digit level, returns to scale are greater than unity for activities such as edible salt, cotton textiles, handloom textiles, knitwear, readymade garments, bamboo and cane products, iron and steel rerolling, and furniture and fixture (Rahman and Islam 2003, 25). All the remaining activities have returns to scale that are lower than unity.

The experience of other developing countries shows that employment elasticities close to unity would be desirable for poor countries, as they do not lead to rapid expansion of low-productivity employment (in case of much higher elasticity) or too little employment (in case of low elasticity). Apart from such historical guidelines, a direct link between employment elasticity (calculated above) and poverty is difficult. In terms of historical experience, the elasticities for most subsectors in Bangladesh seem to be in the desirable range.

From the point of view of poverty reduction, the same amount of employment growth through the growth of low-employment elasticity sectors as through high-elasticity sectors can have a greater degree of poverty alleviation impact. Data presented in Rahman and Islam 2003 (tabs. A.3.16–A.3.19) show that, generally, the subsectors that underwent a decline in employment elasticity experienced higher employment growth than those that didn't. In addition, wage increases generally occur much faster in industries with more employment growth—for example, subsectors such as textile manufacturing, leather and leather products, printing and publishing, and fabricated metals, and the case of four-digit-level subsectors such as bakery, knitwear, readymade garments, and leather. The only exception is the nonmetallic minerals subsector. The above examples indicate some positive prospects of poverty alleviation through growth of the relevant manufacturing subsectors.

To recapitulate, compared to the 1980s, employment elasticities almost invariably declined during the 1990s. Relatively lower values of employment elasticity in the 1990s indicate that the employment-generating capacity of the manufacturing sector from a given rate of output growth has declined over time.

From the perspective of poverty analysis, what matters is not growth alone but also the extent to which it is employment-friendly. For any given growth, employment generation would be higher for growth in activities having higher elasticities. Such activities at the three-digit level are food, tobacco, leather, wood, pottery, nonmetallic minerals, and textiles. Among these, nonmetallic minerals has the highest elasticity. At the four-digit level, the high-elasticity activities are bricks, bakery, tanning, silk textiles, handlooms, grain mills, and ready-made garments. The highest elasticity was found for bricks and the lowest for iron and steel rerolling.

Employment generation per unit of output growth would be limited for those activities having relatively lower elasticities. Such low-elasticity activities at the three-digit level include nonelectrical machinery, iron, fabricated metals, and chemical products. Among these, nonelectrical machinery has the lowest elasticity. At the four-digit level, activities such as soap and steel rerolling are among those showing extremely low values of elasticity. However, along with the generation of employment-friendly growth, it is imperative that productivity, which has a direct bearing on income and hence poverty, also be increased.

Therefore, it may be argued that if total employment can be increased through high growth of sectors where the elasticity of employment has declined, with an associated increase in productivity and wage, this can be an effective step for poverty reduction. Leather and leather products, knitwear, ready-made garments, food manufacturing, and printing and publishing are among such subsectors (see Rahman and Islam 2003, tabs. A.3.18–A.3.21). Leather and leather products, and knitwear and ready-made garments, are the largest export sectors in Bangladesh. Thus the current sectoral growth pattern, if pursued vigorously, can help in both GDP growth and poverty reduction.

■ Wage Rate and Poverty

Trends of Real Wage Rate
Real wage rate indices in construction, manufacturing, and agriculture sectors in Bangladesh are presented in Table 5.12. These data show that there were increases in real wage rate indices in general until 1997–1998. The increase was smaller in the case of construction and agriculture compared to the manufacturing sector (9, 10, and 23 points of increase for the three sectors respectively, over the period 1990/91–1999/00).[10] Moreover, the real wage indices in construction and agriculture went through fluctuations, as demonstrated by annual data.

Table 5.12 Wage Rate Indexes by Sector, Bangladesh, 1990/91–1999/00

	Nominal Indexes				Real Wage Indexes			
	General	Manufacturing	Construction	Agriculture	General	Manufacturing	Construction	Agriculture
1990–1991	1,482	1,575	1,487	1,321	107	114	107	95
1991–1992	1,553	1,641	1,512	1,425	107	113	104	98
1992–1993	1,638	1,724	1,579	1,523	113	119	109	105
1993–1994	1,709	1,828	1,598	1,593	114	121	106	106
1994–1995	1,786	1,947	1,613	1,653	111	121	100	103
1995–1996	1,900	2,064	1,754	1,738	114	123	105	104
1996–1997	1,989	2,161	1,848	1,804	120	130	111	108
1997–1998	2,141	2,395	1,990	1,870	122	137	114	107
1998–1999	2,259	2,522	2,163	1,950	118	131	113	102
1999–2000	2,390	2,702	2,286	2,037	121	137	116	105

Source: Bangladesh Bureau of Statistics, various years.
Note: Base is 1969–1970 = 100.

The rising trend of wage rates in modern sectors is in conformity with a decline of the male underemployment rate, which has already come down to a one-digit level in the urban areas (see Table 5.27), thus reflecting a tightening of the market. With the growing importance of rural nonfarm self-employment, the opportunity cost of labor is rising. Both urban and rural real wage rates have to respond to the rise. Moreover, when employed in the informal sector, workers simultaneously engage in a number of activities and try to enhance earning, which they cannot do when they are employed full-time in manufacturing, and therefore the wage rate in the latter has to be higher.

However, the overall real wage indexes in both agriculture and manufacturing stagnated during the late 1990s (Table 5.12). This explains, at least in part, why GDP growth during the late 1990s failed to achieve poverty reduction during this period. The lesson from this experience is that GDP growth cannot lead to poverty alleviation if it does not generate demand for hired labor and a rise in real wage rate. A decline in the output elasticity of employment, as shown in Chapter 3, is consistent with the observed pattern. Similar research on employment elasticity in rural agricultural sectors should be undertaken.

Table 5.13 presents real wage data for male and female labor calculated on the basis of data from labor force surveys. The data show that between 1989 and 1995–1996, there was a stagnation of the male real wage rate. The real wage rate for male labor, in both rural and urban areas, increased during the late 1990s. However, the increase in male real wage is only 12 percent over 11.5 years. The real wage rate of urban female labor increased by about 60 percent over the entire period. In contrast, women's real wage in the rural areas showed a much smaller increase. One can therefore easily see the rationale behind the recent trend of rural-to-urban migration of female workers.[11]

Gender Differences in Wage Rate and Female Poverty

The analyses of underemployment, structural change in the labor market, wage rates, and poverty in Bangladesh have so far been based on aggregate

Table 5.13   Real Wage Rates in Urban and Rural Areas, Bangladesh, 1989–2000

Sector	1999–2000		1995–1996		1989	
	Male	Female	Male	Female	Male	Female
Agricultural/rural	26.6	14.8	23.0	13.0	23.4	16.8
Nonagricultural/urban	36.9	25.6	32.2	19.3	33.4	15.2

Source: Bangladesh Bureau of Statistics, various years.
Notes: Wage rates are in taka per person per day. For 1995–1996, wage rate is given for rural-urban classification; for other years, by agriculture and nonagriculture (rural and urban consumer price index uses base year of 1985–1986 = 100).

figures for the male and female labor force (though some of the tables contain gender-disaggregated data). Male-female differences in wage rate deserve emphasis because these differences have implications for gender equity and also for the overall functioning of the labor market and poverty levels. Such differences may also highlight the need for a rethinking about the industrial development process based on surplus labor.

The wage rate of female workers is much lower than the wage rate of male workers (see Table 5.14). Between 1984–1985 and 1995–1996, the ratio between the male and female wage rates increased in the rural/agricultural sector, from 1.4 to 1.8, and was found to be at the same latter level in 1999–2000. Thus in the rural areas, the growth of the male wage rate has been much higher than the growth of the female wage rate. In the case of the urban wage rate, the ratio declined during the three periods mentioned above, from 2.38, to 1.67, to 1.4. During this period there was an expansion of employment opportunities for women in the urban areas, which was instrumental in raising their wage rate. Some of the wage increase may have been due to an increase in skills, experience, and education among female workers.

For rural female labor, the real wage rate in 1999–2000 was lower than the real wage in 1989 (Table 5.13). The real wage trend of female workers implies that rural households depending on female wage for a substantial part of their income face a continuation of poverty. This group has hardly benefited from the growth of the rural economy.

A number of factors have contributed to the low wage rate of women. The following reasons deserve attention when formulating policies for women's employment:

1. During the past decade, growth of the female labor force has been much higher than growth of the male labor force. An increase in the female labor force has occurred due to increasing poverty in households who do not have male workers as well as social changes that resulted in a readiness to accept women's employment.

Table 5.14 Male and Female Wage Rates, Bangladesh, 1989–1999/00

Sector	1999–2000		1995–1996		1989	
	Male	Female	Male	Female	Male	Female
Agricultural/rural	63.0	35.0	44.0	25.0	31.6	22.7
Nonagricultural/urban	85.0	59.0	60.0	36.0	46.0	20.9

Source: Bangladesh Bureau of Statistics, various years.

Notes: Wage rates are in taka per person per day. For 1995–1996, wage rate is given for rural-urban classification; for other years, by agriculture and nonagriculture (rural and urban consumer price index uses base year of 1985–1986 = 100).

2. Unemployment and underemployment rates are higher among women compared to men. The difference is much higher in the case of underemployment. The average underemployment rate for men and women together is high because of the high figure for women.
3. The intensity of poverty in the households of female wage laborers and the low wage rate received by women reinforce each other. Since the uneducated female wage laborers usually come from poor households, their bargaining position is weaker than that of male laborers, which in turn makes them vulnerable to low wages and poverty. Once a young woman gets a job, her family pressures her not to lose it, however arduous the work may be and however large the male-female wage difference is.
4. In the rural areas, job segmentation along gender lines is widespread. In most districts, women are not hired for field operations of major crops. Therefore the total demand for female wage labor is small.

The implications of the low female wage rate for the poverty situation becomes clear from Table 5.15. The female wage rate is such that a day's wage cannot maintain a family of three members, even if a woman obtains year-round employment. The situation is worse for rural women. The female wage rate usually supports fewer than two members above the poverty level. The 1999–2000 urban male wage rate supported 3.2 members compared to 2.2 by the female wage rate.

The above observations have far-reaching implications for gender equity in the labor market and women's poverty situation, as well as for the growth of labor-intensive industrialization in Bangladesh. With women's wage rates

Table 5.15 Male and Female Wage Rates Relative to (Moderate) Poverty Line, Bangladesh, 1989–1999/00

	Sector	Wage Rate (taka per day)		Number of Persons Who Can Be Sustained Above Poverty Level by a Day's Wage	
		Male	Female	Male	Female
1989	Agriculture	31.6	22.7	2.1	1.5
	Nonagriculture	46.0	20.9	2.1	1.0
1995–1996	Rural	44.0	25.0	2.2	1.3
	Urban	60.0	36.0	2.5	1.5
1999–2000	Agriculture	63.0	35.0	2.5	1.4
	Nonagriculture	85.0	59.0	3.2	2.2

Source: Bangladesh Bureau of Statistics, various years.

being 45 and 31 percent lower than those of men (in the rural and urban areas respectively), families depending on female labor are subject to more intense poverty. The next section examines whether households with female wage laborers face a greater probability of being poor (Hossain 1996b).

The difference between male and female earning will be even greater than the difference in wage rate, because women obtain employment for a significantly fewer number of days than do men, especially in the rural areas. Table 5.27 shows that the underemployment rate is substantially higher among the female labor force.

▧ Interdependence of the Labor Market and Poverty: Micro-Level Analysis

In labor market analysis for countries with a high population density, the lack of adequate demand for labor, reflected in a surplus labor situation, has been the predominant concern until recently. An analysis of the links between employment of individual workers and poverty requires an understanding of both the supply side of labor and the demand side. The picture of the supply side will be viewed here through an examination of the characteristics of the labor force, especially the educational qualifications of the poor and nonpoor workers, and through the labor force participation rate, the number of workers in a household, and their characteristics.

The situation of the poor in the labor market will also depend on a range of demand-side influences. The demand side will be reflected in the extent of employment, sectoral pattern, and mode and type of employment. The difference between the poor and nonpoor with respect to these characteristics will be examined. Figure 5.1 shows some of these linkages.

Poor Households' Labor Force Characteristics
Though the demographic aspects of households' labor supply are not amenable to policies in the short run, the differences between poor and nonpoor in these respects may be highlighted to provide an idea about whether such characteristics are important contributors to poverty.

Among the characteristics of the supply of labor, the size of the family labor force and gender composition are likely to differ with the poverty status of households. The current hypothesis is that a family with a younger head of household and larger percentage of female workers has a higher probability of being in poverty.

In addition, better skill and better educational endowment of the working-age members should influence their productivity positively and thus enhance the wage rate and earning prospects of the hired workers and self-employed workers respectively. The labor force from poor households is likely to be faced with more disadvantages on this front.

Figure 5.1   Changes of Employment-Poverty Linkage

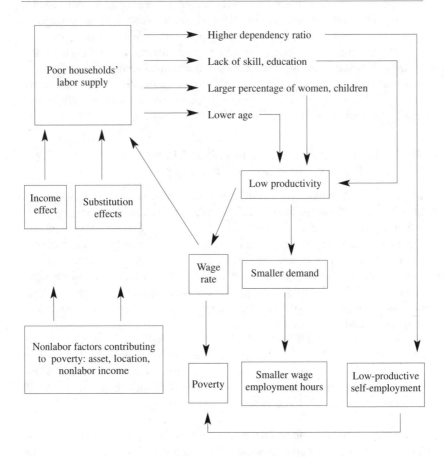

The ownership of assets, especially land, is expected to exert a negative effect on the probability of being below the poverty line. Therefore these characteristics deserve attention. Data on the labor force participation, educational distribution, and type of employment are presented in Tables 5.16 to 5.20.[12]

Workers from poor households are younger (Table 5.16), though the difference is small. The average age of poor workers is 34.4 years, compared to 35.2 years for the nonpoor.

Data presented in Table 5.17 show that the activity ratio among poorer families is higher. The differences are larger in the urban areas, for both men and women. The family size is larger among the poor household, whereas the number of labor force participants is smaller than among the nonpoor (Tables 5.18 and 5.19). The number of family members aged fifteen or older is lower among the poor compared to the nonpoor (Table 5.19). Thus the ratio of av-

137

Table 5.16 Average Age of Poor and Nonpoor Workers by Location, Bangladesh, 1999–2000

Location	Poverty Status	Age (years)
Rural	Poor	34.62
	Nonpoor	35.66
	Total	34.99
Urban	Poor	34.04
	Nonpoor	34.75
	Total	34.45

Source: Bangladesh Bureau of Statistics 1999–2000, 2002.

Table 5.17 Labor Force Participant as Percentage of Total 15+ Age Family Members Among Poor and Nonpoor Households in Urban and Rural Areas, Bangladesh, 1999–2000

Location	Poverty Status	Male Labor Force Participation Rate (%)	Female Labor Force Participation Rate (%)	Male and Female Labor Force Participation Rate (%)
Rural	Poor	92.82	63.86	77.09
	Nonpoor	89.90	66.30	77.09
Urban	Poor	92.40	38.36	64.70
	Nonpoor	86.92	36.46	62.60

Source: Bangladesh Bureau of Statistics 1999–2000, 2002.

Table 5.18 Number of Male and Female Labor Force Members by Poverty Status and Location, Bangladesh, 1999–2000

Location	Poverty Status	Number of Males in Labor Force (age 15+)	Number of Females in Labor Force (age 15+)	Number of Males and Females in Labor Force (age 15+)
Rural	Poor	1.24	0.81	2.05
	Nonpoor	1.36	0.88	2.25
	Total	1.28	0.84	2.12
Urban	Poor	1.20	0.51	1.71
	Nonpoor	1.29	0.49	1.78
	Total	1.25	0.50	1.75

Source: Bangladesh Bureau of Statistics 1999–2000, 2002.

138

Table 5.19   Working-Age Members and Family Size by Poverty Status and Location, Bangladesh, 1999–2000

Location	Poverty Status	Number of Males (age 15+)	Number of Females (age 15+)	Number of Males and Females (age 15+)	Family Size
Rural	Poor	1.38	1.32	2.71	5.05
	Nonpoor	1.59	1.40	2.99	4.57
Urban	Poor	1.35	1.36	2.72	5.15
	Nonpoor	1.59	1.46	3.05	4.51

Source: Bangladesh Bureau of Statistics 1999–2000, 2002.

Table 5.20   Distribution of Poor and Nonpoor Workers by Education, Bangladesh, 1999–2000

Sex of Worker	Education of Worker	Poor (%)	Nonpoor (%)
Female	Never go to school	68.0	42.1
	Classes I–V	21.7	25.8
	Classes VI–VIII	6.3	12.6
	Classes IX–X	2.2	6.8
	Secondary school/high school and equivalent	1.4	8.9
	Bachelor and above, other diploma	0.4	3.7
	Total	100.0	100.0
Male	Never go to school	50.3	22.0
	Classes I–V	27.3	21.0
	Classes VI–VIII	12.6	16.8
	Classes IX–X	4.1	9.0
	Secondary school/high school and equivalent	4.5	18.1
	Bachelor and above, other diploma	1.3	12.6
	Total	100.0	100.0
Male and Female	Never go to school	56.7	28.6
	Classes I–V	25.2	22.6
	Classes VI–VIII	10.3	15.4
	Classes IX–X	3.4	0.3
	Secondary school/high school and equivalent	3.4	15.1
	Bachelor and above, other diploma	1.0	9.9
	All	100.0	100.0

Source: Bangladesh Bureau of Statistics 1999–2000, 2002.

erage nonearners to earners is larger for poor households. The average number of female earners is larger among the poor, and the average number of male earners is smaller. Thus there is evidence of demographic disadvantages adversely affecting the situation of the poor households.

The other important aspect of the difference in labor force characteristics between poor and nonpoor households is the educational endowment of the workers. Such endowment is likely to be lower among the poor. The rationale is that they may not consider it worthwhile to invest in human capital because of their priority for immediate consumption. They may not be in a position to bear the expenses of schooling of children, particularly girl children who will leave the family after marriage. Since such priorities are rational responses to poverty, governments in many countries invest in education, especially primary education. The same is true for Bangladesh. In addition to free primary education, scholarship programs for secondary students have been introduced.

Making education free may not be sufficient for keeping poor children in school. Investment in human capital requires that labor force participation be postponed, indicating that there is an opportunity cost of such an investment. Still, there has been a positive impact of government investment in school education, and enrollment has increased among both the poor and the nonpoor.

How much the composition of education in the labor force differs between the poor and the nonpoor is shown in Figure 5.2 (and Table 5.20). The data show some interesting features. The percentage of workers with secondary or higher education is much smaller among the poor compared to the nonpoor. This holds for both the male and the female labor force. A large percentage of the female labor force, both poor and nonpoor, is without any schooling.

Table 5.21 shows the skill endowment. It must be clarified that in most cases the attainment of skill may occur through on-the-job training and not through institutional training. From the questionnaire used in the labor force survey, these two cannot be distinguished. The percentage of skilled workers is much lower among the poor compared to the nonpoor, and among women compared to men.

Tables 5.22 and 5.23 show the distribution of poor and nonpoor workers by mode of employment and sector of employment respectively. As expected, a larger percentage among the poor are engaged as daily laborers as compared to the nonpoor (24 and 7 percent respectively). A smaller percentage of poor workers being involved as "employers," "salaried workers," and "household workers without pay" accounts for the difference. The extent of self-employment among poor workers shows a different picture between rural and urban areas. In the rural areas, the percentage of wage workers in self-employment is lower among the poor than the nonpoor. The reverse is true for the urban areas.

Sectoral distribution of the labor force by poverty status is shown in Table 5.23. There are higher percentages of workers from poor than nonpoor house-

Figure 5.2 Percentage Distribution of Male and Female Workers from Poor and Nonpoor Households by Education, Bangladesh

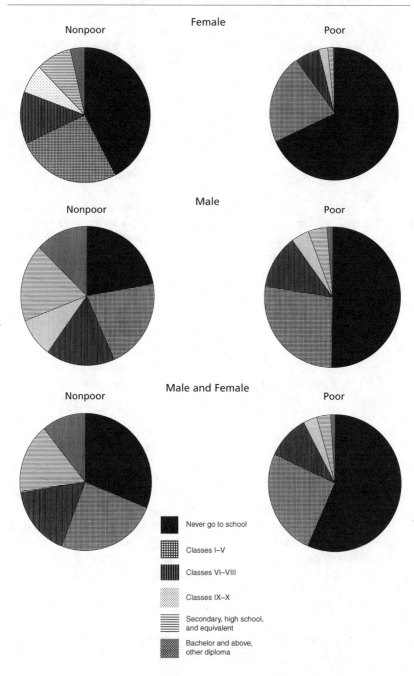

Table 5.21   Distribution of Poor and Nonpoor Labor Force by Skill, Bangladesh, 1999–2000

Location	Sex of Worker	Poverty Status	Skilled (%)	Unskilled (%)
Rural	Female	Poor	8.9	91.1
		Nonpoor	9.0	91.0
		Total	8.9	91.1
	Male	Poor	32.6	67.4
		Nonpoor	45.5	54.5
		Total	37.2	62.8
Urban	Female	Poor	8.5	91.5
		Nonpoor	14.6	85.4
		Total	11.9	88.1
	Male	Poor	26.7	73.3
		Nonpoor	40.4	59.6
		Total	34.6	65.4

Source: Bangladesh Bureau of Statistics 1999–2000, 2002.

Table 5.22   Mode of Employment by Poverty Status, Bangladesh, 1999–2000

		Employment Status in Past Week				
Location	Poverty Status	Self-Employment	Employer	Salaried Worker	Household Worker Without Pay	Daily Labor/ Casual Labor
Rural	Poor	31.1	0.1	6.1	36.0	26.8
	Nonpoor	40.1	0.2	10.7	41.9	7.1
Urban	Poor	40.2	0.1	27.1	14.5	18.1
	Nonpoor	37.7	0.9	39.8	14.3	7.4

Source: Bangladesh Bureau of Statistics 1999–2000, 2002.

holds employed in agriculture, construction, and transport, with a reversal of this situation regarding employment in manufacturing, trade, and other services.

As expected, a much lower percentage of poor compared to nonpoor workers are employed in formal jobs (see Table 5.24).

Factors Determining Households' Poverty Status: Results of Multiple Regression

The determinants of a household's poverty status have been analyzed (whether it is below the poverty level) through logistic regressions using

Table 5.23 Distribution of Employment Sector by Poverty Status, Bangladesh, 1999–2000

Location	Poverty Status	Agriculture (%)	Manufacturing (%)	Construction (%)	Trade (%)	Transport (%)	Financial Service (%)	Other Service (%)
Rural	Poor	74.9	5.8	1.8	8.3	3.8	0.2	5.2
	Nonpoor	68.6	5.9	1.6	11.9	2.2	0.6	9.2
Urban	Poor	23.7	16.5	5.2	20.2	14.3	0.7	19.4
	Nonpoor	16.0	16.7	3.5	25.7	8.6	3.5	26.1

Source: Bangladesh Bureau of Statistics 1999–2000, 2002.

Table 5.24 Distribution of Poor and Nonpoor Labor Force Between Formal and Informal Employment, Bangladesh, 1999–2000

Location	Poverty Status	Informal (%)	Formal (%)
Rural	Poor	89.7	10.3
	Nonpoor	82.1	17.9
Urban	Poor	67.7	32.3
	Nonpoor	49.9	50.1

Source: Bangladesh Bureau of Statistics 1999–2000, 2002.

household data from Bangladesh's 2000 labor force survey. The explanatory variables used in the regressions include:

- Household's characteristics, including demographic features and labor force endowment.
- Household's asset situation, including physical and land assets, education, and remittance receipt.
- Employment characteristics, in terms of mode of employment, sector of employment, and the like.

Household characteristics included in the equation are age of head of household and its square, sex of household head (male = 1), number of working members age fifteen or older, number of child workers, number of dependent members, ratio of female workers, and education of working members of household (consists of two variables: years of education of head of household, and total years of education of other working member).

Several interesting findings result from the regressions (Tables 5.25 and 5.26). The age and square-of-age variables have different signs in both the rural and urban regressions. These variables are significant in the rural equation, but not so in the urban. Coefficients of most of the other variables are similar in the two equations. Both variables representing a household's endowment of education have significant negative coefficients and thus reduce the probability of being in poverty. This is expected, since education enhances productivity and thereby earnings. Sex of head of household has an insignificant coefficient, which is contrary to the current hypothesis and therefore requires an explanation. The current notion is that poverty incidence is higher among the female-headed households. The results of regression obtained in the present case show that households with female heads do not have a higher probability of being in poverty. This has happened because of the wider definition (de jure) of female-headedness. Labor force surveys (and other surveys by the BBS) include within female-headed households those who have male earners living in other places. Therefore these households receive remittance

Table 5.25   Determinants of Poverty Status: Results of Logistic Regression—Rural Bangladesh, 1999–2000

Explanatory Variable	Coefficient	Standard Error	Significance
Age of household head	−0.04	0.02	0.01
Square of age of household head	0.0004	0.0002	0.02
Education of household head	−0.24	0.03	0.00
Education of other household workers	−0.11	0.02	0.00
Sex of household head	−0.18	0.17	0.28
Number of child workers	0.43	0.08	0.00
Whether wage laborer	1.26	0.11	0.00
Whether employee	0.21	0.13	0.11
Whether formal sector	−0.52	0.10	0.00
Whether manufacturing	−0.12	0.09	0.21
Whether construction	−0.46	0.18	0.01
Whether trade	−0.30	0.08	0.00
Whether transport	0.20	0.15	0.17
Whether service	−0.26	0.41	0.52
Whether other sector	−0.22	0.10	0.03
Number of dependents	0.56	0.03	0.00
Number of workers	0.33	0.06	0.00
Ratio of female workers	0.60	0.16	0.00
Whether employer	−0.82	0.80	0.30
Landownership	−0.003	0.0003	0.00
Whether remittance received	−1.99	0.23	0.00
Asset 1	−0.34	0.13	0.00
Asset 2	−.014	0.19	0.46
Asset 3	−1.75	0.54	0.00
Asset 4	−6.42	5.30	0.23
Asset 5	−0.54	0.10	0.00
Constant	0.72	0.40	0.03
−2 log likelihood	4,664.2		
Correct-prediction percentage			
Poor	88.4		
Nonpoor	55.3		
Overall	77.3		

Source: Bangladesh Bureau of Statistics 1999–2000, 2002.

and have a higher chance of being nonpoor. This counterbalances the other fe-male-headed households who do not have male earners and have a greater chance of being poor with a net impact as insignificant.

A larger number of dependent members increases the probability of being poor (the coefficient is positive and significant). This is quite expected. Contrary to expectation are the positive coefficients of two variables: number of working members age fifteen and older, and number of working members age eight to fourteen years. While the presence of more earners is likely to raise income and reduce the chances of being poor, the contrary effect holds: poorer

Table 5.26 Determinants of Poverty Status: Results of Logistic Regression—Urban Bangladesh, 1999–2000

Explanatory Variable	Coefficient	Standard Error	Significance
Age of household head	–0.02	0.02	0.21
Square of age of household head	0.0001	0.0002	0.75
Education of household head	–0.46	0.03	0.00
Education of other household workers	–0.10	0.02	0.00
Sex of household head	0.16	0.17	0.34
Number of child workers	0.09	0.08	0.29
Whether wage laborer	0.47	0.13	0.00
Whether employee	–0.02	0.10	0.82
Whether formal sector	–0.42	0.09	0.00
Whether manufacturing	–0.30	0.08	0.00
Whether construction	–0.55	0.14	0.00
Whether trade	–0.52	0.08	0.00
Whether transport	–0.50	0.10	0.00
Whether service	–1.01	0.26	0.00
Whether other sector	–0.27	0.08	0.00
Number of dependents	0.59	0.03	0.00
Number of workers	0.40	0.08	0.00
Ratio of female workers	0.95	0.17	0.00
Whether employer	–1.21	0.58	0.04
Landownership	–0.005	0.0007	0.00
Whether remittance received	–2.49	0.31	0.00
Asset 1	–0.72	0.11	0.00
Asset 2	0.49	0.20	0.01
Asset 3	–1.51	0.44	0.00
Asset 4	–1.19	0.93	0.20
Asset 5	–0.25	0.13	0.05
Constant	0.24	0.41	0.56
–2 log likelihood	4,501.5		

Correct-prediction percentage
Poor 73.0
Nonpoor 79.2
Overall 76.5

Source: Bangladesh Bureau of Statistics 1999–2000, 2002.

households mobilize more workers. Due to similar reasons, the ratio of female workers to total workers raises the probability of being in poverty.

Mode of employment and sector of employment (of head of household) have been included as explanatory variables, and these variables have the expected signs of the coefficients. Those employed in wage labor have a higher chance of being poor. Formal (versus informal) employment reduces the probability of a household's poverty. Employment in nonfarm sectors reduces the probability, with negative and for most sectors significant, coefficients. The poverty-alleviating role of rural nonfarm activities has been emphasized by other studies as well (Mahmud 1996; Bakht 1996).

A number of other assets have been included as explanatory variables. These variables were included in the questionnaire in binary form, and a household was asked whether or not they possessed it. Values of these assets were not included in the questionnaire. Hence the coefficients have to be interpreted cautiously. For example, in the urban area, the ownership of a rickshaw or sewing machine has positive coefficients that raise the probability of being poor. This implies that these assets are usually owned by poorer groups. The percentage of correct predictions is high, and most of the variables are significant at the 0.00 level.

Unemployment and Poverty: Concepts, Measurement, and Empirical Results

The existence of surplus labor in Bangladesh and other South Asian countries with high population density has been considered almost axiomatic. Such characterization led to the development of theories visualizing that industrialization would proceed through the absorption of surplus laborers from the traditional sectors, where they subsist through work-sharing practices (Lewis 1954). The success of growth strategies based on such a theory and the impact of growth on poverty will to some extent depend on the correctness of the assumption of an elastic supply of labor. Therefore the assumption of "unlimited supply of labor"—or in other words, the existence of unemployment and underemployment—should be reassessed periodically.

If the success of labor absorption by a growing industrial sector is not quite impressive, then the unemployed and underemployed labor force will try to find gainful employment in the other sectors or generate self-employment with varying levels of productivity. Therefore, there is a need for assessment of the earnings of the workers along with their underemployment status. This will help provide a better understanding of the dynamics of the labor market as well as the livelihood strategies of the poor through combinations of wage employment and self-employment.

The vision of the surplus labor theory consists of a transfer of the surplus labor from the "traditional sector" to a "modern industrial sector" and, through the process, generation of surplus for reinvestment. The impact of such a process on poverty was not explicitly formulated because the center of the theory was the process of industrial growth. One important assumption of the theory is that the wage rate will not rise before the surplus labor is exhausted. The "turning point" of the wage rate in the modern sector may take time to arrive, and this will depend on the labor intensity of the industries. Therefore a significant reduction of poverty would not be foreseen during the initial period of industrial growth. It is possible to draw the corollaries of the theory, which predict a slow but continuous improvement of income of the underemployed labor force of the traditional sector. When some of the labor force is withdrawn from the traditional sector, the average consumption of the families where they previously shared the consumption basket will increase and a reduction of poverty is expected.

Before presenting the empirical data on underemployment, it will be useful to examine the available methods of measurement of unemployment and underemployment and suggest suitable indicators for the analysis of the latter in the present context. An assessment of surplus labor in such a predominantly rural economy as Bangladesh cannot be based on the usual concepts and method of measurement of unemployment.

The fact that the usual definition of unemployment developed in the context of the formal labor markets in the industrial economies is not valid for self-employed workers was pointed out by economists long ago (Myrdal 1966). The observation that self-employed workers may not be openly unemployed led to the development of the concept of "disguised unemployment." The empirical application of the concept is difficult, and few attempts of such application were made. The concept of disguised unemployment has nevertheless been useful in directing attention to the fact that many rural workers are engaged in low-productivity employment and many of them are engaged in work sharing on the family farm. With increasing landlessness, the nature of underemployment among self-employed workers has also been changing. Work sharing on a family farm is not an available choice for many such workers. Workers from marginal landowning families resort to a number of nonagricultural jobs with varying levels of productivity. This complicates the identification and measurement of disguised unemployment.

In this situation the following methods have been used for the measurement of underemployment:

- A cutoff point of less than a standard number of hours of employment is chosen, and those who work less than this norm are identified as underemployed. Bangladesh's labor force surveys use thirty-five hours per week as the cutoff point.
- To take into account the extent of variation of underemployment, the time criterion index of an "unemployment equivalent" has been widely used by microstudies. An unemployment equivalent based on a time criterion is measured as the difference between a hypothetical norm of supply of days over a year and a worker's actual days of employment (Krishna 1973; Khan, Islam, and Haq 1981; Rahman 1996; Rahman and Saha 1995).

In the subsequent analysis, we will examine the relationship between poverty and underemployment (based on a cutoff point of thirty-four hours per week, as defined by the labor force surveys). Such measurement of underemployment provides totals of unemployed (those working zero hours), employed (those working more than thirty-four hours), and underemployed (those working one to thirty-four hours).

Table 5.27 provides a distribution of the work force in the poor and non-poor categories by the percentage of underemployment. One of the results that should receive attention is the low magnitude of underemployment among male workers—only 11 percent. Low male underemployment prevails in both rural and urban areas (11.8 and 9.7 percent respectively). This scenario implies that poor workers are not actually without work; rather they are working for long hours, so a more appropriate description of the situation is given by the term "hardworking poor." Employment of fewer than thirty-five hours per week among poor males is 11.4 percent for rural workers and 10.4 percent for urban workers, and the rest (about 90 percent) belong to the category of hardworking poor.

In contrast, the unemployment and underemployment rates are much higher among the female labor force. Among the poor female labor force, 74

Table 5.27   Distribution of Male, Female, and Total Labor Force by Underemployment Situation, Bangladesh, 1999–2000

Gender	Location	Poverty Status	Underemployed (%)		Not Underemployed (%)	
			0–15 Hours per Week	16–34 Hours per Week	35–41 Hours per Week	42+ Hours per Week
Male and female	Rural	Poor	10.6	25.6	15.1	48.7
		Nonpoor	10.3	27.4	14.7	47.6
		Total	10.5	26.2	14.9	48.3
	Urban	Poor	11.1	14.3	12.6	62.1
		Nonpoor	9.0	11.5	12.3	67.2
		Total	9.9	12.6	12.4	65.0
Male	Rural	Poor	3.8	7.6	14.6	74.0
		Nonpoor	4.4	7.9	15.1	72.5
		Total	4.1	7.7	14.8	73.5
	Urban	Poor	6.0	4.4	11.4	78.2
		Nonpoor	6.0	3.1	11.0	79.8
		Total	6.0	3.7	11.2	79.2
Female	Rural	Poor	21.0	52.9	15.9	10.2
		Nonpoor	19.4	57.4	14.0	9.2
		Total	20.4	54.5	15.2	9.8
	Urban	Poor	23.0	37.4	15.3	24.3
		Nonpoor	17.2	33.4	15.5	33.9
		Total	19.8	35.2	15.4	29.6

Source: Bangladesh Bureau of Statistics 1999–2000, 2002.

percent and 60.4 percent are underemployed in the rural and urban areas respectively. However, the interpretation of female underemployment is complicated due to the fact that most of the domestic work is also performed by them.

The average hours of employment for the two groups are shown in Table 5.28. Average employment per week among the poor and the nonpoor is 39.8 and 41.7 hours respectively. Both male and female workers in the nonpoor group work slightly more hours compared to the poor.

With differences in employment per worker being small, differences in earning per hour are likely to account for much of the income differential between the poor and nonpoor. Since a larger percentage of workers of poor households are engaged in wage employment, the low income of such households is also likely to be due to the lower income per hour of wage employment compared to the hourly return from self-employment. In addition, self-employed persons have greater flexibility about the hours they work. As a result, they may choose to work for longer hours.

How much these differences contribute to poverty will be examined through

- a comparison of employment per worker in paid employment and self-employment,
- a comparison of the rate of payment received by poor and nonpoor workers engaged in paid employment, and
- a comparison of earning per hour of self-employment among the workers from poor and nonpoor households.

Relevant data are presented in Tables 5.29 and 5.30 (and Figures 5.3 and 5.4). Data presented in Table 5.29 show that the nonpoor wage workers work for more hours compared to the poor wage workers. In contrast, among the self-employed workers in the rural areas, the difference is small. In the urban areas, self-employment hours among the nonpoor are longer. The differences in hours per week per worker, however, are small. For example, urban self-

Table 5.28   Hours Worked per Week by Male and Female Workers from Poor and Nonpoor Households, Bangladesh, 1999–2000

Poverty Status	Hours Worked		
	Male	Female	Male and Female
Poor	47.7	26.1	39.8
Nonpoor	48.0	28.6	41.7

Source: Bangladesh Bureau of Statistics 1999–2000, 2002.

Table 5.29   Average Hours Worked per Week by Poor and Nonpoor
Workers by Mode of Employment, Bangladesh, 1999–2000

Poverty Status	Location	Weekly Self-Employment Hours	Weekly Employer Working Hours	Weekly Salaried Working Hours	Weekly Unpaid Working Hours	Weekly Wage Employment Hours	Worker Weekly Working Hours
Poor	Rural	46.0464	10.0000	49.6225	25.6253	48.5981	39.57
	Urban	46.8740	33.5000	48.9890	23.5914	49.7736	44.57
	Total	46.3729	20.4444	49.1851	25.2821	48.8958	41.25
Nonpoor	Rural	46.6601	53.6667	48.5390	27.3561	51.6780	39.13
	Urban	49.9560	49.8974	50.2510	29.0466	51.5210	47.20
	Total	48.4228	50.4000	49.9412	27.8516	51.5903	43.57

Source: Bangladesh Bureau of Statistics 1999–2000, 2002.
Notes: Average hours includes employment of all types. Categorization of mode of employment is based on major source of employment.

Table 5.30 Income per Hour from Wage and Self-Employment of Poor and Nonpoor Workers, Bangladesh, 1999–2000

Sector	Location	Poverty Status	Income per Hour from Wage Employment (taka)	Income per Hour from Self-Employment (taka)
Agriculture	Rural	Poor	8.2459	15.6073
		Nonpoor	8.6288	24.1097
		Total	8.2904	19.2813
	Urban	Poor	9.9138	16.2292
		Nonpoor	9.8223	28.5990
		Total	9.8925	22.4131
Nonagriculture	Rural	Poor	11.5863	12.1398
		Nonpoor	12.2665	21.8515
		Total	11.7188	16.0080
	Urban	Poor	11.6962	12.3951
		Nonpoor	12.9735	26.3195
		Total	12.2124	20.2919
Total	Rural	Poor	8.7480	14.0604
		Nonpoor	9.5242	23.1793
		Total	8.8481	17.8676
	Urban	Poor	11.0952	12.9664
		Nonpoor	12.3886	26.5880
		Total	11.5552	20.5711

Source: Bangladesh Bureau of Statistics 1999–2000, 2002.

employment hours among the nonpoor are only 6 percent higher than those among the poor. In other cases, the differences are even smaller.

Moreover, the differences between average hours worked in wage employment and average hours worked in self-employment are small among both the poor and the nonpoor labor force—in the range of 5 to 7 percent. In contrast to the above hypothesis, the self-employed work fewer hours than do those employed as wage laborers. The reason is that the latter have no choice but to accept the prevailing standard hours.

Unpaid family helpers work much fewer hours compared to other categories of workers. The workers in this group are not the main earners of the household, and many of them are engaged in studies or domestic responsibilities along with their income-generating employment.

A comparison of employment hours between poor and nonpoor workers engaged in different "status" of employment, as shown in Table 5.29, reveals a large variation among the "employers," because this is a heterogeneous group of employers from all sectors, from variously sized enterprises, and having various qualifications.

Figure 5.3   Hours Worked per Week by Male and Female Workers in Poor and Nonpoor Households, Bangladesh, 1999–2000

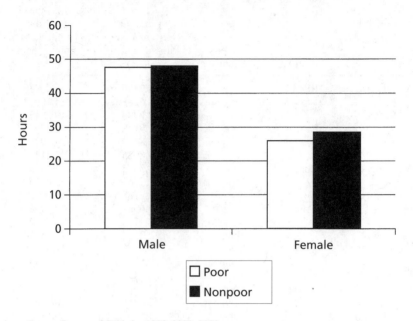

Source: Bureau of Statistics 1999–2000, 2002.

Since the difference between the poor and nonpoor in terms of work hours in wage and self-employment is small, the difference in income per hour from the two sources is likely to contribute most of the difference in income between the two groups. Data on income per hour of wage and self-employment are presented in Table 5.30, separately for agriculture and nonagriculture. Since nonagriculture consists of diverse types of activities, the "income per hour" from this source will also capture the difference in the activities pursued and the qualification of the workers.

The difference between the agricultural wage rate of laborer from poor and nonpoor households is small. The difference is 2.4 taka per day, which is about 4 percent of the wage rate of the poor. As expected, wage rate in non-agriculture shows a larger difference between these two groups (5.6 taka for an eight-hour day). The differences are even larger in the urban areas, which accommodate a much wider range of activities. Moreover, the qualification of workers in the urban areas is more likely to vary with consequent variation in productivity, which is reflected in the difference in wage rates between poor and nonpoor workers. Nonpoor wage workers in urban nonagriculture receive about 12 taka more than do poor workers (for an eight-hour day).

Figure 5.4 Income per Hour from Wage and Self-Employment Among Poor and Nonpoor Workers, Bangladesh, 1999–2000

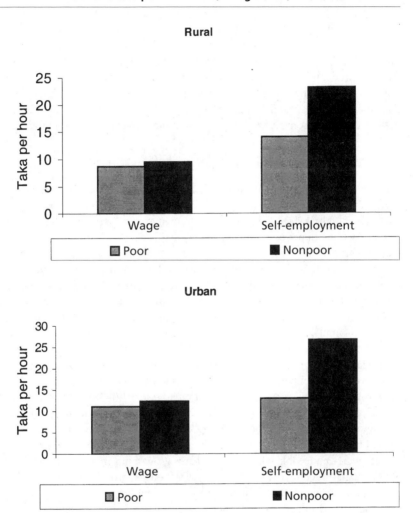

Source: Bureau of Statistics 1999–2000, 2002.

However, average wage rates vary within the small range of 8.2 to 12.9 taka per hour. This contrasts with the pattern of much larger difference in average income per hour for self-employment, which ranges from 12 to 29 taka. In the rural areas, self-employed workers in agriculture, coming from poor and nonpoor groups, earn 15.6 and 24.1 taka per hour respectively. The earnings per hour of their counterparts from nonagriculture in the urban areas are 12.4 and 26.3 taka respectively.

A methodological question is pertinent at the end of this analysis. Earnings per hour from wage employment and self-employment may not be strictly comparable. Wage workers are usually closely supervised, so that the intensity of their work can be expected to be higher than that of self-employed workers. In contrast, some degree (and form) of work sharing is possibly taking place among the self-employed and unpaid family workers. This may reduce the income per hour from self-employment, thus reducing the difference between income from self-employment and income from wage employment.

■ Conclusion

Bangladesh was able to achieve significantly higher rates of economic growth during the 1990s compared to the 1980s. The incidence of income poverty declined during the 1990s. Changes in the human poverty index also show a significant decline in poverty, especially during this decade. It would thus appear that higher rates of economic growth in Bangladesh yielded benefits for the country's poor. Indeed, this conclusion would be valid if a simple comparison of economic growth rates and rates of poverty reduction were made for the 1980s and the 1990s. However, a more careful examination of the economic growth, rates of poverty reduction, changes in the degree of inequality in income/consumption, and employment and labor market outcomes would indicate that economic growth in Bangladesh could be more pro-poor. And employment and labor market variables play an important role in that regard.

Looking at subperiods of the 1990s, one can see that the rate of GDP growth was higher during 1996–2001 compared to 1991–1996, but the annual rate of reduction in poverty was lower. Thus, although the incidence of poverty continued to decline throughout the 1990s, the rate of decline was lower in the second half of the decade, when the rate of economic growth was higher. This is particularly noticeable when one compares growth in agriculture with the rate of decline in rural poverty. During 1996–2001, output growth in agriculture was over 5 percent per annum, compared to 1.5 percent during 1991–1996; and yet rural poverty declined by less than 1 percentage point per annum during 1996–2001, compared to 1.13 percentage points per annum during 1991–1996.

Although the decline in the rate of poverty reduction during the second half of the 1990s should be looked at simultaneously with the observations on alleged problems with the 1995–1996 survey data, other developments in the economy during the 1990s (especially in regard to income inequality and labor markets) appear to be consistent with the lack of a direct correspondence between the economic growth and the rate of decline in poverty.

First, there was no shift in the structure of employment from lower-productivity sectors to those characterized by higher productivity. Indeed, the share of manufacturing employment declined after 1989; and despite a reversal of the trend in the latter half of the 1990s, even the level of 1989 has not been achieved. Second, the employment intensity of growth (measured by the elasticity of employment with respect to output) in manufacturing declined during the 1990s. Third, open unemployment increased during 1996–2002. Fourth, the rate of real wage increase was slower in agriculture compared to other sectors. Indeed, for some years toward the end of the 1990s, real wages in agriculture declined. Finally, inequality in the distribution of income increased during the 1990s.

Analysis of household level data indicates that employment and labor market variables are important among factors influencing the probability of a household being poor. In terms of education, the percentage of the poor who have never gone to school is double that of the nonpoor. The difference is sharper at higher levels of education. Likewise, a higher percentage of the nonpoor labor force is skilled compared to the poor. The poor are more likely to be found in informal employment and are more likely to be casual workers. Employment in nonfarm sectors reduces the probability of a household being poor.

The findings and analysis of this chapter thus point to the possibility that economic growth in Bangladesh could have been more pro-poor in character. Had inequality in the distribution of income not worsened and had there been more positive developments in the employment and labor market situation, perhaps the outcome in terms of poverty reduction could have been more positive. The analysis in this chapter does provide pointers to ways in which growth can be made more pro-poor.

First, high growth in agriculture can contribute to poverty reduction if an environment prevails to ensure that marginal and small farmers participate in such growth, and that demand for hired labor increases. Emphasis has to be on increasing crop intensity and achieving crop diversification. More effective extension service is needed to transfer the results achieved in research stations to the field level.

Second, growth of noncrop agriculture, including livestock, fisheries, and horticultural productions, can have an important impact on growth and poverty reduction. Public investment in infrastructure, availability of credit and support services covering market information, quality control, marketing, and the like would be important for the development of such activities.

Third, rural nonfarm activities can play an important role in lifting the poor out of poverty. But in order for these activities to be effective in doing so, it would be essential to achieve a shift in their productivity and an associated rise in the real wages of workers engaged in them.

While there may be a variety of factors influencing productivity in rural nonfarm activities, the type and size of market, the scale of operation, as well as the type and level of technology appear to be quite important. Interventions (e.g., credit and other support services) aimed at promoting the growth of such activities as part of a poverty reduction strategy need to focus on such factors.

Fourth, both output and employment growth in manufacturing need to be higher than before so that the share of employment in higher-productivity sec: tors can increase. This chapter has identified industries (e.g., food, textiles, leather and leather products, wood products, nonmetallic minerals, etc.) where output growth can be quite employment-intensive, and yet can be associated with rising productivity. Appropriate policies to promote the growth of such industries can contribute to pro-poor growth.

Finally, on the supply side, investment in education and skills can make a significant contribution to poverty reduction. It would of course be essential to ensure that the poor have access to education and skill-development opportunities.

Table 5.31 **Alternative Estimates of Poverty by Ravallion and Sen (1996) Using CBN Method, Bangladesh, 1983/84–1995/96**

	Headcount Ratio (%)	
	Rural	Urban
1983–1984	53.8	40.9
1985–1986	45.9	30.8
1988–1989	49.7	35.9
1991–1992	52.9	33.6
1995–1996	51.1	26.3

Source: Ravallion and Sen 1996.

Table 5.32 **Estimates of Extreme Poverty by DCI Method, Bangladesh, 1983/84–2000**

	Headcount Ratio (%)		
	Rural	Urban	National
1983–1984	36.7	30.4	36.7
1985–1986	26.3	30.7	26.9
1988–1989	28.6	26.4	28.4
1991–1992	28.3	26.3	28.0
1995–1996	24.6	27.3	25.1
2000	18.7	25.0	20.0

Source: Bangladesh Bureau of Statistics, various years.

Table 5.33   Estimates of Extreme Poverty by CBN Method, Bangladesh, 1983/84–2000

	Percentage Households		
	Rural	Urban	National
1983–1984	42.6	28.0	40.9
1985–1986	36.0	19.9	33.8
1988–1989	44.3	21.9	41.3
1991–1992	46.0	23.3	42.7
1995–1996	38.5	13.7	34.4
2000	34.1	16.9	30.0

Source: Bangladesh Bureau of Statistics, various years.

Table 5.34   Trends in Depth and Severity of Poverty, Bangladesh, 1983/84–2000

	Poverty Gap (%)			Squared Poverty Gap (%)		
	Rural	Urban	Total	Rural	Urban	Total
1983–1984	16.8	14.3	16.5	6.7	5.8	6.6
1988–1989	16.0	11.1	15.4	6.1	3.8	5.8
1991–1992	18.1	12.0	17.2	7.2	4.4	6.8
1995–1996	15.4	9.2	14.4	5.7	3.4	5.4
2000	13.8	9.5	12.9	4.8	3.1	4.5

Sources: World Bank 1998; Bangladesh Bureau of Statistics 2001a.

Table 5.35   Relative Inequality in Income Distribution, Bangladesh, 1991–1992 and 2000

	Gini Coefficient	
	Rural	Urban
1991–1992	0.243	0.307
2000	0.271	0.368

Sources: Economic Relations Division 2002; Interim Poverty Reduction Strategy Paper 2002.

Table 5.36   Annual GDP Growth Rate in Agriculture and Manufacturing, Bangladesh, 1986–2003

	Agriculture (% per annum)	Manufacturing (% per annum)
1986	3.49	7.31
1987	−0.25	7.95
1988	−0.88	0.65
1989	−0.38	2.77
1990	10.75	7.68
1991	1.25	6.38
1992	1.39	7.38
1993	1.35	8.62
1994	−0.65	8.15
1995	−1.93	10.48
1996	2.03	6.41
1997	5.57	5.05
1998	1.64	8.54
1999	3.24	3.19
2000	6.92	4.76
2001	5.53	6.68
2002	−0.62	5.48
2003	3.29	6.75

Sources: Bangladesh Bureau of Statistics, various years; Rahman 2005.
Note: Growth rates are at constant 1995–1996 prices.

▨ Notes

1. The dataset has been officially procured.

2. The DCI method uses the calorie intake level of 2,122 kilocalories as the cut-off point for moderate poverty, and 1,805 kilocalories for extreme poverty. In the CBN method, poverty lines represent the level of per capita expenditure at which the members of the household can meet their basic needs (defined by a standard bundle).

3. These data are based on "usual definition." Data for 1983–1984 are available only on the basis of usual definition. On the basis of usual definition, the percentage of labor force in manufacturing (including electricity, construction, etc.) declined from 18.3 percent in 1990–1991 to 12.6 percent in 1999–2000.

4. For some information on the scope and coverage of Bangladesh's manufacturing-industry census and labor force survey, see Rahman and Islam 2003.

5. This has similarity to labor force survey data, which show lower growth of employment during the period 1990/91–1995/96 compared to the previous period.

6. Bangladesh's manufacturing-industry census covers industrial units (subject to the Factories Act of 1934) under Bangladesh Standard Industrial Classification (BSIC). According to the BSIC, various industries are grouped into 38 major industrial groups at the three-digit level (1986), which are again divided into 162 industrial subgroups at the four-digit level (1995–1996). The activities include large enterprises (50+ laborers) and medium-sized enterprises (10–49 laborers), including handloom units with employment of 10+ laborers. See Tables 5.10 and 5.11 for the list of selected subsectors at three- and four-digit levels (Rahman and Islam 2003).

7. See Rahman and Islam 2003, tab. A.3.2–A.3.3; for the employment weights of individual subsectors (with their ranks) at three- and four-digit levels, see Rahman and Islam 2003, tab. A.3.12.

8. In case of individual subsectors, for both value added and output, all the estimates other than for the textile manufacturing and nonelectrical machinery are significant at greater than the 99 percent level. The estimates for these two activities are significant at greater than the 95 percent level.

9. For a similar analysis on output elasticities, see Rahman and Islam 2003, tab. A.3.2.

10. Real wage index (base 1985–1986) has been published by the BBS only for these ten years.

11. It should be mentioned, however, that the real wage trends discussed in this section are based on the BBS's estimates of change in incidence of poverty. Alternative price indexes used by other ongoing studies provide slightly rising trends of agricultural wage rate.

12. Data presented in the tables and figures in this chapter are based on Bangladesh's 1999–2002 labor force survey, published in 2002.

6

Bolivia: Employment-Poverty Linkages and Policies

*Luis Carlos Jemio and
María del Carmen Choque*

In 1985, Bolivia embarked on a comprehensive program of structural reforms aimed at stabilizing its economy and removing structural constraints that prevented sustainable economic growth. As a result, the country achieved economic stability and moderate but stable economic growth during most of the 1990s. Besides, successive governments have implemented various social programs aimed at improving living conditions of the poorest segments of the population. Although there have been noticeable attainments in terms of poverty reduction, as indicated by the improvement in various social indicators in recent years, Bolivia's social indicators still remain weaker than the average for Latin America and are close to levels observed in sub-Saharan Africa. Social conditions are especially acute in rural areas, where 90 percent of the population still lives in poverty.

Different studies have tried to assess the magnitude of poverty in Bolivia and to explain what determines it (World Bank 1990, 1996a, 2002b; Vos, Lee, and Mejía 1998). Various studies analyze the characteristics that determine the probability of individuals and households being affected by poverty. There are certain characteristics related to labor market conditions that explain income differentials among individuals and households, such as the activities from which incomes are obtained, the location of households (i.e., urban versus rural area), the labor category of individual workers or household members, and so forth. Other features are related to certain conditions of individual workers, such as the educational level attained, number of years of labor experience, and the like. However, these various studies all identify human capital (i.e., the educational level of individuals) as being the single most important determinant of income disparities and varied access to basic needs satisfaction among the population.

According to many observers (the World Bank, the International Monetary Fund, the Bolivian government), urban poverty in Bolivia is linked to the problem of employment and low human capital of workers. On average, 85 percent of urban family income is derived from labor activities. Labor income, particularly in the entrepreneurial and semi-entrepreneurial sectors, which has experienced growth rates of around 5 percent a year, stands in contrast to real family income (through self-employment), which has remained virtually stagnant. In the 1990s the shifts in wage disparities were explained mainly by the fact that there was greater demand for skilled labor in more advanced sectors of the economy, while those sectors requiring unskilled labor saw incomes lag behind.

In rural areas, poverty is explained largely by the low productivity of the farm sector and the low price that farm products fetch in the marketplace. Productivity is affected by the use of small-scale production techniques, unskilled labor, water shortages, a lack of basic production infrastructure, the high cost of capital, a lack of definition of ownership rights with respect to the land and natural resources, and other factors that prevent the optimum utilization of the land. Besides, the lack of road infrastructure results in high transport costs, which in turn have an impact on the value of farm products. This hampers the sale of goods and prevents small producers from expanding their operations.

This chapter focuses on analyzing the linkages among output growth, employment, and poverty, at both the macro and micro levels. At the macro level, the linkage between poverty, in its income dimension, and output growth is conceptualized in terms of the average productivity of the employed work force, which is in turn reflected in low levels of real wages and low levels of earnings in self-employment. At the micro level of a household, the same linkage between poverty and employment operates through the type and low productivity of economic activities in which the earning members of a household are engaged, the low level of human capital of the members of the work force, the dependency burden that limits participation in the work force, and the mere availability of remunerative employment.

The chapter begins with an overview of the performance of the Bolivian economy in terms of economic growth and poverty reduction. The aim is to analyze the growth patterns observed in the Bolivian economy, in order to identify the most noticeable structural changes that have occurred over the past two decades. For this purpose, national accounts data, published by the National Institute of Statistics, are utilized. This overview also examines observed trends in poverty indicators over recent decades. We argue that social indicators have improved over time as a result of various social poverty reduction programs undertaken by different administrations in Bolivia. Observed improvements in social indicators are the result not only of the government's social policies and programs, but also of stable economic growth, which has generated employment and income opportunities for the population.

The chapter next focuses on analyzing the linkages among economic growth, employment, and poverty. We address whether the employment intensity of growth reflects the level of development of the country and the imperative for using employment as a route out of poverty. In order to carry out this analysis at the macroeconomic level, data on macroeconomic growth are obtained from national accounts, while data on employment are obtained from household surveys and the population census carried out by the National Institute of Statistics. Additionally, a similar analysis is performed for the specific case of the manufacturing sector. For this purpose, manufacturing-firm surveys carried out by the National Institute of Statistics are utilized.

We also examine the changes that have occurred in the structure of employment and in the productivity of various sectors and occupations—especially of those in which the poor are engaged in large numbers. The aim is to analyze the extent to which economic growth is translated into growth of productive employment, and the extent to which the poor are moving to such high-productivity employment. As real wages and earnings are the main channels through which the benefits of higher output growth and increased productivity are likely to reach the poor, trends in these variables are examined. Data come mainly from various national household surveys carried out by the National Institute of Statistics.

Last, the chapter focuses on the analysis of the linkage between poverty, in its income dimension, and output growth, at the micro level of a household. This linkage operates through the type and low productivity of economic activities in which the earning members of a household are engaged, the low level of human capital of the members of the work force, the dependency burden that limits participation in the work force, and the mere availability of remunerative employment. For this purpose, an econometric Probit model is constructed in order to determine the impact of different variables on the probability of a household being poor.

■ Economic Growth and Poverty

GDP Growth

Bolivia is a landlocked country, and its poorly developed communications infrastructure limits its access to export markets. It is a segmented society, with insufficient investment, weak institutional capacity, and entrenched vested interests hampering the private sector. It is a good example of a country that has achieved successful stabilization and implemented innovative market reforms, yet made only limited progress in the fight against poverty.

During the past two decades, the Bolivian economy clearly exhibited a cyclical behavior, determined by external and domestic shocks and changing domestic conditions. The country moved alternately from a deep economic crisis at the beginning of the 1980s, to a period of recovery and growth during the second half of the 1980s and most of the 1990s, and to a period of deceleration of growth and economic crisis at the end of the 1990s and beginning of the 2000s.

External shocks, such as foreign capital inflows volatility, terms of trade deterioration, and sizable devaluation carried out by neighboring countries, had a significant impact on the country's economic growth, employment creation, income distribution, and poverty incidence.

During the first half of the 1980s, the country experienced a serious economic crisis (see Figure 6.1), as a result of the heavy external indebtedness acquired during the 1970s. Besides, changing climate conditions in 1983, brought about by the Corriente del Niño, resulted in severe droughts and floods that affected economic activity in different regions of the country. As a result, agricultural output fell by 6 percent that particular year and transport infrastructure was heavily damaged. During that period the economy suffered a deep contraction and a severe hyperinflationary process. Between 1980 and 1986, economic growth averaged –2.1 percent a year, and the accumulated drop of GDP amounted to 15 percent. Per capita GDP decreased by 4.1 percent a year and the accumulated drop was as high as 29 percent.

In 1985 a new government took office and implemented a wide-ranging set of reforms aimed at stabilizing the economy and restoring economic growth. The stabilization program focused on a sharp reduction of the nonfinancial public sector deficit and the strengthening of market forces. The policies included trade liberalization, a massive devaluation and unification of the

Figure 6.1   Growth Rates of GDP and per Capita GDP, Bolivia, 1980–2000

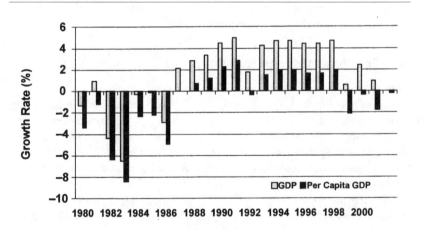

Source: Bolivian National Institute of Statistics.

exchange rate, increases in public sector prices (in particular those of domestic petroleum products), and reductions in government expenditures to levels that could be financed by available funds. As a result of the policies implemented, inflation was reduced from 25 percent a year in 1985 to 16 percent in 1989. From 1987 onward, economic growth was positive, averaging 3.2 percent per annum while per capita GDP grew by 1 percent per annum.

During the 1990s the reform process was consolidated and deepened by the successive governments. Additional structural reforms were implemented, including privatization of state enterprises, pension reforms, decentralization of public administration, and education reforms. Social reforms were introduced at the same time, notably education, health, and pension reforms; basic sanitation and social infrastructure programs; citizen participation; and decentralization of government administration. During most of the decade, economic growth stabilized. GDP growth rate averaged 4.4 percent a year between 1991 and 1998 and per capita income increased on average by 1.7 percent a year.

By the end of the decade, however, economic growth slowed down again as a result of shocks brought about by the international financial crisis. GDP growth decreased to 0.43 percent in 1999. The yearly GDP growth between 1999 and 2002 averaged only 1.6 percent and per capita GDP decreased on average by 1.1 percent a year during this period. Although inflation was maintained very low, the economy faced an increased fiscal deficit and a severe credit crunch in the financial sector.

Sectoral Growth, Structural Changes, and Employment

The cyclical behavior that the Bolivian economy followed led to an uneven growth pattern at a sectoral level (see Table 6.1), producing in turn a structural change in the Bolivian economy.

During the 1980–1986 period, mining experienced the largest reductions in activity, exhibiting a yearly average drop in output equal to 13 percent. In 1985 the collapse in the international tin market meant that most Bolivian mines became unprofitable and their operations had to be discontinued. Comibol, the state mining company, cut its labor force from 30,000 to 7,000. Other sectors that were deeply affected during the economic crisis of the early 1980s were construction and public works (experiencing output contractions of 5.75 percent a year on average), manufacturing (4.17 percent contraction), hydrocarbons (3.41 percent contraction), and activities in the service sector such as commerce (2.86 percent contraction), community, social, and personal services (3.44 percent contraction), and public administration (3.43 percent contraction).

After the stabilization program was implemented in 1985, sectoral output experienced an across-the-board recovery. Mining production exhibited an average output growth equal to 16 percent a year during the 1987–1990 period. Other sectors that presented fast growth during that period were electricity, gas, and water (5.90 percent); construction (4.90 percent); transport

Table 6.1   Average Annual Percentage Change in Sectoral Growth, Bolivia, 1980–2001

	1980–1986	1987–1990	1991–1998	1999–2001	1980–2001
Agriculture	0.89	2.32	3.08	2.44	2.22
Hydrocarbons	−3.41	3.47	5.65	6.33	2.74
Mining	−13.14	16.13	2.29	−2.75	−0.20
Manufacturing	−4.17	3.65	3.82	1.93	1.24
Food, beverage, and tobacco	−0.29	4.28	4.61	3.47	2.98
Other industries	−6.51	3.21	3.15	0.46	0.02
Electricity, gas, and water	3.20	5.90	7.22	2.23	5.11
Construction and public works	−5.75	4.90	9.99	−11.98	1.38
Commerce	−2.86	3.73	3.64	1.00	1.42
Transport and communication	4.58	4.52	6.33	1.10	4.74
Financial servces, insurance, and services to firms	−1.93	1.98	8.15	4.21	3.29
Community, social, and personal services	−3.44	2.54	3.95	3.11	1.45
Restaurants and hotels	−2.47	−0.27	3.57	1.88	0.87
Public administration	−3.43	1.98	2.88	2.15	0.80
Total GDP	−2.03	3.45	4.36	1.34	1.93

Source: Bolivian National Institute of Statistics, various years.

and communication (4.52 percent); manufacturing (3.65 percent); and hydrocarbons (3.47 percent). During this period, sectors were adjusting to the large relative-price shifts brought about by the structural reforms, such as the opening up to foreign trade and the liberalization of domestic prices.

During the 1990s the economy was much better adjusted to the new economic conditions, and output experienced the fastest growth rates of the whole period under analysis. Nontradable sectors exhibited the highest growth rates, such as construction (10 percent on average), electricity (7.20 percent), financial services (8.15 percent), and transport and communication (6.33 percent). Tradable sectors showed more moderate growth. This was the case of agriculture (3.08 percent), hydrocarbons (5.65 percent), mining (2.29 percent), and manufacturing (3.82 percent).

At the end of the 1990s, when Bolivia experienced the negative effects of the international crisis, activity slowed down considerably. The only sector that exhibited fast growth was hydrocarbons (6.33 percent a year on average), because of the increased volumes of natural gas exported to Brazil starting from 2000. Construction presented the largest contractions in output (decreasing on average by 11.9 percent a year), due to the significant drop that occurred in private investment. Other sectors presenting low albeit positive growth rates were agriculture (2.44 percent), manufacturing (1.93 percent), commerce (1.00 percent), transport and communication (1.10 percent), and public administration (2.15 percent). Mining exhibited negative growth (averaging –2.75 percent a year), due to depressed prices observed in international markets for minerals.

Overall, during the two decades under analysis, the sectors presenting a more consistent growth pattern were electricity, gas, and water; transport and communication; and financial and firm services. The sectors that exhibited a more uneven pattern were mining, manufacturing, construction, public administration, and other services, as shown in Table 6.2.

The sectoral trends described above brought about a number of changes in the Bolivian productive structure. Overall, the economy suffered a process of tertiarization, as the sectors that increased their share in GDP were located in the service sector, such as electricity, gas, and water; transport and communication; and financial and firm services. The only commodity-producing sector that increased its share in GDP was hydrocarbons. Other goods-producing sectors, such as agriculture, mining, manufacturing, and construction, decreased their share of total GDP. It is also worth mentioning the significant reduction observed in the share of public administration in total GDP. The drastic process of public sector restructuring that occurred after 1985 explains this trend.

Poverty Indicators and Social Policies
Bolivia is one of the poorest countries in Latin America, with a GDP per capita of around US$1,000 and social indicators similar to those of sub-Saharan African countries. About two-thirds of the Bolivian population is poor, with

Table 6.2 Sector Structure as Percentage of Total GDP, Bolivia, 1980–2001

	1980	1987	1991	1999	2001
Agriculture	14.11	17.28	17.18	14.66	14.94
Hydrocarbons	4.98	4.63	4.41	4.66	5.65
Mining	8.28	4.05	6.25	4.96	4.65
Manufacturing	19.89	18.15	18.10	17.34	17.34
Food, beverage, and tobacco	6.89	8.03	8.43	8.33	8.73
Other industries	13.00	10.11	9.67	9.01	8.61
Electricity, gas, and water	1.10	1.58	1.75	2.15	2.14
Construction and public works	3.78	3.13	3.31	3.91	3.11
Commerce	9.55	9.47	9.63	8.68	8.71
Transport and communication	6.26	9.63	10.11	11.12	11.26
Financial services, insurance, and services to firms	10.96	11.58	10.72	15.09	14.57
Community, social and personal services	5.13	4.95	4.68	4.64	4.75
Restaurants and hotels	4.00	4.08	3.52	3.28	3.27
Public administration	11.96	11.47	10.32	9.50	9.63

Source: Bolivian National Institute of Statistics, various years.

low levels of education, health, and nutrition. The average schooling completed is less than seven years, infant mortality stands at 69 per 1,000 live births, and 10 percent of the children under five are malnourished.

The reform process implemented in the Bolivian economy beginning in 1985 has produced some positive results in terms of stable economic growth, macroeconomic stability, and financial deepening. The dramatic increases in poverty during the early 1980s have been somehow reversed. The reform process, however, has produced far less favorable results in terms of employment generation and poverty alleviation, and Bolivia remains one of the poorest countries in Latin America as measured by most economic and social indicators.

Per capita income is one of the lowest in the Latin American region and has barely increased, from US$561 in 1976 to US$922 in 2001. Poverty incidence is very high as measured by any standard. In 1996, 65 percent of the total population was considered poor because their income levels were below a defined poverty line, equivalent to an amount required to purchase a minimum basket to satisfy basic needs.[1] The poverty incidence decreased between 1996 and 1999, but increased again thereafter, up to 64 percent in 2001. The economic crisis of the late 1990s and early 2000s largely explains this trend. Income disparities are also deeply entrenched. In 1996 poverty incidence among the urban population was 56 percent, while among the rural population the incidence was as high as 81 percent. This situation had not changed significantly in 2001, when poverty incidence was 52 percent in urban areas and 80.1 percent in rural areas. Extreme poverty incidence is also very high. In 1997, 37.8 percent of the total population received incomes below an amount required to purchase a minimum basket to satisfy basic food requirements.

As Table 6.3 illustrates, Bolivia performs very badly in other social indicators as well. Education indicators show that the illiteracy rate is very high, as 12.9 percent of the total population older than fifteen years of age was considered illiterate in 2001. Besides, average years of schooling are relatively low for Latin American standards. In 2000 the average number of years of schooling among the population older than nineteen was 7.5 years. Furthermore, health indicators also portray a situation of generalized lack of access to basic services among the Bolivian population. Life expectancy was only 62.5 years in 2001, and infant mortality was as high as 60.6 per 100,000 live births.

Although most social indicators show that poverty is widespread among the Bolivian population, the relatively long period of macroeconomic stability and continuity of structural reform policies applied by the successive democratically elected governments has yielded some positive results in terms of poverty reduction. Social indicators have generally improved over the past two decades. The illiteracy rate, for instance, was reduced from 36.8 percent in 1976 to 12.9 percent in 2001; the average years of schooling increased from 3.3 years in 1976 to 7.5 years in 2000; life expectancy increased from 58.7

Table 6.3 Poverty Indicators, Bolivia Compared to Latin America and the Caribbean, 1995–2001

	Bolivia	Latin America and Caribbean	Lower Middle Income
Per capita income (US$)	950	3,560	1,240
Poverty (percentage of population below national poverty line)	60		
Urban population (percentage of total population)	64	76	46
Life expectancy at birth (years)	63	70	69
Infant mortality (per 1,000 live births)	61	29	33
Child malnutrition (percentage of children under 5)	7	9	11
Access to improved water source (percentage of population)	75	85	80
Illiteracy (percentage of population age 15+)	14	11	15
Gross primary enrollment (percentage of school-age population)	98	130	107
Male	99	131	107
Female	96	128	107

Source: World Bank 2003b.

years in 1991 to 62.5 years in 2001; and infant mortality decreased from 151 per 100,000 live births in 1976 to 60.6 in 2000. Furthermore, the percentage of households without basic needs satisfaction decreased from 70.2 percent in 1992 to 58.6 percent in 2001.[2] Despite this progress, most social and poverty indicators in Bolivia remain weaker than the average for Latin America and are close to the levels observed in sub-Saharan Africa. Social conditions are especially acute in rural areas, where 90 percent of the population still lives in poverty.

Poverty levels in Bolivia are higher than expected for a low-middle in-come country with a per capita income of nearly US$1,000. There is a three-fold explanation of this phenomenon. First, there is a high degree of inequality in income distribution, especially between urban and rural areas. Table 6.4 provides income shares by quintiles to support this argument. In 1997, at the national level, the bottom quintile obtained 2 percent of total income, while the top quintile obtained 62 percent of total income. This suggests the extremely high degree at income inequality existing in Bolivia, which tends to be very high by any standard. Table 6.4 also provides the Gini coefficients for 1996, 1997, 1999, and 2000, which indicate a high degree of income inequality at the national level, as well as in urban and rural areas. The Gini coefficients also

Table 6.4   Inequality for per Capita Income, Bolivia, 1997

Income Share in 1997	National	Main Cities	Other Urban	Rural
Bottom quintile	2.02	3.87	4.04	1.59
Second quintile	6.23	7.52	7.87	4.98
Third quintile	10.96	11.41	12.73	10.16
Fourth quintile	18.65	18.90	20.19	18.08
Top quintile	62.15	58.28	55.17	65.18
Gini Coefficient	1996	1997	1999	2000
Bolivia	0.58	0.59	0.55	0.60
Urban	0.52	0.54	0.51	0.57
Rural	0.62	0.68	0.44	0.45

Sources: World Bank, Bolivian National Institute of Statistics.
Notes: All measures are based on per capita income, except 1999 and 2000 in rural areas, where per capita consumption is used instead. This may partly explain the large drop in rural inequality.

capture the existing inequality between urban and rural areas, because in all years the national-level Gini coefficients are higher than those measuring urban inequality.

Second, high degrees of poverty in Bolivia can also be explained in terms of the large inequality existing between urban and rural households in the access to basic services, such as health, education, sanitation, drinking water, and housing. The basic needs satisfaction indicators presented in Table 6.5 show that in 1992, 94.2 percent of rural households suffered from unsatisfied basic needs. This indicator was much lower in the case of urban households (51.5 percent). In 2001 there was a significant drop in the share of urban households presenting unsatisfied basic needs (39.0 percent). Conversely, the share of rural households with unsatisfied basic needs stood above 90 percent.

Third, there is a large productivity gap between activities located in the urban and rural areas. Table 6.6 shows that the agricultural sector, which consists predominantly of rural activities, presented labor productivity levels that were a third of the average labor productivity for the economy as a whole. The highest labor productivity sectors in the urban areas, such as mining and electricity, had productivity levels twenty times higher than those observed in the agricultural sector.

Since 1985, different governments have applied social policies aimed at alleviating poverty among the most vulnerable groups. The main social reforms introduced have been education, health, and pension reforms, basic sanitation and social infrastructure programs, citizen participation, decentralization of government administration, and more recently, a universal mother and

Table 6.5 Trends in Poverty Indicators, Bolivia, 1976–2001

	1976	1991	1992	1994	1996	1997	1999	2000	2001
Demographic variables									
Total population (millions)	4.873	6.824	6.983	7.312	7.662	7.847	8.229	8.428	8.631
Growth rate of population (percentage change)	2.05	2.11	2.11	2.74	2.74	2.74	2.74	2.74	2.74
Income indicators									
Per capita income (current US$)	561	783	806	816	964	1,009	1,005	990	922
Poverty incidence (%)					65.0	58.0	56.0	60.0	64.0
Urban					56.0	52.0	44.0	49.0	52.5
Rural					81.0	72.0	75.0	78.0	80.1
Extreme poverty incidence (%)						37.8	35.9	39.8	37.0
Urban									25.9
Rural									55.5
Education indicators									
Illiteracy rate (%)	36.8		20.0		16.6	15.2		13.8	12.9
Urban	15.6		11.8		7.2	7.0		6.3	6.2
Rural	53.2		27.7		32.2	29.7		29.0	25.2
Average years of schooling	3.3		4.4		6.7	7.0	7.3	7.5	
Urban					8.8	9.0	9.4	9.5	
Rural					3.3	2.7	3.3	3.7	
Basic needs satisfaction									
Population with unsatisfied basic needs	85.5	70.6	70.2		60.3	57.3	55.1	55.5	58.6
Urban			51.5		38.7	36.2	32.6	34.9	39.0
Rural			94.2		91.0	89.1	93.0	91.3	90.8
Health indicators									
Life expectancy (years)		58.7	59.1	60.0	60.8	61.2	61.7	62.1	62.5
Infant mortality (per 100,000 live births)	151.0		75.0	75.0	68.5	66.6	62.6	60.6	
Urban				58					
Rural				94					

Source: Bolivian Institute of Statistics.

Table 6.6   Labor Productivity Across Activities, Bolivia, 1997–2001

	1997	1999	2001
Agriculture, hunting, and fishing	2,033	2,133	1,994
Mining	31,339	38,231	47,904
Manufacturing	8,755	8,761	11,119
Electricity, water, and gas	38,137	56,425	43,060
Construction	3,879	3,855	3,721
Commerce and restaurants	3,860	3,428	3,763
Transport and communication	12,868	12,865	14,303
Financial and firm services	31,452	34,762	26,543
Community and personal services	5,671	6,014	6,304
Total	5,735	5,782	5,899

Source: Author estimates based on data published by the Bolivian National Institute of Statistics.
Notes: Figures are in constant 1990 Bolivianos per worker.

child health insurance. Social policies introduced during the 1990s promoted increased investment in human resources, particularly in the areas of education, health, and basic sanitation. Decentralization and popular participation initiatives helped to bring about a redistribution of resources toward poor areas, establishing social control mechanisms, promoting the strengthening of institutions for the decentralized levels of administration, and encouraging greater participation by society.

Social investment was accompanied by a greater need for current expenditures in social sectors. From 1995 to 1999, social expenditures increased from 12.3 percent of GDP to 16.5 percent of GDP. However, the level of social expenditure in Bolivia (35 percent) is still lower than the average for Latin America as a whole (41 percent).

In 1997, Bolivia benefited from the Highly Indebted Poor Countries (HIPC) initiative, which represented a significant relief for the country's external debt service. In 2001 the country entered the HIPC II program, allowing for additional debt service relief. However, the HIPC II program imposed certain conditions on the use of resources made available to the country. The use of these resources was circumscribed within Bolivia's national poverty reduction strategy, which constitutes a framework for focusing policies on poverty reduction and proposes actions to aid the poor (Government of Bolivia 2001).

The efforts made by successive governments and other organizations in the past decade have resulted in an improvement in key social indicators. Besides, steady economic growth observed in the past decade was paramount in explaining the success of poverty reduction programs. Considering that the most effective and sustainable way to fight poverty is to attain sustainable growth, which in turn creates employment and income opportunities for the population, the slowdown in economic activity that occurred at the end of the 1990s and the beginning of 2000 led to a deterioration in some social indicators. For instance, per capita income has fallen, unemployment has increased, and real incomes have decreased since 1999. Moreover, the economic crisis has caused a reduction in fiscal incomes, jeopardizing in turn the continuity of the public sector's social programs aimed at alleviating poverty. In the medium term this could cause a reversal in the past improvements attained in other social indicators.

Linkages Among Economic Growth, Employment, and Poverty

Labor market dynamics depends on the behavior of labor demand and labor supply. This section focuses on analyzing the determinants of labor demand and on the employment-creating capacity of macroeconomic and sectoral growth, while also briefly discussing some aspects that determine labor supply behavior. In this way, a more complete and much clearer perspective of the functioning of the Bolivian labor market is obtained.

Factors Determining Labor Supply

Demographic Trends and Migration. Demographic factors and migration have had a significant impact on the size and structure of labor supply. Bolivia has a relatively high rate of population growth and it has increased over time. Between 1950 and 1976, the estimated growth of the Bolivian population was 2.05 percent. It increased to 2.11 percent during 1976–1992, and to 2.74 percent during 1992–2001. This latest figure represents an increase in the population by about 200,000 persons a year since 2000, which eventually will exert pressure on the labor market.

Migration constitutes another major driving force in determining labor supply. Over time, there has been a clear process of urbanization of the Bolivian population. In 1985, most of the Bolivian people lived in the rural areas (50.6 percent of total population; see Table 6.7). Between 1985 and 2001, the growth rate of the urban population was about 4.08 percent a year, while that of the rural population was very close to zero or even negative. The rate of growth of the population in the main capital cities was about 3.7 percent a year, which was smaller than the rate of growth of the urban population. As a result, in 2001, 65.6 percent of the total population lived in the urban areas, and only 34.9 percent lived in the rural areas.

A strong process of urban migration explains this trend. According to the World Bank, migration is closely linked to the labor markets. Among males who migrated, 47 percent did so for work-related reasons. Among females, "family reasons" is the most quoted explanation for moving. The increased urbanization is explained in terms of income differentials received by work-

Table 6.7   Population Structure, Bolivia, 1985–2001

	1985	1989	1993	1997	2001	Yearly Average Growth Rate
Number of people						
Total population	5,964,223	6,521,464	7,145,252	7,846,679	8,630,904	2.34
Urban	2,946,216	3,487,845	4,110,005	4,822,513	5,658,540	4.08
Capital cities	2,265,142	2,476,123	2,997,955	3,462,880	3,999,905	3.67
Rural	3,018,007	3,033,618	3,035,247	3,024,167	3,013,127	–0.09
Percentage						
Total population	100.0	100.0	100.0	100.0	100.0	
Urban	49.4	53.5	57.5	61.5	65.6	
Capital cities	38.0	38.0	42.0	44.1	46.3	
Rural	50.6	46.5	42.5	38.5	34.9	

Source: Bolivian National Institute of Statistics.

ers in urban vis-à-vis rural occupations. Average real wages in the urban area increased by 92 percent between 1985 and 2001 (see Figure 6.2). Even the legal minimum wage increased in real terms, by 139 percent, during the same period. Domestic terms of trade between rural and urban sectors, on the other hand, measured by the ratio between traditional agriculture prices vis-à-vis consumer prices in the urban area, deteriorated by 17 percent.

Figure 6.2   Real Wage and Domestic Terms of Trade, Bolivia, 1985–2001

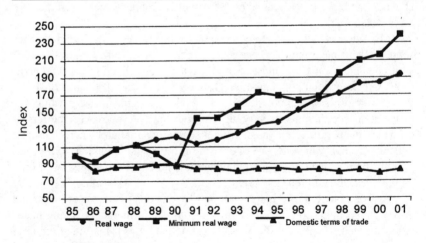

Source: Bolivian National Institute of Statistics.
Note: Index base year 1985 = 100.

Access to basic services, such as education, health, electricity, water, and sanitation, is also important in explaining migration. The limited access that the rural population has to these and other basic services, compared to the much higher access by the urban population, exerts a strong incentive to rural habitants to migrate to the cities.

Migration is also favored by relatively easy access to the urban labor market by recent migrants. According to the World Bank (1996a), generally migrants tend to be young, averaging thirty-two years of age. The unemployment rate among migrants is higher than among the rest of the population. However, once the migrants are working, their wages and participation are similar to the rest of the urban population, indicating little difference in barriers to entry in terms of wages. In self-employment, wages earned by nonrecent migrants tend to be much higher than those received by recent migrants (about 2.7 times).

Participation in the Labor Market. Another factor that played a key role in shaping labor supply was the observed increase in the participation rate. The global participation rate of the population in the labor market, for the main capital cities, augmented from 43.7 percent in 1985 to 56.1 percent in 2000 (see Table 6.8). The largest increases occurred in the second half of the 1980s, when the participation rate increased to 52.8 percent. This is explained by the sharp increase that occurred in the female participation rate after the implementation of the New Economic Policy in 1985. Women's global participation rate increased from 30 percent to 43.8 percent of the total female population of work-

Table 6.8   Labor Indicators for Main Capital Cities, Bolivia, 1985–2000

	1985	1989	1993	1997	2000
Total					
Global participation rate	43.7	52.8	52.6	52.5	56.1
Gross participation rate	32.9	39.4	39.1	40.6	41.5
Employment rate	94.0	89.6	94.0	95.6	92.6
Open unemployment rate	6.0	10.4	6.0	4.4	7.4
Males					
Global participation rate	58.5	62.7	63.0	62.3	65.5
Gross participation rate	43.3	46.0	46.1	47.6	47.6
Employment rate	93.2	90.1	93.5	95.5	93.8
Open unemployment rate	6.8	9.9	6.5	4.5	6.2
Females					
Global participation rate	30.0	43.8	43.2	43.4	47.6
Gross participation rate	22.9	33.2	32.7	33.9	35.9
Employment rate	95.3	89.0	94.7	95.6	91.1
Open unemployment rate	4.7	11.0	5.3	4.4	8.9

Source: Bolivian National Institute of Statistics.

ing age (i.e., more than 10 years of age in the Bolivian case). This is a reflection of the increased need of household members to participate in the labor market, as a means to expand income opportunities for the household, once the market liberalization program was introduced.

As a result of this sizable increase in the number of female participants in the labor market, the open unemployment rate among women increased from 4.7 percent in 1985 to 11.0 percent in 1989. The failure of new female labor market entrants to find job opportunities can be partially explained by their lack of previous working experience and their poor level of human capital in terms of education and other skills demanded by the market. During the 1990s the participation rate among women stood at a relatively stable level and the unemployment decreased as the economy experienced much higher growth rates. Unemployment decreased to 5.3 percent in 1993 and to 4.4 percent in 1997. In 2000, when the economic crisis broke out, unemployment increased again, this time to 8.9 percent of the female labor force.

The global participation rate among men presented a less pronounced increase after the year of the stabilization program. It increased from 58.5 percent in 1985 to 62.7 percent in 1989. As a result, open unemployment among men increased from 6.8 percent of male population in 1985 to 9.9 percent in 1989. As in the case of females, unemployment among men decreased as the economy entered the relatively stable growth process that took place during most of the 1990s. In 2000, when the Bolivian economy experienced the slowdown in economic activity, unemployment increased to 6.2 percent.

Employment Intensity of Growth

The differentiated growth patterns followed by different sectors have had a varied impact on employment creation, depending on the growth patterns themselves and on the technology used in their productive process. As is the case in most developing countries, the Bolivian economy is characterized by the existence of differentiated productive technologies within the same sector—productive units using capital-intensive technologies coexisting with units that are more labor-intensive.

The bulk of the productive sectors that comprise the Bolivian economy have a dual structure, where modern productive units, mostly located in the formal sector, use capital-intensive technology, hire paid workers, and produce for export markets—coexisting with other small-scale units, located in the informal sector, using labor-intensive technologies, relying on unpaid family workers, selling their production in the domestic informal markets, and following household subsistence strategies.

The first column of Table 6.9 presents labor-output ratios calculated for different sectors of the Bolivian economy for 1996. The ratio measures the number of workers employed in each sector per unit of product expressed in

Table 6.9   Sectoral Growth and Employment Creation Capacity, Bolivia, 1980–2001

	Employment/ GDP Ratio,[a] 1996	Average GDP Growth (%), 1980–2001
Agriculture	511	2.22
Community and personal services	463	1.45
Commerce	319	1.42
Construction	244	1.38
Restaurants and hotels	208	0.87
Manufacturing	115	1.24
Transport and communication	73	4.74
Public administration	51	0.80
Electricity, gas, and water	34	5.11
Mining	33	1.27
Financial and firm services	30	3.29

Source: Bolivian National Institute of Statistics.

Note: a. Expressed in number of workers per unit of product, measured in millions of constant 1990 Bolivianos.

millions of constant Bolivianos in 1990. Agriculture shows the highest labor-output ratio, evidencing the widespread existence of small-scale, peasant-type, labor-intensive productive units. Other activities with relatively high employment creation capacity are community and personal services and commerce. Activities with an intermediate employment creation capacity are construction, restaurants and hotels, and manufacturing. Finally, activities with low employment creation capacity are transport and communication; public administration; electricity, gas, and water; mining and hydrocarbons; and financial and firm services.

Based on the classification presented above, Figure 6.3 shows that sectoral growth patterns observed in the Bolivian economy over the past two decades have not been particularly employment-intensive. The sectors with the highest employment-output ratios, like agriculture and commerce and personal services, presented low average growth rates—below 2 percent—over the two decades under analysis. Likewise, the sectors with intermediate employment creation capacities, such as construction, commerce, and restaurants and hotels, also experienced low average growth rates. Conversely, sectors with low employment creation capacity, such as electricity, gas, and water, and transport and communication, exhibited the highest growth rates (above 4 percent a year on average). Financial and firm activities, which have an intermediate employment creation capacity, also experienced intermediate growth—3.4 percent on average. Finally, three sectors that have low employment-output ratios—mining, manufac-

Figure 6.3   Sectoral Growth and Employment Creation Capacity, Bolivia, 1980–2001

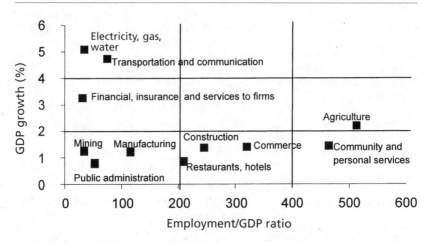

Source: Bolivian National Institute of Statistics.
Notes: Employment/GDP ratio = 1996. GDP growth = 1980–2001.

turing, and public administration—exhibited low average growth rates over the period studied.

Sectoral Growth and Employment During the 1980s and 1990s. The 1980s clearly did not favor the creation of jobs in the Bolivian economy (see Figure 6.4). During most of the decade, almost all economic activities exhibited negative growth rates. Only agriculture, transport and communication, and electricity, gas, and water grew at positive rates. Furthermore, those sectors with the smallest employment creation coefficients, such as transport and communication, and electricity, gas, and water, were the fastest-growing sectors, with average growth rates above 4 percent a year. Agriculture, which has a high employment coefficient, only presented a moderate growth rate—1.1 percent a year on average.

During the 1990s, on the other hand, sectoral growth rates stood at much higher levels (see Figure 6.5). However, growth did not present an employment creation bias. The fastest-growing sectors during that decade—averaging growth rates above 4 percent a year—were those with the smallest employment/GDP ratios. These sectors were financial and firm services; electricity, gas, and water; and transport and communication. Sectors with the highest employment creation capacity, such as agriculture, and communal and personal services, exhibited only moderate growth rates, below 4 percent a year on average.

Figure 6.4   Growth and Employment Creation, Bolivia, 1980s

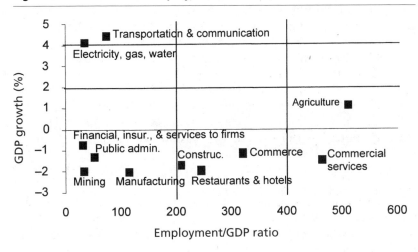

Source: Bolivian National Institute of Statistics.

Figure 6.5   Growth and Employment Creation, Bolivia, 1990s

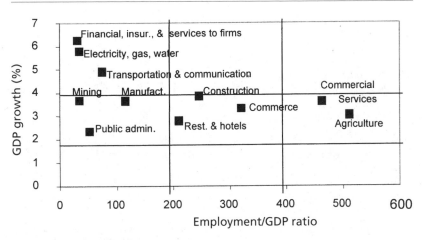

Source: Bolivian National Institute of Statistics.

Employment, Productivity, Real Wage Earnings, and Poverty

As concluded above, economic growth in Bolivia was not specifically favorable to the creation of employment. The 1980s were characterized by relatively low growth rates of GDP, and thus employment creation was almost negligible during that decade. During the 1990s, on the other hand, economic growth recovered, but the fastest-growing sectors were relatively less labor-intensive.

Table 6.10 shows that the overall employment growth rate at the end of the 1980s stood at 1.4 percent a year on average. In that period, the economy had not yet adjusted to the new economic conditions brought about by the stabilization program and structural reforms. Although most economic activities exhibited positive growth rates, there were some sectors that experienced negative growth rates in employment. This was the case of mining; electricity, gas, and water; and commerce and restaurants.

The 1990s presented more favorable conditions in terms of job creation. Between 1992 and 1997 employment expanded at an average growth rate of 3.5 percent a year. Employment in most economic activities, in the primary, secondary, and tertiary sectors, exhibited high positive growth rates.

When the economic crisis broke out at the end of the 1990s, the economy lost its dynamics in terms of job creation. Between 1997 and 1999 employ-

Table 6.10   Average Annual Percentage Change in Labor Force Growth per Activity, Bolivia, 1988–2001

	1988–1992	1992–1997	1997–1999	1999–2001
Agriculture, hunting, and fishing	2.15	2.42	–3.36	12.19
Mining	–5.79	–2.68	–9.12	–12.11
Manufacturing	4.44	4.90	2.67	–18.95
Electricity, water, and gas	–9.96	13.25	–14.81	33.62
Construction	3.12	0.91	6.58	–15.25
Commerce and restaurants	–3.68	15.03	7.55	–6.20
Transport and communication	0.90	0.99	3.07	–6.36
Financial and firm services	12.69	8.18	7.40	30.09
Community and personal services	1.17	–2.18	0.22	–0.24
Total	1.40	3.50	0.76	0.83

Source: Author estimates based on data published by the Bolivian National Institute of Statistics.

Notes: Employment statistics in Bolivia are fragmented and incomplete. Systematic and reliable employment data began to be compiled for both urban and rural sectors only in 1996. Previous rural employment figures can be obtained for 1976 and 1992 only, when population censuses were carried out at the national level, and for 1988, when a national household survey was implemented. Besides, there are some consistency problems in the measurement of employment—the most significant being that, before 1996, family workers were not included as an employment category, and thus they were not counted as part of the employed population. This resulted in very high growth employment rates in sectors where family workers were concentrated (e.g., agriculture, manufacturing, and commerce). This inconsistency had to be corrected in order to calculate the employment growth rates presented in this chapter and therefore the other indicators utilized, namely labor productivity growth and labor elasticities.

ment growth decreased to an annual average rate of 0.76 percent, and to 0.83 percent during the period 1999–2001. The slowdown experienced by the Bolivian economy brought about several job losses and thus unemployment increased significantly. From 1999 to 2001 employment in various economic activities, such as mining, manufacturing, construction, transport and communication, and commerce and restaurants, experienced high negative growth rates.

The above patterns observed in terms of employment creation brought about some interesting changes in the employment structure. Mining, for instance, decreased its share in total employment from 3.2 percent in 1988 to only 1.3 percent in 2001 (see Table 6.11). The manufacturing sector increased its share in employment during the 1990s, from 9 percent in 1988 to 11.4 percent in 1999. However, manufacturing's share in employment decreased again at the end of the 1990s and beginning of the 2000s. Construction also presented the same pattern as manufacturing, increasing its share in total employment between 1988 and 1999, and decreasing its share between 1999 and 2001.

Commerce and restaurants significantly increased their share in employment over time. In 1988 this sector accounted for 12.9 percent of employment and by 2001 its share had increased to 18.8 percent of total employment. This was caused by the large number of workers who were engaged in low-paid, small-scale commerce and related service activities as a means of increasing income opportunities of poor households.

Agriculture is still the sector that has the largest share in total employment, although this share is expected to decrease as long as the rapid process of urbanization of the Bolivian population continues. The share of agriculture

Table 6.11 Percentage Structure of Labor Force Distribution Across Productive Activities, Bolivia, 1988–2001

	1988	1992	1997	1999	2001
Agriculture, hunting, and fishing	43.3	44.6	43.2	39.7	44.2
Mining	3.2	2.4	1.8	1.5	1.3
Manufacturing	9.0	10.1	11.0	11.4	9.2
Electricity, water, and gas	0.4	0.3	0.3	0.2	0.3
Construction	5.5	5.9	5.2	5.9	4.9
Commerce and restaurants	12.9	10.5	17.7	20.2	18.8
Transport and communication	5.4	5.3	4.8	5.0	4.6
Financial and firm services	1.6	2.5	2.2	2.5	3.2
Community and personal services	18.7	18.5	13.7	13.6	13.5

Sources: Author estimates based on data published by the Bolivian National Institute of Statistics. 1992: national census of population and housing. 1988, 1997, 1999, and 2001: national household survey.

in total employment has stood between 43 percent and 45 percent during the period under analysis.

The growth patterns observed in employment and economic activity indicate that during the final years of the 1980s and most of the 1990s, economic growth had a moderate impact in terms of employment creation. At the end of the 1990s and the beginning of the 2000s, economic growth slowed down and employment creation was clearly insufficient. A summary indicator of employment growth that is associated with a given output growth is provided by the output elasticity of employment. A high employment intensity of growth means high employment elasticity. It needs to be noted in this context that employment elasticity reflects the inverse of labor productivity. An elasticity higher than unity implies a decline in productivity, as employment growth is higher than output growth. Conversely, an elasticity lower than unity means that employment expansion is taking place along with an increase in productivity, since employment growth is lower than output growth. A rise in the productivity would lead to a reduction in the employment elasticity. Therefore, as in the case of Bolivia, raising the employment elasticity in individual activities cannot always be welcomed, as that would mean a lowering of the productivity in an economy that is already characterized by widespread low-productivity employment.

A special case occurs when sectors present negative elasticities. In this case there are two possibilities. First, the negative elasticity could be the result of increasing employment and decreasing output. In this case productivity is certainly decreasing. Second, negative elasticity could be the result of increasing output and decreasing unemployment. In this case there is an increase in productivity. This case occurs, for instance, in sectors that have undergone a process of restructuring in order to become more competitive.

Table 6.12 shows the output elasticity of employment for the economy as a whole as well as for the different sectors. Likewise, Table 6.13 presents productivity growth rates for the economy as a whole and for various activity sectors. The analysis of labor elasticities of output confirms the hypothesis that growth in the Bolivian economy was not favorable in terms of job creation. During 1988–1992, employment elasticities stood below unity (0.4), evidencing a very weak employment intensity of growth during that specific period. Employment growth was very low in employment-intensive sectors, such as construction and community and personal services. Other labor-intensive sectors presented large employment decreases, such as mining and commerce. During this period, total productivity for the economy as a whole increased by 2.4 percent a year on average. Productivity increases were particularly high in sectors presenting large employment contractions, such as mining, electricity, and commerce.

During the 1988–1992 period, sectors presenting elasticities higher than unity were agriculture (1.1) and financial services (4.1). Thus these sectors

Table 6.12   Sectoral Output Elasticities of Employment, Bolivia, 1988–2001

	1988–1992	1992–1997	1997–1999	1999–2001
Agriculture, hunting, and fishing	1.1	0.5	3.3	5.1
Mining	–0.9	–0.7	–24.4	–2.4
Manufacturing	1.0	1.1	1.0	–13.3
Electricity, water, and gas	–1.7	1.5	–4.1	34.3
Construction	0.5	0.2	1.1	1.6
Commerce and restaurants	–0.7	4.1	5.6	–4.2
Transport and communication	0.1	0.2	1.0	–3.1
Financial and firm services	4.1	1.1	0.6	–90.2
Community and personal services	0.6	–0.7	0.1	–0.1
Total	0.4	0.8	0.7	0.6

Source: Author estimates based on data published by the Bolivian National Institute of Statistics.

also experienced decreases in productivity. Manufacturing showed an elasticity equal to unity, and thus productivity stood relatively constant. Those sectors that exhibited elasticities lower than unity were construction (0.5), transport and communication (0.1), and community and personal services (0.6). These sectors presented increases in productivity. There were three sectors that presented negative elasticities: mining (–0.9); electricity, gas, and water (–1.7); and commerce and restaurants (–0.7). In all three cases the negative

Table 6.13   Average Annual Percentage Change in Labor Productivity Growth by Economic Activity, Bolivia, 1988–2001

	1988–1992	1992–1997	1997–1999	1999–2001
Agriculture, hunting, and fishing	–0.1	2.2	2.4	–3.3
Mining	12.8	6.9	10.4	11.9
Manufacturing	–0.1	–0.3	0.0	12.7
Electricity, water, and gas	17.5	–4.1	21.6	–12.6
Construction	3.1	4.4	–0.3	–1.8
Commerce and restaurants	9.0	–9.8	–5.8	4.8
Transport and communication	5.1	5.4	0.0	5.4
Financial and firm services	–8.5	–0.7	5.1	–12.6
Community and personal services	0.9	5.5	3.0	2.4
Total	2.4	0.8	0.4	1.0

Source: Author estimates based on data published by the Bolivian National Institute of Statistics.

elasticities were the result of increasing output and decreasing employment. Thus productivity tended to rise in all these cases.

From 1992 to 1997, a period that is characterized by relatively high economic growth, the employment elasticity for the economy as a whole increased to 0.8. This, coupled with rapid economic growth, resulted in an increased employment growth rate and productivity gains. Higher employment growth occurred due to employment creation that took place in the commerce sector. Commerce activities absorbed most of the labor force that was made redundant in sectors such as mining and public services. During these years the Bolivian economy experienced relatively high and stable growth, which was higher than employment growth. Since employment elasticity stood below unity, total productivity for the Bolivian economy increased by 0.8 percent a year on average. This was the result of an uneven pattern across sectors. Those sectors exhibiting reductions or very low increases in employment presented the largest productivity gains (e.g., mining, transport and communication, and community and personal services). Conversely, sectors presenting the highest increases in employment suffered the largest productivity losses (e.g., electricity, gas, and water, and commerce and restaurants).

During that period, sectors presenting employment elasticities higher than unity were manufacturing; electricity, gas, and water; commerce and restaurants; and financial and firm services. Consequently, all these sectors exhibited productivity losses. Conversely, those sectors that showed employment elasticities lower than unity, and consequently obtained productivity gains, were agriculture, construction, and transport and communication.

At the end of the 1990s and beginning of the 2000s, when the economic crisis started, employment elasticities decreased. The overall employment elasticity for the economy as a whole decreased to 0.7 during 1997–1999 and to 0.6 during 1999–2001. A plausible explanation for this is that firms decided to reduce employment as part of their restructuring process in order to confront lower activity and reduced profits. As a result, productivity levels increased, but at a much slower pace.

During the 1997–1999 period, restructuring was very strong in the agriculture, mining, and electricity sectors, and these sectors exhibited very large productivity gains due to sizable employment reductions. Sectors such as construction and commerce did not restructure and suffered productivity losses due to output contractions. The manufacturing and transport and communication sectors presented elasticities close to unity, as moderate output growth rates were matched by employment growth rates. The financial and firm services sector represented a special case, exhibiting large increases in employment and productivity, possibly due to a very strong increase in output.

During the 1999–2001 period, the restructuring process was very strong in sectors such as mining, manufacturing, commerce and restaurants, transport and communication, and community and personal services, where productivity gains were the result of employment rationing policies at the firm level. The electricity, gas, and water sector experienced a sharp reduction in productivity due to high employment growth. Construction constitutes a special case, because the output elasticity of employment increased despite a sizable reduction in employment levels. This is explained by the extremely large contractions that occurred in construction activity and output.

In summary, between 1988 and 2001 the Bolivian economy went from a period of relatively rapid and stable growth to a period of economic crisis characterized by slower growth and lower employment creation. However, overall it can be said that economic growth did not contribute to poverty reduction, because it did not generate enough employment with high levels of productivity, which in turn would provide the basis for sustainable real income increases for workers. First, economic growth tended to be concentrated in sectors of low employment intensity, such as financial services, transport and telecommunication, and electricity, gas, and water. Second, commerce was the only labor-intensive sector that presented stable and relatively high growth rates in employment. However, employment creation in these sectors exhibited low and sharply decreasing productivity. This is explained by the large number of workers who were engaged in low-paid, small-scale commerce and related service activities as a means of increasing income opportunities of poor households. Third, productivity growth across sectors and for the economy as a whole was very limited over the entire period under analysis. This limits the capacity of economic growth to become the basis for higher real wages and incomes for workers.

The Case of the Manufacturing Sector. The analysis carried out above brought about some interesting conclusions. First, it evidenced the process of low productivity growth exhibited by the Bolivian economy during the 1990s, years in which it presented relatively fast and stable growth. Second, because of low productivity growth during the 1990s, at the moment the economy experienced slower growth due to the economic crisis at the end of the 1990s, all activity sectors faced a problem of widespread low productivity, which in turn made it more difficult for firms to cope with lower activity and reduced profits. Finally, as a result of decreased profits and activity levels, once the economic crisis broke out, most firms across sectors embarked on a restructuring process that involved reducing employment levels in order to reverse productivity losses and cope with the crisis.

This above analysis, however, was based on data obtained from different sources (i.e., national census and household surveys). Thus there is room for some data inconsistency due to problems related to different sample sizes and coverage of surveys, vis-à-vis census data that have national and complete coverage. In order to overcome these problems, this section focuses on analyzing the linkages among output growth, employment, and poverty in the case of the

Bolivian manufacturing sector. The data available for this particular sector are
more consistent, as they are obtained through firm surveys, guaranteeing more
stable, consistent, and reliable time-series data. Thus this section analyzes the
trends observed in variables such as production, employment, productivity, real
wages, and output elasticity of employment for the Bolivian manufacturing industry and puts forward some conclusions in relation to existing relationships
among these variables. Data utilized in this section come from the annual manufacturing-firm survey carried out by the National Institute of Statistics, covering the period 1987–2001.

***Output, Employment, Productivity, and Real Wages in the Manufacturing
Sector.*** The trends observed in production, employment, and productivity for
the manufacturing sector, based on data taken from manufacturing-firm surveys, are very similar to those observed in the previous section, based on national accounts data and household surveys. Although there are small differences in the figures observed, the trends followed by the key variables are
quite similar.

Taking the manufacturing sector as a whole, we observe that production increased at an average rate of 4 percent a year during the whole period under
analysis (see Table 6.14 and Figure 6.6). Employment, on the other hand, expanded by 2.6 percent a year, and thus productivity increased by 1.4 percent a
year. The calculated value for the arc output elasticity of employment was therefore 0.6 for the whole period under analysis. It is interesting to note that, during
the whole period covered, nominal wages paid by the manufacturing firms increased faster than the prices of the goods they produced and sold (see Table

**Table 6.14   Average Annual Percentage Changes in Output,
Employment, Productivity, and Real Wages, Bolivia,
1987–2001**

	1987–2001	1987–1990	1991–1998	1999–2001
Total Manufacturing Industry				
Total production	4.0	6.0	4.6	0.5
Employment	2.6	5.8	4.2	–4.7
Employment-output arc elasticity	0.6	1.0	0.9	–9.8
Nominal wages	13.1	18.9	13.4	6.8
Producer prices	8.5	15.7	8.1	2.6
Productivity	1.4	0.2	0.4	5.4
Real wage	3.1	0.2	3.8	4.2
Wage/price ratio	4.2	2.7	4.9	4.0
Food, Beverage, and Tobacco				
Total production	3.5	1.7	4.5	2.8
Employment	3.1	9.6	2.9	–2.4

continues

Table 6.14   Continued

	1987–2001	1987–1990	1991–1998	1999–2001
Employment-output arc elasticity	0.9	5.7	0.6	−0.8
Nominal wages	13.5	23.1	13.8	3.8
Producer prices	7.4	14.6	8.4	−1.6
Productivity	0.4	−7.2	1.6	5.3
Real wage	3.5	3.8	4.2	1.3
Wage/price ratio	5.7	7.4	5.0	5.5
Textiles, Clothing, Leather, and Shoes				
Total production	4.5	−0.9	9.1	−1.8
Employment	3.4	−4.9	8.7	−1.9
Employment-output arc elasticity	0.8	5.2	1.0	1.0
Nominal wages	13.3	13.6	12.7	14.4
Producer prices	7.5	15.6	7.2	0.8
Productivity	1.1	4.2	0.3	0.1
Real wage	3.2	−4.3	3.2	11.7
Wage/price ratio	5.3	−1.7	5.1	13.5
Processed Wood, Paper Products, and Printing				
Total production	2.0	−4.5	1.6	10.1
Employment	1.0	3.0	5.0	−10.6
Employment-output arc elasticity	0.5	−0.7	3.2	−1.1
Nominal wages	9.3	7.4	10.0	9.6
Producer prices	7.4	14.7	9.2	−4.0
Productivity	0.9	−7.3	−3.3	23.2
Real wage	−0.3	−9.5	0.6	7.0
Wage/price ratio	1.8	−6.4	0.7	14.2
Chemical and Plastic Products and Nonmetallic Minerals				
Total production	2.9	6.7	4.3	−4.4
Employment	0.9	4.1	3.5	−8.5
Employment-output arc elasticity	0.3	0.6	0.8	2.0
Nominal wages	13.1	11.7	15.9	7.4
Producer prices	11.0	19.2	8.0	11.2
Productivity	1.9	2.5	0.7	4.6
Real wage	3.1	−5.9	6.0	4.8
Wage/price ratio	1.9	−6.3	7.2	−3.4
Basic Metals, Metallic Products, Machinery, and Equipment				
Total production	6.3	29.5	2.9	−4.9
Employment	3.3	13.3	2.9	−5.1
Employment-output arc elasticity	0.5	0.5	1.0	1.0
Nominal wages	14.6	22.6	15.7	4.4
Producer prices	6.0	14.2	5.7	−0.9
Productivity	2.9	14.3	0.0	0.2
Real wage	4.4	3.3	5.9	1.8
Wage/price ratio	8.1	7.3	9.4	5.3

Source: Bolivian National Institute of Statistics, various years.

188   *Country Studies*

Figure 6.6   Production, Employment, and Productivity in Manufacturing Sector, Bolivia, 1987–2001

Total Manufacturing Industry

Food, Beverage, and Tobacco

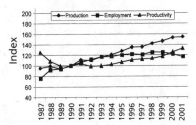

Textiles, Clothing, Leather, and Shoes

Processed Wood, Paper Products, and Printing

Chemical and Plastic Products and Nonmetallic Minerals

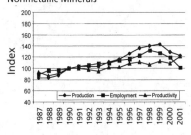

Basic Metals, Metallic Products, Machinery, and Equipment

Source: Bolivian National Institute of Statistics.
Note: Base year 1990 = 100.

6.14 and Figure 6.7). As a result, the wage/price index for the manufacturing sector as a whole grew by 4.2 percent a year.[3] Since growth of the wage/price index was greater than growth of productivity, the manufacturing sector's competitive position weakened, limiting the capacity of manufacturing firms to cope with the economic crisis that broke out at the end of the 1990s.

When analyzing the different subperiods separately, we observe that the av-

Figure 6.7 Real Wages and Productivity in Manufacturing Sector, Bolivia, 1987–2001

Total Manufacturing Industry

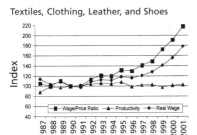

Food, Beverage, and Tobacco

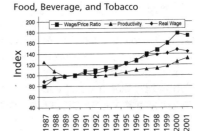

Textiles, Clothing, Leather, and Shoes

Processed Wood, Paper Products, and Printing

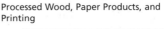
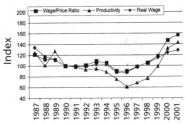

Chemical and Plastic Products and Nonmetallic Minerals

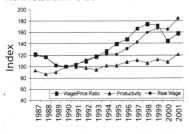

Basic Metals, Metallic Products, Machinery, and Equipment

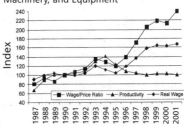

Source: Bolivian National Institute of Statistics.
Note: Base year 1990 = 100.

erage growth rate of output was relatively high during the period of stable growth (i.e., 1987–1998). It was 6 percent between 1987 and 1990, and 4.6 percent between 1991 and 1998. Employment growth, on the other hand, was also high during this period, but slightly lower than output growth (i.e., 5.8 percent on average between 1987 and 1990, and 4.8 percent between 1991 and 1998). Thus the calculated arc output elasticity of employment was slightly below unity, and therefore productivity practically stood constant, increasing at very small growth rates (0.2 percent on average between 1987 and 1990, and 0.4 percent between 1991 and 1998). On the other hand, the wage/price index rose by 2.7 percent a year on average between 1987 and 1990, and by 4.9 percent a year on average between 1991 and 1998, while real wages increased by 0.2 percent and 4.9 percent a year on average during those respective periods. Thus the manufacturing sector was confronted by a situation in which real wages were increasing at a much faster pace in relation to labor productivity, reducing in turn the profitability and competitive position of manufacturing firms. Therefore, because real wages and the wage/price index increased much faster than labor productivity, the manufacturing sector confronted a weak competitive position at the end of the 1990s when the economic crisis broke out.

During the period of economic recession (i.e., 1999–2001) the manufacturing-output growth rate decreased to only 0.5 percent a year on average. Employment, on the other hand, experienced a strong contraction, falling by 4.7 percent a year on average, bringing about a sharp increase in productivity, which grew by 5.4 percent a year on average. Once again, this finding tends to confirm the hypothesis that firms in the manufacturing industry embarked on a restructuring process, making excess labor redundant, in order to confront reductions in sales and profits. Nevertheless, real wages kept increasing at a high rate during this period (4 percent a year on average), albeit at a slower pace than productivity.

In summary, the manufacturing sector experienced a relatively high growth in production and employment during most of the 1990s. This permitted productivity to be maintained at a constant level during that period. Real wages and the wage/price index, on the other hand, increased faster than productivity, reducing in turn the manufacturing sector's profitability and competitive position. During the economic crisis at the end of the 1990s and beginning of the 2000s, manufacturing firms reduced employment in order to attain productivity gains. Real wages, however, still experienced high growth rates during the crisis period.

A disaggregated analysis of the manufacturing sector shows some similarities among the behavior of output, employment, productivity, and real wages for the different branches composing the manufacturing sector vis-à-vis the manufacturing sector as a whole. Most manufacturing subsectors experienced a period—during most of the 1990s—of fast output and employment growth, coupled with productivity losses, followed by a period of slower output growth and negative employment growth, coupled with productivity losses. During the 1990s, in almost all manufacturing subsectors, real wages increased faster than labor productivity. This trend reversed at the end of the 1990s when the economic crisis began. A more detailed analysis on the manufacturing sector behavior concerning the employment-output-productivity linkages can be found in Jemio and Choque 2003.

A Labor Demand Function for the Manufacturing Sector. The previous analysis of employment elasticities of production for the manufacturing sector was based on elasticities calculated through the arc elasticity methodology— that is, by dividing employment growth rates by output growth rates during a given period of time. This methodology, however, could be misleading, because it imputes all employment changes to output changes, and does not consider the effects that other variables, such as real wages, capital utilization, and the like, may have on employment variations. By imputing all changes that occurred in employment purely to output changes, we might be overestimating or underestimating the elasticity values, since we are not considering the effects of other variables.

In order to overcome this problem, in this section we estimate employment elasticities of output for the manufacturing industry using econometric methods. For this purpose, we estimate labor demand functions for the manufacturing sector, which will allow us to analyze the existing linkages among employment, production, real wages, and capital utilization. To this end, a "panel-data" analysis is utilized based on data obtained from the manufacturing-firm survey carried out by the National Institute of Statistics.

The analysis is aimed at estimating labor elasticities of output for the manufacturing sector as a whole, as well as for each of the industrial branches that comprise the manufacturing sector. Furthermore, the model allows us to evaluate the substitution or complementarity effects existing between different productive factors, specifically between labor and capital. Thus a better specification of manufacturing labor demand is obtained, and therefore the estimated labor elasticities of output reflect in a better way the responsiveness of employment to output changes, other effects remaining constant.

The estimated labor demand function has the following specification:

$$L_I = F\left(L_{I,\,t-1},\, Q_I,\, W_I\,/\,P_I,\, CE_I\right)$$

where

L_I = number of workers employed in manufacturing sector I
$L_{I,\,t-1}$ = number of workers employed in manufacturing sector I in period $t-1$
Q_I = output in manufacturing sector I
$W_I\,/\,P_I$ = wage/price index in manufacturing sector I
CE_I = consumption of electricity in manufacturing sector I

In order to obtain labor elasticities directly, we specify the labor demand function in terms of logarithms:

$$\log L_I = \beta_0 + \beta_1(\log L_{I,\,t-1}) + \beta_2(\log Q_I) + \beta_3(\log W_I\,/\,P_I) + \beta_4(\log CE_I)$$

The final specification of the labor demand function includes a lagged value of labor demand, which was included in order to capture an inertial employment creation term, as well as to eliminate autocorrelation problems from the econometric estimates.

Two labor demand functions were estimated econometrically. First was a restricted version in which the β parameters (labor demand elasticities) for all manufacturing branches were restricted to be the same; thus the estimated equations represented a labor demand function for the manufacturing sector as a whole. The second equation type involved nonrestricted versions of labor demand functions in which the β parameters were allowed to vary across different manufacturing branches. Thus, labor demand elasticities for each of the branches are computed and can be compared with the demand elasticity for the manufacturing sector as a whole, as well as among the different sectors.

The results estimated for the restricted labor demand function, which represents the labor demand function for the manufacturing sector as a whole, appears in detail in Table 6.17. These results show that labor demand in period *t* is a function of a lagged value of the same variable, which is highly significant and has a very high demand elasticity (0.97). This means that inertial employment is very significant in explaining employment demand in a given year. Firms do not tend to vary employment levels, either upward or downward, in response to output changes from one year to the other. Besides, labor laws introduce rigidities to the labor market, making it costly for employers to make employment reductions in the short run in response to output contractions. Thus, output fluctuations become less significant in explaining employment changes, once we include a lagged value of employment as an explanatory variable of labor demand. This explains why the output elasticity of employment estimated econometrically is much lower than the arc output elasticity of labor. The econometrically estimated elasticity is only 0.17 compared to 0.6 estimated using the other methodology.

Another finding derived from the econometric exercise is that labor demand appeared to be substitutive vis-à-vis capital utilization. The employment elasticity of electricity consumption, which is taken as a proxy of capital utilization, was –0.15. Moreover, the wage/price relation has a negative impact on employment, making the employment elasticity of wage/price index equal to –0.13.

Another plausible explanation for the large difference found between the arc output elasticity of employment and the elasticity estimated econometrically can be found in the analysis of the results obtained from the unrestricted labor demand function. The unrestricted labor demand function provides separate elasticities for each of the manufacturing industry branches. The results appear in detail in Table 6.18. A disaggregated analysis shows that employment elasticities of output tend to vary across sectors. The estimated labor elasticity for basic metals, metallic products, machinery, and equipment (branches 37 to

39) is very low (0.11). Elasticities in the case of food, beverage, and tobacco (branch 31) and processed wood, wood products, paper, paper products, and printing (branches 33 and 34) are at an intermediate level (around 0.3). Finally, elasticities in the case of textiles, clothing, leather, and shoewear (branch 32) and chemical products, plastic products, and nonmetallic minerals (branches 35 and 36) are much higher (0.68 and 1.00 respectively). Thus the econometrically estimated output elasticity of employment for the total manufacturing sector was influenced significantly by those sectors with the lowest elasticities, namely branches 37–39, 31, and 33–34. Besides, the estimated employment elasticities of output for food, beverage, and tobacco (branch 31) and basic metals, metallic products, machinery, and equipment (branches 37 to 39) were not statistically significant.

Another finding derived from the unrestricted labor demand functions was that in all manufacturing branches, employment was negatively correlated with the wage/price index. However, these elasticities were statistically significant only in the cases of processed wood, wood products, paper, paper products, and printing (branches 33 and 34); chemical products, plastic products, and nonmetallic minerals (branches 35 and 36); and basic metals, metallic products, machinery, and equipment (branches 37 to 39).

Employment, Real Wages, and Poverty. The previous analysis was used to examine employment elasticities of output in order to determine whether growth has tended to promote employment creation. This section focuses on a more detailed examination of whether or not economic growth has led to structural changes that have benefited the poor. In this regard, we first examine the sectors and occupations where the poor are concentrated as well as the trends in earnings in various occupations. Second, we analyze whether there have been discernible shifts in the structure of employment toward occupations with higher productivity and incomes leading to a reduction in poverty incidence. Finally, we concentrate on the analysis of real wages and earnings of wage-paid workers and real earnings of the self-employed, as additional transmission mechanisms of the benefits of growth to the poor.

There is a general agreement among the various studies carried out regarding the sources of income inequalities in the Bolivian labor market. The key factors most often identified as sources of income inequalities are location of workers (i.e., urban versus rural area), activity sector where workers are employed, labor category of workers, and qualification of workers. Including these factors in the analysis of the existing linkage between real wages and productivity will provide us with additional insights into whether the benefits of growth have reached the poor.

Employment and poverty in urban and rural areas. Table 6.15 presents the distribution of workers between urban and rural areas from 1996 to 2001. Clearly the trends show an increase in the share of urban employment to the

Table 6.15   Distribution of Workers, Earning Differentials, and Poverty Incidence Between Urban and Rural Workers, Bolivia, 1996–2001

	1996	1997	1999	2000	2001
Location of workers (%)					
Urban	52.2	52.6	55.4	57.5	55.5
Rural	47.8	47.4	44.6	42.5	44.5
National	100.0	100.0	100.0	100.0	100.0
Average real earnings (constant 2000 Bolivianos)					
Urban	1,107	1,279	1,091	1,099	971
Rural	369	527	234	223	220
National	853	1,024	710	727	637
Poverty incidence (%)					
Urban	47.4	42.8	43.8	34.9	41.1
Rural	87.9	83.8	80.1	93.2	80.9
National	66.7	62.2	60.0	59.7	60.5

Source: Bolivian National Institute of Statistics.

Note: The poverty figures presented here are different from those appearing in Table 6.4 because poverty figures from Table 6.4 are calculated at an individual worker level, while figures in Table 6.15 are at the household level.

detriment of rural employment. In 1996, 52.2 percent of employment was located in the urban areas. In 2001, this share increased to 55.5 percent. As discussed previously, urban migration explains this trend, which in turn was the result of income differentials obtained by workers in urban versus rural areas. In 1996, real incomes received by urban workers were three times those received on average by workers in the rural areas. Between 1996 and 2001, real earnings received by urban workers decreased by 2.6 percent a year on average, while real earnings by rural workers dropped by 9.8 percent a year on average. Besides, the poverty incidence among workers in rural areas is much higher than that prevailing among urban workers. In 1996, 47.4 percent of urban workers perceived incomes that situated them below the poverty line.[4] The poverty incidence among rural workers was as high as 87.9 percent. In 2001, poverty incidence decreased among both urban and rural workers. However, poverty incidence among rural workers decreased faster than it did among their urban counterparts.

Thus there are clear differences in income opportunities between workers in the urban and rural areas. This has an important impact on the magnitudes of poverty incidence, which tends to promote urban migration. Besides, migration is promoted not only by the existing earning gap, but also by observed trends in real earnings over time, which tends to enlarge the existing income gap.

Employment and poverty across activity sectors. Income opportunities and poverty incidence tend to vary across the activity sectors where workers are employed. Figure 6.8 shows that the distribution of workers across activity sectors is quite different between urban and rural areas. In urban areas, workers are mostly engaged in service sectors, such as commerce, restaurants, and hotels (30 percent in 2001); public administration, personal, and communal services (21 percent); transport and communication (8 percent); and financial and firm services (6 percent). The manufacturing sector employs 14 percent of workers, and the agricultural sector employs 11 percent. The structural changes observed in urban employment show that employment in the public administration and communal and personal service sectors decreased from 35 percent in 1985 to 21 percent in 2001. The reform process implemented after 1985 involved a sharp reduction in the size of public sector employment. This reduction has been accompanied by an increase in the share of employment in activities such as commerce, restaurants and hotels, construction, and financial services. Manufacturing reduced its share in total urban employment from 18 percent in 1985 to 14 percent in 2001.

Clearly there are trends leading toward an employment structure where more people are employed in the tertiary sector. The trends followed by real earnings tend to favor the observed structural shifts in employment (see Figure 6.9). Real earnings that increased the most were those of workers engaged in financial and firm services, electricity, and transport and communication. Sectors where real earnings did not increase significantly were manufacturing, commerce, hotels/restaurants, and construction. The explanation for the increased share in total urban employment of sectors where real incomes lagged behind is that these sectors absorbed recent rural migrants, with low levels of human capital, who tended to enter employment in low-paid jobs. Consequently, poverty incidence was much higher in these sectors, which in turn have the highest shares in total urban employment (i.e., manufacturing, commerce, hotels/restaurants, and construction). However, the poverty incidence among workers in practically all activity sectors in the urban areas tended to decrease over time (see Figure 6.10).

Workers in the rural area, on the other hand, tended to be employed in the agricultural sector. About 85 percent of workers were engaged in agricultural activities in 2001, whereas personal and communal services constituted merely 4 percent and commerce, restaurants, and hotels also constituted 4 percent of workers. The observed trend followed by real earnings shows that incomes received by agricultural workers lagged well behind real earnings received by workers engaged in other rural activities. Poverty incidence indicators, on the other hand, show that poverty affects largely workers engaged in agricultural activities. In 2001, 85 percent of agricultural workers in the rural areas obtained incomes below the defined poverty line for that year.

196

Figure 6.8   Percentage of Workers by Economic Activity and Location, Bolivia, 1985–2001 (Urban) and 1996–2001 (Rural)

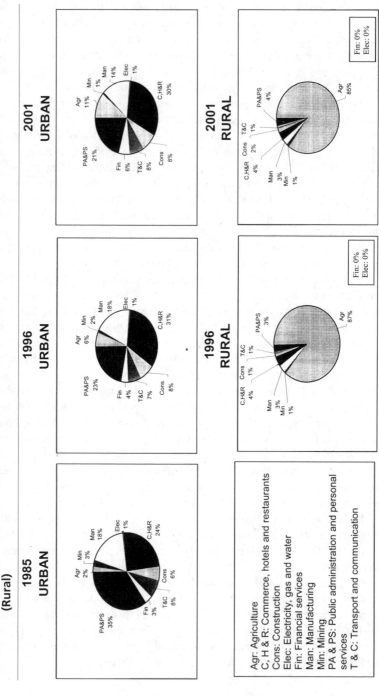

Agr: Agriculture
C, H & R: Commerce, hotels and restaurants
Cons: Construction
Elec: Electricity, gas and water
Fin: Financial services
Man: Manufacturing
Min: Mining
PA & PS: Public administration and personal services
T & C: Transport and communication

Source: Bolivian National Institute of Statistics.

Figure 6.9   Average Real Earnings of Workers by Economic Activity and Location, Bolivia, 1985–2001 (Urban) and 1996–2001 (Rural)

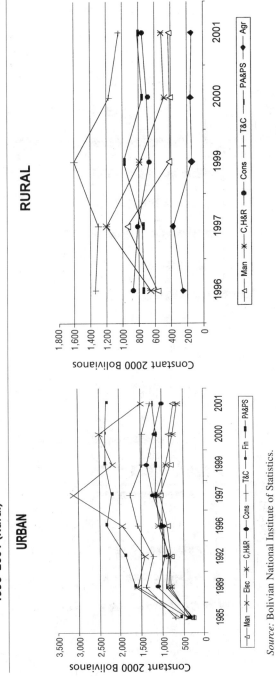

Source: Bolivian National Institute of Statistics.

Figure 6.10   Poverty Incidence by Economic Activity and Location, Bolivia, 1989–2001 (Urban) and 1996–2001 (Rural)

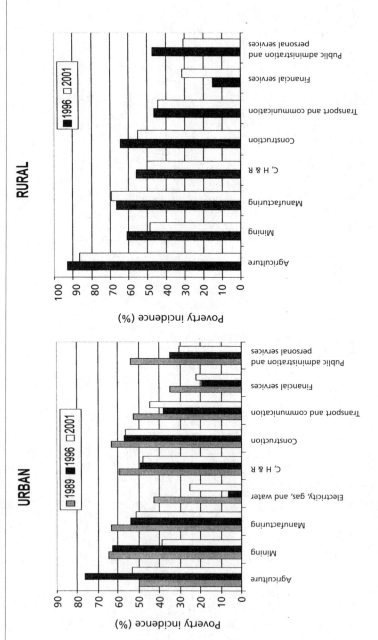

Source: Bolivian National Institute of Statistics.

In summary, although poverty incidence among workers in both the urban and rural areas has tended to decrease recently, the largest share of Bolivian workers tend to be employed in the lowest-paid activities, where poverty incidence is the highest.

Employment and poverty across labor categories. The structure of employment across labor categories is different in urban compared to rural areas. This in turn has an impact on the patterns followed by real earnings differentials and poverty incidences across labor categories.

In 2001 the bulk of urban employment was concentrated among the following labor categories: self-employed (35 percent), employees (32 percent), laborers (12 percent), and family workers (13 percent). Over time, there have been some structural changes. For instance, the share of employees decreased from 41 percent of total urban employment in 1985 to 35 percent in 2001. This decrease is also linked to the contraction in public employment discussed in the previous section. There was also a significant increase in the share of family workers in total employment, as a result of different strategies followed by households to increase their income opportunities. The share of laborers in total urban employment has remained fairly constant over time, increasing from 11 percent in 1985 to 12 percent in 2001. Finally, the share of employers varied between 3 percent and 7 percent over the period studied, and that of professionals stood at a very low level, 1 percent (see Figure 6.11).

The trend exhibited by real earnings among the different urban labor categories varied significantly over time. Real earnings of employers and professionals showed the highest levels and were those that increased the fastest. Real earnings received by employees also presented significant increases, rising by 10 percent a year between 1985 and 2001. Real earnings of laborers, family workers, and self-employed presented the lowest levels and remained largely stagnated over time (see Figure 6.12).

According to previous analysis, poverty incidences among the three last labor categories (i.e. laborers, self-employed, and family workers) were the highest. However, over time there was a decreasing trend of poverty incidence across these labor categories. Poverty incidences in the other labor categories (i.e., employers, employees, and professionals) are much lower and have tended to decrease much faster compared to the other categories (see Figure 6.13).

Workers in rural areas are mainly family workers and self-employed, representing shares of 49 percent and 38 percent respectively in 2001. In the same year the shares in total employment of other labor categories were very small: 7 percent were laborers, 3 percent were employers, and 4 percent were employees.

In terms of real earnings trends, we observe that real incomes of self-employed and family workers were the lowest among rural workers and remained at the lowest levels over the whole period under analysis.

200

Figure 6.11   Percentage of Workers by Labor Category and Location, Bolivia, 1985–2001 (Urban) and 1996–2001 (Rural)

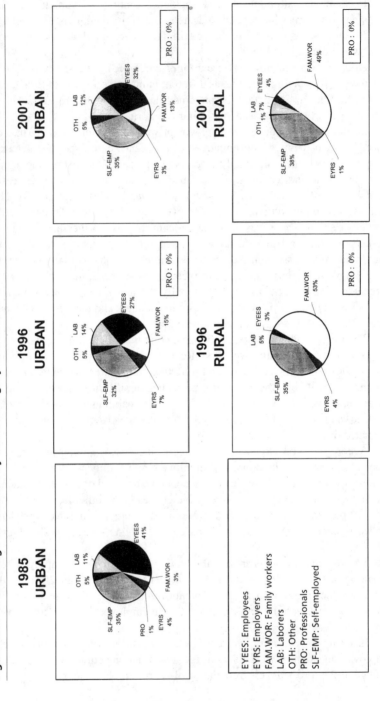

EYEES: Employees
EYRS: Employers
FAM.WOR: Family workers
LAB: Laborers
OTH: Other
PRO: Professionals
SLF-EMP: Self-employed

Source: Bolivian National Institute of Statistics.

Figure 6.12   Average Real Earnings of Workers by Labor Category and Location, Bolivia, 1985–2001 (Urban) and 1996–2001 (Rural)

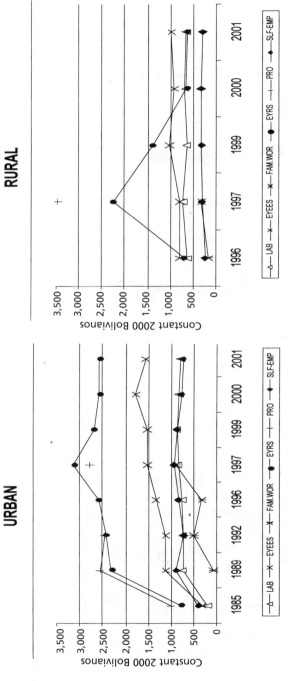

Source: Bolivian National Institute of Statistics.

202

Figure 6.13 Poverty Incidence by Labor Category and Location, Bolivia, 1989–2001 (Urban) and 1996–2001 (Rural)

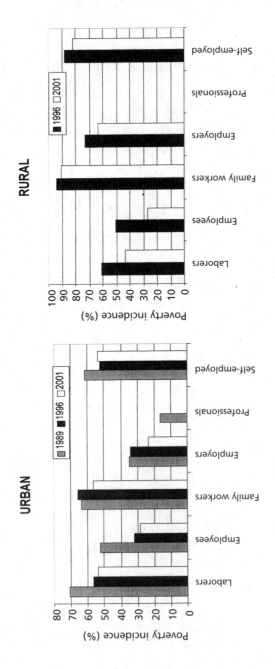

Source: Bolivian National Institute of Statistics.

Finally, in rural areas, poverty incidence affected family workers and self-employed the most. More than 90 percent of family workers and more than 80 percent of self-employed were below the poverty line. Poverty affected to a lesser extent employees, employers, and laborers. In all labor categories we observe a reduction in poverty incidence between 1996 and 2001.

Employment and poverty across educational level. The educational level of workers has been identified, by many studies on the Bolivian labor market, as the single most important variable in explaining income differentials among workers. The structure of workers by educational level tends to be different in the urban and rural areas. The structure of the urban labor force in 2001, based on their educational level, shows that 27 percent of workers had completed basic education, 27 percent had completed middle education, 13 percent had completed intermediate education, 5 percent had completed technical training, 15 percent had completed university education, and 5 percent had no training at all. This structure has remained very much unchanged over time. The most significant change was in the share of workers with university training, which increased from 12 percent of total urban workers in 1985 to 15 percent in 2001 (see Figure 6.14).

As mentioned above, there is a strong correlation between the educational level of workers and their real earning levels. Workers with university training have the highest real income levels and the highest rates of real income growth over time. Workers with technical education come in second, whereas workers with no educational level have the lowest real income levels (see Figure 6.15).

Poverty incidence is also closely linked to educational levels, as can be seen in Figure 6.16. Poverty incidence of workers with no educational level was higher than 60 percent in 2001. This incidence was as low as 10 percent in the case of workers with university training. Again, there is a decreasing trend over time in poverty incidence across all workers with different educational levels.

In the case of rural workers, in 2001, 53 percent had completed basic education, 20 percent had no education, 13 percent had completed intermediate education, and 11 percent had completed middle education. These four educational categories accounted for 97 percent of total rural workers. The share of workers with technical or university education was insignificant.

Educational level has proven to be less important in explaining real income differentials in the rural areas, compared to the case of urban areas. However, workers with university education have tended to earn much more than workers having lower educational levels.

The poverty incidence among rural workers was also very much correlated to their educational level. Poverty incidence was close to 90 percent among workers with no educational level, and it was below 20 percent in the case of workers with university education.

204

Figure 6.14   Percentage of Workers by Education Level and Location, Bolivia, 1985–2001 (Urban) and 1996–2001 (Rural)

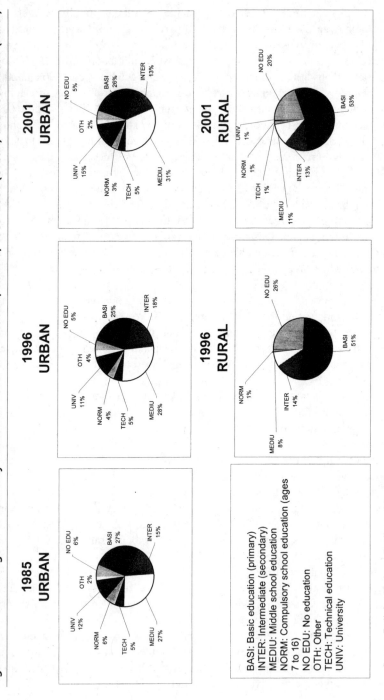

BASI: Basic education (primary)
INTER: Intermediate (secondary)
MEDIU: Middle school education
NORM: Compulsory school education (ages 7 to 16)
NO EDU: No education
OTH: Other
TECH: Technical education
UNIV: University

Source: Bolivian National Institute of Statistics.

Figure 6.15   Average Real Earnings of Workers by Education Level and Location, Bolivia, 1985–2001 (Urban) and 1996–2001 (Rural)

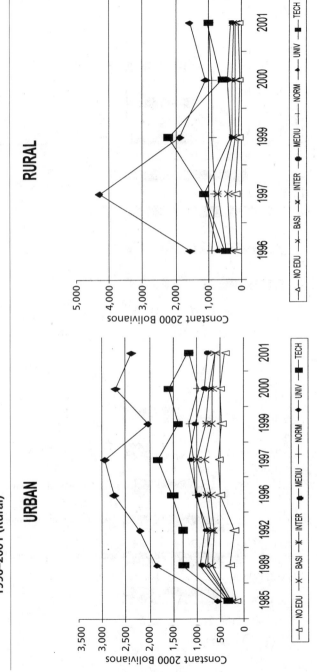

Source: Bolivian National Institute of Statistics.

206

Figure 6.16 Poverty Incidence by Education Level and Location, Bolivia, 1989–2001 (Urban) and 1996–2001 (Rural)

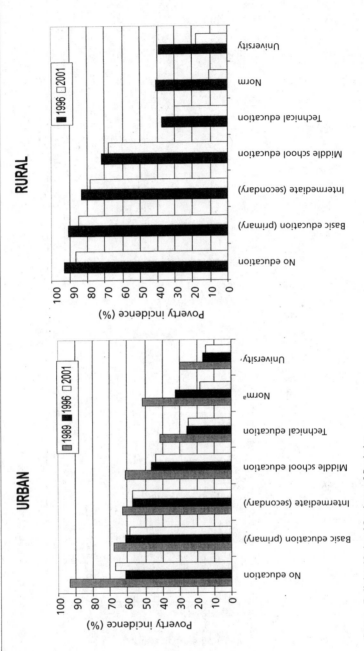

Source: Bolivian National Institute of Statistics.
Note: a. "Norm" is compulsory school education (ages 7–16).

In summary, it is clear that the employment structure in the Bolivian economy has not changed significantly over time, and there have been no discernible shifts of workers toward sectors and occupations with higher productivity and thus with capacity to generate higher real incomes. The most important shift in this direction was the continuous migration from rural to urban areas, which occurred as a means to escape extreme poverty. The large disparities existing between urban and rural incomes, together with the differentiated access by urban and rural households to basic services such as education, health, and water, have also promoted urban migration.

In rural areas, the largest share of workers are engaged in agricultural activities, which in turn generate the lowest-paid jobs and have the highest poverty incidence. Other rural activities generate better-paid jobs, but their incidence in total rural employment is very limited. In urban areas, employment is mostly concentrated in the service sector, which in turn presented the fastest-growing employment creation over time. However, employment created in the service sector (in activities such as commerce, transport, and other services) was of very low productivity and poorly paid.

The share of informal labor categories in total employment—self-employed and family workers—was the highest in both urban and rural areas, being much higher in the case of rural areas. Besides, informal labor categories of employment presented much lower real income levels vis-à-vis formal employment (e.g., employees, employers, professionals, etc.). Real incomes earned by informal workers in turn tended to stagnate over time, presenting only very moderate increases. Consequently, poverty incidence was the highest among informal labor categories.

■ The Role of Employment and the Labor Market in Reducing Poverty: Micro-Level Analysis

The above discussion focused basically on a macro-level analysis of how economic growth could contribute to poverty reduction through increases in employment in higher-productivity sectors and occupations and a rise in real wages. A similar analysis could be carried out at the micro (household) level to examine the impact of employment and labor market variables on poverty. Conceptually, it is possible to link a number of variables that could influence the probability of a household being poor in terms of inadequate income. The variables could be asset-related (e.g., the possession of income-generating assets), human capital–related (e.g., education and skill levels of the working members of a household), or employment-related (e.g., the sector and quantity of employment of the workers, wages, productivity, etc.).

This type of analysis is carried out here based on an econometric Probit-type model, estimated based on data from household surveys. The database utilized corresponds to the household survey for 2000.

The dependent variable is *Fgt_0*, a discrete variable that takes a value of 1 when the household is poor, in terms of inadequate income, and 0 in the case of a nonpoor household. The variables utilized to run the regressions were of the three types discussed above—variables related to human capital, employment, and assets:

Human Capital–Related Variables

sex_1	sex of household head: 0 = female, 1 = male
Age_1	age of household head
Leng	first language of household head: 0 = others, 1 = Spanish
Mem10_1	number of household members between ten and seventeen years of age
Mem18_1	number of household members between eighteen and fifty-nine years of age
Sizhh1	household size
Sizhh2	square power of household size
Edumax	maximum educational level attained by any household member

Employment-Related Variables

Secind_1	1 = household head employed in the secondary sector
Terind_1	1 = household head employed in the tertiary sector
Urbrur_1	location of household: 0 = rural, 1 = urban

Asset-Related Variables

actfis_1	number of physical assets owned by household (max. 5)
	dwelling
	land in the urban area
	land in the rural area
	automobile
	agriculture equipment
actfin_1	number of financial assets owned by household (max. 2)
	bank account
	household's lending to other household
accfin_1	access to formal lending (max. 2)
	bank debt due to mortgages
	credit cards
acnofo_1	access to informal credit

The results obtained appear in detail in Table 6.19. A summary of these results is presented in Table 6.16.

Table 6.16 Summary of Results of Probit Model (Household Survey 2000)

Variables	Model 1	Model 2
Human capital variables		
Sex_1	−0.072	−0.078
Age_1	−0.005	−0.003
Language	−0.457	−0.444
Membr10_1	−0.106	−0.132
Mem18_1	−0.187	−0.187
Sizhh1		0.522
0.525		
sizhh2	−0.016	−0.016
edumaxad	−0.082	−0.084
Employment variables		
secind_1	−0.291	
tercind_1	−0.517	
location		−0.285
Asset variables		
actfis_1	−0.188	−0.171
actfin_1	−0.344	−0.348
accfin_1	−0.365	−0.390
acnofo_1	−0.134	−0.130
constant	0.758	0.603

Human capital–related variables. According to the results obtained, in 2000, human capital–related variables had a significant influence on the probability of a household being poor. The variable sex-of-household-head, for instance, reduces the probability of a household being poor by 7.3 percent when the household head is a man. The age of the household head contributes to reducing the probability of a household being poor by 0.5 percent per additional year of age of the household head. The language spoken by the household head has a significant impact on the probability of whether the household is poor or nonpoor. The fact that the household head has Spanish as his or her first language decreases the probability of the household being poor by 45.7 percent. The number of household members within the working age contributes to reducing the probability of a household being poor. In the case of household members between ten and seventeen years of age, for instance, the household's probability of being poor decreases by 10.6 percent for each of the members fulfilling this condition. In the case of household members who are between eighteen and fifty-nine years of age, the household's probability of being poor is reduced by 18.7 percent for each member fulfilling this condition. The household size reduces the probability of being poor by 1.6 percent for each additional member of the household. Finally, the maximum educational level attained by the household head reduces the probability of the household being poor by an additional 8.2 percent for each incremental educational level attained.

The variable related to human capital conditions plays a significant role in determining the probability of a household being poor or nonpoor. The existence of household members who are within the working age reduces the probability of the household being affected by poverty. Household size has a moderate impact on reducing the probability of the household being affected by poverty. Finally, educational levels attained by the household head again proved to be quite significant in increasing the probability of the household escaping from poverty.

Employment-related variables. Employment-related variables were also tested and proven to have a significant impact in determining the probability of a household being poor. Considering the activity sector where workers are employed produces the following results: The fact that a household head is engaged in both modern secondary and tertiary activity sectors decreases the household's probability of being poor. When a household head is working in secondary sector activities, the probability of the household being poor decreases by 29.1 percent, and decreases by 51.7 percent when the household head is engaged in tertiary sector activities.

The results obtained through the econometric model demonstrated that employment-related variables are important in determining the probability of a household being poor. The most relevant variable was the activity sector where the household head is employed. Variables such as formality of workers and location (i.e., urban versus rural areas) are also important in determining the probability of being poor. However, these variables have a high degree of correlation with the activity sector. Thus their effects tend to cancel out when they are considered together in the same regression. As can be seen in Table 6.16, a second Probit model was estimated, where the location variable was considered instead of the activity sector variable. The results obtained in this second model show that, if the household is located in urban areas, its probability of being poor is reduced by 28.5 percent.

Asset-related variables. Asset-related variables measure to what extent assets owned by the household increase their capacity to generate higher incomes and therefore reduce their probability of being poor. In the Probit model, different asset-related variables were tested. A first group of variables involved the ownership of physical assets by households: dwelling, land in the urban area, agricultural land in the rural area, automobile, and agriculture equipment. The ownership of any of these assets reduced the probability of a household being poor by 18.9 percent. Another variable tested was the ownership by households of financial assets, for which there were two categories: bank accounts, in any of their forms (sight accounts, saving accounts, time deposits, etc.), and informal lending by households to other households. The ownership of these types of financial assets decreases the probability of households being poor by 34.4 percent. This also highlights the fact that only rich households hold financial assets.

Besides physical and financial assets, the Probit model included variables that measure the access of households to credit, through either formal or informal channels. The access of households to formal mechanisms of finance reduces their probability of being poor by 36.5 percent, while access to informal credit channels decreases the probability of the household being poor by 13.4 percent.

* * *

In summary, educational and occupational interventions appear to provide the most important conduct for poverty reduction. Moving workers from low-productivity agricultural activities to more productive jobs in the manufacturing or service sector can contribute to poverty reduction. However, sustained, larger reductions in poverty should be sought through education and therefore through changes in the structure of the labor force made possible by better education. Facilitating household access to productive assets can also have an important impact on reducing poverty. The same applies in the case of a household's access to credit, which can also help to increase the probability of escaping from poverty.

▣ Conclusion

The aim of this chapter has been to analyze the existing linkages among economic growth, employment, and poverty, at both the macro and the micro level, using the Bolivian experience over the past two decades as a case study.

At the macro level, the linkage between output growth and poverty was conceptualized in terms of the average productivity of the employed work force, which in turn was reflected in low levels of real wages and low levels of earnings in self-employment. A first conclusion was that, in general terms, growth in the Bolivian economy has not been particularly favorable in terms of employment creation. During the years of relatively rapid economic growth, the sectors that presented the highest growth rates were those with the lowest employment-output ratios.

The analysis of employment and output growth at the macroeconomic level shows that during the period under study, the Bolivian economy went from a period of relatively rapid and stable growth to a period of economic crisis characterized by slower growth and lower employment creation. However, overall it cannot be said that economic growth contributed to poverty reduction, because it did not generate enough employment with high levels of productivity, which in turn could have formed the basis for sustainable real income increases for workers. First, economic growth tended to be concentrated in sectors with low employment intensity, such as financial services, transport and telecommunication, and electricity, gas, and water. Second, commerce was the only labor-intensive sector that presented stable and relatively high growth rates in employment. However, employment creation in this sector exhibited low and sharply decreasing productivity. This is explained by the large number of workers who were engaged in low-paid, small-scale commerce and related service activities, as a means to increase income opportunities to poor households. Third, productivity growth across sectors and for the economy as a whole was very limited over the entire period under analysis. This limits the capacity of economic growth to become the basis for higher real wages and incomes of workers.

The analysis of manufacturing sector data tells a similar story. In general terms, the manufacturing sector also experienced a period of rapid economic growth during most of the 1990s, and a period of reduced growth at the end of the 1990s and beginning of the 2000s. The high growth rates in production and employment exhibited by the manufacturing sector during most of the 1990s permitted productivity to stay at a constant level during that period. Coupled with the foregoing, real wages and wage/price indexes increased faster than productivity, reducing the manufacturing sector's profitability and competitive position. During the economic crisis at the end of the 1990s and beginning of the 2000s, manufacturing firms reduced employment in order to achieve productivity gains. Real wages, however, still experienced high growth rates.

The analysis of the changes that occurred in the structure of employment and in the productivity of various sectors and occupations—especially of those where poor are engaged in large numbers—shows that economic growth has not translated into growth of productive employment. In general terms, the poor have remained in low-productivity employment. This trend has meant that real wages and earnings—the main channels through which the benefits of higher output growth and increased productivity are likely to reach the poor—have been largely depressed for the poorest and least-qualified segments of the labor force.

The most important shift was the continuous migration of workers from rural to urban areas as a means of escaping from extreme poverty. The large disparities existing between urban and rural incomes, coupled with the differentiated access by urban and rural households to basic services such as education, health, and water, have also promoted urban migration.

In rural areas, the largest share of workers are engaged in agricultural activities, which generate the lowest-paid jobs and the highest poverty incidence. Other rural activities generate better-paid jobs, but their incidence in total rural employment is very limited. In urban areas, employment is mostly concentrated in the service sectors, which present the fastest-growing employment creation over time. However, the employment created in the service sectors was of very low productivity and poorly paid—for instance, in activities such as commerce, transport, and other services.

The share of informal labor categories in total employment—self-employed and family workers—was the highest in both urban and rural areas, being much higher in the case of rural areas. Besides, informal labor categories of employment presented much lower real income levels vis-à-vis formal employment (e.g., employees, employers, professionals, etc.). Real incomes earned by informal workers in turn tended to stagnate over time, presenting only very moderate increases. Consequently, poverty incidence was highest among informal labor categories.

At the micro level of households, the analysis of the existing linkage between poverty and employment was carried out through an econometric Probit model, linking a number of variables that could influence the probability of a household being poor in terms of inadequate income. The variables tested involved three categories: first, human capital–related variables, such as education and skill levels of working members of households, and sex and age of household head; second, employment-related variables, such as the type of activity where the household head is engaged; and third, asset-related variables, such as a household's access to productive assets and to any form of

Table 6.17   Restricted Labor Demand Function

Dependent variable: *LGL?*
Method: Pooled least squares
Date: 03/13/03
Time: 18:07
Sample (adjusted): 1990–2001
Included observations: 12 after adjusting end points
Number of cross sections used: 5
Total panel (balanced) observations: 60

Variable	Coefficient	Standard Error	*t*-Statistic	Probability
C	0.106680	0.220535	0.483734	0.6305
LGL?(–1)	0.970237	0.057365	16.91342	0.0000
LGQ?	0.172912	0.051599	3.351059	0.0015
LGWR?	–0.134446	0.032306	–4.161691	0.0001
LGE?	–0.152975	0.044444	–3.442006	0.0011

R^2	0.930799	Mean dependent variable	4.824341
Adjusted R^2	0.925767	Standard deviation dependent variable	0.182696
Standard error of regression	0.049777	Sum squared resid	0.136277
Log likelihood	97.48605	F-statistic	184.9479
Durbin-Watson statistic	1.012769	Probability (F-statistic)	0.000000

financial credit. The main results obtained were that educational and occupational interventions appear to provide the most important variables in reducing poverty. Moving workers from low-productivity agricultural activities to more productive jobs in the manufacturing or service sector can contribute to poverty reduction. However, sustained, larger reductions in poverty should be sought through education and therefore through changes in the structure of the labor force made possible by better education. Finally, access of households

Table 6.18   Unrestricted Labor Demand Function

Dependent variable: *LGL?*
Method: Pooled least squares
Date: 03/13/03
Time: 18:01
Sample (adjusted): 1990–2001
Included observations: 12 after adjusting end points
Number of cross sections used: 5
Total panel (balanced) observations: 60

Variable	Coefficient	Standard Error	*t*-Statistic	Probability
C	−0.313785	0.440903	−0.711686	0.4809
31—*LGL31*(−1)	0.791183	0.378850	2.088378	0.0433
32—*LGL32*(−1)	0.174964	0.218077	0.802301	0.4272
33—*LGL33*(−1)	0.721715	0.173615	4.156995	0.0002
35—*LGL35*(−1)	−0.354389	0.330269	−1.073030	0.2899
37—*LGL37*(−1)	0.980342	0.228618	4.288133	0.0001
31—*LGQ31*	0.300756	0.653815	0.460002	0.6481
32—*LGQ32*	0.688818	0.155737	4.422955	0.0001
33—*LGQ33*	0.369936	0.121081	3.055280	0.0040
35—*LGQ35*	1.002977	0.312818	3.206260	0.0027
37—*LGQ37*	0.115499	0.168812	0.684187	0.4979
31—*LGWR31*	−0.270459	0.155228	−1.742337	0.0893
32—*LGWR32*	−0.003292	0.093341	−0.035265	0.972
33—*LGWR33*	−0.688852	0.175475	−3.925643	0.0003
35—*LGWR35*	−0.495569	0.164076	−3.020359	0.0044
37—*LGWR37*	−0.126456	0.054587	−2.316580	0.0259
31—*LGE31*	−0.013439	0.486091	−0.027647	0.9781
32—*LGE32*	0.203935	0.316064	0.645233	0.5226
33—*LGE33*	−0.006992	0.122433	−0.057111	0.9547
35—*LGE35*	0.422884	0.347879	1.215606	0.2314
37—*LGE37*	−0.018540	0.279329	−0.066372	0.9474

R^2	0.975371	Mean dependent variable		4.824341
Adjusted R^2	0.962741	Standard deviation		
Standard error		dependent variable		0.182696
of regression	0.035265	Sum squared resid		0.048501
Log likelihood	128.4789	F-statistic		77.22581
Durbin-Watson statistic	1.603635	Probability (F-statistic)		0.000000

Table 6.19 Probit Model to Determine Household's Probability of Being Poor

	Description of Variables
Fgt_0	probability of being poor: 1 = poor, 0 = nonpoor
Human capital variables	
sex_1	sex of household head: 0 = female, 1 = male
Age_1	age of household head
Mem10_1	number of household members between 10 and 17 years of age
Mem18_1	number of household members between 18 and 59 years of age
Sizhh1	household size
Sizhh2	square power of household size
Edumaxad	maximum educational level attained by any household member
Employment variables	
Primin_1	number of household members employed in primary sector
Secind_1	number of household members employed in secondary sector
Terind_1	number of household members employed in tertiary sector
Formal_1	number of household members employed in formal sector
Urb_rur	area of residence: 1 = urban, 0 = rural
Asset variables	
actfis_1	number of physical assets owned by household (max. 5)
	own house
	land in urban area
	land in rural area
	automobile
	agriculture equipment
actfin_1	number of financial assets owned by household (max. 2)
	bank account
	household's lending to other household
accfin_1	access to formal lending (max. 2)
	bank debt due to mortgages
	credit cards
acnofo_1	access to informal credit

Model 1 Results

probit fgt_0_1 sex_1 age_1 tonge_1 edu_19_1 mi10_17 mi18_59 sizehh_1 nro1_
> 1 actfis_1 actfin_1 accfin acnofo secind_j terind_j
Iteration 0:   log likelihood = –3211.8721
Iteration 1:   log likelihood = –2406.7599
Iteration 2:   log likelihood = –2360.1784
Iteration 3:   log likelihood = –2359.4182
Iteration 4:   log likelihood = –2359.4178
Probit estimates
  Number of observations = 4,814
  LR chi^2 (14) = 1,704.91
  Probability > chi^2 = 0.0000
  Log likelihood = –2359.4178
  Pseudo-R^2 = 0.2654

continues

Table 6.19   Continued

fgt_0_1	Coefficient	Standard Error	z	P > |z|	[95% Confidence Interval]	
sexo_1	−0.0725694	0.0551229	−1.317	0.188	−0.1806083	0.0354696
edad_1	−0.0052562	0.001451	−3.623	0.000	−0.0081	−0.0024124
idioma_1	−0.4571199	0.046214	−9.891	0.000	−0.5476977	−0.366542
edu_19_1	−0.0815964	0.0052489	−15.546	0.000	−0.091884	−0.0713088
mi10_17	−0.1059237	0.0293214	−3.613	0.000	−0.1633926	−0.0484548
mi18_59	−0.1866701	0.0277048	−6.738	0.000	−0.2409706	−0.1323697
sizehh_1	−0.0159093	0.0034044	−4.673	0.000	−0.0225819	−0.0092368
nro1_1	0.5216645	0.0378812	13.771	0.000	0.4474188	0.5959103
actfis_1	−0.1889644	0.0248915	−7.592	0.000	−0.2377508	−0.1401781
actfin_1	−0.3436363	0.0549225	−6.257	0.000	−0.4512824	−0.2359902
accfin	−0.3650109	0.0989872	−3.687	0.000	−0.5590223	−0.1709996
acnofo	−0.133739	0.0906275	−1.476	0.140	−0.3113656	0.0438875
secind_j	−0.2906761	0.0803098	−3.619	0.000	−0.4480804	−0.1332719
terind_j	−0.5171673	0.0508132	−10.178	0.000	−0.6167593	−0.4175753
constant	0.7582848	0.1195465	6.343	0.000	0.5239779	0.9925916

Model 2 Results

probit fgt_0_1 sex_1 age_1 tonge_1 edu_19_1 mi10_17 mi18_59 urbrur_1 sizehh_
> 1 nro1_1 actfis_1 actfin_1 accfin acnofo
Iteration 0:   log likelihood = −3211.8721
Iteration 1:   log likelihood = −2439.1559
Iteration 2:   log likelihood = −2398.5838
Iteration 3:   log likelihood = −2398.0293
Iteration 4:   log likelihood = −2398.0291
Probit estimates
    Number of observations = 4,814
    LR chi^2 (13) = 1,627.69
    Probability > chi^2 = 0.0000
    Log likelihood = −2,398.0291
    Pseudo-R^2 = 0.2534

fgt_0_1	Coefficient	Standard Error	z	P > |z|	[95% Confidence Interval]	
sexo_1	−0.0776944	0.0549574	−1.414	0.157	−0.185409	0.0300201
edad_1	−0.0031314	0.0014485	−2.162	0.031	−0.0059704	−0.0002923
idioma_1	−0.4441858	0.046145	−9.626	0.000	−0.5346284	−0.3537432
edu_19_1	−0.0844294	0.0054174	−15.585	0.000	−0.0950472	−0.0738115
mi10_17	−0.1324239	0.0288686	−4.587	0.000	−0.1890053	−0.0758425
mi18_59	−0.1886	0.0275327	−6.850	0.000	−0.2425632	−0.1346369
urbrur_1	−0.2845641	0.0546332	−5.209	0.000	−0.3916433	−0.1774849
sizehh_1	−0.0159114	0.0033971	−4.684	0.000	−0.0225696	−0.0092532
nro1_1	0.5250981	0.0377258	13.919	0.000	0.4511569	0.5990394
actfis_1	−0.1712407	0.0253687	−6.750	0.000	−0.2209625	−0.1215189
actfin_1	−0.3475555	0.0544549	−6.382	0.000	−0.4542851	−0.240826
accfin	−0.3895738	0.0985812	−3.952	0.000	−0.5827895	−0.1963582
acnofo	−0.13023	0.09006	−1.446	0.148	−0.3067444	0.0462845
constant	0.6025107	0.1174966	5.128	0.000	0.3722215	0.8327998

to productive assets and to credit can also help them to improve their living conditions.

The economic and social policy implications derived from the analysis carried out in this chapter can be grouped in actions aimed at expanding employment and income opportunities for the poor, developing the productive capacities of the poor, and increasing participation and social integration. These policies are consistent and have also been included in Bolivia's national poverty reduction strategy.

Specific policies that would contribute to expanding employment and income opportunities for the poor include promoting rural development, developing microfinance, providing support for technical assistance, and expanding infrastructure to support production. In the area of developing the productive capacity and reducing the vulnerability of the poor, the specific policies needed should include improving the quality of education and access to education, guaranteeing ownership of assets of the poor in urban areas, guaranteeing small farmers' landownership rights, and increasing the value of assets of the poor. Finally, in order to increase participation and social integration, policies should be directed at reducing inequalities and barriers based on ethnic discrimination, as well as promoting gender equity.

◼ Notes

1. The consumption-based poverty line calculated by the National Institute of Statistics and the Union of Political, Social, and Economic Analysis, which reflects the expenditure necessary to buy a "minimum food basket" and other necessities, was US$56.11 and US$52.96 in 1999 and 2000, respectively, in the case of the urban area, and US$40.11 and US$38.40 in 1999 and 2000, respectively, in the case of the rural area. Extreme poverty is defined as the proportion of households with income below the level required to purchase the minimum food basket. An Engel coefficient of 0.55 was used to derive the urban poverty line in urban areas. In rural areas, the food budget share among the poor was approximately 75 percent in 1999.

2. The degree of basic needs unsatisfaction is measured by the Unsatisfied Basic Needs Index, which captures the degree of satisfaction of basic needs with regard to minimum standards for quality and access to housing, water supply and sanitation, energy, education, and health. It measures poverty as the share of households with unsatisfied basic needs and other basic necessities.

3. The wage/price index is calculated by dividing the nominal wage—paid by the manufacturing firms—by the producer prices of the goods they produced and sell. Thus it is an indicator of the relative competitiveness of the firms over time. The real wage index, on the other hand, is calculated by dividing nominal wages—paid by the manufacturing sector—by the consumer price index and measure the purchasing power of wages over time.

4. The poverty line utilized was calculated by the National Institute of Statistics and the Union of Political, Social, and Economic Analysis, based on a basket that includes minimum food requirements and other basic expenditures. Baskets tend to vary among regions and between urban and rural areas, depending on the specific particularities of each of the regions.

7

Ethiopia: Growth, Employment, Poverty, and Policies

Mulat Demeke, Fantu Guta, and Tadele Ferede

Global advances in economic development and the progress achieved by developing countries as a whole have largely bypassed the least-developed countries. These countries continue to face appalling conditions of poverty and lack the capacity to break out of the vicious circle of low income, low investment, and low growth. By and large, LDCs have not been able to gain economic and industrial momentum and trigger a sustainable development process (Magarinos 2001).

The economic stagnation in most LDCs and their marginalized position are linked to the insufficient attention paid to the development of productive capacity in industry. It is industry more than any other productive sector that drives the process of economic growth and global integration. Indeed, linking agriculture with industry is the most powerful engine of progress. Industrial development contributes to alleviating poverty by raising productivity, creating employment, reducing risk exposure, and enhancing the physical income-generating assets of the poor.

The labor market is the main channel through which the linkages among economic growth, employment, and poverty can be analyzed. Theoretically, it is common to find a strong relationship between economic growth and changes in the level of poverty. This is so because the majority of the poor derive their main income from wage employment and hence wage income is the critical determinant of their living conditions (Yemtsove 2001). As such, the labor market serves as the main transmission between economic growth and poverty in the sense that growth reduces poverty via increasing employment or reducing unemployment, and increasing labor productivity or rising real wages (O'Connell 1999; United Nations University and World Institute for Development Economics Research 2000). The available evidence suggests that employment status is a strong correlate of poverty (Canagarajah and Mazumdar 2001; Yemtsove 2001; Berck et al. 2000).

Employment, by providing people with access to wages, constitutes one of the most important forces in improving economic equity. Without sufficient growth in employment opportunities, the ability of an economy to eradicate poverty and inequality would be limited.

In Ethiopia, the size of the labor force continues to grow (more quickly) than the ability of the economy to provide new employment opportunities. As a result, the poverty situation in the country is one of the worst in the world and shows no significant sign of improvement over time. According to a recent study, 45.5 percent of the total population lived below the absolute poverty line in 1995–1996 (based on a minimum intake of 2,200 kilocalories per day and provision for some basic nonfood expenditure—i.e., equivalent to US$139 per capita income in aggregate). Despite various policy reforms and efforts to boost agricultural production, the proportion of people living below the absolute poverty line remained 44.2 percent in 1999–2000 (Ministry of Finance and Economic Development [MOFED] 2002). The change between 1995–1999 and 1999–2000 was not statistically significant. Poverty is also more widespread in rural than in urban areas.

It has been argued that the Ethiopian labor market has remained unresponsive to policy reforms (Krishnan, Selassie, and Dercon 1998). The unemployment rate declined slightly with limited increase in private sector employment and self-employment between 1994 and 1997. Real wages stagnated in the private sector but increased slightly in the public sector over the same period. The records in the labor market contrast sharply with the strong recovery of the economy. Previous studies focused on the determinants of poverty, distribution of income, or linkage between growth and poverty alone (on urban areas, see Bigsten and Negatu 1999; K. Yohannes 1996; Mekonnen 1996; Goitom 1996; and Abdulhamid 1996; on rural areas, see Krishnan, Selassie, and Dercon 1998; Dercon 1998, 2001; Bevan and Bereket 1996; B. Yohannes 1996; and Tassew 2002). Recent studies by G. Alemayehu, S. Abebe, and J. Weeks (2003) and S. Bigsten and colleagues (2002) used data on rural and urban household surveys to assess the link between economic growth and poverty in rural and urban areas of Ethiopia. None of these studies address, systematically, the links among growth, poverty, employment, and policies in the country. Hence an in-depth investigation of poverty and its linkage with economic growth and employment is required for informed decisionmaking and redirecting policies and strategies for economic growth in a more pro-poor direction.

It has been argued that employment serves as the principal channel through which the link between economic growth and poverty can be established. As a result, it is important to closely examine wages and earnings, as they help us in assessing how the results of economic growth and increased productivity are transmitted to the poor. The central objective of the study is therefore to establish quantitative relationships among growth, employment, poverty, and policies in the Ethiopian context. The specific objectives of the study are to examine the trends of output, employment, and other social indicators in Ethiopia; break down the impact of growth into employment, productivity, and multiple effects; quantify the likely impacts of alternative public policies on employment and poverty; and suggest policy recommendations.

In order to address these objectives, both descriptive and econometric techniques are employed. The main analytic tool is a type of macro-micro simulation model that is used to analyze the links among growth, employment, poverty, and policies in Ethiopia. This method is outlined later in the chapter. The analysis is based on the 1999–2000 rural and urban household surveys collected by the Department of Economics of Addis Ababa University. The rural sample size consists of 1,576 households in eighteen different sites located in various regions and agro-ecological zones of the country. A sample of 1,500 urban households was drawn from seven major urban centers of the country: Addis Ababa (capital city), Awassa, Bahir Dar, Dessie, Dire Dawa, Jimma, and Mekelle. The distribution of the sample households by urban centers is 900 from Addis Ababa, 125 from Dire Dawa, 75 from Awassa, and 100 from each of the other four cities.

In addition, data for this study have come from various sources, including national accounts statistics; 1995–1996 and 1999–2000 surveys of household income, consumption, and expenditure; the 1999 national labor force survey; and various industrial establishment surveys, welfare monitoring surveys, and population censuses.

■ Economic Growth and Poverty

Ethiopia is among the least-developed countries in the world. Its per capita income, although it varies slightly from one source to another, is estimated at around $100 per annum. Almost half of Ethiopia's more than 60 million people can hardly afford the minimum basic food requirements.

The past regime, which ruled from the mid-1970s to the 1980s, followed a centrally planned economic policy system. The main objectives of this government, also known as the Derge, in taking over the commanding heights of the economy were to ensure promotion of social justice and equity, to generate more resources required to accelerate economic development for improving the living standards of the people, and to undertake construction and management of the economy through planning and a resource allocation system that would ensure steady progress in economic and social development (Eshetu and Manyazewal 1992, 9).

In order to achieve these broad objectives, a number of economic measures were taken, including nationalization of all banks, insurance companies, industrial and commercial firms, and land reform, which made all land the property of the state. Later the economic and social goals incorporated in the Workers Party of Ethiopia were given as accelerating the growth of the productive forces so as to build a strong and internally self-sustaining national economy free from the influences of capitalist markets; expanding, strengthening, and ensuring the dominance of the socialist production relations with a view to creating a conducive environment for the growth of the productive forces, and expanding socialist economic organizations and management; and accelerating sustained growth of the standard of living and cultural well-being of the working people (Eshetu and Manyazewal 1992, 10).

There was also no room for the participation of the private sector under the former government. This was clearly stated in the declaration of 1974, as follows: "resources that are crucial for economic development or that are of such a character that they provide indispensable service to the community, will have to be brought under government control or ownership" (Eshetu and Manyazewal 1992, 9). The ceiling on private investment was set at 250,000 birr for a domestic investor and US$500,000 for a foreign investor. This kind of environment was not very conducive for the private sector, as the economic principles and policies were derived from antimarket and antiprivate ideological motivation.

By and large, the Derge regime presided over an economy that was progressively collapsing as a result of poor macroeconomic policies, economic mismanagement, protracted war and internal instability, and recurrent drought. These, coupled with a population growth rate of around 2.9 percent per annum, led to a decline in the welfare of the society at large. The crisis of the 1980s called for substantial economic, political, and institutional reform to reverse the retrogression.

Following the change of government in 1991, the transitional government of Ethiopia, led by the Ethiopian People's Revolutionary Democratic Forces, adopted stabilization and structural adjustment programs (SAPs) that called for significant policy reforms. Stabilization policies emphasized the reduction of the government budget deficit, credit control, and the like, while structural adjustment policies focused on removing constraints on the supply side and paying close attention to the production of export crops through depreciation of the real exchange rate and other incentives. A number of measures were introduced in the 1990s as part of the SAPs. These included, among others, devaluation of the domestic currency against US currency and interbank determination of exchange rates, abolition of interest rate ceilings, removal of subsidies, tax reform (lowering the marginal tax rates and broadening the tax base), reduction of tariffs and removal of nontariff barriers, simplification of licensing procedures, reorganization of the customs authority, deregulation of prices, and privatization of public enterprises.

The devaluation in September 1992 resulted in an exchange rate of 5 birr for US$1 (i.e., the birr was devalued by about 58.6 percent). The administrative foreign exchange allocation was also replaced by an auction system. The commercial banks can now engage in retail trading of foreign exchange obtained through participation in the auction held by the national bank. The exchange rate of the national currency against the US dollar is thus determined by the daily auction undertaken between the commercial banks in order to encourage production for exports as well as properly managing the extent of imports. This system is considered as a transition from a fixed to a free-floating exchange rate system. While making significant advances toward liberalization in many respects, the government has also retained some policies of the former government. For instance, state ownership of rural land has remained in force, creating tenure insecurity among the farming community. Access to urban land is also secured through lease from the government, which has become bureaucratic and restrictive for private investors. The privatization program has also slowed because of corruption.

Overall Economic Performance

Growth Episodes and Sectoral Structure. The available evidence indicates that the rate of economic growth over the past three decades has been unsatisfactory. Regardless of the policy regimes, real total GDP, agricultural GDP, industrial GDP, and service GDP grew on average by 3.0, 2.1, 2.1, and 4.4 percent per annum, respectively, during the period of 1980–1981 to 2000–2001. On the other hand, the population grew on average by 2.9 percent during the same period, implying a 0.1 percent annual growth rate in per capita income.

Economic performance improved in the 1990s compared to the situation in the 1980s. The growth rate of real GDP, on average, increased from 2.3 percent in 1980/81–1991/92 to 4.6 percent in 1992/93–2000/01. The growth rates of agriculture, industry, and services were, respectively, 1.4, 0.02, and 2.8 percent during the 1980s, compared to 2.5, 5.3, and 7.5 percent during the 1990s (see Table 7.1). But the improvements failed to be sustained as the economy continued to suffer from fluctuations in weather conditions. Figure 7.1 shows that the annual growth rates of GDP, agriculture GDP, industry GDP, and service GDP were subject to substantial fluctuations due to war, drought, mismanagement, and policy failures.

Table 7.1 Growth Episodes, Ethiopia, 1980/81–2000/01

Sector	1980/81–1991/92 (%)	1992/93–2000/01 (%)
GDP at constant factor cost	2.30	4.60
Agriculture	1.40	2.50
Industry	0.02	5.30
Services	2.80	7.50

Source: Author calculations.

Figure 7.1   GDP and Sectoral Growth Rates, Ethiopia, 1981–1999

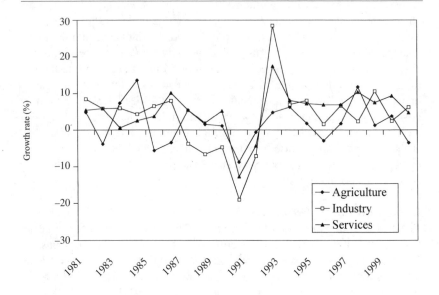

Source: Author calculations.
Note: Figures are at constant factor cost.

With regard to the sector mix of the economy, agriculture accounts for the lion's share of the economy, followed by the service and industrial sectors. Agricultural activities account for almost 50 percent of total GDP, while industry and services have contributed about 11 percent and 38 percent respectively to total GDP over the past two decades. The share of agriculture decreased slightly from 52.9 percent in the 1980s to 48.2 percent in the 1990s. The share of industry declined from 11.9 percent to 10.8 percent over the same period, while the share of services increased from 35.2 percent to 44.0 percent (see Table 7.2).

It appears that the structure of the economy essentially remained unchanged, with the dominance of the subsistence agrarian sector showing no significant sign of declining. Commercial or modern farms belonging to the state or private investors are very few and account for less than 5 percent of the agricultural output. Since 1998–1999, the share of services, including wholesale and retail trade and hotels/restaurants, banking and insurance, transport and communication, and public administration, has been expanding. The service sector also includes very small and informal businesses, which have been growing rapidly as a result of limited employment opportunities in the formal

Table 7.2   Sectoral Shares of GDP, Ethiopia, 1980/81–2000/01

Sector	1980/81–1991/92 (%)	1992/93–2000/01 (%)
Agriculture	52.90	48.20
Industry	11.90	10.80
Services	35.20	44.00

Source: Author calculations.

sector. The industrial sector consists of state-owned large- and medium-scale manufacturing activities that rely on outdated technology and inefficient management. Most of these companies have found it very difficult to compete in a liberalized market environment. Similarly, small-scale manufacturing and handicraft activities lack the capacity to compete with cheap and superior products imported from abroad.

Other Macroeconomic Indicators. Both gross domestic savings and gross domestic investment showed improvements in the 1990s, owing to policy reforms in almost all spheres of the economy. For example, the amounts of domestic private investment and foreign direct investment have increased, albeit sluggishly (MOFED 2002).

The available evidence suggests that inflation has never been out of control in Ethiopia. It has been observed within single digits, usually below 5 percent except in 1994–1995 (MOFED 2002). However, price movements in the country are highly correlated with agricultural production (especially food production). For instance, the inflation rate was 0.9 percent in 1995–1996, while it was 4.2 percent in 1999–2000 (see Table 7.3). The former period was characterized by favorable weather conditions and a bumper harvest, implying low food prices, which is the major element determining the general price level. The period 1999–2000 was marked by drought with low agricultural production and relatively higher food prices. The national inflation rate was below zero (–7.2 percent) in 2000–2001, due to good weather conditions and a better performance of the food subsector.

Table 7.3   Inflation Trends, Ethiopia, 1995/96–2000/01 (percentages)

	1995–1996	1997–1998	1998–1999	1999–2000	2000–2001
National	0.9	3.9	3.9	4.2	–7.2
Urban	—	4.3	4.8	5.7	–3.5
Rural	—	3.8	3.7	3.8	–8.1

Sources: National Bank of Ethiopia 2001; Ministry of Finance and Development 2002.

Ethiopia is also characterized by a very high rate of population growth. The total population more than doubled during the past three decades, increasing from 29.1 million in 1972 to 67.2 million in 2002 (National Office of Population 2000). The sharp increase in the annual growth rate of population from 0.2 percent at the beginning of the century to 3 percent in the 1980s was mainly due to an increase in fertility rate and a decline in mortality.

The impact of rapid population growth on the labor force is twofold. First, a decline in mortality augments survival of the existing labor force. Second, it increases the size of the labor force by adding new entrants into the labor market. The labor force is not only determined by population growth but also by other factors, such as sex, skill, and locational composition of the population. The total labor force increased from 14.7 million in 1984 to 26.5 million in 1994 (see Table 7.4). The total labor force participation rate increased from 0.35 in 1984 to 0.50 in 1994. Both urban and rural labor force participation rates increased between the two census periods.

The trends of wage employment in the modern sector leave much to be desired in Ethiopia. Total wage employment increased from 90,070 (0.6 percent of the labor force) in 1983–1984 to just 95,707 (0.4 percent of the labor force) in 1999–2000. Total wage employment declined by 0.84 percent per annum during the period 1983/84–1991/92. In the reform period 1992/93–1999/00, total wage employment increased by 1.9 percent per year. However, the growth rate was well below the growth rate of the labor force, and unemployment remained rampant in the urban areas.

According to Ethiopia's 1999 national labor force survey, the unemployment rate using the current status approach for the total country was 8.0 percent in 1999. But the unemployment rate for the urban areas was 26.4 percent, about five times higher than in the rural areas (5.1 percent). The incidence of unemployment also varied by sex. In urban areas, unemployment among females was about 34 percent, compared to 18.3 percent among males. The same pattern holds for rural areas, where 8.6 percent of females and 2.4 percent of males were reported to be unemployed.

Trends in Poverty

Poverty reduction is a major national agendum in many developing countries. In Ethiopia, poverty reduction is the priority of development policy, and a poverty reduction strategy paper has been prepared. This section presents the poverty profile based on the Central Statistical Authority's 1995–1996 and 1999–2000 household income, consumption, and expenditure surveys, which were used in the preparation of the PRSP.

Structure of Income and Consumption. The household income, consumption, and expenditure surveys revealed that own-account agricultural enterprise was the main source of income for the rural population, while wages, salaries,

227

Table 7.4 Urban and Rural Labor Forces, Ethiopia, 1984 and 1994

Census Year	Total Population (thousands)			Participation Rate (%)			Labor Force (thousands)		
	Urban	Rural	Total	Urban	Rural	Total	Urban	Rural	Total
1984	4,869.3	37,747.6	42,616.9	0.308	0.352	0.346	1,499.9	13,292.6	14,742.5
1994	7,323.2	46,154.1	53,477.3	0.380	0.517	0.496	2,757.3	23,745.8	26,503.1

Source: Ethiopian Central Statistical Authority, 1984 and 1994.

bonuses, overtime payments, and allowances were important sources of income for the urban households in 1999–2000 (MOFED 2002). Agricultural income proxied by rural income per capita decreased from 1,035.33 birr (US$159.04) in 1995–1996 to 994.71 birr (US$121.31) in 1999–2000, whereas urban income per capita increased marginally from 1,411.32 (US$216.79) to 1,452.54 birr (US$177.14) over the same period. Consistent with the low level of income, food accounted for a significant proportion of households' total expenditure—on average, 60 percent in 1995–1996 and 65 percent in 1999–2000. Rural households spend a higher proportion of their income on food than do their urban counterparts—for example, they spend 60 percent compared to 56 percent of the household budget in 1995–1996 (see Table 7.5). The pattern showed no change in the 1999–2000 surveys (67 percent compared to 56 percent) (Ministry of Economic Development and Cooperation [MEDAC] 1999; MOFED 2002).

The national per capita consumption expenditure in real terms was 1,088 birr (US$167.10) and 1,057 birr (US$128.87) in 1995–1996 and 1999–2000 respectively. In other words, real per capita consumption expenditure tended to decrease over this period. Real per capita consumption expenditure in rural areas declined, compared to a marginal increase in urban areas.

The available evidence indicates that consumption inequality is low in Ethiopia. Consumption inequality at the national level, measured by the Gini coefficient, remained more or less unchanged during the period under consideration. But it increased marginally in urban areas in 1999–2000 as compared to 1995–1996 (0.34 to 0.38) in urban areas, while it decreased marginally in rural areas (0.27 to 0.26). The Gini coefficients of income distribution are relatively higher, especially in urban areas, increasing from 0.55 in 1995–1996 to 0.57 in 1999–2000, with corresponding figures of 0.35 and 0.34 in rural

Table 7.5   Structure of Household Income and Food Consumption, Ethiopia, 1995–1996 and 1999–2000

	1995–1996		1999–2000	
	Income per Capita (birr)	Food Consumption (%)	Income per Capita (birr)	Food Consumption (%)
Rural households	1,035.33 (US$159.04)	60	994.73 (US$121.31)	67
Urban households	1,411.32 (US$216.79)	56	1,452.54 (US$177.14)	56
National	1,087.83 (US$167.10)	60	1,056.71 (US$128.87)	65

Sources: Ministry of Economic Development and Cooperation 1999; Ministry of Finance and Economic Development 2002.

areas. There is a need for a more pro-poor and employment-friendly growth pattern in urban areas.

The distribution of household income/consumption is reported in Table 7.6 using the Addis Ababa University dataset.[1] On average, about 84 percent of the rural sample households and 65 percent of the urban sample households had an annual income per capita of less than 1,800 birr (US$219.51)—equating to a monthly income of less than 150 birr (US$18.29), which was below the minimum wage rate in 1999–2000. Only 7 percent of rural households had an income greater than 2,300 birr (US$280.49), compared to 24 percent of urban households. Income/consumption inequality was relatively high in urban areas (0.53) compared to rural areas (0.37).

Poverty Indexes. As indicated earlier, poverty indexes have been estimated based on the minimum calorie requirement for subsistence (i.e., 2,200 kilocalories per day) and basic nonfood expenditure, which together amount to 1,075 birr (US$165.13) per annum, representing the absolute poverty index. The results show that, in aggregate, none of the indicators of poverty indexes changed significantly between 1995–1996 and 1999–2000 (see Table 7.7). The headcount poverty indexes were 45.5 percent in 1995–1996 and 44.2 percent in 1999–2000 at the national level.

The headcount, poverty gap, and squared poverty gap indexes decreased marginally in rural areas in 1999–2000 compared to 1995–1996. However, this decline in poverty is not consistent with the performance of the agricultural sector. It is important to recall that real agricultural output increased by only 1.9 percent per annum between 1995–1996 and 1999–2000, compared to an increase of the rural population by about 3 percent per annum. This apparent

Table 7.6   Distribution of Annual Income/Consumption per Capita, Ethiopia, 1999–2000

Income Interval (birr)	Rural (%)	Urban (%)
286–786	39.73	32.73
787–1,287	30.77	19.43
1,288–1,788	13.37	12.67
1,789–2,289	7.39	9.13
2,290–2,790	3.44	5.82
2,791–3,291	1.57	3.23
3,292–3,792	1.49	2.60
3,793–4,293	0.52	2.20
4,294–4,794	0.32	1.26
4,795 or above	1.42	10.94
Gini coefficient	0.37	0.53

Source: Author calculations from Addis Ababa University dataset.

Table 7.7   Poverty Trends, Ethiopia, 1995–1996 and 1999–2000

	1995–1996			1999–2000		
	Rural	Urban	National	Rural	Urban	National
Headcount index (P_0)	0.475	0.332	0.455	0.454	0.369	0.442
Poverty gap index (P_1)	0.134	0.099	0.129	0.122	0.101	0.119
Squared poverty gap (P_2)	0.053	0.041	0.051	0.046	0.039	0.045

Source: Ministry of Finance and Economic Development 2002.

decline in per capita output growth is also reflected in the decline of per capita rural income. The Addis Ababa University dataset also indicates that the level of poverty in 1999–2000 was much higher than what is reported in Table 7.6 (based on government data), which shows that the headcount and poverty gap indexes increased while the squared poverty gap index declined in urban areas over the same period. Nevertheless, the changes in all the indexes are not statistically significant (even at 10 percent).[2]

According to MOFED, aggregate poverty among male-headed households, measured by the headcount index, decreased from 0.461 in 1995–1996 to 0.444 in 1999–2000. On the other hand, the headcount poverty index among female-headed families tended to increase (from 0.425 to 0.434) over the same period (see Table 7.8). Surprisingly, the evidence indicates that the headcount poverty index is slightly higher for male- than for female-headed households in rural areas in both periods. It has been documented that customary laws and practices are patriarchal and have significantly constrained women's access to resources both within and outside the home. For instance,

Table 7.8   Gender Dimensions of Poverty, Ethiopia, 1995–1996 and 1999–2000

		1995–1996			1999–2000		
	Gender	Rural	Urban	National	Rural	Urban	National
Headcount index (P_0)	Male-headed	0.477	0.329	0.461	0.455	0.339	0.444
	Female-headed	0.460	0.337	0.425	0.447	0.492	0.434
Poverty gap index (P_1)	Male-headed	0.135	0.09	0.131	0.123	0.086	0.120
	Female-headed	0.129	0.106	0.123	0.118	0.134	0.115
Squared poverty gap (P_2)	Male-headed	0.053	0.039	0.051	0.046	0.030	0.045
	Female-headed	0.051	0.046	0.049	0.044	0.051	0.043

Source: Ministry of Finance and Economic Development 2002.

land is managed and administered at the village level by local officials who operate with traditional gender biases. The problem is compounded by the absence of women's grassroots groups, due to both past experience under the former regime and cultural factors.[3]

As expected, poverty is higher in households headed by farmers than in households headed by nonfarmers. About 48 percent and 45 percent of the farming households lived below the poverty line in 1995–1996 and in 1999–2000 respectively (see Table 7.9), compared to 35 percent and 41 percent of nonfarming households.

Other Basic Welfare Indicators

Apart from income or consumption, education, access to clean water, sanitation, mortality and fertility rates, and life expectancy are important components of welfare. It is widely accepted that human capital accumulation is the engine of socioeconomic transformation or development in any country. It is in recognition of this fact that recent growth models incorporate human capital, proxied by skill acquired from education, as an important element of a production function, endogenous to the system. People in the economy accumulate human capital by spending time learning new skills (Jones 2002). All available evidence indicates that there is an inverse relationship between education and poverty. In Ethiopia, for example, poverty indices are higher for illiterates than for literates, by 45 percent in rural areas and by 85 percent in urban areas (MOFED 2002).

Despite the critical importance of education, Ethiopia has one of the highest adult and youth illiteracy rates in the world as well as in sub-Saharan African countries (see Table 7.10). The adult illiteracy rates for males and females were, respectively, 57 percent and 68 percent in 1999–2000. The youth illiteracy rates for males and females were 46 percent and 48 percent respectively. By contrast, in 1999, the sub-Saharan adult illiteracy rates for males and females were 31 percent and 47 percent, respectively, while youth illiteracy rates for males and females were 18 percent and 27 percent respectively. According to MOFED (2002), the literacy rate among the rural population in 1999 was only 21.8 percent, compared to 70.4 percent in urban areas.

Table 7.9 Employment Dimensions of Poverty, Ethiopia, 1995–1996 and 1999–2000

	1995–1996			1999–2000		
	P_0	P_1	P_2	P_0	P_1	P_2
Farmers	0.475	0.135	0.053	0.452	0.121	0.045
Nonfarmers	0.348	0.024	0.104	0.405	0.112	0.043

Source: Ministry of Finance and Economic Development 2002.

Table 7.10   Country Comparisons in Education Outcomes, 1999

	Adult Illiteracy Rate (%) (age 15+)		Youth Illiteracy Rate (%) (age 15–24)	
	Male	Female	Male	Female
Ethiopia	57	68	46	48
Kenya	12	25	4	6
Tanzania, United Republic of	16	34	7	12
Uganda	23	45	15	29
Sub-Saharan Africa	31	47	18	27

Source: World Bank 2000c.

Gross primary, secondary, and tertiary enrollment rates in Ethiopia are also among the lowest in the world. The situation has not changed significantly, even after the postreform effort to expand enrollment. Both gross enrollment and net enrollment rates were lower for rural areas (52.4 percent gross enrollment and 28.0 percent for net enrollment rates in 1999–2000) than for their urban counterparts (105.4 percent for gross enrollment and 74.5 percent for net enrollment rates). Similarly, females have lower enrollment rates than males in both rural and urban Ethiopia.[4] The government has set a goal of achieving universal primary education by 2015 (MEDAC 1999).

Similarly, health service coverage in Ethiopia is among the lowest in the world. The potential health service coverage, for instance, was limited to 51.2 percent of the population in 2000–2001. There were only 4 physicians per 100,000 people in 2000. The average infant mortality rate per thousand was 106.1, and the total fertility rate was 6.8 percent (Organization for Economic Cooperation and Development 2001). One in every six children dies before celebrating his or her fifth birthday, with 58 percent of these deaths occurring during the first year of life (Ethiopian Economic Association 2000). Child malnutrition, measured by wasting and stunting, is also a very serious problem in the country.

The average life expectancy at birth in Ethiopia was fifty-one years in 1994, compared to fifty-two years in 1984. Life expectancy has declined further in recent years because of the AIDS pandemic, especially among the working-age group. According to the World Bank (2003f), life expectancy at birth was only forty-two years in 2000. HIV/AIDS is now the major development challenge facing the country.

Access to economic infrastructure is very important for the welfare of the population. A person living in rural areas, on average, needs to travel 5.9 kilometers to reach a food market. The average distance to postal service, a telephone booth, an all-weather road, a milling house, and cooking fuel is 21.2, 21.0, 11.4, 4.3, and 1.7 kilometers respectively. Only 3 and 12 percent of the population have access to private and public tap water, respectively. Such safe water sources are largely limited to urban areas: 81 percent in urban areas as opposed to just 5 percent in rural areas. The bulk of the rural population (81 percent) depends on unprotected water sources—wells, springs, rivers, lakes, and ponds.

◼ Linkages Among Economic Growth, Employment, and Poverty

Employment is expected to serve as the principal channel through which the link between economic growth and poverty can work. An employment-intensive growth, accompanied by a rise in labor productivity, is key to reducing poverty via the income effect in the short run and through raising the productive capacity of the future work force in the long run. It is therefore important to examine the trends in employment in relation to output growth, and wages and earnings, as these factors are critical in transmitting the benefits of economic growth and increases in productivity to the poor.

Employment Intensity of Growth
The focus here is to investigate the trends in employment and output for various economic activities. Furthermore, sectoral shares of employment and output and their movements over time will also be assessed, which helps in assessing whether there has been a structural shift in the economy. Finally, estimates of sectoral employment elasticities together with economywide employment elasticities will be examined. Based on the estimates of output elasticity of employment and productivity growth, one can make a case for an employment-intensive growth strategy that is accompanied by a rise in productivity, which helps in demonstrating the importance of such a strategy in reducing poverty over time and also achieving higher economic growth in the future.

Trends in Employment and Output
Employment trends. Employment in the economy grew, on average, by 5.9 percent from 1984 to 1994. Information obtained from the 1984 and 1994 population and housing censuses was used to calculate sectoral and economywide employment growth. An additional source of information on employment was Ethiopia's 1999 national labor force survey, conducted by the Central Statistical Authority. A comparison between the data provided by the 1994 population census and the 1999 labor force survey shows a 0.6 percent annual decline in economywide employment between these two years. Of course, the data from the population census may not be comparable to those from the national labor force survey. The focus of the labor force survey is employment, while that of the population census is population growth and its distribution. If the datasets are

comparable and reliable, the decline in employment between 1994 and 1999 (which can be regarded as the postreform period) seems to be mainly due to the decline in employment in the agricultural sector. Besides, there was a decline in employment in the transport, storage, and communication sectors. On the other hand, it can be seen from Table 7.11 that there was a large increase in employment in the construction, trade, and financial intermediation sectors during the postreform period. Data on employment in the manufacturing sector are available from the annual surveys of large- and medium-scale industries. Such data, presented in Demeke, Guta, and Ferede 2003, indicate a 1.4 percent annual decline in manufacturing employment during the prereform period (1984/85–1991/92) and a 1.8 percent annual increase in the postreform period (1992/93–1999/00). The decline in employment in some sectors and an expansion in other sectors might reflect a structural shift in the economy, but such a conclusion would have to be qualified by what has happened to the pattern of labor productivity and real wages.

Output trends. Real output growth for the prereform program, where output is taken to be gross domestic product at constant factor cost, was on the order of 2.3 percent per annum on a log-linear trend (see Table 7.12). The maximum output growth was attained in 1986–1987, which was 14.1 percent, and the minimum output growth occurred during the 1984–1985 drought. During the prereform years, the mining and quarrying sector attained the maximum output growth (7.8 percent), followed by the distributive and other services sector (6.3 percent). Real output growths were either negative or very low for most years in other economic sectors. The turbulent period of the tran-

Table 7.11   Employment Growth by Major Economic Sector, Ethiopia, 1984–1999

Major Division	1984–1994 (% per annum)	1994–1999 (% per annum)
Agriculture, hunting, forestry, and fishing	6.0	–2.9
Mining and quarrying	4.4	0.8
Construction	7.9	24.2
Electricity, gas, and water supply	7.8	5.9
Wholesale and retail trade, and restaurants/hotels	6.9	17.2
Transport, storage, and communication	8.8	–2.7
Financial intermediation	5.7	37.3
Other services	2.2	3.5
Total	5.9	–0.6

Sources: Author calculations based on data from Ethiopia's 1984 and 1994 population and housing censuses and labor force survey.

Note: Major sector divisions based on International Standard Industrial Classification of All Economic Activities (ISIC—Rev. 2, 1968).

Table 7.12   Growth Rates of Real Output by Major Economic Sector,
Ethiopia, 1984–1999

	1984–1991 (% per annum)	1992–1999 (% per annum)
Agriculture and allied activities	3.6	1.9
Mining and quarrying	7.8	7.5
Manufacturing	–3.0	5.0
Electricity and water	4.6	2.1
Construction	–8.9	5.9
Wholesale and retail trade and hotels/restaurants	–3.1	6.7
Transport and communications	3.7	6.0
Banking, insurance, and real estate	2.4	7.2
Public administration and defense	3.4	11.3
Education and health	3.8	5.5
Domestic and other services	6.3	4.6
GDP at constant factor cost	2.3	4.6

Source: Author calculations.

sition from the command economy (1990–1991) to the market-oriented economy (1991–1992) was marked by a fall in real output.

Sectoral Shares of Employment and Output

Employment share. Agriculture is the leading sector in terms of employment share. According to the 1984 and 1994 population and housing censuses, about 89 percent of the total population were engaged in agricultural activities. The manufacturing sector accounted for about 2 percent of employment, while wholesale and retail trade and hotels/restaurants constituted about 4 percent of employment. The employment share of the domestic and other services sector stood at about 4–5 percent of total employment. The remaining sectors employed about 1 percent of the total work force.

However, the 1999 national labor force survey suggests that the structure of sectoral employment has changed significantly. According to this survey, the agricultural sector accounted for about 80 percent of employment, followed by trade and hotels/restaurants, which stood at about 10 percent. The manufacturing sector, which accounted for only about 2 percent of employment in 1984 and 1994, had a 4.4 percent share in 1999 (see Table 7.13). Between 1994 and 1999, the employment share of the agriculture sector declined from about 89 to 80 percent. It seems that there has been a shift of employment from the agricultural sector of the economy to trade and hotels/restaurants. These facts taken together may be indicative of a slight sectoral shift from occupations with lower productivity to relatively high-paying economic activities. The employment share of trade and hotels/restaurants, for example, rose to 9.6 percent in 1999, compared to a 4.2 percent share in 1994.

Table 7.13   **Employment Share by Major Economic Sector, Ethiopia, 1984–1999**

	1984 (%)	1994 (%)	1999 (%)
Agriculture, hunting, forestry, and fishing	88.6	89.3	79.6
Mining and quarrying	0.1	0.1	0.1
Manufacturing	1.6	1.8	4.4
Construction	0.3	0.3	0.9
Electricity, gas, and water supply	0.1	0.1	0.1
Wholesale and retail trade and hotels/restaurants	3.8	4.2	9.6
Transport, storage, and communication	0.4	0.6	0.5
Financial intermediation	0.1	0.1	0.4
Other services	5.1	3.6	4.4

Source: Author calculations.

Output share. The agricultural sector, which accounted for an average share of about 52 percent during the prereform period, was the largest contributor to the gross domestic product. The next largest contributing sector to GDP (measured at constant factor cost) was wholesale and retail trade and hotels/restaurants, which accounted for an average share of about 9.2 percent. Over the same period, the public administration and defense sector was the third largest contributor to GDP, with a share of 8.7 percent.

The dominance of agriculture continued after the reform program in 1992–1993, when the average share of the sector was about 49 percent, but then declined to about 44 percent in 1999–2000. The share of trade and hotels/restaurants averaged 8.3 percent, compared to 9.2 percent during the prereform period. The output share of the public administration and defense sector surprisingly started to rise after the reform program in 1992–1993. The average output share of the subsector stood at 11.7 percent, against an average share of 8.7 percent during the prereform period. A significant rise in the output share of this sector was registered after the border conflict between Ethiopia and Eritrea, and it was the second largest contributor to GDP during the postreform period (see Table 7.14).

In general, given the trends in sectoral shares of employment and output before and after the reform program, one could conclude that there has been no significant structural shift in the economy. The agricultural sector has remained the source of livelihood for the majority of the working labor force and the largest contributor to GDP.

Employment Intensity of Output. Estimation of output intensity of employment can be carried out either econometrically or using the method of arc elasticities.

**Table 7.14   Percentage Distribution of GDP by Industrial Sector,
Ethiopia, 1983–2000**

	1983–1991	1992–1999	1983–1984	1991–1992	1999–2000
Agriculture and allied activities	51.7	48.6	53.3	56.5	43.6
Mining and quarrying	0.3	0.4	0.2	0.4	0.5
Manufacturing	6.8	6.2	7.2	4.8	6.3
Electricity and water	1.5	1.6	1.3	1.8	1.5
Construction	3.5	2.6	4.0	2.1	2.5
Wholesale and retail trade and hotels/restaurants	9.2	8.3	9.9	6.2	8.7
Transport and communications	5.2	6.0	4.5	5.9	6.4
Banking, insurance, and real estate	6.0	6.6	5.8	5.9	7.1
Public administration and defense	8.7	11.7	7.7	8.0	15.2
Education and health	3.1	3.4	2.9	3.6	3.6
Domestic and other services	3.9	4.8	3.3	5.0	4.8

Source: Author calculations.
Note: Figures are at 1980–1981 constant factor cost.

Arc elasticities. The estimated arc output elasticities of employment fluctuate from period to period for most of the sectors of the economy, reflecting the
variability in employment and output growths. During the period 1984–1994
(the decade that approximates the prereform years), agriculture, manufacturing,
wholesale and retail trade, and hotels/restaurants were the most employment-
intensive sectors of the economy. In these three sectors, a 1 percent increase in
output led to employment increases of about 2, 5, and 16 respectively.

On the other hand, during the period 1994–1999 (the postreform years),
a 1 percent increase in output in agriculture, manufacturing, trade, and ho-
tels/restaurants led to a 1.2 percent fall, a 3.9 percent increase, and a 2.5 percent increase in employment, respectively (see Table 7.15). This shows that
arc output elasticities of employment were very volatile during the two periods. The estimated arc output elasticities of employment for the whole period
of 1984 to 1999 lie between the estimated employment elasticities of output
for the periods 1984–1994 and 1994–1999, with the exception of the estimate
for the construction sector. A very high but negative estimate of the arc output elasticity of employment for the construction sector during 1984–1999 is
due to the fact that the sector's output growth declined marginally while the
corresponding employment growth was very large.

The estimated elasticities for major economic sectors of the economy
suggest that investment in agriculture, manufacturing, wholesale and retail

Table 7.15   Arc Elasticity of Employment by Major Economic Sector, Ethiopia, 1984–1999

	1984–1994	1994–1999	1984–1999
Agriculture, hunting, forestry, and fishing	2.02	−1.21	1.06
Mining and quarrying	0.54	0.07	0.35
Manufacturing	5.06	3.86	4.28
Construction	−2.66	4.45	−54.56
Electricity, gas, and water supply	1.60	3.83	1.91
Wholesale and retail trade and hotels/restaurants	16.18	2.53	4.07
Transport, storage, and communication	1.86	−0.44	0.92
Financial intermediation	1.64	5.30	3.30
Other services	0.41	0.37	0.40
Total	1.91	−0.23	0.94

Source: Author calculations.

trade, and hotels/restaurants sectors would create higher employment opportunities, thereby reducing the prevailing poverty in the country. However, this employment expansion was not accompanied by a rise in labor productivity, as the estimated arc elasticities for these sectors were all above unity. An employment expansion that is not accompanied by a rise in productivity cannot help reduce poverty on a sustained basis. The only sectors in which employment expanded together with a rise in productivity were the mining and quarrying, transport, storage and communications, and domestic and other services sectors (Table 7.15). Interventions and investments in these sectors can be regarded as worthwhile in reducing poverty. As can be seen from Table 7.15, the sectoral arc elasticities fell over time, which may be a sign of revival in output growth after the adoption of the structural adjustment program.

Most of the estimated sectoral arc elasticities show that labor productivity fell over time in those sectors for which employment elasticities of output were greater than unity. Although theoretically, employment elasticities are in fact expected to fall gradually over time, as the country becomes more developed and relatively less labor-abundant, the fall in overall and sectoral employment elasticities of output from the 1984–1994 period to the 1994–1999 period may be a sign of unreliable data (obtained from the 1984 and 1994 population censuses and the 1999 national labor force survey), not an indication of economic maturity.

Econometric estimates. The econometrically estimated output elasticity of employment for the manufacturing sector contrasts sharply with the arc output elasticity of employment.[5] The estimate based on the latter approach is 3.86 for the period 1994–1999, compared to 0.1 using the former estimate (see Table

7.16). This further signifies the volatility of the estimated arc output elasticity of employment.

Employment elasticities of output were econometrically estimated for all the fifteen subsectors of the manufacturing sector, and all the estimated elasticities are below 0.5 and some are even negative, with the exception of the furniture manufacturing subsector, which stood at about unity. The estimated elasticities show that the manufacturing sector of the economy is not as labor-intensive as the arc employment elasticities suggest. However, the manufacturing sector could potentially be labor-intensive depending on the choice of technology.

Econometrically estimated employment elasticities of output for the various subsectors of the manufacturing sector suggest that employment expansion in most of the activities was accompanied by productivity growth, which is the necessary condition for reducing the prevailing poverty via increased real wages and earnings. Investment in those economic activities for which the output elasticity of employment is lower than unity is potentially capable of reducing poverty, which helps households to spend more on education and skill formation of their children. This in turn would help raise the productive

Table 7.16   Econometrically Estimated Sectoral Elasticities, Ethiopia, 1994–1999

Industrial Group	Output Elasticity of Employment	Capital Intensity Elasticity of Employment
Food and beverages	–0.02*	0.18
Tobacco	–0.11*	–0.05
Textiles	0.09	0.10*
Wearing apparel, except fur apparel	0.05*	–0.14
Tanning and dressing of leather	0.07	–0.06*
Wood and products of wood	0.19*	–0.52
Paper, paper products, and printing	0.05*	0.10
Chemicals and chemical products	0.26	0.16
Rubber and plastic products	0.45	–0.10
Other nonmetallic mineral products	0.39	–0.02*
Basic iron and steel	–0.06	–0.10
Fabricated metal products	0.38	0.04*
Machinery and equipment	0.47	0.43
Vehicles, trailers, and semitrailers	0.30	0.58*
Furniture, manufacturing not elsewhere classified	0.97	–0.20
Manufacturing sector	0.07	–0.65

Source: Author calculations.
Note: * = not statistically different from 0 at the 10 percent level of significance.

capacity of the future work force, and thus generate higher economic growth and productivity in the future.

The estimates of employment elasticities of capital intensity for the various subsectors of the manufacturing sector and the overall estimate indicate that, on average, the higher the growth in capital intensity, the lower the growth in employment, which shows an inverse relationship between growth in employment and growth in capital intensity (Table 7.16).[6]

Employment, Productivity, Real Wage Earnings, and Poverty

This section is devoted to discussion of the inverse relationships among employment growth and productivity, sources of output growth, trends in real wage earnings, and poverty. In this connection, employment and productivity effects as sources of output growth for the various sectors of the economy will be assessed. Furthermore, an attempt will be made to estimate agricultural productivity and income. Finally, the nexus of economic growth, employment expansion, and poverty reduction will be assessed.

Sources of Output Growth. During the prereform period, 1984/85–1991/92, sectoral as well as economywide output growths occurred mainly due to employment expansion rather than productivity growth, with the exception of mining and quarrying, construction, wholesale and retail trade, hotels/restaurants, and domestic and other services. During the same period, the construction, trade, and hotels/restaurants sectors experienced a negative employment effect, showing that output expansion in these sectors was caused by productivity effect rather than employment expansion (see Table 7.17). The economywide output expansion during the postreform period, 1992/93–1999/00, was largely driven by productivity growth, which was accompanied by the decline in economywide employment expansion. But the pattern of growth varied from one sector to another. Some of the sectors experienced productivity growth while others faced employment expansion. The sources of output expansion for the agricultural and electricity and water sectors were mainly employment expansion with negative productivity effect. Over the same period, the source of output growth for the remaining sectors of the economy was productivity rather than employment effect. Productivity-led growth in these sectors, with the exception of construction, trade, hotels/restaurants, and domestic and other services, where employment had been slightly rising, was not accompanied by employment expansion as compared to the prereform period.[7] As a result, the growth path during the postreform period has not helped reduce the widespread poverty in the country.

Trends in Income, Productivity, and Poverty. It has been hypothesized that, during the course of development, there is an inverse relationship between

Table 7.17 Breaking Down Output Growth by Major Economic Sector, Ethiopia, Pre- Versus Postreform Period

	Productivity Effect		Employment Effect		Multiple Effect	
	Prereform	Postreform	Prereform	Postreform	Prereform	Postreform
Agriculture and allied activities	0.39	−0.20	0.62	1.21	0.24	−0.24
Mining and quarrying	0.71	0.70	0.29	0.30	0.21	0.21
Electricity and water	0.52	−0.08	0.49	1.09	0.25	−0.08
Construction	1.25	0.63	−0.25	0.38	−0.31	0.24
Wholesale and retail trade and hotels/restaurants	1.71	0.67	−0.72	0.33	−1.23	0.22
Transport and communications	0.39	0.63	0.61	0.38	0.24	0.24
Banking, insurance, and real estate	0.06	0.69	0.95	0.31	0.06	0.22
Public administration and defense	0.35	0.80	0.66	0.20	0.23	0.16
Education and health	0.42	0.60	0.59	0.41	0.25	0.24
Domestic and other services	0.65	0.52	0.36	0.49	0.23	0.25
Total	0.18	0.51	0.98	0.49	0.18	0.25

Source: Author calculations.
Note: Output growth figures based on value added at constant factor cost.

labor productivity and employment growth. To this end, an attempt will be made to assess the relationship between productivity and employment growth using the data for the various sectors of the economy. Four different scenarios can be considered regarding the relationship between productivity and employment growth. First, there may be a positive growth in productivity accompanied by employment expansion, indicating a healthy economic growth. The second scenario is a situation where there may be low or even negative growth in both employment and labor productivity, a sign of sectoral recession or slowdown of economic activities. The third scenario refers to a situation where there may be low or negative productivity growth accompanied by employment expansion, leading to sectoral stagnation—a characteristic of a residual sector. The last scenario refers to a case where there may be negative employment expansion and positive productivity growth, indicating the occurrence of technological shift in the sector. The link between sectoral and economywide employment expansion and output growth will be examined to establish which of the different scenarios apply to the Ethiopian case.

Intertemporal variations in real wages will be examined for employees in the various activities of the manufacturing sector for which sufficient time-series data are available. Time-series data on wages and earnings in the manufacturing sector are obtained from the annual large- and medium-scale manufacturing surveys undertaken by the Central Statistical Authority.

Real Wage Earnings and Productivity in the Nonagricultural Sector. The average economywide real labor productivity growth during the prereform period was only 0.4 percent per annum on a linear trend, with the smallest productivity growth, –11.7 percent, registered in 1984–1985 (the drought year) and the highest productivity growth, 11.6 percent, recorded in 1986–1987. The lower and upper bounds on economywide real labor productivity growth indicate that the growth in labor productivity fluctuated highly during the prereform period. In terms of average real labor productivity, mining and quarrying (5.6 percent), followed by domestic and other services (4.1 percent), were the sectors that registered the highest real labor productivity growth. Employment expansion in these two sectors during the prereform period was 4.4 percent for mining and quarrying and 2.2 percent for domestic and other services. High employment expansion accompanied by high productivity growth in these two sectors indicates a healthy economic expansion. These growth rates are well above the growth in the labor force, and had such growth rates been sustained for a longer period of time they would have helped reduce the prevailing poverty to some extent. During the prereform period, wholesale and retail trade, hotels/restaurants, and construction registered average real labor productivity growth of –11.1 percent and –5.4 percent respectively. The corresponding sectoral employment expansion stood at 7.9 percent and 6.9 percent per annum. A very low or negative labor productivity accompanied by a high employment expansion is a characteristic of a sector that stagnates or serves as a residual sector. Hence, based on the available data, it would be possible to claim that trade, hotels/restaurants, and construction served as such sectors (see Table 7.18). Similarly, the average real labor productivity growth during the prereform period for the manufacturing sector was about −11.3 percent (on a log-linear trend), while the sector's employment growth stood at −1.4 percent (on a linear trend). The low level of average real labor productivity was due to the deficiency of productive capital relative to labor as reflected in the low growth rate of capital intensity of employment, which averages about 1.7 percent per annum. A very low employment expansion accompanied by a very low labor productivity growth is a sign of sectoral recession or slowdown of the economic activities in the manufacturing sector.

However, a different picture is observed during the postreform period (1992–1999). The average economywide real labor productivity growth during the postreform period was about 2.3 percent per annum. This was accompanied by a fall in employment expansion by about 0.6 percent per annum, implying a technological shift or labor-shedding in the economy. The average real labor productivity of the agricultural sector fell by about 0.4 percent during the postreform period. At the same time, agricultural employment declined by about 2.9 percent, indicating a slowdown or a recession in agricultural activities. Public administration and defense, followed by mining and quarrying, were the sectors that registered the highest labor productivity during the postreform

Table 7.18 **Average Annual Percentage Change in Real Labor Productivity Growth by Major Economic Sector, Ethiopia, 1984–1999**

	1984–1991	1992–1999
Agriculture and allied activities	1.4	−0.4
Manufacturing activities	−11.3	9.6
Mining and quarrying	5.6	5.3
Electricity and water	2.4	−0.2
Construction	−11.1	3.7
Wholesale and retail trade and hotels/restaurants	−5.4	4.5
Transport and communications	1.4	3.8
Banking, insurance, and real estate	0.1	5.0
Public administration and defense	1.2	9.1
Education and health	1.6	3.3
Domestic and other services	4.1	2.4
Average labor productivity	0.4	2.3

Source: Author calculations.
Note: Since there are no time-series employment data, all values are computed based on projections using the 1984 and 1994 census data.

period. This indicates a technological shift in the mining and quarrying sector. Most of the economic sectors experienced a healthy expansion, and the source of output growth was mainly due to productivity growth rather than employment expansion during the postreform period. Real labor productivity in the manufacturing sector rose at the rate of 9.6 percent during 1992–1999, while employment expanded at 1.8 percent per annum. Hence the performance of the manufacturing sector during the postreform period was much better than its performance during the prereform period. A positive productivity growth accompanied by employment expansion is an indication of a healthy economic development, although the rate of employment expansion was not as fast as the growth in labor force.

Wages and earnings. During the prereform period, real wages and earnings of the labor force employed in the manufacturing sector grew by about 1.8 percent per annum. Growth rates of real wages and earnings varied markedly, with an average growth rate of –18.6 percent for employees in the chemical industries, but as large as 20.2 percent on a log-linear trend for employees in the machinery and equipment industries. The majority of the economic activities in the manufacturing sector registered a fairly high growth in real wages and earnings during the prereform period (see Table 7.19).[8]

Table 7.19   Average Annual Percentage Change in Real Wage and Salary Growth by Industrial Group in Manufacturing Sector, Ethiopia, 1984–1999

	1984–1991	1992–1999
Food and beverages	2.4	9.7
Tobacco	3.8	9.4
Textiles	1.1	–0.6
Wearing apparel, except fur apparel	9.3	4.8
Tanning and dressing of leather	9.9	6.7
Wood and wood products	6.8	–5.3
Paper, paper products, and printing	5.4	8.2
Chemicals and chemical products	–18.6	16.6
Rubber and plastic products	–3.5	12.3
Other nonmetallic mineral products	–3.1	17.9
Basic iron and steel	9.2	8.2
Fabricated metal products	2.6	5.3
Machinery and equipment	20.2	–2.9
Vehicles, trailers, and semitrailers	–2.9	20.7
Furniture, manufacturing not elsewhere classified	8.9	18.6
Total	1.8	7.5

Source: Author calculations based on time-series data on nominal wages and earnings obtained from Ethiopia's annual survey of large- and medium-scale manufacturing industries.

The average growth rate of real wages and earnings for the labor force employed in the manufacturing industries during the postreform period was 7.5 percent per annum on a log-linear trend (Table 7.19). Real wages and earnings registered an average growth rate of –5.3 percent for employees of the wood industries, as opposed to the average growth rate of 20.7 percent for employees of the vehicle industries. Year-to-year fluctuations in the growth rate of real wages and earnings for the manufacturing sector were also sizable. The largest growth in real wages and earnings was registered in 1992–1993 and the lowest in 1997–1998.

Agricultural Productivity and Income. The agriculture sector attained an average real labor productivity of only 0.5 percent per annum on a linear trend. Labor productivity declined by 20 percent in 1984–1985, the year of catastrophic drought, and by more than 10 percent in 1997–1998. A high degree of volatility, induced by weather, is a major feature of Ethiopian agriculture.

Agriculture registered an employment expansion of 2.9 percent during the period 1984/85–1999/00. Low productivity growth accompanied by employment expansion suggests a sectoral stagnation, a typical feature of a sector of last resort. This is also an indication of underemployment and falling real wages. As pointed out previously, agricultural income proxied by rural income per capita has decreased, reflecting low earnings and/or falling real wages.

Although both labor productivity and output growth were volatile, the trend declined during the pre- and postreform periods. Low labor productivity in the agriculture sector might have been due to loss of soil fertility, land fragmentation, and declining farm size. It has been documented that yields did not change despite increased use of fertilizers mainly due to severe soil degradation (Demeke and Hunde 2003).

■ Modeling the Nexus of Poverty, Employment, Labor Market

This section focuses on modeling the determinants of consumption or poverty. In the process of modeling the determinants of poverty, an attempt is made to identify and quantify the links among economic growth, employment, poverty, and policies in the Ethiopian context. Simulations are also carried out to gauge the impact of socioeconomic factors on poverty.

Specification of the Empirical Model

Two approaches can be distinguished in modeling the determinants of poverty. The first approach could be described as a two-step procedure, with the first step involving modeling the determinants of the log of consumption at the household level.[9] The simplest specification of such a model could be given as:

$$\ln C_j = \beta' X_j + \varepsilon_j \tag{1}$$

where

> C_j = per capita consumption of household j
> X_j = vector of household characteristics or other determinants of consumption
> ε_j = random disturbance term, which is assumed to be normally, independently, and identically distributed with mean 0 and variance σ^2

The second step defines poverty in terms of the household's per capita consumption level, where the poverty measure for household j can be estimated by:

$$\hat{P}_{\theta j} = \left[\max \left(\left(\frac{Z - \hat{C}_j}{Z} \right), 0 \right) \right]^\theta \tag{2}$$

where

> $\hat{P}_{\theta j}$ = estimated poverty measure of household j,
> Z = poverty line
> θ = nonnegative parameter taking integer values 0, 1, and 2

Aggregate poverty of a given population is simply the weighted mean of the above poverty measure, where the weights are given by the household's size. When θ takes a value of 0, the aggregate poverty measure corresponds to the incidence of poverty, or headcount index. Similarly, when θ assumes values of 1 and 2, the aggregate poverty measure corresponds to the poverty gap and the squared poverty gap indexes respectively.[10]

The second approach, which is known as the direct modeling of the household-level poverty measure, is given by:

$$P_{\theta j} = \beta' X_j + \varepsilon_j \tag{3}$$

This direct approach to modeling the determinants of poverty has been popular and often used in research. Despite its popularity, there are several reasons (elaborated in Demeke, Guta, and Ferede 2003) why modeling household consumption is preferable to modeling household poverty levels directly.

Selection of Explanatory Variables of the Model

The set of variables that are hypothesized to determine the level of consumption, and hence poverty, may be categorized into household and community characteristics. Among the set of potential determinants of poverty, an attempt is made to choose those variables that are arguably exogenous to current consumption. For instance, variables such as current school attendance by children are omitted from the regression for the reason that such variables are outcomes, rather than determinants, of current living standards. The set of determinants of consumption may broadly be classified into several categories.

Demographic Characteristics. Included in this category are household size and its composition. Four age groups are distinguished: under 7 years, 7–17 years, 18–64 years, and 65 years and older. The number of adults in the age group 18–64 years is further split by gender, as the marginal returns may differ. To allow for nonlinearities in the relationship between consumption and household size, a quadratic term (in household size) is introduced in the regression model. The other demographic characteristics of households are age and sex of the household head. The other household characteristic that may loosely be categorized as a demographic variable is the number of adults with any physical or mental deficiency in the household.

Education. Several measures pertaining to different levels and dimensions of educational attainment by household members are included in the regression. The number of adult household members who can read and write and the number of adult household members with a primary or higher level of education are among variables hypothesized to influence consumption. Assuming that returns to male and female education may be different, the number of household members with a primary or higher level of education is differentiated by gender.

Employment. Employment characteristics are related to occupations of household members. In this connection, three employment categories are distinguished: agriculture, industry, and distributive and other services. And the number of unemployed persons is included as an explanatory variable for urban areas. To examine the hypothesis that multiple income sources may bring higher income and hence lower risks, a variable related to income diversification within households is included. This variable is constructed by counting the number of income earners among household members from different sources.

Agriculture, Land, and Livestock. Holding size, irrigation method (e.g., whether a household irrigates their land or uses inputs such as fertilizers, pesticides, etc.), and a dummy variable to indicate the relative security of land tenure are included as the determinants of rural household consumption. If land was acquired through an informal means or on a rental basis, then the tenure is considered as relatively insecure. In addition, the type of crop grown (i.e., food crop, horticulture crop, and cash crop) is included, as is a dummy variable indicating the household's possession of livestock.[11] Moreover, the number of residential rooms in urban areas is also included.

Access to Infrastructure. There are a number of potential variables that reflect access to services. Variables related to infrastructure include the presence of particular services in a village: a bank, a market, an agriculture-livestock extension center, a post office, a public telephone, and a paved or improved dirt road. Variables that indicate access to health facilities include the presence of a doctor, a nurse, a midwife, a health center, and a health or sanitary post. As there is no information on most of these variables, participation in the new extension program is taken as a measure of access to infrastructure.

Estimation of the Model

By way of introducing the interpretation and discussion of results, it is important to briefly describe the nature of the dataset used in the estimation of the model. The dataset used is obtained from Ethiopia's 1999–2000 survey of rural and urban households, conducted by the Department of Economics of Addis Ababa University (the household income, consumption, and expenditure survey data produced by the Central Statistical Authority could not be accessed). The rural and urban surveys provide data on a wide spectrum of socioeconomic variables, including household composition and structure, education, household assets, employment and income, consumption expenditure, health status, and other welfare indicators.

The regression model of the determinants of rural poverty is estimated based on 1,339 rural households, while the determinants of urban poverty are estimated based on a sample size of 1,271 urban households.[12] The major estimation issues concern missing values and outliers in the dataset, particularly for adult equivalent real consumption per capita. Households with no information on consumption expenditure are excluded from the dataset. Households whose consumption per capita is below 300 birr (US$35) per year are also excluded, as it is impossible to survive on such a low level of income.

There can be some concerns regarding potential bias in parameter estimates due to either endogenous or omitted variables. For instance, agro-ecological factors that determine the productivity of land may be excluded from the regression model, and hence implicitly subsumed under the error term of the model. If these factors are significant in determining the living standards of the households, the error term of the model will not converge to zero in probability limit, and hence the parameter estimates of the explanatory variables included in the model will be inconsistent. Similarly, if some explanatory variables (for instance, whether a household cultivates horticultural crops or commercial crops) depend on the omitted variables, these explanatory variables will be correlated with the error term. The correlation of explanatory variables with the error term will give rise to inconsistent parameter estimates.

A set of regional and district-level dummy variables has been included in order to solve the problems of endogenous or omitted variables. Dummy variables are introduced into the model to control differences in agro-ecological factors of regions and districts.

Results and Discussion. The initial parameter estimates were subjected to a limited pruning by deleting the interaction terms that are not statistically significant at the 10 percent level of significance. In addition to the interaction terms, regional and *woreda* (district) dummy variables that are statistically insignificant or collinear with other explanatory variables were also excluded from the regression model.

Determinants of Consumption and Poverty in Rural Areas. Table 7.20 presents the parameter estimates, *t*-ratios, and 95 percent confidence interval for the rural determinants of real consumption per capita. For cross-sectional data, the fit of the regression model is good, with an R^2 value of 0.364. The statistical significance of the different variables varies widely; some are statistically significant at the 5 percent level, while others are not significant even at the 10 percent level. Nonsignificant variables (at the 10 percent level of significance) were retained for the reason that they are relevant for the purpose of policy simulation.

With only a few exceptions, the signs on the variables are as expected, and the relative magnitudes are also reasonable. It should be noted that the dependent variable of the model is the natural logarithm of real consumption per capita, and hence the estimated regression coefficients measure the percentage change in real consumption per capita for a unit change in the dependent variable.

Demographic variables. From the estimated regression model, it can be seen that there is a strong negative relationship between real consumption per capita and household size. This is true for the five variables measuring the number of people in the household, disaggregated by age and sex. As expected, there is a negative relationship between consumption per capita and household size, but it is surprising that the estimated coefficients are more negative for adults in the household than they are for children, which suggests that, other things remaining the same, an additional adult in the household will reduce consumption per capita more than an additional child in the household. This result seems to be counterintuitive, if seen from the dimension of dependency ratio.

Table 7.20 Determinants of Rural Poverty, Ethiopia

Logarithm of Real Consumption per Capita (dependent variable)	Coefficient	Robust Standard Error	T	P > |t|
Age of household head	0.002	0.001	1.264	0.206
Persons 0–6 years old	−0.061	0.017	−3.550	0.000
Persons 7–17 years old	−0.115	0.015	−7.844	0.000
Males 18–64 years old	−0.190	0.022	−8.572	0.000
Females 18–64 years old	−0.114	0.026	−4.415	0.000
Persons 65 years and older	−0.153	0.029	−5.344	0.000
Number of persons in agricultural sector	0.002	0.022	0.076	0.939
Number of persons in industrial sector	0.064	0.062	1.029	0.304
Number of persons in service sector	0.036	0.016	2.284	0.023
Number of literate adult males	0.122	0.034	3.573	0.000
Number of literate adult females	−0.014	0.032	−0.427	0.670
Number of adult males who completed primary education	−0.086	0.051	−1.671	0.095
Number of adult females who completed primary education	0.029	0.044	0.654	0.513
Highest level of education of any adult in household	−0.004	0.003	−1.357	0.175
Number of income sources	0.081	0.015	5.504	0.000
Use of any modern agricultural inputs (0/1)	0.004	0.042	0.107	0.915
Security of land tenure (0/1)	0.006	0.083	0.070	0.944
Cultivate food crops (0/1)	−0.022	0.107	−0.204	0.838
Cultivate horticultural crops (0/1)	0.163	0.042	3.863	0.000
Cultivate cash crops (0/1)	0.049	0.052	0.951	0.342
Ownership of substantial livestock (0/1)	0.076	0.033	2.270	0.023
Presence of markets	−0.107	0.037	−2.863	0.004
Participate in the new extension program	0.075	0.048	1.562	0.118
ln of landholding size	0.100	0.020	4.963	0.000
ln of expenditure on assets	0.028	0.007	4.018	0.000
Adult equivalent household size squared	0.003	0.000	7.499	0.000
Dummy variable for Amhara region	0.325	0.073	4.422	0.000
Dummy variable for Oromiya region	−0.349	0.075	−4.640	0.000
Dummy variable for Haressaw district	0.174	0.088	1.965	0.050
Dummy variable for Debreziet district	1.053	0.091	11.628	0.000
Dummy variable for Adel Tike district	0.661	0.081	8.212	0.000
Dummy variable for Sodere district	0.586	0.094	6.240	0.000
Dummy variable for Shashemene district	0.562	0.092	6.101	0.000
Dummy variable for Bako district	0.329	0.094	3.507	0.000
Dummy variable for Endibr district	−0.142	0.091	−1.569	0.117
Dummy variable for Durame district	−0.219	0.071	−3.063	0.002
Constant term	6.767	0.123	54.837	0.000

Regression with robust standard errors
Number of observations = 1,339
$F_{(36, 1302)} = 21.54$
Probability > F = 0.000
$R^2 = 0.364$
Root mean standard error = 0.480

The estimated coefficient of the quadratic term of the household size is positive and statistically significant, suggesting a U-shaped relationship between consumption per capita and household size. The age of head of household does not have a significant effect on consumption per capita at the 10 percent level of significance. However, it does have an effect at the 20 percent level of significance. On the other hand, sex of head of household does not have a significant effect even at 20 percent level of significance; hence the variable is excluded from the set of regressors.

The number of disabled persons in the household was anticipated to have a negative effect on consumption per capita. However, the variable was not significant, and hence it is excluded from the set of explanatory variables.

Education. Among adult education variables, male adult literacy and the number of adult males who completed primary education have a positive association with consumption per capita as expected. However, the impact of male adults who have completed primary education was not statistically significant in influencing consumption per capita.

Employment and income sources. The signs of the three variables for the number of persons employed in the agricultural, industrial, and service sectors of the economy are as expected. The positive signs of adult employment in different economic sectors indicate that, other things being equal, adult employment of any kind leads to a higher level of consumption per capita than unemployment. The incremental gain in per capita consumption is the smallest for those employed in the agricultural sector and the largest for those employed in the industrial sector of the economy. The coefficients of employment in the agricultural and industrial sectors of the economy are not statistically significant. The variable that stands for the diversification of income sources is positive and is statistically significant as expected.

Agriculture and livestock. Among the agriculture and livestock variables, ownership of relatively more farm animals, size of landholding, and expenditure on assets have the expected signs and are statistically significant. The effects of landholding size on consumption per adult equivalent is small, with a 1 percent increase in landholding being associated with only a 0.10 percent increase in consumption per adult equivalent. The effect of all other agriculture and livestock variables (on consumption per capita) is not statistically significant.

Access to infrastructure. Participation in the new extension program is constructed as a binary variable taking a value of 0 if the household does not participate and 1 if it does. Participation in the new extension program has a positive effect on consumption per adult equivalent, but it is not statistically significant (at the 10 percent level).

Determinants of Consumption and Poverty in Urban Areas. Table 7.21 presents results from the estimation of the urban models of the determinants

Table 7.21 Determinants of Urban Poverty, Ethiopia

Logarithm of Consumption per Capita (dependent variable)	Coefficient	Robust Standard Error	T	P > |r|
Constant	7.321	0.159	45.952	0.000
Age of household head	−0.004	0.002	−2.057	0.040
Sex of household head	0.115	0.049	2.362	0.018
Persons 0–6 years old	−0.184	0.044	−4.159	0.000
Persons 7–17 years old	−0.282	0.041	−6.811	0.000
Adult males 18–64 years old	−0.326	0.049	−6.687	0.000
Adult females 18–64 years old	−0.320	0.043	−7.413	0.000
Persons 65 years and older	−0.232	0.058	−4.023	0.000
Household size squared	0.013	0.003	4.198	0.000
Number of rooms	0.098	0.010	9.634	0.000
Number of unemployed persons	−0.044	0.024	−1.833	0.067
Employment in industry	−0.055	0.084	−0.652	0.514
Employment in service sector	0.223	0.067	3.328	0.001
Number of income sources	0.055	0.018	3.099	0.002
Number of disabled persons	0.026	0.027	0.965	0.335
Number of literate adult males	0.069	0.042	1.628	0.104
Number of literate adult females	0.114	0.042	2.726	0.007
Number of adult males who completed primary education	−0.036	0.031	−1.149	0.251
Number of adult males who completed secondary education	0.011	0.048	0.228	0.820
Number of adult males who completed postsecondary education	−0.060	0.111	−0.542	0.588
Number of adult females who completed primary education	−0.075	0.030	−2.526	0.012
Number of adult females who completed secondary education	0.083	0.046	1.783	0.075
Number of adult females who completed postsecondary education	−0.252	0.097	−2.608	0.009
Highest level of education	0.035	0.011	3.127	0.002
Male literacy × employment in industry	0.008	0.021	0.392	0.695
Female literacy × employment in industry	0.001	0.019	0.054	0.957
Male literacy × employment in service sector	−0.014	0.016	−0.861	0.390
Female literacy × employment in service sector	−0.055	0.014	−3.852	0.000
Dummy for Awassa (D1)	0.226	0.090	2.520	0.012
Dummy for Bahr Dar (D2)	−0.164	0.091	−1.795	0.073
Dummy for Dessie (D3)	−0.118	0.109	−1.087	0.277
Dummy for Dire Dawa (D4)	0.171	0.088	1.935	0.053
Dummy for Jimma (D5)	0.099	0.093	1.059	0.290
Dummy for Mekele (D6)	−0.197	0.102	−1.936	0.053

Regression with robust standard errors
Number of observations = 1,271
$F (33,1237) = 10.63$
Probability $> F = 0.0000$
$R^2 = 0.220$
Root mean standard error = 0.784

of real consumption per capita. With only few exceptions, the signs on the parameters are as expected. Note that variables that appeared to be insignificant are retained for simulating the impact of different policies on poverty and economic growth.

Demographic determinants. From the regression results, it is clear that there is a strong negative relationship between real consumption per capita and household size. All indicators of household size appeared to be statistically significant at the 1 percent level. The estimated coefficient of the quadratic term of the household size is positive and statistically significant, suggesting a U-shaped relationship between consumption per capita and household size. This implies that, other things being equal, the addition of a person to the household generally reduces consumption per capita, but at a decreasing rate.

Sex of household head has a significant effect on consumption per capita at the 5 percent level of significance. In other words, households headed by males enjoy greater consumption per capita than households headed by females. Other things remaining the same, the consumption per capita of an urban male-headed household is about 18.0 percent higher than that of its female counterpart. This result is also consistent with the results of the study by MOFED (2002).

Education. Among the education variables, literate adult males, literate adult females, and number of male and female adults who completed secondary education have a positive association with consumption per capita. Except for adult males who completed secondary education, the rest have a positive and significant coefficient at the 10 percent level of significance.

Employment and income sources. The signs of the employment variables for the number of persons employed in the service sectors are positive, except for the case of employment in the industrial sector. This is not to say that employment in the industrial sector is not important, but that the number of people engaged in the industrial sector is very small. Only 25.4 percent of the sample urban households are employed in the industrial sector. Income diversification has a positive and significant effect on per capita consumption. Multiple income sources reduce the risk of consumption volatility.

Other variables that determine consumption per capita are interaction variables—literacy versus employment in different economic sectors. The interaction terms in each case show the differential effect of being a literate employee in a given sector. Of these variables, male literate employees in the agriculture and service sectors, and female literate employees in the service sector, appear to be significant in influencing consumption per capita. The coefficient of the interaction term of male literate employees in the industry shows that consumption per capita of literate adult male employees in industry is 0.08 percent lower than for illiterate adult male employees in the same sector. But consumption per capita of literate adult male employees in the service sector would be

1.4 percent lower than for those illiterate adult male employees in the same sector. Similarly, consumption per capita of literate adult females engaged in the service sector would be 5.5 percent lower than for illiterate adult female employees in the same sector. This indicates that the simultaneous presence of the two attributes (i.e., literacy and employment) reinforce and modify the individual effects of these attributes considered individually.

Poverty Simulation
Simulation Methodology. After estimating the consumption models specified earlier for rural and urban households, an attempt is made to generate predictions of poverty. Using the estimated parameters of the model, predictions of consumption per capita for each household j can be generated as:

$$\hat{C}_j = e^{\beta'X_j} \tag{4}$$

Corresponding to every predicted level of consumption, the probability of a household to be poor is given by:

$$P_{\theta,j} = \int_0^Z \left(\frac{Z - C_j}{Z}\right)^\theta f(C_j)d\,C_j \tag{5}$$

where

$f(C_j)$ = probability density function of per capita consumption of household j
Z = poverty line

Accordingly, the headcount, depth, and severity of poverty can be generated. Predicted national measures of these poverty indexes are finally obtained as the weighted averages of the estimated household probabilities of being poor corresponding to every predicted per capita consumption level.[13]

Results of Simulation. The purpose of these simulations is twofold. The first is to illustrate the impact the changes in the determinants of poverty have on the consumption per adult equivalent and poverty levels. In a situation where explanatory variables are intrinsically related to one another, it may be difficult to trace the relationship between a determinant and the outcome variable by examining the coefficients of the regression model alone. These complications are avoided by assuming that a change in a given explanatory variable will not lead to changes in other explanatory variables. The second purpose of the simulation is to demonstrate the effects that various government policies can have on consumption per adult equivalent and poverty levels. In this respect, our focus will be on altering variables that are amenable to changes, at least to some degree, through public policy. Before running the simulation, it is necessary to establish a reference point or a base simulation against which comparisons can be made. As an empirical model of the determinants of poverty cannot be perfect predictors of consumption per adult equivalent or poverty level, it would not be correct to compare the actual consumption per adult equivalent and poverty level with that of the simulated level. Instead, the correct reference for consumption per adult equivalent is the mean of the predicted values of consumption per adult equivalent obtained from the determinate regression, using the actual values of the regressors as given in equation 4 above. Similarly, the correct reference point for the poverty level is the mean value and the actual value of the explanatory variables denoted by X_j. Table 7.22 presents the comparison of the actual consumption per adult equivalent and poverty level with the results of the base simulation, or reference point. As can be seen, the predicted mean consumption per adult equivalent and the three poverty measures are close to the actual values calculated from the rural and urban household survey data collected by the Department of Economics of Addis Ababa University.

The rural and urban per capita consumption expenditures, based on the Addis Ababa University dataset, are presented in Table 7.22. The average per capita consumption expenditure was 1,092.45 birr (US$127.47) in rural areas and 1,889.49 birr (US$220.48) per year in urban areas in 1999–2000. The headcount poverty indexes for the rural and urban areas of the country are 63.07 percent and 49.18 percent respectively in 1999–2000. These figures are greater than the official poverty statistics of the country (MOFED 2002), which stood at 45.4 percent for the rural and 36.9 percent for the urban areas. There is consistency with the government figures in the sense that poverty is

Table 7.22 Comparison of Actual Measures of Well-Being with Base Simulation, Ethiopia

Statistic	Rural		Urban	
	Actual	Base Simulation	Actual	Base Simulation
Mean adult equivalent per capita consumption per year[a]	1,092.45	959.15	1,889.49	1,453.10
Poverty headcount index	63.07	61.68	49.18	45.27
Poverty gap index	24.25	23.55	20.42	19.22
Squared poverty gap index	11.87	11.73	10.47	10.83

Source: Author model simulation.
Note: a. Expressed in birr at temporally and spatially adjusted 1996 constant prices.

higher in rural than in urban areas. However, the incidence, depth, and severity of poverty are clearly much higher than what is reported in government
statistics. The discrepancy could be ascribed to differences in sample size (the
national statistics are based on a larger sample), measurement problems (believed to be lower in the university survey because of the smallness of the
sample size and closer supervision), and differences in the price used to determine the absolute poverty line. It should be reiterated that there are indica-
tions of data problems in the government reports. One clear problem is the un-
believable calorie figures for the rural areas, in which they have increased
from 1,938 kilocalories in 1995–1996 to 2,723 kilocalories in 1999–2000,
representing an average growth rate of 41 percent.

Table 7.23 shows the change in mean real consumption per adult equivalent resulting from the simulated changes in the explanatory variables, the
changes in the three measures of poverty corresponding to changes in consumption per adult equivalent. The poverty measures capture the distribu-
tional effects of the change in consumption per adult equivalent from the simulated changes in the set of explanatory variables.

One result that is common to all simulations is that the percentage change
in the squared poverty gap index is generally greater than the percentage
change in the poverty gap index, and the percentage change in the poverty gap
index is in turn generally larger than the percentage change in the headcount
index. This is because, at least in part, many of these simulations raise the
consumption levels of the poor, but they do not move the poor above the
poverty line in all cases, as the increase in consumption is small or the household is far below the poverty line. However, improving the well-being of
those households living below the poverty line is an important consideration,
especially in poor countries like Ethiopia. When examining the simulations, it
is worthwhile to keep in mind the quantitative relationship between the determinants of poverty and consumption per adult equivalent.

Education. The effects of increased educational levels on consumption
per adult equivalent and the three poverty measures are presented in simulations 1 and 2 of Table 7.23. Simulation 1 focuses on basic literacy—that is, the
effect on poverty of whether or not a person reads or writes. On the other hand,
simulation 2 examines the effect of higher rates of primary school completion.
In simulation 1, the number of adult males in the household who can read or
write is increased by one. This change applies to households where there is an
adult male who cannot read or write. For the rural and urban households, increasing by one the number of adult males in the household who can read or
write raised the mean adult equivalent consumption per capita by 13 percent
and 8.1 percent respectively, and reduced all poverty indicators. For the entire
population, mean consumption per capita increased by about 12 percent.

Simulation 2 is almost similar to simulation 1, except that it models the
effect of increasing educational attainment. As can be seen from Table 7.23,

Table 7.23 Total Changes in Consumption and Poverty Levels, Ethiopia, 1999–2000

Simulation Number	Description	Percentage Change in Real Consumption per Capita			Percentage Change in Poverty Headcount Index			Percentage Change in Poverty Gap Index	
		Rural	Urban	National	Rural	Urban	National	Rural	Urban
1	Increase by 1 the number of adult males who are literate	13.0	8.1	11.5	-12.8	-7.7	-10.3	-18.9	-10.3
2	Increase by 1 the number of adult females who have completed primary education	2.9	-1.1	0.8	-3.0	5.5	-0.06	-4.6	-6.2
3	Increase landholdings by 0.5 hectare (all holders)	4.6	n/a	2.1	-5.1	n/a	-2.8	-9.1	n/a
4	Increase landholdings by 1 hectare (those with = 2 hectares)	6.6	n/a	3.0	-7.4	n/a	-4.0	-13.0	n/a
5	Households with ≤ 1 hectare adopt modern agricultural inputs	0.1	n/a	0.0	-0.1	n/a	-0.1	-0.2	n/a
6	Households with ≤ 2 hectares adopt modern agricultural inputs	0.1	n/a	0.0	-0.1	n/a	-0.1	-0.2	n/a
7	Households with any land adopt modern agricultural inputs	0.1	n/a	0.1	-0.1	n/a	-0.1	-0.3	n/a
8	Households with ≤ 1 hectare participate in the new extension program	2.6	n/a	1.2	-3.0	n/a	-1.6	-5.4	n/a
9	Households with ≤ 2 hectares participate in the new extension program	4.2	n/a	1.9	-4.6	n/a	-2.5	-7.4	n/a
10	All households participate in the new extension program	6.1	n/a	2.8	-6.2	n/a	-3.4	-9.3	n/a
11	Food crop–producing households start growing horticultural crops	10.2	n/a	4.6	-10.2	n/a	-5.5	-15.5	n/a
12	Food crop–producing households start growing commercial crops	3.4	n/a	1.6	-3.3	n/a	-1.8	-4.3	n/a
13	Move 1 person from the agricultural sector to the industrial sector	5.8	n/a	2.7	-5.8	n/a	-3.2	-8.9	n/a
14	Move 1 person from the agricultural sector to the service sector	3.2	n/a	1.5	-3.2	n/a	-1.7	-5.0	n/a
15	Increase by 1 the number of income sources	8.5	15.3	9.1	-8.5	-5.1	-7.4	-12.8	-6.8
16	Add 1 child to the household	-5.9	-17.5	-11.8	6.1	19.2	12.3	10.1	-27.8
17	Add 1 adult male to the household	-17.3	-27.9	-21.6	18.3	32.5	23.8	32.4	49.2
18	Add 1 adult female to the household	-10.8	-27.5	-18.6	11.3	31.9	19.5	19.1	48.3

Source: Author model simulation.

increasing by one the number of adult females in the household who have completed primary school resulted in a rise in rural consumption per capita by about 3 percent and reduced the headcount index by 3 percent, the poverty gap index by about 5 percent, and the squared poverty gap index by about 6 percent. Increasing by one the number of adult females in the household who have completed primary school has a negative, although very marginal, effect on urban consumption per capita. Mean consumption per capita increased by about 0.8 percent for the whole sample.

Agriculture and livestock (for rural households). Simulations 3 and 4 in Table 7.23 are concerned with an increase in the cultivated area per household by 0.5 hectare for all holders and by 1 hectare for households having 2 or fewer hectares. These simulations resulted in a rise in rural household consumption per capita by 4.6 percent and 6.6 percent respectively. Accordingly, the headcount poverty index declined by 2.8 percent when area per household increased by 0.5 hectare for all holders and by 4 percent when farm size increased by 1 hectare for households with 2 or fewer hectares.

In simulations 5, 6, and 7, the effects of adopting modern agricultural inputs are examined, categorized by households having 1 hectare or less, households having 2 or fewer hectares, and households having any holding size. All these simulations have a marginal effect on per capita consumption or poverty measures.

Simulations 8, 9, and 10 are all concerned with the effects of participating in the new extension program by households. Participation by all households having 1 hectare or less raised rural household consumption per capita by 2.6 percent and reduced the rural headcount poverty index by 3 percent. Participation by households having 2 or fewer hectares raised consumption per capita by 4.2 percent and reduced the headcount poverty index by 4.6 percent. In simulations 11 and 12, the effects of growing horticultural and commercial crops are examined. These simulations raised rural household consumption per capita by 10.2 percent and 3.4 percent and reduced the rural headcount poverty index by 10.2 percent and 3.3 percent respectively.

Simulations 3 through 12 are not applicable to urban households. The national figures for these simulations are computed by assuming that these simulations have no effect on urban households and by taking the urban base simulations.

Employment and income sources. Simulations 13 and 14 in Table 7.23 examine the effects of sectoral shift in the distribution of the labor force, particularly movement of workers from the agricultural sector to the industrial and service sectors of the economy. Simulation 13 models moving one adult from the agricultural sector to the industrial sector, whereas simulation 14 considers the movement of one adult from the agricultural sector to the service sector. Moving one adult from the agricultural sector to the industrial sector for households with one or more adults raised rural household consumption per capita by 5.8 percent and reduced the rural headcount poverty index. Similarly, moving one adult from the agricultural sector to the service sector raised rural household consumption per capita by 3.2 percent and reduced the rural headcount poverty index by the same amount. These results indicate that staying in agriculture does not help in terms of reducing poverty.

Simulation 15 tries to examine the impact of diversifying income sources. Increasing the number of income sources by one raised rural household consumption per capita by 9.1 percent and reduced both the rural and urban headcount poverty indices.

Demographic changes. Simulations 16 through 18 examine the effects that demographic changes have on consumption per capita. Simulation 19 examines the effects of adding one child, which resulted in a reduction of rural and urban household consumption per capita by 5.9 percent and 17.5 percent respectively, and which raised rural and urban headcount poverty indexes by 6.1 percent and 19.2 percent respectively. Simulations 17 and 18 examine the effects of adding one adult male and one adult female to the household respectively. These simulations resulted in a decline in rural household consumption per capita by 17.3 percent and 10.8 percent respectively, and in a corresponding increase in the headcount indexes of 18.3 percent and 11.3 percent respectively. The impact of these simulations on urban households is also significant—that is, consumption per capita declined by about 28 percent and the headcount index increased by 33 percent.

Implications of Economic Growth and Poverty Reduction Simulation

Human capital development can be considered as one of the most important ingredients of the process of development and hence poverty reduction. This section attempts to question the potential of economic growth, whatever its sources, for poverty reduction in the rural as well as the urban population in Ethiopia. It should be noted that the central strategic choice has been between poverty reduction via faster economic growth and reduction through redistribution, though the two may be complementary (Dagdeviren, Hoeven, and Weeks 2001). Poor countries such as Ethiopia need to accelerate their economic growth so that the capital stock grows more rapidly than the already rapidly growing labor force. Based on the national accounts statistics, average real GDP growth (after the reform program) is estimated at about 5 percent per annum, while the population growth stood at about 3 percent per annum, giving a real GDP per capita growth of about 2 percent per annum. The question that may be posed now is, what will be the level of poverty ten years from 1999–2000 if the living standards of the population grow at the same rate as does real GDP per capita, assuming that there will be no change in the relative inequalities among the population? This is equivalent to simulating a distribution-neutral growth scenario in which the adult equivalent consumption per capita is assumed to increase proportionately by the same real GDP growth factor.

Table 7.24 summarizes the findings of this analysis for rural and urban households. It can be seen that a 2 percent distribution-neutral growth in real consumption per capita results in a decline of the headcount poverty index by about 21 percent in ten years' time, which means that such growth could result in a decline in the rural incidence of poverty by about 21 percent and a decline in the rural depth and severity of poverty by about 31 percent and 39 percent, respectively, in ten years' time. In scenario 2 of Table 7.24, the effects of a 3 percent distribution-neutral growth on the real adult equivalent consumption per capita are examined. Such a growth could lead to a decline in the rural and urban incidences of poverty by 32 percent and a decline in rural depth and severity of poverty by 44 percent and 52 percent, respectively, in ten years' time. Similarly, scenarios 3 and 4 of Table 7.24 explore the effects of a faster distribution-neutral rural real consumption per capita growth rate of 5 percent and 7 percent respectively. These growth rates in real consumption per capita would imply a decline in rural incidence of poverty by 49.8 percent and 63.4 percent, respectively, in five years' time. The simulated percentage declines in the rural depth and severity of poverty (as a result of such growth rates) are far larger than the simulated decline in the incidence of poverty. These findings indicate that faster economic growth of a distribution-neutral type could have a significant effect of reducing the prevailing poverty among rural households.

Similar to the rural case, despite differences in magnitudes, all simulations indicate the possibility of a decline in urban poverty following a distribution-neutral growth in urban real consumption per capita. In short, urban simulations indicate that faster economic growth has a significant effect on reducing the prevailing poverty among the urban households, although the effects may not be as strong as in the rural areas.

The simulation exercises indicate that growth of a distribution-neutral type is a precondition for reducing poverty in Ethiopia. Even with a 2 percent per annum distribution-neutral growth in per capita real consumption, there could be a significant reduction in the headcount index of poverty. In reality, there was almost no decline in poverty during the 1990s despite a real per capita GDP growth of about 2 percent per annum. And this, in turn, would imply either that growth was not distribution-neutral,[14] or that output growth did not result in commensurate consumption growth, or both. Irrespectively, expansion of employment alongside productivity growth is important.

◼ Conclusion

The main objective of this chapter has been to examine the quantitative relationships among growth, employment, poverty, and policies in the Ethiopian context, specifically by assessing the sources of output growth and attempting

Table 7.24 Implications of Future Economic Growth for Poverty Reduction in Ethiopia

	Base Value (1999–2000)		2009–2010 Simulated Value		Percentage Change over Ten Years	
	Rural	Urban	Rural	Urban	Rural	Urban
Scenario One: 2% per annum growth in real consumption per capita, distribution-neutral						
Mean adult equivalent real consumption per capita	1,092.45	1,889.49	1,334.63	2,303.27	22.17	21.9
Headcount index	63.07	49.18	49.77	40.75	−21.09	−17.1
Poverty gap index	24.25	20.42	16.79	14.97	−30.76	−26.7
Square poverty gap index	11.87	10.47	7.38	6.9	−37.83	−34.1
Scenario Two: 3% per annum growth in real consumption per capita, distribution-neutral						
Mean adult equivalent real consumption per capita	1,092.45	1,889.49	1,471.31	2,539.31	34.69	34.4
Headcount index	63.07	49.18	42.78	36.85	−32.17	−25.1
Poverty gap index	24.25	20.42	13.69	12.48	−43.55	−38.9
Square poverty gap index	11.87	10.47	5.68	5.42	−52.15	−48.2
Scenario Three: 5% per annum growth in real consumption per capita, distribution-neutral						
Mean adult equivalent real consumption per capita	1,092.45	1,889.49	1,783.42	3,077.77	63.25	62.9
Headcount index	63.07	49.18	31.68	28.7	−49.77	−41.6
Poverty gap index	24.25	20.42	8.68	8.14	−64.21	−60.1
Square poverty gap index	11.87	10.47	3.07	3.09	−74.14	−70.5
Scenario Four: 7% per annum growth in real consumption per capita, distribution-neutral						
Mean adult equivalent real consumption per capita	1,092.45	1,889.49	2,153.76	3,716.91	97.15	96.7
Headcount index	63.07	49.18	23.09	20.12	−63.39	−59.1
Poverty gap index	24.25	20.42	4.80	4.79	−80.21	−76.5
Square poverty gap index	11.87	10.47	1.37	1.53	−88.46	−85.4

Source: Author calculations.

to quantify the likely impacts of alternative public policies on employment and poverty in the country.

The Ethiopian economy grew on average by 2.3 percent and 4.6 percent during the 1980s and 1990s respectively. However, employment (excluding the manufacturing sector) expanded by 5.9 percent during 1984–1994, and declined by 0.6 percent during 1994–1999. It has also been shown that the output growth of the 1980s was driven by an employment expansion that more than offset the negative effects of productivity. Employment expansion thus came at the cost of productivity. On the other hand, the output growth of the 1990s was achieved through a higher productivity that outweighed the negative effects of employment. Increased productivity was not accompanied by an expansion in employment during the 1990s.

The sectoral growth structure is very important in explaining the growth process of the Ethiopian economy. Manufacturing output declined by 3.0 percent in the 1980s, but increased by 5.0 percent in the 1990s. Similarly, employment decreased by 1.4 percent in 1984–1991, but increased by 1.8 percent in 1992–1999. It should be noted that the rate of employment growth was very much below the population growth even in the postreform period. On the other hand, the source of output growth in the manufacturing sector was mainly productivity growth during both the 1980s and the 1990s. The productivity effect outweighed the employment effect and hence growth was mainly productivity-led in the manufacturing sector. However, the productivity effect was low (less than 1 percent) in both periods. A very low employment expansion was accompanied by a very low labor productivity growth, indicating sectoral recession or slowdown.

Agricultural real output increased by 3.6 percent between 1984–1985 and 1991–1992, compared to 1.9 percent between 1992–1993 and 1999–2000. Employment in the agricultural sector increased by 6.0 percent in 1984–1994 according to the 1984 and 1994 censuses of the Central Statistical Authority. This contrasts sharply with the decline in 1994–1999 (by 2.9 percent) as per the data of the 1994 census and the 1999 labor force survey. Although the basis of this comparison can be questioned, the trend appears to be one of declining agricultural employment over time. The source of output growth in the agricultural sector was mainly the employment effect in the 1980s, but the productivity effect in the 1990s. In the earlier period, a negative productivity effect was accompanied by employment expansion, exhibiting a typical feature of a refuge sector, resulting in underemployment and falling real wages. The situation in the 1990s changed, with a slight increase in productivity but a declining employment effect. This could be a reflection of a shift in employment from agriculture to other sectors of the economy during the postreform period. For instance, employment in the other sectors, particularly in the service sector, dramatically increased during the 1990s. Except in the transport, storage, and communication and other services sectors, all service activities experienced a negative productivity growth with significant expansion in employment. Services have become the refuge sector for the rapidly growing labor force.

In Ethiopia, the size of the labor force continues to grow faster than the ability of the economy to provide new employment opportunities. As a result, the poverty situation in the country is one of the worst in the world and shows no significant sign of improvement over time. According to government reports, 45.5 percent of the total population lived below the absolute poverty line in 1995–1996 (based on a minimum intake of 2,200 kilocalories per day and provision for some basic nonfood expenditure—i.e., equivalent to US$139 per capita income in aggregate). Despite various policy reforms and efforts to boost agricultural production, the proportion of people living below the absolute poverty line remained 36.92 percent in urban and 45.4 percent in rural areas in 1999–2000, according to government reports. However, the level of poverty was much higher using the database of the Department of Economics of Addis Ababa University: the proportion of the rural population living below the poverty line was 63.1 percent, and the figure for the urban areas was also much higher, at 49.2 percent. The available evidence thus indicates that the poverty situation may have worsened between 1995–1996 and 1999–2000. Poverty is also more widespread in rural than in urban areas, as reflected in the headcount index and per capita income.

One of the main messages of this chapter is that there is a strong relationship between demographic characteristics and the probability of a household being poor. In other words, households with a larger family size and older heads are more likely to fall into poverty than households with a smaller family size and younger heads. The findings of the chapter also indicate that measures used to reduce dependency at the household level will help reduce poverty. In addition, reducing fertility will have a beneficial impact on women's health, labor force participation, and productivity.

The other key message of the analysis is that education is important in bringing about sustained growth and in reducing poverty in the country. The impact of education in alleviating poverty is significant in both rural and urban areas; households with higher levels of literacy are less likely to fall into poverty than households with lower levels of literacy. Investment in education should be one of the primary elements in reducing poverty in Ethiopia.

The analysis also points to the importance of distribution-neutral economic growth for poverty reduction. Economic growth of such a pattern does hold the promise of significant poverty reduction in the future. For example, a distribution-neutral sustained annual economic growth rate of 7 percent in real per capita terms over the next ten years has the potential of reducing the incidence of poverty in rural and urban areas by about 63.4 percent and 59.1 percent, respectively. The effect of such growth on rural areas is also much greater than in urban areas.

It should be noted that the sectoral pattern of growth is very important in the alleviation of poverty. At current productivity levels, a pattern of growth that favors industry and services will reduce poverty. However, it will also be important to increase agricultural productivity. The analysis shows that transferring labor from agriculture to industry and services will reduce poverty. The relatively high levels of poverty in the agricultural sector reveal a low level of productivity, and releasing labor from the agricultural sector to other sectors is expected to lead to an increase in higher income for the rural population. A successful development strategy should envisage technological advancement in all sectors of the economy, including agriculture. The findings of this chapter also support the argument that increasing the size of landholdings will reduce poverty, and that the reduction in poverty will be greater if it is accompanied by productivity-enhancing investments such as modern inputs.

It is argued that the shift away from agricultural employment is a basic result of increased productivity in other sectors. Agriculture has been the source of volatility in employment and national output. The performance of Ethiopian agriculture is heavily influenced by weather conditions, which have become increasingly unpredictable over the years. Agricultural production increases when the rains are favorable (e.g., 1995–1996 and 2000–2001) only to be followed by a decline when the weather becomes drier (e.g., 1993–1994, 1997–1998, and 2002–2003). Hence the employment strategy for the future should look into sectors other than agriculture. The central focus in agriculture should be to stabilize production using irrigation and other technologies, and to boost agricultural productivity to reduce rural poverty.

The manufacturing sector has to play the leading role in order to inject dynamism into the economy. It should be a leading sector from the viewpoint of productive employment generation. However, rising levels of inequality in urban areas suggest that growth in the nonagricultural sector has not helped poverty reduction. High rates of unemployment in the cities, estimated as 38 percent in Addis Ababa or 26 percent in urban areas in general by the 1999 labor force survey, appear to have depressed wages and contributed to rising income and consumption inequality. Hence the primary focus of the revival strategy in industry should be to ensure that growth is sufficiently employment-friendly and pro-poor. The promotion of vocational and technical training and better financial and infrastructural services for the more labor-intensive small and medium enterprises should constitute important elements of the effort to create an enabling environment. At the same time, the large- and medium-scale manufacturing sector, where the bulk of the industrial output is generated, should receive due attention so that it is able to withstand competition from imports. A well-coordinated industrial strategy is required to make the sector the engine of growth and strengthen its forward and backward linkages with the agriculture and service sectors to ensure sustainable growth.

Finally, the service sector is significant in terms of both national output and employment. The centerpiece of a growth and employment generation strategy should be to increase the productivity of the service sector. With improvement in the transport and communication infrastructure, modernization of the marketing and trade sector, and promotion of the tourism industry, the service industry should be able to generate more productive employment.

Notes

1. The data for urban and rural areas were separately collected in the Addis Ababa University dataset. The sample size does not reflect the large proportion of the rural population (relative to the urban areas). Hence it is impossible to merge the urban and rural dataset to get a national picture.

2. Regional disaggregation of poverty indexes indicates that headcount, poverty gap, and squared poverty gap indexes increased in all regions in 1999–2000 except Amhara; Southern Nations, Nationalities, and Peoples (SNNP); and Harari.

3. See Women's Affairs Office and World Bank 1998.

4. For details, see Demeke, Guta, and Ferede 2003.

5. It should be noted that such econometric elasticities couldn't be determined for the other sectors due to lack of time-series data.

6. Labor productivity, output, and employment growth can be related to output elasticity of employment as follows: Let P = labor productivity, Y = output, N = employment, and $P = Y / N$. Then,

$$dP / dt = P(g_y - g_n)$$
$$g_p = g_y[1 - (g_n / g_y)] \Leftrightarrow g_p = g_y(1 - e_n)$$

where

g_y = output growth
g_n = employment growth
g_p = productivity growth
e_n = output elasticity of employment

7. The symbolic break down of output growth into employment effect, productivity effect, and multiple effect is as follows: Let Y = output, N = employment, and P = productivity. Then $Y = N \times P$. Hence change in output can be written as: $\Delta Y = P\Delta N + N\Delta P + (\Delta N \times \Delta P)$.

Dividing the above equation by ΔY we obtain the following:

employment effect = $P \times (\Delta N / \Delta Y)$
productivity effect = $N \times (\Delta P / \Delta Y)$
multiple effect = $(\Delta N \times \Delta P) / \Delta Y$

8. Time-series data on wages and earnings in manufacturing were all measured in current prices and hence real wages and earnings were obtained by deflating nominal wages by the consumer price index of Addis Ababa—the only available time-series data on consumer price index.

9. The logarithm of consumption is estimated because its distribution more closely approximates the normal distribution than does the distribution of the consumption levels. In other words, this assumption implies that a household's consumption level follows a log-normal distribution.

10. These three measures of poverty belong to the Foster-Greer-Thorbecke class, introduced in Foster, Greer, and Thorbecke 1984.

11. Possession of substantial livestock, in this particular case, is defined as households that possessed above mean possession for all types of livestock.

12. The actual sample size used in the regression model was lower than the total sample size, as some of the households with missing information were excluded.

13. The complete specification of the poverty indexes can be found in Demeke, Guta, and Ferede 2003.

14. Gini coefficients of both consumption and income in urban areas increased during the period 1995/96–1999/00 (from 0.34 to 0.38, and 0.55 to 0.57, respectively). See Demeke, Guta, and Ferede 2003.

8

India: Employment-Poverty Linkages and Policy Options

K. Sundaram and
Suresh D. Tendulkar

At the macro level, the linkage between the prevalence of poverty, in its income dimension, and the average productivity of employed work force that underlies it, is mediated through and explained by the past growth performance. At the micro level of a household, the same linkage between poverty and employment operates through the low productivity of economic activities undertaken by the earning members of a household and the dependency burden that limits work force participation. In this chapter, we explore the macro-level link, as well as the micro-level linkages that emerge from India's national sample surveys on consumer expenditure and employment/unemployment.

We begin with some prefatory observations on the macro-level linkages. In low-income, densely populated, and predominantly agricultural economies like India's, the widespread prevalence of poverty, in its income dimension, can be directly traced to the inadequacy of earnings accruing to the working poor, defined as members of the labor force located in households below poverty line. The inadequacy of their earnings originates in their gainful engagement in low-productivity farm and nonfarm activities with virtual absence or inadequate support of physical or human capital or skills.

How does economic growth impact poverty and employment? Low level of per capita income itself is a reflection of a low average productivity of the work force[1] that is traceable to a backward technology and deficiency of reproducible tangible capital relative to labor. Sustained expansion of productive capacity that constitutes economic growth generates gainful employment opportunities with continuously rising productivity. This makes possible a progressive absorption and integration of the working poor into expanding economic activities often involving rising productivity in their existing occupation with better technology or a shift to new occupations with upgraded skills and productivity. The resulting higher earnings not only improve living

267

standard but also provide the working poor with the means for providing education and skill formation to their children, which paves the way for an intergenerational upward mobility. Empirical studies by G. Fields (1991, 1995) provide ample evidence that episodes of rapid growth in different countries during the post–World War II period have been associated with reduction in income poverty in different countries. In the Indian context also, a study by Suresh Tendulkar and L. Jain (1995) showed that in comparison with the 1970s, marked by slow growth, the doubling of the growth rate of real per capita GDP in the 1980s was associated with reduction in both rural and urban poverty.

Long-Term Economic Growth, 1950/51–1999/00

The long-term average of the annual growth rates of real GDP at factor cost of the Indian economy became stuck around 3.4 percent per annum[2] for three decades, from 1950 to 1980. Over this period, gross domestic savings and investment rates (at current prices) more than doubled, from around 9 percent of GDP at current market prices during the first quinquennium of the 1950s to over 18 percent during 1974–1980 (see Table 8.1). It was an impressive performance in mobilization of resources not equalled by other countries at similar levels of per capita GDP. However, instead of being translated into rapid growth and improved living standards, these high rates of resource mobilization resulted in a high level of (implicit) incremental capital output ratio of around 5.8.[3] Consequently, India remained in the category of "low-income, slow-growing" economies in an international comparison of aggregate rates of economic growth among about forty relatively large less developed countries (population exceeding 10 million) undertaken by L. Reynolds (1985) over the period 1950–1980.

Although functioning markets and associated institutions existed in India, the discretionary policies resulted in a constricting of their operation. At the same time, administered interest rates on institutional credit were kept deliberately low (with a view to inducing investment), and overprotective labor legislation was put in place to protect the existing employment in the organized higher-productivity segment of the economy. The inevitable result was wasteful utilization of successfully mobilized scarce capital in a labor-abundant and capital-scarce economy.

The 1980s saw the emergence of the Indian economy out of the low-growth syndrome of the previous three decades. The average of the annual growth rates for the decade was 5.75 percent, in comparison with 3.4 percent for the previous three decades. However, a strong undercurrent of fiscal profligacy had been brewing during this decade. The consolidated fiscal deficits of the central and state governments (as a percentage of GDP at current market prices) rose from 7.2 percent on average in the first quinquennium of the 1980s to 8.9 percent in the second, ending at a high level of 9.4 percent in 1990–1991.

Table 8.1 Indicators of Aggregate Economic Performance, India, 1951–2003

Simulation Number	Year	Ratios to GDPMP at 2000 Price			GDCF as Percentage of GDP at 1993–1994 Prices	Growth Rate of Gross Domestic Product at Factor Cost at 1993–1994 Prices	Implicit Incremental Capital-Output Ratio
		Gross Domestic Capital Formation	Gross Domestic Saving	Net Capital Inflow			
1	1951–1956	8.96	8.74	0.22	14.72	3.85	3.83
2	1956–1960	13.22	11.10	2.12	19.02	3.38	5.63
3	1961–1965	14.22	11.96	2.26	19.28	5.00	3.86
4	1966–1970	15.00	13.18	1.82	22.04	2.90	7.60
5	1971–1973	15.50	14.67	0.83	21.00	1.90	11.05
6	1974–1980	18.46	18.60	-0.14	22.73	3.40	6.69
7	1981–1985	19.70	18.36	1.34	20.72	5.66	3.61
8	1986–1990	22.60	20.26	2.34	21.96	5.84	3.75
9	1990–1991	26.30	23.10	3.20	25.4	5.30	—
10	1991–1992	22.50	22.0	0.50	22.0	1.3	—
11	1992–1993	23.60	21.80	1.80	22.9	5.1	—
12	1993–1994	23.10	22.50	0.60	23.10	5.9	—
13	1994–1995	26.0	24.8	1.2	26.4	7.3	—
14	1995–1996	26.9	25.1	1.70	27.3	7.30	—
15	1996–1997	24.5	23.2	1.30	25.1	7.8	—
16	1997–1998	24.6	23.1	1.5	25.9	4.8	—
17	1998–1999	22.6	21.5	1.1	24.6	6.5	—
18	1999–2000	25.2	24.1	1.1	27.7	6.1	—
19	2000–2001	24.0	23.4	0.6	26.2	4.4	—
20	2001–2002	23.7	24.0	-0.7	25.6	5.4[a]	—
21	2002–2003	—	—	—	—	4.0[b]	—

Source: Central Statistical Organization 2003, 2004.
Notes: a. Revised estimate.
b. Quick estimate.

A similar trend also existed in the case of revenue deficit. It is possible that these rising fiscal deficits, along with healthy agricultural growth, might have contributed to rising aggregate effective demand that was needed to induce the improved supply response from selective deregulation of controls on private domestic investment and on imports that was undertaken in the mid-1980s.

The basic undercurrent of growing fiscal imbalances of the 1980s not only contributed to worsening current account deficits and led to the external payments crisis that triggered the process of economic policy reforms of July 1991, but also resulted in a double-digit rate of inflation and consequently made the stepped-up rate of economic growth of the 1980s unsustainable. The sustainability of growth required not only a strong dose of fiscal stabilization and exchange rate adjustment but also microeconomic structural adjustment.

The broad contours of the microeconomic structural adjustment policy reforms after July 1991 consisted of the following elements:

1. Total abolition of private industrial investment licensing, except for a clearly defined negative list of industries, currently set at six industries.
2. A drastic reduction in the number of industries exclusively reserved for the public sector after 1991, a list currently confined to just four industries.
3. The abolition of quantitative restrictions on imports of most capital and intermediate goods during the immediate postreform years and those on consumer goods after April 2001.
4. A gradual reduction in the average levels of direct and indirect (customs and excise) tax rates and a reduction in the number of differential rates as well as a plethora of exemptions.
5. A hesitant and as yet highly qualified liberalization of private foreign direct and portfolio investment.
6. A hesitant and as yet not very successful move toward allowing entry of private (domestic and foreign) investment into infrastructure, particularly power, roads, and ports.
7. A gradual transition to a current account convertibility of exchange rate and limited moves toward capital account convertibility.

A sharp dose of fiscal contraction in 1991–1992 predictably resulted in a dip in the growth rate of real GDP to 1.3 percent (Table 8.1), a reduction in both the rate of investment and savings, and a sharp decline in the rate of foreign capital inflow. The economy recovered in 1992–1993, with a growth rate of 5.1 percent. The current account deficit hovered around 1 percent of GDP, despite liberalization of trade and exchange rate policies during the 1990s. The foreign exchange reserves accumulated during the decade, from a precarious level to US$1.2 billion in December 1990 to more than US$100 billion in early 2004. The rate of inflation, too, was brought down to a single-digit level in the second half of the decade. The average of the annual growth rates of aggregate GDP over the decade between 1992–1993 and 2001–2002, at 6.1 percent, was only marginally better than the 5.75 percent average rate achieved during the 1980s. However, this masks the slowdown in the second half of the decade, to 5.5 percent from an impressive 6.7 percent during the first half. The slowdown in the second half was associated with the dilution of fiscal discipline and lower rates of both savings and investments.

Sectoral Employment Structure, 1961–1999/00

The rate and the sectoral pattern of economic growth, along with factor price ratio and sector-specific technologies, determine the sectoral employment structure. Here we examine the changes in the employment structure in India mostly at the one-digit industry level.

International comparisons of long-term changes in employment structure indicate that in the initial stages of economic growth, a decline in share of work force in agriculture and allied activities with lower-than-average productivity per worker is usually matched by a higher share in services, although the share of industrial sector also registers some increase. The economic growth process involves rising average productivity per worker and is characterized by continuing changes in the employment structure involving movements of workers from activities and sectors with lower to higher productivity, combined with an uneven pace of sectoral technological changes. The faster the pace of economic growth, the more rapid are the changes in the employment structure.

Usually, the forty-year period covered here is not long enough for major changes to occur in the average structure of employment by sector of attachment, especially because of the slow growth (much lower than 5 percent per year) since the 1950s. In the subsequent discussion, therefore, we focus on the changes in the structure of incremental employment over successive time points defining the periods.

At the aggregate level, the average annual additions to the work force are 5.1 million between 1961 and 1983 (period 1 henceforth), 6.8 million between 1983 and 1993–1994 (period 2), followed by a slowdown to about 4 million between 1993–1994 and 1999–2000 (period 3). (See Sundaram and Tendulkar 2002, tabs. 1.3–1.5, for the industrial distribution of total, rural, and female workers for 1961, 1983, 1993–1994, and 1999–2000.) With urbanization, the rural share in the additions predictably declined from 71 percent to 68 percent and further to 49.5 percent over periods 1–3. The share of female workers in the incremental work force, too, declined, from 37 percent to 27 percent to as low as 9 percent over the same periods.

At the broad sectoral level, the share of agriculture and allied sectors in the total work force declined slowly (in relation to the length of the period), by a total of 7.4 percentage points over the twenty-two years of slow growth in period 1. The decline in relative terms was faster, by a total of 4.5 percent-age points, over the ten and a half years of period 2, and the pace became even quicker, 4.4 percentage points over a shorter period of the six years in period 3. An interesting point to note is a virtually stagnant absolute size of the work force in the agriculture and allied sectors over the last six years of the twenti-eth century. A marginal decline was also registered in absolute terms in the fe-male work force engaged in this sector in the same six-year period. This is a positive development in view of the lower-than-average productivity in pri-mary production.

Average annual incremental absorption in the secondary commodity-pro-ducing sector (consisting of manufacturing, mining and quarrying, construc-tion and electricity, gas, and water) was slightly over 1 million in period 1 (or only about one-fifth of the average annual additions to the total work force during the low-growth phase, 1961–1983). The pace of additions to the sec-ondary sector work force picked up to 1.45 million per annum in period 2, but still accounted for barely 21 percent of the annual increments to the total work force during 1983–1994. The incremental absorption in the secondary sector rose further, to 1.58 million per annum, or nearly 40 percent of the annual in-crement in total work force, during the last six years of the twentieth century. More interesting is the fact that the rural share in incremental secondary sec-tor employment rose from only 28.9 percent during the first period to a little over 52 percent in the next two periods. This is indicative of increasing em-ployment in nonfarm rural commodity production, albeit largely in the non-formal, nonfactory segment, with a decline in importance of the agriculture and allied sectors. Also, during the last period, there was an interesting shift within this group: total incremental employment of 5.8 million in construction exceeded the 4.8 million added to the manufacturing (factory plus nonfactory) sector.

The average annual additions to the work force in residual services rose and gradually outstripped those in the secondary sector, namely 1.25 million during the first period, and over 2 million per annum in the subsequent two periods. Their share in total incremental work force rose from 24 percent in the first period to a little over one-third in the second period and further to a dominant 57 percent in the final six years.

Examining further the expansion in tertiary sector employment over the 1990s, we observe that the rural share in employment in the incremental ser-vices sector declined from nearly 44 percent in period 1 to 41 percent in pe-riod 2 and further to 28 percent in period 3. In other words, the expansion in tertiary sector employment was mostly an urban phenomenon. Also over this period, expansion of community, social, and personal services practically halted. This is a healthy development, as these services consist of overstaffed public administration and defense and low-productivity personal services. In fact, over the 1990s, employment in both these components underwent an absolute decline. This decline was partly made up by a rise in the number of workers in education and medical and health services. Further, we observe that trade and transport services (29 percent) together accounted for a little over 90 percent of incremental tertiary sector employment in the 1990s, in comparison with 50 to 55 percent in the two earlier periods.

Several interesting features emerge from the foregoing discussion of changes in employment structure. First, the rate of decline in the share of the agriculture and allied sectors (with lower-than-average productivity per worker) was faster in the last two decades of the twentieth century, with absolute number of workers starting to decline. As noted earlier, this is a positive feature. Second, while the share of manufacturing in incremental employment generation in the secondary sector came down from 78 percent to around 58 percent, more than half of this increase in manufacturing employment took place in the rural areas. Combined with a significant growth in real wage rates of rural manual and nonmanual labor in nonagriculture in the 1990s (Sundaram 2001c), this is to be regarded as a positive development. The dominant role of trade and transport services in incremental tertiary sector expansion noted above is consistent with the expansion in rural manufacturing employment and the widely reported efforts of large corporations to reach out to rural areas. It is indicative of competitive pressures released by the reduction in entry barriers (as well as in distortions) introduced by the earlier set of autarkic policies. Finally, the changes in the employment structure have predictably become faster with the rapid growth experienced in the 1980s and 1990s.

Employment and Poverty in the 1980s and 1990s

After 1991 in India, the policy reforms aimed at microeconomic structural adjustment in the industrial sector reduced barriers to entry, relaxed stifling constraints on private sector initiative arising from the need to obtain a number of time-consuming government clearances and sanctions, and reduced the degree of distortions caused by a multiplicity of differential customs and excise duty rates, a plethora of exemptions through their rationalization, and a lowering of their average levels. They led to the emergence of a measure of competition both domestic and external. Also, a fair amount of corporate restructuring took place in the first half of the 1990s (and is still continuing on a smaller scale) through mergers, acquisitions, hiving off noncore activities, and formation of strategic alliances and joint ventures in order to complement and focus on core competencies.

There have been serious apprehensions about the cost of structural adjustment in terms of displacement of labor in this process. In this section, we draw on our earlier studies to examine three issues. First, what has been the impact of adjustment policies on the factory sector employment and output? We draw on Tendulkar 2000a for this purpose. Second, what did the general employment situation look like during the period of reforms? For this purpose we draw on India's quinquennial national sample surveys on employment and unemployment for the years 1993–1994 and 1999–2000 as analyzed in Sundaram 2001c and Sundaram 2001b. Third, how did the structural adjustment policies and macroeconomic management impact the prevalence of poverty? For this purpose we draw on the national sample surveys on consumer expenditure for the years 1993–1994 and 1990–2000 as analyzed in Sundaram and Tendulkar 2003a and Sundaram and Tendulkar 2003b.

Tendulkar 2000a shows that while there was a net decline in manufacturing employment in the 1980s to the extent of nearly 52,000, the 1990s (up to 1997–1998) were marked by an increase in employment in all the industry groups amounting to 1.11 million in the aggregate. This is not to suggest that labor displacement was totally absent in the 1990s. The industry-level aggregates conceal the displacement, which must have taken place at the plant level, but in the net, job gains due to liberalization outweighed job losses. Factory employment in the 1990s grew at 2.9 percent per annum, and the corresponding real consumption wage grew at 1.3 percent.

Regarding the unorganized, nonfactory, nonformal segment, sheltering more than 80 percent of manufacturing, we do not have annual data on these units to monitor employment. However, Sundaram 2001c and Sundaram 2001b examine the movements in real wage rates based on the quinquennial national sample surveys on employment and unemployment and find that adult (age fifteen to fifty-nine) casual male wage laborers in urban manufacturing enterprises experienced 3.2 percent per annum growth in daily real wage rate between 1993–1994 and 1999–2000. This was above the average growth rate of 2.9 percent for all the urban sectors put together. In the rural areas, for the nonmanual labor in nonagriculture, which we take as a proxy for rural manufacturing, the growth rate per annum of daily real wage rate was 3.0 percent for males and even higher, 4.6 percent, for rural females. For the casual labor in rural nonagriculture, the corresponding growth rates were 3.7 percent (males) and 4.1 percent (females). It is plausible to take these survey-based growth rates of real daily wages to be representative of the urban and rural informal manufacturing enterprises. That the growth rates for rural workers are higher than the rates for their urban counterparts is indicative of the tightening of the labor market as well as the rising productivity per worker in the 1990s. What is even more remarkable is that, as noted earlier, 52 percent of the incremental employment in manufacturing in the 1990s took place in the rural areas. The direction of the growth rate differentials in real wage rates indicates the narrowing of rural-urban and factory-nonfactory differentials in real wage levels in the 1990s and a welcome alleviation of long-persistent dualities in these facets of the labor market.

Finally, we turn to the commonly expressed concerns regarding the overall employment situation in the 1990s, as the structural adjustment policies after 1991 had been anticipated to impact adversely on employment. For this purpose, we again draw on Sundaram 2001c and Sundaram 2001b. Three results in particular have been interpreted by some observers to reflect negative outcomes on the employment front:

1. A reduction in the worker-population ratio (WPR) on the principal plus subsidiary usual status,[4] not only in the aggregate but also for all the age groups, between 1993–1994 and 1999–2000 for rural males and females as well as urban males and females. This has been interpreted as a reduction in employment "potential" in the Indian economy.

2. A reduction in the average number of days worked per person per year for the usually employed persons on the principal plus subsidiary status for rural male workers, from 331 to 327, and for urban male workers, from 345 to 343, and a rise in average number of workdays for rural and urban females.

3. A rise in daily status rates of unemployment for rural males, from 5.6 to 7.2 percent, and females, from 5.6 to 6.8 percent, as well as for urban males, from 6.7 to 7.2 percent, in 1999–2000, especially after a decline in 1993–1994 in comparison with 1983. This is taken to reinforce the concern in the first point.

To arrive at an overall assessment of the employment situation in the 1990s, care is needed to interpret the apparent "facts." Thus in a context marked by substantial residual absorption of labor in the mostly self-employed primary sector, changes in overall WPRs reflect primarily changes in labor supply rather than changes in labor demand or employment "potential." In this specific case, the reduction in WPRs between 1993–1994 and 1999–2000 is associated with beneficial improvements in schooling rates in age groups previously recording higher work participation rates. Also, in part, it is associated with a reduction in work participation on the subsidiary status not fully offset by the rise in work participation rates on the principal status. The rise in the unemployment rates on the daily status is also more apparent than real, reflecting an increasing share of casual labor and a reduction in "disguised" unemployment of the erstwhile self-employed. The clearest indicator of a tightening of the labor market is provided by the strong growth in real wages of casual wage laborers in agriculture and in informal sector activities in both rural and urban areas, noted above. What is more, Sundaram 2001c shows that growth in the real wage rate had been strong enough to offset a reduction in WPRs in working-age groups, a (small) reduction in average number of days worked per worker per year for males and the rise in person-day rates of unemployment noted above, and to yield a strong growth in earning per head of population. In respect of the most vulnerable segment of rural agricultural laborers, the average number of days worked per worker per year for this group of workers (at

299 days for males and 239 days for females) was indeed lower than the average for all workers. However, the average annual wage earning per worker showed a healthy growth of 3.1 percent for male and 3.4 percent for female agricultural laborer, and the per capita (including dependents as well as workers) average annual wage earnings for all agricultural labor households rose at a compound annual rate of 2.35 percent between 1993–1994 and 1999–2000. In other words, this group, characterized by the highest prevalence of poverty as well as its numerical dominance among the rural poor population, shared the general improvement in the overall employment situation. Based on this evidence, our overall assessment is one of improvement in the employment situation in India over the 1990s.

How did this improvement impact on the extent of absolute poverty? For this purpose, drawing on Sundaram and Tendulkar 2003a and Sundaram and Tendulkar 2003b, we track the movement of five indicators between 1983 and 1993–1994 (the ten-and-a-half-year prereform period) and between 1993–1994 and 1999–2000: headcount ratio, poverty gap index (reflecting "depth" dimension), squared poverty gap (denoted FGT^*), Sen index (the two indexes representing "severity" dimensions), and absolute size of the poor population (or number of poor) (see Table 8.2). Two estimates for 1993–1994 are given, one with a uniform recall period comparable to estimates for 1983, and another with a mixed reference period comparable to estimates for 1999–2000.

We find a clear and unambiguous decline in absolute income poverty in terms of all the five indicators in rural India and in the country as a whole. In urban areas, this is true for four out of five indicators, the sole exception being the absolute size of the urban population.

Regarding the relative pace of decline (or rise for urban population), we take the total change between the base and the terminal year of the comparable estimates, annualize this change with a simple average over ten and a half years for the estimates between 1983 and 1993–1994 for the prereform period and those for the six years from 1993–1994 to 1999–2000 for the postreform period, and normalize the annual average with reference to the initial level of a given poverty indicator. The relative pace of decline, so defined, was higher in the 1990s than in the earlier period. The results are stark for absolute size of the poor population. Between 1983 and 1993–1994, an average annual decline of 0.64 million for rural population was offset by a 0.65 million increase for the urban population, with absolute size of the poor population remaining virtually unchanged for the country as a whole. For the postreform period, an annual average decline of 2.47 million in the number of rural poor more than offset the annual average urban increase of 0.30 million (less than half the corresponding prereform increase), with a 2.17 million net annual reduction for the country as whole.

Thus, at the all-India level, we have a mutually consistent picture of a higher rate of aggregate GDP growth, an improved employment situation, and

Table 8.2   Alternative Measures of Poverty, India, 1983–1999/00

Segment/Measure	Measures on Uniform Reference Period		Measures on Mixed Reference Period	
	1983	1993–1994	1993–1994[a]	1999–2000
Rural				
Headcount ratio (%)	49.02	39.66	34.19	28.93
Poverty gap index	0.1386	0.0928	0.0728	0.0579
*FGT**	0.0545	0.0315	0.0232	0.0173
Sen index	0.1882	0.1278	0.1014	0.0806
Number of poor (thousands)	268,062	261,369	225,321	210,498
Urban				
Headcount ratio (%)	38.33	30.89	26.41	23.09
Poverty gap index	0.0995	0.0749	0.0600	0.0504
*FGT**	0.0366	0.0265	0.0202	0.0160
Sen index	0.1362	0.1034	0.0833	0.0695
Number of poor (thousands)	65,720	72,586	62,061	63,827
All India				
Headcount ratio (%)	46.47	37.35	32.15	27.32
Poverty gap index	0.1293	0.0881	0.0694	0.0558
*FGT**	0.0502	0.0302	0.0224	0.0170
Sen index	0.1758	0.1214	0.0966	0.0775
Number of poor (thousands)	333,782	333,955	287,382	274,325
Total population (thousands)	718,300	894,006	894,006	1004,086
Share of urban population (%)	23.87	26.28	26.28	27.53

Sources: Estimates of headcount ratio, poverty gap index, *FGT**, and Sen index for 1983 are drawn from Tendulkar, Sundaram, and Jain 1993. Parallel estimates for 1993–1994, with uniform and mixed reference periods, and for 1999–2000, with mixed reference period, have been drawn from unit record data for the fiftieth round of India's national consumer expenditure survey.

Note: a. All numbers in this column are revised estimates.

a more rapid pace of decline or a slower rate of rise in absolute urban poverty in all dimensions during the postreform over the prereform period.

■ The Poor in the Labor Force: Magnitude and Characteristics

We examine the contours of the poor in the labor force in India from two distinct perspectives. In the first perspective, given the poverty line, poor and non-poor households are classified by their principal means of earnings during the previous year. These are "household types" in the terminology of the national survey samples. In the second perspective, individual members of poor and nonpoor households are classified by their labor force and other household characteristics. In particular, the work force activity status of individual members (self-employed, wage and salary employment, casual laborers, and others) overlaps with the description of household types, but is based on the major time criterion and not source of earnings.

Perspective of Principal Means of Household Earnings

In this perspective, we examine the extent of poverty in the 1990s in households classified by their principal means of livelihood or household types in the terminology of the national survey samples. This would highlight the significantly higher headcount ratios, in terms of population, in households that are overwhelmingly dependent on the earnings from irregular, fluctuating, low-wage rural as well as urban manual labor, although poverty has been prevalent in nonmanual labor households as well.

In the rural context, the national sample surveys distinguish five household types by reference to their principal means of livelihood: self-employed in agriculture, self-employed in nonagriculture, agricultural labor, other rural (manual) labor, and residual others. The last category, residual others, covers two types of earnings: those households whose major source of income arises from contractual employment with regular wages and salaries because of skill or educational endowments, and those who earn their living from nonlabor assets without direct participation in economic activity. This nonparticipatory income may accrue from current returns from ownership of immovable assets (rental income accruing from leased-out owned land or real estate) or from past financial investments or receipts from private or public transfers, including remittances and pensions. In urban areas, four livelihood categories are distinguished: self-employed, earnings from regular wages and salaries, earnings from casual labor, and residual others. Since earnings from regular wages and salaries are explicitly distinguished in the urban classification, the category of residual others is taken to include only those households whose major source of income is from nonparticipatory earning as described in the rural context above.

In Tables 8.3 and 8.4 we present comparable all-India estimates of headcount ratios—that is, the proportion of persons below the poverty line by type of household on the major means of livelihood criterion and the share of population located in each type of household in total rural/urban populations and the corresponding poor population for, respectively, the rural and the urban areas for 1993–1994 and 1999–2000.

In order to handle the problems of comparability of poverty estimates over time, we present for 1993–1994 a comparable estimate specially computed (from unit record data) with a mixed reference period that will be com-

Table 8.3 Poverty Prevalence Rates and Distribution of Poor by Means of Livelihood of Household, Rural India, 1993/94–1999/00

Household Type	1993–1994 (Mixed Reference Period)			1999–2000		
	Share in Total Rural Population (per 1,000)	Headcount Ratio (%)	Share in Poor Population (per 1,000)	Share in Total Rural Population (per 1,000)	Headcount Ratio (%)	Share in Poor Population (per 1,000)
Self-employed in agriculture	424	26.08	323	378	21.62	283
Self-employed in nonagriculture	131	29.18	112	138	24.09	115
Agricultural labor	275	52.97	426	311	44.64	480
Other labor	75	35.82	78	74	27.79	71
Others	95	21.69	60	99	14.93	51
All	1,000	34.20	1,000	1,000	28.93	1,000

Sources: Author calculations based on Government of India 1995; data for 1999–2000 computed from Sundaram 2001c.

Table 8.4 Poverty Prevalence Rates and Distribution of Poor by Means of Livelihood of Household, Urban India, 1993/94–1999/00

Household Type	1993–1994 (Mixed Reference Period)			1999–2000		
	Share in Total Urban Population (per 1,000)	Headcount Ratio (%)	Share in Poor Population (per 1,000)	Share in Total Urban Population (per 1,000)	Headcount Ratio (%)	Share in Poor Population (per 1,000)
Self-employed	388	28.51	419	392	26.11	445
Regular wage/salaried	427	15.62	252	400	11.36	197
Casual labor	132	57.25	286	143	49.95	311
Others	54	21.05	43	64	16.85	47
All	1,000	26.41	1,000	1,000	23.09	1,000

Sources: Author calculations based on Government of India 1995; data for 1999–2000 computed from Sundaram 2001c.

parable with the estimates for 1999–2000 (see Sundaram and Tendulkar 2003a, 2003b).

Looking at changes over time, we find a welcome reduction in the headcount ratios in terms of population located in all household types in rural India. The headcount ratio of the most vulnerable agricultural labor households declined sharply, from 53 percent in 1993–1994 to 44.6 percent in 1999–2000, a rate of decline on par with that experienced by all rural households.

In urban India too, the casual labor households that are most vulnerable to poverty experienced a somewhat less sharp decline, of 7 percentage points in headcount ratio between 1993–1994 and 1999–2000.

Despite this decline in headcount or poverty prevalence ratios, the rural (agricultural plus other) labor households, with a 38.5 percent combined share in total rural population, constituted the dominant group (55 percent) among the rural poor population in 1999–2000. Even in urban India, the casual labor households, with a 14 percent share in total urban population, accounted for close to one-third of the urban poor population.

As will be evident from the tables, with a share of nearly 45 percent in the urban poor population and a 40 percent share in the rural poor population, households dependent on the returns from self-employment—in agriculture and outside agriculture—constitute a significant part of the poverty situation in India, such that poverty among population located in (wage-) labor-dependent households can only provide a partial picture about the poor in the labor force.

The Laboring Poor: Time Criterion–Based Perspective

Demographic Determinants.[5] The working poor in the labor force are defined as those who are located in households below the poverty line and are classified as workers (constituting the working poor) as well as unemployed[6] (i.e., those seeking or available for work) on the usual (principal plus subsidiary) status categorization per a long reference period (365 days preceding the survey). This section is focused directly on the second perspective of individual laborers located in households that fall below the poverty line. Two demographic factors shape the overall worker (or labor force) population ratios in the poor and the nonpoor households and therefore also determine the size of the population of the poor in the labor force: the child-dependency ratio and the child-woman ratio. The larger the proportion of children (with lower-than-average participation rates) in the population, the lower, other effects remaining constant, will be the overall (or crude) work force (and labor force) participation rate.

The child-woman ratio, or the ratio of the number of children in the age group 0–4 to the number of women in the reproductive age group 15–49, can also be viewed as a factor that constrains the participation in the labor force of women, who typically have to carry the primary burden of child rearing and for whom, therefore, the demands on their time for child care are often met by reduced participation in the labor force. Table 8.5 (lines 1–5) provides the details of the age-sex composition of the poor and the nonpoor households in rural and urban India for 1999–2000. We have at once a striking result. In both rural and urban India the child-dependency ratios (line 6) are significantly higher—by close to or above 30 percentage points—in the poor relative to the nonpoor households. The child-woman ratios (line 7) in the poor households too are higher (relative to those in the nonpoor households), by about 28 percentage points. In terms of their effect on worker-population ratios (see Table 8.6) for males and for all persons, the WPRs in poor households are lower—by 4–7 percentage points for males—relative to the WPRs in the nonpoor households. This is a consequence of the much higher child-dependency ratios in the poor households.

In the case of women, however, both in rural and in urban India, on average, WPRs of women in the poor households are higher than those in the households above the poverty line, though only marginally so in rural India. In urban India, the differentials have narrowed, but the WPRs for women in poor households continue to be higher than those in the nonpoor households.

Table 8.5   Age-Sex Composition of Population in Poor and Nonpoor Households, Rural and Urban India, 1999–2000

	Share in Rural Population (%)		Share in Urban Population (%)	
	Poor Households	Nonpoor Households	Poor Households	Nonpoor Households
Male child (0–14 years old)	22.83	17.99	21.58	15.05
Female child (0–14 years old)	22.80	15.62	21.33	12.99
Male adult (15–64 years old)	24.81	31.11	26.98	35.71
Female adult (15–64 years old)	26.07	30.43	26.57	31.83
Old (64+ years)	3.49	4.86	3.53	4.42
Child dependency ratio[a] [(1 + 2) / (3 + 4) × 1,000]	897	546	801	415
Child-woman ratio (per 1,000)	685	399	577	291

Sources: Author calculations based on Government of India 1995; data for 1999–2000 computed from Sundaram 2001c.
Note: a. Computed as [(male child + female child) / (male adult + female adult)] × 1,000.

Table 8.6 Worker-Population Ratios (thousands) in Poor and Nonpoor Households by Gender and Rural-Urban Location, India, 1993/94–1999/00

	Rural				Urban			
	Poor Households		Nonpoor Households		Poor Households		Nonpoor Households	
	1993–1994	1999–2000	1993–1994	1999–2000	1993–1994	1999–2000	1993–1994	1999–2000
Males	503	480	578	550	477	464	536	533
Females	330	297	327	299	196	163	139	131
All persons	417	388	458	430	338	315	352	346
Share of female workers in labor force	393	385	341	334	287	256	183	177

Source: Sundaram 2001c.
Note: Worker-population ratios are based on the usual (principal plus subsidiary) status categorization.

That this should occur despite the considerably higher child-dependency ratio and the higher child-woman ratio in the poor households would suggest the presence of a measure of what may be called compelling need-based participation of women in the work force where it is their poverty status that, other effects remaining constant, drives them to greater work participation.[7]

In economic environments characterized by lower returns to labor for women relative to those for men—due to the nature of the industry and occupations in which they are engaged and/or differential returns for the same activity—a larger proportion of women workers to total workers could itself become a factor that raises the probability of a household falling below the poverty line.[8] Seen in this perspective it is significant that the share of women workers to total workers in the poor households is noticeably higher than the corresponding proportion in the nonpoor households. This holds true for both the rural and the urban populations (Table 8.6, last line) in both years. In rural India this differential is of the order of 5 percentage points, while in urban India the share of women workers in the work force in poor households is higher by 8–9 percentage points.

Estimates of Magnitude of the Poor in the Labor Force, 1993–1994. We turn now to a presentation and discussion of the estimated magnitudes of the poor in the labor force in India. At the outset, it is important to stress that all our estimates of the size of the work force, in poor households as well as in all households, fully reflect the results of the 2001 population census in respect of the underlying estimates of population in the four segments—rural males, rural females, urban males, and urban females—for the midpoints (January 1) of the survey years (July–June) 1993–1994 and 1999–2000.

In Tables 8.7 (rural) and 8.8 (urban) we present the distribution of the total population in all households (the poor and the nonpoor) and separately for those located in households below the poverty line—the population of the poor—by gender and labor force status. In each table, panel A presents the estimates for 1993–1994 while panel B presents the estimates for 1999–2000.

Let us first examine the situation as of January 1, 1994. As per our estimates, in rural India there were close to 225 million people living below the poverty line, more or less evenly split between males and females. A little under 42 percent, or about 94 million people located in below-poverty-line households, were in the work force, with another 0.7 million being classified as unemployed. So, in rural India, the size of the poor labor force was estimated to be 94.6 million.

For the corresponding estimates for urban India, the number of poor persons, the number in the work force, and the number in the labor force in poor households are, respectively, 62.0 million, 20.9 million, and 21.6 million. The magnitude of the rural-plus-urban labor poor in the work force is thus estimated to be 116.2 million. After netting out the unemployed, our estimate of

Table 8.7 Distribution of Population (thousands) in All Households and Poor Households by Labor Status and Gender, Rural India, 1993/94–1999/00

Labor Force Category	All Households			Poor Households		
	Males	Females	All Persons	Males	Females	All Persons
Panel A: 1993–1994						
Employed	187,765	104,716	292,481	56,976	36,945	93,921
Unemployed	2,710	831	3,541	550	119	669
Labor force	190,475	105,547	296,022	57,526	37,064	94,590
Outside labor force	149,128	213,875	363,003	55,853	74,796	130,649
Total population	339,603	319,422	659,025	113,379	111,860	225,239
Panel B: 1999–2000						
Employed	198,501	105,635	304,136	50,406	31,530	81,936
Unemployed	3,462	1,107	4,569	818	106	924
Labor force	201,963	106,742	308,705	51,224	31,636	82,860
Outside labor force	172,125	246,781	418,906	53,780	74,364	128,144
Total population	374,088	353,523	727,611	105,004	106,000	211,004

Source: Sundaram 2001c.

Table 8.8 Distribution of Population (thousands) in All Households and Poor Households by Labor Status and Gender, Urban India, 1993/94–1999/00

Labor Force Category	All Households			Poor Households		
	Males	Females	All Persons	Males	Females	All Persons
Panel A: 1993–1994						
Employed	64,592	17,166	81,758	14,918	6,008	20,926
Unemployed	2,726	1,144	3,870	562	161	723
Labor force	67,318	18,310	85,628	15,480	6,169	21,649
Outside labor force	56,634	92,717	149,353	15,819	24,485	40,304
Total population	123,954	111,027	234,981	31,299	30,654	61,953
Panel B: 1999–2000						
Employed	75,326	18,208	93,534	15,235	5,248	20,483
Unemployed	3,554	1,102	4,656	721	116	837
Labor force	78,880	19,310	98,190	15,956	5,364	21,320
Outside labor force	66,645	111,640	178,285	16,881	26,833	43,714
Total population	145,525	130,950	276,475	32,837	32,197	65,034

Source: Sundaram 2001c.

the number of working poor as of January 1, 1994, is 114.8 million, or a little over 30 percent of the total work force.

In terms of gender composition, the share of women among the working poor (37.4 percent) is about 4 percentage points higher than their share in the total work force, reflecting the fact that the poverty prevalence rates among women workers are greater than those for male workers in both rural and urban areas (with headcount ratios of 35.3 percent and 30.4 percent for females and males in rural India, and 35.0 and 23.1 percent in urban India)[9] (see Table 8.13).

Similarly, the workers in rural India are overrepresented among the working poor, because the share of rural workers in the total (rural plus urban) work force is 78.2 percent, while the share of rural working poor, at 81.8 percent, is 4 percentage points higher. The underlying factor is the same: a higher poverty ratio for rural workers (32.1 percent) relative to their urban counterparts (25.6 percent).

Changes Between 1993–1994 and 1999–2000. Comparable estimates for January 1, 2000, are presented in panel B of Tables 8.7 (rural) and 8.8 (urban). The working poor in the labor force in rural India numbered a little under 83 million in 1999–2000, recording a decline of 11.7 million. With a small increase in the number of the unemployed in the below-poverty-line households (of a little under 0.3 million), the decline in the number of the rural working poor (to 81.9 million) was higher, at 12 million over the six-year period 1993/94–1999/00.

In urban India too, the number of both the working poor and the poor in the labor force recorded a decline—albeit a marginal one. This marginal decline for urban persons hides a marginal rise for urban males that is more than offset by the decline in the number of both the working poor and the poor in the labor force among urban females.

Overall, taking both segments together, there is a decline in the number of the working poor in the country as a whole, from 114.8 million in 1993–1994 to 102.4 million in 1999–2000 (i.e., by a little over 12 million). Also, the share of women workers in the working poor has come down—from 37.4 percent to 35.9 percent—over the same period. The rural share too has come down (from 81.8 to 80.0 percent) between January 1, 1994, and January 1, 2000.[10]

Rural Working Poor: Gender and Economic Activity Dimensions. Table 8.9 presents the estimates for 1993–1994 of the rural workers in all households and in poor households classified by gender and economic activity status distinguished in the survey. This information is rearranged in Table 8.10 to obtain the composition of the workers (per 1,000) in the poor and the nonpoor households by gender and broad activity composition. This brings out a significant feature of the working poor in rural India: the proportion of those working in mainly self-employed activities, at 45.5 percent, though lower

Table 8.9 Distribution of Workers (thousands) in All Households and Poor Households by Economic Activity and Gender, Rural India, 1993–1994

Economic Activity	All Households			Poor Households		
	Males	Females	All Persons	Males	Females	All Persons
Self-employed in agriculture	83,927	52,665	136,592	20,614	13,800	34,414
Self-employed in nonagriculture	24,174	8,793	32,967	5,803	2,500	8,303
Self-employed total	108,101	61,458	169,559	26,417	16,300	42,717
Regular wage/salaried in agriculture	2,492	491	3,983	889	154	1,043
Regular wage/salaried in nonagriculture	13,584	2,311	15,895	1,431	426	1,857
Regular wage/salaried total	16,076	2,802	18,878	2,320	580	2,900
Casual labor in public works	620	372	992	316	209	525
Casual labor in agriculture	51,109	36,508	87,617	24,296	18,572	42,868
Casual labor in nonagriculture	11,860	3,575	15,435	3,629	1,283	4,912
Casual labor total	63,589	40,455	104,044	28,241	20,064	48,305
Total work force	187,765	104,716	292,481	56,976	36,945	93,921

Source: Author calculations.

Table 8.10 Distribution of Workers (thousands) in Poor and Nonpoor Households by Economic Activity and Gender, Rural India, 1993–1994

Economic Activity	Poor Households			Nonpoor Households		
	Males	Females	All Persons	Males	Females	All Persons
Self-employed in agriculture	219	147	366	319	196	515
Self-employed in nonagriculture	62	27	88	93	32	124
Self-employed total	281	174	455	411	227	639
Regular wage/salaried in agriculture	9	2	11	8	2	10
Regular wage/salaried in nonagriculture	15	5	20	61	9	71
Regular wage/salaried total	25	6	31	69	11	80
Casual labor in public works	3	2	6	2	0.8	2
Casual labor in agriculture	259	198	456	135	90	225
Casual labor in nonagriculture	39	14	52	41	12	53
Casual labor total	301	214	514	178	103	281
All activities	607	393	1,000	659	341	1,000
Total work force	56,976	36,945	93,921	130,789	67,771	198,560

Source: Author calculations.

than the proportion of those working as casual laborers (51.4 percent), is very substantial in 1993–1994.

In contrasting the activity composition of the working poor with that of the workers located in nonpoor households, two points emerge. First, the share of casual laborers among the working poor is substantially higher (by 23 percentage points) than their share among the work force of nonpoor households. Predominantly, this reflects a much greater proportion of the self-employed among the workers located in above-poverty-line households.

Second, the proportion of those employed as regular wage/salaried employees in nonagriculture is significantly higher (by 5 percentage points) in the nonpoor households relative to those in the below-poverty-line households. As we shall see below, in rural labor households the absence of even one such regular wage/salaried worker in nonagriculture in a household significantly raises the probability of such a household falling below the poverty line.

Parallel estimates of the number of workers in all households and in poor households and of the per 1,000 distribution of workers in the poor and the nonpoor households, by gender and broad activity status in rural India for 1999–2000, are presented in Tables 8.11 and 8.12 respectively.

We noted above an absolute reduction in the number of working poor in rural India of close to 12.0 million between 1993–1994 and 1999–2000. When we examine the changes in the number of working poor by activity categories, we have a striking result. Excepting women workers self-employed in non-agriculture and male casual laborers—also in nonagricultural activities—all other categories distinguished in this exercise experienced a decline in the number of working poor in rural India.

The self-employed, as a group, form the major contributor to the reduction in the number of working poor in rural India. There is a reduction of about 7.4 million in the number of self-employed workers in agriculture who are located in poor households. This reduction is partly facilitated by the reduction in the total number of self-employed workers in agriculture in rural India (from 136.6 million in 1993–1994 to 134.0 million in 1999–2000), with the reduction in headcount ratios in the group by 5 percentage points, from 32 percent to 27 percent, being the key factor (see Table 8.13).

The role of the (sharp) decline in headcount ratios in reducing the number of the working poor can be seen more clearly in the case of the casual laborers engaged in agriculture. Given the fact that between 1993–1994 and 1999–2000 the estimated number of casual laborers in agriculture in rural India increased from 87.6 to 94.6 million, if the headcount ratio among such workers had remained unchanged at the 1993–1994 level of 48.9 percent, the number of such workers in the below-poverty-line households would have increased by a little under 3.5 million. Instead, thanks to a reduction in the headcount ratio among such workers (to 41 percent in 1999–2000), the number of

Table 8.11 Distribution of Workers (thousands) in All Households and Poor Households by Economic Activity and Gender, Rural India, 1999–2000

Economic Activity	All Households			Poor Households		
	Males	Females	All Persons	Males	Females	All Persons
Self-employed in agriculture	83,021	50,972	133,993	16,218	10,833	27,051
Self-employed in nonagriculture	25,956	9,619	35,575	5,445	2,705	8,150
Self-employed total	108,977	60,591	169,568	21,663	13,538	35,201
Regular wage/salaried in agriculture	2,500	615	3,115	735	189	924
Regular wage/salaried in nonagriculture	15,070	2,637	17,707	1,311	335	1,646
Regular wage/salaried total	17,570	3,252	20,822	2,046	524	2,570
Casual labor in public works	430	148	578	137	65	202
Casual labor in agriculture	56,108	38,526	94,634	22,579	16,201	38,780
Casual labor in nonagriculture	15,416	3,118	18,534	3,932	1,066	4,998
Casual labor total	71,954	41,792	113,168	26,648	17,332	43,900
Total work force	198,501	105,635	304,136	50,406	31,530	81,936

Source: Author calculations.

Table 8.12 Distribution of Workers (thousands) in Poor and Nonpoor Households by Economic Activity and Gender, Rural India, 1999–2000

Economic Activity	Poor Households			Nonpoor Households		
	Males	Females	All Persons	Males	Females	All Persons
Self-employed in agriculture	198	133	331	300	181	481
Self-employed in nonagriculture	67	33	100	92	31	123
Self-employed total	265	166	431	392	212	604
Regular wage/salaried in agriculture	9	2	11	8	2	10
Regular wage/salaried in nonagriculture	16	4	20	62	10	72
Regular wage/salaried total	25	6	31	70	12	82
Casual labor in public works	2	1	3	1.3	0.4	2
Casual labor in agriculture	276	198	474	151	100	251
Casual labor in nonagriculture	48	13	61	52	9	61
Casual labor total	326	212	538	204	110	314
All activities	616	384	1,000	666	334	1,000
Total work force	50,406	31,530	81,936	148,095	74,105	222,200

Source: Author calculations.

Table 8.13 Proportion of Persons by Labor Status, and Proportion of Workers by Economic Activity, Located in Households Below Poverty Line, by Gender and Rural-Urban Location, India, 1993/94–1999/00

	1993–1994			1999–2000		
	Males	Females	All Persons	Males	Females	All Persons
Panel A: Rural Headcount Ratio (%)						
Persons by labor status						
Employed	30.35	35.28	32.11	25.39	29.85	26.94
Unemployed	20.29	14.27	18.89	23.63	9.58	20.22
Labor force	30.20	35.12	31.95	25.36	29.64	26.84
Total population	33.39	35.02	34.18	28.07	29.98	29.00
Employed by economic activity						
Self-employed in agriculture	24.56	26.20	25.19	19.53	21.25	20.19
Self-employed in nonagriculture	24.01	28.43	25.19	20.98	28.12	22.91
Self-employed total	24.44	26.52	25.19	19.88	22.34	20.76
Regular wage/salaried in agriculture	35.66	31.44	34.96	29.40	30.73	29.66
Regular wage/salaried in nonagriculture	10.53	18.43	11.68	8.70	12.70	9.30
Regular wage/salaried total	14.43	20.71	15.36	11.64	16.11	12.34
Casual labor in public works	50.95	56.06	52.92	31.86	43.92	34.95
Casual labor in agriculture	47.54	50.87	48.93	40.24	42.05	40.98
Casual labor in nonagriculture	30.60	35.89	31.82	25.51	34.19	26.97
Casual labor total	44.41	49.59	46.43	37.03	41.47	38.67
Total work force	30.55	35.28	32.11	25.39	29.85	26.94
Panel B: Urban Headcount Ratio (%)						
Persons by labor status						
Employed	23.10	35.00	25.60	20.23	28.82	21.90
Unemployed	20.62	14.07	18.68	20.30	10.59	18.05

continues

Table 8.13 Continued

	1993–1994			1999–2000		
	Males	Females	All Persons	Males	Females	All Persons
Labor Force	23.00	33.69	25.28	20.23	27.89	21.74
Total population	25.25	27.61	26.37	22.56	24.59	23.52
Employed by economic activity						
Self-employed in agriculture	33.65	33.22	33.47	27.43	34.19	29.86
Self-employed in nonagriculture	22.67	34.60	24.85	20.26	30.46	22.19
Self-employed total	24.08	34.16	26.33	20.94	31.22	23.09
Regular wage/salaried in agriculture	33.33	35.71	33.64	23.16	17.50	21.92
Regular wage/salaried in nonagriculture	12.54	16.90	13.22	10.42	11.88	10.66
Regular wage/salaried total	12.76	17.06	13.43	10.54	11.95	10.77
Casual labor in public works	37.04	40.00	37.40	41.15	48.15	42.59
Casual labor in agriculture	67.10	70.62	68.72	59.64	57.91	58.83
Casual labor in nonagriculture	42.77	47.59	43.95	39.00	44.52	40.00
Casual labor total	47.40	56.52	50.13	41.74	49.60	43.59
Total work force	23.10	35.00	25.60	20.23	28.92	21.90

Source: Author calculations.

Note: Headcount ratio in each labor force activity category is defined by the number in a given category who are located in below-poverty-line households as a proportion of the total number in that category located in all (poor plus nonpoor) households.

casual laborers in agriculture in below-poverty-line households declined by a little over 4 million between 1993–1994 and 1999–2000. As observed earlier, this significant reduction in headcount ratio among casual workers in rural India has been made possible by the strong growth in real wages experienced by casual laborers in rural India.

In terms of the broad activity composition of the working poor, the situation in 1999–2000 (Table 8.12) reflects the growing share of casual laborers in the total rural work force. In the total rural work force, for casual laborers in agriculture and casual laborers in nonagriculture, this increase was on the order of about 1 percentage point each. This is partially offset by a marginal decline in the share of casual laborers in public works, so that we have an overall increase of a little over 2 percentage points in the share of casual laborers as a group. In the case of the working poor in rural India, the share of casual laborers, as a group, has increased from about 51.4 percent to 53.8 percent (Tables 8.10 and 8.12), with a 2-percentage-point rise in the share of casual laborers in agriculture among the working poor. This is despite the sizable reduction in the poverty ratios for this class of workers noted above.

With an unchanged share of the regular wage/salaried workers of a little over 3 percent, the rise in the share of casual laborers in the rural working poor is matched by a decline in the share of the self-employed as a group. The broad pattern of change—a rise in the share of casual laborers and a fall in the share of the self-employed—for the working poor also holds true for the workers located in above-poverty-line households.

The significantly higher share of the regular wage/salaried employees in the nonagricultural sector among the workers in above-poverty-line households (relative to their share in the working poor) continues to be true in 1999–2000; if anything, this divergence has increased slightly.

Urban Working Poor: Gender and Economic Activity Dimensions. We turn now to an examination of the activity composition of the working poor in urban India and the changes therein between 1993–1994 and 1999–2000 (see Tables 8.14–8.17).

Unlike in rural India, it is the self-employed as a group (and not casual laborers) who contributed the largest share, 45 percent, to the working poor in urban India in 1999–2000. These are mostly urban informal sector self-employment activities having very low productivity and absorbing unskilled workers with inadequate physical or human capital endowment. With a share of 36 percent, casual laborers have a distinctly lower share among the working poor. Also, as one would expect in the urban context, workers in nonagricultural activities, with a 83 percent share, dominate the working poor (Table 8.17).

Another significant feature of the activity composition of the working poor in urban India is the fact that regular wage/salaried employees account

Table 8.14 Distribution of Workers (thousands) in All Households and Poor Households by Economic Activity and Gender, Urban India, 1993–1994

Economic Activity	All Households			Poor Households		
	Males	Females	All Persons	Males	Females	All Persons
Self-employed in agriculture	3,453	2,456	5,909	1,162	816	1,978
Self-employed in nonagriculture	23,423	5,237	28,660	5,311	1,812	7,123
Self-employed total	26,876	7,693	34,569	6,473	2,628	9,101
Regular wage/salaried in agriculture	288	42	330	96	15	111
Regular wage/salaried in nonagriculture	26,945	4,955	31,904	3,380	838	4,218
Regular wage/salaried total	27,233	5,001	32,234	3,476	853	4,329
Casual labor in public works	108	15	123	40	6	46
Casual labor in agriculture	2,021	1,739	3,760	1,356	1,228	2,584
Casual labor in nonagriculture	8,354	2,719	11,073	3,573	1,294	4,867
Casual labor total	10,483	4,473	14,956	4,969	2,528	7,497
Total work force	64,592	17,167	81,759	14,918	6,009	20,927

Source: Author calculations.

Table 8.15 Distribution of Workers (thousands) in Poor and Nonpoor Households by Economic Activity and Gender, Urban India, 1993–1994

Economic Activity	Poor Households			Nonpoor Households		
	Males	Females	All Persons	Males	Females	All Persons
Self-employed in agriculture	56	39	95	38	27	65
Self-employed in nonagriculture	254	87	340	298	56	354
Self-employed total	309	126	435	336	83	419
Regular wage/salaried in agriculture	5	0.7	5	3	0.4	4
Regular wage/salaried in nonagriculture	162	40	202	387	68	455
Regular wage/salaried total	166	41	207	390	68	459
Casual labor in public works	2	0.3	2	1	0.15	1
Casual labor in agriculture	65	59	123	11	8	19
Casual labor in nonagriculture	171	62	233	79	23	102
Casual labor total	238	121	358	91	32	123
All activities	713	287	1,000	817	183	1,000
Total work force	14,918	6,009	20,927	49,674	11,158	60,832

Source: Author calculations.

Table 8.16 Distribution of Workers (thousands) in All Households and Poor Households by Economic Activity and Gender, Urban India, 1999–2000

Economic Activity	All Households			Poor Households		
	Males	Females	All Persons	Males	Females	All Persons
Self-employed in agriculture	2,993	1,676	4,669	821	573	1,394
Self-employed in nonagriculture	28,234	6,585	34,819	5,719	2,006	7,725
Self-employed total	31,227	8,241	39,488	6,540	2,579	9,119
Regular wage/salaried in agriculture	285	80	365	66	14	80
Regular wage/salaried in nonagriculture	31,120	5,978	37,098	3,243	710	3,953
Regular wage/salaried total	31,405	6,058	37,463	3,309	724	4,033
Casual labor in public works	209	54	268	86	26	112
Casual labor in agriculture	1,665	1,461	3,126	993	846	1,839
Casual labor in nonagriculture	10,820	2,374	13,194	4,220	1,057	5,277
Casual labor total	12,694	3,889	16,583	5,299	1,929	7,228
Total work force	75,326	18,208	93,534	15,235	5,248	20,483

Source: Author calculations.

Table 8.17 Distribution of Workers (thousands) in Poor and Nonpoor Households by Economic Activity and Gender, Urban India, 1999–2000

Economic Activity	Poor Households			Nonpoor Households		
	Males	Females	All Persons	Males	Females	All Persons
Self-employed in agriculture	40	28	68	30	15	45
Self-employed in nonagriculture	281	98	379	307	63	370
Self-employed total	321	126	447	337	78	915
Regular wage/salaried in agriculture	3	0.7	4	3	1	4
Regular wage/salaried in nonagriculture	159	35	194	381	72	453
Regular wage/salaried total	162	36	198	384	73	457
Casual labor in public works	4	1	5	1.7	0.4	2
Casual labor in agriculture	49	41	90	9	8	18
Casual labor in nonagriculture	207	52	259	90	18	108
Casual labor total	260	95	355	101	27	128
All activities	743	257	1,000	823	177	1,000
Total work force	15,235	5,248	20,483	60,091	12,960	73,051

Source: Author calculations.

for a little under one-fifth (19.8 percent) of the working poor. However, as in the case of rural India, the share of such workers among the working poor is distinctly smaller (by 26 percentage points) than their share among nonpoor workers.

In terms of changes over the 1990s, as noted earlier, there is a decline—albeit marginal—in the number of the working poor in urban India for both sexes taken together. In terms of the three broad activity groups (self-employment, regular wage/salaried employment, and casual labor) for both sexes together, there is a slight (1 percentage point) rise in the share of the self-employed offset by a similar decline in the share of the regular wage/salaried employees, with the share of the casual labor households remaining virtually constant. However, the share of women in the working poor, and of those among them working as casual laborers, has declined by slightly under 3 percentage points. This decline is compensated by a similar rise in the share of male casual laborers in nonagricultural activities among the working poor in urban India.

Working Poor: Educational Characteristics. Before concluding this discussion of the working poor in India, we wish to focus on the differences in the educational characteristics of the working poor and the workers in the above-poverty-line households. We present in Table 8.18 a distribution of usual status (principal plus subsidiary) workers located in poor and nonpoor households by level of education, gender, and rural-urban location for 1993–1994. The contrasts by poverty status (given gender and location), by gender (given location and poverty status), and by rural-urban location (given gender and poverty status) are rather striking.

Consider first the poor-nonpoor contrast. In rural India, the proportion of illiterate workers in poor households (i.e., among the working poor) is 20 percentage points greater than that among the workers in nonpoor households. Further, among workers in nonpoor households, the proportion with education up to and above the secondary level of education (24 percent) is much higher—relative to the 10 percent share among the working poor.

These contrasts in the education levels of the working poor and of the workers in the nonpoor households are even sharper in urban India. Thus, while 48 percent of the working poor are illiterates, the proportion of illiterates among workers in nonpoor households is much lower, at 18 percent. Equally if not more significant is the fact that while the proportion of workers with education above the secondary level is less than 4 percent among the working poor, close to 27 percent of workers in nonpoor households have this level of education.

The gender contrasts, too, are rather stark. Among the working poor in rural India, the proportion of illiterates among women workers (at 88 percent) is higher than the corresponding proportion among males, by nearly 30 per-

Table 8.18 Distribution of Usual (principal plus subsidiary) Status Workers in Poor and Nonpoor Households by Education, Gender, and Rural-Urban Location, India, 1993–1994

Level of Education	Poor Households			Nonpoor Households		
	Males	Females	All Persons	Males	Females	All Persons
Panel A: Rural India (%)						
Illiterate	59.74	87.82	70.81	37.38	72.96	49.55
Literate up to primary	25.87	9.54	19.43	30.94	17.60	26.38
Up to secondary	12.38	2.46	8.47	24.33	8.07	18.77
Above secondary	2.01	0.19	1.29	7.36	1.36	5.31
Panel B: Urban India (%)						
Illiterate	37.88	71.16	47.50	13.04	37.27	17.52
Literate up to primary	33.96	19.99	29.92	23.81	20.73	23.24
Up to secondary	23.45	7.35	18.79	35.10	20.13	32.33
Above secondary	4.72	1.51	3.79	28.05	21.87	26.91

Source: Author calculations.

centage points. Even among workers in nonpoor households in urban India, the share of illiterates among women workers is nearly three times as large as the proportion of illiterates among male workers in these households.

Across the rural-urban divide, for both males and females and in both poor and nonpoor households, the proportion of illiterate workers is smaller, and the proportion of those with education up to or above secondary level is sharply higher in urban India.

As we shall see below, the level of a worker's education matters in conditioning the probability of a household falling below the poverty line. So the redressing of inequalities in worker education levels across gender and location is important—not only as a goal by itself but also as a key instrumental variable in reducing poverty.

■ Labor Market Characteristics of Households and Poverty

Starting with the premise that, for a given household, the probability of it being poor is conditioned by its physical and human capital resource base and the extent and nature of its participation in the labor market, we examine, using a Probit model framework, the relationship between the household-level characteristics in general and in particular their labor market characteristics on the one hand and the probability of the household being poor on the other. Focusing on the rural labor households in Madhya Pradesh, the model is evaluated by reference to the unit record data from the 1993–1994 consumer expenditure and employment/unemployment survey.

We turn now to the key labor market characteristics that impact the probability of a household being poor. The first and the most obvious factor here is the earner strength of the household normalized for household size. In our analysis we capture this by the usual (principal plus subsidiary) status worker-population ratio in the household *(wprupss)*. And, other effects remaining constant, the higher the worker-population ratio, the lower the probability of the household being poor.

Previously we outlined the hypothesis that, given the number of workers, a higher ratio of female workers could, per se, be a factor raising the probability of the household being poor. Care is needed in interpreting this hypothesis and the empirical results confirming it. One additional female worker in the household would directly lower the probability of the household being poor by raising the earner strength *(wprupss* in the model) of the household. However, the extent of this favorable effect would be moderated or partially offset (if the hypothesis is confirmed by data) by the widely observed lower returns to female labor relative to those for males.

Our analysis of the activity composition of workers among poor and the nonpoor households highlighted the fact that the proportion of workers who are regular wage/salaried employees in nonagricultural activities was significantly higher in the nonpoor households than among the working poor. Since the absence of such workers is the norm among the poor households, we introduce this as a binary dummy variable, which takes the value 1 if such a worker is not present in the household, and 0 otherwise. It is hypothesized that, other effects remaining constant, this factor would raise the probability of the household being poor. It would surprise no one to find that, in our sample of labor households in rural Madhya Pradesh, a little over 94 percent of such households do not have even a single worker who is employed as a regular wage/salaried employee in nonagricultural activities.

Finally, we have from the survey the activity status classification of the members of the household on each of the seven days preceding the date of survey, on the basis of which the current daily status estimates are generated. From this information we can compute, for each household, the number of days at work in the week preceding the survey. This is normalized by reference to the number of workers in the household as per the usual (principal plus subsidiary) status categorization. This variable, *perdwkd* (person-days worked during the reference week per usual status worker in the household), is hypothesized to carry a negative sign—that is, the higher the number of days worked per worker in a household, the lower the probability of such a household being poor.

The other variables entering the model include:

Social group affiliation—that is, whether the household is a scheduled caste or a scheduled tribe.

Child-woman ratio as a factor constraining the nature and extent of labor market participation of the women in the household.

Possession of milk cattle and/or draught animals and per capita land possessed, reflecting the physical asset base of the household and capturing the human capital resource base.

Proportion of usual status workers with education up to or above the secondary level.

In presenting the results, we have reported both the regression coefficients as well as *dF/dx* values, where *dF* indicates the marginal change in the probability of being poor and *dx* stands for a unit change in the explanatory variable—1 hectare for *PCLDPOS,* a 1-percentage-point change in the child-woman ratio, and so forth. In the case of dummy variables—*SC/ST* and *REGNONAG* (region/subround dummies)—*dF/dx* is for the discrete change from 0 to 1. We also report, for each of the variables, values of Z (analogous to the *t*-value in OLS regression) and P > |z|, which test for the underlying coefficient being 0 (see Table 8.19).

Test statistics indicate that the overall fit of the model is good and almost all the variables are statistically significant. Focusing on the results in respect of

Table 8.19   Probit and Dprobit Coefficients of Household-Level Regressions, Rural Madhya Pradesh

Variable	Probit Coefficients	Marginal Coefficients (dF/dx)	X-bar
D_SCST	0.31096		
	(0.000)	0.12319	0.6187
PCLDPOS	−0.64798		
	(0.003)	−0.25829	0.118
D_MILCH	0.11558		
	(0.117)	0.04601	0.6258
P_WKREDU	−0.00887	−0.00354	2.5890
	(0.003)		
CHIL_WOM	0.003436		
	(0.000)	0.00137	68.0026
P_FEM_RAT	0.00149		
	(0.189)	0.000595	45.9777
D_RNAG	0.54036		
	(0.001)	0.02498	0.9429
P_WPRUPSS	−0.0516		
	(0.000)	−0.00206	54.1557
PER_DWKD	−0.0528		
	(0.030)	−0.021067	5.9264
D_SUBR1	0.29607		
	(0.003)	0.117631	0.2581
D_SUBR2	0.19938		
	(0.040)	0.079408	0.2445
D_SUBR3	0.10079		
	(0.303)	0.040187	0.2575
D_REG1	0.58552		
	(0.000)	0.229475	0.2840

continues

the labor market variables, it is seen that all the labor market variables carry the predicted sign and, except for the variable relating to the ratio of female workers to total workers on the usual (principal plus subsidiary) status categorization, are highly significant. Even the female ratio variable is significant at the 20 percent level of significance. Of these variables, in terms of marginal impact, the absence of even one regular wage/salaried worker in nonagriculture raises the probability of the household being poor by a little over 20 percent.

Next in order of impact is the effect of raising the number of days worked in a week by a usual status worker in the household by one day. This lowers the probability of the household being poor by a little over 2 percent. It would take a rise of 10 percentage points in the usual (principal plus subsidiary) sta-

Table 8.19   Continued

Variable	Probit Coefficients	Marginal Coefficients (*dF/dx*)	X-bar
D_REG2	0.83753		
	(0.000)	0.314158	0.1368
D_REG3	1.14395		
	(0.000)	0.402205	0.1115
D_REG4	0.16812		
	(0.292)	0.06698	0.1427
D_REG5	0.79097		
	(0.000)	0.29954	0.1511
D_REG6	1.33367		
	(0.000)	0.44397	0.0921
CONSTT	−1.25502		
	(0.000)		
Number of observations	1,542		
Wald chi^2	241.46		
Log likelihood	−926.22217		
Percentage of cases correctly predicted	77.65		
Percentage of poor households correctly classified as poor	65.07		
Percentage of nonpoor households correctly classified as nonpoor	70.47		
Observed probability	0.4883268		
Predicted probability (at x-bar)	0.4837734		

Notes: Figures in parentheses are the p-values (i.e., P > |z|), which constitute the test of the underlying coefficient being 0. *dF/dx* is for discrete change of dummy variable from 0 to 1. The X-bar values represent the mean values of the characteristic among the sampled households in the case of the continuous variables. In the case of the binary dummy variables, the X-bar values relate to the proportion of sample households with the specified characteristic. Thus an X-bar value of 0.6187 for *D_SCST* indicates that a little under 62 percent of the surveyed households, in the sample analyzed, are scheduled caste or scheduled tribal households.

tus worker population ratio in the household (from an average of a little over 54 percent) to match the effect of one additional day of work per week by a usual status worker, in terms of the effect on lowering the probability of the household being poor. A similar rise of 10 percentage points in the proportion of adult workers with secondary or higher level of education would lower the probability of the household being poor by 3.5 percent.

■ Dynamic Employment Policy

The employment policy following from the analysis presented in this chapter has the objective of meeting the twin challenge of productively absorbing prospective average annual additions of 8 million or more to the Indian labor force while progressively raising the levels of productivity per worker, which alone can ensure rising real returns to labor. The focus on real returns to labor is derived from the fact that a large proportion of the current Indian work force in general and of the working poor in particular is located in low-productivity activities and sectors with low returns to labor being diagnosed as the basic cause of income poverty. It also follows that raising real returns to labor based on rising productivity necessarily implies low or declining gross employment elasticities with respect to real output. So the central concern of employment policy has necessarily to be the rapid volume growth of real output based on sustained expansion of productive capacity, which defines economic growth (Kuznets 1973). Thus, rapid economic growth plays a powerful instrumental role in dynamic employment policy that takes care not just of the "quantity" of employment or the number of "jobs" or employment opportunities but also of the "quality'" of employment in terms of rising real returns to labor.

The dynamic employment policy flowing from this perspective has four basic ingredients: raising the rate of investment by generating private inducement to invest; improving resource-use efficiency; inducing faster growth in relatively more labor-intensive sectors; and addressing the urgent need for putting in place effective safety nets, including government-organized direct antipoverty programs for self-employment and wage-employment generation. International comparisons of rapidly growing economies (defined by well-above-average growth in real GDP in international comparisons) (see Hayami 1997, chap. 8; Tendulkar and Sen 2003; and Tendulkar 2000b) show that rapid growth results from a combination of high rates of investment with a high resource-use efficiency that is ensured by an aggressively open economy, with government playing a market-complementing role of providing physical and social infrastructure and following market-friendly policies. The first two ingredients are thus integral parts of well-known, standard growth-promoting policies. The third, to be consistent with continuing efficiency and productivity improvements, requires an aggressively open economy, and the fourth is required to alleviate short-term problems of "pains" of adjustment and prevalence of income poverty.

While the general dynamic employment policy explored in this chapter applies to all low-income countries with widespread prevalence of poverty and low productivity, it has to take account of specific initial conditions in each country. In this section we briefly discuss the major elements of such a policy in the Indian context. There has been a broad political consensus across a wide ideological spectrum of Indian polity on the need to put the economy on a rapid growth trajectory in order to eradicate poverty. The latest (tenth) five-year plan (2003–2008) postulates a growth rate of 8 percent—the highest projected in any Indian planning document.

Raising the Rate of Investment

Post-1991 economic policy reforms in investment, trade, and financial sector policies aim at generating a market-friendly environment for private investment by reducing policy-induced entry barriers in various economic activities. They will have to be complemented by reducing government dissavings and reversing the dilution of fiscal discipline that occurred in the second half of the 1990s, which was marked by a slowdown in rates of investment and savings. This would require drastic reduction in recently rising national and local revenue deficits so that government can pursue a responsible macroeconomic policy and play an effective role in providing safety nets and antipoverty programs as also present in the provision of physical and social infrastructural investments.

Improving Resource-Use Efficiency

Competition—both domestic and international—remains the best available instrument for reducing wasteful utilization of resources and generating newer and more productive employment opportunities, despite its attendant problems of differential speeds of adjustment in different markets and sometimes persistent disequilibria. Reforms since 1991 have managed to reduce entry barriers and introduce competition. However, Indian policymakers have continued to pursue asymmetric policies with respect to consequences of increased competition. While they welcome and have been supportive of the new employment opportunities in newly emerging sunrise industries, they have been wary of permitting a phase-out of sunset industries as well as inefficient units in sunrise industries. Consequently, the resulting improvements in resource-use efficiency have been undercut by organized labor market rigidities arising from overprotective labor legislation, and the continuation of exit barriers for enterprises while the overall economic performance continues to be constrained by the persistence of bottlenecks in physical (power, transport, communications, ports), social (education and health), and financial institutional infrastructure, and the limited access of small and medium enterprises to the institutional credit market. Corrective steps are clearly needed in these critical areas to ensure rapid expansion of productive employment.

Sectoral Policies

These policies consist of inducing faster growth in relatively labor-intensive sectors as part of the overall rapid growth strategy. Such a policy is distinct from the conventional "labor and employment" policy that lays single-minded emphasis on quantitative expansion of employment without making simultaneous efforts at raising the efficiency and productivity and aggressively tapping external markets to correct the domestic supply-demand mismatch. It is the latter efforts that form an important ingredient of the dynamic employment policy, for which aggressive opening up of the economy plays a critical role—

and had been missing in the earlier policy. Incidentally, this is equally important for improving the resource-use efficiency in the manufacturing sector in
the labor-using direction, as has been effectively done by China.

Four specific areas have been identified in the labor-intensive categories
by India's Task Force on Employment, set up by the Planning Commission
(see Government of India 2001b).

1. *Agriculture and allied activities.* The focus ought to be on raising
   productivity of land and livestock through improved technology
   along with diversification of crop and noncrop agriculture-related activities with a view to reducing widespread underemployment and
   improving real returns to labor. Here the Task Force on Employment
   correctly mentions statutory restrictions, originally socially well-
   intentioned but economically misplaced, on movements of primary
   commodities that have prevented the emergence of unified national
   markets, increased transaction costs, and resulted in their misuse by
   vested interest groups to restrict competition. The government has
   only very recently begun to address these activities.

2. *Food-processing industries.* Despite India being the largest producer
   of food grains and the second largest producer of fruits, vegetables,
   and milk, these products are mostly consumed in unprocessed forms,
   because of the absence of preservation infrastructure, statutory restrictions on movements, and complete insulation from external markets. Given a large international and growing domestic market with
   rising per capita incomes for processed food, appropriate restructuring of the industry with an eye on changing tastes would generate
   considerable productive employment in these as yet little-tapped
   labor-intensive activities.

3. *Small-scale industries.* This aspect had been the major plank of the
   conventional employment policy, with a plethora of concessions that
   have generated incentives to remain small even if inefficient and provided protection by restricting competition from domestic large-scale
   units by reserving a large number of industries for exclusive small-
   scale production. Many of these are labor-intensive exportables,
   which require a large-scale operation to be able to successfully compete in growing international markets for labor-intensive products.
   The inefficiencies and perverse incentives resulting from these policies have been pointed out (see Tendulkar and Bhavani 1997 and
   Bhavani and Tendulkar 2000). Adverse consequences of reservation
   policy have also been documented by the Abid Hussain Committee
   (Government of India 1997) as well as the Task Force on Employment (Government of India 2001b). Phased abolition of reservation

has also been recommended by official committees (Government of India 2001a, 2000). Progress, however, has been slow.

4. *Services.* The Task Force on Employment has identified a variety of service activities with considerable productive labor-absorbing potential. They include travel and tourism, which is constrained by service-specific infrastructure, and construction, real estate, and housing development, whose potential is constrained by small-scale operation and outdated laws on land development and rent control, which additionally also constrain labor-intensive, distributive trades in general and large-scale organized retailing in particular. All these activities would generate additional demand for a large variety of unskilled, semiskilled, and highly professional labor through direct and indirect linkages. Directly skill-intensive services in information technology as well as educational and health services require that the educational and skill base of a less educated and low-skilled labor force of 400 million be upgraded.

The Indispensable Complement of Effective Safety Nets and Antipoverty Programs

A dynamic employment policy centered on rapid growth as the key instrument has to reckon with an inescapable concomitant of the latter, namely the short-term dislocation and displacement resulting from unemployment and obsolescence and potential conflicts from rising earning disparities between sunrise and sunset industries, whose composition keeps changing continuously in the process of structural change (Kuznets 1972). These conflicts arise from differential speeds of adjustment to market signals in competitive markets. However, job losses in the process of sectoral reallocation of labor are more than offset by job gains in newly emerging activities. So long as the tempo of rapid growth is maintained, net employment will increase with rising productivity per worker to take care of both the quantity and quality dimensions of employment. This feature indicates a clear need for effective safety nets to alleviate hardships of displaced/unemployed workers, complemented by a facilitation of their movement to areas, industries, or units experiencing expansion. These safety nets may consist of strictly time-bound protections, providing reasonable compensation in the event of layoff, retrenchment, or closures; expanding facilities for skill acquisition; offering training and education; and facilitating their industrial, occupational, and locational mobility. Evolving these safety nets requires a decisive shift of past policy away from the legislative protection of existing employment, which has slowed the generation of new and more productive employment opportunities besides endangering the sustainability of protected employment in competitive product markets.

Programs for generating self-employment and wage employment for targeted households below the poverty line have been in operation since the end of the 1970s, with their numbers multiplying over the years with uneven effectiveness. There has been a welcome rationalization of these programs since 1999. Innovative features of the rationalized antipoverty programs for enhancing income-earning potential through self-employment include the provision of multiple doses of credit to help a poor household attain viability gradually in the newly undertaken activity, and the introduction of microcredit to self-help groups that undertake collective monitoring of the supported activities as well as repayment of loans. Similarly, two types of programs to generate wage employment have been devised and are in operation. The first aims at generating additional wage employment on demand during a slack agricultural season or in the event of an agricultural harvest failure by providing manual work with a view to providing income supplement to the poor households. The primary objective of the second program is the creation of demand-driven community infrastructure at the village level for generating sustained employment opportunities for the rural poor. The distinguishing feature of both is their demand-driven character in place of the earlier and much less effective supply-driven employment programs.

*   *   *

We have outlined above the four major ingredients of a dynamic employment policy for India, with more detailed discussions of the new ingredients (sectoral policies, and safety nets and antipoverty programs) and brief discussions of the better-known and recognized growth-promoting components (raising the rate of investment and improving resource-use efficiency). The logic is simple. On the supply side, the basic idea is to raise the productivity of human resources through skill and educational development of the expanding labor force by enhancing the public and private provision of health and educational services. Simultaneously, it is necessary to expand the demand for an increasing and better-skilled and educated and hence potentially more productive labor force. For this purpose, a rapid pace of economic growth with a sectoral substrategy for inducing faster growth in relatively more labor-intensive industries assumes a critical role with domestic and external competition as powerful instruments. Finally, the indispensable need for evolving effective safety nets and antipoverty programs as integral components of the suggested employment policy is highlighted. While simple in logic, the suggested approach poses important challenges for the Indian society and polity in terms of significant departures from the past policy of "labor and employment." However, if the basic need for tackling the quantity as well as the quality dimensions of employment for a growing labor force is conceded, the underlying challenges are inescapable and have to be squarely faced.

Notes

We are grateful to Sanjeev Sharma for competent assistance and Anjali for efficient typing.

1. Notice that per capita income is a product of average productivity of work force multiplied by work force-to-population ratio, which varies within narrow bounds between 0 and unity (1.0) during the growth process.

2. Calculated from column 7 of Table 8.1.

3. This can be derived by using the ex post Harrod-Domar identity of growth rate, equaling the ratio of rate of investment (at constant prices) to the incremental capital output ratio. See Harrod 1959.

4. We focus on principal plus subsidiary usual status in preference to principal usual status, because cross-tabulations of employment characteristics by monthly per capita total expenditure are available only with respect to principal plus subsidiary usual status. We rely on these cross-tabulations to link poverty and employment in the subsequent discussion.

5. All estimates regarding the laboring poor are based on unit record data pertaining to India's employment-unemployment surveys for 1993–1994 (the fiftieth round) and 1999–2000 (the fifty-fifth round). Unlike in the fiftieth round, the fifty-fifth-round employment-unemployment survey was canvassed on an independent sample of households but drawn from the same universe of households as India's consumer expenditure survey, with a highly abridged worksheet for recording the household consumer expenditure. In order to identify the poor households in the employment-unemployment survey for studying the size and structure of the working poor—and to do so in a manner consistent with the poverty ratios computed from the detailed consumer expenditure survey—the following two-step procedure has been used. In the first step, from the fifty-fifth-round consumer expenditure survey, the proportion of households below the poverty line is estimated. In the next step, the level of monthly per capita expenditure at which the same proportion of households (rounded to the nearest integer) fall below the poverty line as estimated from the consumer expenditure survey is computed from a ranking of households on consumer expenditure recorded on the basis of the abridged "worksheet" in the fifty-fifth-round employment-unemployment survey. The poverty line so derived is used to identify the poor households in the employment-unemployment survey to study their labor force characteristics.

6. Though the usual status unemployment rates are not high, especially in the poor households, currently the unemployed add about 1 million each in rural and urban India to the size of the laboring poor.

7. For an early exploration of the relationship between female labor force participation rates, fertility burden, average level of living, and asset base, see Sundaram 1989b.

8. Our Probit model analysis of household-level data on the poverty status of labor households in Madhya Pradesh in fact confirms this hypothesis, as discussed later in the chapter.

9. See note to Table 8.13 for a definition of headcount ratio in each labor force or work force category.

10. Since the share of women (and of rural areas) in the total work force has also come down to 31 percent (76.4 percent) over the same period, both women and the rural areas continue to be overrepresented among the working poor with higher headcount ratios than the comparator groups.

9

Indonesia: Poverty, Employment, and Wages

Iyanatul Islam

There is ample evidence to support the view that, in Indonesia, the linkages among economic growth, employment, the labor market, and poverty are robust. In the rapid growth phase of the Suharto period (1966–1998), income poverty fell on a sustained basis as workers moved from agriculture to the more productive nonagricultural activities, the size of the wage employment sector expanded, some degree of skill deepening took place, and real wages generally rose in line with increases in productivity. On average, real wages grew at a rate of 5 percent per annum over the 1976–1997 period. Furthermore, one can detect a close correlation between real wage growth and changes in poverty. Thus poverty fell as real wages rose and vice versa— although there are some exceptions to this general pattern. The precrisis experience of Indonesia thus provides a good example of high rates of economic growth of an employment-intensive character leading to a rapid rate of poverty reduction.

The 1997 financial crisis temporarily reversed this process. While the crisis did not wipe out all the gains of the precrisis period, and while some degree of recovery has been in progress since 1992, the Indonesian labor market is still characterized by rather modest employment outcomes. And the poverty reduction process witnessed during the precrisis period also seems to have remained stalled.

Given the above background, an analysis of the linkages among poverty, employment, and the labor market in Indonesia can be useful in at least two respects. First, as the precrisis experience of Indonesia is a good example of high economic growth taking an employment-intensive character, and thus contributing to rapid reduction of poverty, an analysis of that experience would be of relevance to countries that need and aspire to embark on a similar poverty-reducing growth path. Second, given the country's modest recovery in recent years—in terms of both economic growth and performance on the employment front—an important issue is that of adopting an employment-focused policy framework that can make a significant contribution to poverty reduction.[1]

This chapter provides an analysis of the linkages among poverty, employment, and the labor market with both of these perspectives in view. After presenting a brief overview of the trends in income/consumption poverty, nonincome dimensions of poverty, and vulnerability, I examine the linkage between poverty and employment, including an examination of the degree of employment intensity of economic growth in Indonesia and the relationship between poverty and the employment characteristics of households. I next visit the important debate on how labor market flexibility helped in mitigating the impact of the economic crisis on poverty, then analyze the linkages among productivity, real wages, and poverty. Last, I attempt to delineate the key features of an employment-focused policy framework that could help the country in returning to the path of poverty reduction.

◼ The Multiple Dimensions of Poverty in Indonesia: Pre- and Postcrisis Perspective

Income/Consumption Poverty: Precrisis Period

Perhaps the most researched, and publicized, aspect of poverty in Indonesia draws on the so-called income/consumption approach. The latter entails the use of expenditure distribution data to derive a "poverty line" below which people are classified as poor—that is, people who have inadequate purchasing power to acquire the basic necessities of life. When expressed as a proportion of the population, such a statistic becomes the well-known and widely used "headcount ratio." In the case of Indonesia, current consumption expenditure, rather than current income, is used to estimate the headcount ratio.

Estimates of consumption poverty are routinely provided by the Central Bureau of Statistics (CBS) and may be regarded as the official estimates for Indonesia. Long-term trends in precrisis poverty in Indonesia, based on the income/consumption approach, are shown in Figure 9.1. Both CBS and alternative estimates are shown.[2] The sharp fall in poverty between 1976 and 1996 is evident, whether the CBS or the alternative approach is used. The only exception seems to be the 1976–1978 period, when the alternative estimates suggest a slight increase in the headcount ratio, but with the CBS measures showing a discernible decline.[3]

Income/Consumption Poverty: Postcrisis Period

There is widespread acknowledgment that the 1997 financial crisis led to a sharp jump in the incidence, depth, and severity of income poverty.[4] This is

Figure 9.1 Consumption Poverty, Indonesia, 1976–1996

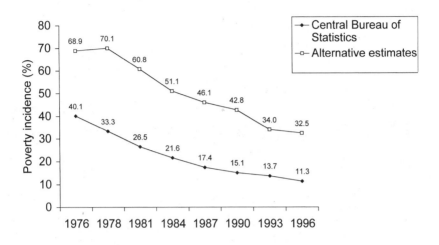

Source: UNDP 2003.

clear from Figures 9.2–9.4. As can be seen in Figure 9.2, income/consumption poverty increased conspicuously between 1996 and 1999.[5] It has since then tapered off and—as measured in 2002—is apparently fairly close to the pre-crisis threshold.

A more ambiguous picture emerges when one uses alternative international poverty lines to establish the incidence of poverty—the so-called dollar-a-day and two-dollar-a-day poverty lines (both measured in terms of purchasing power parity).[6] Thus, while the dollar-a-day poverty line suggests that income/poverty in 2002 was a little lower than the 1996 benchmark, the higher poverty line (US$2 a day) suggests that it was still a little above (by 5.9 percent) the precrisis level (see Figure 9.3). The circumspect nature of the evidence on the nature of the reversal in the sharp increase in poverty due to the 1997 crisis is made apparent in Figure 9.4, which shows that both the depth and the severity of poverty, while lower than what they were during 1999, were in 2002 still noticeably above their precrisis norms.

Another important anomaly that one can note is that even in subperiods of the precrisis era (1990–1993), both the depth and the severity of poverty rose while the incidence of poverty fell (contrast Figure 9.2, exhibiting the incidence of poverty, with Figure 9.4, showing the depth and severity of poverty).[7] In other words, while the proportion below the poverty line declined, income distribution among subgroups in poverty worsened.

316

Figure 9.2   Percentage of Population Below National Poverty Line, Indonesia, 1990–2002

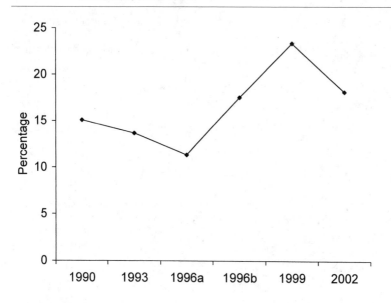

Source: UNDP 2003.

Figure 9.3   Income Poverty, Indonesia, 1990–2002

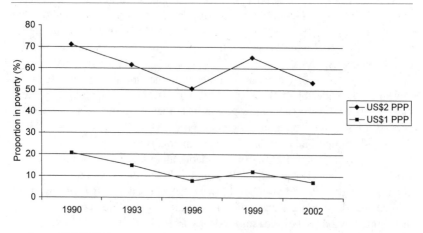

Source: UNDP 2003.

Figure 9.4   Depth and Severity of Poverty, Indonesia, 1990–2002

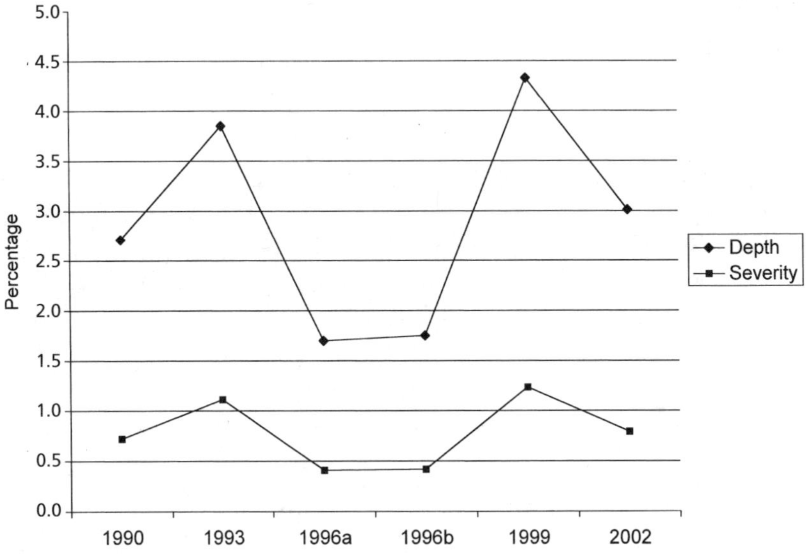

Source: UNDP 2003.

Nonincome Dimensions of Poverty and the Millennium Development Goals

Income/consumption poverty is only one aspect of the multidimensional nature of poverty in Indonesia and corresponds to only one of the declared Millennium Development Goals.[8] As is well-known, the MDGs were endorsed by 189 member states at the Millennium Summit of the United Nations in September 2000. They represent eight consolidated goals pertaining to eradicating extreme poverty and hunger; achieving universal primary education; promoting gender equality; reducing child mortality; improving maternal health; combating HIV/AIDS, malaria, and other diseases; ensuring environmental sustainability; and developing a global partnership for development. Seven of the eight goals were translated into targets that could be monitored over a given period, with 1990 as the base year and 2015 as the terminal year. These targets correspond to a range of deficient capabilities whose alleviation directly impinges on the well-being of the poor and enables them to function as productive members of society.

How has Indonesia fared in coping with deficient capabilities, especially in the postcrisis era? Figures 9.5 to 9.10 seek to shed light on this issue. As can be seen, there have been improvements in child health as measured in terms of the decline in undernutrition and infant mortality rates (Figures 9.5

318

Figure 9.5   Child Malnutrition (under 5 years), Indonesia, 1989–2002

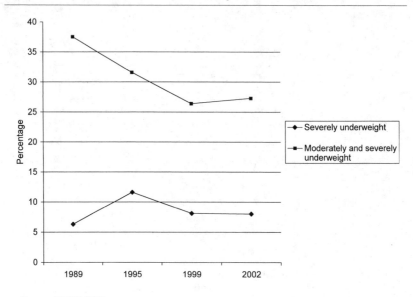

Source: UNDP 2003.

Figure 9.6   Infant and Under-5 Mortality Rates, Indonesia, 1989–2002

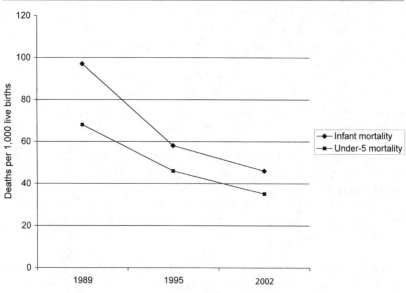

Source: UNDP 2003.

and 9.6). Progress in maternal health as measured in terms of declines in maternal mortality rate is quite evident (Figure 9.7). There has been considerable progress toward attaining universal net enrollments in primary and secondary education (Figure 9.8) and significant improvement in access to sanitation facilities and safe drinking water (Figures 9.9 and 9.10). For ease of reference, Table 9.1 highlights the state of play in terms of the key indicators as they prevailed in 2002 vis-à-vis the 2015 targets.

It thus appears that the 1997 crisis has not adversely affected the positive trend toward reductions in deficient capabilities. Indeed, a cross-country analysis reveals that Indonesia is among the relatively small number of countries that are on track to attain the MDGs by 2015.[9] Nevertheless, some concerns remain. The country lags behind regional norms in terms of the various indicators that are pertinent to the MDGs.[10] The standard of achievement in particular areas, such as access to safe drinking water, is modest; in 2002 only 50 percent of Indonesians enjoyed this privilege and only 18 percent of households had access to piped water. Progress in child health appears to have stalled after 1999. Net enrollments in junior education are rather low (61.7 percent) and, if current trends prevail, the country will struggle to attain universal junior secondary education for boys and girls by 2015. There is also considerable disquiet about the quality of education that Indonesians receive.[11]

Figure 9.7   Maternal Mortality Rate, Indonesia, 1992–2002

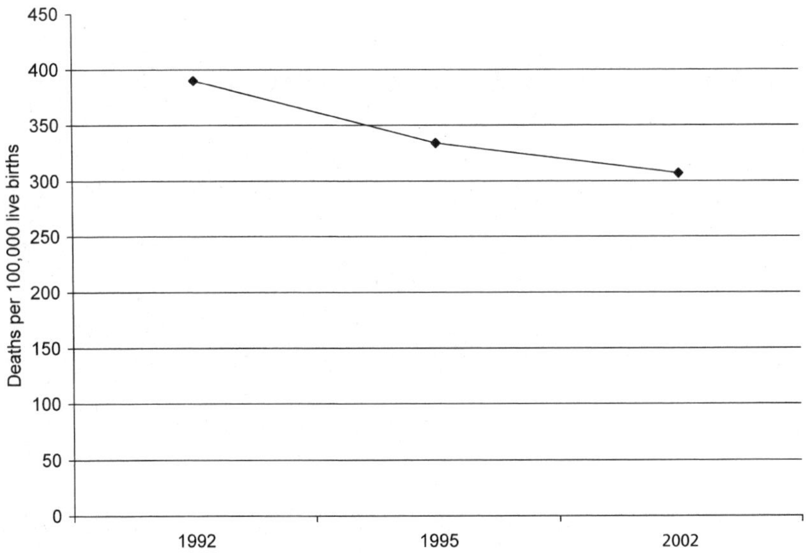

Source: UNDP 2003.

320

Figure 9.8   Net Enrollment Ratios in Primary and Junior Secondary
             Education, Indonesia, 1992–2002

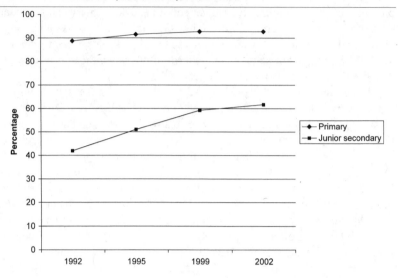

Source: UNDP 2003.

Figure 9.9   Percentage of People with Access to Improved Sanitation,
             Indonesia, 1992–2002

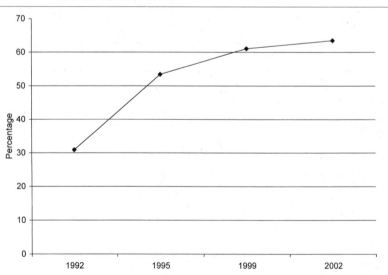

Source: UNDP 2003.

Figure 9.10 Percentage of People with Access to Safe Drinking Water, Indonesia, 1992–2002

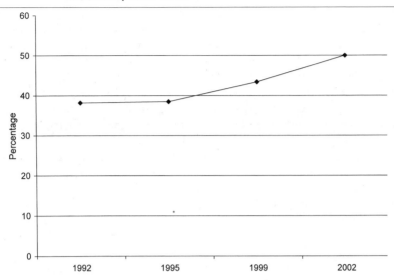

Source: UNDP 2003.
Note: Safe drinking water originates from improved water sources controlled for excreta disposal.

Table 9.1 Key Indicators of Deficient Capabilities in Indonesia Relative to 2015 Targets

Indicator	2002	2015 Target
Extreme poverty: percentage of population living below national poverty line	18.2	7.5
Child malnutrition: percentage of children moderately and severely underweight	27.3	18.3
Under-5 mortality rate	46	32
Infant mortality rate	35	17
Maternal mortality rate	307	124
Net enrollment rate (boys and girls)		
Primary	92.7	100
Secondary	61.7	100
Access to safe water		
Percentage of households with piped water	18.3	57.3
Percentage of households with access to improved water sources[a]	50	69.1

Source: United Nations Development Programme 2003.
Note: a. Ten meters or farther from excreta disposal.

Vulnerability in Indonesia

It is now widely recognized that estimates of the incidence of poverty overlook the crucial fact that individuals and households may move in and out of poverty.[12] Both the poor and nonpoor may thus be vulnerable to at least transient episodes of impoverishment. For the currently poor, this means falling deeper into poverty; for the currently nonpoor, this means slipping below the poverty line. Such vulnerability could be triggered by economywide shocks, such as the 1997 financial crisis that engulfed Indonesia and other countries in East Asia; location-specific shocks, such as a crop failure in a rural community; or traumatic individual events, such as the sudden loss of a breadwinner in the family.

Several studies have been conducted in Indonesia that draw on sophisticated methods of measurement to identify the proportion of the population that are vulnerable to at least a temporary episode of poverty.[13] These measures seek to identify the risk or probability that an individual or household could either slip below or move further away from the poverty line. A simple yet appealing approach to measuring vulnerability is to arbitrarily upgrade the existing poverty line by a discrete amount and work out how many additional people are likely to fall below it. The results of such a simple exercise for Indonesia are quite telling. Expressed in dollar terms (on a PPP basis), the national poverty line in 2002 turns out to be approximately US$1.6 a day, yielding a headcount ratio of 18 percent (see Figure 9.11). If the poverty line is raised by 40¢ a day (to US$2 a day), then the incidence of poverty jumps to a conspicuous 53.5 percent. Thus, by this method, 35.3 percent of the population (53.5 less 18.2 percent) are vulnerable to falling below the poverty line. This is quite a large number and falls within the estimates established by other studies. The evidence reveals the troubling fact that a significant proportion of Indonesians hover just above the poverty line. This makes them nonpoor at a point in time, but it simultaneously makes them vulnerable to any shock that can push them below the poverty line, even if such an episode could turn out to be transient in nature.

Crisis, Recovery, and the Indonesian Labor Market: The Persistence of Structural Weaknesses

As poverty shot up during the peak of the crisis, there was an involuntary reallocation of labor to the agricultural sector and an enlargement in the size of the urban informal sector, thus creating a phase of "deindustrialization."[14] Real wages also collapsed by about 40 percent.

As noted, some form of recovery seems to have taken place. As of 2002, income/consumption poverty had fallen from its peak in 1998–1999 to close to the level recorded in 1996. Real wages are growing again and in 2002 were 10–30 percent above their precrisis values.[15]

Modest Employment Outcomes in the Postcrisis Era. Despite such promising signs of recovery, employment outcomes have been quite modest. Consider

Figure 9.11   Vulnerability as Measured by Changes in Incidence of Poverty Resulting from Raised Poverty Line, Indonesia, 1992–2002

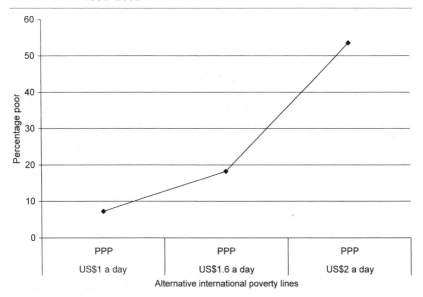

Source: Indonesia's national labor force surveys (SAKERNAS), various years.

some important statistics. The employment share of the agricultural sector fell to 40.1 percent in 1997, but by 2001 it still stood at 43.3 percent. The share of wage employment peaked at 35.5 percent in 1997, but by 2001 it had tapered off to 33.3 percent. The available evidence suggests that capacity utilization rates in the manufacturing sector fell to a low of 66 percent in 2001 from their peak of 78 percent in 1996, while the growth of manufacturing employment fell from 2.8 percent in the 1994–1997 period to 0.6 percent for the 1998–2001 period. Employment elasticity in manufacturing is much lower now than in previous decades.[16] In other words, there is no compelling evidence that the adverse changes in the employment structure that one witnessed during 1998 in the wake of the crisis-induced recession have dissipated.

Attention should also be drawn to the fact that the open unemployment rate has gone up quite sharply in recent years. It was recorded in excess of 9 percent in 2002 compared to 4.7 percent in 1997.[17] Admittedly, open unemployment in Indonesia is concentrated among the relatively well educated, but the fact that it is dominated by very high youth unemployment rates is a source of some concern. The youth unemployment rate in 2001 stood at 24.1 percent compared to 15.5 percent in 1997, and accounted for more than 60 percent of the total unemployed. Such visible manifestations of lack of productive employment opportunities for young Indonesians could turn out to be a source of social unrest.

Gender Disparities in the Labor Market. Gender disparities persist in the Indonesian labor market. While the male-female wage gap has decreased in recent years, a cursory inspection of the relevant data shows that, on almost every significant indicator of the labor market, female workers lag behind male workers.[18] In 2001, for example, the labor force participation rate (in the 15–64 age bracket) for females was 53.3 percent compared to 87.3 percent for males. Female workers are also underrepresented in the wage-employment sector (29.3 percent versus 35.6 percent in 2001), overrepresented in part-time employment (56.4 percent) and the urban informal sector (49.9 percent versus 42.2 percent), exhibit higher involuntary underemployment (11.5 percent versus 7.6 percent), and have lower educational attainments (15.5 percent of female workers have secondary education versus 21.1 percent of male workers).[19]

Gender disparities in the labor market are also reflected in the multiple constraints faced by women entrepreneurs. They lack adequate access to training in marketing, bookkeeping, and management skills. They lack the networks and business information that would equip them to better compete and to meet changes in consumer demand and technology. They face difficulties obtaining credit, particularly when their requirements exceed what cooperatives and other microcredit sources can offer women.

Implications of a Vast and Diverse Informal Economy. Other aspects of the Indonesian labor market deserve scrutiny. To start with, any understanding of the poverty–labor market nexus in Indonesia requires a clear recognition of the vast and diverse nature of the informal economy that straddles both urban and rural activities and accounted for 67 percent of the Indonesian work force in 1999. Official statistics suggest that the size of the urban informal sector has increased since 1997. Work in the informal economy is too often characterized by low levels of skill and productivity, low or irregular incomes, long working hours, small or undefined workplaces, unsafe and unhealthy working conditions, and lack of access to information, markets, finance, training, and technology. Workers in the informal economy are not recognized, registered, regulated, or protected under labor legislation and social protection, often because their employment status is ambiguous. A large proportion of those who suffer these conditions are women and children.

■ Poverty and the Labor Market: The Role of Employment

As mentioned previously, the precrisis experience of Indonesia is an example not only of high economic growth, but also of growth of an employment-intensive character that contributed to the impressive rate of poverty reduction. In order to substantiate this contention, it is necessary to examine whether the structure of employment changed in the expected direction (i.e., from low-productivity and high-productivity sectors and categories) over time, and how employment-intensive growth was. The purpose of this section is to examine these aspects, and to explore the extent to which the evolution of consumption poverty (and consumption-based indicators of vulnerability) can be reconciled with developments in the labor market, where such developments are assessed from the perspective of a range of employment indicators. The discussion is reinforced by developing a cross-section profile of the employment/skill and demographic characteristics of the poor. Finally, the section revisits some important debates in the Indonesian context. Do employment adjustments during the crisis represent a high degree of labor market flexibility that, in turn, mitigated the impact of the crisis on consumption poverty?

Changes in Employment Structure: Overview and Implications for Poverty

Drawing on a variation of key indicators of the labor market (KILM) devised by the ILO, a brief account is offered of the following employment indicators in the Indonesian context: labor force participation rate, employment-to-population ratio, status in employment, part-time workers, the size of the urban informal sector, unemployment and underemployment, the sectoral composition of employment, and the skill levels of the work force.[20] These indicators enable one to develop an understanding of the structure of the Indonesian labor market. This in turn sets the context for appreciating the poverty-employment nexus.

Table 9.2 captures the various ways in which one can track the transformation of the Indonesian labor market over the 1990s. The Indonesian labor force grew from 75 million in 1990 to 96 million in 2000, entailing an average annual growth rate of 2.5 percent. In terms of absolute numbers, this suggests an addition of 2 million members to the work force annually. Hence the challenge is to ensure that the economy—through a combination of the natural processes of growth and policy interventions—is able to generate at least 2 million jobs to maintain "flow equilibrium" in the labor market.

In some respects, one cannot detect a great deal of change in the labor market; in other respects, the changes are evident. Thus the labor force participation rate—as well as the employment-to-population ratio—remained relatively stable, the former entailing modest fluctuations between 66 and 68 percent over the period 1990–2000. The gender composition of the work force was also steady, remaining at around 38 percent female, as was the proportion of young workers among the total labor force, which fluctuated between 21 and 23 percent.

As a contrast to the stable features of the labor market noted above, one observes significant urbanization and formalization of the work force. The relative size of formal sector employment rose from 28 percent in 1990 to 38 percent on the eve of the crisis in 1996, while the relative size of the urban labor force increased from 26 percent to 36 percent.

326

Table 9.2 Overview of Indonesian Labor Market, 1990–2000

	1990	1993	1996	1998	1999	2000
Size of labor force (millions)	75.4	79.2	88.2	92.7	94.8	95.7
Labor force participation rate (%)	66.4	67.8	66.9	66.9	67.2	67.7
Employment-to-population ratio (%)	64.7	63.8	63.6	63.3	62.9	63.6
Female labor force (%)	38.8	38.6	38.5	38.8	38.4	38.6
Youth labor force (%)	23.1	22.2	22.3	21.3	21.3	21.6
Urban labor force (%)	25.5	29.5	33.9	36.0	38.1	38.0
Formal employment (%)	28.1	32.1	37.9	35.4	36.9	35.3
Urban informal sector employment (%)	44.2	43.7	42.5	45.7	45.8	44.7
Part-time employment (%)	28.0	29.1	33.3	28.6	27.3	27.9
Female part-time employment (%)	59.8	57.0	57.4	57.7	56.8	57.2
Time-related underemployment rate (%)	8.7	9.0	9.9	8.5	9.1	9.2
Youth unemployment rate (%)	8.0	8.9	15.5	17.1	19.9	17.5
Overall unemployment rate (%)	2.5	2.8	4.9	5.5	6.4	6.1

Sources: Estimated from Indonesia's national labor force surveys (SAKERNAS), various years. Some indicators also extracted from Puguh, Ahmed, and Islam 2000, statistical appendix. Some indicators for 2000 (part-time employment, time-related underemployment, youth unemployment rate, size of the urban informal sector) are estimates based on historical trends. Direct computations of these indicators will require special tabulations based on unpublished SAKERNAS data.

These developments are consistent with the sustained decrease in consumption poverty documented previously. A reallocation of labor from low-productivity, low-paid jobs in the rural economy to better-paid employment in the urban and formal economy is one well-known route via which ordinary workers and their dependents can improve their living standards.

As far as different indicators of underutilization and "casualization" of the work force are concerned, the picture is mixed. Part-time employment remained roughly steady between 1990 and 1993 (28 to 29 percent) and rose moderately thereafter (33 percent). The relative size of the urban informal sector hardly changed (gravitating around 45 to 43 percent). There is also no clear trend of an increase in the proportion of women who worked part-time. Thus these measures of casualization of the work force do not show any consistent deterioration in the precrisis period. There is little evidence as well that, prior to the crisis, involuntary underemployment (or "time-related" underemployment) was widespread, being around 8–9 percent. This suggests that the sustained decline in consumption poverty in the rapid-growth Suharto era represented genuine social gains.

What about unemployment and its implications for poverty? In the precrisis period, it was below 5 percent. The conventional wisdom is that the aggregate unemployment rate is an inappropriate indicator of the state of the Indonesian labor market, given its stage of development. In the absence of a comprehensive unemployment benefits scheme, joblessness for protracted spells is an option that only few can afford. Not surprisingly, the long-term unemployment rate (defined as those unemployed for a year or more) was around 1 percent between 1990 and 1996. The available statistics—to be discussed more fully later—typically suggest that unemployment in Indonesia is largely a voluntary phenomenon, concentrated among educated youth. Certainly, as can be seen, the youth unemployment rate is far above the overall unemployment rate. In 1997 nearly 70 percent of the unemployed were represented by young members of the work force.

The current debate on youth unemployment has tried to disentangle "choosy youth" from "unwanted youth."[21] While some commentators suggest that the youth unemployment rate largely reflects a case of young graduates queuing for reasonably secure public sector jobs,[22] others have warned that not all the unemployed young members of the work force should be classified as "choosy youth" coming from reasonably affluent backgrounds. There is a cohort, which are the victims of penurious socioeconomic circumstances.

Table 9.2 also enables one to focus on the impact of the crisis on the Indonesian labor market. A scrutiny of the table would suggest that, in terms of some indicators, the impact of the crisis on the labor market was modest and hence seemingly at odds with the view that there was a sharp increase in poverty when the crisis was at its worst, in 1998. Thus the unemployment rate rose only moderately (from 4.9 percent in 1996 to 5.7 percent in 1998), although there was a more discernible increase in 2000 (over 6 percent).[23] The incidence of involuntary underemployment actually decreased between 1996 and 1998, while the incidence of part-time employment hardly changed. On the other hand, the size of the urban informal sector increased noticeably—from 43 percent to 46 percent between 1998 and 1996—and by 2000 had not reverted to the precrisis level. At the same time, there was an alarming increase in the incidence of youth unemployment between 1996 and 1999, probably reflecting constrained job opportunities in the public sector induced by the growth slowdown in the postcrisis period.

A clearer perspective on the impact of the Indonesian crisis on the labor market can be gleaned from Table 9.3, which exhibits the sectoral composition of the work force over the 1990s. The employment share of the agricultural sector, after falling on a sustained basis from 55 percent in 1990 to 43.5 percent in 1996 (and 41 percent in 1997), experienced an abrupt reversal: its employment share increased to 45 percent (approaching the level achieved in 1995). Employment in the manufacturing sector contracted as well: the employment share of the sector declined from 12.6 percent to 11 percent between 1996 and 1998. Thus the impact of the crisis was reflected not through a big jump in unemployment, underemployment, or even part-time employment, but in an involuntary shift of the work force into agricultural activities as well as into the informal economy of the urban sector.

It remains to be seen whether some of these sectoral reallocations of labor will be persistent. As the estimates for 1999 show, the changes in the employment share of agriculture resumed their historical pattern, but estimates for 2000 show it slipped back to 45.1 percent.[24] On the other hand, manufacturing employment grew to the point where its employment share increased to 13 percent. It is also noteworthy that by 2000 (Table 9.2), the share of formal sector employment had not yet reached its precrisis level, suggesting the muted but lingering impact of the 1997 crisis on the Indonesian labor market.

Table 9.3   Sectoral Composition of Work Force, Indonesia, 1990–2000 (percentages)

	1990	1993	1996	1998	1999	2000
Agriculture	55.1	50.0	43.5	45.0	43.2	45.1
(Food crop)	41.6	35.1	26.4	29.9	28.0	28.3
Industry	10.9	11.9	13.5	12.1	13.8	13.5
(Manufacturing)	10.2	11.1	12.6	11.3	13.0	13.0
Services	34.0	38.1	43.0	43.0	43.0	41.4
(Trade)	14.8	16.0	18.9	19.2	19.7	20.6
(Nontrade)	19.2	22.2	24.1	23.8	23.3	20.8

Source: Estimated from Indonesia's national labor force surveys (SAKERNAS), various years.

A discussion of the Indonesian labor market would be incomplete without some reflection on a key aspect of the employment structure: the extent to which rapid growth in the precrisis era was accompanied by a deepening of the skills of the labor force. Table 9.4 enables one to offer a commentary. While recognizing that the process skill formation emanates from multiple sources, this table uses the educational attainment of the work force as a credible approximation of the skills embodied in the work force. It is clear that the rapid-growth, precrisis era was accompanied by substantial upgrading of the educational profile of Indonesian workers. The proportion of less educated/less skilled workers (defined as those who have primary education and less) fell from 87 percent to 79 percent between 1990 and 1996, with a corresponding increase in the share of the educated/skilled work force (defined as those with at least secondary education) from 14 percent to 21 percent.

These structural changes in the Indonesian labor market juxtapose rather well with the sustained decline in poverty witnessed during the precrisis period. As a subsequent discussion will demonstrate more explicitly, there is a strong correlation between educational attainment and poverty incidence at the household level. Thus, as more Indonesians gained access to the education system, it provided them with an escape route from impoverishment.

Changes in Employment Elasticity: Overview and Implications for Poverty

An important question pertains to the extent to which the employment intensity of rapid economic growth, especially in the manufacturing sector, played

Table 9.4 Educational Attainment of Work Force, Indonesia, 1990–2000 (percentages)

	1990	1993	1996	1998	1999	2000
Less educated/skilled work force	86.5	83.7	78.8	77.4	76.3	77.8
No schooling	15.0	12.2	9.7	8.6	8.0	7.9
Primary schooling (incomplete)	25.3	23.3	18.9	18.2	17.0	16.1
Primary schooling (complete)	36.1	36.8	37.2	36.4	36.0	38.2
Lower-secondary schooling	10.1	11.3	13.0	14.2	15.3	15.6
Educated/skilled work force	13.5	16.3	21.2	22.6	23.7	22.4
Upper-secondary schooling	11.5	13.6	17.4	18.4	19.1	17.9
Tertiary schooling	2.0	2.7	3.8	4.2	4.6	4.5

Source: Estimated from Indonesia's national labor force surveys (SAKERNAS), various years.

a role in influencing trends in poverty in the Suharto era. Provided a stable relationship exists between output growth and the job creation rate—a variation
of the so-called Okun's law observed in industrialized countries—it should be
possible to estimate employment elasticity.[25] The latter, as is well-known, is a
useful summary statistic for computing the employment intensity of economic
growth. From the perspective of poverty analysis, what matters is not growth
of output per se, but the extent to which it is employment-friendly. Higher employment elasticity translates to the fact that, for any given growth rate, the
job creation rate is higher. However, care should be taken in interpreting the
normative implication of this proposition. It is possible to have "excessive"
employment creation at the expense of growth of productivity. For example,
an employment elasticity that exceeds unity means a proliferation of low-productivity jobs. Thus, employment-friendly growth should really mean the expansion of durable and productive work opportunities.

Bearing such analytic caveats in mind, consider Table 9.5, which shows
employment elasticity in manufacturing for three subperiods: 1975–1980,
1981–1985, and 1986–1992. Employment elasticity was quite low (0.3) in the
1970s, rose appreciably in the 1980s (0.8), and tapered off a little with the
onset of the 1990s (0.7). These estimates are consistent with conventional interpretations of the evolution of the employment-poverty linkage in the Indonesian context. In the 1970s, Indonesia's oil wealth was used to fund public
infrastructure and rural development, but the manufacturing sector remained
small, inefficient, and protected. This constrained its capacity to act as a loco-
motive for employment creation, although the oil wealth–driven public investment policy of the 1970s did reap some social dividends, given that it heralded
the onset of a remarkable decline in mass poverty. As the oil price boom dissipated in the early 1980s, the Suharto government was forced to turn to an
outward-oriented industrialization strategy that began in earnest from the mid-
1980s. The much higher values of manufacturing employment elasticity in the
1980s support the notion that the manufacturing sector was beginning to play
a more significant role in spearheading employment creation by drawing in
less skilled workers from the rural and informal economy to the more formal
economy.

**Table 9.5   Evolution of Employment Elasticity in Indonesian
Manufacturing, 1975–1992**

Period	Employment Elasticity in Manufacturing
1975–1980	0.33
1981–1985	0.76
1986–1992	0.66

Source: Extracted from Islam 2001, 4, tab.

Some studies have documented the fact that manufacturing employment elasticity declined appreciably in the latter half of the 1990s, raising the possibility that the capacity of industrialization to sustain large-scale job creation was becoming constrained. Table 9.6 conveys pertinent information. As can be seen, employment elasticity in the formal sector (represented by large- and medium-scale enterprises) was an average of 0.5 for the 1985–1997 period, but fell from 0.8 in the 1985–1988 period to 0.3 in the 1993–1997 period. Whether this represents the onset of a durable trend remains to be seen. Table 9.6 also provides useful information on employment elasticities in subsectors within manufacturing. For the 1985–1997 period as a whole, the subsectors with "high" employment elasticities (above 0.5) are garments, furniture, electrical goods, and footwear. It is noteworthy that these are also subsectors with a good deal of export orientation.

Current research on the employment intensity of economic growth in Indonesia has also reflected on methodological complications entailed in the estimation of employment elasticity. One study has shown that the conventional way of estimating employment elasticity, which is simply an ex post procedure, may engender unreliable estimates.[26] They seem to fluctuate widely depending on the time periods used. Econometric estimates of employment elasticity using pooled province-level data generate more stable estimates and suggest an employment elasticity of approximately 0.7 for the 1977–1996 period.

Linking Poverty to the Employment Characteristics of Households: A Profile

The overview of changes in the Indonesian labor market, as captured in a range of employment indicators, suggests that formalization and urbanization

Table 9.6   Sectoral Employment Elasticities Based on Medium- and Large-Scale Enterprise Survey, Indonesia, 1985–1997 (three-digit International Standard Industrial Classification)

Sector	1985–1988	1988–1993	1993–1997	1985–1997
All medium- and large-scale manufacturing	0.8	0.6	0.3	0.5
Food manufacturing	1.1	0.2	0.2	0.3
Textile	0.7	0.5	0.1	0.4
Garment	0.8	0.5	–0.6	0.7
Furniture	0.8	0.9	0.4	0.8
Electrical goods	–0.2	0.6	0.4	0.6
Transport equipment	0.4	0.2	0.4	0.3
Metal	0.4	0.5	0.4	0.5
Footwear	1.3	0.9	1.1	1.0

Source: Islam and Nazara 2000b, 18, tab. 7.

of the work force, together with an upgrading of the educational attainment of workers, are fully consistent with the sustained declines in poverty in the pre-crisis period. At the same time, there is little evidence that "casualization" of the work force became pronounced, while other indicators, such as the gender composition of the work force and the relative employment share of young workers, remained roughly stable. There is also some evidence that growth under the Suharto regime became more employment-friendly.

The 1997–1998 crisis reversed the poverty-reducing structural changes in the Indonesian labor market, with a forced movement of workers into the agricultural sector and into the informal segment of the urban economy. It remains to be seen whether these reversals will turn out to be persistent, with data for 1999 showing a resumption of historical trends, but data for 2000 indicating otherwise. The unemployment rate has increased moderately, largely reflecting a high incidence of youth unemployment. Involuntary underemployment was not widespread in the Suharto era. The crisis does not seem to have brought about a lasting worsening in the incidence of underemployment.

An overview of the structural changes in the Indonesian labor market thus sets the context for further analysis of the poverty-employment linkage at the household level. Pertinent information on this issue is displayed in Tables 9.7–9.9. In Table 9.7, one is able to discern the incidence of poverty by main sector of occupation and the relative importance of each sector of occupation in nationwide poverty. Table 9.8 replicates the estimates, this time from the

Table 9.7 Poverty Incidence by Main Sector of Occupation, Indonesia, 1996–1999

	February 1996		February 1999	
	Poverty Incidence (%)	Contribution to Total Poor (%)	Poverty Incidence (%)	Contribution to Total Poor (%)
Agriculture	26.3	68.6	39.7	58.4
Trade	8.0	8.1	17.6	11.1
Manufacturing	10.7	5.7	22.9	7.7
Civil, social, and private services	5.7	5.7	13.1	7.4
Transport and communication	8.9	3.3	24.0	5.6
Construction	14.0	5.4	29.0	5.5
Receiving transfer	6.6	1.9	15.6	2.7
Mining and quarrying	15.3	1.0	29.8	1.00
Others	13.3	0.1	32.0	0.3
Finance	1.2	0.1	5.2	0.2

Sources: Pradhan et al. 2000; unpublished estimates. Original data from Indonesia's national socioeconomic survey (SUSENAS).

Table 9.8   Poverty Incidence by Educational Level of Household Head, Indonesia, 1996–1999

	February 1996		February 1999	
	Poverty Incidence (%)	Contribution to Total Poor (%)	Poverty Incidence (%)	Contribution to Total Poor (%)
Illiterate and incomplete primary education	31.2	27.7	47.5	19.9
Incomplete primary education but literate	21.6	35.1	36.7	31.8
Completed primary education	15.0	30.2	29.7	35.4
Completed junior secondary education	7.0	4.8	16.9	7.6
Completed senior secondary education	2.4	2.2	8.6	5.1
Completed tertiary education	0.4	0.1	2.0	0.3

Sources: Pradhan et al. 2000; unpublished estimates. Original data from Indonesia's national socioeconomic survey (SUSENAS).

perspective of the educational level of households. Table 9.9 draws together a wide array of information on the demographic, skill, and employment status of poor households and compares it with information on nonpoor households.

The information in these tables is supplemented by Figures 9.12–9.15, which depict the employment and skill characteristics of households at different

Table 9.9   Demographic, Skill, and Employment Status of Poor and Nonpoor Households, Indonesia, 1999

	Poor Households	Nonpoor Households
Average family size	4.6	4.0
Percentage female-headed	16.3	14.0
Mean age (years) of household head	44.8	45.6
Mean years of schooling of household head	6.0	7.4
Percentage of household heads as own-account workers and unpaid family workers	56.8	54.2
Percentage of household heads as employees	30.6	34.6
Average hours worked per week	33.4	35.9

Sources: Sutanto and Irawan 2000; unpublished estimates. Original data from Indonesia's national socioeconomic survey (SUSENAS).

points on the expenditure distribution. More specifically, a quintile approach is used in which the employment and educational attributes of households in different quintiles—poorest 20 percent to richest 20 percent—are compared. The figures are undergirded by the plausible assumption that the poorest quintile largely coincides with the population of households officially classified as poor.

The information in the various tables does not hold surprises. The bulk of the Indonesian poor can be found in the agricultural sector. For example, in 1999 the poverty incidence in agriculture was approximately 40 percent compared to a poverty rate of only 5 percent for household heads who identified finance as their main sector of occupation. Furthermore, 58 percent of nationwide poverty could be accounted for by the agricultural sector. Thus, any strategy of poverty reduction in Indonesia will have to recognize the widespread existence of poor households in agricultural activities.

Table 9.8 examines the linkage between poverty incidence and the educational attainment of household heads. There is a strong correlation between the two variables, although one should hasten to add that correlation based on cross-section data does not necessarily imply causality. The bulk of poverty in Indonesia resides among household heads who have attained primary education or less. For example, in 1999, poverty rates varied between 39 percent and 48 percent for groups with primary education or less. Such groups in turn accounted for the bulk of nationwide poverty in Indonesia. At the other extreme, poverty among household heads with tertiary education was 2 percent in 1999, while for those with secondary education or more, the incidence varied between 5 and 8 percent. It thus seems that the upgrading of the Indonesian work force during the 1990s was an important mechanism in bringing about the impressive decline in poverty prior to the crisis. This also means that ensuring broad access to the education and training system, particularly at the secondary level, will remain a major policy goal for the Indonesian government.

Table 9.9 compares the demographic, employment, and skill characteristics of poor households with characteristics of nonpoor households. The former have a somewhat larger household size (4.6 persons versus 4.0 persons in 1999), but there is no evidence that poor households are either substantially younger or older than nonpoor households. There is also no clear evidence of "feminization" of poverty in the sense that a moderate 16 percent of households headed by females are classified as poor.

In terms of employment status, it appears that informal self-employment is a major characteristic of poverty. Thus, 56 percent of household heads who were self-employed in 1999 were classified as poor, compared to 30 percent of household heads who were classified as employees being regarded as poor.

In terms of hours worked per week, there is some difference between poor and nonpoor households. Thus, poor households in 1999 worked an average of thirty-three hours per week compared with thirty-six hours per week for nonpoor households.

Table 9.10 shows a discernible gap between poor and nonpoor households in the area of education. Mean schooling for poor households was 6.0 years in 1999 versus 7.4 years for nonpoor households.

Figures 9.12 to 9.15 revisit the linkage between poverty and the employment and educational attributes of workers from the standpoint of quintiles of households. They are generated from estimates derived from the 1999 national socioeconomic survey (SUSENAS). These estimates were compiled by a Jakarta-based research agency using special tabulations.[27] The figures add

Table 9.10   Unemployment Rate and Poverty Incidence by Educational Attainment, Indonesia, 1999

	Unemployment Rate (%)	Poverty Incidence (%)
No schooling	0.4	47.5
Less than primary	1.5	36.7
Primary	4.8	29.7
Secondary	15.9	13.0
Tertiary	12.7	2.0

Source: Based on previous tables in this chapter.

Figure 9.12   Percentage of Work Force in Informal Sector by Quintile, Indonesia, 1999

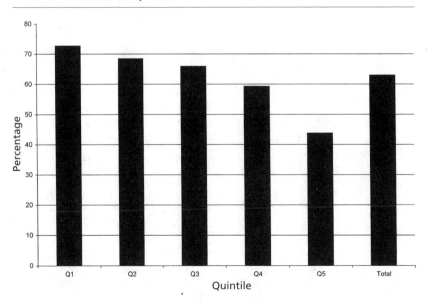

Source: Indonesia's 1999 national labor force survey (SAKERNAS).

336

Figure 9.13   White-Collar Workers by Quintile, Indonesia, 1999

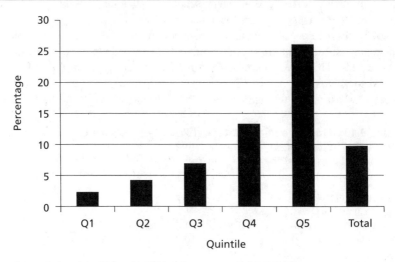

Source: Indonesia's 1999 national labor force survey (SAKERNAS).

Figure 9.14   Educational Attainment by Quintile, Indonesia, 1999

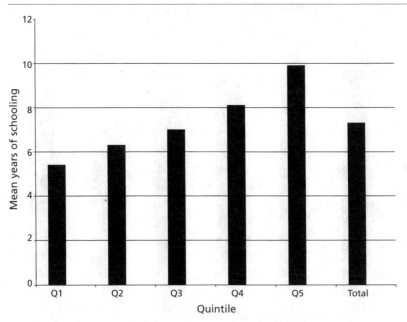

Source: Indonesia's 1999 national labor force survey (SAKERNAS).

to the information embodied in the previous tables in the sense that they enable one to see the relationship between poverty and employment characteristics from the perspective of households at different points on the expenditure distribution. As can be seen, there is a preponderance of the poorest 20 percent of households in the informal sector (Figure 9.12), while the proportion of white-collar workers is rather low for the bottom quintile (Figure 9.13). Furthermore, in terms of mean years of schooling, the gap between the bottom quintile and top quintile is quite substantial: the poorest 20 percent have a little over five years of schooling compared to ten years for the richest quintile (see Figure 9.14). It is noteworthy that the average educational attainment of the poorest 20 percent is well below the long-held goal of the government that all Indonesians should obtain at least nine years of schooling. Thus, upgrading the educational attainment of poor Indonesians at least to the national standard remains a major policy challenge.

Figure 9.15 shows the distribution of households by quintile in terms of low hours of work per week (less than twenty). A discernible pattern emerges: the incidence of low hours of work diminishes as one moves to a richer quintile, this tendency becoming more marked for the top two quintiles. Thus, inadequate hours of work is one attribute of Indonesian poverty.

Figure 9.15   Hours Worked per Week (<20) by Quintile, Indonesia, 1999

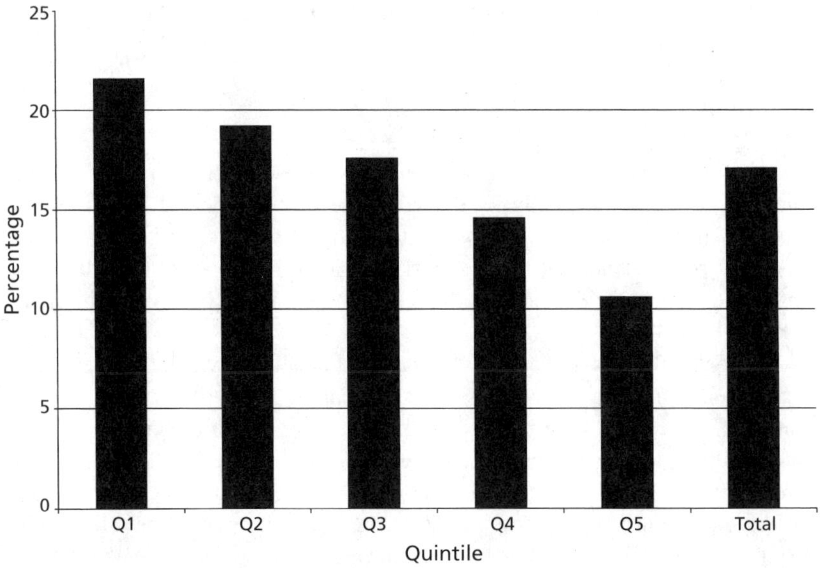

Source: Indonesia's 1999 national labor force survey (SAKERNAS).

Unemployment and Poverty

What the above figures and tables do not show is the extent to which unemployment can be related to poverty. Recall from the previous discussion the conventional wisdom that unemployment has limited relevance to the understanding of poverty in Indonesia. How much is this contention borne out by the available data?

It is clear from Table 9.10 that unemployment in Indonesia is largely concentrated among educated workers. In 1999, secondary school leavers had an unemployment rate of 16 percent, the highest in the country. This is followed by tertiary graduates, who exhibited an unemployment rate of 13 percent. At the same time, the poverty rate for this group was well below the national average and ranged from 13 percent (secondary school graduates) to 2 percent (tertiary graduates). This experience contrasts sharply with the case of less educated workers, encompassing those with up to a primary education. The unemployment rate for this cohort varied from 5 percent (primary school graduates) to less than 1 percent (no schooling). In 1999 the poverty rates for this group were the highest in the country (37 percent to 48 percent). Thus the contention that unemployment has limited relevance in understanding poverty in Indonesia seems to be borne out by the available evidence. In general, the poor cannot afford to stay unemployed for too long and have to seek work of any kind to eke out an existence. It would be useful, as part of future research strategy, to probe more fully the relationship between poverty and unemployment. For example, it should be possible to identify unemployment rates for different quintiles and highlight the extent to which unemployment is a luxury for richer quintiles, but is unaffordable for poorer quintiles. A more careful scrutiny of unpublished SUSENAS and SAKERNAS data along such directions is worth pursuing.

Employment, Labor Market Flexibility, and Poverty: Revisiting the Debate

An important debate that has emerged in the Indonesian context pertains to the role that labor market flexibility played in the precrisis period in facilitating sustained improvements in the living standards of workers and in mitigating the social consequences of the Indonesian crisis. It is important to understand this debate in order to develop a fuller appreciation of the poverty-employment nexus.

Labor market flexibility may be regarded as a synonym for the textbook case of a competitive or neoclassical labor market. The virtue of the latter is that workers are free to adjust the work force in response to shifting relative wage and employment opportunities, while firms are free to adjust the work force in response to shifting profit opportunities. In such a framework, collective bargaining driven by trade unions, strongly enforced hiring and firing decisions, unemployment benefits, minimum wages, and so forth, are regarded as undesirable institutional arrangements, as they constrain the free choice of

workers and firms. More important, arrangements meant to protect the interests of workers paradoxically hurt employment opportunities by raising the
price of labor above what the market will bear.

Despite its appealing simplicity, the analytic construct of labor market
flexibility in precrisis Indonesia was adapted to the requirements of paternalistic authoritarianism. Thus the emphasis was on the provision of centrally
mandated benefits for workers (especially minimum wages, and later, a formal social security system). This was juxtaposed with a political framework
that tightly circumscribed labor rights, while informal systems of social protection through the network of friends and families were seen as playing an
adequate and complementary role for workers in the informal economy. The
rapid growth of the precrisis period and its ability to absorb new entrants to
the work force appeared to justify such a strategy.[28]

The notion of labor market flexibility reemerged in postcrisis Indonesia.
Some observers argue that such flexibility enabled workers to cope with the
crisis with a degree of resilience that ensured that the social impact of the crisis was contained. Had labor markets been rigid, as in the case of a so-called
Keynesian labor market, one would have witnessed large-scale unemployment and poverty.[29]

Both the precrisis characterization of the Indonesian labor market and its
postcrisis resurrection overlook a number of problems. To start with, some observers, while sympathetic to the notion of labor market flexibility, drew attention to the stresses and strains afflicting the precrisis period. Thus one study
highlighted the limits of a paternalistic system that offered substantial centrally
mandated minimum wage increases in the 1990s to appease workers.[30] The
consequence was a threat to employment opportunities and falling international competitiveness—although subsequent evaluations have not reached a
clear-cut position on this issue.[31]

Another study highlighted the problems caused by the lack of a credible
industrial relations system. The mid-1990s were infamous for a sharp increase
in labor unrest.[32] Both these studies argued for the revamping of the industrial
relations system and recommended democratic forms of enterprise-level bargaining.

As for the use of the notion of labor market flexibility in explaining the
evolution of poverty both during and after the crisis is concerned, one can ex-
press reservations about its validity.[33] In a so-called Keynesian labor market, the
primary vehicle for a rise in poverty following a demand shock (such as the one
induced by the Indonesian crisis) is a rise in unemployment (given that wages
are rigid). In a neoclassical labor market operating in a dualistic, developing
economy—presumably the Indonesian case—the primary vehicle for a rise in
poverty as a consequence of a demand shock is a decline in real wages reflecting a reallocation of labor to low-productivity activities. Indeed, employment
adjustments during the Indonesian crisis followed this classic pattern (as dis-

cussed previously) and were accompanied by a steep fall in real wages (discussed later). Whether the unemployment-driven increase in poverty (the Keynesian case) will be higher than the real wage–driven increase in poverty (the neoclassical case) is ultimately an empirical issue that cannot be determined a priori.

A better way of coming to grips with the understanding of the evolution of poverty during the crisis is to eschew preconceived notions of the virtues of labor market flexibility and carefully revisit the current state of knowledge on what could have happened to the poor. It now appears that the sharp increase in consumption poverty and the plummeting of real wages during the crisis period were a tragic manifestation of a collapse in the purchasing power of Indonesians as a result of the "inflation shock" of 1998.

If one combines the 1998 episode with the fact that a significant proportion of Indonesians are clustered around the poverty line, then relatively small shifts in the latter may lead to large changes in the incidence of consumption poverty. However, the sharp rise in poverty (and the steep fall in real wages) during 1998 turned out to be transient as inflation abated (and became deflation for a while), reflecting the restoration of macroeconomic stability. In addition, the government launched a comprehensive, donor-supported social safety program. Some elements of the program worked well, others did not. On balance, it appears that the social safety net interventions managed to reinforce the resilience of ordinary Indonesians in the face of unprecedented adversity. The evidence suggests that social safety net interventions probably prevented an additional 7–11 percent of the population from sliding below the poverty line.[34]

It is clear from the preceding discussion that the notion of labor market flexibility, while useful, can only represent the beginning rather than the end of any analysis of the linkage between poverty and the structure of the labor market. The paradigm of labor market flexibility is essentially silent on, or pays insufficient attention to, a range of complex issues. How does one give primacy to employment concerns in macroeconomic management? Should such primacy be given? Are there basic worker rights? If so, how does one embed them within the industrial relations system? Is there any role for public deliberation in the formulation of labor market policy? What role is there for the state in dealing with labor market risks, such as suboptimal employment adjustments and falling real wages, triggered by economic shocks?

■ Poverty and the Labor Market: The Role of Wages

So far, the discussion of the poverty-labor market nexus has focused primarily on issues in employment.[35] There is, of course, another critical dimension that affects the welfare of workers, namely the rewards to their labor services in the form of real wages. Accordingly, this section will review the long-term behavior of real wages in Indonesia; highlight episodes of falling/stagnating real wages, with specific reference to the 1997 financial crisis; suggest a framework that can explain the behavior of real wages in Indonesia and highlight the role that changes in productivity have played in underpinning wage growth; and explore the relationships among real wages, productivity, and poverty at both the sectoral and the aggregate level.

Trends in Nominal and Real Wages: Overview

Nominal earnings of wage employees increased by 15 percent per annum on average in the 1976–1997 period, before the crisis, according to the national labor force surveys (see Table 9.11). Earnings did not grow evenly during this period, however, slowing down to 10 percent and 7 percent per annum during 1976–1978 and 1987–1989 respectively. During this twenty-one-year period, consumer prices rose by an average of 10 percent per annum, resulting in real growth in earnings of 5 percent per annum. For the two lower-nominal-growth periods, real earnings stagnated during 1976–1978, while declining by 2 percent per annum during 1986–1989.

The East Asian financial crisis, which began in Indonesia in mid-1997, had a major impact on real earnings. In the first year, consumer prices rose by 100 percent, while nominal earnings grew by 20 percent, causing real earnings to decline by over 40 percent. In the following two years, nominal earnings continued to grow by 20 percent per annum, while inflation was brought under control, rising by just 5–10 percent per annum. Real earnings began to climb slowly again to around 90 percent of their precrisis level by 2000.

Published earnings data from the labor force surveys by gender and urban-rural location are available only since 1982. The real earnings of females grew faster than for males in the 1982–1997 period, before the crisis (6 versus 4 percent per annum). This acceleration took place during 1982–1986 and 1989–1997. Rural real earnings also grew faster than urban earnings during this period (4 versus 3 percent per annum), particularly during the 1982–1986 period. These differential growth rates led to the narrowing of gender and urban-rural earnings, suggesting tighter labor market conditions during these two periods of relatively rapid wage growth.

Real Wage Trends by Sector

Real earnings of employees grew more rapidly in agriculture and manufacturing than in other sectors before the crisis. They grew by 5 percent per annum in these two sectors, compared with 4 percent per annum in utilities, construction, transport, and services; 3 percent in trade; and just 2 percent in mining and finance between 1976 and 1997 (see Table 9.12). Since earnings in the agricultural and manufacturing sectors were lower than average, while those in mining and finance were higher than average, these differential growth rates led to the narrowing of earnings differentials observed in the previous section.

Table 9.11 Trends in Nominal and Real Earnings, Indonesia, 1976–2000

	Index (1997 = 100)							Average Annual Growth Rate[a] (%)						Precrisis	
	1976	1978	1982	1986	1989	1997	2000	1976–1978	1978–1982	1982–1986	1986–1989	1989–1997	1997–2000	1982–1997	1976–1997
Nominal earnings															
Indonesia	5	6	16	26	32	100	179	10	27	13	7	15	21	13	15
Male			17	27	33	100	180	—	—	13	7	15	22	13	
Female			12	22	28	100	178	—	—	16	8	17	21	15	
Urban			20	31	34	100	170	—	—	12	—	15	19	12	
Rural			18	32	33	100	183	—	—	16	—	15	22	13	
Urban change in poverty incidence	14	17	30	41	53	100	203[b]	10	16	8	9	8	27[b]	8	10
Real earnings (1997 = 100)															
Indonesia	37	37	53	64	61	100	88	0	9	5	–2	7	–4	4	5
Male			55	67	63	100	89	—	—	5	–2	6	–4	4	
Female			40	54	53	100	88	—	—	8	–1	8	–4	6	
Urban			65	74	63	100	84	—	—	3	—	6	–6	3	
Rural			58	77	63	100	90	—	—	7	—	6	–4	4	

Sources: For earnings, Indonesia's national labor force survey (SAKERNAS), annual publication for 1990–2000; living standards indicators and women's social indicators, various years, for 1976–1989; and special tabulations from raw data produced by Indonesia's Central Bureau of Statistics (CBS) for 1982 and 1986–1989. For consumer prices, weighted average consumer price index of forty-three cities (twenty-seven before 1994); annual average indexes; monthly CBS bulletin.

Notes: a. Growth rates for 1976–1978, 1982–1986, and 1998–2000 are point-to-point compound growth rates.

b. Growth rates for 1986–1989 and 1989–1997 are average annual growth rates.

In general, real earnings moved in the same direction across sectors, though at different rates, during the subperiods of rapid growth of 1978–1982, 1982–1986, and 1989–1997. Similarly, the overall decline observed during 1986–1989 was shared by most sectors. The exception was the 1976–1978 period, which registered real earnings increases in some sectors such as manufacturing, transport, and services, and declines in others such as agriculture and trade.

Real Wage Trends by Education
Labor force survey data constitute the only source of information on wages by education level. These data show that the real earnings of employees with primary school education or less rose relatively more rapidly than for those with junior and senior secondary education (3 percent versus 1 percent and 2 percent respectively), leading to the narrowing of wage differentials by educational level before the crisis noted previously (see Table 9.13). Their real wages also fell less rapidly during the crisis period 1998–2000. At higher education levels, however, the real earnings of diploma and university graduates rose in line with the average during periods of rapid growth, while continuing to grow in the periods of constant overall earnings.

Long-Term Trends in Real Wages: Summary
Following a period of relative wage stagnation during most of the 1970s, which was otherwise a period of rapid economic growth, real wages grew by 5 percent per annum on average during the twenty-year period between 1978 and 1997, and where equally shared by the agricultural and nonagricultural sectors. Real wage improvements took place in all years except the mid-1980s, paradoxically also otherwise known as a period of rapid economic growth. The financial crisis of 1997–1998 had a major impact on real earnings. Real wages declined by 40 percent in the first year, and remained at 10 percent below their precrisis level three years later, in 2000.

Before the crisis, females in rural areas improved their wages relative to males in urban areas. Workers in the agricultural and manufacturing sectors, where wages were lower than in other sectors, improved their position relative to workers in other sectors. Workers with less than primary education improved their position relative to those with junior and secondary school education. This led to the narrowing of wage differentials. Wage differentials were unaffected by the crisis.

Understanding the Long-Term Behavior of Real Wages in Indonesia: Toward a Demand-Supply Framework
Although changes in definitions, questionnaires, and coverage over such a long time frame introduce many comparability problems in employment data from different time periods, a careful assessment of the labor force survey

Table 9.12 Real Earnings by Sector, Indonesia, 1976–2000 (percentage average annual growth)

	1976–1978	1978–1982	1982–1986	1986–1989	1989–1997	1997–2000	Precrisis 1976–1997
Agriculture	−1	8	4	0	7	−4	5
Mining, quarrying	−19	6	—	—	4	−3	2
Manufacturing	8	7	4	−3	8	−7	5
Utilities	−14	8	—	—	8	−11	4
Construction	0	6	—	—	6	−7	4
Trade, hotel, restaurant	−5	7	2	−1	6	−7	3
Transport	4	4	—	—	5	−5	4
Finance and banking	2	0	—	—	6	−6	2
Services	5	6	0	0	6	−4	4
Other[a]	—	—	—	−3	—	—	—
All sectors	0	9	5	−2	7	−6	5

Sources: For earnings: Indonesia's national labor force survey (SAKERNAS), annual publication for 1990–2000; living standards indicators and women's social indicators, various years, for 1976–1989; and special tabulations from raw data produced by Indonesia's Central Bureau of Statistics (CBS) for 1982 and 1986–1989. For consumer price data: weighted average consumer price index of forty-three cities (twenty-seven before 1994); annual average indexes; monthly CBS bulletin.

Notes: Growth rates are deflated by urban consumer price index, and are point-to-point compound growth rates.

a. "Other" included mining, construction, transport, and finance sectors in one category in the 1986–1988 questionnaires.

Table 9.13 Real Earnings by Education Level, Indonesia, 1976–2000 (percentage change per annum)

	1976–1978	1978–1982	1982–1986	1986–1989	1989–1997	1997–2000	Precrisis 1976–1997
No schooling	—	—	—	—	5	-2	—
Incomplete primary[a]	-2	10	3	1	6	-7	5
Primary	5	4	1	-3	6	-9	3
Junior secondary	4	2	-1	-5	4	-8	2
Senior secondary, general	8	-1	-2	-4	5	-8	2
Senior secondary, vocational[b]	7	2	1	-2	5	-6	3
Diploma I and II	—	—	—	1	4	-5	—
Diploma III	—	—	—	—	5	-7	—
University	7[c]	-5[c]	-1[c]	3	4	-7	2
All levels	0	9	5	-2	7	-6	5

Sources: For earnings: Indonesia's national labor force survey (SAKERNAS), annual publication for 1990–2000; living standards indicators and women's social indicators, various years, for 1976–1989; and special tabulations from raw data produced by Indonesia's Central Bureau of Statistics (CBS) for 1982 and 1986–1989. For consumer price data: weighted average consumer price index of forty-three cities (twenty-seven before 1994); annual average indexes; monthly CBS bulletin.

Notes: a. No schooling and incomplete primary together until 1989.
b. Senior secondary, general and vocational together.
c. Diploma and university graduates together.

data does suggest that the demand for labor grew somewhat more rapidly than its supply to produce the observed real wage increases during most of this period. The key factors responsible for the moderate tightening of the labor market may be summarized from supply- and demand-side perspectives.

On the supply side, two important measures were undertaken. First, the nationwide family planning program launched in the early 1970s succeeded in slowing the growth of the working-age population, from around 4.0 percent to 2.6 percent per year between the late 1970s and the late 1990s. Second, the large-scale school building program and education campaign led to increased enrollment at double the rate of the working-age population. Enrollments were particularly rapid in the late 1970s and first half of the 1980s, averaging 14 percent and 8 percent per annum respectively, and at a higher rate for female youth. At its peak, the population attending school increased by 0.7 million children and teenagers per annum during 1978–1982, and by 0.5–0.6 million per annum in the 1980s. This resulted in the slower growth rate of the labor force relative to the working-age population over this whole period (2.4 versus 2.8 percent per annum).

On the demand side, strong and sustained economic growth in labor-intensive sectors, particularly manufacturing and construction, led to a corresponding demand for labor. Nonoil GDP growth averaged 8 percent per year in this twenty-one-year period, led by the manufacturing and construction sectors, which grew at 13 percent and 10 percent per annum respectively. Most other sectors grew by 7–10 percent per annum, with the exception of the agricultural sector, which averaged just over 3 percent per year.

The windfall revenues from the first and second oil booms of the mid-1970s and late 1970s were plowed back into an ambitious public infrastructure program that included the rehabilitation and construction of new irrigation canals and the construction of school buildings, roads, and health centers, thereby creating substantial demand for construction labor. Agricultural production grew as a direct result of improved rural infrastructure and investment in disseminating the green revolution package of rice varieties and fertilizer from the International Rice Research Institute, providing ample demand for rural labor. In addition, strong, sustained, and broad-based economic growth, particularly of relatively labor-intensive sectors such as manufacturing, construction, and transport, created additional demand for unskilled labor in both urban and rural areas.

Real wages first increased in the late 1970s, when agricultural production grew faster than in earlier periods. This coincided with rapid expansion of the construction sector when some wage employees were drawn away from agriculture, even though the end of the oil boom in 1981–1982 led to a sharp drop in construction labor thereafter. After momentarily stagnating due to the further contraction of construction labor in the second half of the 1980s, the demand for wage labor once again picked up in the construction sector, which, coupled with continued strong demand for unskilled wage labor in the manufacturing and other sectors, allowed the agricultural sector to gradually reduce its work force during most of the 1990s, leading to sustained real wage increases.

Agricultural and nonagricultural wages moved together, because wage movements in different sectors reinforced each other due to a high degree of labor mobility and integration between sectors. The moderate tightening of the labor market led to narrower wage differentials by gender and education attainment, and between urban and rural areas.

Some observers have highlighted the point that institutional factors also played a major role in influencing the behavior of wages in the 1990s.[36] In 1992 the Suharto regime began an aggressive pursuit of minimum wage policy. Such a policy stalled for a while during the crisis, but seems to have picked up with renewed vigor since then. Minimum wage increases, it is argued, pushed up average wages as well. Statistically, it has been difficult to substantiate this proposition. While no one doubts that minimum wages have gone up substantially in real terms, the circumstances of precrisis Indonesia also need to be taken into account. A general tightening of the labor market led to a real wage boom that in turn provided a conducive environment for minimum wages to be pushed up.

The Wage-Productivity Relationship: Overview

Table 9.14 offers an overview of the trends in real wages for various subperiods covering 1976–2000 and compares them with changes in productivity. For the economy as a whole, real wage growth kept pace with productivity growth for the 1976–1997 period. Furthermore, periods when productivity growth was buoyant were also accompanied by real wage growth, but this was not always the case. For example, rapid productivity growth in the 1986–1989 period stands in stark contrast to the decline in real wages. Considering the fact that this period also coincides with the trade liberalization cum deregulation reform agenda, one could raise doubts about the short-term consequences of such an agenda for the welfare of workers. However, by the beginning of the 1990s, and until the eve of the 1997 financial crisis, real wages grew a little above productivity growth. Note that there were other subperiods (1978–1986) in which real wage growth exceeded productivity growth—sometimes by quite substantial margins.

At the sectoral level, one can discern significant variations. Real wages grew at roughly twice the rate of productivity growth in agriculture in the 1976–1997 period, but the converse was the case in manufacturing. In the trade and services sector, real wage growth also exceeded productivity growth during the precrisis period.

Table 9.15 shows the trends in real wages, productivity, and poverty. The information is also depicted in Figure 9.16.

Table 9.14 Wage-Productivity Relationship, Indonesia, 1976–2000 (percentage change)

	1976–1978	1978–1982	1982–1986	1986–1989	1989–1997	1997–2000	1976–1997
All							
GDP per worker	3.8	5	1.9	4.7	5.8	-4.3	4.9
Real wage	0.7	9.1	4.8	-1.7	6.6	-6.1	5
Agriculture							
GDP per worker	-0.9	4.9	-1.2	0.3	4.4	-2.8	2.4
Real wage	-1	7.9	4	0	6.6	-3.9	4.7
Manufacturing							
GDP per worker	17.3	1.6	13.3	2.7	7.5	-6	7.7
Real wage	8.5	6.8	4.4	-3.1	7.7	-11.1	3.5
Trade							
GDP per worker	0.3	6.2	0.3	5.1	1.3	-6.7	2.5
Real wage	-4.8	7.1	2.3	-0.9	5.6	-7.3	3.3
Services							
GDP per worker	-3.1	5.7	-3	12	-0.5	-1.1	1.7
Real wage	4.5	5.6	0	-0.4	5.9	-3.6	3.7

Sources: Indonesian national accounts and labor force survey (SAKERNAS).
Notes: Worker by sector = total employment – family workers. Employment in all sectors is for ages 15+; in other sectors age is 10+ until 1997, 15+ thereafter.

49

Table 9.15 Real Wages, Productivity, and Poverty in All Sectors Combined, Indonesia, 1976–2000 (percentage change)

	1976–1978	1978–1982	1982–1986	1986–1989	1989–1997	1997–2000	1976–1997
GDP per worker	3.8	5.0	1.9	4.7	5.8	-4.3	4.9
Real wage	0.7	9.1	4.8	-1.7	6.6	-6.1	5.0
Poverty	-7.0	-6.0	-10.0	-2.0	-4.0	6.0	-29.0

Sources: Indonesian national accounts and labor force survey (SAKERNAS).

Figure 9.16   Co-movements Among Real Wages, Productivity (GDP per worker), and Poverty Incidence, Indonesia, 1976–2000

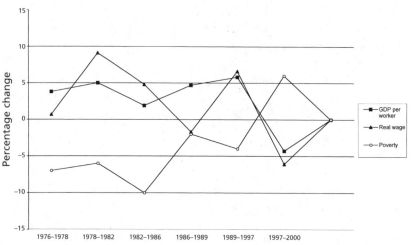

Source: Indonesia's national labor force surveys (SAKERNAS), various years.

Over the precrisis period (1976–1997), real wages and productivity grew at 5 percent annually while poverty declined by 29 percent. At the same time, in the crisis period and its aftermath (1997–2000), the increase in poverty of 6 percent was accompanied by a collapse in both real wages and productivity. Yet there are subperiods during which the linkages among indicators of consumption poverty, real wages, and productivity diverge. This is most conspicuous in the 1986–1989 period, when poverty fell at a steep rate but real wages actually declined at an annual rate of 2 percent. This divergence is also conspicuous in the 1976–1978 period, when real wages barely grew (at about 1 percent) but consumption poverty fell rather steeply. Apart from these anomalous episodes, the co-movements in real wages, productivity, and consumption poverty are quite apparent, with the substantial declines in poverty being accompanied by rising productivity and real wages, and vice versa.

An important study on real wages in Indonesia has also explored the wage-poverty linkage. Pertinent information derived from that study is provided in Table 9.16. As can be seen, there is, on the whole, a reasonably good correspondence between the movement in real wages for agricultural workers (in Java) and the changes in poverty incidence. The conspicuous exceptions seem to be 1978–1980 and 1987–1990, when poverty fell even when real wages declined.[37]

Table 9.16   Comparison of Changes in Poverty and Real Wages, Indonesia, 1976–1998

	Change in Number of Poor Based on Official Poverty Line (%)	Agricultural Real Wages in Java (%)
1976–1978	−12.9	4.4
1978–1980	−10.4	−1.8
1980–1984	−17.3	4.4
1987–1990	−9.3	−5.7
1990–1993	−4.8	19.2
1993–1996	−13.1	14.2
1996–1998	52.0	−33.0

Source: Adapted from Papanek and Handoko 1999, tab. 2.

The link between poverty and wages at the sectoral/occupational level is exhibited in Table 9.17 using data for 1999 and 2000. As can be seen, agriculture, which is the least-paid sector (with wages being 54 percent of the national average) and also among the least-productive sectors, had the highest concentration of poverty and accounted for nearly 60 percent of the total population in poverty. At the other extreme, finance, in which average wages were 75 percent above the national average and contained a high incidence of

Table 9.17   Relationship Between Poverty and Relative Wages by Sector of Occupation, Indonesia, 1999 and 2000

	February 1999	2000	
	Poverty Incidence (%)	Contribution to Total Poor (%)	Relative Wage (national = 100)
Agriculture	39.7	58.4	54
Trade	17.6	11.1	93
Manufacturing	22.9	7.7	93
Civil, social, and private services	13.1	7.4	127
Transport and communication	24.0	5.6	127
Construction	29.0	5.5	98
Receiving transfer	15.6	2.7	
Mining and quarrying	29.8	1.0	152
Others	32.0	0.3	
Finance	5.2	0.2	175
Electricity, gas, and water	14.5	0.2	145

Source: Calculated by the author.

white-collar workers, had the lowest poverty incidence in the country. However, the relationship between wages and poverty at the sectoral level is by no means exact. For example, the mining and quarrying sector has relative wages at 52 percent above the national level. Yet it has a poverty rate (29 percent) that is higher than the manufacturing sector (23 percent), which has relative wages that are 7 percent below the national standard.

■ Poverty Reduction Through the Creation of Broad-Based Employment Opportunities: Some Policy Issues

The salient dimensions of the nature of poverty in Indonesia and the systemic nature of labor market weaknesses highlighted in the previous sections set the context for enunciating the view that employment creation ought to be a core element of a national poverty reduction strategy.[38] More specifically, there is a need to create enough durable jobs annually (2.5 to 3 million according to current estimates) to absorb new entrants to the work force and to clear the backlog of the unemployed and the underemployed. Embedded within the overarching goal of employment creation are a series of policy issues that need to be explored.

The Need for a Return of Rapid, Sustainable, and Equitable Growth. Over the 1999–2002 period, the average growth rate was 3.2 percent. Contrast this with a 7.0 percent growth rate for 1994–1997.[39] The growth rate in the second quarter of 2003 was 3.8 percent.[40] Such modest growth is being driven by domestic consumption rather than investment and exports, as was the case in the precrisis period.

The postcrisis growth rate recorded so far is not enough to create jobs to cope with the 2 million entrants to the work force annually and to cope with the backlog of the unemployed and the underemployed. Based on current estimates of employment elasticity, a growth rate of 5–6 percent in the short to medium term appears critical in underpinning any employment-focused strategy for mitigating the incidence of poverty in postcrisis Indonesia.[41]

A caveat is in order. While growth is a necessary condition for reducing poverty through the employment channel, this virtuous linkage can be easily offset if inequality rises at the same time. For example, there is evidence that income distribution deteriorated between 1999 and 2002. If such adverse changes in inequality had not taken place, then the available evidence suggests that the incidence of poverty in 2002 would have been at least 4 percentage points lower.[42] In sum, one needs both rapid and equitable growth that can be sustained over time. This will strengthen the poverty-employment nexus.

Reflecting Employment Goals in Macroeconomic Policy.[43] It is difficult to
be serious about employment-led recovery from the 1997 financial crisis and
its terrible aftermath unless employment concerns are formally incorporated
as part of macroeconomic policy goals and targets. Indonesian monetary authorities, in common with such authorities in many countries, are entrusted
with the task of reining in inflation to an agreed target. In the medium term,
the aim is to maintain the inflation rate below 5 percent.[44] At the same time,
fiscal policy is constrained by the need for "fiscal consolidation" in order to
rein in a crisis-induced explosion of public debt. This has understandably created a macroeconomic policy framework geared toward monitoring financial
and fiscal variables.

In the 2001–2002 period, Indonesia experienced double-digit inflation (in
the 11.5–11.9 percent range), while the nominal interest rate, as recorded in
mid-2001, was the highest among Southeast Asian economies. From mid-
2001 to late 2003, the nominal interest rate fell by 350 basis points and at the
latter date the inflation rate stood at 6.6 percent.[45] At some point, the monetary authorities need to resolve some fundamental issues. What are the ex ante
social gains of keeping inflation persistently below 5 percent, or conversely,
what are the social costs of allowing inflation to drift above 5 percent in the
medium term?[46] Have monetary authorities taken on board the lessons of international evidence that a moderate rate of inflation (below 15 percent) is not
harmful to growth or prejudicial to the poor?[47] Unless there are convincing
answers to such basic questions, inflation targeting in a stringent fashion may
cause more problems than it will resolve.

Consider also the implications of running a tight fiscal policy at a time
when economic growth seems to be quite anemic. The balanced-budget prin-
ciple remains enshrined in law, requiring that public expenditure should not
exceed domestic budgetary revenue plus foreign aid inflows. The 2003 budget
deficit met its fiscal goal, owing to successful efforts to restrain spending and
slow disbursement in key infrastructure and development projects. However,
the continued failure to lower fuel subsidies and overambitious projected
growth rates has led to concern among some observers who argue that this
will render future budget revisions unrealistic.[48]

More important, one could argue that, while the composition of the
budget is important, its overall size in relation to the financing needs of a national poverty reduction strategy cannot be ignored. For example, preliminary
estimates reveal that attaining universal basic education for all Indonesians
(currently fixed at nine years of education) will require an investment of 5.6
trillion rupiah per annum.[49] Establishing a primary road network that is comprehensive in nature will also require an annual investment of 6.5 trillion rupiah. Current estimates suggest that the shortfall in relation to these spending
requirements is 15–20 percent for provincial roads and 30 percent for rural

roads.[50] It also appears that it would cost around 6.2 trillion rupiah annually to deliver targeted health care programs to the districts.[51]

It appears that there is a case for balancing the focus on financial and fiscal variables in macroeconomic management with a credible commitment to the provision of productive and durable employment opportunities for all Indonesians. Such a commitment could occur in the form of an annual "jobs summit" staged in the context of public deliberations on issues pertaining to employment creation at both the national and the local level. It would entail setting explicit job creation targets that would be consistent with absorbing new entrants to the work force and making a significant dent on the current stock of the unemployed (given assumptions about the structural parameters of an economy). This key target would then set the context for working out the corresponding growth rate and requisite policy initiatives, and for specifying a pro-poor budgetary framework. The use of employment creation targets as the locus of macroeconomic management in turn provides scope for exploring ways in which the growth process can be made employment-intensive, thus reducing the burden on the growth rate alone to engender the required number of jobs to meet policy goals.

Strengthening the Labor Market Information System to Complement Employment-Focused Macroeconomic Management. Any attempt to craft an employment-focused policy framework needs to be undergirded by an appropriate statistical framework that can enable the government to monitor the labor market. To start with, it is necessary to regularly update key indicators of the labor market with due attention to gender disaggregation. In addition, it may be worthwhile to consider suggestions made in Dhanani 2002 for improving the labor market information system. These include improvements in the design and collection of labor market data; greater efforts to collect information on the self-employed (who account for 40 percent of the work force); early warning systems to monitor the living standards of the working poor by focusing on monthly wage data of vulnerable groups in the labor force; integrating labor market data with poverty indicators; reduction in the lags among data generation, processing, and dissemination; strengthening the capacity of district-level officials to produce relevant labor market data; and ensuring that the collection and production of labor statistics are fully funded from regular budgetary resources of the government. In addition, pertinent labor market information should be developed for job seekers, students, trainees, and employers.

Identifying Sectors with Employment Potential. Any credible poverty reduction strategy in Indonesia will have to focus on the agricultural sector. It dominates the national employment scene, with 41 million workers, of whom 80 percent are attached to the informal economy. Furthermore, poverty is very much a rural phenomenon, as about 75 percent of the total poor households reside in the rural areas and depend on the agricultural sector for their main livelihood.

The rural poor are often confronted with disadvantages stemming from remoteness, lack of education and health care, insecure and unproductive jobs, high fertility, and discrimination against women or ethnic minorities. Thus, poverty reduction policies and programs must give strategic focus on rural development and must create more opportunities for women and men to find work in the rural areas. Such policies not only promote economic growth but also help alleviate urban poverty by restraining rural-urban migration to a more sustainable rate.

Given this close connection between the rural economy and poverty, it is not surprising that the Indonesian government has made a formal commitment to rural development by seeking to implement measures that will stimulate off-farm employment opportunities. In particular, a recent government white paper focused on the development of small-scale agribusiness activities. This is a welcome initiative, but appropriate policy details need to be delineated.[52] Examples of judicious interventions that the government could consider include improvements in land tenure security, enabling farmers to diversify into agribusiness through provision of greater information and capacity building, and nourishing linkages between small and large businesses.

Another plank of rural development is investment in rural infrastructure. The recent white paper made some welcome announcements in this sphere, such as the development of village infrastructure, the Kecematan Development Program, the Urban Poverty Eradication Program, and the provision of clean water and sanitation.

The Role of Enterprise Development in Employment Generation and Poverty Reduction. Official statistics suggest that the vast bulk of Indonesian workers are employed in small and medium-sized enterprises (SMEs). Hence it is not surprising that SME development represents a core plank of Indonesia's poverty reduction strategy. The government could undertake a variety of initiatives in SME development, including strengthening the policy coordination framework, harnessing the entrepreneurial talent of young men and women, revisiting the cooperative model, and building capacity for local employment and development.

Strengthening the Policy Coordination Framework. In order to take advantage of the opportunities to promote SME development initiatives, it is imperative that there be stronger coordination of policies and programs among the national players, as well as among local governments and the private sector. Furthermore, it is important that the national government use its convening powers to ensure that local programs and policies are both economically sound and friendly to SMEs. Such initiatives should systematically draw on international best practices and on the expertise of local businesses and their associations.

Employment Generation Through Public Investments in Infrastructure. A recent study suggests that there are significant weaknesses in the provision of infrastructure facilities in Indonesia.[53] Around 50 percent of Indonesian households do not have access to electricity, and there are only 9.1 telephones per 100 people. These indicators compare rather unfavorably with regional norms.

Consider the following statistics that highlight the nexus between poverty incidence and access to infrastructure facilities. Approximately 50 percent of Indonesians in the poorest quintile do not have access to an asphalt road as the main road in the place in which they reside. Between 6 and 11 million Indonesians do not have any reliable connection to any decent road or motorized transport network. These people are likely to reside in some of the least accessible and most disadvantaged areas of the country.

Future public spending allocations need to focus on the provision of rural infrastructure facilities. Connecting the rural poor to markets and services through a rural road network of a reasonable standard will form an important plank of the government's poverty reduction strategy.

Public investment in infrastructure facilities—both in rural areas and elsewhere—can be readily crafted as an important tool of employment policy. One ILO study has shown that labor-based production methods in infrastructure investment in Indonesia can generate as many as 1.2 million durable jobs over four years without compromising standards of quality that one associates with equipment-intensive production techniques. This means that, if general growth-induced employment creation is on the order of 2 million jobs annually, it has the potential to rise to 2.3 million annually with the adoption of labor-based production methods in public investment policy.[54]

International evidence confirms these positive findings. Studies show that labor-based infrastructure programs are 10–30 percent less costly in financial terms than more equipment-intensive techniques, reduce foreign exchange requirements by 50–60 percent, and create up to five times as much employment for the same investment.[55]

Conclusion

This chapter has reviewed the multidimensional nature of poverty in Indonesia and recent developments in the labor market. As is now widely acknowledged, the 1997 financial crisis led to a sharp but temporary reversal in the sustained progress against poverty in the rapid growth of the precrisis era. This era witnessed the movement of workers from agriculture to the more productive nonagricultural activities and an expansion in the size of the formal wage-employment sector. Furthermore, some degree of skill deepening took place and real wages generally rose in line with increases in productivity.

Not all the available indicators in the precrisis era paint an unambiguously positive picture. Thus, for example, the depth and severity of poverty rose in the 1990–1993 period even as the incidence of poverty declined. Real wages generally rose in line with declines in poverty, but there were some conspicuous exceptions. Despite such episodic anomalies, the decline in consumption poverty in Indonesia in the precrisis period was accompanied by significant and sustained improvements in various nonincome dimensions of poverty, most notably in terms of improvements in child and maternal health, access to safe drinking water and sanitation facilities, and improvements in access to basic education. The 1997 financial crisis does not seem to have had a persistently adverse impact on the nature of deficient capabilities. Projections based on past trends suggest that Indonesia is on track to meet, by 2015, the Millennium Development Goals pertaining to target reductions in both income and nonincome dimensions of poverty.

Nevertheless, Indonesia faces a major challenge in coping with the problem of deficient capabilities. Progress in child health has stalled since the mid-1990s. Half of households still do not have access to safe drinking water, while the goal of attaining universal basic education is constrained by poor outcomes at the junior secondary level, where the net enrollment rate is still around 62 percent. There are also persistent concerns about the low quality of education that the average Indonesian receives. What is particularly striking is that, in a large and regionally diverse country, at least a third of the provinces are unlikely to meet at least one of the MDGs based on an extrapolation of recent trends.

The strength of the poverty-labor market nexus in Indonesia was quite evident in the aftermath of the 1997 financial crisis. As consumption poverty shot up, real wages collapsed by about 40 percent. The size of the informal and agricultural sector expanded as shrinking job opportunities in the formal sector induced an involuntary reallocation of labor. Since then, the interaction between poverty and the labor market has turned out to be more complex. Thus, while consumption poverty fell from its crisis-induced peak, and real wages as measured in 2002 have recovered from their trough, employment outcomes have been much more muted, and formal sector job opportunities remain largely sluggish. Indeed, employment growth in manufacturing has slowed sharply and employment elasticity in this sector is much lower now than in previous decades. This in turn reflects sluggish growth of the economy, which has primarily relied on domestic consumption rather than investments and exports, which were the engines of growth in the precrisis period. The predictable consequence is that the informal economy and the agricultural sector are now larger than they were in the past. The open unemployment rate is higher now than in the pre-1997 period, while youth unemployment is endemic. Gender disparities persist in the labor market despite some progress in the past. A high degree of geographic mobility of labor acted as a safety valve for the poor in the past, but the emergence of a large number of internally displaced persons and an increase in the number of vulnerable migrants have marred this mechanism. Indeed, vulnerability is a conspicuous feature in Indonesia, as it affects at least a third of the population.

In terms of critical policy issues, this chapter has posited the view that employment creation on a durable basis is key to the sustainable reduction of Indonesian poverty. This would entail the need to incorporate employment concerns in macroeconomic policy, which is currently preoccupied with inflation targeting and fiscal consolidation to rein in a crisis-induced explosion in public debt. Indonesian policymakers can certainly claim credit for engendering macroeconomic stability, but one now needs to go well beyond that narrow premise and focus on initiatives that will unleash rapid, sustainable, and equitable growth. Current growth is still below the 5–6 percent rate that is required to underpin creation of the 2.5 to 3 million jobs on an annual basis that are needed to absorb new entrants to the labor force.

At some stage, Indonesian policymakers need to respond to the financing needs of a comprehensive and credible poverty reduction program, even after allowing for the elimination of waste and inefficiency in the current budgetary framework. About 18 trillion rupiah in new funds and initiatives will be needed on an annual basis in three critical areas—the provision of universal basic education, the delivery of primary health care services, and the provision of a comprehensive road network. The latter, in turn, is a specific manifestation of systemic weaknesses in the quality and standard of infrastructure facilities, which are retarding growth and hobbling the capacity of policymakers to reduce poverty.

There are a number of options that could be explored in making the growth process more employment-friendly, including identifying sectors with high employment potential, nurturing and nourishing a policy environment friendly to the development of SMEs, and adopting labor-based programs in designing and developing public investments in infrastructure. Furthermore, policymakers need to consolidate the benefits that flow from a high degree of geographic mobility of labor by easing impediments to travel, regulating the "migration" industry, ensuring access to secure and cost-effective means of remittances, and looking after vulnerable migrants.

Finally, given Indonesia's regional diversity and the current program of democratic decentralization, any poverty reduction strategy will need to focus on ensuring that all the country's regional communities share in the fruits of growth. This may well entail the need to monitor the attainment of the Millennium Development Goals at a district level.

▓ Notes

1. The Indonesian government finalized its poverty reduction strategy paper in late 2004.

2. The alternative estimates take the 1996 poverty line and project it backward and forward using the prevailing inflation rates. The procedure is described in Dhanani and Islam 2002. The CBS poverty lines in Figure 9.1, on the other hand, pertain to poverty lines derived for each period of observation.

3. Note that the estimates presented in Figure 9.1 vary in one significant respect from new estimates by the CBS. In Figure 9.1 the headcount ratio is shown to be 11.3 percent for 1996, while it is shown to be 18 percent for 1996 in new estimates by the CBS. This discrepancy is due to the fact that CBS used two different poverty standards, the so-called old poverty standard based on 1996 data (embodied in Figure 9.1) and a new poverty standard based on 1998 data (embodied in the new estimates). The latter are readily comparable across time, as they are based on a common poverty line. On the other hand, the statistics in Figure 9.1 are less comparable across time, because they are based on period-specific poverty lines.

4. The estimates reported here are based on special tabulations by the Central Bureau of Statistics in connection with the compilation of a report on the Millennium Development Goals. I am grateful to the United Nations Support Facility for Indonesian Recovery, a Jakarta-based project of the United Nations Development Programme, for providing access to these tabulations.

5. The Central Bureau of Statistics upgraded the national poverty line in 1998.

6. It is customary to refer to US$1 a day as the "extreme" poverty line and US$2 a day as the "moderate" poverty line applicable to a middle-income economy. L. Pritchett (2003) maintains that in global comparisons of poverty, three benchmarks (measured in terms of PPP) should be used: US$1 a day measuring the incidence of destitution, US$2 a day measuring extreme poverty, and US$15 a day measuring poverty based on living standards of the poor in rich countries.

7. Note too that the incidence of severe undernutrition among children in Indonesia increased between 1989 and 1995—see Figure 9.5.

8. The estimates reported in this section are based on special tabulations by the Central Bureau of Statistics prepared in connection with the compilation of a report on the Millennium Development Goals. I am grateful to the United Nations Support Facility for Indonesian Recovery for providing access to these tabulations.

9. United Nations Development Programme 2003.

10. World Bank 2003d.

11. See International Labour Organization (ILO) 2003b.

12. The vulnerability estimates presented in this section draw on World Bank 2003a.

13. These studies are reviewed in Islam 2002.

14. The labor market statistics reported in this section are based on special tabulations by the Central Bureau of Statistics using the ILO's key indicators of the labor market (KILM). Puguh Irawan bears formal responsibility for managing the KILM project in the CBS.

15. Alisjahbana and Manning 2002.

16. The statistics were kindly supplied by Shafiq Dhanani, a Jakarta-based consultant for the United Nations Industrial Development Organization. They were prepared as part of a forthcoming book on industry and labor in Indonesia.

17. Asia Recovery Information Centre database for 2003 (http://www.aric.adb.org).

18. The male-female wage gap is explored in Dhanani and Islam 2001a.

19. The only exception seems to be female workers with tertiary education, who are on par with their male counterparts (5.0 percent).

20. See Irawan, Ahmed, and Islam 2000 for an application of the ILO's KILM framework to Indonesia.

21. See Manning and Junankar 1998.

22. Dhanani 2001.

23. Preliminary estimates for 2001 suggest that the unemployment rate was 8.1 percent (Dhanani 2002, tab. 2).

24. Preliminary estimates for 2001 suggest that the employment share of agriculture is 43.8 percent, while the employment share of manufacturing is 13.3 percent (Dhanani 2002, tab. 2.8).

25. See Padalino and Vivarelli 1997.

26. See Islam and Nazara 2000b. The "ex post" procedure really entails dividing observed GDP growth by observed employment growth.

27. See Insan 2000. In Figures 9.12 to 9.15, Q1 = poorest 20 percent, up to Q2 = richest 20 percent.

28. Prominent examples of studies on Indonesia that work within the analytic tradition of labor market flexibility include Manning 1998; Wiebe 1996; and Mason and Baptist 1996.

29. As C. Manning (2000, 108) observes: "I conclude that labor markets remained highly flexible despite the rapid economic transformation. *I suggest that this flexibility is a key explanation for why unemployment and poverty did not rise more than they did during the crisis*" (emphasis added). See also Tubagus 2000.

30. See Agrawal 1995.

31. For an evaluation of the evidence on the impact of minimum wages on employment in Indonesia, see Islam and Nazara 2000a, in which it is argued that minimum wage increases in the 1990s were benign in terms of their impact on employment, but Social Monitoring and Early Response Unit (SMERU) 2001a reaches an alternative conclusion.

32. See Edwards 1996.

33. See Dhanani and Islam 2001b.

34. See Dhanani and Islam 2002 for a thorough review.

35. This section draws on Dhanani and Islam 2001a. See Papanek and Handoko 1999 for a seminal study on wages and poverty in pre- and postcrisis Indonesia.

36. See SMERU 2001b.

37. Regression analysis using quarterly Indonesian wage data in Papanek and Handoko 1999 suggests that real wages respond positively to output growth and negatively to inflation.

38. This section draws on ILO 2003b, chap. 1. The author of this chapter is also the principal author of the ILO study.

39. Asia Recovery Information Centre database for 2003 (http://www.aric.adb.org).

40. The latest growth estimates are available at the website of the Central Bureau of Statistics (http://www.bps.go.id).

41. The 5 percent figure was highlighted in ILO 1999b. See also Islam and Nazara 2000b.

42. See World Bank 2003d, chap. 5.

43. The United Nations Development Programme has played an active role in advocating the adoption of "pro-poor macroeconomic policy" in developing countries. Indonesia is one of eight Asian countries that has recently been studied to validate the

ideas embedded in pro-poor macroeconomics. See McKinley 2003. The key message is that there should be a focus on public investment–led fiscal policy complemented by accommodating monetary policy. The need for public investment in infrastructure is emerging as a major policy issue in Indonesia.

44. The challenges and constraints of implementing "inflation targeting" in Indonesia are explored in Alamsyah et al. 2001.

45. Asia Recovery Information Centre, July 2003 update (http://www.adb.aric. org); World Bank 2003e.

46. See Akerlof, Dickens, and Perry 1996, in which it is argued that the social costs of moderate inflation have been exaggerated.

47. The evidence is reviewed in I. Islam 2003.

48. See Economist Intelligence Unit 2005.

49. These are unpublished estimates prepared by the Indonesian Ministry of Education.

50. See World Bank 2003a, chap. 3.

51. See Chowdhury 2003.

52. See Government of Indonesia 2003. This is typically known as the white paper.

53. See World Bank 2003a. See also *Jakarta Post,* December 3, 2003.

54. See ILO 1999c.

55. See ILO 2000a.

10

Uganda: Economic Growth, Employment, Poverty, and Pro-Poor Policies

Kabann I. B. Kabananukye,
Adrine E. K. Kabananukye, J. Krishnamurty,
and Daisy Owomugasho

Uganda is a landlocked East African country bordered by Kenya to the east, Rwanda to the southwest, Tanzania to the south, Sudan to the north, and the Democratic Republic of Congo to the west. It is a former British protectorate that became independent on October 9, 1962.

Lying astride the equator, the country is well endowed with natural resources, with some 18 million hectares of arable land, although less than one third is under cultivation. Uganda is an agro-based country, with over 90 percent of the population deriving its livelihood from agriculture and related activities and contributing about 40 percent to the GDP.

Uganda was characterized by political instability between the mid-1960s and mid-1980s. Economic mismanagement, civil strife, and armed conflicts left most of the country's infrastructure in a sorry state. This followed a military coup in 1971. The military government's eight-year rule was characterized by brutal murders and a mass exodus of the expatriates and Asians who had previously dominated Uganda's manufacturing and business sectors of the economy, and resulted in a general breakdown of infrastructure. Between 1979 and 1986, Uganda went through five political regimes. This had far-reaching social, political, and economic implications that translated into unemployment, poverty, and overall economic decline.

In 1986 the National Resistance Movement (NRM) took over the government. Since then, there have been remarkable changes in economic developments and political stability, although some insecurity and insurgency still persist in northern and eastern parts of the country, where people are living in "protected camps." Infrastructure facilities became largely run-down in the conflict areas, roads fell into disrepair, agricultural farms were abandoned, and schools and health units closed. It is probable that poverty and unemployment in the country were high. However, the NRM government forged peace initiatives in the war-torn regions, alongside attempts to restore peace in a bid to promote economic growth and eradicate poverty and unemployment.

The economic recovery program (ERP), launched in 1987,[1] registered significant progress in various sectors of the economy, including construction, manufacturing, as well as mining and quarrying. Despite Uganda's impressive macroeconomic performance, it is still one of the poorest countries in the world. Poverty reduction is therefore a fundamental objective of Uganda's development strategy.

The poverty eradication action plan (PEAP), introduced in 1997, is a guiding framework for the achievement of poverty eradication in Uganda.[2] It adopts a multisectoral approach, recognizing the multidimensional nature of poverty and linkages among underlying factors. It aims at promoting good governance and security, economic growth and transformation, the ability of the poor to raise their incomes, and a better quality of life for the poor. Uganda also has an aspiration to attain a highly trained, competent, and knowledgeable labor force that is motivated, responsible, efficient, enterprising, innovative, and industrious. The people as well aspire for secure and well-remunerated employment.

It is against this backdrop that we seek to explore issues and dynamics in economic growth, employment, poverty, and pro-poor policies in Uganda since the 1980s. It is now generally recognized that despite a most difficult recent history of disorder, civil war, insecurity, destruction of assets, and outflow of capital, Uganda managed over much of the 1990s to maintain a very creditable record of economic growth and poverty reduction. This chapter seeks to enhance our understanding of what happened, looking at income growth, poverty reduction, and employment changes.

We begin by examining trends and patterns in economic growth between 1987 and 2002, with key features of structural change identified for two subperiods, 1992–1997 and 1998–2002. We analyze available evidence on poverty and inequality, looking at both income-related measures and other indicators of poverty.

Next we examine the main features of growth and structural change in the labor force over the 1990s, providing estimates of employment elasticities, exploring links between employment expansion and poverty reduction, and examining features of economic growth that contributed to poverty reduction. Finally, we attempt to model the main determinants of employment and poverty with a view to quantifying the likelihood of certain types of employment growth having stronger impacts on poverty.

▓ Analysis of Economic Growth and Poverty Reduction

We begin by reviewing trends in economic growth and their links to the process of structural transformation of the economy; this analysis then leads into a discussion of poverty trends and the extent of social transformation in Uganda, in which we consider both income and other poverty measures. The basic question being investigated is the extent to which growth has resulted in poverty reduction over the years.

Economic growth rates in Uganda have been relatively well monitored since the 1980s, while poverty data became easily available starting in the 1990s, following the increased prioritization of poverty reduction within the national development framework. It was not until 1995 that policymakers in Uganda started realizing that economic growth is a necessary but not sufficient condition for reducing poverty in the country and therefore carefully analyzed the existing data in order to develop in 1997 a poverty eradication action plan. Implementation of the PEAP since that time has led to periodic monitoring of poverty trends in the country and attempts to assess their links to economic growth.

Economic Growth and Structural Change

Growth Trends. According to the available statistics, Uganda's national GDP and per capita GDP have been growing since 1986, although the rates have varied greatly from year to year. The country has an impressive sustained growth record over the period. In 2002–2003, national GDP was 2.4 times its 1987–1988 level and per capita GDP was 1.5 times its 1987–1988 level. However, there is some evidence that growth has recently slowed in both aggregate and per capita terms. Thus over the six-year period 1991/92–1996/97, national GDP increased by 42 percent and per capita GDP by 20 percent. Over the subsequent six-year period, 1997/98–2002/03, the increase was much lower, by 34 percent and 13 percent respectively (see Table 10.1).

The relatively good performance of GDP growth in the first phase, 1991–1992 to 1996–1997, was due to several factors. Important among these were the restoration of peace, the elimination of internal conflicts, and the restoration of law and order. Public spending priorities shifted away from military and police expenditure and toward road construction. Measures were taken to rebuild investor confidence, to simplify procedures, and to attain macroeconomic stability and implement economic liberalization. In the area of liberalization, of particular importance were trade liberalization, liberalization of coffee marketing, and privatization of public enterprises. This period also witnessed a coffee boom, when international prices were favorable, enabling farmers to earn high profits.

Table 10.1   Trends in Total GDP and GDP per Capita at Factor Cost, Uganda, 1987–2003

	GDP (million shillings)	GDP per Capita (shillings)	GDP Growth Rate (%)	Per Capita GDP Growth Rate (%)
1987–1988	3,786,258	247,468	7.3	4.4
1988–1989	4,020,985	255,447	6.2	3.2
1989–1990	4,241,117	261,878	5.5	2.5
1990–1991	4,473,376	268,510	5.5	2.5
1991–1992	4,639,669	269,343	3.7	0.3
1992–1993	5,010,004	281,156	8.0	4.4
1993–1994	5,279,982	286,442	5.4	1.9
1994–1995	5,807,790	304,585	10.0	6.3
1995–1996	6,292,700	319,028	8.3	4.7
1996–1997	6,597,080	323,323	4.8	1.3
1997–1998	6,888,596	326,369	4.4	0.9
1998–1999	7,393,862	338,643	7.3	3.8
1999–2000	7,828,950	346,632	5.9	2.4
2000–2001	8,274,376	354,155	5.7	2.2
2001–2002	8,772,644	362,980	6.0	2.5
2002–2003	9,199,814	367,951	4.9	1.4

Source: Ugandan Bureau of Statistics data and worksheets, September 2003 (unpublished).
Note: Figures are in constant 1997–1998 prices.

However, from around 1997, the impact of these measures may have begun to wear off; also, international prices for the major export commodities, notably coffee, declined. Luckily, Uganda's export diversification strategy had taken off, with nontraditional export commodities such as fish, hides and skins, and horticulture coming onto the market. Unfortunately, the growth of the economy was impeded by the European Union–imposed ban on fish exports from Uganda due to quality concerns. Even though this ban was subsequently lifted, the fish industry has yet to recover to the levels that were attained in 1998 in terms of volume. The growth of the economy has slowed due to, among other factors, deterioration in the terms of trade and the reemergence of insecurity in the northern region of the country.

GDP per capita has followed a pattern similar to that of overall growth, rising relatively faster in the first phase under study and slowing down over the second phase, up to 2003. As we attempt to show later, not all regions and socioeconomic categories gained equally from the benefits of growth.

Key Features of Structural Change. Economic growth in Uganda was initially accompanied by substantial structural changes in GDP. The percentage shares of three major sectors, agriculture, industry, and services, shown in Table 10.2, indicate that a sharp fall between 1992 and 1997 in the agriculture sector, from 49 to 41 percent, and a sharp rise in the industrial sector, from 13

Table 10.2 Sectoral Contributions to GDP, Uganda, 1992–2002
(percentages)

	1992	1997	1998	2002
Agriculture	48.8	41.3	41.8	39.8
Industry	13.1	18.5	18.6	19.4
Services	38.1	40.1	39.6	40.8

Source: Ugandan Bureau of Statistics data by calendar year.

to nearly 19 percent, were the only two major changes. Also, the decline in agriculture and the rise in industry were of a much smaller order in the latter period, 1998–2002, when compared to the former period, 1992–1998. Looking at agriculture proper, the production of field crops, its share declined from 36.9 to 31.1 percent between 1992 and 1997. Over the same period the share of manufacturing rose from 6.4 to 9.3 percent. Between 1998 and 2002 the share of agriculture proper declined a little, from 32 to 30.6 percent, while that of manufacturing rose modestly, from 9.4 to 9.7 percent. These results suggest that the pace of structural change also diminished alongside deceleration in the growth of GDP, reported earlier. This is not unexpected, for the pace of structural change is dependent on the pace of economic growth.

Summarizing this picture of growth and structural change over the decade after 1992, growth remained positive, but slowed to some extent in later years, and this deceleration was also reflected in the pace of structural change. This conclusion is supported by a growth accounting exercise by D. Dunn in 2002, which found that total factor productivity rose by 3 percent per year between 1992 and 1997 and then fell back to 0.5 percent per year. While the positive impact of improved security and the elimination of macroeconomic distortions may have not been fully exhausted, increasingly economic growth will require significant increases in the rate of investment.[3]

The end of the coffee boom, trade restrictions and deterioration in the terms of trade, the impact of weather conditions, and other factors that affected agriculture all contributed to the relative slowdown of economic growth in recent years. Also, the slowdown is partly explained by the recent poor performance of the northern region, where insurgency has affected security. Unfortunately, regional estimates for GDP do not exist. These events are reflected, as we shall see later, in estimates of poverty and wage rates.

The rapid growth of population may have also acted as a constraint on economic growth. The 2001 census has revealed that population is growing at the rate of 3.4 percent annually. This has led to a very high dependency ratio, with over half the population being under the age of fifteen.

The immediate challenge lies in speeding economic growth and structural transformation in the Ugandan economy, if the expected poverty outcomes, as reflected in the PEAP, are to be achieved. In the meantime, it is desirable to know whether the economic growth that has been achieved so far has translated into benefits for the majority of Ugandans through reduced poverty. This is the thrust of the rest of this chapter.

The Poverty Scenario

As a result of Uganda's national household surveys and 1998 and 2002 participatory assessments, there is a general consensus that defines poverty as a lack of basic needs and services such as food, clothing, shelter, basic health care, education, markets, roads, information, and communication. Lack of adequate productive assets such as land, poor access to credit and other productive inputs, a situation of powerlessness, and social exclusion are other dimensions of poverty. Often, lack of adequate productive employment opportunities is a major cause of poverty, and this is reflected in income and other measures of poverty. While most of these poverty dimensions are monitored periodically through the household surveys, some, particularly those relating to qualitative aspects, are difficult to measure and hence data on them do not exist.

In order to obtain a fuller picture of poverty conditions in Uganda over the years, this section explores progress in poverty reduction, looking at the income as well as other relevant dimensions of welfare. Income poverty, which is usually measured in terms of average personal consumption expenditure, relies heavily on data obtained from national household surveys. These data are used to estimate the proportion of the population below poverty line, defined in terms of the money value of a basket of commodities. Other dimensions of poverty may be assessed in terms of the level of access or deprivation of basic services, and through indicators such as mortality rates and asset levels.

Income Poverty. Poverty may be defined in terms of inadequacy of income in relation to essential consumption needs. This in turn requires that the latter be defined and quantified. The poor in Uganda are defined as those members of the population whose personal consumption expenditure is below the poverty line. S. Appleton (1999) sets the poverty line at 16,012 Ugandan shillings (1989 prices) per adult equivalent per month, computed on the basis of the price of an average food basket for the poor population and an adult male food consumption of 3,000 kilocalories per day plus estimated consumption of nonfood items.[4]

Overall and regional poverty trends. High rates of growth of national GDP and per capita GDP are clearly an essential requirement for reducing poverty. The benefits from Uganda's economic growth have been reasonably broad-based, with overall income poverty declining from 56 percent in 1992 to 35 percent in 2000. This implies that in 2000, 35 percent of the Ugandan population were unable to meet their basic needs and were living below the poverty line. However, these benefits have not been equally distributed among regions and socioeconomic groups, as further explored below. Table 10.3 shows the incidence of poverty for the period 1992/93–2002/03.

As Table 10.3 indicates, the proportion of population below the poverty line declined consistently throughout the 1990s. The period 1992/93–1996/97, which saw relatively rapid GDP growth, also witnessed a sharp decline in the poverty rate, from 56 to 44 percent. This decline continued through to 1999–2000, but the results for 2002–2003 suggest that the decline reversed, with the poverty proportion rising again, to 38.8 percent. In part, this may be a lagged impact of the slowing of GDP growth after about 1997. Of course, one would have to await results for a few more years before being sure that a rising trend in poverty has appeared, and factors other than the growth rate of GDP could have played a role in causing this outcome.

For all the region-residence components, there was a decline in the poverty percentage over the period 1992/93–1999/00. However, between 1999–2000 and 2002–2003, it appears that the poverty proportion rose in central, eastern, and western Uganda and fell marginally in northern Uganda. Poverty proportions declined in both rural and urban areas until 1999–2000, but again, in 2002–2003, the reported proportions were higher in all region-residence categories, except for rural northern Uganda, where a decline was reported.

Of all the regions, the north had the highest poverty incidence in 1992–1993, but until 1996–1997 it shared in the general pattern of declining poverty. However, the most recent estimates, for 1999–2000 and 2002–2003, suggest a reversal of this pattern. Between 1996–1997 and 1999–2000 the poverty proportion in rural areas of the north rose from 60 to 67 percent, and declined slightly to 65 percent in 2002–2003. The problems of the north need to be addressed effectively if the trend of poverty reduction is to be maintained. The proportion of the poor living in the north remained fairly constant at 22 percent until 2000, which reported an increase to about 36 percent.[5]

The observed fall in poverty countrywide occurred at a time when the benefits of stable conditions and a liberalized economy were unfolding. Until about 1997, there was a spurt in international coffee prices to the benefit of Ugandan growers, who were able to take advantage of liberalization in coffee-marketing systems.

Further analysis of existing data on households interviewed in 1992–1993 and 1999–2000 (Lawson, Mekay, and Okidi 2003) throws more light on poverty dynamics in Uganda and regional disparities. It has been found that despite all the policy interventions put in place by the government since the beginning of the 1990s, a core number of households remained in poverty during the eight-year period, known as the chronically poor, and a substantial number of households moved back into poverty (see Figure 10.1). An estimated 18.9 percent of households were poor in both 1992 and 1999, while 10.3 percent of households that were not poor in 1992 had moved into poverty by 1999.

Table 10.3 Poverty Incidence, Uganda, 1992–2003 (percentages)

Survey Area	1992–1993	1993–1994	1994–1995	1995–1996	1997–1998	1999–2000	2002–2003
All Uganda	55.7	52.2	50.1	48.5	44.0	35.1	38.8
Residence							
Urban	27.8	20.6	22.3	19.5	16.3	10.1	14.4
Rural	59.7	56.7	54.0	53.0	48.2	39.0	42.7
Region							
Central	44.7	35.6	30.3	30.1	27.7	20.1	22.3
Eastern	59.5	58.0	64.9	57.5	54.3	37.3	46.0
Northern	71.4	69.2	63.5	68.0	58.8	64.8	63.7
Western	52.5	56.0	50.4	46.7	42.0	28.0	32.9
Central rural	52.9	43.4	35.9	37.1	34.3	25.6	27.6
Central urban	21.2	14.2	14.6	14.5	11.5	7.0	7.8
Eastern rural	61.2	60.2	66.8	59.4	56.4	39.2	48.3
Eastern urban	42.6	30.5	41.5	31.8	24.8	17.4	17.9
Western rural	53.6	57.4	51.6	48.3	43.2	29.4	34.3
Western urban	34.4	24.9	25.4	16.2	19.9	5.6	18.6
Northern rural	72.7	70.9	65.1	70.3	60.7	66.7	65.0
Northern urban	49.7	46.2	39.8	39.6	32.6	30.6	38.9

Sources: Uganda's 2002–2003 national household survey; Appleton 1999.

Figure 10.1 Poverty Dynamics, Uganda, 1992–1999

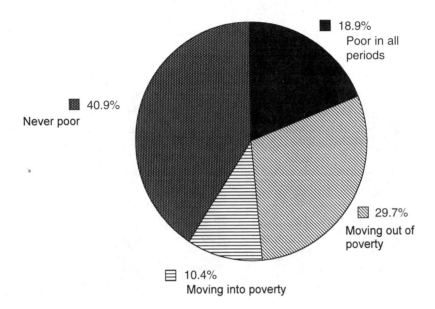

Source: Uganda's 1999–2000 national household survey.

Almost one-third (30.1 percent) of the chronically poor and one-quarter (25.4 percent) of households moving into poverty reside in northern Uganda. This, as noted earlier, is a region where the problem is particularly serious.

But this is not to say that there were no chronically poor households or no households moving into poverty in the other regions of the country, as can be seen in Figure 10.2. Attempts to explain the causal factors for these trends show that households that are persistently in poverty or that are moving into poverty are characterized by the following factors:

- Presence of household heads and family members who are less educated.
- A low asset base, particularly in regard to land and livestock.
- Residence in insecure or conflict-affected areas.
- Large family size.
- Limited access to basic infrastructure and social services.
- Engagement largely in subsistence agriculture.

This implies that future efforts to ensure a more equal distribution of regional economic growth must focus more on securing peace and security in the

372   *Country Studies*

Figure 10.2   Proportion of Chronic/Transient Poverty by Region, Uganda, 1999

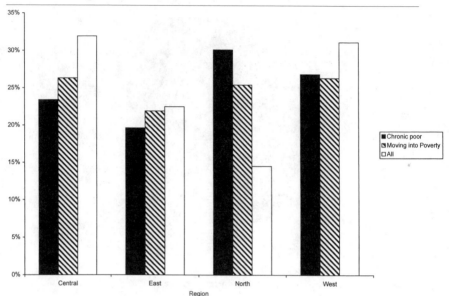

Source: Uganda's 1999–2000 national household survey.

north, strengthening the human resource base, promoting nonagricultural wage-employment activities, and increasing access to basic and social services, especially by the poor, among other factors.

While percentages of the population below the poverty line fell until 1999–2000, the same cannot be said of inequality. As Table 10.4 shows, it appears that overall inequality declined during the phase of growth, from 1992–1993 to 1997–1998, but then increased until 2002–2003, during the phase of slowdown in GDP growth. Both rural and urban inequality declined until 1997–1998 and rose subsequently.

Table 10.4   Gini Coefficients, Uganda, 1992/93–2002/03 (percentages)

	Rural	Urban	National
1992–1993	32.6	39.4	36.4
1997–1998	31.1	34.5	34.7
2000–2001	32.2	40.4	38.4
2002–2003	36.3	47.7	42.8

Sources: Appleton in Reinikka and Collier 2001; Uganda's 2002–2003 national household survey.

In Figure 10.3, which relates to the period 1992/93–1999/00, apart from the obvious rural-urban differences, there are high proportions of low-income earners in both rural and urban areas as well as nationally. Although the percentage of people with income equal to or less than 50,000 shillings per month declined in Uganda, the percentages still remained high. Most Ugandans, especially in rural areas, were in this category in 1992–1993. There was a notable reduction in this group of people by 1997, and the decline continued, at a somewhat reduced pace, to 1999–2000.

Poverty by socioeconomic group. Further analysis reveals the types of households that benefited most from the economic growth. All income groups enjoyed higher consumption levels in 2000–2001 compared to 1992–1993, but the gains were largest for the richest 10 percent of the population, who saw their real per capita consumption levels increase by 20 percent. Consumption levels of the poorest decile grew by just 8 percent during this period.[6] Table 10.5 shows the incidence of consumption poverty among different socioeconomic groups in rural areas.

Most socioeconomic groups benefited from the broad-based growth experienced during the 1990s. However, poverty continues to be higher among groups that reside in rural areas than those in urban areas. And in particular, poverty remains particularly high among households engaged in agriculture, despite the observed decline in poverty among them. In fact, households engaged in noncrop agriculture—representing about 3 percent of the rural pop-

Figure 10.3 Percentage of People in Lowest Income Class, Uganda, 1992/93–1999/00

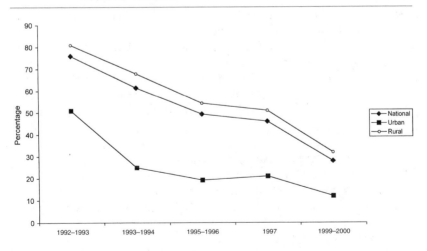

Source: Appleton in Reinikka and Collier 2001; results of Uganda's 2002–2003 national household survey.

Table 10.5   Incidence of Consumption Poverty by Socioeconomic Category, Uganda, 1992–2000

| | Percentage of Poor Below Poverty Line | | | | | |
| | 1992–1993 | | 1996–1997 | | 1999–2000 | |
	Rural	Urban	Rural	Urban	Rural	Urban
National	60	28	54	20	39	10
Food crops	64	—	63	—	46	—
Cash crops	63	—	47	—	34	—
Agriculture	—	55	—	36	—	23
Noncrop agriculture	57	—	43	—	44	—
Mining, manufacturing, utilities, and construction	45	38	40	25	35	8
Private sector services	40	16	31	12	22	7
Government services	41	26	36	22	22	6
Not working	65	32	68	18	53	15

Sources: Appleton in Reinikka and Collier 2001.

ulation—experienced increased poverty between 1996 and 2000. This was attributed to the European Union–imposed ban on fish imports from Uganda during this period and the persistent drought that affected livestock production in the north and west.

A recent participatory poverty assessment, conducted in 2001–2002,[7] confirms that the productive sectors (crops, livestock, and fisheries) continue to perform poorly and that this has negatively affected household income levels. Some of the key factors behind these observed trends were reported to include low prices offered in a liberalized environment, lack of markets, the depreciating quality of land and the environment, poor farming practices coupled with limited access to extension advice, high and multiple taxes, and insecurity and human displacement affecting the north and east. These trends were reported in nine out of the twelve districts sampled in the assessment. These trends are worrying given the fact that the majority of households in rural areas derive their livelihood from agriculture and yet about half of them are still poor. Policy initiatives to remove constraints to agricultural production must become central points in the poverty reduction strategies.

The high observed growth rates in manufacturing, utilities, construction, and private sector services translated directly into poverty reduction in households engaged in these activities, especially in the urban areas. For example, in urban areas, poverty among households engaged in private sector services, constituting over 50 percent of the population, fell from 16 percent in 1992–1993 to 7 percent in 2000.

It is possible to compare changes in the proportion of households below the poverty line, classified on the basis of the head of household's occupation. The estimates are presented in Table 10.6. This table must be interpreted with some caution, however, as the reported sectoral attachment of a household head may differ from that of household members, and the latter may include the principal contributor to household income. An increase in the incidence of poverty among households engaged in crop agriculture appears to have occurred between 1999–2000 and 2002–2003, and this is in marked contrast to declines that occurred from 1992–1993 to 1999–2000. Again, a similar pattern obtains for the service sector, with the conspicuous exception of government services. In government services, staff reductions combined with improved pay probably account for this result.

Most vulnerable among the poor. But even within any given socioeconomic group, there are categories of the poor who are more vulnerable and disadvantaged than others. By virtue of their numbers, children and youth are heavily represented among the poor in Uganda. They constitute about 76 percent of the population based on Uganda's 2002–2003 national household survey. Poverty among youth is exacerbated by HIV/AIDS, orphaned children, lack of basic necessities, lack of health care and education, and living in conflict areas. On the other hand, youth lack employment opportunities, as they have inadequate skills, have limited access to productive assets like land, and suffer from problems associated with early marriages.

Table 10.6   Percentage of Household Heads Below Poverty Line by Sector, Uganda, 1992–2003

	1992–1993	1996–1997	1999–2000	2002–2003
National	55	49	35	38
Crop agriculture	—	—	—	50
Food crops	64	62	45	—
Cash crops	60	46	34	—
Noncrop agriculture	55	40	41	34
Mining	32	74	43	26
Manufacturing	44	27	25	28
Public utilities	34	11	—	12
Construction	36	35	23	23
Trade	25	20	13	17
Hotels	26	19	17	21
Transport and communications	32	15	15	18
Miscellaneous services	27	28	18	28
Government services	36	30	17	13
Not working	58	62	44	38

Sources: Appleton in Reinikka and Collier 2001, tabs. 4.12–4.13; Uganda's 2001 and 2002–2003 national household surveys.

Women and widows in all socioeconomic categories are heavily represented among the poor due to lack of rights and lack of control over major productive assets, resulting from the traditional roles ascribed by society, the burden of many dependents, and land- or property-grabbing by relatives upon the death of a spouse. Other extremely vulnerable and poor people include those who are physically disabled, the elderly, internally displaced persons, and refugees.

Other Dimensions of Poverty. Reducing poverty is not only about enhancing private consumption, but also should encompass improvement in social welfare indicators. The other poverty measures investigated here focus on publicly provided goods and services including health care, education, and water; HIV/AIDS prevalence rates; access to assets and finance, particularly land and microcredit; and outcome/impact indicators on mortality, health, and nutrition. Selected information on trends in key social developments in Uganda during 1991–2000 is provided in Table 10.7.

Table 10.7   Social Development Indicators, Uganda, 1991–2000

	1991	1995	2000	Target	Target Year
Poverty and inequality					
Poverty level (%)	56	44	35	10	2017
Gini coefficient (inequality)	0.364	0.366	0.384	—	—
Demographics					
Total population (millions)	16.7	19.3	22.2	—	—
Female population (millions)	8.5	9.8	11.2	—	—
Male population (millions)	8.2	9.5	11.0	—	—
Population growth rate (%)	2.5	—	2.9	—	—
Education and literacy					
Gross primary enrollment (millions)	2.3	2.6	6.8	—	—
Net primary enrollment (%)	—	84	77	90	2007–2008
Gender: Ratio of girls' enrollment to boys' (%)	—	—	99	—	—
Pupil-teacher ratio	—	—	65:1	—	—
Pupil-textbook ratio	—	—	6:1	—	—
Pupil-classroom ratio	—	—	106:1	—	—
Adult literacy rate (%)	54	62	68	—	—
Female literacy rate (%)	—	50	57	89	2007–2008
Male literacy rate (%)	—	73	74	90	2007–2008
Health and nutrition					
Under-5 mortality (per 1,000 live births)	180	147	152	103	2005
Infant mortality (per 1,000 live births)	122	81	88.4	68	2007–2008
Maternal mortality (per 100,000 live births)	700	506	505	354	2007–2008
Percentage of children stunted (low height for age)	—	25.5	22.5	—	—

continues

Education. The government's policy of universal primary education, initiated in 1997, has led to an upsurge in gross primary enrollment, from 2.6 million in 1997 to 7.3 million in 2002. However, net primary enrollment rates actually fell, from 84 percent in 1997 to 77 percent in 2000, possibly as a result of pupil dropout rates, particularly poor children and girls. The two most critical factors for the success of the education policy have been the government's commitment to increase education financing and timely and concerted donor support.

To illustrate the rapid expansion in funding for education, public education spending increased from 2.6 percent of gross national product in 1996 to 4 percent in 2000, equivalent to an increase of 24 to 32 percent of the total discretionary recurring budget. In 2002 the share of primary education in the total education budget reached 70 percent (World Bank 2002a). The main challenges are poor quality of education, low primary retention rates, and low rates of transition from primary to secondary or vocational education. The increased enrollment has necessitated additional strategies aimed at ensuring in-

Table 10.7   Continued

	1991	1995	2000	Target	Target Year
Health and nutrition (*cont.*)					
Percentage of children wasted (low weight for height)	—	38.3	38.6	—	—
Immunization (DPT3) (%)	—	61	48	90	2007–2008
Deliveries at health facility (%)	—	35.4	19	50	2007–2008
Births with medical assistance (%)	38	38	39	—	—
Malaria (proportional morbidity) (%)	—	25	37	—	—
Price of dose of antibiotics (shillings)	—	1,900	1,100	—	—
Price of dose of malaria drugs (shillings)	—	1,500	1,099	—	—
Sexual and reproductive health					
HIV/AIDS prevalence (%)	—	14	6.1	5	2007–2008
Fertility rate (children per woman)	—	6.9	6.9	—	—
Contraceptive prevalence rate (%)	—	15	23	—	—
Unmet need for family planning	52	29	35	—	—
Water and sanitation					
Rural access to safe drinking water (%)	—	39	53	90	2007–2008
Urban access to safe drinking water (%)	—	—	62	100	2007–2008
Households with latrine or toilet (%)	—	79.9	82.3	—	—

Sources: Uganda's 1995 and 2000–2001 surveys of demographics and health; Appleton in Reinikka and Collier 2001; Ugandan Ministry of Water, Lands, and Environment; Uganda's 2001 and 2003 poverty status reports; Uganda's 2002 report on its poverty reduction strategy paper.

Note: "Target" refers to the government of Uganda's target.

creased access to postprimary schooling. Most government efforts have thus far focused on increasing access, countrywide, to secondary, vocational, and technical education.

In line with the Millennium Development Goal to eliminate gender disparity in primary and secondary education preferably by 2005 and to all levels of education no later than 2015, the gender gap at the primary level has already been eliminated, with as many boys now in school as there are girls. The gender gap improved from 93 percent in 1992 to 97 percent in 1997 and 99 percent in 1999–2000 (Government of Uganda 2001). According to the Ministry of Education Statistics, the gender gap at the secondary level has yet to be closed: there are between 20 and 35 percent more boys than girls in the first four grades at the secondary level, and over 60 percent more boys in the fifth to sixth grades (Levin 2002). More action needs to be undertaken to overcome this challenge.

Regionally, large parts of northern Uganda, particularly those affected by conflict, lag behind the rest of the country in literacy. Children in camps for the internally displaced are unable to access meaningful education on a consistent basis, due to the inadequacy of facilities and a lack of trained teachers. Women are even more affected, having much lower literacy levels than their male counterparts. For example, in 2000 the illiteracy rate among women in the north stood at 67 percent, almost double that of their male counterparts, at 36 percent (Government of Uganda 2001).

Health and HIV/AIDS. Improving the health status of the Ugandan population remains a major challenge for the government. We examine here the trends in one of the most important outcomes from health and other sectoral interventions: infant, maternal, and under-five mortality rates based on Uganda's 1995 and 2000 surveys of demographics and health and its 1999–2000 national household survey. The prevalence rates of HIV/AIDS, a key determinant of infant mortality, are also presented.

Infant mortality is defined as the probability of dying between birth and age one, while under-five mortality is the probability of dying between birth and the fifth birthday. Levels of infant, under-five, and maternal mortality decreased significantly during the 1991–1995 period, but then either deteriorated or stagnated by 2000 (see Table 10.7). The pattern of high and increasing mortality rates between 1995 and 2000 is surprising and disturbing, because Uganda experienced high economic growth and poverty reduction over much of the period from 1992. Of course, it takes time for improved income levels to have an impact, and other factors may also be relevant.

Although the causal factors are not fully known, there seems to be a strong correlation between infant mortality and income and wealth. Based on data from national household surveys, infant mortality is highest among the poorest 20 percent of the population, according to the recent participatory assessment. Other explanatory factors include the high levels of HIV/AIDS and malaria, which have direct impact on mortality rates.

There are regional differences in mortality rates, as illustrated by the occurrence of infant mortality (see Figure 10.4). From 1995 to 2000, infant mortality fell in both the central and eastern regions, while it increased in the northern and western regions. This corresponds to the fall in poverty in the central and western regions during this period, and the corresponding rise in poverty in the northern region. It is has not been established why infant mortality rose in the west when income levels were rising, but some evidence points to a poor response to immunization in the region and malnutrition arising from sale of poor-quality food.

In the recent participatory assessment, ill health has been identified by poor people as the main cause of poverty in Uganda. Malaria is one of the leading causes of morbidity and mortality, as is HIV/AIDS. The HIV sero prevalence declined from 14 percent in the mid-1990s to 6.5 during 2001–2002, which is still unacceptably high. Although the proportion of the affected people and the rate of spread of HIV/AIDS are decreasing, due to the aggressive strategies to minimize effects of the scourge, many people are still affected by the epidemic and its devastating health, psychosocial, and economic consequences.

Figure 10.4 Infant Mortality by Region, Uganda, 1995–2000

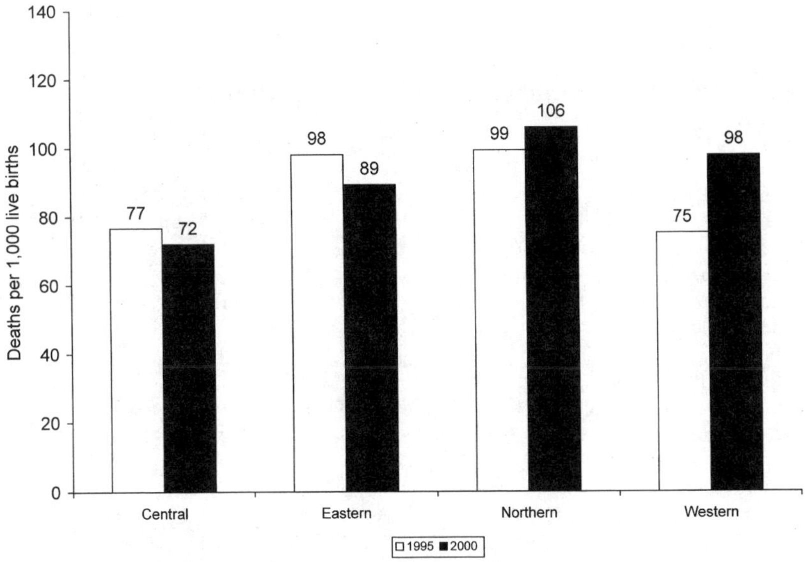

Source: Uganda's 1995 and 2000–2001 national household surveys.

Key factors for the stagnation of HIV/AIDS levels include poverty, prostitution among men and women, and movements caused by displacement in conflict-affected areas in the north. Most ministries have integrated HIV/AIDS strategies and developed appropriate budgets to address this challenge. In addition, resources have been mobilized by the government and civil society to help run HIV/AIDS programs at the district level, and to help the poor access such services.

The removal of cost sharing in government-funded health centers and hospitals has resulted in large populations, particularly the poor, seeking health services elsewhere. The main challenge now is the lack of drugs to sufficiently treat these patients. Unfortunately, as Table 10.8 shows, a significant section of the population (34.9 percent), especially in rural areas, does not receive any medical attention, due to distance and cost barriers. For those who do, the majority again receive treatment from private hospitals or clinics.

Summary of Poverty Trends

A key message that emerges from examining poverty trends in Uganda is that despite macroeconomic success and a significant fall in income poverty over the 1990s, progress in social and human development has been relatively modest. Some negative trends have been observed, in the form of a slowing in growth rates and patterns of structural change, a rise in inequality after 1997, as well as an increase in poverty between 2000 and 2002. The picture in terms of social development indicators is also mixed, with some achievements and some disturbing trends.

Table 10.8   Medical Attention for Sickness, Uganda, 1998

	Rural (%)	Urban (%)	National (%)
No medical attention	36.2	25.1	34.9
Home treatment	21.0	25.7	21.6
Outdoor treatment at government health facility	15.4	13.0	15.1
Outdoor treatment at private health facility	22.0	30.2	23.0
Treatment with private doctor	1.3	1.9	1.4
Treatment through pharmacy	1.6	2.2	1.7
Treatment with traditional doctor	0.8	0.4	0.8
Indoor treatment at government health facility	0.7	1.0	0.8
Indoor treatment at private health facility	0.3	0.3	0.3
Others	0.5	0.3	0.5

Source: Keefer 2000.

It is evident that not all regions and groups have benefited equally from growth, and post-1997 trends in northern Uganda indicate some reversal of the achievements in poverty reduction. As Uganda is predominantly an agricultural country and this sector accounts for the majority of the poor, the pace of poverty reduction is clearly tied to developments within it. The success in establishing peace and security and in deregulation and liberalization certainly led to economic growth and to a reduction in poverty until about 1997, but it appears that the effect on growth has begun to wear off. The coffee boom is over, and the situation in terms of peace and security as well as economic development appears to be unsatisfactory in northern Uganda, where the proportion of the poor has started to rise. For Uganda as a whole as well, the most recent results suggest that poverty is rising.

◼ Employment, Growth, and Poverty

In the absence of regular labor force surveys, it is not possible to provide satisfactory estimates of the labor force on an annual basis. Some figures are available from Uganda's integrated household surveys of 1992–1993, 1999–2000, and 2002–2003, and for 1997 from Uganda's pilot labor force survey. The estimates for 1992–1993 and 1997 are based on a rather inclusive concept of work,[8] and assign priority to work over nonwork. On the other hand, the estimates for 1999–2000 and 2002–2003 are based on the concept of main activity and hence have a much more restrictive definition of work.[9]

Hence it is not possible to compare the estimates for the period after 1997 with those for the earlier period. Even when more recent results are available, lack of comparability with 1997 will be a constraint, but this could be overcome by reclassification of both 1999–2000 and 2002–2003 data so as to include as workers not only those for whom it is the main activity, but also those for whom it is the secondary activity. Experience elsewhere suggests that this could result in a reasonable degree of comparability with the earlier estimates of the work force.[10]

Changes Between 1992–1993 and 1997

The economically active population, comprising workers and those who are described as not working, rose sharply, from 6.2 million to 9.1 million, over the period from 1992–1993 to 1997, representing a 46 percent increase. Among those who were reported as working, the increase was 45 percent (see Table 10.9). The share of agriculture rose nominally, from 76.6 percent to 77.0 percent, and this masked a shift within the agricultural work force from food crops toward cash crops. The share of the industrial sector (comprising mining, manufacturing, public utilities, and construction) declined slightly, relative to the work force, from 5.3 to 4.9 percent. It is indeed surprising that economic growth in this period did not lead to a rise in the share of the industrial

Table 10.9   Changes in Structure of Work Force by Sector, Uganda, 1992/93 and 1997

	1992–1993		1997		Percentage Increase in Number of Workers
	Number of Workers (thousands)	Percentage of Work Force	Number of Workers (thousands)	Percentage of Work Force	
Agriculture	4,544	76.7	6,625	77.0	45.8
Industry	316	5.3	425	4.9	34.5
Services	1,066	18.0	1,556	18.1	46.0
Total workers	5,926	100.0	8,606	100.0	45.2

Source: International Labour Organization 2002, tab. 2.13, based on Uganda's 1992–1993 integrated household survey and 1997 report on the pilot labor force survey.

sector. The share of the service sector (comprising trade, hotels, transport and communications, miscellaneous services, and government services) remained steady, at 18 percent. Generally, the sectoral shares remained characteristic of an economy at the early stage of development.

An examination of sector shares in more detail is provided in Table 10.10, which shows that agriculture's share rose slightly, and that of manufacturing fell slightly. The shares of all the service sectors rose, but that of government

Table 10.10   Structure of Work Force, Uganda, 1992 and 1997

	Number of Workers (thousands)		Percentage of Work Force	
	1992	1997	1992	1997
Crop agriculture	4,383	6,444	74.0	74.9
Noncrop agriculture	161	181	2.7	2.1
Mining	6	18	0.1	0.2
Manufacturing	223	307	3.8	3.6
Public utilities	6	9	0.1	0.1
Construction	81	91	1.4	1.1
Trade	415	606	7.0	7.0
Hotels	31	81	0.5	0.9
Transport and communications	93	172	1.6	2.0
Miscellaneous services	105	190	1.8	2.2
Government services	422	507	7.1	5.9
All workers	5,926	8,606	100.0	100.0

Sources: Table 10.9; Ugandan Bureau of Statistics GDP worksheets, September 2003 (unpublished).

services fell sharply. The relative decline in government services probably reflects the sharp reductions made in staffing as part of the restructuring undertaken by the government. The general rise in services, on the other hand, is not unexpected in a country undergoing economic development.

Looking at the growth of the work force and comparing it with that of GDP at factor cost, we find that the work force increased by 45 percent while real GDP at factor cost grew by about 40 percent. The slower growth of GDP in relation to work force was particularly marked in the agriculture sector (see Table 10.11). The share of this sector in GDP fell from 60 percent to 43 percent, while its share in the work force hardly changed. At the same time, GDP growth outpaced work force growth in the industrial sector: GDP rose from 14 to 19 percent, while the corresponding share to the work force remained around 5 percent. In the case of the service sector, GDP rose from 36 to 38 percent, while its work force share remained around 18 percent. Hence, in terms of relative output per worker, the agriculture sector saw a sharp relative fall, and the industrial and service sectors fairly sharp relative rises.

Employment Elasticities

When we compare GDP growth with that of the work force, we find that while GDP in the agriculture sector increased by 19 percent, the work force rose by 46 percent. This means that GDP per worker in agriculture actually fell. In the industrial sector, GDP grew 98 percent while the work force increased by about 35 percent. In the service sector, GDP increased 46 percent while employment

Table 10.11   Sectoral Shares in Work Force and GDP, and Relative Output per Worker, Uganda, 1992–1993 and 1997

	1992–1993	1997
Agriculture		
Percentage share in work force	76.7	77.0
Percentage share in GDP	59.6	42.8
Output per worker in agriculture	0.66	0.56
Industry		
Percentage share in work force	5.3	4.9
Percentage share in GDP	13.6	19.2
Output per worker in industry	2.57	3.92
Services		
Percentage share in work force	18.0	18.1
Percentage share in GDP	35.8	38.0
Output per worker in services	1.99	2.10

Source: Table 10.9.

Notes: Average output per worker = 1 (1990 base year). Output per worker = total GDP of the sector (agriculture or industry or services) divided by the number of workers in that sector. Expressed as a ratio when compared to average output per worker (economywide).

grew by nearly 48 percent. Hence the industrial sector saw a rise in GDP per worker and the service sector saw a slight fall. While bearing in mind that the work force figures do not necessarily relate to full-time employment through the year and that all the figures have to be taken as approximate, it is nevertheless clear that the 1992–1997 period saw economic growth accompanied by labor absorption. In the case of the agriculture sector, this appears to have led to an absolute decline in output per worker.

The relationship between output growth and employment growth is best expressed in terms of the relevant elasticities. In this section we report on estimates of arc growth elasticities of employment with respect to output growth. These estimates, presented in Table 10.12, are based on the GDP at factor cost figures and the work force estimates used in Table 10.11.

Between 1992 and 1997 the overall elasticity of employment with respect to output was about 1.1. The agriculture sector and the service sector, to a lesser extent, are responsible for this high overall elasticity. The high labor absorption by the agriculture sector is reflected in an elasticity of 2.5 and that of the service sector in an elasticity of 0.9. On the other hand, the industrial sector had a relatively low elasticity of 0.4. While evidence for the post-1997 period has comparability problems and does not lend itself to a similar analysis, it cannot be assumed that the employment elasticities remained at the levels shown in Table 10.12 after 1997. In particular, agriculture may not have been able to keep absorbing workers, and industry and services may have become more labor-absorbing in response to new policies and programs and with the end of the policy of downsizing government employment.

Employment elasticities may not be very reliable, as the employment estimates are based on a rather inclusive concept of work and one person reported to be working is not the same as a person-year of full-time work. The problem is most acute in agriculture, where considerable underemployment is known to exist, but it is not entirely absent in the other two sectors, especially in their informal components. An attempt is therefore made to measure the employment elasticities in manufacturing establishments for which data are available for 1992 and 1998 from Uganda's Bureau of Statistics and reported in a recent ILO

Table 10.12   Sectoral and Aggregate Employment Elasticities, Uganda, 1992–1997

Sector	Elasticity of Employment with Respect to Output
Agriculture	2.46
Industry	0.35
Services	0.94
Aggregate	1.13

Sources: Tables 10.9 and 10.11.

study.[11] This covers 119 manufacturing establishments in 1992 and 123 manufacturing establishments in 1998, employing 113,000 and 119,000 workers respectively. The details are provided in Table 10.13.

One could of course ask how dependable the elasticity estimates reported in Table 10.13 are, especially in using them as guides for the relationship between output growth and employment growth in the future. For one thing, the period covered by the estimates is rather short. Moreover, this was the period during which the economy of Uganda in general and the manufacturing sector in particular were going through structural adjustment and economic reforms. Unusually high values of elasticity (especially the negative ones) may be indicative of a sector going through sharp adjustments rather than a real long-term relationship between output and employment growth. Furthermore,

Table 10.13 Elasticities of Employment with Respect to Output in Selected Manufacturing Establishments, Uganda, 1992–1998

Sector	Employment Elasticity
Processed milk	0.27
Edible oils and soap	0.76
Wheat flour	10.40
Sugar	–0.76
Sugar confectionery	0.00
Other food products	–0.15
Uganda (Warangi tribe)	–0.83
Beer	–0.03
Soft drinks	0.00
Cigarettes	4.70
Cotton fabrics	–5.90
Blankets	1.20
Fishnets	0.00
Leather	–0.36
Footwear	–0.14
Paper and paper products	0.10
Foam products	0.24
Paints	0.53
Oxygen and acetylene	2.96
Motor vehicle batteries	–0.02
Cement	0.04
Blocks, bricks, and tiles	–0.02
Steel and its products	–0.38
Corrugated iron sheets	7.89
Cables	0.49
Toothbrushes, plastics, and ball pens	–10.00

Source: Elasticities calculated from Ugandan Bureau of Statistics primary data reported in International Labour Organization 2002, tab. 2.10.

given the small overall sample size, figures for the subsectors may be based on data from a small number of units, and hence may not be truly representative. However, despite the limitations mentioned above, the figures presented in Table 10.13 may be taken as indicative of what happened to manufacturing employment in Uganda during a period when output growth was high.

Looking at the sectors that are large in terms of output and employment, edible oils and soaps had high and positive employment elasticity, but both employment and output declined. Sugar had a high and negative elasticity of 0.76, a considerable increase in output being accompanied by a sharp decline in employment. Other food products had a low but negative elasticity, as did beer. Soft drinks had an elasticity of about 0. Cotton fabrics had a very large and negative elasticity of 5.9, as employment plummeted alongside a modest output increase. Another fairly large sector, cement, had elasticity near 0, as did blocks, bricks, and tiles. Steel ingots and products had a negative elasticity of 0.38. Surprisingly, corrugated iron sheets had a phenomenal elasticity of 7.89, due to a massive increase in employment accompanying a modest expansion in output. In general, the reported employment elasticities are often negative for the larger sectors of activity and the overall picture is of output expansion not accompanied by employment growth, and in fact accompanied in several cases by employment decline.

Another sector for which some useful information is available on its employment-creating capacity is labor-based road works. According to a study by Gary Taylor and M. Bekabye (2000), the overall use of labor-based methods created three times as many jobs as did equipment-based methods, due to the "multiplier" effects. Furthermore, labor-based methods generate about two times more GDP through indirect effects than do equipment-based methods, and although the direct benefit of labor-based methods on public revenue (taxes, duties, etc.) is smaller than that of equipment-based methods, this is more than offset once indirect benefits are included.

Uganda has devoted a significant share of its public investment expenditure to road construction and continues to do so at present. Roads and works accounted for about 4.3 percent of the allocation of public funds in 1994–1995, and by 2001–2002 their share had risen to 9.3 percent. However, it is not clear whether all this construction was done in a manner that would enhance employment creation. The use of labor-based methods could significantly add to employment creation and poverty reduction. If the country is to exploit these potential benefits, a significant shift to the use of more labor-based methods for construction is indicated. The implications of these results for Uganda's macroeconomic framework are compelling. Labor-based methods generate more income to households, increase GDP faster, save money (e.g., see Table 10.14), and have a strong stimulus on local private investment.

The Taylor and Bekabye study illustrates that the greater use of labor-based methods has a high potential for creating productive employment both

Table 10.14 Financial and Economic Comparison of Labor- and Equipment-Based Methods for Feeder Road Rehabilitation, Uganda, 1993–1997

	Labor-Based Methods	Equipment-Based Methods	Difference
Average financial cost[a] per kilometer (US$)	8,000	9,770	+22%
Average economic cost[b] per kilometer (US$)	5,080	8,150	+60%

Source: Taylor and Bekabye 2000.
Notes: a. Financial cost is actual cost.
 b. Economic cost is true cost to the economy, considering all costs exclusive of taxes, considering exchange rate distortions and labor price.

directly and indirectly. Through a policy of greater use of labor-based methods, households would have increased incomes, which would enable them to afford the basic requirements for their livelihoods. Since greater use of labor-based methods also provides a stronger stimulus to the local economy, this would also lead to increased economic growth, with the accompanying improvement in national poverty trends. Strong government policies together with a reform of the regulatory framework will be needed if Uganda is to significantly tap the potential socioeconomic benefits of more labor-based methods.

Links Between Employment and Poverty

Surveys in Uganda do not cross-classify employment and unemployment of individuals by the average personal consumption expenditure of the household to which the person belongs. This would have enabled a much more thorough analysis of the links among poverty, employment, and unemployment.

However, it is possible to look at poverty in relation to the employment sector of the head of the household. It carries the unverified assumption that most, if not all, working household members are in the same sector as their head of household. The relevant data have already been presented in Table 10.6.

The results show that a high percentage of households with heads engaged in food production are poor, although it must be noted that the percentage fell sharply between 1992–1993 and 1999–2000, from 64 to 45 percent. This decline probably did not continue to occur in 2002–2003, but we cannot confirm this in the absence of a separate figure for food crops. Declines in poverty percentages are much sharper for those engaged in cash crop production and noncrop agriculture. However, in the case of cash crops, some increase may have occurred between 1999–2000 and 2002–2003.

Most of the other categories appear to have fairly low poverty incidence. Trends for the category of those who are not working are very difficult to interpret, as the data relate to heads of households that may have working members. Also, the really poor households cannot afford to remain out of work and their members may end up taking any work that is available, including work that is poorly remunerated. Hence, those reported as not working are not necessarily poor, while those in such sectors as food crop production might be facing heavy underemployment and low earnings. Open unemployment is a luxury that the really poor may not be able to afford.

The government of Uganda (2003d) stressed another dimension of poverty and employment. In urban areas, people emphasize that poverty is characterized by the escalating unemployment and poor wages for those who are employed. Unfortunately, very few data are available on wage rates that can be used for analysis of changes over time. Some data on wage rates have been collected in Uganda's 1999–2000 national household survey, relating to wage rates per day in the major regions for agricultural and nonagricultural remuneration and for men and women separately. These data point to large gender differentials and to the fact that the northern region tends to have much lower wage rates, reflecting, no doubt, the difficult economic situation there.[12]

In the case of unemployment, the analysis has to be restricted to 1997, when Uganda's pilot labor force survey was undertaken. The figures relate to persons in the labor force who are not working. These data have been analyzed in the ILO report *Investment for Poverty-Reducing Employment in Uganda,*[13] which finds that the unemployment rate in 1997 was 7.4 percent, with the rural rate being lower, 5.1 percent, and the urban rate being much higher, 21.7 percent. Gender differences appear to have been small: the unemployment rate for men was 6.7 percent and for women, 7.0 percent. Kampala had very high unemployment, at 31 percent. The northern region reported low unemployment, at 3.9 percent. In this instance, and in general, the reported rates, which relate to open unemployment, do not appear to reflect poverty differentials or even the real situation in the labor market.

Summary of the Linkage Between Employment and Poverty

The evidence on employment is limited and not comparable beyond 1997, and links with growth and poverty are difficult to establish conclusively. Nevertheless, it is clear that the agriculture sector managed to absorb much of the increase in numbers entering the labor market up to 1997. Industry, on the other hand, tended to show low employment elasticity. It appears that road construction has the potential to create considerable employment, provided labor-based technologies are used. Given that agriculture absorbed much of the growing addition to the labor force, it is not surprising that food production is the activity where the poor appear to be concentrated. The remarkable progress in the cash crop sector has not been matched by developments in food production, and the most recent data suggest that 50 percent of households with heads engaged in crop production are below the poverty line.

Some Features of Growth and Poverty Reduction in Uganda

The steady reduction during the 1990s in the percentage of people below the poverty line highlights Uganda as an important example of poverty reduction happening through recovery from a long period of civil war and disorder and a period of economic growth. The success must be attributed to the adoption of policies and programs that enabled economic growth to take place in a manner that was poverty-reducing. The process of reform of the economy, combined with developments in the world market, made it possible for the economy to grow, drawing relatively poorer farmers and others into the process. Government expenditure also played a positive role. However, not all parts of Uganda shared in the sharp decline in poverty, and the north in particular continues to have a high proportion of people below the poverty line. The start of the new century appears to have seen a setback to poverty reduction. Evidence for the most recent period, 2000 to 2002, suggests that the process has stalled. We examine here the role of the establishment of law and order, agriculture and exports, government expenditure patterns, and regional variations in explaining the Ugandan experience.

Return of Law and Order

The period from about 1972 to 1986 was marked by a breakdown in the political and socioeconomic system due to civil wars and chaotic and dictatorial rule. This resulted in the destruction of productive assets, diversion of resources toward the military and away from development, widespread uncertainty, disruption of markets and information flows, and heightened risk, making private economic actors less willing to invest in the production sectors. There was also the flight of capital and enterprise, including that of the expelled expatriate Asian community. Widespread physical and economic insecurity was accompanied by arbitrary exactions by individuals and groups holding power or with arms at the local level; lack of protection for private assets including land, cattle, and produce; lack of credit sources and capital; poor infrastructure and communications; and little investment in education, health, and social services. Several of these obstacles to productive participation in economic activity were removed by 1992.

The return of law and order after 1986 helped to create an enabling environment for economic growth. It resulted in a return of capital and enterprise and started the process of recovery. Several important achievements were recorded. The demobilization and reintegration of combatants were achieved. Public spending was drastically reordered and expenditures were progressively directed toward infrastructure and education. The tax system and the banking system were reformed. After 1992, programs to secure the return of capital began to work, especially as investment approval procedures were simplified, macroeconomic stability was achieved, and economic liberalization measures began to have an impact. Trade, particularly exports, was liberalized, export duties on products like coffee were eliminated, and the marketing system was deregulated. Large numbers of state enterprises were privatized. With the reforms, private foreign capital and foreign aid began to flow in.

As law and order and public security were restored and the rule of law was established, the measures for deregulation and promotion of freer markets; the elimination of export taxes; investments in transport, communications, and infrastructure;[14] reorganization of banking and credit; investments in education, health, and social services; and other measures made it possible for the poor to take advantage of new market opportunities alongside other, better-off groups. Hence the recovery process was accompanied by a sharp reduction in poverty. Agriculture was a major beneficiary of the developments up to 1992 and many smallholders were able to benefit from the new environment for economic activity, including foreign trade.

Agriculture and Exports

In 1992, Uganda was predominantly rural, with about 88 percent living in rural areas. Most rural households were engaged in agriculture. Agriculture was carried out mainly on small farms. Available estimates indicate that by 2000 there were about 3 million smallholder households in rural areas having crop production as their predominant activity, followed by livestock keeping and fishing.[15] In terms of sector of household heads in 1992, food crop, cash crop, and noncrop agriculture (which together accounted for 73 percent of the population) had 64, 60, and 55 percent respectively under the poverty line.[16] Hence agriculture was large and had a large number of relatively small producers, many of whom were below the poverty line. Growth in agriculture had therefore the potential to significantly impact on poverty.

Figure 10.5 shows the trends in exports of Uganda's four major crops: coffee, tea, cotton, and tobacco. In the case of coffee, the impact of deregulation and improved access to domestic and world markets were most marked. Export taxes were eliminated in time to take advantage of a boom in the world coffee market that lasted until the mid-1990s. As a result of reforms to coffee marketing, the share of Ugandan farmers in the export price of robusta coffee increased from 42 to 63 percent between May 1991 and June 1997; of arabica coffee, from 39 to 65 percent; and of tea, from 29 to 37 percent.

Coffee was the preeminent cash crop, accounting for the bulk of the area under cash crops and for about 70 percent of all exports until 1995–1996. The price of coffee exports rose from US$0.86 per kilogram in 1991–1992 to a peak of $2.55 in 1994–1995, and continued to remain high in 1997–1998.[17] Uganda was well positioned to take advantage of this fortuitous development—a tripling of the export price—and it is likely that the beneficiaries included many of the relatively poor who grow coffee on small farms. A decomposition exercise suggests that about half of the reduction in poverty

Figure 10.5 Exports of Principal Agricultural Produce, Uganda, 1986–2002

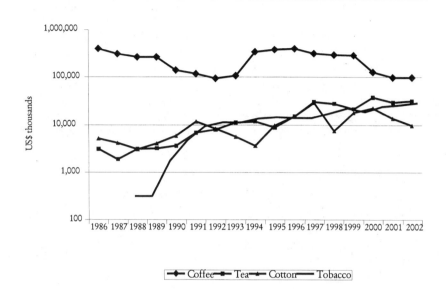

Source: Author's calculations.

between 1992 and 1995–1996 could be attributed to improvements in the condition of cash crop farmers.[18]

The production and export of many other agricultural or rural products— including fish, maize, hides and skins, and high-value horticultural crops— expanded in the 1990s, and this probably also benefited the poor. Coffee accounted for about 58 percent of exports in 1997–1998, but the share declined to 43 percent by 1999. Since about 1999, exports in general have been affected by the volatility of international prices of primary commodities as well as by bad weather and rising oil prices. Export prices for three other traditional items, cotton, tobacco, and tea, also fell from 1998 to 1999.

Hence the period from 1992 until about 1996 was marked by large income increases accruing to coffee growers and, to a lesser extent, to producers of cotton, tobacco, and tea. Many beneficiaries were small producers below the poverty line. As export-based incomes rose in the countryside, not only did they reduce the poverty of many small producers, but they are also likely to have provided, through increased spending by these producers, more income-earning opportunities for the rural poor who were not engaged in the exported products.

After about 1997 the export prices of all these traditional products declined, and some of the earlier gains in terms of poverty reduction were probably lost.

This setback was only partially compensated by the growth of nontraditional exports. Between 1998–1999 and 2001–2002, coffee exports declined by US$222 million, while nontraditional exports rose by US$145 million. The major commodities in the rise of nontraditional exports from US$251 million to US$300 million were fish and fish products, maize, hides and skins, and flowers.

The period up to about 1996 had been marked by economic growth accompanied by structural change as well as a reduction in poverty and inequality. After this, growth slowed down, and inequality began to increase. Recent evidence suggests that poverty levels have risen, albeit with a time lag, since 2000. This slowdown may be associated with the end of the coffee boom and the emergence of adverse movements in the country's terms of trade from 1998 to 1999.

Public Expenditure

The government has been using a medium-term expenditure framework to allocate resources and align priorities in line with the objective of poverty reduction. Within this framework, the government has created a poverty action fund to channel expenditure, especially donor funds, to directly poverty-reducing public services, including primary education, primary health care, agricultural extension, feeder roads, water and sanitation, and law and order. The impact of this mechanism to shift expenditures toward poverty reduction can be judged by the fact that the share of the action fund in total spending rose from 17 percent in 1997–1998 to 31 percent in 2000–2001.[19]

Looking at the composition of public expenditure, the impact has occurred principally in raising the share of roads and works, from 4.9 percent in 1997–1998 to 8.2 percent in 1999–2000. This is likely to have created a considerable volume of employment and, through that route, impacted on poverty. It may also have improved access of the poor to resources and markets. It is more difficult to assess the impact on poverty of a significant reduction in the share of public administration, from 24.9 to 20.5 percent, over the period, as we do not know the status of those who gained or lost jobs or faced increases or decreases in earnings.

Regional and Spatial Dimensions

The decline in the incidence of poverty between 1992 and 2000 and the increase between 2000 and 2002 were not uniform over the country. The experiences of the different regions were significantly different, reflecting the impact of events and conditions prevalent in different parts of the country.

Poverty proportions were much higher in rural than in urban areas. In both there was a sharp decline: from 59.7 and 27.8 percent in rural and urban areas respectively in 1992–1993, to 42.7 and 14.4 percent respectively in 2002–2003 (see Table 10.3). As urban poverty proportions are generally lower than rural proportions, and as poverty proportions have declined in both segments, the increase in the weight of the urban sector over time would have accentuated the decline in poverty at the aggregate level.

There is considerable variation in the levels and trends in poverty incidence in the different regions of Uganda. In 1992–1993 the central region, and to a lesser extent the western region, had levels of poverty lower than the national average, while the northern and eastern regions had levels above the national average. In 2002–2003 the poverty incidence was less than in 1992–1993 and again the central and western regions had levels below the national average, while the northern and eastern regions had levels above the national average.

Not only did northern Uganda in 2002–2003 have a poverty proportion much higher than the national average, but the proportion actually rose after 1997, while it continued to fall for the country as a whole until 1999–2000. In this region the poverty proportion declined from the high level of 71 percent in 1992–1993 to 59 percent in 1997–1998, only to rise again to 65 percent in 1999–2000 and fall slightly to 64 percent in 2002–2003. It is also worth noting that in 1999–2000, about 44 percent of the poorest 20 percent of Ugandans lived in the north.[20]

The pace of poverty reduction, particularly in central Uganda, where the poverty proportion has been halved, and eastern Uganda, where the proportion has dropped from a half to a third, may be difficult to maintain over time. Sharp reductions in poverty are needed in eastern Uganda, but clearly the high level of poverty in northern Uganda, 64 percent in 2002–2003, has to be addressed on a priority basis if Uganda hopes to continue recording aggregate declines in poverty.

The problems of northern Uganda are indeed complex and not easily addressed, including civil strife, insecurity, low levels of literacy and education, poor health and sanitation, and the presence of refugees from nearby conflict areas. The rise in poverty in northern Uganda has been largely associated with two factors: the long-standing war and conflicts in the north since the late 1980s, which have led to massive deaths, loss of property, and internal displacement; and the fall in price and area under production of the major commodities traded in the north, particularly cotton. The price of cotton more than halved between 1992 and 1999, as a result of the dismantling of government marketing boards. Apart from the disruptions and displacements to production and the functioning of markets caused by conflict and insecurity, other factors include harsh climatic conditions, environmental mismanagement, corruption, low productivity, and inefficient service delivery.[21]

■ Modeling the Determinants of Poverty

In this section we focus on modeling the determinants of consumption or poverty. In the process of modeling the determinants of poverty, an attempt will be made to identify and quantify links that can be established between consumption levels and selected sociodemographic characteristics relating to household size and composition, education, and employment. The analysis here has the advantage of being based on a single dataset that permits us to link variables relating to the same set of sampled households. The dataset used in the estimation of the model is obtained from Uganda's 1999–2000 national household survey, which was conducted by the Bureau of Statistics.

Specification of the Empirical Model

Two approaches may be distinguished in modeling the determinants of poverty. The first approach could be described as directly modeling the determinants of poverty status (poor or not poor).[22] We model the poverty status to being poor (as opposed to being not poor) as:

$$H_j = \beta'X + \varepsilon + u_j \tag{1}$$

where

j = household number
X = explanatory variable
ε = unobserved heterogeneity at the household level
u_j = transitory variation

We assume the standard normalizing assumption that $u_j \sim N(0,1)$. We also assume that the heterogeneity component is distributed normally, $\varepsilon \sim N(0,\sigma_\varepsilon^2)$. The probability of being in a given poverty status for household j is:

$$H_j = \begin{cases} 0 \\ 1 \end{cases}$$

where

$H_j = 0$ indicates poor
$H_j = 1$ indicates not poor

The second approach to modeling the determinants of poverty levels involves, as a first step, taking the log of consumption at the household level.[23] The simplest specification of such a model could be given as:

$$\ln C_j = \beta'X_j + \varepsilon_j \tag{2}$$

where

C_j = per capita consumption of household j

X_j = vector of household characteristics or other determinants of consumption

ε_j = random disturbance term, which is assumed to be normally, independently, and identically distributed with mean 0 and variance σ^2

The second step is to define poverty in terms of the household's per capita consumption level, where the poverty measure for household j can be estimated by:

$$\hat{P}_{\theta j} = \left[\max \left(\left(\frac{Z - \hat{C}_j}{Z} \right), 0 \right) \right]^{\theta} \tag{3}$$

where

$\hat{P}_{\theta j}$ = estimated poverty measure of household j

Z = poverty line

θ = nonnegative parameter taking integer values 0, 1, and 2

Aggregate poverty of a given population is simply the weighted mean of the above poverty measure, where the weights are given by household sizes. When θ takes a value of 0, the aggregate poverty measure corresponds to the incidence of poverty or headcount index. Similarly, when θ assumes values of 1 and 2, the aggregate poverty measure corresponds to the poverty gap and the squared poverty gap indexes respectively.[24]

This direct approach to modeling the determinants of poverty, using equation 1, which is adopted in this exercise, is popular and has often been used by researchers in the area of poverty analysis. The approach models the probability of households being poor by employing the Probit model.[25] In the Probit model, an attempt is made to allow for rural-urban heterogeneity by estimating separate models.

Selection of Explanatory Variables of the Model

The set of variables that is hypothesized to determine poverty status may be categorized into household and community characteristics. Among the set of potential determinants of poverty, an attempt is made to choose those variables that are not outcomes of poverty. For instance, variables such as current school attendance by children are omitted from the regression for the reason that such variables are outcomes, rather than determinants, of being poor or nonpoor. The set of determinants used may broadly be classified into three categories: background characteristics, education, and employment.

Background Characteristics. Included in this category are household size and its composition. Four age groups are distinguished: 7 years or younger, 7–17 years, 18–64 years, and 65 years or older. The number of adults in the age group 18–64 is further split by gender, as the marginal returns may differ. To allow for nonlinearities in the relationship between consumption and household size, a quadratic term (in household size) is introduced in the Probit model. The other background characteristics of households are age and sex of the household head.

Education. Several measures pertaining to different levels and dimensions of educational attainment by household members are included in the regression. The number of adult household members who can read and write and the number of adult household members with primary or higher level of education are among variables hypothesized to influence consumption. Assuming that returns to male and female education may be different, the numbers of household members with primary or higher level of education are differentiated by gender.

Employment. Employment characteristics are related to occupations of household members. In this connection, two employment categories are distinguished: those in the agriculture sector and those in the service sector. To examine the hypothesis that multiple income sources may bring higher income and hence lower risks, a variable related to income diversification within households is included. This variable is constructed by counting the number of income earners among household members from different sources.

Estimation of the Model: Description of Dataset

As mentioned, the dataset used in the estimation of the model is obtained from Uganda's 1999–2000 national household survey. The sample size for households is 10,696. A total of 8,344 households were from rural areas, while 2,352 households were taken from urban areas. All four regions of the country were included in the study: central, east, north, and west.

The Probit regression model of the determinants of rural poverty is estimated based on 8,311 rural households, while the determinants of urban poverty are estimated based on a sample size of 2,332 urban households. The major estimation issues related to some missing values and outliers in the dataset, particularly for adult equivalent real consumption per capita. Households whose consumption per capita is below 6,000 shillings (US$3) per month are also excluded, as it is impossible to survive on such a low level of income. The dataset was divided into poor and nonpoor based on the UN's 2003 statistical report (http://unstat.un.org), in which poverty is defined in terms of a consumption expenditure for an individual of less than one US dollar a day.

Results and Discussion

The initial parameter estimates were subjected to a limited pruning by deleting the interaction terms that are not statistically significant at the 10 percent level. In addition, the interaction terms that were statistically insignificant or collinear with other explanatory variables were excluded from the regression model.

Determinants of Consumption and Poverty in Rural Areas. Table 10.15 presents the parameter estimates, z-values, and 95 percent confidence intervals for the rural determinants of real consumption per capita. For cross-sectional data, the fit of the regression model is good, with an R^2 value of 0.1792. The statistical significance of the different variables varies widely; some are statistically significant at the 5 percent level while others are not significant even at the 10 percent level. Nonsignificant variables (at the 10 percent level) were retained for the reason that they are relevant for the purpose of policy simulation.

With only a few exceptions, the signs on the variables are as expected, and the relative magnitudes are also reasonable. It can be noted that the dependent variable of the model is binary in nature and hence measures the probability of households being in a status below the poverty line.

Background characteristics. Age and sex of household head are highly significant at the 5 percent level. Results from the model show that female-headed households are more likely to be found below poverty levels compared to male-headed households. Results also show that with increase in age of household head, the probability of eventually falling in the poor category is high. This result is more likely to be true if the household head becomes too old to provide for the family.

From the estimated Probit regression model, it can be seen that there is a strong negative relationship between poverty status and the different age categories in the household. Results show that there is a negative relationship between poverty status and children aged seventeen years and younger. It is not surprising that estimated coefficients for children under seven years of age were more negative than for children aged seven to seventeen years. This implies that an additional child under eighteen years of age is more likely to put the household into a poor status. These results seem to be plausible, for older age groups have the possibility of providing production power, especially in the case of adult males between eighteen and sixty-four years of age.

The estimated coefficient of the quadratic term of the household size is positive and statistically significant, suggesting a U-shaped relationship between consumption per capita and household size.

Education. Among adult education variables, adult males who completed secondary education have a positive association with poverty status. This im-

Table 10.15 Determinants of Rural Poverty, Uganda

Poor/Nonpoor	Coefficient	Standard Error	z	P > |z|	[95% Confidence Interval]	
Age of household head	-0.0053747	0.0013136	-4.09	0.000	-0.0079492	-0.0028001
Sex of household head	-0.1669378	0.0409393	-4.08	0.000	-0.2471774	-0.0866981
Persons aged 0-6	-0.3495804	0.0244913	-14.27	0.000	-0.3975825	-0.3015782
Persons aged 7-17	-0.258725	0.0231433	-11.18	0.000	-0.3040851	-0.2133649
Adult males aged 18-64	0.1086653	0.0440076	2.47	0.014	0.022412	0.1949187
Household size squared	0.0053396	0.0014969	3.57	0.000	0.0024056	0.0082735
Employed in agriculture	-0.1088854	0.0206882	-5.26	0.000	-0.1494335	-0.0683373
Employed in service sector	-0.0600429	0.0901618	-0.67	0.505	-0.2367568	0.116671
Number of income sources	0.108061	0.0153159	7.06	0.000	0.0780424	0.1380796
Number of literate adult males	-0.236985	0.0568962	-4.17	0.000	-0.3484995	-0.1254706
Number of literate adult females	-0.1222564	0.0546923	-2.24	0.025	-0.2294513	-0.0150615
Number of adult males who completed primary education	-0.1439013	0.0849101	-1.69	0.090	-0.3103221	0.0225194
Number of adult males who completed secondary education	0.2605732	0.1090459	2.39	0.017	0.0468471	0.4742993
Number of adult females who completed primary education	-0.2601318	0.1355131	-1.92	0.055	-0.5257325	0.0054689
Number of adult females who completed secondary education	0.1122604	0.1738037	0.65	0.518	-0.2283886	0.4529094

continues

Table 10.15 Continued

Poor/Nonpoor	Coefficient	Standard Error	z	P > |z|	[95% Confidence Interval]	
Dummy for east	-0.4032288	0.0431359	-9.35	0.000	-0.4877737	-0.318684
Dummy for west	-0.1205609	0.0419396	-2.87	0.004	-0.202761	-0.0383608
Dummy for north	-0.114194	0.0479554	-23.81	0.000	-1.235931	-1.047949
Male literacy × employment in agriculture	0.0536218	0.0457227	1.17	0.241	0.035931	0.1432366
Female literacy × employment in agriculture	0.0949158	0.0778203	1.22	0.223	0.0576091	0.2474407
Male literacy × employment in service sector	0.1224965	0.1448388	0.85	0.398	-0.1613824	0.4063753
Female literacy × employment in service sector	-0.1067298	0.3037533	-0.35	0.725	-0.7020753	0.4886158
Constant	1.796095	0.118151	15.20	0.000	1.564523	2.027667

Probit estimates
  Number of observations = 8,311
  Wald chi^2 (22) = 1,508.40
  Probability > chi^2 = 0.0000
  Pseudo-R^2 = 0.1792
  Log likelihood = -4,579.7038

Notes: Adult females aged 18–64 dropped due to collinearity. Persons aged 65+ dropped due to collinearity. 0 = poor and 1 = nonpoor completely determined.

plies that educated adult males are more likely to be found above the poverty line. Results also show an abnormal pattern with the number of literate adult males and females associated with a negative coefficient.

Employment and income sources. The probability of being above the poverty line increases when the number of income sources a family has increases. Results also show that persons employed in the agricultural sector are more likely to be associated with poor poverty status. However, the variable of those employed in the service sector is not significant at the 5 percent level.

Regional differences. Results show big differences in poverty levels among the different regions. The central region is significantly different from the north, east, and west regions, in that order.

Determinants of Consumption and Poverty in Urban Areas. Table 10.16 portrays the results from the estimation of the urban model of the determinants of real consumption per capita. Note that variables that appeared to be insignificant are retained for simulating the impact of different policies on poverty and economic growth. However, compared with the case of rural setting, there is some marked difference in the variables found to be significant in the urban setting.

Background determinants. Age and sex of household head are not significant determinants at the 5 percent level. However, age is significant at the 10 percent level and negative. The presence of members within the household below age eighteen is a negative and significant determinant. As with the case in rural areas, an increase in persons who are below age eighteen is more likely to push the household to a poor status.

Education. Among the education variables, adult females who have completed secondary education are more likely to be associated with nonpoor status. This is contrary to the findings for the rural areas, where the adult males are associated with nonpoor status.

Employment and income sources. The signs of the employment variables for the number of persons employed in the agriculture sector are negative. However, employment in the service sector is not significant even at the 10 percent level.

Regional differences. As in the case with rural areas, the central region poses a big difference from the north and east, in that order. However, the variable for the west is insignificant even at the 10 percent level.

Determinants of Poverty: Summary

The modeling exercise highlights several important and strong relationships between social and economic variables and poverty. In rural areas, it appears that female-headed households are more likely to be poor than are their male counterparts. Again, the older the household head, the greater the chance that the household is below the poverty line. More children in the household ap-

Table 10.16 Determinants of Urban Poverty, Uganda

Poor/Nonpoor	Coefficient	Standard Error	z	P > |z|	[95% Confidence Interval]	
Age of household head	-0.0066974	0.0034469	-1.94	0.052	-0.0134532	0.0000584
Sex of household head	-0.1041309	0.0882888	-1.18	0.238	-0.2771737	0.068912
Persons aged 0–6	-0.2818808	0.0348359	-8.09	0.000	-0.3501579	-0.2136038
Persons aged 7–17	-0.0945171	0.0291873	-3.24	0.001	-0.1517232	-0.0373109
Adult males aged 18–64	0.1855634	0.1307553	1.42	0.156	-0.0707123	0.441839
Household size squared	-0.0004847	0.0012524	-0.39	0.699	-0.0029393	0.00197
Employed in agriculture	-0.2254278	0.0487368	-4.63	0.000	-0.3209502	-0.1299055
Employed in service sector	-0.0510564	0.0938789	-0.54	0.587	0.2350556	0.1329428
Number of income sources	0.0198881	0.0274767	0.72	0.469	-0.0339652	0.0737414
Number of literate adult males	-0.1611214	0.1412888	-1.14	0.254	-0.4380423	0.1157995
Number of literate adult females	-0.0802552	0.1425624	-0.56	0.573	-0.3596723	0.1991619
Number of adult males who completed primary education	-0.0984006	0.2198297	-0.45	0.654	-0.5292589	0.3324577
Number of adult males who completed secondary education	0.0074594	0.1186782	0.06	0.950	-0.2251455	0.2400643
Number of adult females who completed primary education	-0.2511441	0.2683889	-0.94	0.349	-0.7771767	0.2748884
Number of adult females who completed secondary education	0.3766653	0.1449953	2.60	0.009	0.0924798	0.6608508

continues

Table 10.16 Continued

Poor/Nonpoor	Coefficient	Standard Error	z	P > |z|	[95% Confidence Interval]	
Dummy for east	-0.3308831	0.0911944	-3.63	0.000	-0.5096209	-0.1521453
Dummy for west	-0.0877647	0.1030078	-0.85	0.394	-0.2896564	0.114127
Dummy for north	-0.9680511	0.0934091	-10.36	0.000	-1.15113	-0.7849727
Male literacy × employment in agriculture	0.1234349	0.0634074	1.95	0.052	-0.0008414	0.2477112
Female literacy × employment in agriculture	-0.0708028	0.1021855	-0.69	0.488	-0.2710828	0.1294771
Male literacy × employment in service sector	0.0230992	0.1563926	0.15	0.883	-0.2834246	0.329623
Female literacy × employment in service sector	0.1208842	0.4345624	0.28	0.781	-0.7308424	0.9726109
Constant	2.144891	0.2141577	10.02	0.000	1.72515	2.564633

Probit estimates
Number of observations = 2,332
Wald chi^2 (22) = 292.62
Probability > chi^2 = 0.0000
Pseudo-R^2 = 0.1749
Log likelihood = -833.44212

Notes: Adult females aged 18–64 dropped due to collinearity. Persons aged 65+ above dropped due to collinearity.

pears to be associated with poverty, as is belonging to an agricultural household. On the other hand, the more diversified the structure of income sources for a household, or the more educated males it has, the less likely it is to be poor. In urban areas, poverty appears to be associated with a larger number of children in the household, and the presence of educated female members is associated with the household being out of poverty. The regional dimensions of growth and poverty are also important features. Future reductions in poverty will require more attention being paid to the northern region, where high levels of poverty continue.

■ Conclusion

This chapter has examined the case of Uganda, where, following peace and the restoration of law and order, it was possible through policies and programs to liberalize the economy, link it up with world markets, and create conditions where capital began to flow into the country again and domestic and international actors began investing in development. This process took place over the 1990s, though there is some evidence of deceleration after 1997. The first period, 1991–1992 to 1996–1997, was marked by fairly rapid average rates of economic growth of a little under 7 percent per year, with GDP per head increasing at an annual average rate of about 3 percent. The second period, 1997–1998 to 2002–2003, saw economic growth average about 5 percent and per capita income growth about 2 percent.

In terms of structural change, the share of agriculture in GDP fell sharply between 1992 and 1997, and that of manufacturing rose sharply. Over the subsequent period, 1998 to 2002, there was very little change in the sectoral shares. In the case of the economically active population, between 1992–1993 and 1997 there appears to have been little structural change, and comparable figures are not available for more recent years.

The percentage of people below the poverty line appears to have declined quite steadily between 1992–1993 and 1999–2000, from 55.7 to 35.1 percent. However, the results for 2002–2003 indicate a rise again in the poverty proportion to 38.8 percent. The decline up to 1999–2000 occurred in both rural and urban areas, as well as in most of the regions, with the important exception of rural areas in the north, where poverty initially declined but again rose after 1997–1998. Insurgency and declining cotton prices help to explain why the north again saw an increase in the poverty proportion. The increase after 1999–2000 occurred in both rural and urban areas, as well as in all the regions except the north, where there was a nominal decline.

Inequality also declined between 1992 and 1997–1998, but appears to have increased between 1997–1998 and 2002–2003. In fact, the national level of the Gini coefficient in 2002–2003 is higher than it was in 1992–1993 in respect to both rural and urban areas.

In terms of dimensions of poverty other than personal consumption expenditure, the evidence suggests that expansion in primary education was substantial between 1997 and 2002, but low retention rates were a serious problem. Several indicators of health status improved between 1991 and 1995, but appear to have either deteriorated or stagnated since. HIV/AIDS and malaria remain serious problems. Agricultural extension services still remain thin on the ground, and credit in rural areas is still limited in availability. Environmental problems have also surfaced in the form of declining soil fertility, deforestation, rangeland degradation, and declining fish stocks.

Based on estimates for sectoral GDP and employment, arc growth elasticities of employment with respect to output growth have been obtained. While overall elasticity appears to be around 1.0, the elasticity for the agriculture sector is extremely high, and the elasticity for the industry sector is low. This indicates that agriculture has been able to absorb large amounts of labor over the process of output growth. It should be noted that the measured elasticity does not take adequate account of the fact that many who work in agriculture may not be working at full intensity.

Estimates for elasticities in manufacturing are probably more reliable. In several lines of production the elasticities turn out to be negative between 1992 and 1998: output expansions have led to employment declines. It is not surprising, then, that manufacturing growth has not generated much in terms of work opportunities.

Among other sectors, road construction is a potential employment spinner and it is significant that 9 percent of public funds were invested in this activity in 2001–2002.

While it is not possible to fully map the relationships among employment, unemployment, and poverty, it is clear from data on poverty by employment sector of the head of household that food crop–producing households were often poor in 1992–1993, and many continued to be poor in 1999–2000 and 2002–2003. This is perhaps a reflection of the fact that agriculture, particularly subsistence agriculture run as a family enterprise, is where many new entrants to the labor force go when there are few jobs available elsewhere in the economy. In the case of cash crop households, there has been a remarkable drop in the poverty proportion, as indeed in most other employment sectors.

Some data are available for unemployment, but the reported rates probably do not reflect poverty, as the really poor cannot afford to be unemployed for long periods of time. Data on wage rates are unfortunately not available on a comparable basis over time. This is a major gap in the information system, for movements in wage rates can be a useful barometer of the changing employment situation.

There is little doubt that sound macroeconomic policies and a stable economic framework were important factors responsible for the success in growth and poverty reduction. The success in poverty reduction was due in part to favorable conditions in the world economy for Uganda's coffee production, which had just emerged from a regime of controls and limitations on trade and marketing. This favorable conjuncture of circumstances may not occur again.

In the future, the constraints on the food crop sector may have to be more directly addressed. Also, economic growth needs to lead to productive employment opportunities outside subsistence agriculture. Unless this happens, the process of poverty reduction may be difficult to sustain. This requires greater employment creation in the short and medium term in both private and public investments, which in turn calls for investments that intensively utilize local resources, including labor, and that have strong multiplier effects on the domestic economy. Policies and strategies that promote intensive utilization of local resources would create employment especially for the poor, and would be complementary to other poverty reduction efforts.

The problems caused by insecurity and insurgency in northern Uganda are having an adverse effect on growth, poverty reduction, and employment expansion in that region and, to some extent, on the national average. A solution to the problems of this troubled region is an urgent necessity.

There is a need to underscore the importance of livelihood policies and programs that increase access of the poor, especially men and youth, to productive land and affordable credit. There is also a need to address related issues such as production skills, including entrepreneurship.

While trade liberalization has certainly been an important factor in promoting growth, there is a need to address the potential negative effects on the poor from trade liberalization and privatization, as in the case of tobacco farmers in Arua and elsewhere.

There is a case for looking more closely at the availability of traditional social safety nets, which may be weakening, and the possibility of strengthening them and also developing new systems of social protection in the face of the impacts of the volatile world economy.

More generally, the problems of rapid population growth, inadequate spread of education, lack of diversification in agriculture, and slowdown in the process of structural change may be responsible for limiting the achievements in terms of poverty reduction in Uganda. Of course, the progress made in spreading education and some diversification in income sources may have helped to reduce poverty

There is considerable scope for strengthening the information system by collecting more data on the links between poverty and employment at the household level. In fact, more frequent and fuller labor force surveys are needed. A system of data collection on wage rates in selected locations for particular categories of skilled and unskilled workers is urgently needed. This will provide early warning of possible deteriorations in the economic system, long before the results of surveys become available.

Finally, this chapter points to the need to look at growth, poverty, and employment trends and patterns at the regional or subnational level. This is an area where not only more data are needed, but also much more analysis. Many of the policies and programs that are needed may have to be directed at the northern region, where adverse trends are beginning to manifest themselves.

◼ Notes

1. The ERP marked the beginning of structural adjustment in Uganda. The program, whose main objectives were to resume economic growth, attain fiscal stability, and control inflation, adopted the standard approach of economic liberalization and privatization, financial sector liberalization, and trade and foreign exchange liberalization. Trade policy included the removal of trade restrictions, especially allowing trading in agricultural products outside the framework of marketing boards. For details on the ERP, see Kabananukye et al. 2004.

2. An important part of the PEAP was the review of a public investment plan undertaken to reorient public spending toward the objectives of the PEAP. The key policy instrument that has been used to switch resources toward strategic poverty reduction program areas has been a medium-term expenditure framework. In addition, a poverty action fund was established in 1998 as an instrument for allocating resources released under the Highly Indebted Poor Countries debt relief initiative. For information on how the poverty eradication action plan and poverty action fund were utilized and which sectors benefited from reallocation of resources, see Kabananukye et al. 2004.

3. For an excellent discussion of this issue, see Berthelemy et al. n.d.

4. For a fuller discussion, see Appleton 2001, esp. annex 4.1.

5. See Government of Uganda 2002b for details and a fuller discussion.

6. See Government of Uganda 2001.

7. See Government of Uganda 2002a.

8. A worker was anyone who was in paid or self-employment for at least one hour during the reference period of seven days prior to the date of enumeration. Major time spent during this period was not taken into account in determining whether or not a person was a worker.

9. Main activity is the usual or normal activity situation of a person in respect of his or her participation in gainful or nongainful activities during the past 365 days. It is based on major time spent.

10. For a discussion, see Krishnamurty 1987.

11. International Labour Organization (ILO) 2002, tab. 2.10.

12. See Uganda National Household Survey 2001, tab. 1.26.

13. See ILO 2002, 181–188.

14. During the 1990s, about 38 percent of public expenditure was devoted to construction, buildings, and roads. See ILO 2002, 37.

15. See ILO 2002, 82.

16. See Appleton 2001, tab. 4.12. These estimates are not strictly comparable with the estimates given in Table 10.14 in this chapter, although both are based on data collected in surveys undertaken by Uganda's Bureau of Statistics.

17. See Appleton 2001.

18. Ibid.

19. See Government of Uganda 2001.

20. The figure is from Government of Uganda 2002b.

21. See Government of Uganda 2002b.

22. Poor when consumption expenditure per day is defined to be below US$1 based on the UN's 2003 statistical report (http://unstat.un.org). Individual countries do not necessarily adopt this line. Many, like Uganda, have their own nationally derived poverty lines.

23. The logarithm of consumption is estimated because its distribution more closely approximates the normal distribution than does the distribution of the consumption levels. In other words, this assumption implies that a household's consumption level follows a log-normal distribution.

24. These three measures of poverty belong to the Foster-Greer-Thorbecke class, introduced in Foster, Greer, and Thorbecke 1984.

25. See Demeke, Guta, and Ferede 2003, 39, for a discussion of the two approaches.

11

Vietnam: Employment-Poverty Linkages and Policies for Pro-Poor Growth

Pham Lan Huong, Bui Quang Tuan, and Dinh Hien Minh

In the mid-1980s Vietnam was among the world's forty poorest countries, with about 75 percent of its population living in poverty. However, with the opening of the economy in the late 1980s, Vietnam's economy became one of the ten fastest-growing economies in the world. Impressive success in poverty reduction was also achieved during the 1990s. Worldwide experience suggests that a high and sustained rate of economic growth is necessary for achieving a significant reduction in poverty. The nature and pattern of growth, as well as the way its benefits are distributed, are extremely important in determining whether economic growth succeeds in reducing poverty. In this regard, the importance of employment of labor (the most abundant endowment of the poor) should not be forgotten, as it provides the key link between growth and poverty reduction. As poverty persists in many parts of the world, the experience of Vietnam in attacking poverty and providing employment opportunities for the poor may be relevant to other developing countries.

This chapter explores how rapid growth has been translated into substantial poverty reduction through output growth, employment generation, productivity, structural shifts in employment, and changes in labor incomes. Descriptive and comparative analytic methods, including econometric methods, are adopted to examine these linkages at both macro and micro levels using cross sections and time-series data.

Following an overview of economic performance and poverty reduction and examination of causal relationships between them, the chapter discusses linkages among economic growth, employment, productivity, and poverty at the macro level, and then examines the impact of different labor market variables in reducing poverty at the household level.

■ Economic Growth and Poverty During the 1990s

The Trend in Economic Growth Performance

The Vietnamese economy of the 1980s was a kind of "modified" planned economy. By 1988 the failure of efforts to stabilize the economy as well as the expectation of the drying up of aid from the former Soviet Union had created enormous pressure on reform. In March 1989, Vietnam adopted radical and comprehensive economic reforms aimed at stabilizing and opening the economy, enhancing freedom of choice for economic units, and introducing competition so as to create supportive policies and an institutional environment for growth and poverty reduction in Vietnam. The reform measures included:

- More or less complete price liberalization.
- Large-scale devaluation and unification of the exchange rate.
- Increases in interest rates to positive levels in real terms.
- Substantial reduction in subsidies to the state-owned enterprise sector.
- Agricultural reforms.
- Encouragement of the private sector.
- Removal of domestic trade barriers and creation of a more open economy.

The economic reform package of 1989 created the basic conditions required for the transformation of Vietnam into a market-oriented economy. The success of the reforms resulted in spectacular economic growth over the period before the Asian crisis. During the 1990s the annual GDP growth rate averaged 7.2 percent, with a period of rapid growth between 1991 and 1997, when it averaged 8.5 percent per annum. Per capita GDP rose by 1.8 times and the ratio of domestic savings to GDP increased by 3.2 times (Le et al. 2002). All sectors grew, albeit at different rates (see Table 11.1). At the same time, inflation was kept under control, at a single-digit level. Industry grew at an average annual rate of 9.6 percent, thereby enhancing entrepreneurial income and creating employment opportunities for unskilled labor. The service sector performed well too, and the quality of services improved dramatically to support growing private sector activities. From 1991 to 2000, the value of financial services increased by 3.2 times, education and training services rose by 2.2 times, health and related social services increased by 1.7 times, and the transport, storage, and communication sector increased by 1.8 times (Socialist Republic of Vietnam [SRV] 2002).

Between 1989 and 1995, growth was driven by services that contributed in 1990 to about 82 percent of the GDP increase. After 1995, manufacturing took the lead, although it had already begun making a good contribution to GDP since 1992. As is evident from Figure 11.1, there was a significant change in the industrial structure of the economy. The share of industry in

Table 11.1 Major Macroeconomic Indicators, Vietnam, 1990–2001

	1990	1991	1992	1993	1994	1995	1996	1997	1998	1999	2000	2001
GDP growth (%)	5.1	5.8	8.7	8.1	8.8	9.5	9.3	8.1	5.8	4.8	6.8	6.8
Agriculture	1.0	2.2	6.9	3.3	3.4	4.8	4.4	4.3	3.5	5.2	4.0	2.7
Industry[a]	2.3	7.7	12.8	12.6	13.4	13.6	14.5	12.6	8.3	7.7	10.1	10.4
Services	10.2	7.4	7.6	8.6	9.6	9.8	8.8	7.1	5.1	2.3	5.6	6.1
Inflation (%)	67.1	67.6	17.5	5.2	14.5	12.7	4.6	3.6	9.2	0.1	-0.6	0.8
FDI (US$ millions)[b]	839	1,322	2,165	2,900	3,766	6,531	8,497	4,649	3,897	1,568	2,000	2,503
Export (US$ millions)	2,404	2,087	2,581	2,985	4,054	5,449	7,256	9,185	9,360	11,540	14,483	15,027
Annual growth (%)	23.5	-13.2	23.7	15.7	35.8	34.4	33.2	26.6	1.9	23.3	25.5	3.8
Import (US$ millions)	2,752	2,338	2,541	3,924	5,826	8,155	11,144	11,592	11,499	11,742	15,637	16,162
Annual growth (%)	7.3	-15.1	8.7	54.4	48.5	40.0	36.6	4.0	-0.8	2.1	33.2	3.4

Source: Vietnamese General Statistical Office, various years.
Notes: a. Including construction.
b. Total commitments, including Vietnam's contribution.

GDP increased from 2.3 percent in 1990 to 10.1 percent in 2000, reflecting a pattern similar to that experienced by Indonesia, Malaysia, and Thailand during the early stages of their industrialization. Although the relative importance of the agricultural sector in GDP declined, it made impressive progress, with an average annual growth rate of 5.6 percent over the 1990s. Since 1989, Vietnam has not only been able to ensure food security at the national level, but has also turned from a net food importer into one of the largest exporters of rice, coffee, pepper, and cashew nuts.

As demonstrated in Table 11.1, the expansion of international trade has been one of the most important factors in Vietnam's economic growth. Vietnam boosted its exports from US$2,404 million in 1990 to US$15,027 million in 2001, with a substantial shift away from member countries of the Council of Mutual Economic Assistance and toward the rest of the world. The high growth rates of the economy during 1992–1997 were associated with substantial annual rates of export growth of over 20 percent during 1992–2002. In terms of its share of GDP, exports made a significant contribution, rising from 22.2 percent in 1990 to 25.1 percent in 1995 to 45.6 percent in 2001. This was the result of a more outward-looking trade policy and export promotion measures. The foreign investment sector became an integrated part of the economy and played a limited role in transferring technology, management, and working skills.

The economy suffered some slowdown over the period 1998–1999 as the impact of the regional economic crisis was felt. There has been steady recovery since, although growth rates continued to be lower than in the first half of

Figure 11.1   Structure of GDP by Sector, Vietnam, 1986–2001

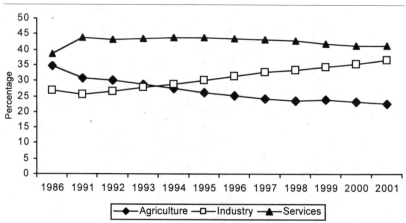

Source: Vietnamese General Statistical Office, various years.

the 1990s. In the late 1990s the pace of sectoral shifts was also slower than in the early 1990s. The service sector, which accounted for the largest single component of GDP, reversed its trend in the second half of the 1990s, and began a relative decline from 43.8 percent in 1995 to 41.0 percent in 2001.

Several major factors contributed to the economic recovery, including some improvement in the quality of growth and the efficiency of resource allocation,[1] mainly as a result of the dynamic performance of the private sector and the internal structural transformation of the agricultural, forestry, and fishery sector through diversification and shifts from low-value staple foodstuffs to cash crops, livestock, and aquaculture. Other major factors included increased investment and acceleration of international economic integration.

But the economy's competitiveness remains low compared with other countries in the region. The pace of reforms in the state-owned enterprise (SOE) sector and banking system was so slow that it impeded improvement in the business climate in general. Vietnam has been facing difficulties in international trade, as the prices of major export commodities, such as rice, coffee, black pepper, cashew nuts, rubber, and tea, have dropped since 2000,[2] while prices of agricultural inputs have risen.

It may not be possible for Vietnam to sustain its postcrisis growth unless a new wave of deeper reforms is introduced. The reform program should include the following key components:[3]

- Institutional reforms, which comprise reform of the legal framework and public administration, and strengthening of people's participation.
- Improvement of macroeconomic policies in conjunction with trade liberalization and the gradual opening of capital account.
- Structural reforms, including reform of the SOE sector, the banking system, and trade. Measures to promote private sector development and attract foreign direct investment (FDI) are also essential parts of the structural reforms.
- Agricultural development and poverty reduction in rural areas. The focus should be on strengthening farmers' rights to land use, expanding their choices relating to diversification of production, reducing the risks associated with agricultural product markets, ensuring the food security at household level, providing basic services, and developing rural industries.
- Reform of the education and training system, and science and technology.

These reform measures would create a stable and favorable environment to conduct business and enhance human capital, which together would lead to more businesses coming into operation, accompanied by growth, employment, and income expansion.

The Trend in Poverty Reduction

Poverty Definition and Measurement. Poverty is a multidimensional concept that extends beyond material deprivation. It is now generally agreed that the dimensions of poverty include not only income-based variables, but also capabilities—such as nutrition, health, education, vulnerability, voicelessness, and powerlessness (World Bank 2000e). Such a view of poverty, which explicitly recognizes the interaction and causal relationship among these dimensions, broadens the scope of poverty analysis and extends the range of policy measures that may be considered for reducing poverty. This chapter adopts this broad definition of poverty. However, the focus of the quantitative analysis will be on income poverty (material deprivation) and other indicators of human development, which are more readily quantifiable.

There are currently two approaches to the measurement of income/expenditure poverty in Vietnam. The first is used by the General Statistical Office (GSO) (with World Bank technical assistance, hence sometimes referred to as the World Bank poverty line); and the other is that calculated by the Ministry of Labor, Invalids, and Social Affairs (MOLISA) (often referred to as the official or national poverty line). The GSO calculates two poverty lines for Vietnam: a food poverty line and a general poverty line. The food poverty line is calculated as expenditures required, given Vietnamese food consumption patterns, to deliver 2,100 kilocalories per person per day. This is based upon the minimum individual requirement of calories that would ensure good nutritional status. The general poverty line is based upon the food poverty line, but it allows for the inclusion of a minimum quantum of nonfood expenditure. These measures constitute absolute poverty lines and are taken as constant in real terms over time. The basket of goods used to calculate the poverty lines is not varied, with adjustments made only to the prices used to estimate the expenditure required to purchase that basket.

The GSO estimates the rate of poverty using Vietnam's national survey of living standards, which has been conducted twice: in 1992–1993 and in 1997–1998. There are two poverty lines (in 1998 prices) estimated for the 1998 living standards survey: a food poverty line of 1,286,833 dong (US$92) per person per year,[4] and a general poverty line of 1,789,871 dong (US$128) per person per year. The GSO approach is commonly referred to as the international poverty line, since it is based upon an internationally accepted methodology.

The poverty lines that have been used by MOLISA are more of the nature of relative poverty lines. From time to time, MOLISA revises the national poverty line. The current MOLISA (national) poverty line, adopted in 2001, is 80,000 dong (US$5.7) per month in rural mountainous and island regions (960,000 dong [US$68] per year), 100,000 dong (US$7) per month in the rural plains areas (1.2 million dong [US$85] per year), and 150,000 dong (US$10.7) per month in urban areas (1.8 million dong [US$128] per year).

The MOLISA poverty line is often lower than the GSO general poverty line (Centre for International Economics 2002).

The poverty approach used in this chapter is that of the GSO. It has the following advantages: it takes into account both food and nonfood expenditure norms, it does not change in real terms over time, and it permits cross-country comparison. The discussion here largely draws on the *Vietnam Development Report 2000* (Poverty Working Group 1999) and the *Vietnam Development Report 2004* (Asian Development Bank [ADB] et al. 2003), comprehensive analytic works on the critical issues in attacking poverty in the years to come.

Overall Poverty Reduction Progress. Vietnam made substantial progress in poverty reduction over the 1990s. Figure 11.2 indicates that there has been a sharp fall in both rural and urban poverty in the postreform period for both the GSO poverty measures used. The general poverty proportion declined from over 70 percent at the end of the 1980s to 58 percent in 1993, 37 percent in 1998, and 29 percent in 2002 (Poverty Working Group 1999; ADB et al. 2003). During 1993–2002 the proportion of the food-poor fell from 25 percent to 11 percent. Figure 11.2 and Table 11.3 also reveal that poverty is being reduced at

Figure 11.2   Incidence of Poverty, Vietnam, 1993, 1998, and 2002

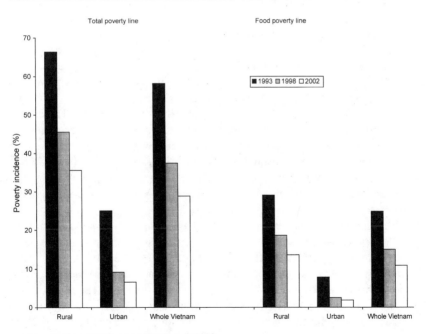

Source: Asian Development Bank et al. 2003.

a slower rate. During 1993–1998, poverty fell at an average of more than 4 percentage points per year. For the period 1998–2002 it was reduced by only 2 percentage points per year. Nevertheless, except for China and Indonesia in the 1980s, almost no other country in recent years has recorded such a sharp decline in poverty.

Available studies suggest that the decline in poverty in Vietnam reflects rising household per capita expenditures and GDP per capita due to an increase in real income during the 1990s. According to Vietnam's living standards surveys, the average annual real household per capita expenditure rose by 7.4 percent over the period 1993–1998, and 4.0 percent over the period 1998–2002, indicating a considerable improvement in living standards. During this period the average annual growth in GDP was about 7.2 percent, which was much faster than the average annual growth in population, 1.6 percent, implying thereby a 5.6 percent annual growth in per capita income in aggregate. Table 11.2 demonstrates that Vietnam's GDP per capita increased considerably, from US$98 in 1990 to US$404 in 2000 in current prices, or about 1.7 times in real terms.

Poverty Reduction by Region, 1993, 1998, and 2002. Poverty has declined in all seven regions of Vietnam, but at different rates (see Table 11.3). The proportion of the population living under the poverty line in 2002 varied from 11 percent in the southeast to 52 percent in the central highlands.

The three regions with the highest poverty rates in 1993, 1998, and 2002 were the northern uplands, the northern central region, and the central highlands. The northern uplands has seen the greatest reduction in poverty and the central highlands the least. Table 11.3 reveals that poverty is also more severe in these three regions; the persistence of high levels of poverty reflects the many constraints that these regions face in participating in the growth process, including the difficult terrain, which limits agricultural development and hinders access to infrastructure, and the low level of human capital. The central highlands, among other things, also suffered from the fall in coffee prices. As the rates of poverty reduction among the regions have been unequal, this would have contributed to growing income disparity over the 1990s. When the economic reforms began to take effect, poorer regions, usually the mountainous and remote regions, generally gained less from growth than did richer regions.

A first detailed poverty map of Vietnam using combined data from the 1999 population census and the 1998 living standards survey shows two contrasting representations of the maps in Figure 11.3. The left panel indicates poverty rates (share of the poor in the total population), while the right panel shows the density of poverty (number of the poor per area). The figure points to the trade-off in policies focusing on the poorest regions (uplands) or targeting regions with the highest concentration of poverty (lowlands) (ADB et al. 2003).

Table 11.2 GDP per Capita, Vietnam, 1990–2000

	1990	1991	1992	1993	1994	1995	1996	1997	1998	1999	2000	1990–2000
Value (US$)												
Nominal GDP per capita	98	119	145	190	228	289	337	364	354	375	404	
Real GDP per capita (PPP)	1,046	1,086	1,158	1,228	1,313	1,414	1,521	1,619	1,695	1,741	n/a	
Growth (%)												
Nominal GDP per capita	4.7	21.4	21.8	31.0	20.0	26.8	16.6	8.0	-2.7	5.9	7.7	15.2
Real GDP per capita (PPP)	n/a	3.8	6.6	6.0	6.9	7.7	7.6	6.4	4.7	2.7	n/a	5.8

Source: General Statistical Office 2001.

Table 11.3 Poverty by Region, Vietnam, 1993–2002

	Share of Population in 2002 (%)	Contribution to Total Poverty (%)			Headcount Index (poverty line)			Poverty Gap Index			Poverty Gap Squared Index		
		1993	1998	2002	1993	1998	2002	1993	1998	2002	1993	1998	2002
By urban-rural													
Rural	75	91	94	94	66	46	36	22	12	9	0.092	0.044	0.030
Urban	25	9	6	6	25	9	7	6	2	1	0.024	0.005	0.004
By region													
Northern uplands	15	19	25	22	82	64	44	29	19	12	0.131	0.071	0.046
Red River Delta	22	26	18	17	63	29	22	18	6	4	0.070	0.021	0.012
North central	13	16	18	20	75	48	44	25	12	11	0.105	0.041	0.036
Central coast	9	8	8	7	43	35	25	17	10	6	0.085	0.045	0.021
Central highlands	6	4	5	10	70	52	52	26	19	17	0.140	0.096	0.070
Southeast	15	10	5	5	37	12	11	10	3	2	0.040	0.012	0.008
Mekong Delta	21	18	21	17	47	37	23	14	8	5	0.056	0.027	0.014
All Vietnam	100	100	100	100	58	37	29	19	10	7	0.079	0.036	0.024

Source: Pham, Minh, and Long 2004.

Figure 11.3   Geographical Distribution of Poverty, Vietnam, Late 1990s

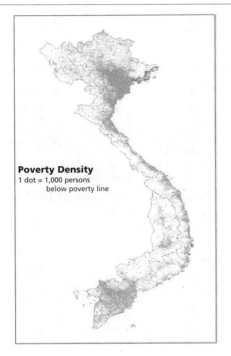

Source: Asian Development Bank et al. 2003.

Poverty Reduction by Other Dimensions. Table 11.3 also shows that all the poverty indicators were significantly higher for rural areas and that poverty reduction was slower than in cities. Poverty is highly concentrated in rural areas, which are home to 94 percent of the poor, with 36 percent of the rural population living below the poverty line in 2002. Rural poverty is strongly associated with farming households, as rural industries are relatively unimportant in Vietnam. As Table 11.4 demonstrates, the poorest workers in the economy are farmers, who accounted for 84 percent of the poor in Vietnam in 2002. The table also shows that poverty among the working population in all sectors declined substantially over the period 1993–2002.

Poverty in Vietnam also has an ethnic dimension. There are fifty-four ethnic groups in Vietnam, of whom the Kinh ethnic group, primarily living in the lowlands, comprises about 85 percent of the population and constitutes the dominant ethnic group. The remaining ethnic groups are ethnic minorities, and most of them, except the Chinese, reside in the uplands. Ethnic minorities had substantially higher poverty rates and witnessed much smaller reductions, from 86 percent to 69 percent, while for the rest of the population the rate fell

Table 11.4 Poverty by Main Sectoral Occupation for People Age 15+ Who Have Had a Job in the Past 12 Months, Vietnam, 1993–2002

	Poverty Incidence (%)			Share of Total Poverty (%)			Share of Population (%)		
	1993	1998	2002	1993	1998	2002	1993	1998	2002
Agriculture, forestry, fishery	66.1	44.4	38.9	85.7	84.3	84.0	73.9	67.1	58.7
Mining, manufacturing, construction	37.8	20.9	15.3	7.4	8.0	8.5	11.1	12.8	17.0
Services	28.1	12.7	9.9	5.7	6.4	6.4	11.6	15.5	18.6
Others	20.8	9.1	4.9	1.2	1.3	1.1	3.4	4.7	5.7
Total	57.0	34.8	27.6	100.0	100.0	100.0	100.0	100.0	100.0

Source: Pham, Minh, and Long 2004.

from 54 percent to 23 percent between 1992 and 2002. While economic gains were widespread, they barely reached the remote areas where the ethnic minorities are concentrated, and consequently ethnic people are beginning to lag behind. In 1993 they constituted 20 percent of the poor, but by 2002 the figure had risen to more than 30 percent (ADB et al. 2003).

Last but not least, these impressive achievements in poverty reduction in Vietnam over the period 1990–2002 remain fragile. As Figure 11.4 shows, in 1993 a large proportion of the population was just below the poverty line. Even a small increase in their income would have lifted them out of poverty. In 2002 a large proportion of the population remained clustered closely around the poverty line. These households are very vulnerable, as any shock that reduces income slightly could push many back into poverty.

Human Development Indicators

Several of the key social dimensions of poverty also showed an improvement during the 1990s. Access to public health centers, clean water, electricity, and roads substantially improved between 1993 and 1998, indicating that the poor benefited from the economic reforms (see Table 11.5). Improved access to basic services improved the life expectancy at birth and the adult literacy rate. By 2000, Vietnam had achieved universal primary education.[5] Already high primary school enrollment rates further improved between 1993 and 2002 (see Table 11.6). Lower secondary enrollment rates more than doubled for both girls and boys. The number of children enrolled in lower secondary school dipped to a low level of 2.7 million in 1990, but this figure climbed to 6.4 million in late

Figure 11.4 Distribution of Expenditure per Capita, Vietnam, 1992–1993, 1997–1998, and 2002

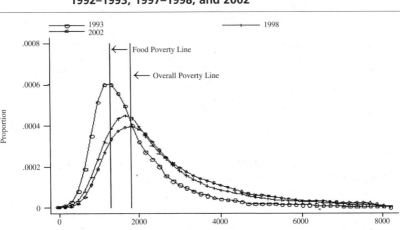

Source: Asian Development Bank et al. 2003.

Table 11.5   Access to Infrastructure, Vietnam, 1993–2002
(percentage of total)

	1993	1998	2002
Share of rural population with access to public health center within the community	93	97	97[b]
Share of rural population with access to clean water[a]	18	29	40
Share of urban population with access to clean water[a]	58	77	76
Share of population using electricity as a main source of lighting	48	77	80[c]

Sources: Poverty Working Group 1999; Steering Committee of Comprehensive Poverty Reduction and Growth Strategy 2003; General Statistical Office secondary data from Vietnam's 1992–1993, 1997–1998, and 2001–2002 living standards surveys.

Notes: a. Clean water is defined to include piped water, deep wells with pumps, and rainwater.
b. Share of communes with a health center.
c. Figure for 2002 estimated by authors.

2002. Upper-secondary enrollment rates increased dramatically for both girls and boys, rising from 6 to 27 percent for girls and from 8 to 30 percent for boys over the period 1993–1998. About 2.45 million children were enrolled in upper-secondary school in late 2002, reversing the downturn in enrollments

Table 11.6   Social Indicators, Vietnam, 1993–2002 (percentages)

	1993	1998	2002
Education			
Primary enrollment rate (net)	—	—	91.6
Female	87.1	90.7	91.0
Male	86.3	92.1	91.7
Lower-secondary enrollment rate (net)			
Female	29.0	62.1	67.0
Male	31.2	61.3	67.2
Upper-secondary enrollment rate (net)			
Female	6.1	27.4	—
Male	8.4	30.0	—
Child nutrition			
Incidence of stunting among children aged 0–59 months	51	34	33
Female	51	33	34
Male	50	35	32
Adult nutrition			
Incidence of moderate and severe malnutrition in adults (body mass index less than 18.5)	32	28	—
Female (nonpregnant)	32	30	—
Male	32	25	—

Sources: Poverty Working Group 1999; United Nations Development Programme 2003; Steering Committee of Comprehensive Poverty Reduction and Growth Strategy 2003.

seen in the late 1980s and early 1990s (Poverty Working Group 1999; Steering Committee of Comprehensive Poverty Reduction and Growth Strategy 2003).

Child malnutrition also declined dramatically, from about half the population to a third between 1993 and 2002. The under-five child mortality rate fell from 58 in 1990 to 38 per 1,000 live births in 2002, and the maternal mortality rate declined from 249 in 1990 to 165 per 100,000 live births in 2002 (United Nations Development Programme [UNDP] 2003). Life expectancy increased from 65.2 years in 1992 to 68.6 years in 2001. These indicators are high even by the standards of countries in the region, which have much higher per capita income levels. Vietnam's Human Development Index has shown a remarkable improvement since the early 1990s, rising from 0.611 in 1992 to 0.688 in 2001 (see Table 11.7).

Studies conducted by Action Aid Vietnam (1999), the Mountain Rural Development Program (1999), Oxfam (1999), and Save the Children UK (1999) reveal that poor households in Vietnam feel more confident about their livelihoods in recent years. With the introduction of market-oriented reforms, the poor are able to obtain higher prices for goods and services they supply, leading to an improvement in their living standards. They have reported reduced stress and fewer domestic and community disputes as life becomes better and easier. The gains from reforms appear to have been widespread, as all regions and groups have experienced a fall in poverty, although at different rates.

Linkage Between Growth and Poverty

Vietnam was a very poor country in 1980s, but subsequently growth has been high and broad-based, and poverty reduction has been widespread and substantial. Since Vietnam is a capital- and land-scarce country, the growth has impacted upon poverty reduction mainly through employment creation, and changes in income levels have come from the more efficient use of existing factors. Among the different types of main employment, nonfarm self-employment grew most rapidly during 1993–1998 (see Table 11.8), with a much higher

Table 11.7   Human Development Index, Vietnam, 1992–2001

	1992	1993	1994	1995	1997	1998	1999	2000	2001
Life expectancy at birth (years)	65.2	65.5	66.0	66.4	67.4	76.8	67.8	68.2	68.6
Adult literacy (%)	91.9	92.5	93.0	93.7	91.9	92.9	93.1	93.4	92.7
Combined enrollment rate (%)	49	51	55	55	62	63	67	67	64
HDI (value)	0.611	0.618	0.634	0.639	0.666	0.671	0.682	0.688	0.688
HDI (rank)	120	121	121	122	110	108	101	109	109

Sources: National Centre for Social Sciences and Humanities 2001; United Nations Development Programme 2002, 2003.

Table 11.8   Employment Growth Rates by Type of Main Employment, Vietnam, 1993–1998 (percentages)

	Farm Self-Employment	Nonfarm Self-Employment	Wage Employment	Total Employment
All Vietnam	0.4	5.4	3.5	1.8
By rural-urban				
Rural	0.8	6.7	3.3	1.7
Urban	–8.7	3.9	3.7	2.0
By gender				
Male	–0.3	8.3	4.6	2.1
Female	0.9	3.2	2.0	1.5

Source: Poverty Working Group 1999.

growth in rural areas than in urban areas. Wage employment grew as well, but in contrast to nonfarm self-employment, growth in cities was higher than in the countryside.

Although the average annual rural farm self-employment growth rate was not large (0.8 percent), the living standards of rural households improved substantially between 1993 and 1998, due to agricultural productivity improvement coming from intensification and diversification away from low-value outputs (staple crops) to higher ones (livestock, aquaculture, perennial crops, and fruits) and high export orientation of the sector. While real revenues from rice cultivation increased by 21.2 percent over this period, revenues from livestock and aquaculture rose by 52.3 percent, from other food crops by 55.0 percent, from industrial crops by 65.6 percent, from fruit trees by 112.3 percent, and from perennial crops by 127.1 percent (Poverty Working Group 1999). This confirms that the agricultural reform and the 1993 Land Law had a crucial impact on patterns of agricultural production, and points to the importance of crop diversification in increasing rural living standards.

The reforms opened the economy to the world, raised the relative prices of agricultural products relative to both agricultural inputs and other nonagricultural prices, and improved efficiency. While fertilizer price increased only less than 1.2 times, and even dropped for nitrogen, phosphorous, and potassium, producer crop price almost doubled, especially for nonrice crops over the period 1993–1998 (Benjamin and Brandt 2001).[6] Most households in Vietnam are rural and net sellers of agricultural products. They benefited substantially from this rise. Favorable agricultural terms of trade at the time Vietnam opened up the economy further reinforced the gains. Between 1992 and 1998, Vietnam's rice export price increased on average by 9.2 percent per year in nominal terms.[7] It has been estimated that almost half of this increase was due to realignment of the exchange rate, a fifth due to increases in international rice prices, and the remainder due to improved marketing efficiency and quality (Poverty Working Group 1999). Most rural households had land and knowledge to respond to the improved price incentives. As a result, agricultural export earnings rose by 14.3 percent per annum over 1990–1998, more than fourfold from US$1 billion in 1990 to US$4.3 billion in 2000 (General Statistical Office 2000; SRV 2002). Consequently, rural agricultural income grew by over 60 percent between 1993 and 1998.

In turn, higher household income generated in agriculture created increasing demands for goods and services, which were met by the private sector, thereby boosting the growth of nonfarm jobs. In addition, agro-processing businesses, which were established to serve large-scale agricultural production areas, raised value added, created additional jobs, and raised the income of the rural poor. Production activities in traditional craft villages were restored to respond to the policy encouraging private sector development. The rural economy shifted from subsistence production to commercial production to meet domestic and export demands, and at the same time household income rose significantly. All these activities resulted in the growth of rural nonfarm self-employment by 6.7 percent from 1993 to 1998, compared to the increase in rural income from this source of 30.5 percent. This must have contributed to poverty reduction.

Major increases in income in the cities came from nonfarm self-employment and wage employment, mostly in the private sector. As Vietnam's living standards surveys show, during 1993–1998, overall underemployment was less severe, decreasing from 66 percent of total employees to 57 percent.[8] Unemployment also declined, from 3.7 percent to 2.2 percent. SOE redundant workers could find jobs relatively easy in the private sector, which grew rapidly in response to strengthened property rights, a changing attitude toward it, and a more supportive environment.

Furthermore, higher real income growth relative to employment growth means that the major source of poverty reduction came from substantial improvement in real income. Indeed, overall declines in poverty are associated with declining poverty rates within each sector, rather than from shifts in employment from low-wage sectors such as agriculture to high-wage ones. An empirical study by S. Bales, D. T. Phung, and S. C. Ho (2001) suggests that over 90 percent of the reduction in poverty occurred because earnings rose within each sector, with the largest gains (55–60 percent) of the poverty reduction accounted for by improvement in income within the agricultural sector. The intersectoral employment shift accounts for only 6.0 to 8.8 percent of the reduction in poverty.

Rapid growth and increasing export earnings raised government revenues, more of which were spent on infrastructure, education, and health. All these services are essential for the poor in creating economic opportunities, improving their capacities, and reducing their vulnerability to poverty. During the 1990s the road network was improved considerably and a large number of modern bridges were built to replace old ones. Many ferry landings and wharves have been upgraded and expanded to meet increased demand over the past few years. Post and telecommunication services also have expanded rapidly, and the domestic telecommunication network has been modernized. In 2000, 89.4 percent of communes had access to electricity, 94.6 percent were accessible by car, 98.9 percent had primary schools, and 99.0 percent had a health center (GSO 2002 *Statistical Yearbook* data).

Another factor that may have contributed to impressive poverty reduction outcomes in Vietnam is that poverty reduction has been always among the highest priorities of the government. Along with its reform policies to sustain high economic growth, the government has provided special financial resources for a national program for hunger eradication and poverty reduction, which, although implemented in 1998, dates back to the very first initiative taken by Ho Chi Minh City in 1992. The government also launched a number of nationwide hunger eradication and poverty reduction measures, such as a program to regreen barren hills and wasted land and sedentarize nomadic ethnic minorities, and a program for employment generation. A separate program to support the poorest mountainous and remote communes was launched in 1998, despite budget constraints. Between 1992 and 2000, the government made a total investment of approximately 21,000 billion dong (US$1.5 million) for poverty reduction–related measures. The Bank for the Poor has been established to provide concessional credit, with the total amount of funds loaned out reaching 5,500 billion dong (US$392,000). In addition, the government has provided considerable support to programs for ethnic minorities, fixed cultivation, sedentarization, and resettlement. Local people have contributed to infrastructure development projects, mainly in kind, by providing construction materials and their labor, valued at 150 billion dong (US$10,714) between 1992 and 2000. Line ministries and agencies, mass and social organizations, provinces, and large cities have also raised funds and sent their staff to assist the poorest communes (State Committee for Ethnic Minorities and Mountainous Areas Affairs 2001).

Vietnam's poverty reduction campaign has received strong support from many nations, international organizations, and nongovernmental organizations in various ways (experience sharing, technical assistance, development funds) under the framework of grant aid and concessional credit. This has helped to speed up the pace of poverty reduction in Vietnam.

However, the pace of poverty reduction has slowed since 1998.[9] This may be due to several factors:

- In the early 1990s, because Vietnam was a very poor country, rapid and broad-based growth could lift many people out of poverty. Now the phase of easy gains in poverty reduction is probably over, and Vietnam will have greater difficulty in reducing its poverty rate substantially in the future, even if economic growth continues to be high (Haughton 2001).

- Because there is an element of fragility in the gains in poverty reduction, the price fall between 1999 and 2001 for major agricultural products that Vietnam exported to the world (rice, coffee, rubber, cashew nuts, and pepper) reduced the income of farmers and pushed many of them back into poverty. The index of domestic prices of nonfood relative to that of food also reversed its trend, turning against farmers. It dropped to 98.8 percent between December 1997 and December 2001, compared with 102.5 percent for the period 1992–1997.[10]

- The lower economic growth as a consequence of the regional crisis and new problems arising during the first round of the reforms translated into a slowdown in poverty reduction. High and sustainable rates of economic growth are a necessary (but not sufficient) condition for rapid poverty reduction.

- The positive impacts of the agricultural reforms in particular and the economic reforms in general in early 1990s are now exhausted, and agriculture is reaching its limits under current circumstances. Constraints that the sector faces include low productivity, difficulties in marketing its products, falling prices of the agricultural products that Vietnam exports to the world, and an acute shortage of cultivable land, which limits the number of full-time jobs that can be created in agriculture. The underemployment prevailing in agriculture and a slow shift in employment from agriculture to manufacturing and services have their roots in the government's industrial policy (discussed in great detail below).

- The poor who escaped from poverty in the early 1990s are those who had the capacity to take advantage of opportunities that the reforms created. The people who remain poor are those who are harder to reach, even if rapid economic growth were to continue. Some of them are people with low human capital, who do not have enough knowledge and health to earn good income. Many of the hard-to-reach poor live in the uplands and remote areas, where infrastructure is poor, so access to the market and information is not easy to obtain. This group also includes ethnic minorities who need support specifically aimed at their problems, such as language barriers and low literacy, limited opportunities to acquire new functional and technical skills, lack of access to the mass media, and low level of interaction with outsiders. Such groups within the poor often face physical and social isolation, remoteness, powerlessness, and vulnerability. The government has adopted a range of targeted policy measures to reach these groups of the poor, but the measures have had a negligible impact so far due to low spending, low coverage, and poor targeting (Van de Walle 2001).

*   *   *

Rapid and sustained economic growth over most of the 1990s, as a result of the comprehensive reform package implemented in the late 1980s, has brought remarkable progress in poverty reduction. Between the mid-1980s and 2002, Vietnam reduced its poverty rate by more than 60 percent. Major channels through which the benefits of growth reached the poor include improvement in real earnings and income of workers, thanks to agricultural reform in rural areas and changes in the attitude toward the private sector that raise demand for products that the poor can supply. However, there still exist disparities in poverty reduction between rural and urban areas and among regions, sectors of employment, and ethnic groups. The economic slowdown, and consequently the decline in the rate of poverty reduction in the late 1990s, indicate new emerging problems and weaknesses of the economy that call for another wave of reforms.

■ Linkages Among Economic Growth, Employment, and Poverty

Employment Intensity of Growth

A measure relating employment growth with economic growth is the growth of output elasticity in employment. It is measured as the proportionate change in employment divided by the proportionate change in GDP during a given period. A higher employment elasticity means a higher rate of growth of employment for a given increase in output. The employment elasticity should be interpreted with caution, however. It is possible to have "excessive employment creation that is at the expense of growth of productivity" (Islam 2002). Thus, elasticities greater than unity imply declining labor productivity, and an elasticity of less than unity means that employment expansion is taking place alongside an increase in productivity.

Despite some qualifications of this measure, it is still worth examining the trend in employment elasticity with respect to output growth. One important reason is that from the perspective of poverty analysis, while the growth of output is an important concern, it is also important to determine whether output growth creates employment.

There have been no studies, until now, of nexus between output growth and employment growth in Vietnam. P. Belser (1999), while trying to analyze the impact of output growth on employment growth in various ownership sectors, estimated the arc growth elasticity of employment for the industry sector between 1993 and 1998. This single coefficient does not adequately determine whether a sector is experiencing a rising or falling productivity over time, and does not accurately measure how much employment growth is associated with a particular level of output growth over time. This section attempts to fill this gap by conducting elasticity estimation and examining its level as well as changes over time.

Theoretical Framework and Data. There are two methods for the estimation of growth elasticity of employment. First is a simple method measuring the arc elasticity—that is, the elasticity is computed between two different points in time, rather than at one point in time. Thus, arc elasticity, ε, is calculated as follows:

$$\varepsilon = \frac{\Delta L / L}{\Delta Y / Y} \tag{1}$$

where

L = employment
Y = GDP

The numerator is the proportionate change in employment, or the employment growth rate, while the denominator is the proportionate change in GDP, or the growth rate of GDP.

Second is an econometric estimation of a double-log linear equation relating employment and GDP:

$$\ln L = \beta_0 + \beta_1 \ln Y \tag{2}$$

The regression coefficient β_1 is the employment elasticity:

$$\beta_1 = \frac{d \ln L}{d \ln Y} = \frac{dL / L}{dY / Y}$$

For estimation of the employment elasticity, time-series data are compiled using various published and unpublished data provided by the GSO and MOLISA.

It should be noted that classification of economic activities in Vietnam is different from that in other countries. Particularly, the primary sector (often referred to in Vietnam as the agricultural sector) includes agriculture, forestry, and fisheries; the secondary sector (industrial sector) consists of mining and quarrying, manufacturing, electricity, gas, water supply, and construction; and the tertiary sector (service sector) covers the remaining industries.

Employment Elasticity, 1986–2001. Based upon the relationships defined above, employment elasticities for the period 1986–2001 were estimated. Estimates of the annual arc employment elasticities of GDP growth by the simple method for the whole economy are shown in Table 11.9 and Figure 11.5, and their econometric estimation for the whole economy as well as by sector is presented in Table 11.10. The elasticity estimates by both methods are consistent and very similar, although arc elasticities are somewhat higher for the periods 1987–1991 and 1998–2001. Generally, the overall employment elasticities for Vietnam during the 1986–2001 period are relatively low (around just 0.26 to 0.37) when compared with those for other Asian countries.

It can be seen from Figure 11.5 that the employment elasticity fluctuates a great deal: it is of relatively high value during the subperiod 1987–1991, more or less stable and low for the subperiod 1992–1997, and varies greatly and is relatively high again for the subperiod 1998–2001. As annual employment growth rates for the whole period, 1987 to 2001, do not fluctuate much (they range between 1.63 percent and 2.66 percent),[11] this movement is principally caused by considerable variations in annual GDP growth rates, which are moderate for the first and last subperiod (5.05 percent and 6.04 percent respectively), and high between 1992 and 1997 (8.77 percent). It appears that the employment elasticity and GDP growth move in opposite directions.

The differences in employment elasticity of GDP growth among the three subperiods correspond to different stages in reforms in the economy.

The Subperiod of Adjustment, 1986–1991. The period before 1989 was the one of partial (micro and financial) reforms to respond to depletion of the economy. The major objectives of these reforms included creation of new incentives in the agriculture and SOE sectors to produce more output, stabilization, and revitalization of the economy. However, as the reforms were undertaken within the framework of a centrally planned economy, without addressing the fundamental problems of resource misallocation and macroeconomic imbalances, after some initial positive outcomes resulting from better utilization of existing resources, GDP growth was modest again. The subperiod 1987–1991, which was one of fluctuating and high employment elasticity, may be seen as an episode when the impacts of the partial reforms were fully realized.

During this subperiod the employment elasticity of GDP growth was high but declining, implying that the economy was relatively labor-intensive but becoming less so. However, growth during this subperiod appears to have been marked by greater efficiency compared to the period before 1987. Workers who were employed had to work harder and utilize their time well, and as a result their productivity was higher. On the other hand, there were those without jobs as a result of the reforms.

Due to the lion's share of agriculture in total employment (about 73 percent) and its large share to GDP (about 32 percent at 1994 prices) in this subperiod, the overall employment elasticity is greatly influenced by the employment elasticity of the agricultural sector. The high employment elasticity

Table 11.9 GDP and Employment Annual Growth Rates (percentages) and Arc Elasticities, Vietnam, 1987–2001

	1987	1988	1989	1990	1991	1992	1993	1994	1995	1996	1997	1998	1999	2000	2001	1987–1991	1992–1997	1998–2001
GDP growth	3.63	6.01	4.68	5.09	5.81	8.70	8.08	8.83	9.54	9.34	8.15	5.76	4.77	6.79	6.84	5.05	8.77	6.04
Employment growth	2.08	1.82	1.63	1.63	2.46	2.39	2.34	2.35	2.19	2.21	2.17	2.14	2.11	2.02	2.66	1.92	2.28	2.23
Elasticity	0.57	0.30	0.35	0.32	0.42	0.28	0.29	0.27	0.23	0.24	0.27	0.37	0.44	0.30	0.39	0.39	0.26	0.38

Source: Author calculations based on data from Vietnamese General Statistical Office.

Figure 11.5   Annual Growth Rates and Arc Elasticities of GDP and Employment, Vietnam, 1987–2001

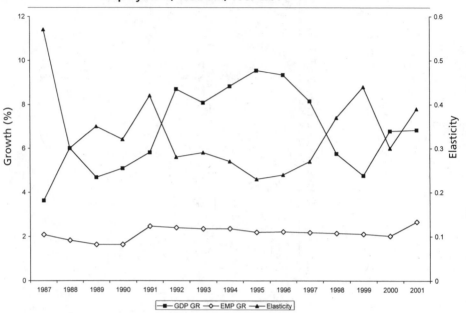

Sources: Vietnamese General Statistical Office, various years; data provided by Vietnamese Ministry of Labor, Invalids, and Social Affairs. Author calculations.

of the sector in this period (0.553) reflects, on the one hand, its high labor intensity, which is very encouraging, but on the other hand it may reflect other forces at work. A more detailed examination suggests that the agricultural sector during this period was very labor-intensive and did not generate high value added compared with the other two sectors. Agriculture, despite the serious constraint on the availability of cultivable land, had been forced to accommodate rural youth who had not been able to find jobs in sectors outside agriculture, as well as workers retrenched due to SOE reform. This resulted in higher

Table 11.10   Employment Elasticity Using Econometric Method, Vietnam, 1986–2001

	1986–1991	1992–1997	1998–2001	1986–2001
Total economy	0.369	0.260	0.366	0.305
Agricultural sector	0.533	0.394	–0.177	0.374
Industrial sector	–0.590	0.229	0.944	0.180
Manufacturing	n/a	0.294	0.790	0.371[a]
Service sector	0.820	0.500	1.910	0.710

Source: Author estimations based on data from Vietnamese General Statistical Office.
Note: a. For the period 1990–2001.

rural underemployment (around 60–70 percent) and lower productivity in agriculture than in the other two sectors. Agriculture has always been the sector with the lowest growth rate, averaging 2.5 percent for the period 1986–1991. Sluggish growth of agriculture, combined with a large number of agricultural workers, made the sectoral employment elasticity relatively high. However, because of its low growth rates, the high labor intensity of the sector did not lead to a large increase in employment.

The estimated employment elasticity for the industrial sector during this period was negative, which was probably caused by the negative output growth rate of the sector in 1989 (–2.6 percent) alongside the still positive (although negligible) growth in employment. The sector underwent a difficult phase with low growth rates, which averaged 4.2 percent for this subperiod. In fact, the sector also did not perform well in terms of employment, which decreased by 7 percent in central SOEs, by 16 percent in provincial SOEs, and by 28 percent in private enterprises. This sharp drop was caused by several factors. First, some enterprises lost state-budget subsidies and became inefficient. Second, others found access to credit more restrictive. Third, as a result of a reduction in market distortions, the structure of relative prices changed dramatically and the profitability of many firms were affected. Finally, the contraction also resulted partly from the collapse of trading partners in the socialist countries, while new markets were not established (Le et al. 2002).

In the early 1990s, in sharp contrast to agriculture, the service sector was relatively small in terms of employment, but the largest in terms of GDP. However, it grew rapidly, much faster than the agriculture and industrial sectors. The growth of output elasticity in employment in the service sector was high, with rapid expansion of the sector having a strong positive impact on employment. As Table 11.10 shows, an output growth rate of 1 percent can create a 0.82 percent growth rate of employment. The service sector was able to absorb (or was forced to absorb, as in the case with agriculture) a significant proportion of redundant workers from the industrial sector. This was fortunate for the economy, which was undergoing structural reforms.

The Subperiod of High and Stable Growth, 1992–1997. In 1989 Vietnam adopted a radical and comprehensive reform package aimed at stabilizing and opening the economy, enhancing freedom of choice for economic units, and promoting competition so as to fundamentally change the system of economic management. Implementation of the reform measures had positive impacts on the economy during this subperiod. GDP growth rates were high and stable, averaging 8.77 percent per annum. The industrial sector took the lead in terms of output growth, with an average annual growth rate of 13.25 percent and a rising share in overall GDP, while the opposite happened with agriculture. The service sector also grew at high and stable rates, but its share in GDP was almost stable. Taking the three sectors together, it is rather surprising that high growth was not accompanied by significantly higher employment growth rates over this subperiod. The employment growth rate was just 2.3 percent, compared with 1.9 percent in the previous subperiod. This situation is mirrored in lower overall as well as sectoral employment elasticity compared with the previous subperiod. Several possible explanations may be put forward.

The labor force in Vietnam was growing at a stable rate of 2–3 percent per annum. Significantly higher GDP growth in this subperiod should have enabled the economy to absorb all the increments to the labor force at the lower level of the employment elasticity. Furthermore, declining employment elasticity also meant productivity improvement, and hence rising income.

However, a closer look at sectoral developments shows that the high growth of the industrial sector was not accompanied by commensurate employment growth, because certain selected industries, most of which were state-owned, capital-intensive, and import-substituting, were promoted at the cost of the rest of the economy, through investments, subsidies, concessional taxes, and high tariffs for their import-competing products. Small- and medium-scale private enterprises and export-oriented industries, which were often very labor-intensive, could not compete on this uneven playing field and were crowded out by SOEs or import-substituting industries.

The dominance of capital-intensive industries can be seen in the very limited impact of strong industrial output growth (13.4 percent per annum) on employment (4 percent per annum) between 1992 and 1997, implying an employment elasticity of under 0.3 for the industry sector (Belser 1999). In sharp contrast, the Republic of Korea, Singapore and Taiwan, China during the 1970s and 1980s, and Indonesia in the early 1990s were able to raise manufacturing employment annually at rates close to 80 percent of their manufacturing output growth rates (Poverty Working Group 1999).

Labor-intensive agriculture experienced the lowest output growth, and its GDP share was declining. This development path is common for many developing countries, but what is notable for Vietnam is the sluggish "Lewis transition"—that is, the movement of labor out of agriculture to the other two sectors was too slow, particularly as manufacturing failed to absorb surplus labor. Rural underemployment continued to exist.

The Subperiod of Post–Asian Crisis, 1998–2001. The post–Asian crisis period was the time when Vietnam entered into a new stage of development: the potential benefits of the past reforms were nearly exhausted and Vietnam took significant steps toward integrating itself into the regional and world economy. The regional crisis in 1997–1998 had had an adverse impact on the Vietnamese economy, especially on FDI flows.

For this subperiod, overall employment elasticity increased from 0.260 in the 1992–1998 period to 0.366 in the 1998–2001 period. This was the result of both lower GDP growth (averaged at 6.04 percent) and a slight acceleration in labor reallocation among the three sectors, reducing labor engaged in the agricultural sector and increasing employment in the other two sectors. This is to a large extent attributable to the government policy since 1998 of reprioritizing in favor of agriculture and rural development. In addition, though capital-intensive and import-substituting SOEs still continued, evidence of their failure became more apparent. There was a growing opinion against their protection. A big push for the private sector was made when the Enterprise Law was promulgated in 1999.[12] In just two years, 2000–2001, over 35,000 new enterprises were registered, with over 600,000 jobs being created. This figure does not include new jobs generated in newly registered individual business households and those jobs that came from the expansion of existing enterprises. A striking increase in employment elasticities for industrial and service sectors reflects these changes. The negativity of the employment elasticity for agriculture was due to an absolute reduction of its work force in 2001.

However, some caution should be exercised in interpreting these elasticities. In the service sector, employment grew more rapidly than output between 1998 and 2001, so the employment elasticity increased substantially and far exceeded unity (1.91), which implies the growth of low-productivity employment. This process of movement has been under way for some time, because agricultural productivity and worker incomes are still much lower than in services. In fact, the service sector in Vietnam now appears to serve as a pool of self-employed and casual labor that has moved out of agriculture and cannot be absorbed in the formal sector.

Employment, Productivity, and Poverty

As demonstrated in Table 11.11, rapid growth has been accompanied by a significant change in the structure of the economy in terms of both GDP and employment, with the share of industry increasing and that of agriculture declining. This reflects a common pattern of development in which workers gradually move out of agriculture to industry and services, where they can earn more. But the changes in the employment pattern were slower than the changes in GDP structure. Between 1991 and 2001, the share of industry in GDP increased by almost 11 percentage points; in sharp contrast, its share in employment increased by only 3 percentage points. In 2001 the overwhelming majority of the work force (62.77 percent) was still in agriculture, while it produced only 22.40 percent of the GDP. Most of the workers moving out of agriculture were absorbed by the service sector. By and large, the shift in the work force followed only one route, from agriculture to services, but not to manufacturing, and therefore it was rather slow.

Figure 11.6 presents sectoral productivity (strictly product per worker) for the period 1987–2001. The figure and Table 11.12 reveal the following:

Table 11.11   Structural Changes, Vietnam, 1986–2001

	GDP at 1994 Prices (%)			Employment Structure (%)		
	Agriculture	Industry	Services	Agriculture	Industry	Services
1986	34.74	26.82	38.44	72.91	13.87	13.22
1991	30.74	25.63	43.64	72.70	11.25	16.05
1992	30.22	26.59	43.19	72.40	11.26	16.34
1993	28.88	27.71	43.41	72.06	11.28	16.66
1994	27.43	28.87	43.70	71.64	11.36	17.00
1995	26.24	29.94	43.82	71.25	11.37	17.38
1996	25.06	31.34	43.60	70.72	11.52	17.77
1997	24.17	32.64	43.20	70.15	11.66	18.20
1998	23.66	33.43	42.91	69.55	11.80	18.65
1999	23.76	34.36	41.88	68.91	11.95	19.13
2000	23.28	35.41	41.30	68.24	12.11	19.65
2001	22.40	36.57	41.03	62.77	14.42	22.82

Source: Author derivations based on data from Vietnamese General Statistical Office and Ministry of Labor, Invalids, and Social Affairs.

- Agriculture has the lowest productivity in terms of both growth rate and level, with its productivity level relative to industry declining from one-fourth to one-ninth and, relative to services, from one-sixth to one-seventh.
- The industrial sector enjoys the highest productivity growth rates and levels, and it surpassed that of services in the second half of the 1990s. Nevertheless, its growth suffered a sharp slowdown after 1998.
- The service sector experienced steady and high productivity growth rates and levels, but its performance after 1998 was not particularly robust.
- Overall, productivity is driven by agricultural productivity, which is also significantly lower than productivity of the industry and service sectors.
- The gaps between industry and services productivity on the one hand and agricultural productivity on the other widened up to the late 1990s. The situation improved after that (see Figure 11.7), because agriculture experienced higher growth rates while the opposite happened with industry and services.

Patterns and levels of sectoral productivities are closely associated with sectoral growth performance and the relative sluggishness in shifts in the sectoral employment structure in relation to the shift in sectoral GDP. Slow growth in agriculture, combined with the slow movement of the labor force from agriculture to the other two sectors, resulted in both a low level and a

Figure 11.6   Productivity, Vietnam, 1987–2001

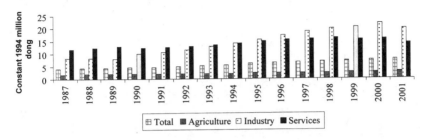

Source: Vietnamese General Statistical Office, various years; data provided by the Vietnamese Ministry of Labor, Invalids, and Social Affairs.

low growth rate of agricultural productivity relative to that in the rest of the economy. In turn, levels and patterns of overall and sectoral growth and employment are for the most part driven by the industrial policies that the country adopts. Some explanations for the sectoral patterns of employment and productivity can be found in the government's industrial policies during the 1990s, as well as the quality of the labor force, both of which will be discussed below.

Productivity is closely associated with qualifications of the labor force, which have experienced some improvement. As Table 11.13 and Figure 11.8 indicate, there was some improvement over the period 1997–2002 with a change in the composition of the work force away from unskilled workers (unskilled and semiskilled) toward workers with qualifications. But this shift was small, and by 2001 an overwhelming majority of the employed labor force (84 percent) still had no relevant skills. The number of skilled workers without certificates almost doubled between 1999 and 2001, and there was also a big increase in skilled persons with certificates. Despite a large increase in the number of workers with postgraduate qualifications, this group only formed 0.07 percent of the employed labor force in 2001. Another important issue is whether qualifications and skills on the supply side match demand in the labor market.

Table 11.14 shows that agricultural workers have much lower skill levels and are less educated than workers in manufacturing and services. The lower level of skills and qualifications in agriculture hinders the use of new technology and thereby makes agricultural productivity grow slowly relative to that of manufacturing and services. This has the effect of depressing rural income.

Regarding industrial policies, the government appears to be following a combination of import-substitution and export-oriented strategies. Its main objective, however, is the substitution of domestic production for imports of manufactured goods so that the economy can become more self-sufficient.

Table 11.12 Employment Growth and Productivity, Vietnam, 1987–2001

	Employment Growth Rate (%)				Productivity Growth Rate (%, 1994 prices)			
	Total	Agriculture	Industry	Services	Total	Agriculture	Industry	Services
1987	2.08	2.22	1.87	1.55	1.50	-3.30	6.50	3.00
1988	1.82	1.17	3.46	3.75	4.10	2.50	1.50	4.80
1989	1.63	1.15	0.75	5.11	3.00	5.80	-3.30	2.60
1990	1.63	2.78	-18.09	15.47	3.40	-1.70	24.90	-4.60
1991	2.46	2.01	2.56	4.46	3.30	0.20	5.00	2.80
1987–1991	1.92	1.87	-1.89	6.07	3.06	0.68	6.91	1.73
1992	2.39	1.97	2.47	4.26	6.20	4.80	10.10	3.20
1993	2.34	1.86	2.53	4.34	5.60	1.40	9.80	4.10
1994	2.35	1.76	3.11	4.40	6.30	1.60	10.00	5.00
1995	2.19	1.64	2.26	4.49	7.20	3.10	11.10	5.10
1996	2.21	1.44	3.51	4.51	7.00	2.90	10.60	4.10
1997	2.17	1.35	3.42	4.62	5.90	2.90	8.90	2.40
1992–1997	2.27	1.67	2.88	4.44	6.35	2.79	10.04	3.98
1998	2.14	1.27	3.39	4.71	3.50	2.20	4.80	0.40
1999	2.11	1.17	3.45	4.74	2.60	4.00	4.10	-2.40
2000	2.02	1.02	3.37	4.77	4.70	3.60	6.50	0.50
2001	2.66	-5.58	22.19	19.21	4.10	8.90	-9.70	-11.00
1998–2001	2.23	-0.53	8.10	8.36	3.73	4.67	1.41	-3.12
1987–2001	2.15	1.15	2.68	6.03	4.56	2.59	6.71	1.34

Source: Author derivations based on data from Vietnamese General Statistical Office and Ministry of Labor, Invalids, and Social Affairs.

Figure 11.7   Productivity Gap Between Sectors, Vietnam, 1986–2001

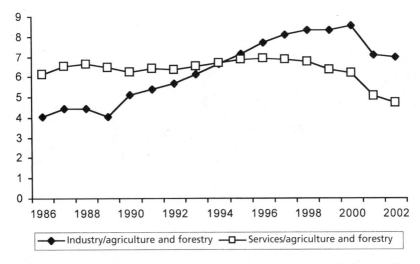

Sources: Vietnamese General Statistical Office, various years; data provided by the Vietnamese Ministry of Labor, Invalids, and Social Affairs.

The rationale that appears to support this policy is that, due to major weaknesses of the economy in terms of production inefficiencies, technological levels, capital availability, and managerial skills, a significant number of domestic businesses cannot compete internationally unless they develop for some time under some degree of protection (the so-called infant industry argument). But protection provided to selected capital-intensive industries draws away scarce resources (capital and skilled labor) from agriculture and

**Table 11.13   Qualification of Labor Force, Vietnam, 1996–2002
(percentages)**

	1996	1997	1998	1999	2000	2001	2002
Unskilled workers	87.69	87.75	86.70	86.13	84.36	82.93	80.28
Semiskilled workers	1.77	1.51	1.46	1.52	1.48	1.33	3.22
Skilled workers without certificate	2.12	2.34	2.16	2.33	2.26	4.56	3.91
Skilled workers with certificate	2.26	2.05	2.59	2.35	3.00	3.89	4.58
Vocational college education	3.84	3.80	4.05	4.22	4.96	3.61	3.86
Tertiary education	2.31	2.56	3.05	3.46	3.95	3.67	4.16

Source: Vietnamese Ministry of Labor, Invalids, and Social Affairs.

Figure 11.8   Growth Rates of Labor Force by Skill Level, Vietnam, 1997–2001

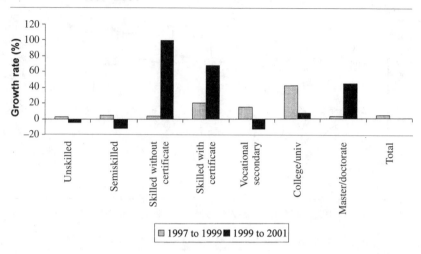

Sources: Vietnamese General Statistical Office, various years; data provided by the Vietnamese Ministry of Labor, Invalids, and Social Affairs.

labor-intensive manufacturing into capital-intensive industries, leaving the former, especially agriculture, with unskilled labor and little capital. The rapid development of the manufacturing and service sectors was largely concentrated in urban areas due to good infrastructure and availability of skilled labor. The urban bias and heavy focus on large-scale manufacturing projects in the public investment program before 1998 have contributed substantially to rural backwardness and agricultural underfunding, especially in research and extension.

Compared with some other countries in the region, such as the Philippines, Thailand, and Indonesia, agriculture receives substantially less public expenditure support than it contributes to GDP. Given the relative importance of public expenditure among all agricultural investment sources, this makes it difficult to achieve the major advances in agricultural output and productivity that would enable agriculture to catch up with other sectors and restructure its production. The *Vietnam Public Expenditure Review* (UNDP 1996, 10–22) suggested that only public investment in irrigation and water resource management was adequate; public investment in other agriculture-related components was far short of needs.

Further, the state and FDI sectors dominated industry (accounting for 78.1 percent of the total industry output in 1998), but employed relatively fewer workers (35.7 percent of the industrial employees) than did the private sector, which is much smaller in terms of the total output, but much more

Table 11.14 Composition of Labor Skills by Sector, Vietnam, 2001 (percentages)

	Unskilled	Semiskilled	Skilled Without Certificate	Skilled with Certificate	Vocational Secondary Education	College/ University Education	Master's Degree/ Doctorate
Agriculture	97.10	0.60	0.50	0.45	1.06	0.28	0.00
Industry	52.84	2.13	21.67	15.79	3.35	4.17	0.05
Services	61.64	2.85	5.41	6.11	11.07	12.67	0.26
Total	82.63	1.33	4.67	3.96	3.68	3.67	0.07

Source: Vietnamese Ministry of Labor, Invalids, and Social Affairs.

labor-intensive. This suggests that the lack of growth in industrial employment to a large extent results from the small size of the private sector. As suggested previously, poverty is a rural phenomenon and is more prevalent in mountainous and remote areas, where nonfarm activities are underdeveloped. This points to the need to generate more opportunities for the labor of the rural poor.

On the other hand, it should be noted that although the service sector in Vietnam provides higher income levels for workers compared to agriculture, its capacity to absorb labor is probably reaching its limit under the current industrial policy. This has resulted in an increasing number of new jobs in services at declining productivity since 1998. Although the sector has recovered steadily since 2000, services are mainly concentrated in social infrastructure (education and health), domestic retail trade, repairs, and other low-value personal services for households and tourists. High value-added services to support the development of highly competitive manufacturing, such as financial and banking services, insurance, telecommunications, business consulting services, and information technology, are underdeveloped. These activities can contribute significantly to the future growth of output, employment, and productivity of the sector, provided the right incentives are in place.

Wages and Salaries

Although real wages and earnings are important channels through which the benefits of rapid output growth and improved productivity are likely to reach the poor, discussion on this issue is limited due to the lack of long time-series data on wages and earnings in Vietnam.

Real wages and earnings appear to be rising. Empirical studies conducted in 2001 by Van Hoang and colleagues, and D. Haughton and colleagues, found that most changes in household wealth, among those who could improve their income substantially between 1993 and 1998, were due to increases in earnings per hour worked. The effects of working more, or having a higher proportion of the household working, or receiving more remittances, were comparatively minor. During 1991–2002 the growth rate of real income was higher than that during 1996–1999 (5.8 percent versus 4.6 percent per year). As income inequality worsened slightly over the 1990s,[13] the benefits of growth accruing to the poor were probably less availing than those accruing to the rich.

This finding is verified by the real situation in the public sector, where real wages and earnings for employees increased thanks to upward adjustments of the monthly nominal minimum wage between 1997 and 2001.[14] The government adjusted the monthly minimum wage from 144,000 dong (US$10.3) in 1997, to 180,000 dong (US$12.8) in 2000, 210,000 dong (US$15) in 2001, and 240,000 dong (US$17) in 2002.[15] As the consumer price index increased by about 80 percent while the minimum wage rose about 170 percent during this period, the adjustments resulted in an increase in real wages for public servants.

It should be borne in mind that because of differences in multipliers, senior staff enjoy a greater improvement of real wages than do their juniors. However, looking at the longer period from 1993 to 2004, adjustments in the minimum wage seem to have just compensated workers for the overall increase in prices.

For foreign companies and joint ventures, the minimum wage is usually about three or four times higher than that in domestic enterprises. This situation leads to differences in wages and earnings between domestic (including state and private) and foreign enterprises. It has been estimated that in 2001, the average monthly income in the state sector and the average monthly income in the private sector were approximately 900,000 dong (US$60) and 375,000 dong (US$25) respectively, while the counterpart income in the foreign-invested sector was 1,029,000 dong (US$74).[16]

Wage and earning disparities also exist between rural and urban areas. Wage income in rural areas accounted for only 21.9 percent of rural household income in 1993, and the proportion declined to 17.1 percent in 1998 (Poverty Working Group 1999). Given that agricultural wage employment, the dominant type of rural wage employment, declined by 4.7 percent per annum over the period 1993–1998, the unchanged level of rural wage income in real terms implied an improvement in rural wages. Nevertheless, this improvement appears to have been smaller than that for urban workers, for over this period per capita expenditure in rural areas increased by 30 percent (or 5.4 percent per annum), while in urban areas it grew twice as fast, at 61 percent (or 9.9 percent per annum).

*   *   *

Vietnam's achievements in poverty reduction during the 1991–2001 period of renovation were remarkable, but more impressive outcomes could have been achieved if it had utilized its comparative advantage, namely the abundance of labor. A certain proportion of the poor, particularly those residing in the countryside, mountainous, and remote areas, was not able to move out of low-income low-productivity agriculture and into manufacturing, because the latter was largely urban-based and many of its enterprises were too capital-intensive to generate many jobs as they grew. At the same time, agriculture, constrained by the availability of cultivable land, severely underfunded, and burdened with low human capital and inadequate infrastructure, was not able to provide enough jobs or high enough income for rural people. Rural industry, dominated by labor-intensive small- and medium-scale enterprises, was not able to compete on an uneven playing field to provide many employment opportunities.

At the macro level, declining poverty in Vietnam has been associated with improved real income and earnings in each sector, rather than intersectoral employment shifts toward high-productivity occupations. Striking improvements in productivity in the industry sector between 1992 and 1997 reduced poverty, mainly for existing workers, but did not generate many additional jobs, and did not facilitate the employment movement of workers out of agriculture.

■ Employment-Poverty Linkages: An Estimation Using a Probit Model

Despite impressive economic growth in Vietnam over most of the past decade, in 1998, 45 percent of the rural population were still below the poverty line, and almost one-third of the population were poor even in 2002. How important are factors such as household human capital, employment, and other variables in explaining the poverty status of households? Identification of the causes of poverty is important for policymakers seeking to design appropriate measures to attack poverty.

There are several studies attempting to explain household levels of wealth or poverty in Vietnam. Using a regression of the logarithm of real per capita consumption of rural households on a vector of household and community characteristics, as well as regional dummy variables, D. Dollar and P. Glewwe (1998) found that in addition to regional differences, rural income in 1992–1993 was determined by quantity of land farmed, the household head's level of education, and access to infrastructure (irrigation, electricity, and passable roads). The study focused on rural income but did not determine factors affecting the poverty status on households.

Thomas Wiens (1998) adopted another approach, examining simple correlations between household poverty and each factor that was believed to affect poverty. His study suggested that rural poverty in 1992–1993 was associated with the paucity of productive resources (land, savings, and other liquidity assets, as well as physical capital), their low quality (lack of irrigation, an unfavorable natural environment, lack of education, lack of decent public infrastructure), lack of access to markets (for inputs, credit, outputs, and off-farm employment opportunities), and the high number of dependents relative to productive resources. Wiens's study is illuminating in respect of poverty determinants, but his approach has a serious drawback. It is impossible to disentangle the effects of each separate factor in influencing household poverty.

There are two studies that estimate multinomial logistic regression models applying data from Vietnam's 1992–1993 and 1997–1998 living standards surveys to determine poverty-related factors. The first, by P. Glewwe, M. Gragnolati, and H. Zaman (2000), investigates the factors that determine movements in and out of poverty by splitting the panel sample into four categories: households that were poor in both years ("remain poor"), households that were poor in 1992–1993 but not in 1997–1998 ("escape poverty"), households that were not poor in 1992–1993 but were in 1997–1998 ("fall back into poverty"), and households that were not poor in both years ("never poor"). Glewwe and colleagues found that factors such as better education, favorable location (in urban areas, or in the Red River Delta and the southeast region), a white-collar worker household head, and improvement in the productivity of rice appear to enable households to escape poverty. The study permits tracking of changes in poverty between 1993 and 1998, but does not directly quantify the probability of a household being poor according to different attributes.

Thien Do and colleagues (2001) also applied multinomial logistic regressions to model determinants of poverty/wealth in both 1992–1993 and 1997–1998. The major shortcoming of this work is that it omits several variables that are essential for poverty reduction, such as asset-related variables (household income, landholding, and durable assets), variables indicating level of agricultural diversification (perennial crop cultivation, aquaculture), and variables relating to a supporting environment to conduct business (access to credit and to technical information).

Our empirical work in this section tries to overcome all the weaknesses of the above studies in analyzing quantitatively the factors that influence the poor and nonpoor status of households in Vietnam. In quantifying the impact of the factors on a household's poor/nonpoor status, we differentiate the effect of income, household characteristics (which somehow are controllable by households), and variables representing environmental factors (which are out of control of households). The study exploits a Probit model to ascertain the distinct effect of each of these factors. We conduct hypothesis tests relating to the significant role of the factors and the signs of the effect, and interpret the impact of these factors on household poor/nonpoor status.

Model Specification

To conduct an empirical study on economic and social issues dealing with responses of categorical or ordinal data, general linear models are often inappropriate, because they do not maintain their desirable asymptotic properties when the errors are heteroscedastic, or nonnormal. For this reason, general linear models often provide misleading answers. For this kind of problem, discrete choice models and limited dependent variable models have proven to be more effective and more suitable for the task of analysis. Here we use a Probit model, which is among the class of discrete choice models.

As the focus of the analysis is the impact of the determinants on the poverty situation of households, it is useful to employ a model with a dependent variable that takes only two values, representing the poor and the nonpoor status of households. Let variable Y denote household poor/nonpoor status; if the ith household is among the poor category, then $Y_i = 1$, and if it is not, then $Y_i = 0$. Now let P_i be probability that $Y_i = 1$ (the event occurs), and let $(1 - P_i)$ be the probability that $Y_i = 0$ (the event does not occur).

Define a latent variable Y^* such that:

$$Y_i = X_i\beta + \varepsilon \tag{1}$$

where

X = vector of factors that determines Y

We do not observe Y^*, but rather Y, which takes only two values, 1 and 0, according to the following rule:

$Y_i = 1$ if $Y_i > 0$
$Y_i = 0$ otherwise

If it is assumed that Y_i is normally distributed with the same mean and variance, it is possible not only to estimate the parameters of equation 1, but also to obtain some information about the unobservable Y_i itself. This gives rise to a standard Probit model:[17]

$$P_i = \text{prob}\ (Y_i = 1) = \Phi\ (X_i, \beta/\sigma) \tag{2}$$

Estimating the Probit model is straightforward, even though the model is non-linear and no closed-form expression for function Φ exists.

The Probit regression measures the association between probability of being poor/nonpoor and a whole range of factors, including characteristics of the household, the income and mean of production, and the socioeconomic environment (development level of the area where the household lives). The dependent variable of poor/nonpoor status is created based upon the poverty line calculated by the Poverty Working Group (1999), as previously detailed. The independent variables determining the probability of a household being poor/nonpoor are discussed below.

A prominent feature of households in Asian developing countries, especially in Vietnam, is their multigenerational makeup.[18] Moreover, under the influence of Confucianism, a typical household in Vietnam keeps a quite strict hierarchy. The head of a household, as an "old person," often has a final decision in family matters. As the household head plays a crucial role in the business of the household, the demographic characteristics of the household can be represented by characteristics of the household head. In other words, in our analysis, the characteristics of the household head can be good proxies for the characteristics of the household. Such characteristics would include variables of age, education, gender, and working sector status.

Age of the household head (denoted by the variable *AGE* in the model) can represent experiences of the household. The older the household head, the more experience he or she tends to have and the wider the range of investment opportunities for the household. For farmwork and for households involved in agricultural activities, experience seems to be very important, because crop cultivation is affected by many factors, such as climate conditions, quality of soil, irrigation, and the timing of the harvest. The success of a harvest depends greatly on skill and the art of cultivation. Accumulated experience and knowledge transfers from generation to generation determine these factors. Consequently, households with more experience are more likely to succeed and escape poverty.

The rationale behind the use of the education variable *(EDUC)* in the model comes from several sources. On one hand, education may affect income according to the concept of M. Friedman's permanent income (1957). Since education usually plays a very important role in ensuring a certain life-cycle income, it is argued that education will result in a more stable income to individuals and households. Hence, higher education may have a positive effect on the probability of escaping poverty. On the other hand, if one takes the precautionary motive and liquidity constraints into account, a higher education level raises the household head's ability to assess the economic environment and balance the budget of the family to its best interest. In developing countries, where uncertainty is high and liquidity constraints are severe, education could help an individual or household cope better with various sources of uncertainty of income and constraints upon borrowing, thus raising saving and assets. Therefore, via this channel, the education level may also have a positive impact on reducing the probability of being poor. In both channels, education is conventionally argued as an important input for generating income and creating assets, and improving the poor/nonpoor status of the household. In Vietnam, poverty rates tend to decline with higher levels of education, and those who have an education level of lower secondary or less make up almost 90 percent of the poor. The highest incidence of poverty (57 percent) is for those who have not even completed primary education (Poverty Working Group 1999).

In addition, education often has a characteristic of spillover effect. This means that the knowledge of a household member attending school or college could be spread and used for the common welfare of the household. It is very likely that a household head can be influenced by education of other adult members of the household. For example, the education and knowledge of an adult member of a household can help the household head apply better seeds, pesticides, and fertilizers. As a result, crop yield can be improved, and the income of the household can be raised. Because of this characteristic, the analysis uses an additional variable of education, defined as an average number of years of schooling of household members who are older than sixteen (denoted *AVEREDUC* in the model). This is the age at which ideas and knowledge of an individual could be regarded as helpful to the household head in decision-making. The variable can also capture the education level of the household head because he or she is supposed to be older than seventeen.

Gender *(GENDER)* often plays an important role in the organization and conduct of the business of the family. Quantitative data from both rounds of Vietnam's living standards survey show that female-headed households are usually materially better off than their male-headed counterparts. The incidence of poverty as well as its depth are lower in the former than in the latter. This may not be the case in many other developing countries.

Whether the household head works in the farm or the nonfarm sector may also influence the level of wealth and income stability of households. As discussed previously, the incidence of poverty is the highest among farming households, with 84 percent of the poor in Vietnam working in agriculture in 2002. Working in nonfarm activities is often thought to result in higher and more stabilized income, because in the farm sector, crops depend greatly on uncontrollable factors such as weather and natural conditions. Therefore, the working status of a household head *(FARM)* may also have an effect on the probability of poor/nonpoor status of the household. Besides the variable *FARM,* an additional variable that presents nonfarm productive activities carried out by any member of a household *(NONFARMONE)* is also used. The reason for using this variable arises from the fact that households often have multigenerational characteristics. Any member of the household who is involved in nonfarm activities could share the benefits with all other members of the household. As a result, involvement of a household member in nonfarm activities may help to reduce the poor status of the household.

Regarding household demographic characteristics, household size *(HHSIZE)* often matters for family businesses. This is because a larger household size is often related to a greater number of children in the household, creating more financial pressure on household expenditure. Household size also can have a positive effect on household income, due to the nature of the economy of scale. These two effects work in opposite directions and the net effect can only be determined by empirical studies. The dependency ratio *(DEPRA-TIO)* is also important for the change of the probability of poor/nonpoor status of a household. The dependency ratio is very often used in the literature at both macro and micro levels. It is defined in this analysis as the ratio of the number of children under fifteen plus the number of people sixty-five and older to the total number of household members. Children under fifteen are dependent, since most of them are in school. People sixty-five and older are included as dependents for the reason that labor force participation drops sharply for that age group, to less than 50 percent. The rationale for the use of this variable in the model comes from the fact that the likelihood of household budget deficits will be higher when the number of dependents increases, because dependents deplete household resources rather than create them. Therefore, an increase in the dependency ratio can raise the probability of the household falling into poverty. Data from Vietnam's living standards surveys confirm that the number of children is highest in households in the poorest quintile, and drops as per capita expenditure rises (Poverty Working Group 1999; ADB et al. 2003).

The poor/nonpoor status also depends on a set of factors related to physical assets and income of households. In this analysis, three variables are used to represent physical assets of a household. The first variable is income *(INCOME)*. The rationale for using this variable is the phenomenon of the vicious circle of poverty. A household that is poor, having a low level of income and often having to borrow, would have less opportunity to invest for the future. The productivity of future business (e.g., future crops) would be low. In some cases in Vietnam, poor agricultural households have to sell their crops at low prices, before they harvest, in order to pay back their debts to lenders. As a result, their income is low, and the investment opportunities for the future are limited. A lower income level of a household can therefore result in a rise in the probability of being poor. The second variable in the set is land (in the model, two variables, per capita irrigated land, *PCIRRLAND,* and per capita land, *PCLAND,* are used). These are the important means of production for farming households. The participatory poverty assessments (Action Aid Vietnam 1999; Oxfam 1999; Mountain Rural Development Program 1999) suggest that the quantity and quality of landholdings are critical determinants of well-being. Poor households are often those whose landholdings are either too small or of such poor quality that they cannot support household self-consumption needs and grow cash crops. The third variable is durable assets *(DURABLE)*. This is a proxy for assets of households. A higher value of assets of households can have a positive impact on investment opportunities and can result in reducing the probability of being poor.

The set of variables discussed above relates to the financial capacity of households. In this analysis, an additional set of variables, which represents technical capacity of households, is used. This includes the characteristics of household products and the capacity of households to diversify crops and products. Vietnam's experience suggests that those households that diversify their products can improve production efficiency and hence raise their income. The set of these variables includes a dummy for perennial industrial crops *(PERINDCROP),* which represents household involvement in growing perennial industrial crops, and a dummy for aquaculture *(AQUACULTURE),* which represents household involvement in aquaculture activities. It is expected that involvement of households in these activities would reduce the probability of their being poor, because agricultural diversification often brings higher income for households.

As the dataset contains information on credit and borrowings, a variable representing access to credit in the formal sector *(CREDACC)* is also included. The reason for including this variable in the model is the argument that access to formal credit could help households to better increase investment and stabilize consumption, and consequently would help to reduce the

probability of being poor. In addition, a variable representing technical support in the form of state-provided dissemination of information *(INFORSP)*
for farm households is included. This kind of support facilitates improvement
of productivity and farming household income, and is therefore expected to
reduce the probability of being poor.

The importance of location for opportunities to improve income and
move out of poverty in Vietnam is highlighted in many reports and studies.[19]
This is the justification for the inclusion of dummy variables for regions
(REG) and for urban/rural areas *(URBAN)* where households live. Definitions
of the variables used in this model and a summary of their statistics are provided in Tables 11.17 and 11.18.

Data

The data for this empirical analysis are taken from the living standards survey
conducted by the World Bank and the General Statistical Office and State
Planning Committee of Vietnam between 1997 and 1998. It is a survey at the
household and individual level with a sample of 6,000 households located in
all regions of Vietnam.

Due to the sampling procedure, there is a sampling bias. The sample size
selected for the 1997–1998 survey was projected to be 6,000 households. The
majority of the sample comprises the selected households interviewed in
1992–1993, during the first living standards survey (4,800 households). An additional 1,200 households were required to attain a sample size of 6,000. This
was done by selecting households from the total sample of Vietnam's 1995
multipurpose household survey, conducted by the GSO.

In order to provide an adequate sample to disaggregate results into the
seven major regions, the selection of the additional households was not pro-
portional to population, but instead was chosen so that the total sample of
6,000 households oversampled certain specific domains. Therefore, to correct
for the bias, we used weighted data for estimation in our analysis (see Table
11.19).

Result Estimation and Interpretation

Two Probit models were used to estimate the effect of the determining variables on the poor/nonpoor status of households. The second model is different from the first model in using the variables of access of any member of a
household to nonfarm activity *(NONFARMONE)* and average years of schooling of adult members of household *(AVEREDUC)* instead of the activity
(FARM) and education *(EDUC)* of the household head, respectively.

The estimated results of the Probit models are presented in Tables 11.15
and 11.16. These results were obtained after the problem of heteroscedasticity
had been solved. The pseudo-R^2 (i.e., the measure of overall fitness of the
model) shows that both models perform well. In addition to the estimation of

the model coefficients, values of derivatives at the mean values (meaning the partial change) of all the variables in the sample were computed. The coefficients of this model (Dprobit models, third columns in Tables 11.15 and 11.16) help to explain the effect of a change in the explanatory variables on the probability of outcome and thus measure partial changes or marginal effects in the probabilities. The hypothesis that an explanatory variable has an insignificant effect on the outcome is tested using the z-test. The Z-statistic and, equivalently, P-values show the significant/insignificant level of the estimated coefficient of an independent variable. For a general rule of interpretation of the Probit model, a positive (negative) sign of an estimated coefficient in the model shows that a higher value of the variable increases (decreases) the likelihood that the event occurs.

In general, the estimated results of the Probit models support very well the hypotheses presented previously. Tables 11.15 and 11.16 show that, in models 1 and 2 respectively, in terms of the statistically significant level, 14 out of 21 and 15 out of 21 estimated coefficients are significant at the 5 percent level.

Table 11.15   Probit and Dprobit Regression Results (Model 1)

Variable	Probit Coefficients	Marginal Effect (dP/dx)	z	$P > |z|$
INCOME	−0.0001	−0.00001	−5.69	0.00
DURABLE	−0.0001	−0.00001	−4.05	0.00
HHSIZE	0.35	0.05	13.62	0.00
GENDER	−0.08	−0.01	−1.23	0.20
FARM	0.35	0.05	4.53	0.00
URBAN	−0.72	−0.08	−6.81	0.00
AGE	−0.02	−0.002	−6.65	0.00
EDUC	−0.07	−0.01	−7.96	0.00
DEPRATIO	0.63	0.09	5.12	0.00
REG1	0.47	0.08	4.87	0.00
REG2	0.38	0.06	3.94	0.00
REG3	0.26	0.04	2.56	0.01
REG4	−0.04	−0.005	−0.40	0.69
REG5	0.17	0.03	1.54	0.12
REG6	−1.01	−0.09	−8.27	0.00
CREDACCFM	−0.01	−0.001	−0.14	0.90
PCLAND	0.00003	0.000004	1.40	0.16
PCIRRLAND	−0.0001	−0.00002	−3.79	0.00
AQUACULTURE	−0.31	−0.05	−2.66	0.01
PERINDCROP	−0.09	−0.01	−1.52	0.13
INFORSP	−0.09	−0.01	−1.43	0.15
CONST	−0.44		−2.31	0.02

Number of observations = 4,856
Wald chi^2 = 700.72
Pseudo-R^2 = 0.35

Table 11.16   Probit and Dprobit Regression Results (Model 2)

Variable	Probit Coefficients	Marginal Effect (*dP/dx*)	*z*	P > |z|
INCOME	−0.001	−0.00001	−6.23	0.00
DURABLE	−0.001	−0.00001	−4.36	0.00
HHSIZE	0.38	0.05	16.02	0.00
GENDER	−0.16	−0.02	−2.64	0.01
NONFARMONE	−0.39	−0.05	−5.99	0.17
URBAN	−0.80	−0.08	−7.88	0.00
AGE	−0.01	−0.001	−2.68	0.01
AVEREDUC	−0.23	−0.03	−7.71	0.00
DEPRATIO	0.32	0.04	2.77	0.01
REG1	0.29	0.04	3.40	0.00
REG2	0.19	0.03	2.12	0.03
REG3	0.12	0.02	1.25	0.21
REG4	0.02	0.003	0.22	0.83
REG5	0.19	0.03	1.79	0.07
REG6	−1.02	−0.08	−8.74	0.00
CREDACC	−0.02	−0.003	−0.42	0.69
PCLAND	0.00003	0.00003	1.40	0.16
PCIRRLAND	−0.0001	−0.00002	−4.50	0.00
AQUACULTURE	−0.24	−0.03	−2.31	0.02
PERINDCROP	−0.15	−0.02	−2.53	0.01
INFORSP	−0.11	−0.01	−1.71	0.09
CONST	−0.69		−4.21	0.00

Number of observations = 5,413
Wald chi^2 = 833.34
Pseudo-R^2 = 0.35

The signs of the coefficients are as expected. Income *(INCOME)* and assets *(DURABLE)* were important to poor/nonpoor status. Other things being the same, as income increases, the likelihood that the household is poor would be reduced. An increase in income by 1 million dong (US$71), holding all other variables constant at their mean, would reduce the probability of the household being poor by 10 percentage points. Similarly, the positive coefficient of *DURABLE* suggests that, as durable assets increase, other things being the same, the probability of the household being in the nonpoor category is likely to increase. An increase in durable assets by 1 million dong, holding all other variables constant, would reduce the probability of the household being poor by 1 percentage point. These results support well our hypothesis that the set of asset variables can help households improve their life and escape from the vicious circle of poverty.

For the set of characteristics of households, household size *(HHSIZE)* is an important factor determining poor/nonpoor status. The result shows that a one-unit increase in household size, other things being the same, would result in an increase of probability of the household being poor by 5 percentage points. This result implies that the effect of the household size on poverty via the channel of demographic dependency may be larger than the effect via the channel of economies of scale. In the channel of the demographic dependency, an increase in the number of nonworking people (dependents) could increase the expenditure of the household and thus increase the likelihood that the household is poor. In the channel of economies of scale, the per capita cost of living and the production scale of households can be reduced by the increase in the number of dependents. The effect via the first channel outweighs the effect via the second channel, making the net effect of household size on the likelihood of the poor/nonpoor status positive. The result of the estimated coefficient of the variable of dependency ratio *(DEPRATIO),* in fact, confirms this suggestion. An increase by one unit in the dependency ratio, other things being the same, would result in an increase in the range of 4–9 percentage points in the probability of the household being poor.

The age of the household head *(AGE)* seems to have a negative effect on the probability that the household is poor. As the household head's age increases by one year, holding all other variables constant, the probability of the household being poor is reduced by a range of 0.1–0.2 percentage point. The variable of education of the household head is also important. Holding all other variables constant, a one-year increase in attending school by the household head *(EDUC)* would result in reducing the probability of the household being poor by 1 percentage point (model 1). Similarly, a one-year increase in the average years of schooling of adult members in the household *(AVEREDU)* would reduce the likelihood of the household being poor by 3 percentage points (model 2).

Access to nonfarm employment is clearly associated with the poor/nonpoor status of households. The household head working in the farm sector *(FARM)* would increase the probability of a household being poor by 5 percentage points, in comparison with working in the nonfarm sector (model 1). By contrast, if a household has at least one member *(NONFARMONE)* who is involved in nonfarm activity, the probability of the household being poor is 5 percentage points lower (model 2).

While per capita land area *(PCLAND)* is unimportant, the variable of per capita irrigated land *(PCIRRLAND)* is positive in reducing the probability of the household being poor. The result shows that as the area of per capita irrigated land of a household increases by one hectare, other things being the same, the probability that the household is poor would be reduced by 20 percentage points. This result confirms the argument that a household having more means of production and irrigated land would have more and better opportunities to work and invest and thus have a better chance to reduce poverty.

However, as land and irrigated land area are limited, the issue of using techniques to intensify land use is more important. In the models, the variables associated with the technical issues are diversification of crops (such as culti-vating perennial crops, raising fish and shrimp) and technical and information support from the government. The coefficient of the dummy variable *AQUA-CULTURE,* which represents household involvement in raising fish and shrimp, is found significant at the 5 percent level. As a household becomes in-volved in aquacultural activities, its probability of being nonpoor is reduced by 3–5 percentage points. Similarly, as a household grows perennial industrial crops (*PERINDCROP* = 1), the probability of the household being poor is re-duced by 2 percentage points, in comparison with a household that does not.

The dummy variable *INFOSP,* which represents a household's having re-ceived information and technical support from government agencies, is im-portant at the 9 and the 15 percent level in model 2 and model 1 respectively. This means that the evidence of the effect is weaker than that of the other vari-ables. A positive value of the coefficient implies that if a household receives technical and information support from government agencies, this would re-duce the likelihood that the household falls into the category of poor. The vari-able of access to credit in the formal sector is insignificant even at the 10 per-cent level. This suggests that the formal credit system for poor people may not function well enough and does not yet have a significant role in poverty alle-viation. The informal sector may be the major source supplying credit for the poor.

The dummy variables of regions *(REG)* are also important, except for two regions, the central coast and the central highlands. This indicates that, apart from the southeastern region, in comparison to the households in the Mekong Delta (the base region), the probability of households being poor in other re-gions seems to be higher. This result seems reasonable, since the southeastern region and the Mekong Delta are the two most developed regions of the coun-try. The significance level of the coefficient of the dummy variable of areas *(URBAN)* suggests that there are differences between urban and rural areas. The negative sign of the coefficient of this variable shows that households liv-ing in urban areas would have a lower likelihood of being poor than house-holds in rural areas. This result confirms the higher opportunity of improving life conditions for people in urban areas and is supported by the evidence of widening the urban-rural income gap.

*   *   *

The results of this empirical analysis support the argument that the poor/non-poor status of a household can be affected by many factors. The analysis con-firms the importance of factors such as farm and nonfarm income, assets, the demographic characteristics of households (such as household size, age, edu-cation level, and dependency ratio), agricultural diversification, the availabil-ity of irrigated land, technical and information support from government agencies, and location. Among these factors, the most influential appear to be multiple sources of household income from farm and nonfarm activities, household size, dependency ratio, education, household location, and technical and information support from the government.

◼ Conclusion

Rapid and sustained growth in Vietnam over most of the 1990s has resulted in notable achievements in poverty reduction. Vietnam's experience over the 1990s suggests that market-oriented reforms and economic integration, by and large, do not hurt the poor; instead they help the poor by increasing the demand for the goods and services that they sell. The broad-based rapid growth brought by the reforms has in fact increased opportunities for the poor. Since Vietnam is a poor country with abundant labor but scarcity of land and capital, growth accompanied by intensive use of labor is the key to achieving the goal of poverty reduction.

The implementation of major government policies, especially industrial policies, has resulted in a relatively slow shift in the employment structure when compared with the GDP structure. It has also resulted in disparities in levels of development among regions, and differentials in sectoral productivities. Agriculture has suffered from low productivity as well as sluggish growth relative to the other sectors. As most of the poor are farmers, the performance of agriculture has to some extent constrained progress in poverty reduction. Also, during the past decade, major improvements in household income came from increases in earnings per hour worked within each sector rather than from the movement of labor out of low-productivity sectors (e.g., agriculture) and into sectors with higher productivity. This was probably due to the relatively highly capital-intensive nature of the latter. Where structural shifts in employment did occur, for instance, to services in the recent past, productivity declined, as the sector's capacity to absorb labor without loss of productivity was limited. These structural features are reflected in wide variations in the pace of poverty reduction between rural and urban areas, and among regions, sectors, and occupations. The period of easy gains in poverty reduction in Vietnam appears to be over. It will be much more difficult for government policies and programs to have an impact on those among the poor who live in the countryside, mountainous, and remote areas; who have low levels of endowments; or who belong to ethnic minorities with their specific ways of life, culture, language, and custom. It is also important to stress that the achievements in poverty reduction in Vietnam remain fragile, for a large proportion of the population remains clustered around the poverty line and continues to be highly vulnerable.

A key point emerging from this chapter is the essential role of employment expansion and high productivity for rapid and sustainable poverty reduction. Every pro-poor policy, directly or indirectly, seeks to create employment opportunities for the poor or improve productivity on a sustainable basis, especially in the sector employing the poor. Both elements raise the incomes of the poor and hence speed up the pace of poverty reduction. Policies for poverty reduction therefore should focus on two issues: accelerating the shift in employment from agriculture to higher-productivity sectors, and further improving productivity in all sectors, with a special focus on agriculture, which employs most of the poor.

Two broad groups of pro-poor policies to deal with these issues may be distinguished: policies at the macro level, and those at the household level.

Macro-Level Policies

We have argued that a necessary requirement for poverty reduction is high and sustainable economic growth. Vietnam's experience before the Asian crisis shows that high growth could benefit many of the poor, directly or indirectly, through improved productivity and a higher level of employment creation. However, a high level of growth is not sufficient. The pattern of growth is also an important factor in accelerating the pace of poverty reduction. The high incidence of poverty in rural areas points to the need for the government to review its industrial policy and accord greater priority to rural development.

At the macro level, the pace of poverty reduction is determined crucially by the way the structure of the economy shifts over time, and this in turn depends on government industrial policies. Over the period 1993–1998, rural living standards in Vietnam improved, driven predominantly by a diversification of on-farm activity as a strong response to the agricultural reforms. However, in the future, Vietnam may not be able to replicate this land-based, agricultural diversification success story, which is now reaching its limits (Poverty Working Group 1999).

Growth in the medium term will probably come from the establishment of labor-intensive industries to generate rural off-farm employment for semi-skilled and unskilled labor. Given these realities, to promote growth and poverty reduction in rural areas, policies should promote intensive investment in agriculture to improve land productivity, by diversification of agricultural production away from rice and toward high-value crops, livestock, and aquaculture, and through intensifying agricultural research and development and the dissemination of research results through agricultural extension. Expanding domestic markets are essential for agriculture, which in the past has been exporting a large part of its output of certain products to other countries. A more radical way to improve rural income is through the generation of supplementary off-farm employment, particularly if rural-urban migration is not viewed as a good alternative.

In urban areas, living standards have risen faster than in rural areas, but the opportunities provided by economic growth have been less evenly distributed. The state industrial sector has grown rapidly, but created relatively few jobs, as it continues to be dominated by capital-intensive enterprises. The urban unemployment problem has to be tackled. Further reform of SOEs is required so as to address the problem of SOE inefficiency. There is a need to abolish all explicit and implicit subsidies and protection that have created overwhelming advantages for SOEs and have crowded out investment in the private sector. Incentives for the expansion of labor-intensive industries and the private sector development should be provided. The Enterprise Law serves as a good example of this kind of incentive to promote a dynamic private sector, and could provide significant opportunities for employment creation in the years to come.

The process of structural change in employment will continue, with further shifts in the future away from agriculture and toward manufacturing and service sectors. Therefore the ability of the economy to maintain its impressive record of achievement in poverty reduction would depend critically on what happens to wages and earnings in the service sector. For the time being, this sector is very labor-intensive, providing low-value-added services that do not create much income. The sector should move toward high-value services that support manufacturing, and it should grow faster and become more competitive. Services that would have great scope include finance and banking, information technology, telecommunications, legal advice, insurance, and consulting. They could generate many jobs and generate high incomes, but this would require that the relevant training be provided.

Household-Level Policies
At the household level, past experience shows, and this chapter has confirmed, that some of the poor were able to escape poverty because they utilized their labor and took full advantage of the opportunities created by the reforms. These were people who had labor, land, and economic assets; they could borrow to invest in their farm and nonfarm businesses; and they had the education and knowledge required to be able to respond to market demands. They lived in areas with good infrastructure and developed nonfarm activities; they had access to information about markets and new techniques; and they were very close to markets, or had convenient access to them, to buy and sell products.

But not all the poor could benefit in this way. Many were constrained by their low human capital (poor health, limited education and knowledge); large numbers of dependents (children, elderly or disabled family members); limited endowment of land, capital, and assets; and the remoteness of their location. Government pro-poor policies directed at the household level therefore should aim to improve the capability of the poor, create a productive environment for them to do business in, and provide safety nets for those who are not capable of taking advantages of opportunities created for them, or who suffer from unexpected substantial falls in income due to natural disasters or loss of jobs. The most important policies that would have an impact at the household level include:

1. Policies to enhance the human capital of the poor through providing basic services such as health care, clean water, education, training and retraining, and technology transfer through agricultural extension activities, so that the poor have the knowledge and intellectual and physical capability to take up opportunities created by the economic reforms. As Vietnam's 1997–1998 and 2001–2002 living standards surveys demonstrate, people with an education level of lower secondary or less make up 97 percent of the poor in Vietnam. In 2002 the highest incidence of poverty (40 percent) was for those who have not completed primary education (GSO data). Education and training to acquire necessary skills, and general and functional knowledge, usually provide good opportunities for securing stable jobs and understanding and applying new techniques. Education also helps households take advantage of other infrastructure services such as irrigation, communication, electricity, and transport. In China, spending on education helped to bring the greatest number of people out of poverty (Fan, Zhang, and Zhang 2002). Better health care will improve the health status of the poor, which in turn will reduce the costs incurred by illness and diminish the risk of lost earnings.

2. Policies to improve physical infrastructure such as electricity, road, irrigation, and communication can contribute to increasing the access of the poor to markets. Physical isolation caused by remoteness and poor infrastructure reduces economic opportunities and makes access to markets, basic social services, credit, information, and mass media more difficult. Poor infrastructure creates major obstacles for agricultural diversification and results in the underdevelopment of off-farm activities. Adequate irrigation services have in the past contributed substantially to productivity improvement of rice and other crops and enabled more rapid rotation of crops and harvests from 1.3 up to 2–2.7 harvests during the year (Poverty Task Force 2002). Good infrastructure is also crucial for improving the welfare of the poor in many other economic and social aspects, such as nutrition, health, literacy, political and social exclusion, and vulnerability. A recent empirical study (Fan, Hazell, and Thorat 2000) suggests that the Indian government's expenditure on road construction contributed more to poverty reduction than did its other investments.

3. Policies to promote research and development, especially in agriculture, can significantly raise productivity. Returns to investment in agricultural research are very high worldwide, and its impact on poverty reduction is substantial. Two recent studies (Fan, Hazell, and Thorat 2000; Fan, Zhang, and Zhang 2002) show that agricultural research and development expenditures ranked second in India as well as in China (after road construction in the former and education in the latter), in terms of poverty reduction through greater

agricultural yields, which generated higher income for farmers, declines in food prices for consumers, and improved wages in nonfarm activities.

4. So far, only a small number of private businesses have access to formal credit due to complicated administrative formalities and other implicit barriers. If investment opportunities are forgone due to capital shortage, all other investments and policies to create a favorable environment for businesses and improve human capital for the poor will not be successful. Policies that facilitate easy access to credit for doing business, especially for the poor, are therefore needed, and this will require further reform of the banking sector.

5. Protection from external shocks is essential for poverty reduction in Vietnam, where a large proportion of households is clustered around the poverty line. An important need is to establish safety nets, including social protection for the disabled, retrenchment payments, and emergency relief. Vietnam's new round of reforms, together with the further growth and reduction in poverty that are expected, will lead to structural changes in the economy. Some sectors will expand and some will contract. Some people in the declining sectors may lose their jobs or sources of income and fall back below the poverty line. SOE and trade policy reforms are the most likely set of measures that would have direct implications for the level of poverty in Vietnam. SOE reforms are likely to have an adverse impact upon employment. The adverse effects of the layoffs that may result will have to be mitigated by a well-designed safety net that provides funding for retraining and severance pay. Retraining and an ability to quickly relocate to fast-growing areas will assist displaced workers in taking advantage of opportunities that may be generated by the reform program. The magnitude of the adverse effects of layoffs will ultimately and crucially depend on the establishment of safety nets, and quality and relevance in relation to needs of the training and retraining provided. In a disaster-prone country like Vietnam, social safety nets can also help the poor obtain relief.

* * *

A special targeted program is needed in Vietnam to help upland people and ethnic minorities to escape from poverty. People belonging to ethnic minorities often face not only physical but also social isolation from the world outside their community. This isolation is associated to a significant extent with their linguistic, cultural, and educational differences, as well as with differences in cultivation practices. These impede their interaction with the outside world and limit their access to new and improved information, techniques, and ideas. Again, the regional dimension should be accorded greater importance in both macro- and household-level policies. There is a trade-off in resource allocation between areas with the highest financial returns and those with the greatest

460

Table 11.17   List of Variables Used for Probit and Dprobit Models

Variable	Meaning
INCOME	Real income of a surveyed household readjusted by price indexes of regions and months (January 1998 = 1) that can compare to year 1993 (thousand dong)
DURABLE	Values of durable assets of a surveyed household (thousand dong)
HHSIZE	Number of household members
GENDER	Dummy variable, equals 1 if household head is male, 0 otherwise
FARM	Dummy variable classifying household head's job in agricultural and nonagricultural sectors, equals 1 if the job is agricultural, 0 otherwise
NONFARMONE	Dummy variable, equals 1 if household has at least one member involved in nonagricultural sector, 0 otherwise
AGE	Age of household head (years)
EDUC	Number of schooling years of household head (years)
AVEREDUC	Average number of schooling years of all household members over age 16 (years)
URBAN	Dummy variable, equals 1 if household lives in urban area, 0 otherwise
DEPRATIO	The ratio of number independent members (under age 15 and over age 64) to number of dependent members (age 15–64)
CREDACC	Dummy variable, equals 1 if one or more member of household borrowed from formal credit organizations, 0 otherwise
PCLAND	Per capita land area (square meters)
PCIRRLAND	Per capita irrigated land area (square meters)
AQUACULTURE	Dummy variable, equals 1 if household is involved in aquacultural activity, 0 otherwise
PERINDCROP	Dummy variable, equals 1 if household grows perennial industrial crops, 0 otherwise
INFOSP	Dummy variable, equals 1 if household receives information and technical support from government agencies, 0 otherwise
REG1	Dummy variable, equals 1 if household lives in northern uplands
REG2	Dummy variable, equals 1 if household lives in Red River Delta
REG3	Dummy variable, equals 1 if household lives in northern central region
REG4	Dummy variable, equals 1 if household lives in central coast
REG5	Dummy variable, equals 1 if household lives in central highlands
REG6	Dummy variable, equals 1 if household lives in southeastern region
REG7	Base dummy variable, equals 1 if household lives in Mekong Delta

Table 11.18   Summary of Statistics of Variables Used in Probit Models

Variable	Mean	Standard Deviation	Minimum	Maximum
POOR	0.26	0.44	0.00	1.00
INCOME	15,734.48	23,654.56	−29,524.42	1,110,928.00
DURABLE	7,121.47	34,696.48	0.00	1,069,000.00
HHSIZE	4.75	1.95	1.00	19.00
GENDER	0.73	0.44	0.00	1.00
AGE	48.01	13.77	16.00	95.00
URBAN	0.29	0.45	0.00	1.00
FARM	0.57	0.49	0.00	1.00
DEPRATIO	0.39	0.25	0.00	1.00
CREDACCFM	0.30	0.46	0.00	1.00
EDUC	7.09	4.42	0.00	22.00
AVEREDUC	0.51	1.49	0.00	22.00
NONFARMONE	0.50	0.50	0.00	1.00
PCLAND	1,931.87	2,157.81	14.25	28,250.00
PCIRRLAND	1,256.39	1,640.46	0.00	28,250.00
PERINDCROP	0.30	0.46	0.00	1.00
AQUACULTURE	0.74	0.44	0.00	1.00
INFOSP	0.41	0.49	0.00	1.00
REG1	0.14	0.35	0.00	1.00
REG2	0.20	0.40	0.00	1.00
REG3	0.12	0.32	0.00	1.00
REG4	0.13	0.33	0.00	1.00
REG5	0.06	0.24	0.00	1.00
REG6	0.17	0.38	0.00	1.00
REG7	4.02	2.15	1.00	7.00

Table 11.19   Factors for Oversampling

Domain	Relative Sampling Fraction
Urban	
Hanoi, HCMC	2
Other cities	2
Other urban areas	1.5
Rural	
Northern uplands	1
Red River Delta	1
North central	1
Central coast	1.5
Central highlands	3
Southeast	2
Mekong Delta	1

needs. Evidence from many countries suggests that resource allocation under pro-poor policies should be directed more toward poorer regions with greater needs, rather than serving to reinforce current regional disparities.

Last but not least, implementation of different policies in isolation from one another is not enough. An integrated package of interventions embodying complementary policies is desirable in order to reap greater benefits from available resources. Vietnam's comprehensive poverty reduction growth strategy (SRV 2002) and its development goals reflect the government's determination to adopt an integrated approach toward the poor. But these policy measures will succeed only if a massive effort is undertaken, with close coordination on all fronts among all stakeholders.

▪ Notes

1. Improvement in quality of growth is reflected in increasing contribution of total factor productivity in 2000 and 2001, which accounts for more than 30 percent of GDP compared to the average level of 20 percent during the 1997–1999 period (Central Institute for Economic Management [CIEM] 2002).

2. Rice prices fell by over 40 percent between 1998 and 2001, and Robusta coffee (which in 2000 accounted for 99 percent of Vietnam's coffee production) in 2001 traded at only a third of its 1998 price. See World Bank 2001b and CIEM 2002 for more details.

3. See Le et al. 2001.

4. The 1993 and 1998 living standards surveys were conducted by the General Statistical Office with funding from the Swedish International Development Agency and the United Nations Development Programme, and technical assistance from the World Bank. These nationally representative sample surveys provide data on a wide range of topics, including expenditures and incomes; education; health, fertility, and nutrition; employment; migration; housing; agricultural activities; and small household businesses, credit, and savings. In addition to the household questionnaires, the surveys included commune questionnaires (for rural areas only), price questionnaires, and for 1998, modules on school and health facilities. Some 4,800 households were included in the first living standards survey and about 6,000 households were covered in the most recent survey. Approximately 4,300 households were included in both the first and the second survey, providing a large panel of household data useful for analyzing how living standards have changed over time. Since 2001, Vietnam's living standards survey and its multipurpose household survey have been combined into a biannual survey (of "household living standards") that has substantially larger coverage, of 75,000 households.

5. According to current standards, universal primary education is achieved in a province if 80 percent (70 percent) of the fourteen-year-olds in 90 percent (80 percent) of its communes for provinces in the lowland areas (mountainous areas) have completed primary education.

6. J. Haughton (2001) estimated that between 1993 and 1998 the price of rice rose by 62 percent, while the price of nonfood items increased by just 23 percent. The price of other food items rose even faster than the price of rice, so that food prices increased by 68 percent overall.

7. Derived from the General Statistical Office's *Statistical Yearbook* (various years).

8. Underemployment here is defined as working less than forty hours per week.

9. The changes in poverty reduction in Vietnam are very similar to those in China, which embarked on economic reforms ten years earlier than did Vietnam. The economic reforms and rapid growth in China led to a rapid fall in poverty in the 1980s, followed by a period when poverty hardly fell any further (Haughton 2001).

10. CIEM estimate.

11. It should be noted that employment data in Vietnam in the late 1980s and early 1990s might disguise some distinction between employment and underemployment, with the latter probably being reduced gradually during this period. On the other hand, in response to the SOE reform measures introduced since 1989, SOE employment decreased significantly. This situation led to overall decelerating employment growth rates, but improving labor productivity.

12. The Enterprise Law was passed by the National Assembly on June 12, 1999, and came into effect on January 1, 2000.

13. The Gini coefficient for per capita expenditure increased from 0.33 in 1993 to 0.35 in 1998, and Gini for per capita income increased from 0.390 in 1999 to 0.391 in 2001–2002. It should be borne in mind that the Gini coefficient for per capita income is always higher than that for consumption expenditure, due to differences in savings.

14. In the public sector this minimum wage is used as a base on which nominal salaries are calculated as a multiplier of the minimum wage. Thus, any increase in the minimum wage automatically leads to an increase in the salaries of all public servants.

15. Since 2005 the minimum monthly wage for public sector employees has been set at 290,000 dong (US$21).

16. *Vietnam Economic Times,* August 18, 2000.

17. See Long 1997, or Johnston and Dinardo 1997, for example.

18. This chapter uses "household" and "family" interchangeably, although in fact there are a number of definitions that distinguish these two concepts. In the literature, a variety of functions are usually associated with the household: coresidence, joint production, shared consumption, and kinship links. These functions define different sets of individuals. Generally, given the varied and complex nature of human society, no definition of the household completely fits all circumstances. The definition of the household should be given depending on the particular purpose of research. The household in this chapter is defined in terms of shared consumption, income, and kinship links and thus is very close to the family.

19. See, for example, Asian Development Bank et al. 2003; Poverty Working Group 1999; Haughton 2001; Do et al. 2001; Haughton et al. 2001; Deichmann et al. 2001; National Centre for Social Sciences and Humanities 2001; Glewwe, Gragnolati, and Zaman 2000; and Centre for International Economics 2002.

Part 3

Conclusion

12

Implications for Public Policy

Rizwanul Islam

The main message emerging from this book can be summed up as follows: A high rate of economic growth is a necessary condition for poverty reduction, but not sufficient. There is no invariant relationship between economic growth and poverty reduction; similar growth rates can be associated with different outcomes on poverty reduction. Developments in employment and labor markets that take place as a result of growth play an important role in producing such varying results regarding poverty reduction. For economic growth to be pro-poor, it has to result in a transformation of the economic and employment structure toward high-productivity activities and the poor benefiting from that through higher real wages and earnings.

The chapters here contain two types of empirical analysis of the linkages among economic growth, employment, and poverty. In Chapters 3 and 4, Rizwanul Islam and Azizur Rahman Khan provide cross-country analysis, while Chapters 5–11 present country-level analysis. Islam's cross-country analysis is presented in two parts, the first of which employs regression analysis using cross-country data, while the second is based on the country studies presented in this volume. In the former, he demonstrates that the employment intensity of growth is an important explanatory variable in explaining the variation in the rates of poverty reduction. He also shows the impact of employment and labor market variables on poverty reduction. Developments that are shown to make significant contribution to poverty reduction include the structural transformation of employment toward manufacturing and other nonfarm sectors, education, and the degree of labor force participation.

Khan's analysis of the linkages among growth, employment, and poverty reduction is cast in terms of differences in performance between various developing regions of the world, with due attention to variations within regions also. He shows that with the exception of Philippines, countries of East and

Southeast Asia have, by and large, been the most successful, not only in achieving high rates of economic growth but also in achieving a strong linkages among growth, employment, and poverty reduction, and thus in translating high growth into impressive rates of poverty reduction. In countries of South Asia, growth has been quite steady, but the rate of poverty reduction has not been so; and linkages among growth, employment, and poverty linkage have not worked in the same manner as in the countries of East and Southeast Asia. Within sub-Saharan Africa, there are very few examples where these linkages work successfully—except perhaps Uganda and Ghana. Likewise, in Latin America also, the evidence is rather mixed. While the 1990s witnessed a restoration of economic growth in many countries of that region, growth has not been particularly employment-friendly. Chile is one country where the linkages among growth, employment, and poverty operated satisfactorily.

Regarding mechanisms through which output growth translates into employment growth and poverty reduction, a few points emerging from Khan's chapter are worth highlighting. First, in countries of East and Southeast Asia that succeeded in achieving a very significant reduction in poverty, the incentive structure in the market, and institutions, did not have many distortions to encourage the use of inappropriate technologies in production, to discourage investment in sectors that are employment-intensive, or to lead to other employment-averse behavior on the part of employers. This enabled output to be appropriately employment-intensive. Second, the countries mentioned above, by and large, adopted policies to endow their labor force with human capital. This enabled the poor to acquire skills needed in rapidly changing labor markets. Third, in some countries (e.g., the Republic of Korea), conditions were created (through land reform and other support services) to enable small farmers and landless laborers to develop themselves into productive entrepreneurs. Fourth, increased labor productivity led to increased demand for wage labor, which in turn led to increased employment or higher wages or both. Thus the poor who depend on wage labor could benefit from the results of high economic growth.

Although demographic transition does not feature explicitly in the analytic frameworks presented in this volume (i.e., in Chapters 2–4), change in the demographic structure of the population, reflected in the proportion of population in the economically active age group, does constitute an important factor influencing poverty. As fertility falls, the dependency ratio falls, and during this phase of demographic transition a country can enjoy a favorable participation ratio that in turn can be a positive factor in terms of both income generation and investment in human capital. Indeed, if employment-intensive economic growth coincides with this phase of demographic transition, the poverty-reducing effect of growth can be strong. This point is illustrated by the experiences of the Southeast Asian countries during the 1980s and the 1990s. The importance of the demographic factor is also illustrated by the fact that the dependency ratio comes out as a strong explanatory variable in the regression exercise undertaken in Chapter 3.

The country studies in the book yield a number of interesting conclusions, some of which are very much in line with those of Islam and Khan mentioned above. Most of these countries witnessed economic reforms during the 1980s and the 1990s. The reform packages contained a number of common (and rather familiar) elements, although there were differences in details and timing. The common elements included measures for monetary and fiscal stabilization, trade liberalization, exchange rate depreciation, liberalization of the domestic economies, and privatization. Such reforms, by and large, created environments for high economic growth, as has been witnessed in countries as diverse as Bolivia, Ethiopia, India, Uganda, and Vietnam. However, there were differences in the rates of growth achieved and in the extent to which they were sustained. Uganda and Vietnam provide examples of high growth, while growth in Bolivia and Ethiopia has not been so high. In terms of sustainability also, the records of Uganda and Vietnam have been better—although growth in Uganda started faltering after 2000. Bolivia, on the other hand, witnessed a decline in GDP growth already in 1998.

Apart from the rate of economic growth, what is important from the point of view of poverty reduction is the pattern of growth engendered by economic reforms. And it is in this respect that differences are found. Such differences, in turn, produce different performances in poverty reduction. The result is the absence of an invariant relationship between economic growth and poverty reduction. Utilizing data on the seven countries covered here, Islam (Chapter 3) brought this out quite clearly.

Contrasts in the patterns of growth and different outcomes in terms of growth can be illustrated by using the examples of Bolivia on the one hand and Uganda and Vietnam on the other. In Vietnam, reforms in agriculture led to an improvement in agriculture's terms of trade. And as most households in rural Vietnam are net sellers of agricultural products, the poor households also benefited from an improvement in the sector's terms of trade. A similar situation obtained in Uganda, where a combination of the boom in the world coffee market and liberalization of marketing helped the growers. Being an activity based on smallholders, cultivation of coffee thus helped raise the incomes of poor farmers. In Bolivia, on the other hand, high growth took place in capital-intensive sectors like electricity, gas and water, financial services, and transport and communication. Growth in agriculture (the most labor-intensive sector) was rather modest during the 1990s.

The importance of the employment intensity of growth in reducing poverty is also illustrated by the country studies presented here. Khan, in Chapter 4, shows that growth in countries of East and Southeast Asia has been more employment-intensive than growth in countries of South Asia; and the record of poverty reduction has also been more impressive in the former. A comparison of the study of Indonesia (Chapter 9) with the studies of Bangladesh and India (Chapters 5 and 8 respectively) throws additional light on this development. Employment elasticity with respect to output growth in Indonesia's manufacturing sector was quite high during the 1980s and started declining only during the 1990s. Bangladesh, on the other hand, had a lower average employment elasticity in manufacturing that had already started declining—although the incidence of poverty remained at a very high level. And the record of poverty reduction in Bangladesh was also modest compared to Indonesia. Likewise in India, although economic growth during the 1990s was higher than in the 1980s, the employment and labor market situation did not appear to register a corresponding improvement. The rate of poverty reduction also remained modest.

A high employment intensity of growth is also not sufficient for poverty reduction, because many of the world's poor are not unemployed. And poverty in such cases is more due to the inability of many jobs to ensure decent levels of income and living. A major challenge, therefore, is to increase productivity and income alongside increases in employment. Country studies assembled in the book demonstrate this quite well. The preeconomic crisis experience of Indonesia provides a good example of high employment intensity coupled with increases in labor productivity creating the foundations for increases in real wages and earnings. Except for short periods, labor productivity and real wages in Indonesia moved hand in hand, and as a result, income poverty registered an impressive decline. In Ethiopia, on the other hand, there were improvements in productivity growth, but a decline in overall employment during the 1990s. Of course, in manufacturing, improvement in productivity was associated with a healthy growth of real wages. But given the small size of the sector relative to the overall economy, and slow employment growth in the sector, real wage growth in Ethiopia was not able to create much impact on the poverty situation. Bolivia's experience provides an extreme case of real wage increases in manufacturing without much improvement in productivity; such a pattern could not be sustained. The upshot of these examples (among others) is that for high economic growth to result in corresponding rate of poverty reduction, growth must be employment-intensive and at the same time, productivity, real wages, and earnings (of both wage workers and the self-employed) must rise.

Another important factor that contributes to poverty reduction is diversification of the economy and the sources of livelihoods of poor households. The importance of a structural shift of employment toward higher productivity sectors was noted in the analytic frameworks presented in Chapters 2–4, especially in Chapter 3. The country studies lend support to this contention. First, in the econometric exercises undertaken to examine the importance of different variables in explaining the probability of a household being poor, the variables relating to diversified sources of income often turn out to have significant explanatory power. Two distinct aspects of diversification need to be noted. In some situations, poor households use multiple occupations as a strategy for survival and getting out of poverty. On the other hand, in fast-growing, dynamic economies, nontraditional economic activities with higher productivity should open up possibilities for the poor to move out of the traditional low-productivity activities. Indonesia's experience before the Asian economic crisis (of 1998) and Vietnam's recent experience provide examples of the latter type of diversification playing a major role in reducing poverty, especially in rural areas. In Vietnam, while there were shifts to higher-value crops within agriculture, nonfarm self-employment in rural areas also registered high growth during the 1990s. The econometric exercises undertaken in the various country studies also demonstrate the important role of employment in nonfarm sectors in reducing the probability of a household being poor.

A related factor is access to assets. The ability of a household to diversify its sources of income and to move to higher-productivity activities depends critically on its access to productive assets and credit from formal institutions. This is especially the case because of a slow growth of wage employment in the modern sector, which appears to have become a common pattern in the current economic growth regime in many countries. The econometric exercises reported in the country studies also indicate the importance of access to assets and credit in influencing the probability of a household moving out of poverty.

The analytic framework outlined in Chapters 2–4 places a good deal of importance on the capacity of the poor to integrate into the growth process through the labor market channel. And in this respect, education and skills can play an important role. Indeed, development literature points out the role that investment in human capital formation plays in boosting economic development that benefits the poor. The empirical analyses presented in the book also indicates the importance of education in reducing poverty. For example, cross-country regressions reported in Chapter 3 indicate the strong influence of literacy on poverty, and the country studies also show that education contributes positively to poverty reduction.

The case studies assembled here have important implications for public policy. There can be two broad types of public policy aimed at poverty reduction. First, policies can be aimed not just at raising the rate of economic growth, but also at influencing the pattern of growth—or at giving growth a more pro-poor orientation. The second category of policies would include direct interventions, some of which are often targeted at the poor. Direct interventions could, in turn, be of two types: one linked to development-oriented programs, and the other intended to provide safety nets for the poor. Development-oriented direct interventions (which would include, for example, targeted programs in the areas of credit, technology, extension services, etc.) have an interface with the first category of policies, because such interventions can be important in shaping economic growth in a pro-poor direction.

The policy implications that arise from the volume belong to both categories, although it must be added that the country studies do not aim at providing a detailed discussion of such policies.

First, as employment is a key element in linking economic growth to poverty reduction, policies for pro-poor growth would mean policies for employment-intensive growth. Strategies for poverty reduction must therefore integrate strategies for high rates of output growth with those for a rapid expansion of productive employment. And that would require making employment an integral element in the process of formulating macroeconomic policies.[1] In other words, employment concerns must be incorporated into macroeconomic policy goals and targets, and the employment and labor market impact of various elements of macroeconomic policies will need to be analyzed before a policy package is adopted. Apart from the implications of the debate on fiscal prudence and inflation targeting for economic growth, human development and social protection, macroeconomic policies can have a significant outcome on the employment outcome of a given rate of economic growth through their effects on the different sectors and subsectors of the economy. It should be possible to have a pro-employment macropolicy regime by taking into account the possible employment effects of tariffs, exchange rates, and taxation policies on the growth of sectors and subsectors that are, by their nature, more labor-intensive than others.

Second, as similar packages of economic reforms appear to be producing different results in terms of the rate and sustainability of economic growth as well as its employment-generating and poverty-reducing effects, this has important implications for public policy in this area. Clearly, a one-size-fits-all approach is not very useful. Reform-induced growth appears to have been pro-poor in situations where agriculture has benefited from the reforms, because agriculture, in many poor countries, still accounts for a sizable share of the GDP as well as the country's poor. Likewise, if reforms can lead to the growth of nonfarm activities in rural areas and labor-intensive manufacturing, the poor are likely to benefit from such growth. These aspects need to be taken into consideration while formulating and implementing measures of economic reforms (especially in the sequencing of their various elements).

Third, a number of measures on the supply side can be useful in producing a conducive environment and necessary incentive structures for investment in employment-intensive sectors. Investment in physical infrastructures (e.g., roads, irrigation and water management) is one such measure. The critical importance of infrastructure in catalyzing development is well known. By opening up and linking hitherto isolated remote areas, roads and improved transport can play a critical role in facilitating the growth of employment-intensive (and hence pro-poor) economic activities. From the point of view of poverty reduction, there are at least two more reasons for providing particular attention to investment in infrastructure. The first relates to the weight of this sector in a typical developing-country economy, and the second to options available in terms of choice of technology. Very large proportions of public investment in such countries are devoted to infrastructure. And for a sizable segment of the sector (e.g., feeder roads, maintenance, irrigation, water management, etc.), labor-intensive methods can be applied without compromising quality and efficiency.[2] These considerations, along with the potential multiplier effects and development-catalyzing impact of infrastructure, make investment in infrastructure a top priority in strategies for pro-poor growth.

Fourth, apart from infrastructure, other supply-side measures mentioned in almost all the country studies include support for higher-level technology and extension service. Clearly, these are areas where governments have an important role to play, especially in the context of poverty and the inability of the poor to pay for support services. The other element mentioned (not surprisingly) is credit. It is well known that NGOs are active in this area—with useful positive results—in many developing countries. But even in this area, governments can play a useful role in providing the necessary policy environment within which microcredit operations would be carried out.

Fifth, the country studies reaffirm the role of human capital (in terms of education and skills) in reducing poverty. Indeed, education and skills are among major factors influencing the ability of the poor in obtaining access to opportunities that are created by the process of economic growth. And public policy has a critical role to play in this regard, especially in providing basic education and skills. Apart from directly creating necessary infrastructure in these areas, governments also have an important role to play in putting in place a conducive environment and framework for private investment to take place and for enterprises to come forward in areas of skill development.

Sixth, in a number of countries (Bolivia and Vietnam, for example), poverty may be linked to ethnicity, which in turn may also have a regional dimension. In these cases, targeted measures aimed at the disadvantaged groups and regions would be needed.

Seventh, safety net measures will be needed even when a country achieves high and employment-intensive growth. There are several reasons for this. One is the existence of poor households who do not have adequate labor endowment, and hence would need direct income transfers. The second reason why safety nets are needed is the possibility of short-term dislocations and displacement of workers in the context of structural changes in market economies. Changes that take place in the sectoral composition of such economies are likely to cause job losses in some sectors for some workers, although new jobs can be expected to be created elsewhere in the economy. Safety nets are needed to enable workers to cope with such adjustment processes. Third, in a globalized world with increasing interdependence among countries, the possibility of external economic shocks and their adverse effects on employment and labor markets need to be taken into account. Experience with the aftermaths of such shocks during economic crises in different parts of the world (e.g., East Asia in 1997–1998 and Argentina in 2001–2002) clearly shows the importance of effective safety nets. Finally, safety nets are also needed in countries that are vulnerable to shocks due to natural disasters. A large number of the world's low-income developing countries fall into this category; and it is the poor in such countries who face the greatest difficulties in coping with such shocks. Preparedness to protect the poor in such crisis situations is an important part of pro-poor public policy.

■ Notes

1. The World Commission on the Social Dimensions of Globalization (International Labour Organization 2004) also calls for the development of instruments and methods that can promote coherence between economic and social goals.

2. For more details on the two points mentioned here, see Islam and Majeres 2001.

Bibliography

Abdulhamid, B. K. (1996): "Poverty and Nutritional Status in Urban Ethiopia." In K. Bereket and T. Mekonnen (eds.), *Proceedings of the Fifth Annual Conference on the Ethiopian Economy*. Ethiopian Economic Association, Addis Ababa.

Acemoglu, D., and R. Shimmer (2000): "Productivity Gains from Unemployment Insurance." *European Economic Review* 44(7): 1195–1224.

Action Aid Vietnam (1999): *Ha Tinh Province: A Participatory Poverty Assessment*. Action Aid, Hanoi.

Adam, C., and D. Bevan (2003): "Aid, Public Expenditure, and Dutch Disease." Centre for the Study of African Economics working paper. Oxford University Press, Oxford.

Adams, D. W. (1988): *The Conundrum of Successful Credit Projects in Floundering Rural Financial Markets*. University of Chicago Press, Chicago.

Adelman, I., and C. T. Morris (1973): *Economic Growth and Social Equity in Developing Countries*. Stanford University Press, Stanford.

Agenor, P. (2002): "Macroeconomic Adjustment and the Poor: Analytical Issues and Cross-Country Evidence." Mimeo. World Bank, Washington, D.C., January 14.

Agrawal, N. (1995): "Indonesia: Labour Market Policies and International Competitiveness." Background paper for *World Development Report 1995*. World Bank, Washington, D.C.

――― (1996): "The Benefits of Growth for Indonesian Workers." Policy Research Working Paper no. 1637. World Bank, Washington, D.C.

Ahluwalia, M. S., N. Carter, and H. Chenery (1979): "Growth and Poverty in Developing Countries." *Journal of Development Economics* 6: 299–341.

Akerlof, G., W. Dickens, and G. Perry (1996): "The Macroeconomics of Low Inflation." *Brookings Papers on Economic Activity* (1): 1–76.

Alam, M. S. (2002): "Poverty Profile of Bangladesh 1999: Selected Socio-Economic Indicators." Paper presented at the regional seminar *Poverty Monitoring Survey 1999*. Centre on Integrated Rural Development for Asia and the Pacific and Bangladesh Bureau of Statistics, Dhaka.

Alamsyah, H., et al. (2001): "Towards Implementation of Inflation Targeting in Indonesia." *Bulletin of Indonesian Economic Studies* 37(3): 309–324.

Alemayehu, G., S. Abebe, and J. Weeks (2003): "The Pattern of Growth, Poverty, and Inequality: Which Way for a Pro-Poor Growth?" Paper presented at the first international conference on the Ethiopian economy. United Nations Conference Centre, Addis Ababa, January 3–5.

Alisjahbana, A. S., and C. Manning (2002): "Survey of Recent Developments." *Bulletin of Indonesian Economic Studies* 38(3): 277–305.

Amjad, R., and A. R. Kemal (1997): "Macroeconomic Policies and Their Impact on Poverty Alleviation in Pakistan." *Pakistan Development Review* 36(1) (Spring): 36–38.

Appleton, S. (1999): "Changes in Poverty in Uganda, 1992–1997." Centre for the Study of African Economics Working Paper no. 106. Mimeo. Oxford University Press, Oxford.

———— (2001): "Changes in Poverty and Inequality." In Ritva Reinikka and Paul Collier (eds.), *Uganda's Recovery: The Role of Farms, Firms, and Government.* World Bank, Washington, D.C.

Appleton, S., and A. Balihuta (1996): "Education and Agricultural Productivity: Evidence from Uganda." *Journal of International Development* 8(3): 415–444.

Asia Recovery Information Centre (2001): "Asia Recovery Report." Asian Development Bank, Manila, September 2001.

———— (2002–2003): "Asia Recovery Report." Updates. Asian Development Bank, Manila.

Asian Development Bank, Australian Agency for International Development, UK Department for International Development, German Agency for Technical Cooperation, Japan International Cooperation Agency, Save the Children UK, United Nations Development Programme, and World Bank (2003): Joint donor report to the Consultative Group Meeting, Hanoi, December 2–3.

Atingi-Ego, M., and R. Sebudde (2001): "Uganda's Equilibrium Real Exchange Rate and Its Implications for Non-Traditional Exports." *Bank of Uganda Staff Papers* 1(1). Paper no. RP 140.

Badan Pusat Statistik, Badan Perencanaan Pembangunan Nasional, and United Nations Development Programme (2001): *Indonesia Human Development Report 2001: Towards a New Consensus—Democracy and Human Development in Indonesia.* United Nations Development Programme, Jakarta.

Bagachwa, M. D., and F. Stewart (1990): "Rural Industries and Rural Linkages in Sub-Saharan Africa: A Survey." Ld'A-QEH Development Working Paper no. 23. Queen Elizabeth House, Oxford.

Bakht, Z. (1996): "The Rural Non-Farm Sector in Bangladesh: Evolving Patterns and Growth Potential." National workshop on *Stimulating Growth Through the Rural Non-Farm Activities in Bangladesh: Review of the Experience and Search for a Policy Agenda.* Bangladesh Institute for Development Studies and World Bank, Dhaka.

Bales, S., D. T. Phung, and S. C. Ho (2001): "Sectoral Changes and Poverty." In D. Haughton, J. Haughton, and P. Nguyen (eds.), *Living Standards During an Economic Boom.* Statistical Publishing House, Hanoi.

Bangladesh Bureau of Statistics (BBS) (various years): *Labour Force Survey.* Dhaka.

———— (various years): *Report on Bangladesh Census of Manufacturing Industries.* Dhaka.

———— (various years): *Statistical Yearbook of Bangladesh.* Dhaka.

———— (1999–2000): *Report on Labour Force Survey.* Dhaka.

———— (2001a): *Bangladesh Economic Survey.* Ministry of Finance, Dhaka.

———— (2001b): *Household Income Expenditure Survey 2000.* Dhaka.

———— (2002): *Report of Poverty Monitoring Survey.* Ministry of Planning, Dhaka.

Bangladesh Institute for Development Studies (BIDS) (2001): *Fighting Human Poverty: Bangladesh Human Development Report 2000*. Dhaka.

Bangsal, K., and B. Sari (2000): "Indonesian Study on Voices of the Poor." In *World Development Report 2000/2001*. Oxford University Press, New York.

Bank of Indonesia (2000): "Economic, Monetary, and Banking Developments, 2nd Qtr." Mimeo. Jakarta.

Bank of Uganda (1993): "Credit for Small Enterprises: Enterprise Development Projects." Development Finance Department, Kampala.

Beattie, R. (2000): "Social Protection for All: But How?" *International Labour Review* 139(2): 129–148.

Behrman, J. R., N. Birdsall, and M. Szekely (2000): "Economic Reform and Wage Differentials in Latin America." Research Working Paper no. 435. Inter-American Development Bank, Washington, D.C.

Bell, C., S. Devarajan, and H. Gersbach (2003): "The Long-Run Costs of AIDS: Theory and an Application to South Africa." Mimeo. World Bank, Washington, D.C.

Belser, P. (1999): "Vietnam: On the Road to Labour-Intensive Growth." Background paper for *Vietnam Development Report 2000*. United Nations Development Programme, Hanoi.

Belshaw, D., P. Lawrence, and M. Hubbard (1999): "Agricultural Tradeables and Economic Recovery in Uganda: The Limitations of Structural Adjustment in Practice." *World Development* (27): 673–690.

Benjamin, D., and L. Brandt (2001): "Agriculture and Income Distribution in Vietnam During the Reform Period." Mimeo. World Bank, Washington, D.C.

Berck, P., C. Costello, L. Fortman, and S. Hoffman (2000): "Poverty and Employment in Timber-Dependent Countries." Discussion Paper no. 00-52. Resource for the Future, Washington, D.C.

Berry, A., E. Rodriguez, and S. Hoffman (2001): "Small and Medium Enterprise Dynamics in Indonesia." *Bulletin of Indonesian Economic Studies* 37(3): 363–384.

Berthelemy, J. C., L. Soderling, J. M. Salmon, H. B. Solignac, L. Bevan, et al. (n.d.): "Economic Growth, Investment, and Export Expansion." Discussion paper prepared for the Ugandan Ministry of Finance, Planning, and Development. Kampala.

Bevan, D., J. Okidi, and F. Muhumuza (2003): "Poverty Eradication Action Plan Revision 2002–03: Discussion Paper on *Economic Growth, Investment, and Export Promotion.*" Mimeo. Kampala, July.

Bevan, P., and K. Bereket (1996): "Measuring Wealth and Poverty in Rural Ethiopia: A Data-Based Discussion." In K. Bereket and T. Mekonnen (eds.), *Proceedings of the Fifth Annual Conference on the Ethiopian Economy*. Ethiopian Economic Association, Addis Ababa.

Bhagwati, J. N. (1988): "Poverty and Public Policy." *World Development* 16(5): 539–654.

Bhalla, S. (2003): "India's Rural Economy: Issues and Evidence." Joint Overseas Development Institute–Institute for Human Development working paper. New Delhi.

Bhat, M. (2001): "Indian Demographic Scenario, 2025." Institute of Economic Growth Discussion Paper no. 27. Institute of Economic Growth, New Delhi, June.

Bhattacharya, D. (2001): "Bangladesh Economy in FY 2000: Macro-Economic Outlook." In *Changes and Challenges: A Review of Bangladesh's Development 2000*. Centre for Policy Dialogue and University Press Limited, Dhaka.

Bhavani, T. A., and S. D. Tendulkar (2000): "Determinants of Firm-Level Export Performance: A Case Study of Indian Garment Industry." *Journal of International Trade and Development* 10(1) (March): 65–92.

Bigsten, A., and M. Negatu (1999): "The Anatomy of Income Distribution in Urban Ethiopia." *African Development Review* 11(1): 1–30.

Bigsten, A., et al. (1999): "Exports of African Manufactures: Macro Policy and Firm Behaviour." *Journal of International Trade and Development* 8(1): 53–71.

Bigsten, S., K. Bereket, S. Abebe, and T. Mekonnen (2002): "Growth and Poverty Reduction in Ethiopia: Evidence from Household Panel Surveys." Working Paper in Economics no. 65. Department of Economics, Göteborg University, Sweden.

Bloom, D., and A. Mahal (1997): "Does the AIDS Epidemic Threaten Economic Growth?" *Journal of Econometrics* (77): 105–124.

Bloom, D., and J. Sachs (1998): "Geography, Demography, and Economic Growth in Africa." *Brookings Papers on Economic Activity* (2): 207–295. (Includes comments by P. Collier and C. Udry.)

Boltho, C. (1994): *China's Emergence: Prospects, Opportunities, and Challenges.* International Economics Department, World Bank, Washington, D.C.

Bonaglia, F., and K. Fukasaku (2002): *Trading Competitively: Trade Capacity Building in Sub-Saharan Africa.* Organization for Economic Cooperation and Development, Paris.

Bonnel, R. (2000): "Economic Analysis of HIV/AIDS." African Development Forum background paper. World Bank, Washington, D.C.

Booth, A. (1999): "Survey of Recent Developments." *Bulletin of Indonesian Economic Studies* 35(3): 3–38.

——— (2000): "Poverty and Inequality in the Soeharto Era: An Assessment." *Bulletin of Indonesian Economic Studies* 36(1).

Breman, J. (2000): "The Impact of the Asian Crisis on Work and Welfare in Village Java." Dies Natalis 2000 address delivered at the forty-eighth-anniversary assembly of the Institute of Social Studies. The Hague, October 12.

Brett, E. A. (1992): "Providing for the Rural Poor: Institutional Decay and Transformation in Uganda." Research Report no. 23. University of Sussex, Institute of Development Studies, Sussex.

Campbell, D. (1999): "Globalization and Change: Social Dialogue and Labour Market Adjustment in the Crisis-Affected Economies of East Asia." Mimeo. International Labour Organization and East Asia Multidisciplinary Advisory Team, Manila.

Canagarajah, S., and D. Mazumdar (2001): "Employment, Labour Markets, and Poverty in Ghana: A Study of Changes During Economic Decline and Recovery." Unpublished background paper for Economic Sector Work. World Bank, Washington, D.C.

Central Institute for Economic Management (CIEM) (2002): *Vietnam's Economy in 2001.* National Political Publishers, Government of Vietnam, Hanoi.

Central Statistical Authority (various years): *Annual Survey of Large and Medium Scale Manufacturing Industries.* Government of Ethiopia, Addis Ababa.

Central Statistical Organization (2003): *National Accounts Statistics 2003.* Government of India, New Delhi.

——— (2004): "Press Note on Quick Estimates of National Income, Consumption Expenditure, Saving, and Capital Formation, 2002–2003." Government of India, New Delhi, January 30.

Centre for International Economics (2002): "Vietnam Poverty Analysis." Report prepared for the Australian Agency for International Development. Canberra.

Chaudhuri, S., J. Jalan, and A. Suryahadi (2001): "Assessing Household Vulnerability to Poverty: A Methodology and Estimates for Indonesia." Paper presented to the workshop *Poverty and Vulnerability: Third Asia Development Forum.* Bangkok.

Chen, S., and M. Ravallion (2001): *How Did the World's Poorest Fare in the 1990's?* Development Research Group, World Bank, Washington, D.C.

Chenery, H., M. S. Ahluwalia, C. L. G. Bell, J. H. Duloy, and R. Jolly (1974): *Redistribution with Growth.* Oxford University Press, New York.

Chirmatsion, G. (1996): "Aspects of Poverty in the City of Addis Ababa: Profile and Policy Implications." In K. Bereket and T. Mekonnen (eds.), *Proceedings of the Fifth Annual Conference on the Ethiopian Economy.* Ethiopian Economic Association, Addis Ababa.

Chowdhury, A. (2003): "Financing Human Development." Mimeo. United Nations Support Facility for Indonesian Recovery, Jakarta.

Cloudeaul, A., J. Henstchel, and Q. Wodon (2001): "Well-Being Measurement and Analysis." Draft prepared under poverty reduction strategy paper. World Bank, Washington, D.C., April.

Collier, P., and D. Dollar (2002): "Aid Allocation and Poverty Reduction." *European Economic Review* (46): 1475–1500.

Comisión Económica para América Latina (CEPAL) (2000): *Social Panorama in Latin America.* Santiago.

——— (2001): *Preliminary Overview of the Economies of LAC.* Santiago.

Dagdeviren, H., R. Hoeven, and J. Weeks (2001): "Redistribution Matters: Growth for Poverty Reduction." Employment Paper no. 2001/10. International Labour Office, Geneva.

——— (2002): "Poverty Reduction with Growth and Redistribution." *Development and Change* 33(3): 383–413.

Dasgupta, P. (1993): *An Inquiry into Well-Being and Destitution.* Clarendon Press, Oxford.

Datt, G. (1997): *Poverty in India and Indian States: An Update.* International Food Policy Research Institute, Washington, D.C.

——— (1999): "Has Poverty Declined Since Economic Reforms?" *Economic and Political Weekly* 34(50): 3516–3518.

Datt, G., S. Kenneth, M. Sanjukta, and D. Gabriel (2000): "Determinants of Poverty in Mozambique: 1996–97." International Food Policy Research Institute, Washington, D.C.

Datt, G., V. Kozel, and M. Ravallion (2003): "A Model-Based Assessment of India's Progress in Reducing Poverty in the 1990s." *Economic and Political Weekly,* January 25.

David, I. P., A. Asra, and M. De Castro (1999): "Poverty Incidence in the Asian and Pacific Region: Data Situation and Measurement Issues." Mimeo. Asian Development Bank, Manila.

de Hann, A., and A. Dubey (2003): "Characteristics Behind Chronic Poverty." Paper presented at the Chronic Poverty Research Centre. University of Manchester, April 2003.

Deaton, A. (2003): "Adjusted Indian Poverty Estimates." *Economic and Political Weekly,* January 25.

Deaton, A., and Jean Dreze (2002): "Poverty and Inequality in India: A Re-examination." *Economic and Political Weekly,* September 7.

Deichmann, J., D. Haughton, P. Nguyen, and D. T. Phung (2001): "Correlates of Living Standards: A Graphical and Statistical Analysis." In D. Haughton, J.

Haughton, and P. Nguyen (eds.), *Living Standards During an Economic Boom.* Statistical Publishing House, Government of Vietnam, Hanoi.

Deininger, K., and J. Okidi (2002): "Growth and Poverty Reduction in Uganda, 1992–2000: Panel Data Evidence." Research Series no. 29. Makerere University, Economic Policy Research Centre, Kampala.

Demeke, M., F. Guta, and T. Ferede (2003): "Growth, Poverty, and Employment Policies in Ethiopia: An Empirical Investigation." Issues in Employment and Poverty Discussion Paper no. 12. Recovery and Reconstruction Department, International Labour Organization, Geneva.

Demeke, M., and B. Hunde (2003): "Population Pressure and Intensification of Agricultural Practices in Ethiopia: An Enquiry into Sustainability of Farming Practices." Paper presented at the first international conference on the Ethiopian economy. United Nations Conference Centre, Addis Ababa, January 3–5.

Demery, L., and L. Squire (1995): "Poverty in Africa: An Emerging Picture." Mimeo. World Bank, Washington, D.C.

Department for International Development (DFID) (1997): *Eliminating World Poverty: A Challenge for the 21st Century.* CM 3789. Stationery Office, London.

——— (2002): *Making Globalisation Work for the Poor.* White paper. London.

Dercon, S. (1998): "Changes in Poverty in Rural Ethiopia, 1989–1995: Measurement, Robustness Tests, and Decomposition." WPS/98-8. Centre for the Study of African Economics, UK.

——— (2001): "Economic Reforms, Growth, and the Poor: Evidence from Rural Ethiopia." WPS/2001-8. Centre for the Study of African Economics, UK.

Dercon, S., and P. Krishnan (2000): "Vulnerability, Seasonality, and Poverty in Ethiopia." *Journal of Development Studies* 36(6): 25–53.

Dhanani, S. (2001): "Unemployment and Underemployment in Indonesia Before and During the Financial Crisis." Background paper prepared for the InFocus Socio-Economic Security Programme of the International Labour Organization. Geneva.

——— (2002): "Strengthening the Indonesian Labour Market Information System." Paper prepared for the Recovery and Reconstruction Department of the International Labour Organization. Geneva.

Dhanani, S., and W. Diah (2001): "Indonesian Reform Agenda and Employment Prospects." Mimeo. International Labour Organization Area Office, Jakarta.

Dhanani, S., and I. Islam (2000): "Poverty, Inequality, and Social Protection: Lessons from the Indonesian Crisis." United Nations Development Programme/United Nations Support Facility for Indonesian Recovery Working Paper no. 00/01. United Nations Development Programme, Jakarta.

——— (2001a): "Indonesian Wage Structure and Trends, 1976–2000." Background paper prepared for the InFocus Socio-Economic Security Programme. International Labour Organization, Geneva.

——— (2001b): "Labour Market Adjustment to Indonesia's Economic Crisis: A Comment." *Bulletin of Indonesian Economic Studies* 37(1): 113–115.

——— (2002): "Poverty, Vulnerability, and Social Protection in a Period of Crisis: The Case of Indonesia." *World Development* 30(7): 1211–1231.

Dhar, P. N. (1990): *Constraints on Growth, Reflections on the Indian Experience.* Oxford University Press, New Delhi.

Division for the Advancement of Women and United Nations (1999): *1999 World Survey on the Role of Women in Development: Globalization, Gender, and Work.* Division for the Advancement of Women, Department of Economic and Social Affairs, United Nations, New York.

―――― (2001): "The Situation of Rural Women Within the Context of Globalization." Report of the Expert Group Meeting held in Ulaabbaatar, Mongolia, June 4–8. Division for the Advancement of Women, Department of Economic and Social Affairs, United Nations, New York.

Do, T. K., D. M. Le, T. D. Lo, N. M. Nguyen, Q. Tran, and X. D. Bui (2001): "Inequality." In D. Haughton, J. Haughton, and P. Nguyen (eds.), *Living Standards During an Economic Boom.* Statistical Publishing House, Government of Vietnam, Hanoi.

Dollar, D., and P. Glewwe (1998): "Poverty and Inequality in the Early Reform Period." In D. Dollar, P. Glewwe, and J. Litvack (eds.), *Household Welfare and Vietnam's Transition.* World Bank Regional and Sectoral Studies. World Bank, Washington, D.C.

Dollar, D., and A. Kray (2001): "Growth Is Good for the Poor." Policy Research Working Paper no. 2587. World Bank, Washington, D.C.

Dunn, D. (2002): "Economic Growth in Uganda: A Summary of the Post-Conflict Experience and Future Prospects." Mimeo. International Monetary Fund, Washington, D.C.

Economic and Social Commission for Asia and the Pacific (2000): "Social Security and Safety Nets." In *Economic and Social Survey of Asia and the Pacific.* ESCAP Publishing, Bangkok.

Economic Commission for Latin America and the Caribbean (2003): *Social Panorama of Latin America, 2001–2002.* Santiago.

Economic Relations Division (2002): *Bangladesh: A National Strategy for Economic Growth and Poverty Reduction.* Government of Bangladesh, Dhaka.

Economist Intelligence Unit (2005): *Indonesia Country Profile: Main Report—October 29th, 2004.* Available online at http://www.eiu.com.

Edwards, S. (1996): "Labour Regulations and Industrial Relations in Indonesia." Paper presented to the Ministry of Manpower/World Bank workshop *Indonesian Workers in the 21st Century.* Jakarta, April 2–4.

Eshetu, C., and M. Manyazewal (1992): "The Macroeconomic Performance of the Ethiopian Economy." In K. Bereket and T. Mekonnen (eds.), *Proceedings of the First Annual Conference on the Ethiopian Economy.* Ethiopian Economic Association, Addis Ababa.

Ethiopian Economic Association (2000): *Annual Report on the Ethiopian Economy.* Vol. 2. Addis Ababa.

Ettema, W. (1992): *Agricultural Policies in Developing Countries.* Cambridge University Press, Cambridge.

Fan, S., P. Hazell, and S. Thorat (2000): "Government Spending, Growth, and Poverty in Rural India." *American Journal of Agricultural Economics* 82(4): 1038–1051.

Fan, S., L. Zhang, and X. Zhang (2002): *Growth, Inequality, and Poverty in Rural China: The Role of Public Investments.* Research Report no. 125. International Food Policy Research Institute, Washington, D.C.

Fields, G. (1980): *Poverty, Inequality, and Development.* Cambridge University Press, New York.

―――― (1991): "Growth and Income Distribution." In G. Psacharopolous (ed.), *Essays on Poverty, Equity, and Growth.* Pergamon Press, New York.

―――― (1995): "Income Distribution in Developing Economies: Conceptual, Data, and Policy Issues in Broad Based Growth." In M. G. Quibria (ed.), *Critical Issues in Asian Development: Theories, Experiences, and Policies.* Oxford University Press, Hong Kong.

Foster, J., J. Greer, and E. Thorbecke (1984): "A Class of Decomposable Poverty Measures." *Econometrica* (52): 761–766.

Friedman, M. (1957): *A Theory of the Consumption Function.* Princeton University Press, Princeton.

Galbraith, J., and V. G. Cantu (1999): "Inequality in American Manufacturing Wages, 1920–1998: A Revised Estimate." Draft, University of Texas Inequality Project. Available online at http://utip.gov.utexas.edu.

Gautier, B. (2002): "Exchange Rate Impact on the Production and Productivity of Firms in Uganda." Mimeo. Department for International Development, London.

Gemini (1995): "Employment and Income in Micro and Small Enterprises in Kenya: Results of a 1995 Survey." Technical Report no. 92. Development Alternatives, Bethesda.

General Statistical Office (GSO) (various years): *Statistical Yearbook.* Statistical Publishing House, Government of Vietnam, Hanoi.

———— (2000): *Socio-Economic Statistical Data of Vietnam, 1975–2000.* Statistical Publishing House, Government of Vietnam, Hanoi.

———— (2001): *Vietnam's Economy During the Years of Renovation Mirrored in Aggregate Economic Indicators of the System of National Accounts.* Statistical Publishing House, Government of Vietnam, Hanoi.

Ghose, A. (2000): "Trade Liberalization and Manufacturing Employment." Employment Paper no. 2000/3. International Labour Organization, Geneva.

Ghura, D., C. Loiter, and C. Tsangarides (2002): "Is Growth Enough? Macroeconomic Policy and Poverty Reduction." Working Paper no. WP/02/118. International Monetary Fund, Washington, D.C.

Glewwe, P., M. Gragnolati, and H. Zaman (2000): *Who Gained from Vietnam's Boom in the 1990s? An Analysis of Poverty and Inequality Trends.* Development Research Group Working Paper no. 2275. World Bank, Washington, D.C.

Goitom, C. (1996): "Aspects of Poverty in the City of Addis Ababa: Profile and Policy Implications." In K. Bereket and T. Mekonnen (eds.), *Proceedings of the Fifth Annual Conference on the Ethiopian Economy.* Ethiopian Economic Association, Addis Ababa.

Goudie, A., and P. Ladd (1999): "Economic Growth, Poverty, and Inequality." *Journal of International Development* (11): 177–195.

Government of Bolivia (2001): *Estrategia Boliviana de Reducción de la Pobreza, Diálogo Nacional.* La Paz.

Government of India (1995): "NSS 50th Round (1993–1994) Consumer Expenditure Survey." National Statistical Service (NSS), New Delhi.

———— (1997): *Report of the Expert Committee on Small Scale Industries.* Department of Small Scale Industries and Agro-Based Industries, Ministry of Industries, New Delhi.

———— (2000): *Mid-Term Appraisal of the Ninth Five-Year Plan (1997–2002).* Planning Commission, New Delhi.

———— (2001a): *Economic Reforms: A Medium-Term Perspective.* Recommendations of the Prime Minister's Economic Advisory Council. Planning Commission and Economic Advisory Council, New Delhi.

———— (2001b): *Report of Task Force on Employment Opportunities.* Planning Commission, New Delhi.

Government of Indonesia (2003): "Economic Policy Package in Conjunction with the Completion of the Government's Program with the IMF." White paper. Jakarta.

Government of Uganda (2001): *Uganda Poverty Status Report.* Ministry of Finance, Planning, and Economic Development, Kampala.

———— (2002a): "Challenges and Prospects for Poverty Reduction in Northern Uganda." Discussion Paper no. 5. Ministry of Finance, Planning, and Economic Development, Kampala, March.

———— (2002b): *Second Participatory Assessment Report: Deepening the Understanding of Poverty.* Ministry of Finance, Planning, and Economic Development, Kampala.

———— (2003a): "Government Interventions to Promote the Production, Processing, and Marketing of Selected Strategic Exports." Progress report, September 2001–March 2003. Ministry of Finance, Planning, and Economic Development, Kampala.

———— (2003b): *Poverty Status Report 2003.* Ministry of Finance, Planning, and Economic Development, Kampala.

———— (2003c): "Strategies to Promote Economic Growth." Paper presented to the 2003 Consultative Group Meeting. Ministry of Finance, Planning, and Economic Development, Kampala.

———— (2003d). *Uganda Participatory Poverty Assessment Report (UPPAP) National Report.* Ministry of Finance, Planning, and Economic Development, Kampala.

Hanmer, L., and F. Naschold (2000): "Attaining the International Development Targets: Will Growth Be Enough?" *Development Policy Review* 18(1): 11–36.

Harrod, R. (1959): "Domar and Dynamic Economics." *Economic Journal* 49 (September): 451–464.

Haughton, D., J. Haughton, T. T. L. Le, and P. Nguyen (2001): "Shooting Stars and Sinking Stones." In D. Haughton, J. Haughton, and P. Nguyen (eds.), *Living Standards During an Economic Boom.* Statistical Publishing House, Government of Vietnam, Hanoi.

Haughton, J. (2001): "Introduction: Extraordinary Changes." In D. Haughton, J. Haughton, and P. Nguyen (eds.), *Living Standards During an Economic Boom.* Statistical Publishing House, Government of Vietnam, Hanoi.

Hayami, Y. (1997): *Development Economics: From Poverty to the Wealth of Nations.* Clarendon Press, Oxford.

Heckscher, Eli (1991): "The Effect of Foreign Trade on the Distribution of Income." In Bertil Ohlin and Eli Heckscher, *Heckscher-Ohlin Trade Theory.* Massachusetts Institute of Technology Press, Cambridge.

Hernani, W. (2002): "Mercado Laboral, Pobreza y Desigualdad en Bolivia, in Estadísticas y Análisis, Revista de Estudios Económicos y Sociales." Mecovi Bolivia, Gesellschaft für Technische Zusammenarbeit and Instituto Nacional de Estadisticas, La Paz.

Hiedholm, C., and J. Parker (1980): "Small Scale Business in Africa: Initial Evidence." Working Paper no. 33. Presented to the conference *Policy Approaches Towards Technology and Small Encounter Person Development.* Kampala.

Hoang, Van Kinh, B. Baulch, Q. D. Le, V. D. Nguyen, D. G. Ngo, and N. K. Nguyen (2001): "Determinants of Earned Income." In D. Haughton, J. Haughton, and P. Nguyen (eds.), *Living Standards During an Economic Boom.* Statistical Publishing House, Government of Vietnam, Hanoi.

Horton, S. (1994): "Bolivia." In S. Horton, R. Kanbur, and D. Mazumdar (eds.), *Labor Markets in an Era of Adjustment,* vol. 2. World Bank, Washington, D.C.

Hossain, M. (1992): "Determinants of Poverty." In H. Z. Rahman and M. Hossain (eds.), *Rethinking Rural Poverty: A Case for Bangladesh.* Bangladesh Institute for Development Studies, Dhaka.

———— (1996a): "Rural Income and Poverty Trends." In H. Z. Rahman, M. Hossain, and B. Sen (eds.), *1987–1994: Dynamics of Rural Poverty in Bangladesh.* Mimeo. Bangladesh Institute for Development Studies, Dhaka.

———— (1996b): "Structure of the Labour Market: Unemployment Poverty in Bangladesh." Paper presented at the regional seminar *Labour Market and Industrial Relations in South Asia: Emerging Issues and Policy Options.* Indian Society of Labour Economics and Indian Industrial Relations Association, New Delhi, September 18–20.

Huong, P. L., B. Q. Tuan, and D. H. Minh (2003): "Employment Poverty Linkages and Policies in Vietnam." Issues in Employment and Poverty Discussion Paper no. 9. Recovery and Reconstruction Department, International Labour Organization, Geneva.

Huong, P. L., B. Q. Tuan, D. H. Minh, and T. Q. Long (2003): "Decent Work Strategies for Poverty Reduction in Vietnam." Draft paper. Central Institute of Economic Management, Government of Vietnam, Hanoi.

Impact Monitoring and Evaluation Cell (1999): "Proshika's Impact Assessment Study 1998–99." Proshika, Dhaka.

Insan, H. Sejahtera (2000): "Provincial Poverty and Social Indicators, SUSENAS 1993–1999." Report prepared for the Asian Development Bank. Jakarta.

Interim Poverty Reduction Strategy Paper (2002): "A National Strategy for Economic Growth and Poverty Reduction." External Resource Division, Ministry of Finance, Government of Bangladesh, Dhaka.

International Fund for Agricultural Development (2001): *Rural Poverty Report 2001: The Challenge of Ending Rural Poverty.* Oxford University Press, London.

International Labour Organization (ILO) (1999a): *Demystifying the Core Conventions of the ILO Through Social Dialogue: The Indonesian Experience.* Jakarta.

———— (1999b): *Indonesia: Strategies for Employment-Led Recovery and Reconstruction.* Jakarta.

———— (1999c): Project document for technical support and training targeting the creation of 1.2 million jobs. Australian Agency for International Development, Canberra, and International Labour Organization, Geneva.

———— (1999–2000): *Key Indicators of the Labour Market.* Geneva.

———— (2000a): *Employment-Intensive Investment in Infrastructure: Jobs to Build Society.* Geneva.

———— (2000b): *World Labour Report: Income Security and Social Protection in a Changing World.* Geneva.

———— (2001a): "Poverty and Employment in Africa: Issues and Evidence." Recovery and Reconstruction Department, Geneva.

———— (2002): *Investment in Poverty-Reducing Employment in Uganda.* Jobs for Africa Programme and Area Office for East Africa, Dar es Salaam.

———— (2003a): "Working out of Poverty." Report of the director-general for the International Labour Conference. Geneva.

———— (2003b): "Working out of Poverty: An ILO Submission for the Indonesian PRSP." Jakarta.

———— (2004): *A Fair Globalization: Creating Opportunities for All.* World Commission on the Social Dimensions of Globalization, Geneva.

International Labour Organization et al. (2003): "Macroeconomics of Poverty Reduction: The Case of Bangladesh." Paper presented at regional workshop *Macroeconomics of Poverty Reduction,* organized by the United Nations Development Programme. Kathmandu, January 4–6.

International Monetary Fund (1996): *Vietnam: Recent Economic Developments.* Washington, D.C.

———— (1999): "Bolivia." Staff report for the 1999 Article IV Consultation and Request for Second Annual Arrangement Under the Poverty Reduction and Growth Facility. Washington, D.C.

—— (2000): "Bolivia: Interim Poverty Reduction Strategy Paper." Report prepared by the Bolivian authorities. Washington, D.C.

Irawan, P., I. Ahmed, and I. Islam (2000): *Labour Market Dynamics in Indonesia: An Analysis of 18 Key Indicators of the Labour Market, 1986–1999.* International Labour Organization, Jakarta.

Islam, I. (2000): "Beyond Labour Market Flexibility: Issues and Options for Post-Crisis Indonesia." *Journal of the Asia Pacific Economy* 6(3): 305–334.

—— (2002): "Poverty, Employment, and Wages: An Indonesian Perspective." In *Labour Market Policies and Poverty Reduction Strategies in Recovery from the Asian Crisis.* Report of a seminar held in Jakarta, April 19–May 1. International Labour Organization, Bangkok.

—— (2003): "Avoiding the Stabilisation Trap: Towards a Macroeconomic Policy Framework for Growth, Employment, and Poverty Reduction." Employment Paper no. 2003/54. International Labour Organization, Geneva.

Islam, I., and S. Nazara (2000a): "Minimum Wages and the Welfare of Indonesian Workers." Occasional Discussion Paper no. 3. International Labour Organization Area Office, Jakarta.

—— (2000b): "Technical Note on the Indonesian Labour Market: Estimating Employment Elasticity for the Indonesian Economy." International Labour Organization Area Office, Jakarta.

Islam, R. (1990): "Rural Poverty, Growth and Macroeconomic Policies: The Asian Experience." *International Labour Review* 129(6): 693–714.

—— (1998): "Indonesia: Economic Crisis, Adjustment, Employment, and Poverty—Issues in Development." Issues in Employment and Poverty Discussion Paper no. 23. Recovery and Reconstruction Department, International Labour Organization, Geneva.

—— (2001): "Poverty Alleviation, Employment, and the Labour Market: Lessons from the Asian Experience." Paper presented at the Asia and Pacific forum *Poverty: Reforming Policies and Institutions for Poverty Reduction,* organized by the Asian Development Bank. Manila, February 5–9.

—— (2003a): "Labour Market Policies, Economic Growth, and Poverty Reduction: Lessons and Non-Lessons from the Comparative Experience of East, Southeast, and South Asia." Issues in Employment and Poverty Discussion Paper no. 8. Recovery and Reconstruction Department, International Labour Organization, Geneva.

—— (2003b): "Revisiting the East Asian Model of Economic Growth and Poverty Reduction: A Labour Market Perspective." Paper presented at the conference *Economics for the Future,* organized by the Cambridge Journal of Economics. Cambridge, UK, September 17–19.

Islam, R., and J. Majeres (2001): "Employment-Intensive Growth for Poverty Reduction: What Can Labour-Based Technology in Infrastructure Contribute?" In *Work 2001: Proceedings of an International Conference on Employment Creation in Development.* University of Witwatersrand, Johannesburg.

Jemio, L. C. (1999a): "Reformas, Crecimiento, Progreso Técnico y Empleo en Bolivia" [Reforms, Growth, Technical Progress, and Employment in Bolivia]. *Reformas Económicas* (33): 1–59.

—— (1999b): "Reformas, Políticas Sociales y Equidad en Bolivia" [Reforms, Social Politics, and Equity in Bolivia]. *Reformas Económicas* (38): 1–84.

Jemio, L. C., and M. D. C. Choque (2003): "Employment-Poverty Linkages and Policies: The Case of Bolivia." Issues in Employment and Poverty Discussion Paper no. 11. Recovery and Reconstruction Department, International Labour Organization, Geneva.

Jo, B., and D. T. Ellwood (1983): "Slipping into and out of Poverty: The Dynamics of Spells." Working Paper no. 1199. National Bureau of Economic Research, Cambridge, Mass.

Johnston, J., and J. Dinardo (1997): *Econometric Methods.* 4th ed. McGraw-Hill, New York.

Jones, C. (2002): *Introduction to Economic Growth.* W. W. Norton, New York.

Jorgensen, S. L., and J. V. Domelan (1999): "Helping the Poor Manage Risks Better: The Role of Social Funds." Paper presented at the Inter-American Development Bank conference *Social Protection and Poverty.* Brookings Institution and Inter-American Development Bank, Washington, D.C., February 4–5.

Kabananukye, K., et al. (2004): "Economic Growth, Employment, Poverty, and Pro-Poor Policies in Uganda." Issues in Employment and Poverty Discussion Paper no. 16. Recovery and Reconstruction Department, International Labour Organization, Geneva.

Kaija, D. (1995): "The Role of NGOs in Poverty Alleviation in Uganda: Case Study of Nakanyonyi World Vision Project in Mukono District." Master's thesis. Makerere University, Kampala.

Kakwani, N., and H. Son (2002): "Pro-Poor Growth and Poverty Reduction: The Asian Experience." Paper presented at the workshop *Poverty Alleviation,* organized by the United Nations Development Programme. Kathmandu, October.

Kanbur, R., and L. Squire (1999): "The Evolution of Thinking About Poverty: Exploring the Interactions." Mimeo. World Bank, Washington, D.C.

Kayizzi-Mugerwa, S. (2003): *Reforming Africa's Institutions: Ownership, Incentives, and Capabilities.* United Nations University and World Institute for Development Economics Research, Helsinki.

Keefer, P. (2000): "Growth and Poverty Reduction in Uganda: The Role of Institutional Reform." Mimeo. World Bank, Washington, D.C.

Khan, A. R. (1997a): *Philippines: Employment in a Globalizing and Liberalizing World.* International Labour Organization and Southeast Asia and the Pacific Multidisciplinary Advisory Team, Manila.

——— (1997b): *Reversing the Decline of Output and Productive Employment in Rural Sub-Saharan Africa.* Issues in Development Discussion Paper no. 17. Development Policies Department, International Labour Organization, Geneva.

——— (2000a): "Economic Development: From Independence to the End of the Millennium." In Rounaq Jahan, *Bangladesh: Promise and Performance.* University Press, Dhaka.

——— (2000b): "Globalization and Development: Opportunities and Hazards." Public lecture delivered at the Bangladesh Institute for Development Studies. Dhaka, September 12.

——— (2000c): *Globalization and Sustainable Human Development: An Assessment of Challenge Facing Nepal.* United Nations Conference on Trade and Development, Geneva.

——— (2001a): "Bangladesh Economy 2000: Selected Issues—A Review." *Bangladesh Development Studies* (2) (June): 7–26.

——— (2001b): "Employment Policies for Poverty Reduction." Issues in Employment and Poverty Discussion Paper no. 1. Recovery and Reconstruction Department, International Labour Organization, Geneva.

Khan, A. R., R. Islam, and M. Huq (1981): *Employment, Income, and the Mobilizing of the Local Resource: A Study of Two Bangladesh Villages.* Asian Employment

Programme, International Labour Organization–Asia Regional Team for Employment Promotion, Bangkok.

Khan, A. R., and M. Muqtada (1997): *Employment Expansion and Macroeconomic Stability Under Increasing Globalization.* International Labour Organization Studies Series. Macmillan, London.

Khan, A. R., and C. Riskin (2001): *Inequality and Poverty in China in the Age of Globalization.* Oxford University Press, New York.

Kikonyogo, C. (1999): "Micro-Finance and Poverty." *New Vision* (Kampala), November 26.

Krishna, R. (1973): "Unemployment in India." *Economic and Political Weekly* 9(8): 375–484.

Krishnamurty, J. (1987): "Unemployment in India: The Broad Magnitudes and Characteristics." In T. N. Srinivasan and Pranab K. Bardhan (eds.), *Rural Poverty in South Asia.* Columbia University Press, New York.

Krishnan, P., T. G. Selassie, and S. Dercon (1998): "The Urban Labour Market During Structural Adjustment: Ethiopia 1990–1997." Working Paper no. 98-9. Centre for the Study of African Economies, Oxford University Press, Oxford.

Kuznets, S. (1955): "Economic Growth and Income Inequality." *American Economic Review* (45): 1–28.

———— (1972): "Innovations and Adjustments in Economic Growth." *Swedish Journal of Economics* 74(4) (December): 431–451.

———— (1973): "Modern Economics Growth: Findings and Reflections." *American Economic Review* 63(3) (June): 247–258.

Law and Development Partnership (2002): "Monitoring the Uganda Medium Term Competitive Strategy, Phase 1: Strategic Monitoring Programme." Draft report. Mimeo. Economics Department, Nottingham University, Nottingham, December.

Lawson, D., A. Mekay, and J. Okidi (2003): "Uganda: Explaining the Dynamics, Growth, and Poverty Reduction in Uganda." Economic Policy Research Center, Makerere University, Kampala.

Le, D. D., V. T. Thanh, P. L. Huong, D. H. Minh, and N. Q. Thang (2002): *Explaining Growth in Vietnam.* In *Global Research Project (Country Studies).* Statistical Publishing House, Hanoi.

Lee, E. (1998): *The Asian Financial Crisis: The Challenge for Social Policy.* International Labour Organization, Geneva.

Levin, K. (2002): "Options for Post Primary Education and Training in Uganda: Increasing Access, Equity, and Efficiency Within Sustainable Budgets." Commissioned study for the Ministry of Education and Sports for the Education Sector Review. Kampala, April 12. [Unpublished; available at the Ministry of Education and Sports headquarters, Kampala.]

Levitsky, J. (1989): *Micro Enterprise in Developing Countries.* 4th ed. Intermediate Technology Development Group, London.

Lewis, W. Arthur (1954): "Economic Development, with Unlimited Supplies of Labour." *Manchester School of Economic and Social Studies* (22): 139–191.

Lindbeck, A., and D. J. Snower (1989): *The Insider-Outsider Theory of Employment and Underemployment.* Massachusetts Institute of Technology Press, Cambridge.

Lipton, M., and M. Ravallion (1995): "Poverty and Policy." In *Handbook of Development Economics,* vol. 3B. North-Holland, Amsterdam.

Long, J. S. (1997): *Regression Model for Categorical and Limited Dependent Variables.* International Educational and Professional Publishers, London.

Magarinos, C. (2001): "General Statement of UNIDO on the Third United Nations Conference on the Least-Developed Countries (LDC III)." Brussels.

Mahalanobis, P. C. (1955, 1963): "The Approach of Operational Research to Planning in India." *Indian Journal of Statistics* 16, pts. 1–2 (1955): 3–130. [Reprinted under the same title by Asia Publishing House, Bombay, and Statistical Publishing Society, Calcutta, 1963.]

——— (1960, 1961): "Labour Problems in a Mixed Economy." *Indian Journal of Labour Economics* 3(1) (April 1960): 1–8. [Reprinted as *Talks on Planning* by Asia Publishing House, Bombay, and Statistical Publishing Society, Calcutta, 1961.]

Mahmud, W. (1995): "Recent Macroeconomic Developments in Experience with Economic Reform." In *A Review of Bangladesh's Development, 1995.* Centre for Policy Dialogue and University Press Limited, Dhaka.

——— (1996): "Employment Patterns and Income Formation in Rural Bangladesh: The Role of Rural Non-Farm Sector." Paper presented to the national workshop *Stimulating Growth Through Rural Non-Farm Activities in Bangladesh.* Bangladesh Institute for Development Studies and World Bank, Dhaka.

——— (1997): "Macroeconomic Update in Growth or Stagnation?" In *A Review of Bangladesh's Development, 1996.* Centre for Policy Dialogue and University Press Limited, Dhaka.

Majid, N. (2000): "Pakistan: Employment, Output, and Productivity—Issues in Development." Discussion Paper no. 333. International Labour Organization, Geneva.

——— (2001): "The Size of the Working Poor Population in Developing Countries." Employment Paper no. 2001/16. International Labour Organization, Geneva.

Makerere University Institute of Environment and Natural Resources (2000): *Biodiversity Status Report 2000.* Kampala.

Manning, C. (1998): *Indonesian Labour in Transition: An Indonesian Success Story?* Cambridge University Press, Cambridge.

——— (2000): "Labour Market Adjustments to Indonesia's Economic Crisis: Contexts, Trends, and Implications." *Bulletin of Indonesian Economic Studies* 36(1): 105–136.

Manning, C., and P. N. Junankar (1998): "Choosy Youth or Unwanted Youth? A Survey of Unemployment." *Bulletin of Indonesian Economic Studies* 34(1): 55–93.

Mason, A., and J. Baptist (1996): "How Important Are Labour Markets to the Welfare of the Poor?" Paper presented to the Ministry of Manpower/World Bank workshop *Indonesian Workers in the 21st Century.* Jakarta, April 2–4.

McCawley, P. (2000): "Poverty in Indonesia: The Role of the State in the Post-Soeharto Era." Paper presented to the fiftieth-anniversary conference of the Faculty of Economics. University of Indonesia, Jakarta, October 4–5.

McGee, R. (2000): "Meeting the International Poverty Targets in Uganda: Halving Poverty and Achieving Universal Primary Education." *Development Policy Review* 18(1): 85–106.

McKay, A. (1997): "Poverty Reduction Through Economic Growth: Some Issues." *Journal of International Development* 9(4): 665–673.

McKinley, T. (2003): "The Macroeconomics of Poverty Reduction: Initial Findings of the UNDP Asia-Pacific Regional Program." Bureau for Development Policy, United Nations Development Programme, New York.

Mekonnen, T. (1996): "Food Consumption and Poverty in Urban Ethiopia: A Preliminary Assessment." In K. Bereket and T. Mekonnen (eds.), *Proceedings of the Fifth Annual Conference on the Ethiopian Economy.* Ethiopian Economic Association, Addis Ababa.

Milanovic, B. (1999): "True World Income Distribution, 1988 and 1993: First Calculation Based on Household Surveys Alone." World Bank, Washington, D.C. Available at http://www.worldbank.org/research/transition.

Milner, C., O. Morrissey, and N. Rudaheranwa (2000): "Policy and Non-Policy Barriers to Trade and Implicit Taxation of Exports in Uganda." *Journal of Development Studies* 37(2): 67–90.

Mingat, A., and C. Winter (2002): "Education for All by 2015." *Finance and Development* 39(1): 1–8.

Minhas, B. S. (1991): "Public Versus Private Sector: Neglect of Lessons of Economics in Indian Policy Formulations." R. R. Kale Memorial Lecture. Gokhale Institute of Politics and Economics, Pune.

Ministry of Economic Development and Cooperation (MEDAC) (1999): *Survey of the Ethiopian Economy: Review of Post-Reform Developments.* Government of Ethiopia, Addis Ababa.

Ministry of Education (various years): *Annual Educational Statistics Abstract.* Government of Ethiopia, Addis Ababa.

Ministry of Finance and Economic Development (MOFED) (2002): *Ethiopia: Sustainable Development and Poverty Reduction Program.* Government of Ethiopia, Addis Ababa.

Ministry of Health (2000): "Health and Health Related Indicators." Planning and Programming Department, Government of Ethiopia, Addis Ababa.

Ministry of Labor, Invalids, and Social Affairs (MOLISA) (various years): *Statistical Data of Labour-Employment in Vietnam.* Labour-Social Publishing House, Government of Vietnam, Hanoi.

——— (various years): *Status of Labour-Employment in Vietnam.* Statistical Publishing House and Labor and Social Affairs Publishing House, Government of Vietnam, Hanoi.

Ministry of Water, Lands, and Environment (2002): *The National Forest Plan 2002.* Government of Ethiopia, Addis Ababa.

Mishra, S. (2001): "History in the Making: A Systemic Transition in Indonesia." Working Paper no. 01/02. United Nations Support Facility for Indonesian Recovery, Jakarta.

Morduch, J. (1999a): "Between the Market and the State: Can Informal Insurance Patch Up the Market?" Stiglitz summer research workshop on poverty. World Bank, Washington, D.C., July 6–8.

——— (1999b): "The Microfinance Promise." *Journal of Economic Literature* (37): 1569–1614.

Morris, J. R. (1983): "Reforming Agricultural Extension and Research Services in Africa." Agricultural Administration Network Discussion Paper no. 2. London Development Institute, London.

Mosley, P. (2002): "The African Green Revolution as a Pro-Poor Policy Instrument." *Journal of International Development* (14): 695–724.

Mountain Rural Development Program (1999): *Lao Cai Province: A Participatory Poverty Assessment.* Vietnam-Sweden Mountain Rural Development Program and Vietnam-Sweden Health Cooperation Program, Hanoi.

Muhumuza, R. (1999): "Efforts of World Vision Towards Small Scale Business Development." *New Vision* (Kampala), November 19.

Muhwezi, D. (1994): "Growth Potential in Small Scale Manufacturing Enterprises in Kampala." Master's thesis. Makerere University, Kampala.

Mujeri, M. K. (2000): "Poverty Trends and Agricultural Growth Linkages." Food Management and Research Support Project Working Paper no. 26. Government of Bangladesh, Dhaka.

——— (2001): "Macroeconomic Developments in the 1990s." In A. Abdullah (ed.), *Bangladesh Economy 2000: Selected Issues.* Bangladesh Institute for Development Studies, Dhaka.

Mukherjee, N. (2000): "Consultations with the Poor." Background paper to *World Development Report 2000/2001.*

Muqtada, M. (2003): "Macroeconomic Stability, Growth, and Employment: Issues and Considerations Beyond the Washington Consensus." Employment Paper no. 2003/48. Employment Sector, International Labour Organization, Geneva.

Myint, H. (1959): "The 'Classical Theory' of International Trade and the Underdeveloped Countries." *Economic Journal* 68(270): 317–337.

Myrdal, G. (1972): *Asian Drama: An Inquiry into the Poverty of Nations.* Random House, New York.

Narayan, D., et al. (2000): *Voices of the Poor: Can Anyone Hear Us?* Oxford University Press, New York.

National Bank of Ethiopia (2001): *Quarterly Bulletin* 16(4).

National Bureau of Statistics (2000): *China Statistical Yearbook 2000.* China Statistical Press, Beijing.

National Centre for Social Sciences and Humanities (2001): *National Human Development Report 2001: Doi Moi and Human Development in Vietnam.* Political Publishing House, Government of Vietnam, Hanoi.

National Office of Population (2000): *The Ethiopian Population Profile.* Ministry of Economic Development and Cooperation, Government of Ethiopia, Addis Ababa.

Nissanke, M. (2002): "Donors' Support for Microcredit as Social Enterprise: A Critical Appraisal." World Institute for Development Economics Research Discussion Paper no. 2002/127. United Nations University and World Institute for Development Economics Research, Helsinki.

Nurkse, R. (1953): *Problems of Capital-Formation in Underdeveloped Countries.* Basil Blackwell, Oxford.

O'Connell, P. (1999): "Astonishing Success: Economic Growth and the Labour Market in Ireland." Employment and Training Paper no. 44. International Labour Organization, Geneva.

Ohlin, Bertil (1991): "The Theory of Trade." In Bertil Ohlin and Eli Heckscher, *Heckscher-Ohlin Trade Theory.* Massachusetts Institute of Technology Press, Cambridge.

Okidi, J., G. Bahiigwa, and G. Kempeka (2002): "Costing the Millennium Development Goals: Uganda Country Study." Economic Policy Review Commission Occasional Paper no. 18. Kampala.

Okidi, J., and A. McKay (2003): "Poverty Dynamics in Uganda, 1992 to 2000." Paper presented at the 2003 annual conference *Chronic Poverty Research.* University of Manchester, UK.

Okidi, J., P. Okwi, and J. Ddumba (2000): "Welfare Distribution and Poverty in Uganda, 1992–1997." Paper presented at the African Economic Research Consortium workshop *Poverty, Income Distribution, and Labor Market Issues in Sub-Saharan Africa.* Nairobi, May.

Onyach, Alaa (1992): "Industry in Uganda: Current State, Problems, and Prospects." Paper presented at the 1992 Uganda Economic Association policy meeting. Kampala.

Organization for Economic Cooperation and Development (1996): *Shaping the 21st Century: The Contribution of Development Cooperation.* Development Assistance Committee, Paris.

——— (2001): *African Economic Outlook.* Paris.

Osmani, S. R. (2000): "Growth Strategies and Poverty Reduction." *Asian Development Review 2000* 18(2): 85–130.

——— (2002): "Exploring the Employment Nexus: Topics in Employment and Poverty." Mimeo. United Nations Development Program, New York, and International Labour Organization, Geneva.

——— (2004): "The Employment Nexus Between Growth and Poverty: The Asian Experience." Mimeo. Report prepared for the Swedish International Development Cooperation Agency and the United Nations Development Programme. Stockholm and New York.

Osmani, S. R., et al. (2003): "Macroeconomics of Poverty Reduction: The Case of Bangladesh." Paper presented at the regional workshop *Macroeconomics of Poverty Reduction,* organized by the United Nations Development Programme. Kathmandu, January 4–6.

Oxfam (1999): *Tra Vinh Province: A Participatory Poverty Assessment.* Hanoi.

Padalino, S., and M. Vivarelli (1997): "The Employment Intensity of Economic Growth in G-7 Countries." *International Labour Review* 136(2): 191–214.

Papanek, G., and B. Handoko (1999): "The Impact on the Poor of Growth and Crisis: Evidence from Real Wage Data." Paper presented at the conference *Economic Issues Facing the New Government.* Jakarta, August 18–19.

Parikesit, D., and B. Hudayana (1999): "Socio-Economic Summary of Review of Labour-Based Programmes, Phase 2." Working Paper no. 1. Australian Agency for International Development, Canberra, and International Labour Organization, Geneva.

Pham, L. H., D. H. Minh, and T. Q. Long (2004): "Decent Work Strategies for Poverty Reduction in Vietnam." Draft background paper prepared for the International Labour Organization. Central Institute of Economic Management, Hanoi.

Plumptre, A., et al. (2001): *Chimpanzee and Large Mammal Survey of Budongo Forest Reserve and Kibaale National Park.* Oxford University Press, Oxford.

Poverty Task Force (2002): *Localising IDTs for Poverty Reduction in Vietnam: Enhancing Access to Basic Infrastructure.* Government of Vietnam, Hanoi.

Poverty Working Group (1999): *Vietnam Development Report 2000: Attacking Poverty.* Joint report of the Government-Donor-NGO Poverty Working Group, Consultative Group Meeting for Vietnam. Hanoi, December 14–15.

Pradhan, M., A. Suryahadi, S. Sumarto, and L. Pritchett (2000): "Measurements of Poverty in Indonesia, 1996, 1999, and Beyond." Social Monitoring and Early Response Unit (SMERU), Jakarta. World Bank Working Paper no. 2437. World Bank, Washington, D.C.

Pritchett, L. (2003): "Who Is Not Poor? Proposing a Higher International Standard for Poverty." Working Paper no. 33. Center for Global Development, Washington, D.C.

Pritchett, L., A. Suryahadi, and S. Sumarto (2000): "Quantifying Vulnerability to Poverty: A Proposed Measure, Applied to Indonesia." Social Monitoring and Early Response Unit (SMERU), Jakarta. World Bank Working Paper no. 2437. World Bank, Washington, D.C.

Private Sector Foundation Uganda (2003): "Private Sector Concerns and Proposals." Mimeo. February 2003.

Rahman, R. I. (1996): "Unemployment Wages Rate and Poverty, 1987–94: Dynamics of Rural Poverty in Bangladesh." Bangladesh Institute for Development Studies, Dhaka.

——— (2000): *Poverty Alleviation and Empowerment Through Microfinance: Two Decades of Experience in Bangladesh*. Bangladesh Institute for Development Studies Research Monograph no. 20. Dhaka.

——— (2001): "Tractor Use, Irrigation, and Productivity in Bangladesh Agriculture." In A. A. Abdullah (ed.), *Bangladesh Economy 2000: Selected Issues*. Bangladesh Institute for Development Studies, Dhaka.

——— (2002): "Pattern of Economic Growth and Its Sustainability." Paper presented at the seminar *Performance of the Bangladesh Economy*. Bangladesh Institute for Development Studies, Dhaka.

——— (2005): "Economic Growth, Investment Pattern, and Employment Generation: How to Achieve Pro-Poor Growth." Paper presented at a seminar on the 2005–2006 national budget and poverty reduction strategy. Bangladesh Institute for Development Studies, Dhaka.

Rahman, R. I., and S. R. Khandker (1994): "Role of Targeted Credit Programmes in Promoting Employment and Productivity of the Poor in Bangladesh." *Bangladesh Development Studies* 22(2–3): 37–63.

Rahman, R. I., and K. M. Nabiul Islam (2003): "Employment Poverty Linkages: Bangladesh." Issues in Employment and Poverty Discussion Paper no. 10. Recovery and Reconstruction Department, International Labour Organization, Geneva.

Rahman, R. I., and B. K. Saha (1995): "Impact of Grameen Krishi Foundation on the Socio-Economic Condition of Rural Households." Mimeo. Bangladesh Institute for Development Studies, Dhaka.

Rama, M. (2001): "Globalization and Workers in Developing Countries." Mimeo. World Bank, Washington, D.C., July 24.

Ravallion, M. (1995): "Growth and Poverty: Evidence for Developing Countries in the 1980s." *Economic Letters* 48(3–4): 411–417.

——— (1997): "Can High-Inequality Developing Countries Escape Absolute Poverty?" Policy Research Working Paper no. 1775. World Bank, Washington, D.C.

——— (1998): "Appraising Workfare Programs." Working Paper no. 1955. World Bank, Washington, D.C.

——— (2001): "Growth, Inequality, and Poverty: Looking Beyond Averages." *World Development* 29(11): 1803–1815.

Ravallion, M., and B. Sen (1996): "When Method Matters: Monitoring Poverty in Bangladesh." *Economic Development and Cultural Change* 44(4): 761–792.

Reddy, S., and T. Pogge (2002): "How Not to Count the Poor." Unpublished working paper. Columbia University, New York.

Reinikka, R., and P. Collier (eds.) (2001): *Uganda's Recovery: The Role of Farms, Firms, and Government*. World Bank, Washington, D.C.

Reynolds, L. (1985): *Economic Growth in the Third World, 1950–1980*. Yale University Press, New Haven.

Sadaah, F., H. Waters, and P. Haywood (1999): "Indonesia: Undernutrition in Young Children, East Asia, and the Pacific Region." *Watching Brief* (1) (January). World Bank, Washington, D.C.

Save the Children UK (1999): *Ho Chi Minh City: A Participatory Poverty Assessment*. Hanoi.

Sekkat, K., and A. Varoudakis (2000): "Exchange Rate Management and Manufactured Exports in Sub-Saharan Africa." *Journal of Development Economics* 61(1): 237–253.

Sen, A. K. (1999): *Development as Freedom*. Alfred A. Knopf, New York.

Shamunnay, U. (2000): *The Budget and the Poor*. University Press, Dhaka.

Skoufias, E., A. Suryahadi, and S. Sumarto (2000): "Changes in Household Welfare, Poverty, and Inequality During the Crisis." *Bulletin of Indonesian Economic Studies* 36(2): 97–114.

Social Monitoring and Early Response Unit (SMERU) (2001a): "Education Difficulties for the Poor: If They Can Be Exploited, Why Not?" *SMERU Newsletter* (3) (May–June): 1–8.

——— (2001b): "Wage and Employment Effects of Minimum Wage Policy in the Indonesian Urban Labour Market." Mimeo. SMERU Research Institute, Jakarta, October.

Socialist Republic of Vietnam (SRV) (2002): *The Comprehensive Poverty Reduction and Growth Strategy*. Hanoi.

Squire, Lyn (1993): "Fighting Poverty." *American Economic Review,* May 1993. [Papers and proceedings of the 105th annual meeting of the American Economic Association.]

Srinivasan, T. N. (2001): "Growth and Poverty Alleviation: Lessons from Development Experience." Working Paper no. 17. Asian Development Bank, Tokyo.

Ssekatawa, J. H. (2002): "Country Employment and Poverty Profile: Uganda." Mimeo. International Labour Organization Country Office, Kampala.

Ssendawula, G. (1998): "The Role of Micro-Finance Projects in Extending Credit." Budget special. Uganda Ministry of Finance, Planning, and Economic Development, Kampala, June 11.

State Committee for Ethnic Minorities and Mountainous Areas Affairs (2001): *Preliminary Report on Implementation of the National Program for Socio-Economic Development in Communes Suffering Special Hardship in Mountainous and Remote Areas During Two Years, 1999–2000, and the Plan for 2001*. Report prepared for the national conference summing up two years of implementation of the program and realization of the 2001 plan. Government of Vietnam, Hanoi, May 10–12.

Steering Committee of Comprehensive Poverty Reduction and Growth Strategy (2003): *Vietnam Growth and Reduction of Poverty: Annual Progress Report of 2002–2003*. Government of Vietnam, Hanoi.

Subbarao, K., et al. (1997): "Safety Net Programs and Poverty Reduction: Lessons from Cross-Country Experiences." Directions in Development. World Bank, Washington, D.C.

Sundaram, K. (1989a): "Agriculture Industry Inter-Relations in India: Issues of Migration." In S. Chakravarty (ed.), *The Balance Between Industry and Agriculture in Economic Development*. Macmillan in association with the International Economic Association, Basingstoke.

——— (1989b): "Inter-State Variations in Work Force Participation Rates of Women in India: An Analysis." In A. V. Jose (ed.), *Limited Options: Women Workers in Rural India*. International Labour Organization, Geneva.

——— (2001a): "Employment and Poverty in 1990s: A Postscript." *Economic and Political Weekly,* August 25.

——— (2001b): "Employment and Poverty in 1990s: Further Results from NSS 55th Round Employment-Unemployment Survey, 1999–2000." *Economic and Political Weekly* 36(32) (August 11): 3039–3049.

———— (2001c): "Employment-Unemployment Situation in the Nineties: Some Results from NSS 55th Round Survey." *Economic and Political Weekly* 36(11) (March 11): 931–940.

Sundaram, K., and S. D. Tendulkar (2002): "The Working Poor in India: Employment-Poverty Linkages and Employment Policy Options." Issues in Employment and Poverty Discussion Paper no. 4. Recovery and Reconstruction Department, International Labour Organization, Geneva.

———— (2003a): "Poverty Has Declined in the 1990s: A Resolution of Comparability Problems in NSS Consumer Expenditure Data." *Economic and Political Weekly* 38(4) (January 25–31): 327–337.

———— (2003b): "Poverty in India in the 1990s: Revised Results for All India and 15 Major States for 1993–94." *Economic and Political Weekly* 38(46) (November 15–21): 4865–4871.

Suryahadi, A., Y. Suharso, and S. Sumarto (1999): "Coverage and Targeting in the Social Safety Net Programs: Evidence from 100 Village Survey." Research working paper. Social Monitoring and Early Response Unit (SMERU), Jakarta.

Suryahadi, A., Y. Suharso, S. Sumarto, and L. Pritchett (2000): "The Evolution of Poverty During the Crisis in Indonesia, 1996 to 1999 (Using Full Susenas Sample)." World Bank Research Working Paper no. 2435. Social Monitoring and Early Response Unit (SMERU), Jakarta.

Suryahadi, A., and S. Sumarto (2001): "The Chronic Poor, the Transient Poor, and the Vulnerable in Indonesia Before and After the Crisis." Working paper, May. Social Monitoring and Early Response Unit (SMERU) Research Institute, Jakarta.

Sutanto, A., and P. B. Irawan (2000): "Regional Dimensions of Poverty: Some Findings on the Nature of Poverty." Paper presented at the international conference *Poverty Measurement in Indonesia*. Central Bureau of Statistics, Government of Indonesia, and World Bank, Jakarta, May 16.

Tassew, W. H. (2002): "Off-Farm Employment and Income Inequality: The Implication for Poverty Reduction Strategy." In Gebrehiwot Ageba, Jemmal Mohammed, and Solomon Tesfaye (eds.), *Proceedings of the Eleventh Annual Conference on the Ethiopian Economy*. Ethiopian Economic Association, Addis Ababa.

Taylor, G., and M. Bekabye (2000): "An Opportunity for Employment Creation: Labour-Based Technology in Roadworks—The Macro-Economic Dimension." Working paper. International Labour Organization, Geneva.

Tendulkar, S. D. (2000a): "Employment Growth in Factory Manufacturing During the Pre- and Post-Reform Periods." Presentation to a conference in honor of Professor K. L. Krishna at the Delhi School of Economics. New Delhi, December.

———— (2000b): "Indian Export and Economic Growth Performance in Asian Perspective." Working Paper no. 54. Indian Council for Research in International Economic Relations, New Delhi.

Tendulkar, S. D., and T. A. Bhavani (1997): "Policy on Modern Small Scale Industries: A Case of Government Failure." *Indian Economic Review* 32(1) (January–June): 85–110.

Tendulkar, S. D., and L. R. Jain (1995): "Economic Growth, Relative Inequality and Equity: The Case of India." *Asian Development Review* 13(2): 138–168.

Tendulkar, S. D., and B. Sen (2003): "Markets and Long-Term Growth in South Asia, 1950–97." In I. J. Ahluwalia and J. G. Williamson (eds.), *The South Asian Experience with Growth*. Oxford University Press, New Delhi.

Tendulkar, S. D., K. Sundaram, and L. R. Jain (1993): "Poverty in India, 1970–71 to 1988–89." Report prepared for the International Labour Organization Asia Regional Team for Employment Programme. New Delhi.

Thiesenhusen, W. C., and J. Melmed-Sanjak (1990): "Brazil's Agrarian Structure: Changes from 1970 Through 1980." *World Development* 18(3): 393–415.

Tran, V. T., N. D. Nguyen, V. C. Nguyen, and Q. Nguyen (2000): *Kinh Te Viet Nam 1955–2000* [Vietnam's Economy 1955–2000]. Statistical Publishing House, Government of Vietnam, Hanoi.

Tubagus, F. (2000): "The Impact of the Crisis on the Labour Market in Indonesia." Report prepared for the Asian Development Bank. Manila, March 22.

Tulip, A., and M. Bitekerezo (1993): Paper presented at the conference *Uganda Small Scale*. International Conference Centre, Kampala. [Unpublished; available at the World Bank offices in Kampala.]

Tumwebaze, H. K. (1992): "Excess Capacity in Uganda Manufacturing Sector." Master's thesis. Makerere University, Kampala.

Uganda Coffee Development Authority (2001): *Annual Report*. Kampala, October–September.

Uganda National Household Survey (2001): *Report of the Community Survey*. Diskette. Government of Uganda, Kampala, January 2001.

Union of Political, Social, and Economic Analysis (2002): "Bolivia's Strategy of Poverty Reduction: Advance Report and Perspectives." La Paz.

United Nations (2003): *Millennium Development Goals: Closing the Millennium Gaps*. UN Vietnam Office, Hanoi.

United Nations Conference on Trade and Development (2002): *Trade and Development Report*. New York.

United Nations Development Programme (UNDP) (1991): "Promotion of Rural Small Scale Industry." Project Document no. DP/UGA/90/017/01/37. New York.

———— (1996): *Vietnam Public Expenditure Review*. Vol. 1. Hanoi.

———— (1998): *Human Development Report 1998*.

———— (2000): *Human Development Report 2000*. New York.

———— (2002): *Human Development Report 2002*. Oxford University Press, New York.

———— (2003): *Human Development Report 2003*. Oxford University Press, New York.

United Nations Support Facility for Indonesian Recovery (1999): "The Social Implications of the Indonesian Economic Crisis: Perceptions and Policy." Discussion Paper no. 1. United Nations Development Programme, Jakarta.

United Nations University (UNU) and World Institute for Development Economics (WIDER) (2000): "Rising Inequality and Poverty Reduction: Are They Compatible?" Unpublished paper prepared for the UNU/WIDER meeting in Helsinki. December 11–13, 1999.

Van de Walle, D. (2001): *The Static and Dynamic Incidence of Vietnam's Public Safety Net*. World Bank, Washington, D.C.

Van Ginnekan, W. (ed.) (1999): *Social Security for the Excluded Majority*. International Labour Organization, Geneva.

Vos, R., H. Lee, and J. A. Mejía (1998): "Structural Adjustment and Poverty." In P. Van Dijck (ed.), *The Bolivian Experiment: Structural Adjustment and Poverty Alleviation*. Cedla, Amsterdam.

Vroman, W. (1999): "Unemployment and Unemployment Protection in Three Groups of Countries." Social Protection Discussion Paper no. 9911. World Bank, Washington, D.C., May.

Welfare Monitoring Unit (1999): *Poverty Situation in Ethiopia*. Ministry of Economic Development and Cooperation, Government of Ethiopia, Addis Ababa.

White, H., and E. Anderson (2001): "Growth Versus Distribution: Does the Pattern of Growth Matter?" *Development Policy Review* 19(3): 267–289.

Widyanti, W., S. Sumarto, and A. Suryahadi (2001): "Short-Term Poverty Dynamics: Evidence from Rural Indonesia." Working paper. Social Monitoring and Early Response Unit (SMERU) Research Institute, Jakarta, September.

Wiebe, F. (1996): "Income Insecurity and Underemployment in the Indonesian Informal Sector." Paper presented to the Ministry of Manpower/World Bank workshop *Indonesian Workers in the 21st Century.* Jakarta, April 2–4.

Wiens, T. (1998): "Agriculture and Rural Poverty in Vietnam." In D. Dollar, P. Glewwe, and J. Litvack (eds.), *Household Welfare and Vietnam's Transition.* Regional and Sectoral Studies. World Bank, Washington, D.C.

Women's Affairs Office and World Bank (1998): *Implementing the Ethiopian National Policy for Women: Institutional and Regulatory Issues.* Washington, D.C.

Wood, A. (1997): "Openness and Wage Inequality in Developing Countries: The Latin American Challenge to East Asian Wisdom." *World Bank Economic Review* 11(1): 33–57.

Wood, A., and K. Jordan (2000): "Why Does Zimbabwe Export Manufactures and Uganda Not? Econometrics Meets History." *Journal of Development Studies* 37(2): 91–116.

Wood, A., and J. Mayer (2001): "Africa's Export Structure in a Comparative Perspective." *Cambridge Journal of Economics* 25(3): 369–394.

World Bank (1990): *World Development Report 1990: Poverty.* Washington, D.C.

——— (1993): *Uganda: Growing out of Poverty.* Washington, D.C.

——— (1995): *World Tables 1995.* Washington, D.C.

——— (1996a): "Bolivia: Poverty, Equity, and Income—Selected Policies for Expanding Earning Opportunities for the Poor." Report no. 15272-BO. Washington, D.C.

——— (1996b): *Labour Market Policies for Higher Employment in Bangladesh.* Dhaka.

——— (1997): *World Development Indicators 1997.* CD-ROM. Washington, D.C.

——— (1998): *Bangladesh: From Counting the Poor to Making the Poor Count.* Dhaka.

——— (2000a): "Indonesia: Managing Government Debt and Its Risks." East Asia and the Pacific Region. Washington, D.C., May 22.

——— (2000b): "Poverty Reduction in Indonesia: Constructing a New Strategy." Draft for discussion. Jakarta.

——— (2000c): *World Development Indicators 2000.* Oxford University Press, Washington, D.C.

——— (2000d): *World Development Report: Attacking Poverty.* Oxford University Press, Washington, D.C.

——— (2000e): *World Development Report 2000/2001.* Oxford University Press, New York.

——— (2001a): *Engendering Development: Through Gender Equality in Rights, Resources, and Voice.* Washington, D.C.

——— (2001b): *Implementing Reforms for Faster Growth and Poverty Reduction: Vietnam Development Report 2002.* Hanoi.

——— (2001c): "Indonesia Update." Washington, D.C., October.

——— (2002a): "Achieving EFA in Uganda: The Big Bang Approach." Washington, D.C.

——— (2002b): "Bolivia: Poverty Diagnostic 2000." Report no. 20530-BO. Washington, D.C.

——— (2002c): *Globalization, Growth, and Poverty: Building an Inclusive World Economy.* Washington, D.C.

——— (2002d): *Poverty Assessment in Bangladesh.* Dhaka.

——— (2003a): *Averting an Infrastructure Crisis: A Framework for Policy Action.* Jakarta.

——— (2003b): *Bolivia at a Glance.* Washington, D.C. Available online at http://www.worldbank.org/data/countrydata/aag/bol_aag.pdf.

——— (2003c): *Global Economic Prospects and the Developing Countries.* Washington, D.C.

——— (2003d): *Indonesia: Beyond Macroeconomic Stability.* Jakarta.

——— (2003e): *World Development Indicators 2003.* Oxford University Press, Washington, D.C.

——— (2003f): *World Development Report 2003.* Washington, D.C.

Yemtsove, R. (2001): "Labour Markets, Inequality, and Poverty in Georgia." Discussion Paper no. 251. World Bank, Washington, D.C.

Yohannes, B. (1996): "Common Property Rights, Poverty, and Environmental Degradation in the Borena Plateau." In K. Bereket and T. Mekonnen (eds.), *Proceedings of the Fifth Annual Conference on the Ethiopian Economy.* Ethiopian Economic Association, Addis Ababa.

Yohannes, K. (1996): "Demographic Characteristics of Poor Households in Urban Ethiopia." In K. Bereket and T. Mekonnen (eds.), *Proceedings of the Fifth Annual Conference on the Ethiopian Economy.* Ethiopian Economic Association, Addis Ababa.

The Contributors

María del Carmen Choque obtained her master's in regional development and planning at the Institute of Social Studies, The Hague, Netherlands. She has worked as an international consultant for the Economic Commission for Latin America and the Caribbean, the International Development Bank, the World Bank, and the International Labour Organization.

Mulat Demeke is associate professor, Department of Economics, Addis Ababa University, Ethiopia. His research interests include poverty and labor market issues, strategy and policy in rural and agricultural development, agricultural markets and food security, regional economic integration, and sustainable use of natural resources.

Tadele Ferede is lecturer, Department of Economics, Addis Ababa University, Ethiopia. His research interests include SAM-based general equilibrium modeling, intersectoral linkages, labor market analysis, poverty and food security, macro-micro linkages, regional economic integration, and commodity market analysis.

Fantu Guta is lecturer, Department of Economics, Addis Ababa University, Ethiopia. His research interests include SAM-based general equilibrium modeling, intersectoral linkages, labor market issues, growth and poverty, macro-micro linkages, and regional economic integration.

Pham Lan Huong is deputy director, Department for Trade Policy and International Integration Studies, Central Institute for Economic Management, Hanoi, Vietnam. Her research interests include income distribution and poverty, trade policy, public expenditure issues, agricultural and rural development, and computable general equilibrium modeling.

Iyanatul Islam is professor of international business, Griffith University, Brisbane, Australia. His research interests include labor market–poverty linkages in Indonesia, globalization and macroeconomic conservatism, and the East Asian political economy.

K. M. Nabiul Islam is a research fellow at the Bangladesh Institute of Development Studies (BIDS). His research activities include policy-oriented research in the areas of technology choice; employment and growth in industries; disasters and poverty management; and water, flood, and environment management. He is the author of *Flood Loss Management* and coauthor of three books on choice and transfer of technology in large industries in Bangladesh. He is currently involved as project director in one of the study components of the Integrated Coastal Zone Management Plan of Bangladesh.

Rizwanul Islam is director, Employment Strategy Department, International Labour Office, Geneva, Switzerland. His research interests include the nexus of economic growth, employment and poverty, and policies for pro-poor growth. Islam's recent publications include *East Asian Labour Markets and the Economic Crisis: Impacts, Responses, and Lessons* (coedited with Gordon Betcherman of the World Bank).

Luis Carlos Jemio obtained his doctorate in economics at the Institute of Social Studies, The Hague, Netherlands. He has worked as an international consultant for the Economic Commission for Latin America and the Caribbean, the International Development Bank, the World Bank, and the International Labour Organization, and is a former finance minister of Bolivia.

Adrine E. K. Kabananukye is research associate, Makarere Institute of Social Research, Makarere University, Kampala, Uganda. Research interests include education, career guidance, mentoring and apprenticeship training for development, entrepreneurial skills, labor market analysis, informal employment and women's participation, and project appraisal, monitoring, and evaluation.

Kabann I. B. Kabananukye, a social anthropologist, is lecturer and researcher, Makarere Institute of Social Research, Makarere University, Kampala, Uganda. His research interests include replicable models of poverty alleviation, child labor dynamics in the development process, indigenous knowledge systems and practices for ethnic minorities, and pro-poor formal and informal initiatives and social capital.

Azizur Rahman Khan is professor of economics, University of California,

Riverside, United States. His research interests include development, income distribution, employment, and poverty. Khan's recent publications include *Inequality and Poverty in China in the Age of Globalization* (coauthored with Carl Ruskin).

J. Krishnamurty, a former official of the International Labour Organization, obtained his doctorate in economics from Delhi University, India. His research interests include labor markets and employment, crisis response and reconstruction, and recent Indian economic history.

Dinh Hien Minh is deputy director, Department for Trade Policy and International Integration Studies, Central Institute for Economic Management, Hanoi, Vietnam. Her research interests include macroeconomic policy analysis, economic growth, trade, investment and poverty reduction, and econometric modeling.

S. R. Osmani is professor of development economics, University of Ulster, United Kingdom. His research interests include poverty, inequality, hunger, famine, nutrition, and rights-based development. Osmani's recent publications include *Economic Inequality and Group Welfare* and *Nutrition and Poverty.*

Daisy Owomugasho is lecturer and senior researcher, Makarere Institute of Economics, Makarere University, Kampala, Uganda. Her research interests include poverty, gender, entrepreneurship and group dynamics, and macro- and microeconomic policy.

Rushidan Islam Rahman is research director, Bangladesh Institute of Development Studies, Dhaka. She obtained her doctorate in economics from Australian National University. Her research interests include poverty measurement, unemployment and underemployment, growth prospects of the Bangladesh economy, microcredit, rural nonfarm activities, and gender dimensions of the labor market. Rahman's recent publications include *Performance of the Bangladesh Economy: Selected Issues.*

K. Sundaram is professor, Delhi School of Economics, Delhi University, India. His research interests include the nexus of labor, employment, and poverty, and he is currently jointly coordinating a project to develop a macroeconomic model for India.

Suresh D. Tendulkar obtained his doctorate in economics from Harvard University. Since his retirement as professor, Delhi School of Economics, Delhi University, India, he has been a member of the university's Centre for Development Economics. His research interests include employment, poverty, international trade, and labor.

Bui Quang Tuan is director, Department of Development Studies, Institute of World Economics and Politics, Hanoi, Vietnam. His research interests include development, international trade and investment, and integration.

Index

About the Book

While it has become abundantly clear that neither overall economic growth nor targeted micro-level interventions inevitably reduce poverty in developing countries, much of the development literature continues to focus on these two approaches. Exploring a third, and more promising, avenue, *Fighting Poverty* offers a systematic analysis of the link between employment and pro-poor economic growth.

The authors provide both conceptual frameworks and rich empirical evidence to demonstrate precisely how employment can serve to link growth with poverty reduction. They include in-depth case studies of Bangladesh, Bolivia, Ethiopia, India, Indonesia, Uganda, and Vietnam.

Rizwanul Islam is director of the Employment Strategy Department of the International Labour Organization.